Contents

THE BEST OF SOUTHEAST ASIA: TOP ATTRACTIONS

A selection of the top sights of the region, from superlative beaches to cosmopolitan cities and handsome old towns, mountain resorts and fascinating ancient sites.

◁ **Gunung Bromo**. This majestic, smoke-belching volcano high above the padi fields of eastern Java lies within a far larger and more ancient caldera, 10km (6 miles) across. Get there at dawn for stupendous views – but remember to wrap up warm. See page 321.

◁ **Boracay**. This beautiful island, with probably the highest-profile of any of the 7,107 in the Philippines, has a deserving reputation for powder-fine white sand of crushed coral, tall swaying palms and an aquamarine sea where diving is a sheer delight. See page 369.

▷ **Bangkok**. From the magnificent Grand Palace to the floating markets and superb food, cosmopolitan Bangkok is a fascinating city. See page 47.

▽ **Angkor Wat**. One of the world's premier ancient sights and the high point of classical Khmer architecture. This massive temple, surrounded by a square moat, is covered in miles of bas reliefs. See page 171.

△ **The Andaman Coast**. Some of the world's most perfect tropical beaches can be found on Thailand's west coast, from Phuket to stunning Krabi and Ko Phi Phi. See page 63.

▷ **Intramuros, Manila**. This old walled city encompasses the 16th-century Spanish town and lies amid the animated Philippine capital. See page 353.

◁ **Singapore's Chinatown market**. Night markets are a feature of Southeast Asia, and the one in Singapore's Chinatown is always worth visiting. During the day, teahouses and medicinal emporia are full of delights, too. See page 285.

▽ **George Town**. The main centre on the Malaysian island of Penang is a lovely old town with a Chinese heart. The food is fantastic, too. See page 251.

▽ **Yogyakarta, Java**. Ancient temples, royal palaces, batik, gamelan, dances, and puppet performances are the attractions of this traditional Javanese town. See page 316.

∧ **Bali**. The icon of tropical resorts, this mountainous Indonesian island is known for its friendliness, and its outstandingly rich culture of music and arts that come together during its many vibrant festivals. See page 323.

△ **Hue and Hoi An**. Surrounded by high walls and a moat, the Imperial City beside the Perfume River in Hue, central Vietnam, is a romantic highlight. Nearby are the magnificent tombs of the Nguyen emperors, while a short journey to the coast brings you to the picturesque town of Hoi An. See page 209.

▽ **Borobudur**. Java is home to the world's largest Buddhist monument, built between AD 778 and 856 and for centuries concealed beneath volcanic ash. The magnificent stupa is a geometrical aid for meditation, which pilgrims climb, passing extraordinary sculptures to reach its zenith. See page 319.

△ **Northern Thailand**. The mountains, jungle, rivers and waterfalls of the far northwest offer some of the best trekking and rafting in Asia. Meet the hill tribes, and ride on elephants. See page 59.

▽ **Shwedagon Pagoda, Yangon**. Pagodas don't come much more fanciful than the Shwedagon, built as a keepsake for eight hairs of Gautama Buddha. See page 97.

▷ **Luang Prabang**. The former royal capital of Laos on the banks of the Mekong, Luang Prabang is a beautiful city crowded with temples – notably the winged-roof Wat Xieng Thong. Don't miss the Royal Museum. See page 135.

△ **Northern Highlands, Luzon**. Twisting mountain roads lead from the city of Baguio through the forested highlands of the Philippines' far north to reach the spectacular rice terraces of Banaue. See page 362.

△ **Baliem Gorge, Papua**. Fly to the New Guinea Highlands – there is no road in or out – for some memorable hiking and meeting the Dani tribe. See page 336.

▽ **Hanoi Old Quarter**. Attractive French colonial architecture, narrow shopfronts and commercial frenzy combine to create urban Asia at its most romantic, and most exciting. See page 201.

△ **Phnom Penh**. Cambodia's capital of wide boulevards and chic riverside restaurants maintains its traditions. The royal palace in the Silver Pagoda is a place of riches, and still home to King Norodom Sihanouk and his family. See page 162.

▽ **Plain of Jars, Laos**. Why these giant vessels are scattered across the lonely plateaux of northeastern Laos, nobody really knows. See page 141.

THE BEST OF SOUTHEAST ASIA: EDITOR'S CHOICE

Outstanding cultural attractions, glittering temples and ancient sites, colourful markets, wildlife-rich forests, mountains and some of the world's premier dive sites...here, at a glance, are our recommendations on what to prioritise to make the most of your trip.

Bagan temples, Myanmar.

ANCIENT SITES

Bagan, Myanmar. Ancient pagodas bear witness to the time when Bagan was one of the richest capitals in the region. See page 108.

Ayutthaya, Thailand. This former capital city on a loop in the Chao Phrao River was once dubbed 'the Venice of the East'. See page 53.

Ta Prohm, Angkor. The jungle setting makes this arguably the most magical temple complex in

Cham ruins deep in the jungle at My Son, Vietnam.

Cambodia's famous ancient site. See page 174.

My Son, Vietnam. Tucked under the green slopes of Cat's Tooth Mountain, My Son is the most important Cham site in Vietnam. See page 212.

Wat Phu, Laos. The 'mountain temple' complex contains palaces built by Champasak royalty. See page 143.

Central and East Java. The lush green fertile plains of Java nurtured ancient sites, most notably at the great stupa of Borobudur. See page 319.

Pura Besaki, Bali. The most important temple in Bali has an impressive total of 30 public temples and hundreds of shrines. See page 328.

NIGHTLIFE

Ho Chi Minh City. Vietnam's largest city and river port, still often called Saigon, is a hive of activity day or night. The city has the best nightlife in Indochina. See page 217.

Nha Trang, Vietnam. An incomparable bay with shining white sand, Nha Trang has full tourist facilities and Vietnam's best beach nightlife scene. See page 213.

Ko Samui, Thailand. The largest island in the lovely Samui Archipelago is also the chief destination in

East-central Thailand. Samui stays up late! See page 68.

Bangkok, Thailand. Not only a selection of everything Thailand has to offer, but much of Asia as well. Bangkok is a megalopolis of restaurants, bars and clubs. See page 47.

Kuta-Legian-Seminyak, Bali, Indonesia. This village threesome remains one of the most popular beach resorts and nightspots on the island. See page 325.

Key-rings depicting Aung San Suu Kyi for sale at Yangon's Bogyoke market.

SPECTACULAR NATURE

Halong Bay, Vietnam. With 3,000 limestone island outcrops and a tranquil indigo sea, this is one of nature's great gifts to the world. See page 206.

Mount Kinabalu, Sabah. Climbers hiking up this revered, jagged mountain (reaching 4,093 metres / 13,428ft) are rewarded with fantastic scenery. See page 257.

Bukit Timah Nature Reserve, Singapore. A surprising chunk of primary rainforest remains in Singapore, complete with trails and a canopy walk. See page 291.

Komodo National Park, Indonesia. This large national park, spread over several islands, is home to the extraordinary Komodo dragon. See page 332.

Bunaken Marine Park, Sulawesi. With beautiful clear, deep warm water, this Indonesian marine park is a favourite for divers and naturalists. See page 335.

Banaue rice terraces, Philippines. These breathtaking terraced hillsides have achieved Unesco World Heritage status. See page 362.

St Paul's Subterranean River flows through Palawan in the Philippines.

BEACHES AND RESORTS

Krabi, Thailand. Many of the islands on the Krabi peninsula, such as Ko Phi Phi and Ko Lanta, have marvellous beaches. See page 66.

Langkawi, Malaysia. Duty-free shopping helps the island's economy, but most come for the perfect beaches. See page 255.

Kuta, Bali. Close to Bali's main airport, with a broad sandy beach, Kuta is a lively resort with every facility. See page 325.

Boracay, Philippines. Home to what is often voted 'the best beach in the world'. See page 369.

Vang Vieng, Laos. Amid startlingly beautiful natural terrain on the banks of the Nam Song, Vang Vieng offers swimming, kayaking and rafting. See page 133.

Cenang beach on Langkawi.

GREAT ARCHITECTURE

Burmese pagodas. Outstanding architectural gems in 'The Land of the Pagodas' can be seen in Yangon at Botataung and Sule, as well as at the famous Shwedagon. See page 94.

Wat Xieng Thong, Luang Prabang. The most elegant temple in Laos has a swooping roofline locals equate with chicken wings. See page 138.

Bayon, Angkor, Cambodia. This

12th-century temple, highly decorated with bas reliefs, is the most celebrated structure in Angkor after Angkor Wat. See page 170.

Imperial City, Hue, Vietnam. This haunting ensemble stands by the Perfume River, where you can take a boat to the royal tombs. See page 209.

Manila Cathedral, Philippines. Rebuilt after World War II bombing, this is the fifth church on the site, though its colonial Spanish origins remain steadfast. See page 355.

Petronas Towers, Kuala Lumpur. The world's tallest twin buildings were completed in 1994: walk the linking Skybridge, if you dare. See page 249

The Petronas Towers, Kuala Lumpur.

LOCAL CUISINE

Thailand. One of the world's great cuisines, which has influenced the whole region, but you may be surprised at the local variations that go from hot to cool. See page 38.

Myanmar. *Danpauk* or Burmese biriyani, is a curry dish often served at religious festivals. Chicken is cooked together with the local rice, *paw hsan hmwe*, which is highly regarded.

Cambodia. *Galangal* is a root similar to ginger but with less of a bite. Pounded into a paste, it is often found in Khmer cooking, and single slices are sometimes added to a dish to give a 'roasted' flavour. See page 401.

Vietnam. *Pho* is a ubiquitous soup, eaten at breakfast lunch, dinner, or as a late night snack. Steaming hot broth is poured over a bowl of rice noodles topped with chicken or beef, fresh herbs and onion. See page 407.

Malaysia. Peranakan (Straits Chinese) in origin, *laksa* is a coconut-based curry soup made with thick rice noodles, and may have tofu and shrimps. When noodles are made from yellow *mee*, it is known as *curry mee*. Assam *laksa* is made with fish. See page 416.

Singapore. Fusion rules in one of the world's great food cities: Chinese, Indian, Indonesian, Malay, and Western influences have made a great melting pot, celebrated in the annual Food Festival in July. See page 427.

Indonesia. Fried rice is *nasi goring*, sometimes with added tamarind and chilli spice that is typically served with eggs, chicken, prawns or sate (skewered beef or mutton). See page 433.

Philippines. Not heavily spiced, dishes typically mix sweet and salty tastes, as in *dinuguan* (pig's blood stew) served with *puto*, a sweet steamed rice cake. See page 441.

Pho, noodle soup, is a staple dish in Vietnam.

BEST MUSEUMS, GALLERIES AND MONUMENTS

National Museum, Bangkok. Housed in palatial buildings, the museum has one of the best collections in Asia. See page 48.

National Museum of Cambodia, Phnom Penh. The magnificent architecture of Cambodia's chief museum houses religious art and statuary from Angkor and other civilizations. See page 163.

Singapore Art Museum. This elegant building, originally built as a school, has the world's largest collection of contemporary Southeast Asian art. See page 288.

National Museum, Jakarta. Based on a Dutch colonial collection, this museum showcases an impressive array of artefacts from the distant past. See page 313.

Art museums of Ubud, Bali. The island's cultural capital, Ubud, has been an arts centre since the 1930s. Several renowned museums are located here, including Puri Lukisan See page 327.

Vigan Heritage Architecture district in the Philippines' Ilocos Sur.

Laksa, a Malaysian speciality.

BEST FOR FAMILIES

Waterfront, Vientiane, Laos. Take a stroll down beside the Mekong River, with cafes and stalls offering food, fruit shakes and beer. See page 131

Kuching waterfront, Borneo. A delightful kilometre-long stretch of recreational areas, gardens, walkways, stalls and restaurants by the Sarawak River in northwest Borneo. See page 258

Underground River, Palawan, Philippines. Deep in the jungle, visiting St Paul Subterranean National Park is an unforgettable experience. See page 370.

Vigan Heritage Village, Philippines. Philippine architecture uniquely fuses Spanish and Asian influences in this well-preserved, cobblestoned heritage village. See page 362.

Dalat, Vietnam. This mountain resort in south-central Vietnam has elegant architecture and is surrounded by lovely scenery and a wealth of activities. See page 214.

Neka Art Museum in Bali's Ubud.

Bangkok is the place to go for lively nightlife.

BEST MARKETS

Bogyoke Aung San market, Yangon, Myanmar. An atmospheric and animated city market, a great place to look for souvenirs. See page 97.

Phnom Penh markets, Cambodia. Cambodia's capital has a wonderful choice of markets, including the Art Deco Central Market. See page 138.

Night Market, Luang Prabang, Laos. This traditional evening market is the centrepiece of the town at night and one of the finest craft markets in Southeast Asia. See page 138.

Pasar Seni Art Market, Ubud, Bali. the large market offers superior crafts and souvenirs in Bali's cultural capital. See page 327.

Ben Thanh Market, Ho Chi Minh City. Vietnam's most famous market offers something of everything (everything being mostly tourist souvenirs) at the heart of the city. See page 221.

MONEY-SAVING TIPS

Budget airlines. There are numerous budget airlines, such as Jet Star Asia and Tiger Airways, operating out of Singapore, Bangkok and other regional hubs. Do your research, as using these can save you a small fortune. See page 376.

Taxis, tuk-tuks, cyclos etc. Don't get ripped off! Always agree a fare before you embark on your journey. See page 376.

Save on phone calls. If you are spending more than a few days in a country and need to make calls, either buy a SIM card for your phone locally, or pre-paid international phone cards that can be used in public phone boxes.

Bargaining. The art of haggling comes quickly to most people travelling around the region. It is most often called for when buying souvenirs in a market, but savvy travellers should also try their luck at hotels – simply asking for a reduced rate at more expensive hotels often works wonders. Off-season discounts can be worth investigating, too.

Outside a pottery workshop in Kyaukmyaung, Myanmar.

Crowding into a Jeepney, the symbol of the Philippines.

Shopping in Malaysia's Cameron Highlands.

Taman
Negara
National Park
Transfer by
Mini Van & Boat
* Boat Ticket Included
RM 65
Per Pa
Hill

Fresh bounty at Tan An Market in Can Tho.

SOUTHEAST ASIA

From the northern hills of Vietnam to the dragons of Komodo, frenetic Manila to laid-back Vientiane, the sands of Ko Samui to Balinese temples and the ruins of Angkor, Southeast Asia offers an unrivalled range of experiences and unforgettable sights.

A carved detail on Prambanan Temple in central Java.

Southeast Asia's complexity and diversity, as well as its natural beauty, has always made it intoxicating to travellers. The region has been a fixture on the backpacker circuit for as long as there have been backpackers – and even though many areas are well and truly 'discovered' these days, there are still enough remote, beautiful corners – notably in Laos, Cambodia, Vietnam, the Philippines and Myanmar – to satisfy the most adventurous itinerant. Those with less time on their hands jet in for two weeks in the sun at beach resorts in Thailand or Bali, while others come to see ancient landmarks such as Angkor and Borobudur, or fascinating, fast-changing cities like Hanoi or Bangkok.

Rival empires

Southeast Asia has always been on the edge; a luxuriant rim caught between Asia and the Pacific Ocean. This diverse collection of nations has historically been pulled between powerful forces. The region was a key battleground in World War II, and a decisive point of Cold War conflict during the Indochina wars from the 1950s to the 1970s. Today, the influence of the United States and Japan, and the growing clout of China, compete to shape the economic and political landscape.

Long ago, Southeast Asia played host to powerful civilisations that are little understood today. The Khmer kingdom that built Angkor in the 9th to 13th centuries expanded from its Cambodian homeland to cover large sections of Thailand, Laos, and Vietnam. Angkor's capital had a population in excess of one million and was home to sophisticated architecture and engineering technology. Further south on the island of Sumatra, Srivijaya was a maritime empire that controlled trade in the 7th century between China and Europe through the vital Straits of Malacca.

From the 16th century onwards, these rich lands became attractive to European merchants. Control of the hugely lucrative spice trade from Indonesia (the 'East Indies') was followed later by formal colonisation and profits from plantation crops and hardwoods from Myanmar to the Philippines. British, French, Portuguese, Spanish and Dutch empires grew to cover most of the region by the late 19th century, with Thailand alone remaining aloof. Japan's conquest of Southeast Asia in World War II (driven in part by the need for raw materials) brought this period to an abrupt end, with independence following for all in the years ahead.

The 'tiger' economies

Into the 21st century, Southeast Asia remains in delicate equilibrium between powerful forces. The United States and China are duelling key players in the region. Geographic proximity and the strong ties due to the large number of Chinese emigrants in many Southeast Asian countries have been a major factor in the region's economic development. There are still some areas of unrest, such as separatist movements in Mindanao (southern Philippines) and parts of Indonesia, tensions arising from Muslim fundamentalism and politics in Malaysia, and occasional riots and uprising in Thailand. However, the end of the Cold War, and the decreasing of political tensions in the region, has largely switched the focus to economics.

A Legong dance performance in Ubud.

Much of the world's industry uses Southeast Asia as an inexpensive manufacturing base for accessing both China's growing market and for producing goods. Whilst it is true that Southeast Asian nations have suffered under the recent global economic downturn, the impact has arguably not been as grave as the financial crisis that hit the region in the late 1990s. The region's tourism industry has been hit, too, as travellers in Europe and North America pinch pennies on their travel budgets and stay closer to home. On the other hand, the dynamism of Southeast Asia's so-called 'tiger economies' – which, led by Singapore, emerged so suddenly in the 1960s and '70s – is resilient, and early signs of returning economic growth and prosperity can be seen region-wide.

Disparities

Binding together a region of this size and disparity is a difficult, if not impossible, undertaking. It is home to hundreds of languages, people of every major religion, governments ranging from a freewheeling democracy to a recovering military dictatorship and various forms of monarchy, Marxism and political dynasties. An area this large is also bound to suffer vast inequalities of wealth. Singapore's per capita GDP is about US$52,000, while that of Laos is approximately four percent of that figure.

There remains no single voice for the region, although the Association of Southeast Asian Nations (ASEAN) has attempted to fill this role. ASEAN was formed in the 1960s at the height of the Cold War as a security alliance backed by the United States. The consensus-based nature of the organisation has traditionally earned it the reputation of being a toothless talk-shop and regional problems, such as human rights violations, have often been met with silence by ASEAN.

The spirituality of Southeast Asia is as diverse as other aspects of the region. It is home to the world's largest Muslim nation, Indonesia, as well as Asia's largest Christian country, the Philippines. The northern areas are predominantly Buddhist, their societies infused with Buddhist culture, the towns and cities home to golden temples that epitomise the exotic east.

Geography

The region can be divided into two distinct areas. 'Mainland' Southeast Asia includes Thailand, Laos, Myanmar, Cambodia and Vietnam, a region roughly corresponding to what was known as Indo-China. Insular Southeast Asia includes Malaysia, Singapore, and the island nations of Indonesia and the Philippines.

Southeast Asia's land mass covers about 4.5 million sq km (1.8 million sq miles), making it half the size of China and 18 times that of Great Britain. The region's combined population of 593 million people is just under half that of India's and almost twice that of the United States. Indonesia alone has more than 242 million people, including the largest Muslim population on earth. The metropolitan areas of Jakarta, Manila and Bangkok each have populations in excess of 20 million – by some estimates, these cities are respectively the world's 2nd-, 6th- and 28th-largest. Jakarta and Manila continue to grow rapidly.

The southern and eastern margins of Southeast Asia sit along the volcanically active 'ring of fire' – and have witnessed some of history's most dramatic eruptions. In 1883, a volcano disintegrated the Indonesian island of Krakatoa in one of the largest eruptions ever recorded. Volcanic flows engulfed ships passing up to 40km (25 miles) away, and, remarkably, the eruption could be heard in places some 4,500km (2,800 miles) distant. More recently, in 1991, Mount Pinatubo in the Philippines erupted and spewed 10 billion metric tonnes of magma into the atmosphere, causing a planet-wide layer of haze that lowered global temperatures by nearly one degree. The cataclysmic 2004 tsunami that killed hundreds of thousands in Sumatra and Thailand was a brutal reminder of the region's exposure to violent forces of nature. The weather also plays its part: each year, the Philippines, and to a lesser extent Vietnam, are battered by typhoons.

Around the region

Thailand is the best-known and most visited Southeast Asian nation amongst Westerners. While Thai beaches of interest have shifted over the decades – from Pattaya, to Phuket, to Samui – the architectural delights of Bangkok and Chiang Mai persist, as does the appeal of the scenery and hill-tribe cultures of the northwest. Thailand is not without its troubles however: political uprisings, flooding and crime against tourists get much attention in the press and are taking their toll on tourism in some areas.

Myanmar (**Burma**) is a magical country rapidly emerging from an appalling military dictatorship into a very bright future. Since human rights activist Aung San Suu Kyi was released from prison in 2010, conditions have improved immensely and tourism is developing quickly. To the north, *Monks collecting alms at Luang* Mandalay has chimed like music to the Western ear, ever since *Prabang, Laos.* Rudyard Kipling wrote of its magic. And if Yangon once seemed stalled in time, Bagan was and always will be frozen in time, its thousands of ancient pagodas peppering the expansive plain as testimonial to the great kings that rose and fell.

Laos and Cambodia, wedged in amongst powerful neighbours, are – with Myanmar – the region's poorest countries. The Lao capital, Vientiane, is indisputably Asia's most quiet and laid-back capital city, while the royal centre of Luang Prabang to the north is not only quiet, but adorned with glorious architecture. Both cities line the banks of the Mekong, one of the world's great rivers, which flows south into Cambodia and Vietnam. Cambodia's historical anchorage lies at the fabulous site of Angkor, representative of the great Khmer kingdom that long ruled the region. Its capital, Phnom Penh, also has a great deal to offer, while the southern beaches and islands are attracting more and more visitors.

Vietnam has the distinction of having been a divided country for much of its modern history, and best known in the West for the brutal war of the 1960s and 70s. Today, its people's entrepreneurial skills have pushed it to the forefront of economic growth in the region. Travellers to Hanoi, Vietnam's capital, or Ho Chi Minh City, the former Saigon, can't help but be impressed by the youthful vibrancy of the country. There are fascinating sights in abundance all over Vietnam – the ancient city of Hue and the beautiful towns of Hoi An and Dalat to name but three.

Southeast Asia is blessed with many perfect beaches, as here on Phu Quoc Island.

Like Myanmar, **Malaysia** was once part of the British Empire. Unlike Myanmar, Malaysia has turned itself into one of the region's most important economies. Graced with a blend of colonial, Islamic and ultramodern architecture, Kuala Lumpur keeps getting more prosperous – and more congested. Further north, Penang has an intoxicating mix of atmospheric Chinese alleys and white-sand beaches. Across the sea to the east on the island of Borneo, the Malaysian states of Sabah and Sarawak are synonymous with the exotic and adventurous. Wedged in between is **Brunei**, ruled by a sultan who is one of the world's wealthiest men. Back on the mainland, the southern tip of the Malaysian peninsula (and indeed of the entire Eurasian land-mass) is occupied by **Singapore**, the city-state governed like a corporation and perhaps the most efficient place on earth.

Indonesia is Southeast Asia's largest country both in size and popula-tion. Its vast capital, Jakarta, is on Java, one of the world's most densely populated islands. Some of the region's great ancient empires arose here, leaving behind incredible cultural sights, overlooked by a spine of vol-canic mountains. East of Java is the smaller island of Bali, increasingly developed, but still intriguing with its hybrid Hindu culture and history. The remainder of the country extends across thousands of islands large and small, with equatorial rainforests, volcanoes, unique wildlife and ultra-remote areas such as Papua – one of the world's last true frontiers.

Finally, the **Philippines** is the most unusual of Asian nations, with nearly five centuries of Spanish and American influence that has rendered it in some ways more reminiscent of Central America than the rest of Southeast Asia. In Manila, cathedrals rise to rival those of Europe, although elsewhere in the archipelago – notably in the north of Ilocos and the southern islands of the Visayas – these Western textures are less in evidence.

Planning your trip

Today, the region is largely at peace, and the booming economies have produced roads, bridges and border crossings that have opened it up to tourism as never before. The overland trip from Phnom Penh to Ho Chi Minh City used to be a hair-raising two-day journey over bone-jarring roads, through military checkpoints, and wallet-emptying border guards. Today, it is a smooth 5-hour ride in a comfortable air-conditioned bus.

But despite the growing ease of travel in Southeast Asia, the region has not developed to the point that it has lost its sense of adventure. What was true in the past still holds today: your neatly planned travel itinerary won't usually last more than a few days. It will melt in the boiling sun and sweat of a Bangkok sidewalk restaurant, or be used as a coaster in a Manila folk music bar, or be left on the beach in Malaysia. Southeast Asia goes its own way. And when you're in it, so do you.

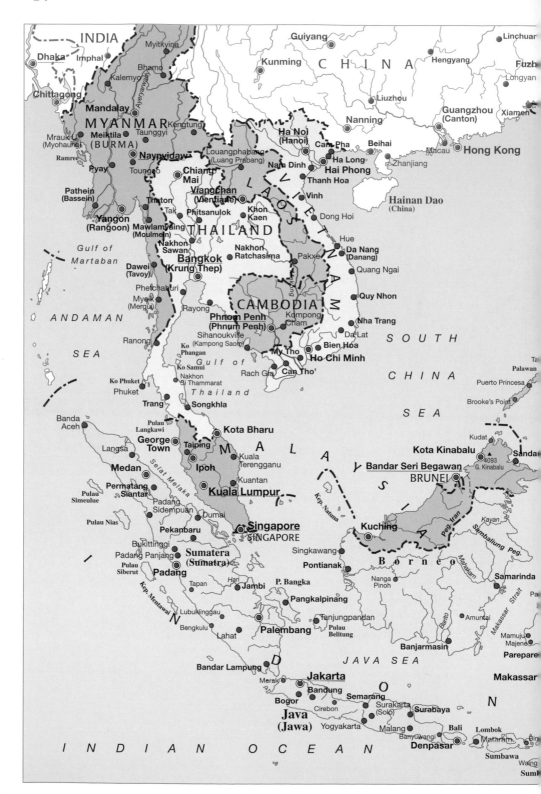

enzou

Okinawa

(Japan) shoto

Nansei

iwan

Io-Jima
(Japan)

Batan
Islands

Babuyan
Islands

Tangatan

P H I L I P P I N E

**N O R T H E R N
M A R I A N A
I S L A N D S**
(U S A)

ag

Ilagan

uio **Luzon**

S E A

Dilalongan

Jpan

PHILIPPINES

Manila

alamba

Guam
(USA)

Lucena Naga

atangas Legaspi

pan **Samar**

Masbate

P A C I F I C

oro Calbayog

Panay

Sagay Tacloban

Iloilo **Cebu**

egros Butuan

O C E A N

LU Pagadian **Mindanao**

A

Babelthuap

Zamboanga Davao

General
Santos

P A L A U

ELEBES

S E A

Manado

Gorontalo Ternate **Halmahera**

Pulau Waigeo

Pulau
Biak

Manokwari

Maluku (Moluccas)

Pulau
Misool

Pulau
Yapen

Jayapura

Kepulauan
Sula

SERAM SEA

Sulawesi

Seram **Papua
(Irian Jaya)**

New

PAPUA

Buru Ambon

Amamapare

A **Guinea**

NEW

GUINEA

Muna Buton

BANDA SEA

Kepulauan
Aru

E

S

ORES SEA Wetar

res

Pulau Yamdena

Pulau Dolak

**TIMOR
LESTE** Dili

Kupang **Timor**

**TIMOR
LESTE**

ARAFURA SEA

Torres Strait

Melville
Island **AUSTRALIA**

Wat Arun from the river, Bangkok.

THAILAND

**More than any other Southeast Asian country, Thailand
has long epitomised the region's unique qualities.**

*A guardian demon at the
Temple of the Emerald
Buddha in Bangkok.*

Thailand conjures up images of warm tropical seas,
cascading waterfalls and fiery chillies. The Thai
people have a graciousness and sense of fun rarely
found elsewhere. Tourist brochures don't call this the
Land of Smiles for nothing.

Thais have a strong sense of community and pride in
their country that underlies their ability to smile at the
vicissitudes of life. This natural warmth combines with
their country's many attractions – including some of the
world's most beautiful beaches, historic sites, wonderful
food, fabulous Buddhist architecture and art – to make the
kingdom irresistible to many. With so much wonder on
tap, tourism is inevitably a key component of the economy.

Thailand has a population approaching 70 million and
a land area twice that of England. The capital, Bangkok,
bears little relation to the rest of the country; it is a vast,
energised city with a vibe of its own.

Thailand is divided into four regions: the Central
Plains (including Bangkok), and the North, Northeast
and South. From the country's 2,600km (1,600 mile)
of coastline, elevations rise to a peak of 2,600 metres
(8,500ft) in the North. The North is a region of verdant
hills is clad in teak forests and valleys carpeted in bright
green padi fields and orchards of fruit trees. The northeast, or Isaan, has one of the strongest regional identities
and is dominated by the dry Khorat Plateau, where farmers cultivate
rice, tapioca, jute and other cash crops.

*A tuk-tuk negotiates the
Bangkok traffic.*

The Chao Phraya River flows through the Central Plains, carrying
produce and people south to Bangkok and flooding the rice fields during the monsoon season. The South runs down a long, narrow arm of
land leading to Malaysia. Seductive tropical beaches extend along the
Gulf of Thailand (east) and Andaman Sea (west) coasts and fringe the
numerous islands.

With an aged king and continuous political tensions, Thailand is
approaching a crossroads. Change is certain, but with the nation's bright
past and present bursting with potential, Thailand remains a deservedly
popular tourism destination.

DECISIVE DATES

Pre-Thai civilisation

3600–250 BC
Ban Chiang bronze culture flourishes in northeastern Thailand.

c.250 BC
Suvannabhumi trading with India.

4th–8th centuries AD
Influence of Mon and Khmer empires spreads into Thailand.

9th–13th centuries
Khmer Empire founded at Angkor.

Sukhothai era

1238
Khmer Empire wanes. Kingdom of Sukhothai founded.

1281
Chiang Saen kingdom founded in north.

1296
Lanna Kingdom founded at Chiang Mai.

1280–1318
Reign of Ramkamhaeng in Sukhothai. This 'Golden Age' sees the first attempts to unify the Thai people and a flourishing of the arts.

1438
Sukhothai is virtually deserted; power shifts to Ayutthaya.

Kingdom of Ayutthaya

1350
City of Ayutthaya founded by Phya U-Thong, who proclaims himself Ramathibodi I.

1369
Ramesuan becomes king and later captures Chiang Mai and Angkor in Cambodia.

1569
Burmese capture and loot Ayutthaya.

1590
Naresuan becomes king, throws off Burmese suzerainty. Ayutthaya expands rapidly.

1656–88
Reign of King Narai. British influence expands. Reputation of Ayutthaya as a magnificent city spreads.

1767
Burmese King Alaungpaya captures and sacks Ayutthaya. Seven months later General Phya Tak Sin expels the Burmese occupiers. He moves the capital to Thonburi, near Bangkok.Beginning of the Chakri dynasty.

1767
Phya Taksin crowned as King Taksin.

1779
Generals Chao Phya Chakri and his brother Chao Phya Sarasin conquer Chiang Mai and expel the Burmese.

1782
The erratic Taksin is deposed and executed. Chao Phya Chakri ascends to the throne, founding the Chakri dynasty and later assumes the name Rama I. Capital is moved to Bangkok.

1868
Chulalongkorn (Rama V) reigns for the next four decades. Chulalongkorn ends the custom of prostration in royal presence, abolishes slavery, and modernises infrastructure, schools, military and government.

Siamese King Naresuan fighting the Burmese crown prince Mingyi Swa at the battle of Yuthahatthi in January 1593.

King Chulalongkorn, or Rama V.

End of the absolute monarchy

1932
A coup d'état ends the absolute monarchy and ushers in a constitutional monarchy.

1939
The country's name changes from Siam to Thailand, 'Land of the Free'. King Ananda (Rama VIII) ascends to the throne.

1942
Japan invades Thailand with the acquiescence of the military government, but a spirited if small resistance movement thrives.

1946
A mysterious gunshot kills King Ananda; Bhumibol Adulyadej (Rama IX) ascends to the throne.

1973–91
Bloody clashes between army and demonstrating students bring down the military government. Various military-backed and civilian governments come and go for almost 20 years.

1991
Another clash between military and civilians results in the leaders of both factions kneeling in contrition before the king. Civilian politicians gain power.

2001
Billionaire tycoon Thaksin Shinawatra and his Thai Rak Thai party win the election.

2004
The Boxing Day tsunami claims 8,000 lives along Thailand's Andaman coastline, devastating several resorts around Phuket.

2006
King Bhumibol Adulyadej celebrates 60 years on the throne, the world's longest-reigning monarch. The Royal Thai Army stages a bloodless coup, deposing Thaksin.

2008
Thaksin goes into exile while facing corruption charges. Anti-Thaksin demonstrators shut Bangkok's Suvarnabhumi Airport. Two pro-Thaksin Prime Ministers are forced to resign.

2009
Red Shirt protests disrupt the ASEAN Summit, causing several heads of state to be airlifted to safety; Songkran riots erupt in Bangkok; Yellow Shirt leader Sondhi Limthongkul is shot.

2010
Courts find Thaksin guilty of abuse of power. Thousands of Red Shirt demonstrators occupy parts of Bangkok. Eighty-five people are killed and nearly 1,500 injured in clashes with the army.

2011
The Thaksin proxy Pheu Thai Party wins a landslide election. His sister Yingluck becomes Thailand's first female prime minister.

2012
Police stop protest of 10,000 in Bangkok calling for overthrow of Prime Minister Yingluck Shinawatra.

2013
The Government and southern Muslim separatists sign first-ever peace talks deal.

Around 20,000 Red Shirt demonstrators attend a rally in Bangkok in 2013.

Traditional Thai dress.

PEOPLE AND CULTURE

Warm-hearted smiles, a pleasant disposition and a sense of calm: these are the qualities that are readily found in the Thai people. But Thais can also be fiercely patriotic – it is illegal, for example, to criticise the Thai monarchy.

One of the first things that visitors to Thailand notice is the smiles, warmth and friendliness of local people. There is always amiable concern and an openness seldom found elsewhere. The standard greeting is *pai nai*, or "Where are you going?" Thais aren't really worried about your destination; it's just their way of saying "How are you?"

One of the guiding precepts of Thai life is *sanuk*, which means fun. The quantity and quality of *sanuk* in both work and play will often determine whether something is worth pursuing. Almost as important is the concept of *sabai*, best translated as 'contented'. Thais consider that the ideal life should be a mix of *sanuk* and *sabai*. The antithesis of *sanuk* is *seriat* – from the English word 'serious'. Underpinning this light-hearted pursuit of happiness are the Buddhist values of tolerance and acceptance.

The Thai jigsaw

Thailand has a population of over 64 million, more than 90 percent of whom are Theravada Buddhists (see page 87). Muslims make up around six percent of the population and are mostly concentrated in the southern regions. Around 14 percent of the population are descendants of Chinese immigrants who relocated from China during the 19th and first half of the 20th century. The Chinese have assimilated remarkably well into Thai society.

Each region has its own language variant, cultural traits and distinctive cuisine. The central Thai dialect is the language spoken by educated Thais throughout the country. In the hills of the North, people speak a Thai variant called *kham meuang* and share certain cultural and culinary traits with neighbouring

Thai boxing, or Muay Thai.

Burma. People in the Northeast speak Isaan (also spelled Isan or E-san), a language closely related to Lao, and eat their meals with sticky rice. The Northeast is also Thailand's poorest region; many people from this region are seasonal migrants.

The South is a more prosperous region, its economy driven by tourism along its lengthy coastlines, which also support fishing and fruit orchards. Aside from a small group of Malay-speaking Muslims, most people in this region speak a southern dialect of Thai. In the three southernmost provinces of Yala, Pattani and Narathiwat, civil unrest between Muslims and the Thai government has been escalating for the past few years.

A revered monarch

At the heart of Thai society is the kingdom's reverence for their monarch, His Majesty King Bhumibol Adulyadej (see page 31). The national anthem is played before cinema screenings and the audience stands as a mark of respect. Even when the anthem is played at 8am and 6pm on radio and TV each day, many Thais also stand still as a mark of respect. At offices, shops and homes throughout the land, the king's portrait is prominently portrayed.

When the king celebrated 60 years on the throne in 2006, well-wishers wearing yellow scene is confined mainly to Bangkok and is frequently depicted in the society pages of the city's newspapers and magazines, such as *Thailand Tatler*, with immaculately attired women sporting large, expensive jewels and big hair.

Most Thai people make up the agrarian segment who live in villages and farm the land. Village life has changed radically over the past few decades as poverty has forced many to find work in the big cities as taxi drivers, construction workers – and as prostitutes.

Gender inequality is deeply embedded into Thai society, and women are generally expected

The country is known for its fabulous street food.

shirts (the colour of Monday, the day he was born) jammed the roads leading to the Royal Plaza. Criticism of the king and royal family is extremely rare and *lése majesté* laws prevent public critique of the king.

Hi-So and Lo-So

Thai society is markedly hierarchical, with an individual's roles and duties defined by his or her social status. Thai language uses personal pronouns which indicate whether the speaker is addressing a younger or elder person, or a person of lower or higher status. The top end of society is known as 'Hi-So' (from the English phrase 'high society'), and comprises Thai nobility and wealthy Sino-Thai families. The Hi-So

to be socially submissive to Thai men. A high proportion of Thai men are *chao choo*, or adulterers. If a women is unfaithful, it is ample grounds for divorce, but it is not, however, when a man cheats on his wife. On the other hand, many women hold the family purse-strings and today are often prominent in tourism, real estate and advertising.

Sexual attitudes

Thailand has a reputation as a sexual playground for foreign visitors (see page 382), but the Thais themselves remain the industry's main clients. Outside of a few areas in Bangkok, such as Patpong and Nana Plaza, or Pattaya's notorious sex scene, prostitution in

The practice of Thai men dressing as women began around 40 years ago. Today, lady boys, known pejoratively as katoey, are not only found in bars – many have normal jobs (some are TV presenters and models).

Thailand is similar to elsewhere in the world: brothels exist on the margins of almost every medium-sized town.

Within society as a whole, Thais dress conservatively and public displays of affection are rare. Homosexuality is tolerated, as are transvestites and transsexuals (or lady boys).

Socialising the Thai way

The Thai love of fun, or *sanuk*, infuses all social gatherings. Thais enjoy group activities and it is always a case of the more the merrier. Surnames are rarely used and even relative strangers will refer to each other by their nicknames, or *cheu len*. These are most often one-syllable monikers based on animals like Moo (pig), Noo (mouse), or Poo (crab) or anglicised adaptations such as X, Boy or Benz.

Another cultural trait is *kraeng jai*, which denotes an unwillingness to impose on other people. This often means that emotions such as anger or displeasure are hidden away, and conflict avoided at all cost. Thais do not like saying 'no' too directly for fear of causing offence.

Connected to this is the idea of *jai yen*, or 'cool heart'. To lose your temper or to raise your voice in public is seen as a severe loss of face. Those who lose their cool are considered to be *jai ron*, or 'hot-hearted'.

Organised crime and corruption

Beneath the placid and happy-go-lucky surface of Thai society lies a darker underbelly. Organised crime is prevalent throughout the country as powerful mafia clans thrive on illegal gambling, drugs and prostitution. Known as *jao phor*, the godfathers often operate legal businesses and may even participate in provincial politics.

Corruption is as rife in politics as it is in day-to-day interactions on the street. Government and big businesses have nepotistic values; construction contracts, for instance, will often be offered to favoured companies. At the other

end of the spectrum, a policeman will nearly always forget about a traffic offence in return for a 200-baht bribe.

Adapting to new influences

Historically, Thailand has always welcomed outside influences, yet despite long-standing trading connections with the West, it remains the only nation in Southeast Asia to have avoided colonisation by a European power. Thais are happy to embrace some foreign ways but remain deeply loyal to their own culture and beliefs. Today, this mentality can

Thailand has a venerable tradition of woodcarving.

THAI-STYLE GREETING

Thais greet each other by raising and clasping their hands together in a prayer-like gesture called the *wai*. While the *wai* may look like a simple movement, it is loaded with social nuances. The hands must be held at certain levels between the chest and the forehead, depending on the social standing of each person. When greeting a person of higher rank, the hands must be raised higher to show respect. In response to a child's greeting, an adult may keep their hands at chest level. Modern adaptations include an informal one-handed *wai*, used among friends – and no one bats an eye when a mobile phone is held in the other hand.

be seen all over the country, from the presence of international chain-stores in the cities, to the idea that beauty is often personified by the *luk kreung* – literally 'half child' – mixed-race children who have one Thai and one Caucasian parent.

Hill tribes

Thailand's hill tribes (*chao khao* – 'mountain people') are a major draw for tourists heading to the northern hill country, but make up less than two percent of the population. Thailand is home to at least 20 hill tribes, which belong

An Akha man plays a wooden flute.

to six principal groups: Karen, Hmong, Lahu, Mien, Akha and Lisu. They mainly originate from Tibet, Burma, Laos and China.

Karen

With a population of over 320,000, the Karen are the largest hill tribe in Thailand. They comprise two sub-groups, the Sgaw and Pwo, whose dialects are not mutually intelligible. The Karen have been settling in Thailand since the 18th century and they are still trickling in, fleeing human-rights abuses in military-ruled Myanmar (Burma). In Myanmar there are around 6 million Karen, and a Karen army has been fighting for independence from Myanmar for over 50 years. The Karen were

early converts to Christianity when Burma was a British colony. But whether professing Christian, Buddhist or animist beliefs, the Karen place a great emphasis on monogamy and trace their ancestry on the maternal side of the family.

Hmong

Numbering about 120,000, the Hmong are the second-largest hill tribe in Thailand. The majority immigrated in the 1950s and 1960s, fleeing the civil war in Laos. Hmong are renowned for their independent spirit and relations with Thai authorities have often been uneasy. Opium use is common and polygamy is permitted. The White Hmong and Blue Hmong can be identified by their dialects and clothing. Blue Hmong women wear indigo pleated skirts and tie their hair up in huge buns, while White Hmong women wear white hemp skirts and black turbans.

Lahu

Some of the 73,000 Lahu in Thailand are Christian, but they are also animists and have a long history of messianic leaders who are believed to possess supernatural powers. The traditional dress of the four groups – Red Lahu, Black Lahu, Yellow Lahu and Lahu Sheleh – are all slightly different, but red and black jackets are common. Lahu are skilled makers of baskets and bags. The Lahu are experts at catching wild pigs, deer, snakes and birds with their rifles and crossbows.

Mien

Like the Hmong, most Mien (also known as Yao) probably came to Thailand from Laos, but there are large numbers in Burma, Vietnam and China's Yunnan Province. Many Chinese elements, such as ancestor worship and Taoism, are evident in their animist religious beliefs. Though many of Thailand's 40,000 Mien have taken to the Thai dress of T-shirts and sarongs or jeans, women traditionally wear black jackets with red fur-like collars and large blue or black turbans. They also create dense, intricate embroideries on bags and clothing.

Akha

Probably the poorest and shyest of the hill tribes, the 48,000 Akha have been the most resistant to assimilation. Yet the Akha are the tribe most tourists want to see, drawn by the ornate headdress of silver discs, coins, beads and feathers that Akha women wear. Unlike other tribal women who save their finery for ceremonies, Akha women wear their headdress even while tending the fields. Animist beliefs are mixed with ancestor worship and the Akha can trace their ancestry back 20 generations.

Lisu

The 28,000 Lisu in Thailand are easily identified by their penchant for bright colours. Women wear long green or blue cotton dresses

have immigrated to Thailand in recent times to escape the upheavals in Burma. The Shan may have been the first Tai inhabitants of northern Thailand in the 9th or 10th century.

The **Kayan** (also known as Padaung) are a Karennic people residing in Burma. Kayan women are famous for the heavy brass neck rings they wear; these typically weigh 5kg (11lbs) and make their necks appear elongated. Though the practice had almost died out in Burma, a number of Padaung women there, forced by grinding poverty to chase the tourist dollar, have since donned the coils.

The unmarried women of the Red Karen tribe wear white.

with striped yokes. Men wear baggy loose pants of the same colours. Animist beliefs are combined with ancestor worship. The Lisu are good silversmiths and make jewellery for the Akha and Lahu – and are regarded as sharp businesspeople.

Other minorities

Two other groups deserve mention, as their villages are frequent stops on trekking tours, though strictly speaking they are not Thai hill tribes. The **Shan** are very similar to the Thais with their settled communities, rice-growing practices and Theravada Buddhism beliefs. They are an ethnic Tai group and their language is close to the northern Thai dialect. Many Shan

Threats to hill tribes

Thailand's hill tribe cultures are threatened by land shortages, resettlement, lack of land rights and citizenship, illiteracy and poor medical care. Living in villages at higher elevations, most practise slash-and-burn agriculture, and traditionally grow opium, discouraged by the Thai authorities: some of the crop substitution programmes sponsored by the government, the UN and foreign governments have been very successful. The intention is that the villagers will be dissuaded from growing opium if they can make a living from more profitable crops, such as tea, coffee or fruit. Many have changed their ways, but others have resisted because of the capital investment involved.

THAILAND'S CUISINE

It can be spicy, it can be sweet, it can be almost anything you want. There is nothing bland about Thai cuisine, which most likely explains its universal appeal.

Thai cuisine is world-famous for its inventive mix of pungent, robust and delicate flavours. From seafood markets to floating restaurants to hawker stalls – fantastic food can be found pretty much anywhere around the country and prices are very low. There is a huge variety on offer, and while there are very spicy regional dishes – certain southern Thai curries are notable – not all Thai food is laden with chillies.

A traditional Thai meal will include at least one spicy dish, a few that are less hot, and some that are comparatively bland, flavoured with only garlic or herbs. Common ingredients include *nam plaa* (fish sauce), soy sauce, oyster sauce, lime, tamarind juice, lemongrass, basil, garlic, ginger and coconut cream. Combinations of these produce flavours that are fresh and strong, but not always spicy.

Spicy and hot dishes

Kaeng means curry. This group includes the spiciest of Thai dishes and forms the core of Thai cooking. Thailand's famous green curry, *kaeng khiaw waan*, employs a hand-ground, cumin-based curry paste braised with coconut milk and chunks of meat (usually chicken or beef) and tiny pea-sized eggplants. *Kaeng phet* is a hotter red version popular with beef or pork. A close relative is *kaeng phanaeng*, a 'dry' curry with peanuts added for a creamier texture. Yellow with turmeric, *kaeng karee* is a milder Indian-style curry typically made with chicken and potatoes. Southern-style curries include heavily spiced *kaeng masaman* (peanuts, potatoes and either chicken or beef) and the very pungent fish-based *kaeng leuang. Kaeng som*, or 'sour curry', consists of a chilli-based soup laced with plenty of tamarind juice and

A fragrant massaman curry.

A surprise to some visitors is that most Thais use a spoon and fork, not the chopsticks regularly found in Thai restaurants located in Europe and North America.

kapi (shrimp paste), along with pieces of either fish or shrimp.

Among other fiery favourites is *tom yam kung*, a lemongrass-scented soup teeming with shrimp. *Po taek* ('the fisherman's net bursts') is a cousin of *tom yam kung*, containing squid, mussels, crab and fish, and redolent with fresh Thai basil. *Yam* is a hot and spicy salad combining meat or seafood and vegetables. Popular throughout Thailand, it is one of the hottest dishes available.

If you have overdone the spice, try the cucumbers that come as a free side salad to most meals – they will help to dampen the fire.

Mild curries

Tom khaa kai, a thick coconut-milk soup of chicken pieces with lemongrass and galangal (a spicy and fragrant root in the ginger family) is milder than the average Thai dish. *Plaa-meuk thawt kratiam phrik thai* is squid stir-fried with garlic and black pepper. Sub-

in Thai restaurants abroad. Northern cuisine is the mildest of Thai food.

Northerners generally eat *khao nio* (sticky rice), kneading it into a ball to dip into sauces and curries such as the Burmese-inspired *kaeng hanglay*, a sweet-and-tamarind-sour pork dish. The noodle dish called *khao soi* is also found in Myanmar, but it is possibly of Chinese origin. Usually made with chicken, it has fresh egg noodles swimming in a mild coconut curry, with crispy noodles sprinkled on top.

Other northern Thai specialities include sausages, such as the spicy pork sai oua

Choosing skewers of street food in northeast Thailand.

stitute *muu* (pork) for *plaa-meuk* (squid) if you prefer. Another milder dish is *kaeng juet*, a non-spicy clear broth filled with glass noodles, minced pork, tofu and Chinese lettuce. *Neua phat nam-man hawy* is beef stir-fried in oyster sauce and garnished with chopped onion and green vegetables.

Regional distinctions

Each of Thailand's four regions has its own distinctive cuisine. Northern and northeastern (Isaan) dishes are closely related to Lao cooking, and are generally eaten with sticky rice. Meanwhile, southern Thai food is flavoured with the tastes of Malaysian cooking. Central cuisine corresponds broadly to the food found

DINING ETIQUETTE

At the start of the meal, heap some rice onto a plate and then take a spoonful or two of curry. It is considered polite to take only one spoonful at a time, consuming it before ladling another dish onto the rice. Thais eat with the spoon in their right hand and fork in their left, the fork pushing the food onto the spoon. Chopsticks are only for noodle dishes. For soupy noodle dishes, use the chopsticks to pile noodles onto the spoon. Thais take their time over meals, talking and making an entire evening of the affair. Since dishes are typically shared by all, take several friends so that you can order and sample more dishes.

(roasted over a coconut husk fire to impart aroma and flavour) and *naem* (fermented raw pork and pork skin seasoned with garlic and chilli). *Laab* is a popular salad dish of minced pork, chicken, beef or fish served with mint leaves and raw vegetables to reduce the heat of the spices. It is also commonly served in the Northeast.

The food of the **northeastern** (Isaan) region is generally simple peasant fare, usually spicy, and eaten with mounds of sticky rice kept warm in bamboo baskets. Spicy dishes include the ever-popular *som tam* (shredded green papaya, garlic, chillies, lime juice, and variations of tomatoes, dried shrimp, preserved crab and fermented fish) and a version of *laab* sausage, which is spicier and sourer than its northern counterpart.

> *When eating noodle soup, there will be a collection of four small plastic bowls nearby, for seasoning. These represent the basic flavours of Thai food: sweet, sour, salty and spicy.*

Frying bananas to create a typical Thai dessert.

THAI FOOD FOR SWEET-TOOTHS

In Thailand, desserts and sweets *(khanom)* come in a bewildering variety; from custards, cakes and ice creams to an entire category based upon egg yolks cooked in flower-scented syrups. Bananas and coconuts make an appearance in just about every single dessert.

Anyone walking through a Bangkok market is bound to come across a sweets vendor selling anything from candied fruits to mega-calorie custards made from coconut cream, eggs and palm sugar, generally sold in the form of three-inch squares wrapped in banana leaves. Try sampling *sangkhya maphrao awn*, a custard made from coconut cream, palm sugar and eggs, or *khao laam*, a glutinous rice mixed with coconut cream, sugar and either black beans or other goodies. *Kluay tort* uses bananas sliced lengthwise, dipped in a coconut-and-rice flour batter and then deep-fried until crisp. Many of these sweets are amazingly inventive. You may finish off a rich pudding, for example, before realising that its tantalising flavour came from crisp-fried onions. Perennial favourites include *katih*, a rich and heavenly coconut ice cream and the unsurpassed mango with sticky rice.

Thailand has all manner of fruits eaten as desserts. As well as the ubiquitous banana, there are pineapples, watermelons and papayas, plus the less-familiar rambutans, mangosteens and stinky durians.

But perhaps the most popular Isaan food, *gai yang*, is not spicy at all. This is chicken grilled in an aromatic marinade of peppercorns, garlic, fish sauce, coriander and palm sugar, then chopped into bite-sized pieces and served with both spicy and sweet dipping sauces.

Central cuisine, influenced by the royal palaces, includes many of the dishes made famous at Thai restaurants abroad. It is notable for the use of coconut milk and garnishes such as grapes, which mellow the chilli heat of the fiery dishes and add a tinge of sweetness. Trademark dishes include *tom kha gai* (a soup

A gourmet take on sticky rice and mango.

of chicken, coconut milk and galangal) the celebrated *tom yum goong* (hot and sour shrimp soup) and *kaeng khio waan* (green curry with chicken or beef, Thai basil leaves and pea-sized aubergines). Another influence on the regional cuisine is the large Chinese presence; stir-fries and noodle dishes are commonplace.

Southern cuisine – notable for some of Thailand's most fiery dishes – also has gentler specialities such as *khao yam*, a mild salad of rice, vegetables, pounded dried fish and a southern fish sauce called *budu*. Slightly spicier is *phad sataw*, a stir-fry usually of pork or shrimp, and *sataw*, a large lima bean look-alike with a strong flavour and aroma. *Khao moke gai* is delicious roasted chicken with turmeric-seasoned

yellow tinted rice, like an Indian-style biryani, often sprinkled with crispy fried onions.

Spicy southern dishes include *kaeng tai plaa*. Fishermen who needed food that would last for days out at sea are said to have created this dish by blending the fermented stomachs of fish with chillies, bamboo shoots, vegetables and an intensely hot sauce. An even hotter dish is *kaeng leuang* (yellow curry), a variant of the central Thai *kaeng som* curry, with fish, green papaya and bamboo shoots or palm hearts.

Vegetarian

Despite most Thais being Buddhist, (and so theoretically non-meat eaters), vegetarians can find their options are limited. Most restaurants in tourist areas will cater to their needs, but elsewhere menus tend to be more carnivore-friendly. Among the best veggie dishes are *pad thai*, (tasty fried noodles), *kaeng jood* tao huu (tofu soup) or *pad woon sen* (stir-fried clear noodles). Vegans should ask for their food to be cooked without fish or oyster sauce, things which are usually added as a matter of course. It is also possible to simply order normal dishes minus the meat.

Hawker centres

Much like street food vendors, Thailand's hawker centres, or food courts, sell a wide range of delicious, authentic and inexpensive local dishes for dining in or take-away. They may be found in shopping centres or stand-alone centres in busy areas of town.

Drink

Thais are big beer and whisky drinkers. Locally-made spirits such as *Sang Som* and Mekong are among the cheapest and most popular. Western whiskies, such as *Johnnie Walker* and *100 Pipers*, are also easy to find. When served, the whisky is heavily watered down with ice and soda water, and omnipresent hostesses ensure glasses are always filled to the brim. Most restaurants allow you to bring your own bottle of whisky. *Tiger*, *Singha*, *Leo*, Chang and Heineken are the most common beers, and are nearly always served with ice to keep them cool.

Some vineyards produce wine of varying quality, but it is treated as a luxury item and so comes with a hefty price tag. Upmarket restaurants catering to foreign customers usually have wine lists.

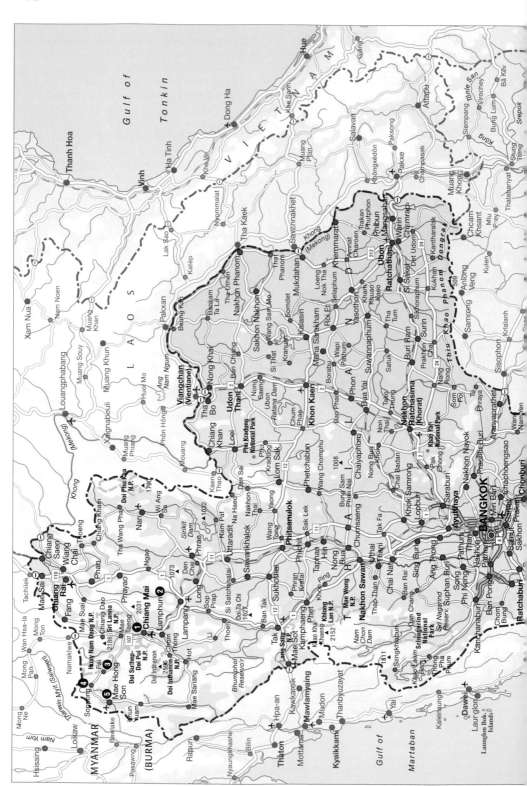

Thailand

100 miles
100 km

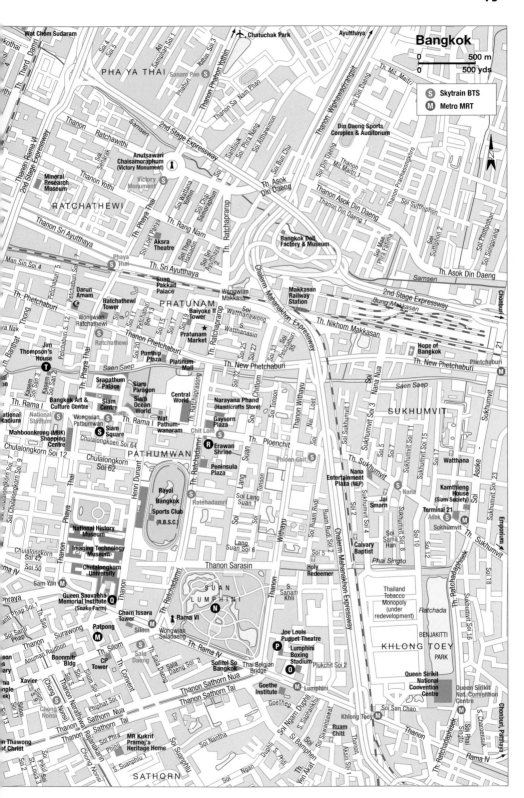

Bangkok

0 — 500 m
0 — 500 yds

Ⓢ Skytrain BTS
Ⓜ Metro MRT

Wat Chom Sudaram
Wat Chom Sudaram
Chatuchak Park
Ayutthaya

PHA YA THAI
Sanam Pao

Din Daeng Sports
Complex & Auditorium

Mineral
Research
Museum

Anutsawari
Chaisamoraphum
(Victory Monument)

Victory
Monument

2nd Stage Expressway

RATCHATHEWI

Thanon Sri Ayutthaya

Th. Asok
Din Daeng

Thanon Asok Din Daeng

Thanon Din Daeng

Th. Asok Din Daeng

2nd Stage Expressway

Aksra
Theatre

Phaya
Thai

Th. Sri Ayutthaya

Bangkok Doll
Factory & Museum

Makkasan
Railway
Station

Suan
Pakkad
Palace

Wongwian
Makkasan

Bung Makkasan

Th. Nikhom Makkasan

Ratchathewi
Tower

PRATUNAM

Baiyoke II
Tower

Pratunam
Market

Wongwian
Ratchathewi

Ratchathewi

Thanon Phetchaburi

Hope of
Bangkok

Th. New Phetchaburi

Phetchaburi

Jim
Thompson's
House

Panthip
Plaza

Platinum
Mall

Th. New Phetchaburi

Saen Saep

SUKHUMVIT

Srapathum
Palace

Siam
Paragon

Siam
Centre

Siam
Ocean
World

Central
World

Narayana Phand
(Handicrafts Store)

Bangkok Art &
Culture Centre

National
Stadium

Wongwian
Pathumwan

Siam
Square

Wat
Pathum-
wanaram

Gaysorn
Plaza

Chit Lom

Watthana

Mahboonkrong (MBK)
Shopping
Centre

Th. Rama I

Chulalongkoen Soi 64

PATHUMWAN

Erawan
Shrine

Th. Ploenchit

Phloen Chit

Nana
Entertainment
Plaza (NEP)

Nana

Kamthieng
House
(Siam Society)

Peninsula
Plaza

Jai
Smarn

Terminal 21

Asok

Sukhumvit

National History
Museum

Royal
Bangkok
Sports Club
(R.B.S.C.)

Ratchadamri

Imaging Technology
Museum

Chulalongkorn
University

Calvary
Baptist

Queen Saovabha
Memorial Institute
(Snake Farm)

SUAN
LUMPHINI

Holy
Redeemer

Thailand
Tobacco
Monopoly
(under
redevelopment)

Ratchada

BENJAKITTI

KHLONG TOEY
PARK

Charn Issara
Tower

Rama VI

Patpong

Thanon Sarasin

Joe Louis
Puppet Theatre

Lumphini
Boxing
Stadium

Wongwian
Saladaeng

Th. Rama IV

Sala
Daeng

Sofitel So
Bangkok

Thai Belgian
Bridge

Queen Sirikit
National
Convention
Centre

Queen Sirikit
Nat. Convention
Centre

Boonmitr
Bldg

CP
Tower

Th. Silom

Goethe
Institute

Lumphini

Xavier

Chong
Nonsi

Thanon Sathorn Nua

Thanon Sathorn Tai

Khlong Toey

Ruam
Chitt

MR Kukrit
Pramoj's
Heritage Home

SATHORN

Rama IV

BANGKOK

This is one of the most confounding, challenging, and yet rewarding cities in the world. Amidst its traffic-clogged roads and towering buildings are some of the most exquisite historical edifices anywhere.

At first glance, this city of 10 million people seems a bewildering blend of new and old, exotic and commonplace, all merged into one metropolitan melange sprawling for mile after mile on either side of the Chao Phraya River. If Bangkok seems to lack order, it is because it has never had any, save for the royal core of the city where the kings built their palaces and royal temples. Although the city is around 400 years old, it only became the nation's capital in 1782, when the current royal dynasty was established.

The long and winding Chao Phraya River is the city's anchor. Bangkok's founding king dug a canal between two of the river's bends and sliced off a parcel of land into an artificial island called **Rattanakosin**. With glittering highlights including the Grand Palace and Wat Phra Kaew, it is an essential part of any city tour.

Southeast (downriver) from Rattanakosin are the enclaves where foreigners originally settled – **Chinatown**, **Little India** (or Pahurat), and **Thanon Silom**, where the European riverfront community resided. Today, Silom, together with **Thanon Sathorn** and **Thanon Sukhumvit** further east, have become important business and commercial centres. To the north of Rattanakosin is **Dusit**, centred on the wide boulevard of

Khao San Road is backpacker central.

Thanon Ratchadamnoen and one of the oldest parts of Bangkok.

Across on the opposite bank of the Chao Phraya is **Thonburi**, with canals still threading through colourful neighbourhoods.

Royal Bangkok

The southern side of Thanon Na Phra Lan is lined by the white crenulated walls of **Wat Phra Kaew** and the **Grand Palace** Ⓐ complex (www.palaces.thai.net; daily 8.30am–4.30pm, tickets sold until 3.30pm; charge),

Main Attractions
Riverboat Trips
Grand Palace / Wat Phra Kaew
Wat Arun
National Museum
Wat Suthat
Chinatown
Erawan Shrine
Siam Square

A glass mosaic on the wall of Wat Phra Kaew.

Chutachak market.

Bangkok's most famous sight. The only entrance and exit to the complex is in the middle. On the right are the offices of the Royal Household, to the left is the ticket booth.

The first stop within the palace grounds is **Wat Phra Kaew** (Temple of the Emerald Buddha), the royal chapel of the Grand Palace. Passing though the gate, you will confront 6-metre (20ft) -tall demon statues inspired by the *Ramakien*, the Thai version of the Indian epic *Ramayana*. You must walk the glittering length of the *bot* (ordination chapel) to reach its entrance. In front are scattered Chinese-style statues, which function as stand-ins for incense offerings to the Emerald Buddha inside. The 75cm (30-inch) -tall jadeite statue is perched high on an altar, clothed according to the season and enclosed in a glass case, and shielded by a towering nine-tiered umbrella.

Visitors must be dressed smartly – no shorts, short skirts or revealing tops, open-toed sandals or flip-flops. Suitable clothing may be borrowed from an office near the Gate of Victory.

Wat Arun

Directly opposite the Grand Palace on the other side of the Chao Phraya River is **Wat Arun** Ⓑ (www.watarun.net; daily 8am–5.30pm; charge), one of the river's oldest and most distinctive landmarks, dating back to the Ayutthaya period. Also known as the Temple of Dawn, its 82-metre (270ft) -high *prang* (tall spire) is bedecked with millions of tiny pieces of Chinese porcelain. The five-towered temple represents Mount Meru, spiritual centre of Buddhist/Hindu cosmology.

Getting across the river is simple thanks to a fleet of long-tail boats stationed at various piers, or *tha*. As well as short trips from one side to the other, it is also possible to book a cruise along the river and the canals that branch off it. Such trips show the extremes of Bangkok, passing by five-star hotels on one side, then moving off to the wooden riverside shacks where young children play in the brown water.

Once back on the Grand Palace side, turn left on Thanon Maharat and walk south past Thanon Thai Wang, which runs into the Tha Tien river-taxi dock after passing a fresh market surrounded by early 20th-century shophouses.

Turn left (ie east) onto Soi Chetuphon and head for the gate to **Wat Pho** Ⓒ (www.watpho.com; daily 8.30am–6pm; charge), Bangkok's largest and oldest temple, predating the Bangkok dynasty. Its first buildings were constructed in the 16th century. Few statues are more impressive than its 46-metre (150ft) -long **Reclining Buddha**, which occupies the entirety of a building in the northwestern corner of the extensive palace complex. Mother-of-pearl on the soles of the feet details the 108 signs of a true Buddha.

A treasure trove of Thai and Southeast Asian riches, the **National Museum** Ⓓ (Wed–Sun 9am–4pm except public holidays; charge) comprises a half-dozen old and new buildings. One of the oldest is at the rear of the compound, the Wang Na, dating from 1782. This vast palace once

extended across to **Khlong Lot** and up to the Grand Palace, and its name refers to the palace of the so-called second king, a deputy king of sorts. When King Chulalongkorn's heir-apparent – the second king – attempted a violent overthrow, Chulalongkorn abolished the office in 1887 and tore down most of the buildings. The Wang Na is one of the remnants, serving as the National Museum and housing *khon* masks, gold and ceramic pieces, palanquins, weapons, instruments and an elephant riding-seat made from ivory.

East of the Grand Palace

At the next cross-street, Thanon Ratchabophit, turn right to visit one of the most attractive temples off the beaten tourist path. Before crossing over the canal, however, notice immediately to the north what appears to be a golden pig lording over a construction site, actually an archaeological excavation. The **Pig Memorial** was built in 1913 as a birthday present from friends to Queen Saowapha, Chulalongkorn's favourite wife, who was born in the Year of the Pig.

Across the bridge, **Wat Ratchabophit E** (daily 8am–5.30pm; free) is easily recognisable by its distinctive doors, carved in relief with jaunty soldiers wearing European uniforms. Built in 1870 by Rama V (1868–1910), the design was intended to meld Western and Thai art forms. The *bot's* windows and entrance doors are works of art. Inlaid mother-of-pearl depicts the insignias of the five royal ranks.

Continue north up Thanon Fuang Nakhon and turn right at the second corner onto Soi Suthat. Two short blocks on is **Wat Suthat F** (daily 8.30am–3pm; charge). Completed during the reign of Rama III, it is noted for its enormous stupa, said to be the tallest in Bangkok. The doors are among the wonders of Thai art. Carved to a depth of 5cm (2 inches), they follow the Ayutthayan tradition of floral motifs, with tangled jungle vegetation hiding small animals.

Immediately north is a giant red and wooden gateway, all that remains of the 200-year-old **Giant Swing** (Sao Ching Cha), once the centrepiece of an annual ceremony honouring the

TIP

Be sure to keep your admission ticket to the Wat Phra Kaew and Grand Palace. This allows free access to many of Dusit's sights, like the Ananta Samakhom Throne Hall, Vimanmek Mansion, Abhisek Dusit Throne Hall and the Royal Elephant Museum.

The golden Buddha in Wat Suthat.

A visitor in Wat Pho.

A noodle stand in Talad Kao Market, Chinatown.

Hindu god Shiva. In the past, a bench bearing teams of two to four standing young men was suspended from the crosspiece and the men would attempt to catch (with their teeth) a bag of gold suspended from on high. The swing was taken down in 2006 for safety reasons.

North of the old royal city

Northward to Dusit, crossing the *khlong* (canal), Thanon Ratchadamnoen turns into a pleasant, tree-lined boulevard that leads to an immense square with a statue of King Chulalongkorn on horseback. To the left of the square lies the spacious **Amporn Gardens**, complete with fountains, trees and an air of grandeur.

At the back of the square is the former National Assembly (Parliament) building, built in 1907 by Chulalongkorn. To the east is **Dusit Zoo ⒼG** (www.zoothailand.org; daily 8am–6pm; charge), the city's main animal park and one of the most popular places in Bangkok for family outings. An aviary and enclosures containing exotic wildlife surround a lake with boats for rent.

Behind the **old National Assembly** is **Vimanmek ⒽH** (www.vimanmek.com; daily 9.30am–4pm, tickets sold until 3.15pm; charge, or free with Grand Palace entrance ticket), billed as the world's largest golden teak building. Vimanmek was built by Chulalongkorn as a residence for his family in what was, in 1900, a suburb of Bangkok. The 100-room home is filled with exquisite European objects.

Just past the railway line on the north side of Thanon Sri Ayutthaya are the grounds of the **Chitralada Palace ⒤I** (closed to the public). Surrounded by a moat and high fencing, the grounds include grazing cattle, milk churns and fishponds.

Wat Benjamabophit ⒥J (daily 8.30am–5.30pm; charge), the Marble Temple, lies on the other side of Thanon Sri Ayutthaya. The last major temple built in Bangkok, construction was initiated by Rama V in 1900 and finished 10 years later. Designed by Prince Naris, a half-brother of the king, the temple's features are largely a departure from the traditional style. The most obvious of these must be the enclosed courtyard, the Carrara marble

used to cover the main buildings, and the curved, yellow Chinese roof tiles. Behind the *bot* is a gallery holding 51 Buddha images from around Asia.

Chinatown

Chinese merchants originally settled the area that now comprises the old royal city, but they were compelled to move to the present **Sampeng Lane**  when construction began on the Grand Palace in the 1780s. In 1863, King Mongkut built Charoen Krung (New Road), the first paved street in Bangkok, and Chinatown soon began to expand northward towards it. Chinatown was followed at Khlong Krung Kasem by a Muslim district that, in turn, was followed by an area occupied by *farang* (Westerners) where the Oriental Hotel now stands on the river's east bank.

The area has had a rowdy history. What began with mercantile pursuits soon degenerated into a lusty entertainment area. By 1900, alleys led to opium dens and houses whose entrances were marked by green lanterns (*khom khiaw*). A green-light district functioned like a Western red-light district, and while the lanterns have disappeared, the term *khom khiaw* still signifies a brothel. Today, Chinatown's main attractions are along Yaowarat Road. Off from the busy main thoroughfare, dozens of narrow alleyways lead to animated markets, kerb-side tea stalls and dim sum cafés.

Bangrak and Silom

Further south and just east of the Chao Phraya River is Bangrak, a vibrant modern district that has expanded greatly in the past three decades. Anchoring the western end is the grand **Oriental Hotel** (www.mandarinoriental.com/bangkok), directly on the bank of the Chao Phraya. From the Oriental, stroll inland past the gaggle of *tuk-tuk* drivers, long-tail-boat touts and 'copy watch' sellers to the end of the *soi*, turn right and you'll soon be at the less exciting end of one of Bangkok's most dynamic (after dark, at least) thoroughfares, Thanon Silom.

Love it or hate it, and few have any other opinion, the notorious **Patpong** (actually two streets – Patpong I and Patpong II) at the opposite end

The Giant Swing.

Patpong night market.

of Thanon Silom has an electric, sinful arrogance. It is hard to imagine a starker contrast to the serene temples and palaces and the gracious smiles and *wai* of hotel staff than the raucous touting and outrageous sex shows of this part of town. The night-time market here is so hectic it occasionally threatens to outshine even the neon lights of the go-go bars.

At the end of Thanon Silom, just east of Patpong, is a huge and busy intersection that can take what seems an eon to cross. To the northeast across the intersection lies **Suan Lumphini** Ⓝ (Lumphini Park; daily 5am–8pm; free), a tranquil and tropical oasis of greenery with boating lakes and open-air cafés.

Come nightfall, things along Thanon Rama IV are far less serene at **Lumphini Boxing Stadium** Ⓞ (Tue, Fri, Sat evenings; charge), where explosive bouts are held between the country's top pugilists. A more cultured evening venue along Thanon Rama IV is the **Joe Louis Puppet Theatre** Ⓟ (www.joelouistheatre.com; daily; charge), the last of the country's small puppet troupes.

Also along Thanon Rama IV is the

Queen Saovabha Memorial Institute Ⓠ (www.saovabha.com; Mon–Fri 8.30am–4pm, Sat–Sun and holidays 8.30am–noon; charge), or as it is better known, the **Snake Farm**. Operated by the Thai Red Cross, it produces anti-venom serum to be used on snakebite victims.

Heading north along Thanon Ratchadamri towards the intersection with Thanon Rama I, one passes two of the city's most opulent hotels, the Four Seasons (formerly the Regent) and the Grand Hyatt Erawan. At the intersection, the **Erawan Shrine** Ⓡ (daily 8am–10pm) draws visitors and locals. To improve their fortunes or to pass exams, believers make offerings at a statue of a four-faced deity. Originally built by the Erawan Hotel (now the Grand Hyatt) to counter a spate of bad luck, the shrine is an atmospheric place, filled with the scent of incense smoke and jasmine. To repay the god for wishes granted, supplicants place floral garlands or wooden elephants at the god's feet, or hire a resident troupe to perform a traditional dance.

The intersection of Rama I and Phayathai, around **Siam Square** Ⓢ, is one

A policeman attempts to direct Bangkok's chaotic traffic.

of the best areas to shop, especially for those who like a little local colour and chaos (see page 53). But there are other attractions besides shopping and eating in this area. On Khlong Mahanak at the north end of Soi Kasemsan II is **Jim Thompson's House** ❶ (www.jimthompsonhouse.com; daily 9am–5pm; charge). This Thai-style home comprises six Thai houses acquired throughout the country and joined together by the remarkable American, who revived the Thai silk industry. In 1967, while on a visit to the Cameron Highlands in Malaysia, Thompson mysteriously disappeared; despite an extensive search, no trace has ever been found of him. His legacy however lives on in the beautiful silk sold at the Jim Thompson boutiques in Bangkok.

Rama I continues east to become **Thanon Sukhumvit**, Thailand's longest street, which continues all the way to the Cambodian border. The efficient Skytrain provides the fastest means of transport between the plethora of upmarket shops, restaurants, spas and entertainment venues that line this major artery.

Outside of Bangkok

Bangkok's hinterland is filled with a rich variety of sights and experiences that can be visited as day trips or overnighters from the capital. Among the highlights, 80km (50 miles) north of Bangkok, is the old royal city of **Ayutthaya**, Thailand's capital from 1350 to 1767. The ruined city is immense, comprising several sites that should not be missed.

The nearest mountains to Bangkok are in the extensive **Khao Yai National Park** (www.dnp.go.th), which sprawls across parts of four provinces northeast of the capital; wildlife includes a small number of tigers and elephants.

Around 150km (90 miles) south of the capital is the upmarket beach resort of **Hua Hin**. Horse-rides along the beach, a frenetic night market and quality spas are among the highlights.

Damnoen Saduak floating market is located about 100km (62 miles) southwest of Bangkok or 4hrs round-trip by bus. Swamped at times by tourists, it is best to arrive early in the morning to avoid the crowds.

TIP

The **Bangkok Skytrain** (www.bts.co.th) consists of two lines which intersect at Siam station. Trains operate from 6am to midnight (3 minutes peak; 5 minutes off-peak). Single-trip fares vary according to distance, and tourists may find it more useful to buy the unlimited ride 1-Day Pass, available at station counters.

A plethora of signs on Khao San Road.

SHOPPING IN BANGKOK

Whether you want to buy a designer dress or a monkey, Bangkok has just about everything for sale. From luxury boutiques to street-side stalls offering fake watches, this is a shopper's paradise. Those with cash to flash disembark at the BTS Skytrain's Siam stop and head for the glitzy **Siam Paragon**, **Central World** or **Siam Discovery**. Opposite, Siam Square is a great place to people-watch as trendy students browse the funky clothes shops or sip mochas in the coffee bars. The best market, **Chatuchak**, is near the Mo Chit BTS stop. This vast site is packed at weekends and sells furniture, amulets, artwork, antiques, clothes and even live lizards. Prices are fixed in the malls but out on the street be prepared to haggle hard, but always with a smile.

Elephant trekking, at Ban Ruammit, near Chiang Rai.

CHIANG MAI AND THE NORTH

In the northern mountains, Chiang Mai is a pleasant base from which to explore the many hill tribes and national parks that retain Thailand's more traditional textures.

D espite increasing urbanisation, 700-year-old **Chiang Mai** remains a relaxed, cool alternative to the energy-sapping humidity of Bangkok. Situated 300 metres (1,000ft) above sea level in a broad valley divided by the picturesque **Ping River**, the city lorded it over the north for seven centuries as the capital of the Lanna kingdom. During its splendid isolation, Chiang Mai developed a culture quite removed from that of the central plains, with wooden temples of exquisite beauty and a host of unique crafts, including lacquerware, silverwork, woodcarvings, ceramics and umbrella-making. Today, much of its heritage is still evident, with remnants of the original walls and moats surrounding the city and dozens of temples that enhance the city's character and charm.

Origins

Chiang Mai's story actually begins further north, in the town of Chiang Rai. Its founder and king, Mangrai, ruled a sizeable empire that ran as far north as Chiang Saen, on the Mekong River. When Kublai Khan sacked the Burmese kingdom of Bagan in 1287, Mangrai formed an alliance with the rulers of Sukhothai, then Siam's capital, to protect his realm. With his southern boundaries secure, Mangrai extended his territory by annexing the old Mon

kingdom of Lamphun, before establishing a new base in the Ping Valley in 1296. He named this capital Chiang Mai, or New City.

Legend has it that the location was chosen due to the auspicious sighting of white deer along with a white mouse with a family of five, all at the same time. Rather than building on the banks of the Ping, which often floods, he built his city – with the help of 90,000 labourers – half a kilometre to the west, surrounding it with sturdy brick walls.

Main Attractions

Wat Phra Singh
Wat Phan Tao
Night Bazaar
Wat Phra That Doi Suthep
Trekking Around ,Mae Hong Son

In Chiang Mai.

Less than a century after Chiang Mai's founding, Ayutthaya replaced Sukhothai as the capital of Siam. This new kingdom had its own expansionist ambitions, including designs on its neighbour to the north – and for the next 400 years, there was fierce competition and periods of open warfare. In the 16th century, Ayutthaya crushed an invasion by Chiang Mai, and Chiang Mai's power waned. To compound its troubles, the same Burmese enemy who were laying siege to Ayutthaya invaded the region in the early 1700s.

Although the Burmese were finally defeated, Chiang Mai was badly damaged and soon abandoned. It remained deserted until 1796, when the Burmese army was defeated. New nobles then began restoring the city to its former prominence. It continued to enjoy autonomy from Bangkok until the railway brought meddling central government administrators. In 1932, following the death of the last king of Chiang Mai, the north was finally fully incorporated into the Thai nation.

Shopping at Chiang Mai Night Bazaar.

Old Chiang Mai

The commercial centres of downtown are along Thanon Thaphae, with numerous hotels, shops and guesthouses. Hotels and shops have also sprung up along Thanon Huai Kaeo, which leads out to Doi Suthep.

A tour of the city should begin with **Wat Chiang Man** (daily 9am–6pm; free), which translates as 'power of the city'. It was the first *wat* to be built by Mangrai, who resided there during the construction of the city in 1296. Located in the northeast part of the old walled city, it is the oldest of Chiang Mai's 300-plus temples.

Two ancient, venerated Buddha images are kept in the abbot's quarters. The first image, Phra Sae Tang Tamani, is a small 10cm (4-inch) -high crystal Buddha image taken by Mangrai to Chiang Mai from Lamphun, where it had reputedly resided for 600 years. It is paraded through the streets at Songkran, the Thai New Year (April). The second image, a stone Phra Sila Buddha in bas-relief, is believed to have originated in India around the 8th century. Both statues

are said to possess the power to bring rain and to protect the city from fire.

Also in the temple complex is Chang Lom, a 15th-century square *chedi* buttressed by rows of stucco elephants.

Imperiously positioned at the head of Thanon Ratchdamnoen is **Wat Phra Singh** (daily 9am–6pm; free), noted for three monuments: a library, *chedi* and the Wihan Lai Kham. The magnificent Lanna-style wooden library, on the right side of the compound, is raised on a high base decorated with lovely stucco guardians. Behind the main *wihan* (central hall housing Buddha images), built in 1925, is a beautiful wooden *bot* (ordination chapel), and behind this, a *chedi* built by King Pha Yu in 1345 to hold the ashes of his father.

But Wat Phra Singh's most beautiful building is the small Phra Wihan Lai Kham, to the left of the *bot*. Built rather late in the Lanna period, in 1811, the wooden building's front wall is decorated in gold flowers on a red lacquer base. Intricately carved wooden window frames accent the doors, while the interior walls are decorated with murals. Although focusing on the Buddhist stories of Prince Sang Thong (on the north wall) and the Tale of the Heavenly Phoenix (south wall), they also record in fascinating detail aspects of early 19th-century Lanna society and exhibit clear indications of persisting Burmese cultural influence.

Calamity is associated with **Wat Chedi Luang** (daily 9am–6pm; free), built in 1401 to the east of Wat Phra Singh on Thanon Phra Pokklao. A century and a half later, a violent earthquake shook its 90-metre (295ft) pagoda, reducing its height to 42 metres (140ft). It was never completely rebuilt, although it has been impressively restored. Even in its damaged state, the colossal monument is majestic. For 84 years the Emerald Buddha, now in Bangkok, was housed here before being moved to Vientiane in Laos (see page 130).

Close to the wat's entrance stands an ancient and tall gum tree. When it falls, says a legend, so will the city. As if serving as counterbalance, the *lak muang*, or city boundary stone in which the spirit of the city is said to reside, stands near its base.

Wat Chedi Luang: stunted by earthquake-damage, but still impressive

A food stall selling soup at the night market.

The *wihan* of **Wat Phan Tao** (daily 9am–6pm; free), adjacent to Wat Chedi Luang, formerly a palace, is a masterpiece of wooden construction. Its doorway is crowned by a beautiful Lanna peacock framed by golden *naga* (serpents).

Located 1km (0.6 miles) northwest of the city walls, **Wat Jet Yot** (daily 9am–6pm) was completed by King Trailokaraja in 1455. It was built as a vague replica of the Mahabodhi Temple in India's Bodhgaya, where the Buddha gained enlightenment while spending seven weeks in its gardens. It was badly damaged during the Burmese invasion of 1566.

Close to the Ping River is the Night Bazaar, a market with everything from designer goods to fabrics made by some of the many ethnic groups in the area. The Sunday night market on the 'Walking Street' (Ratchadamnoen Road in the Old City; 4pm–midnight) is a much bigger, though very crowded event.

Outside Chiang Mai

A steep series of hairpin curves rises up the flanks of **Doi Suthep** – 15km

Wat Phra That Doi Suthep, an orgy of gold.

(9 miles) northwest of the city – to Chiang Mai's best-loved temple, **Wat Phra That Doi Suthep** (daily 8am–6pm; charge). The site was selected in the mid-1300s by an elephant that was turned loose with a Buddha relic strapped to its back; where it stopped, it was believed, a temple should be built. Having climbed the slopes of Doi Suthep to the site, the story goes that it promptly dropped dead on the spot.

The scenery en route to the temple is beautiful, with the winding road passing the entrance to the **Huai Kaew Falls**. Seven-headed *naga* serpents undulate down the balustrade of a 290-step stairway that leads from the parking lot to the temple. For the weary, a cable train makes the same ascent for a few baht. Below from the *wat*, Chiang Mai is spread at one's feet.

From the upper terrace, a few more steps lead through the courtyard of the temple itself. In the late afternoon light, there are few sights more stunning than that which greets one at the final step. Emerging from cloisters decorated with murals depicting scenes from the Buddha's life, one's eyes rise to the summit of a 24-metre (80ft) -high gilded *chedi*, partially shaded by gilded bronze parasols. An iron fence surrounds it with pickets culminating in praying *thevada* (guardians). Appearing in the east and west ends of the compound are two *wihan*. At dawn, the eastern one shelters chanting nuns in white robes. At sunset, the western one holds orange-robed monks chanting their prayers.

From the car park, a road ascends a further 5km (3 miles) to **Phu Ping Palace**, the winter residence of the royal family. When they are absent, the public may stroll through the gardens (daily 8.30–11.30am, 1–3.30pm; charge).

From the entrance of Phuping Palace, the road continues through pine forests to the commercialised Hmong hill-tribe village of **Doi Pui**. It's all rather tacky, but improvements over the past decades have brought substantial material benefits to its inhabitants, including a paved street (lined with souvenir stands). It is possible to wander by the houses to get glimpses of how local people live.

The **Night Safari** (www.chiangmai nightsafari.com), 15km (9 miles) northwest of Chiang Mai, is part of Doi Suthep National Park and offers bus rides across a pseudo-savannah where you can get close, but not too close, to lions, rhinos and crocodiles.

Once an agricultural region, the **Mae Sa Valley**, 35km (22 miles) west of Chiang Mai, cultivates a new money-earner – tourism. Waterfalls, working elephant camps, butterfly farms, orchid nurseries and a charming private museum called **Mae Sa House Collection** (with prehistoric artefacts and Sukhothai ceramics, among many things) vie for the visitor's attention. Quiet resorts line the river.

South to Lamphun

The road south from Chiang Mai is one of the most beautiful in northern Thailand. **Lamphun ②**, 25km (14 miles) along the way, dates from the mid-6th century and is famed for two old *wat* and its young and prolific *lamyai* fruit trees.

For the best perspective on Lamphun's **Wat Pra That Haripunchai**, enter through its riverside gate, where large statues of mythical lions guard its portals. Inside the large compound, monks study in a large Buddhist school set amidst monuments and buildings, which date as far back as the late 9th century. A kilometre west of Lamphun's old moat stands **Wat Kukut** (also known as Wat Chama Devi), dating from the 8th century. The temple has a superb pair of unusual *chedi*. Erected in the early 1200s, the larger *chedi* consists of five squared tiers, each of which contains three nichcs. Each niche holds a Buddha statue.

To the southwest of Chiang Mai is Thailand's highest peak, the 2,596-metre (8,516ft) **Doi Inthanon**, its forests rich in wildlife.

North of Chiang Mai

Follow Route 107 north from Chiang Mai (beginning at Chang Phuak Gate) towards Chiang Dao and Fang. The road passes through rice fields and small villages, then begins to climb past Mae Taeng into the Mae Ping Gorge, which forms the southern end of the Chiang Dao Valley. Ahead, on the left as one follows the river through scenic countryside, is the imposing outline of Chiang Dao mountain.

At the 56km (35-mile) marker is the **Chiang Dao Elephant Training Centre** (www.chiangdaoelephantcamp.com; daily 8am–3pm; charge), on the bank of the Mae Nam Ping. Twice daily, a line of elephants walk into the Ping to be bathed for the amusement of tourists, who reward the baby elephants with bananas.

About 60km (40 miles) from Chiang Mai on Route 107, a dirt road branches left to reach **Doi Chiang Dao**, which at 2,186 metres (7,175ft) is Thailand's third-highest peak. A jeep or a trail bike is needed to negotiate this 9km (5.5-mile) track, which leads to the Hmong village of Pakkia up

TIP

Chiang Mai is best visited during winter, late November through early February, when it is abloom with an astounding variety of beautiful flowers. Numerous resorts in Mae Sa Valley carpet the hillsides with flower gardens. A Flower Festival takes place each February.

Girls of the Lisu tribe, near Mae Hong Son.

Rice paddy field workers.

The beautiful Wat Chong Klang in Mae Hong Son.

the mountain. Entry to the sanctuary is restricted and permission must be obtained from the wildlife headquarters near Wat Pa Bong.

Further north, Route 107 enters the quiet town of **Chiang Dao**, located 70km (45 miles) from Chiang Mai. At the far end of town, a simple road leads off to the left for 5km (3 miles) to **Tham Chiang Dao** (daily; charge), a complex of caves filled with Buddha statuary. In a deeper section is a large, reclining limestone Buddha.

The far northwest

A minor road (Route 1095) branches off northwest from Route 107 at Mae Malai to reach the towns of Pai and Mae Hong Son, the main tourist centres of this beautiful region of forested hills and minority peoples.

Some 90km (56 miles) northwest, ensconced in a wide, fertile valley and surrounded by mountain peaks, **Pai** ❸ is a town of around 5,000 people which has become a magnet for hippies, artists and musicians from all over the world.

Further northwest is the Shan market town of **Soppong** ❹, 70km (42 miles)

northeast from Mae Hong Son, which functions as the main jump-off point for visits to **Tham Lot** (daily 8am–5.30pm; charge), some 8km (5 miles) away. This is the most famous limestone cavern complex in northern Thailand.

Continue on to **Mae Hong Son** ❺, the provincial capital surrounded by tall green peaks and populated by Karen, Hmong, Lawa, Shan, Lisu and Lahu tribespeople, who, taken collectively, easily outnumber the ethnic Thais. Doi Kong Mu, a hill that rises a steep 250 metres (820ft) above the town, affords a commanding view. Two picturesque Burmese-Shan temples, **Wat Chong Klang** and **Wat Chong Kham** (both daily 8am–6pm; free), flank a serene town centre lake, **Nong Chong Kham**.

Tour agencies, hotels and guesthouses in Mae Hong Son can arrange treks to mountain valleys, limestone caves and hill tribe villages in the vicinity. Many Mae Hong Son visitors travel to controversial nearby 'longneck villages' to meet Padaung refugees from Burma, whose women traditionally wear heavy brass coils around their necks to make them appear elongated.

HILL TRIBES

At one time the hill tribes that live in and around Chiang Mai were largely subsistence farmers. Agriculture still plays a crucial role, but the advent of tourism has undeniably changed some communities. Trekking to see the tribespeople can be a rewarding experience for all concerned, but these days some villages look more like souvenir centres. There is therefore a delicate balance between preserving traditional values and allowing access. Visitors should go with a guide and understand a few dos and don'ts before entering a village. Always ask permission before taking photographs, never touch spiritual items and if you want to take a gift, make it something practical such as pencils and paper for children. Better still, give a donation to a charity that helps the tribespeople.

From Buddhism to modern wellness

Massage, with its Buddhist origins, is an inherent part of normal life in Thailand and this makes spa treatments a natural Thai experience.

Travelling monks arrived in Thailand in the 2nd or 3rd century AD, bearing not only Buddhism, but also *nuad paen boran* (ancient massage); legend says it was developed from Indian Vedic treatments by Shivakar Kumar Baccha, the Buddha's own medical adviser. Nearly 2,000 years after it entered the country, the world now calls it simply Thai massage. It is just one of many treatments now available in modern spas – an enticing feature of the Thailand beach holiday.

The association with the country's religious philosophy means that the most dedicated masseurs still perform the service within the Buddhist concept of mindfulness. Before they start, true adherents will make a *wai* (a slight bow with hands clasped together) to pay respects to their teacher and focus on *metta* (loving kindness), thought to be the ideal state of mind in which to give massage.

For centuries, throughout Thailand, temples were places of healing, and they administered many of the treatments we now associate with modern spas, such as herbal compresses and herbal medicines.

Massage techniques

As it is based on ancient Indian teachings, Thai massage includes the stretching elements of yoga alongside acupressure and reflexology. There should also be a meditative quality, although low-budget shops may have music or TV playing that scupper this. The massage principle revolves around 10 energy lines, called *sip sen*, believed to carry physical, emotional, and spiritual energy between meridian points around the body. When the lines become blocked, illness or emotional stress occurs, so they must be reopened.

The experience is usually vigorous, employing push-and-pull stretching of tendons and joints and deep-tissue kneading with elbows, knees, feet and fingers. It is not a suitable treatment for people with back, neck or joint problems. *Bow bow, kap/ka* is a useful phrase, meaning 'softer, please'. Sometimes an ointment is used on painful muscles – Tiger balm is the most famous brand – but generally there are no oils Involved.

Where to enjoy Thai massage

The most common operations are in small houses consisting of little more than several mattresses on the floor, curtained off from each other. These places can be found on many streets, particularly in tourist areas, and provide exquisite relaxation for as little as B200 an hour. But there are many other pampering environments to suit most tastes and all budgets.

Urban spas, often in traditional teak houses, may include beauty elements such as body scrubs and facial treatments, while luxurious resort spas offer the gamut of 'wellness' options, from massage to Traditional Chinese medicine, reiki, meditation, hypnotherapy and New Age treatments such as crystals and floral essences.

A massage at the Northern Traditional Healing Hospital, Chiang Mai.

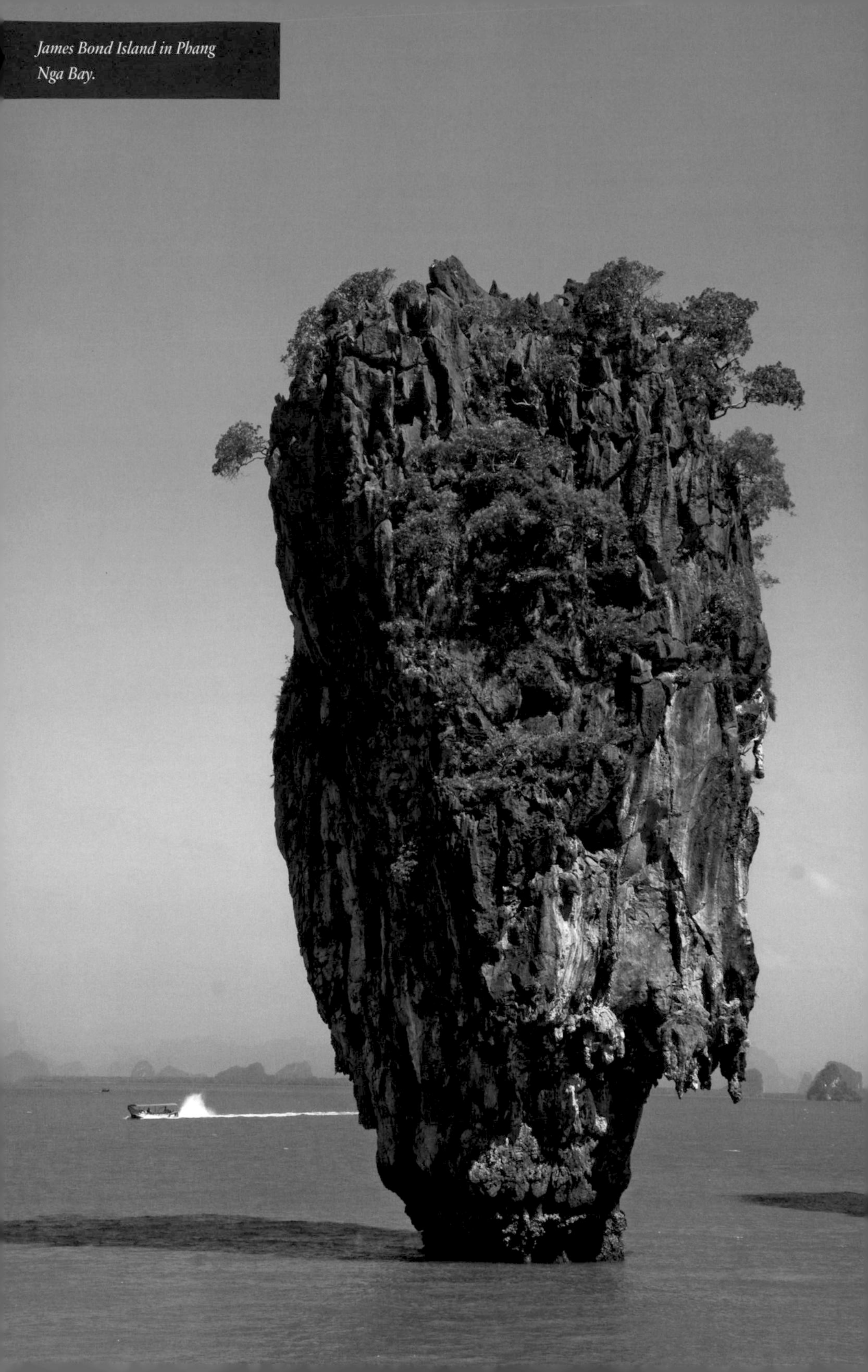

James Bond Island in Phang Nga Bay.

SOUTHERN BEACHES AND ISLANDS

Most tourists travel to Thailand for its seductive southern islands – Phuket, Samui, Phi Phi and others. Whether they want to be pampered or find rustic ambience, the beautiful beaches will not disappoint.

Thailand's deep south is the perfect place to head for some sun, sea and relaxation. Its powder-soft sand, idyllic beaches and warm waters make it a world-class destination.

The south contains 14 provinces and is teeming with scenic hideaways and unspoiled beaches. In many ways this peninsular region is far removed from the rest of the country, with significant differences in climate, culture and religion. Groves of rubber trees are more common than rice fields, and the gilded dome of a Muslim mosque is a more familiar sight than the sloping orange roof of a Buddhist temple.

The earthquake-generated tsunami of 2004 caused tragic loss of life and damage along Thailand's Andaman coast. Remarkably, given the scale of the destruction, most tourist destinations were back to near-normal conditions within six months, and today it is business as usual.

Phuket

The undeniable physical beauty of **Phuket ❻** extends beyond its palm-fringed beaches to its picturesque villages, coconut groves, rubber plantations and forested hills. It languished in relative isolation for decades despite its natural resources of tin, rubber and coconut due to a number of factors. Its distance from Bangkok, the lack of a bridge across the causeway, bad roads

on the island itself, and a seeming lack of interest in developing it for recreation all played their parts. That has all changed now and today it is a flourishing tourist island. Though development has had some drawbacks, it remains a worthy holiday destination.

The road from Phang Nga on the mainland crosses the 600-metre (2,000ft) Thaothep Kasetri Bridge, from where a busy dual carriageway soon reaches the heart of the island. The crossroads at **Ban Tha Rua ❹**, with roads leading off to Surin Beach

Main Attractions

Phuket beaches
Phang Nga islands
Ko Phi Phi
Ko Samui
Ang Thong National Marine
  Park
Ko Phangan

A long tail boat in the clear waters off Phuket.

and Khao Phra Taew National Park, is dominated by two bronze statues of female warriors, swords in hands. The pair are sisters: Chan and Muk, who once led an army of villagers to repel Burmese invaders.

Unlike many Thai provincial centres, the town of **Phuket B** on the island's southeast coast has a rich identity of its own. The charm of the old buildings is complemented by the many colourful Chinese shrines – notable examples include the brightly-painted **Jui Tui Temple** (daily 8am–6pm; free) and the smaller **Put Jaw** (daily 8am–6pm; free) next door, which sit just past the market on Thanon Ranong. Like many Chinese shrines elsewhere in Asia, their central altars are dedicated to Kuan Yin (Guanyin), the goddess of mercy. Jui Tui is the starting point for the five days of colourful and bizarre parades that mark the annual Phuket Vegetarian Festival in October (see page 65).

Southeast along the coast is **Rawai C**, whose foreshore is a mass of rocks that lies exposed during low tide, when clam hunters venture out, turning over the stones in search of

Karon Beach, Phuket.

dinner. Rawai holds one of the island's handful of *chao lay*, or sea gypsy, villages. It also has the **Phuket Sea Shell Museum** (www.phuketseashell.com; daily 8am–6pm; charge), a beautiful collection of shells from Thailand and beyond, including the world's-largest golden pearl. The most exclusive hotel in the area is the newly-renovated InterContinental Phuket Rawai Beach Resort (formerly **Evason Resort and Spa**), which has its own private beach on the nearby island of **Ko Bon.**

Phuket's principal attraction, however, is its many splendid beaches. From Rawai the coastal road continues over the north–south ridge of hills, offering great views for 45km (28 miles) – as far as Ko Phi Phi. Continue around the southernmost tip at **Laem Promthep,** where the sunsets are spectacular, to **Nai Harn D**, one of the island's prettiest stretches of sand. Further north are the smaller, picturesque bays of **Kata Noi** and **Kata E**. There are good snorkelling opportunities at the northern end of Kata and the southern end of Kata Noi beach. **Karon Beach F** is the second-largest

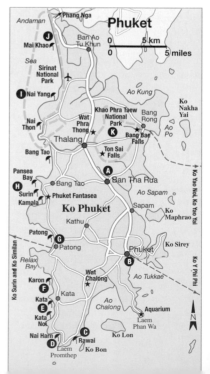

of the island's beach resorts, with hotels and restaurants at its top, middle and bottom. Both Karon and Kata have a growing choice of hotel, dining and watersport facilities. Relax Bay, with its luxury hotel, **Le Meridien Phuket**, offers some snorkelling along its northwestern rocks.

The most-developed beach by some way is **Patong ⑥**, due west of Phuket Town on the opposite side of the island, and north of Karon. In the early 1970s, Patong was little more than a huge banana plantation wedged between the mountains and a wide crescent of sand. The erstwhile plantation is now a tourist city-by-the-sea, with multi-storey condominiums and hotels rising above night markets, seafood emporiums, bars, nightclubs and tourist shops. During the day the 4km (2.5 miles) of beach is packed with sunbathers, hawkers – and banana boats and jet-skis on the water.

Dive shops offer trips into the bay or northwest to the **Similan Islands National Marine Park**, considered one of the best diving areas in the world, with crystal-clear waters and spectacular corals populated by brightly coloured tropical fish and rays.

Some 3km (2 miles) north of Patong, **Kamala Bay** has charming Islamic hamlets with well-kept gardens against a backdrop of forested hills rising to over 500 metres (1,600ft). Its former tranquillity has been broken at the northern end, where a giant Disney-like theme park has been built, called **Phuket Fantasea** (www.phuket-fantasea. com; Fri–Wed 5.30-11.30pm, showtime 9pm; charge). The 3,000-seat theatre uses elephants, lasers and illusions to tell of Thai legends through the ages.

The attractive coastal road north to **Surin Beach ⑪** passes beautifully compact **Singh Beach,** its sandy cape hedged by verdant headlands. Larger Surin Beach, with its seafood shacks, soon gives way to the idyllic **Pansea Bay**, dominated by two proprietary resorts, the Chedi and the Amanpuri. The long beach at **Bang Tao** is dominated by the immense Laguna Phuket, which shelters five large resorts.

Nai Yang Beach ⑫, just south of the airport, is under the jurisdiction of **Sirinat National Park**. There are a few

Practising with power snorkels for a look at the local sea life.

Phuket Fantasea.

VEGETARIAN FESTIVAL

Phuket's 10-day Vegetarian Festival is one of the most extreme events on the Thai calendar. Part of this Chinese-inspired event involves locals piercing their faces and bodies with sharp metal objects in displays of devotion. Other activities include fire-walking and climbing ladders with razor-sharp rungs – while barefoot. Pregnant women and those who are mourning, are banned from watching any rituals. Those who do take part make merit at the temples, wear white and abstain from eating meat, having sex or drinking alcohol throughout the 10 days. The festival, held every October, began in 1825 when a visiting Chinese opera company fell sick. After they recovered by holding ceremonies and not eating meat, locals were so impressed that they held their own festival each year.

Buddha detail on Phra Yai temple, Ko Samui.

The sea gypsies are becoming more assimilated into Thai culture.

Spartan bungalows for rent in the 90-sq-km (35-sq-mile) park. With a good map it is possible to drive along Phuket's scenic west coast from Nai Yang to the island's southern tip, Prom Thep.

North of Nai Yang is Phuket's longest beach, **Mai Khao ❶**. Extending for 9km (5.6 miles), it is relatively undeveloped. Giant sea turtles come ashore from December through February to lay their eggs.

The forested hills that provide a backdrop to much of Phuket can be experienced on hikes through **Khao Phra Taew National Park ❶** (www.dnp.go.th; daily 6am–6pm; charge). Two pretty waterfalls fringe the park: Ton Sai on the west, and Bang Bae on the east.

Phang Nga and Krabi

Back on the mainland, **Phang Nga ❼** is a lovely, peaceful township somehow left behind in Thailand's development surge. The main objective of any first-time trip here should be to the geological wonderland of **Phang Nga Bay.**

Just before the mouth of Phang Nga River, the boat approaches the base of

Khao Kien Mountain, where a cavern contains primitive paintings depicting human and animal forms. Such rock art is quite common in the limestone caves in the area and date from around 2,000 years ago. The floors of many caves in Phang Nga and Krabi are still scattered with the discarded seashells of prehistoric people, but tide fluctuations have compromised archaeological evidence.

Ko Ping Kan is perhaps the most spectacular and most-visited of Phang Nga's islands. Behind the beach, the mountain seems to have split in two, the halves leaning against each other, inviting inevitable comparisons with two lovers. The island and nearby monolith Ko Tapu are now known as **James Bond Island** as they are featured in the Bond movie *The Man with the Golden Gun*, when the famous spy takes on the evil Scaramanga. Daily boat trips bring hundreds of tourists to the island.

About 50km (30 miles) south of Phang Nga, **Thanboke Koranee National Park** (tel: 0 7568 1071; www. dnp.go.th; daily 6am–6pm; charge), near Krabi, is one of the most beautiful in Thailand. The mainland town of **Krabi**

SEA GYPSIES

Phuket and some surrounding islands are home to groups of sea gypsies, once nomadic fishing families, who have their own culture and language. They are skilled fishermen above and below the water. From a young age, they learn to dive up to 20 metres (70ft) in search of lobsters, prawns, and crabs, staying below for up to three minutes. Inevitably, modern life in the form of pollution and diminishing stocks has robbed the sea gypsies of most of their traditional fishing grounds. These people, also called Moken or Chao Lay, have their own language and live in their own communities, but are slowly being assimilated into Thai culture. They are friendly and approachable, but their villages can be remote, so a guide is useful if visiting.

8 itself is a small but bustling service centre built opposite mangrove swamps on a sort of peninsula along the Krabi River. From town, Krabi River mangroves can be explored by renting a long-tail boat, first stopping off to visit the huge cavern inside the Khanab Nam twin peaks, which flank the river. Traditionally, the leaves, bark, fruit and mosses of the surrounding mangroves provided folk cures for the alleviation of lumbago, kidney stones and menstrual pains. The trees also provided a source of weak alcohol and leaves for wrapping tobacco. Two rare bird species inhabit the mangroves: the mangrove pitta and the brown-winged kingfisher.

To the west of Krabi town is Ao Nang, an upmarket resort where most visitors base themselves. From here, longtail boats head out on trips to nearby islands. Ko Gai, Ko Poda and Railae are the most popular destinations, and are remarkably unspoilt despite the large numbers of visitors. Ko Gai and Ko Poda are a 20-minute boat ride from Ao Nang. Both these small islands have pristine sands and warm, cobalt waters. The islands have only a handful of wooden shacks, so development, for now, is limited. Even closer to Ao Nang is Railae beach, an isthmus where giant limestone karsts offer an incredible backdrop.

Ko Phi Phi

With palm-fringed beaches and lofty limestone mountains as a backdrop, **Ko Phi Phi** **9** is arguably one of the most beautiful islands in Asia. Turquoise waves caress a beach so dazzlingly white it is almost painful to the eye. The water is so crystalline, colourful fishing boats seem suspended in mid-air. Phi Phi lies equidistant, about 45km (30 miles), from both Phuket and Krabi. The island is in fact two islands: the smaller **Phi Phi Ley**, a well-preserved craggy limestone monolith similar to the other shrub-covered peaks of Phang Nga Bay, and **Phi Phi Don**, an epicentre of tourism development with only a few remaining unspoiled beaches at its northern tip. Should the diving bug bite, Phi Phi Island has several dive shops where visitors can earn their Open Water scuba certification.

TIP

From Krabi, visitors can catch long-tail boats sailing out to Railae Beach, with larger ones leaving daily for Ko Phi Phi, and for Ko Lanta from November to May.

Maya Bay, Ko Phi Phi.

Floral garlands (phuang malai) are a part of Thai culture – traditionally hung in front of houses or used for religious offerings. Jasmine blooms feature in most.

On the beach at Ko Samui.

Ko Samui

Over 4 million tourists arrive at **Ko Samui** ❿ every year, and the relatively small island – a beautiful, if slightly tarnished, tropical vision of white-sand beaches, palm trees and jungle-clad mountains – is fully equipped to accommodate them. There are luxury hotels, upmarket restaurants, a modern airport, easy transport, a few chaotic commercial strips, and the full panoply of watersports and other diversions.

Scattered around elsewhere on the island are a go-kart track, snake farm, butterfly aviary and many snooker parlours. The numerous signs for 'monkey shows' are opportunities to see pig-tailed macaques engaged in their usual jobs on coconut farms. They twist coconuts from the treetops, then retrieve and deposit them in burlap bags. In the interior are several waterfalls descending from the heights of **Khao Phlu,** the island's highest point at 635 metres (2,080ft).

There is no need to linger among the drab cement blocks of Samui's biggest town, the western port of **Na Thon**, other than to wait for the ferry to Ko Phangan, Ang Thong National Marine Park or back to the mainland.

Instead, head over to the east coast. Long ago, the original beachcombers were drawn by a 6km (4-mile) swathe of soft, silky sand at **Chaweng**. The sand at its half-sized southern neighbour, **Lamai**, is slightly lower grade. South of Lamai, the smaller beaches of **Ban Hua Thanon** and **Ban Bangkao** are unremarkable, but the coral reef is healthy near the former and the latter is a charming Muslim village. From either, make a day trip inland and swim at the two-tiered waterfall at **Na Muang**. On the western side of the island, **Ban Taling Ngam** offers a couple of deluxe resort retreats.

Three lovely bays occupy almost the entire northern coast of Ko Samui. For a panorama, head along the north shore to **Maenam**. The sand is coarser than that of the east, but the 4km (2.5-mile) stretch is relatively undeveloped. East of Maenam, **Bo Phut** is much narrower, but relatively protected; it is a short walk from the little fishing village of Ban Bo Phut. **Bangrak**, better known as **Big Buddha Beach**, is a busy, bustling resort that suffers from the din from the adjacent road and the jets roaring overhead. Quieter **Choeng Mon**, on the island's northeastern spur, has decent sand and water, and is within quick access of Chaweng's commercial facilities.

Lastly, located 30km (20 miles) west of Ko Samui, are the attractions of 41 brilliant isles comprising **Ang Thong National Marine Park.** Day-long package trips voyage to Ko Wua Talab, park headquarters, and Ko Mae Ko, although they allow little time to investigate any more than a viewpoint, the cave on Wua Talab, and the clear, pea-green saltwater lake on Mae Ko. On both islands, the designated swimming spots have limited coral and fish. For a closer look around the islands and more time snorkelling, you can charter a speedboat.

Ko Phangan

If Ko Samui is increasingly the island of package tours and brief vacations, its neighbour 15km (9 miles) to the north, **Ko Phangan**, is a refuge for backpackers on leisurely world tours and Europeans lazing away winter-long holidays. From the cacophonous southern port town of **Thong Sala**, a ferry port for Ko Samui and Ko Tao, there is a paved 10km (6-mile) road that runs due north to the village of **Chalok Lam**. East of Chalok Lam, the justly prized **Hat Kuat** (Bottle Beach), is most easily accessible by sea.

Continuing eastward and down the coast, things become more remote. **Hat Sadet** has a waterfall and jumbo rocks bearing the graffiti of Thai royalty, while **Thong Nai Pan Bay** has wonderful cliff viewpoints, a double-barrelled bay and a coral reef. Eventually you will reach the pretty southern cove of **Hat Thian**, which offers more beaches on either side. Pick one and drop anchor.

Just 10 minutes away by long-tail boat is **Hat Rin,** famed for its all-night 'full-moon' party (www.fullmoonparty-thailand.com). The biggest bashes of the year

take place in December and January, when leading British DJs fly in. Most months there are 5,000 or more revellers who wander, and occasionally stagger, between the giant sound systems set up along the beach. So successful are the events that there are now parties for each of the moon's phases. All-night boats run between Hat Rin and Samui.

The road joining Hat Rin and Thong Sala is paved and so it is possible to visit the intervening villages and beaches of **Ban Tai** and **Ban Khai**. An easy stroll up a hill from Ban Tai is **Wat Khao Tham** (daily; charge), where Buddhist meditation courses are sometimes held.

Ko Tao

This small, simple island north of Ko Phangan attracts diving enthusiasts of all levels, thanks to its shallow coral reefs and budget prices. Most guesthouses offer significant discounts for those who sign up for a diving programme, but there are several relaxed beaches to enjoy for those who prefer to stay on top of the water. Hat Sai Ri on the west coast has a good beach and plenty of facilities.

TIP

Songthaew – small pick-up trucks converted to taxis – serve Ko Samui. They rarely refuse a fare and will load up until passengers are hanging from the tailgate and roof. Negotiate a fee before you set off.

Protecting the fragile environment at Ko Tao.

BUDDHIST TEMPLE ARCHITECTURE

To please Buddha and in search of nirvana, his followers have created some wonderful buildings.

Buddhist culture is based on the temple, and across the region there are examples dating back to around the 8th century. In Thailand, Laos and Cambodia, Buddhist temples are called *wat*; Indonesian temples are *vihara* or *candi*, in Vietnam they are *dong tu or den*, while the usual Chinese term is *si*. At their height, these were often like monastic enclosures, and could vary in size from a small village temple to a vast compound, the largest encompassing royal palaces. Traditionally, they took on the role of school, community centre, hospital and entertainment venue, as well as being a place of worship and teachings about Buddhism.

A typical *wat* has two enclosing walls that separate it from the secular world. The monks' quarters (*kuti*) are situated between the outer and inner walls. In larger temples, the inner walls may be lined with Buddha images and serve as cloisters for meditation.

Within the inner walls at the heart of the temple is the **ordination hall** (*bot*, or *sim* in Laos), surrounded by eight stone tablets and set on consecrated ground. This is the most sacred part of the temple – ordinations and special ceremonies are held here, and only monks can enter. The **sermon hall** (*viharn*), open to all, contains the principal Buddha images and sometimes takes the form of an open-sided pavilion.

Also in the inner courtyard is the bell-shaped **stupa** (also known as *chedi*, *zedi* or *that* – see page 71) containing the relics of the Buddha, and sometimes towering spires as well.

A view from the road of the Bodhi Tataung giant statues in Mandalay underlines their impact.

The Silver Pagoda, part of Cambodia's Royal Palace in Phnom Penh, has what is probably the most expensive floor in the world, made of more than 5,000 silver tiles each weighing 1kg Unlike other cultural treasures, it was preserved by the Khmer Rouge to show the richness of the Khmer culture.

These towering prang (tall, slim stupas in the Ayutthaya or Khmer style) at Wat Pho, Thailand are decorated with coloured tiles.

The Shwedagon in Rangoon, the region's most spectacular stupa. Pilgrims walk up through the lower terraces to reach enlightenment.

REGIONAL VARIETY

There is a great overlap of religions and architecture throughout the region. Stupas, for example, are often of Hindu origin, while Buddhas sit alongside Confucian and Taoist images in Chinese-style pagodas. Buddhism itself is divided into two branches in Southeast Asia: Therevada Buddhism, in which the aim is to reach nirvana after many reincarnations, spread east from Sri Lanka, and influenced Burma, Thailand, Laos and Cambodia. Mahayana Buddhism, which places less emphasis on nirvana, spread south from Tibet and China, influencing Vietnam. Local architecture was clearly affected by these outside influences.

This reclining Buddha at Ta Cu Mountain is the largest in Vietnam. The position – lying on the right side – is called 'Realising Nirvana' and represents Buddha's release from the mortal realm.

The Tree of Life Mosaic made of coloured glass on the Wat Xieng Thong temple in Luang Prabang.

Chinese influence is obvious in most of the Mahayana Buddhist temples in Vietnam, such as here at the octagonal Thien Mu Pagoda (Celestial Lady Pagoda) in Hue.

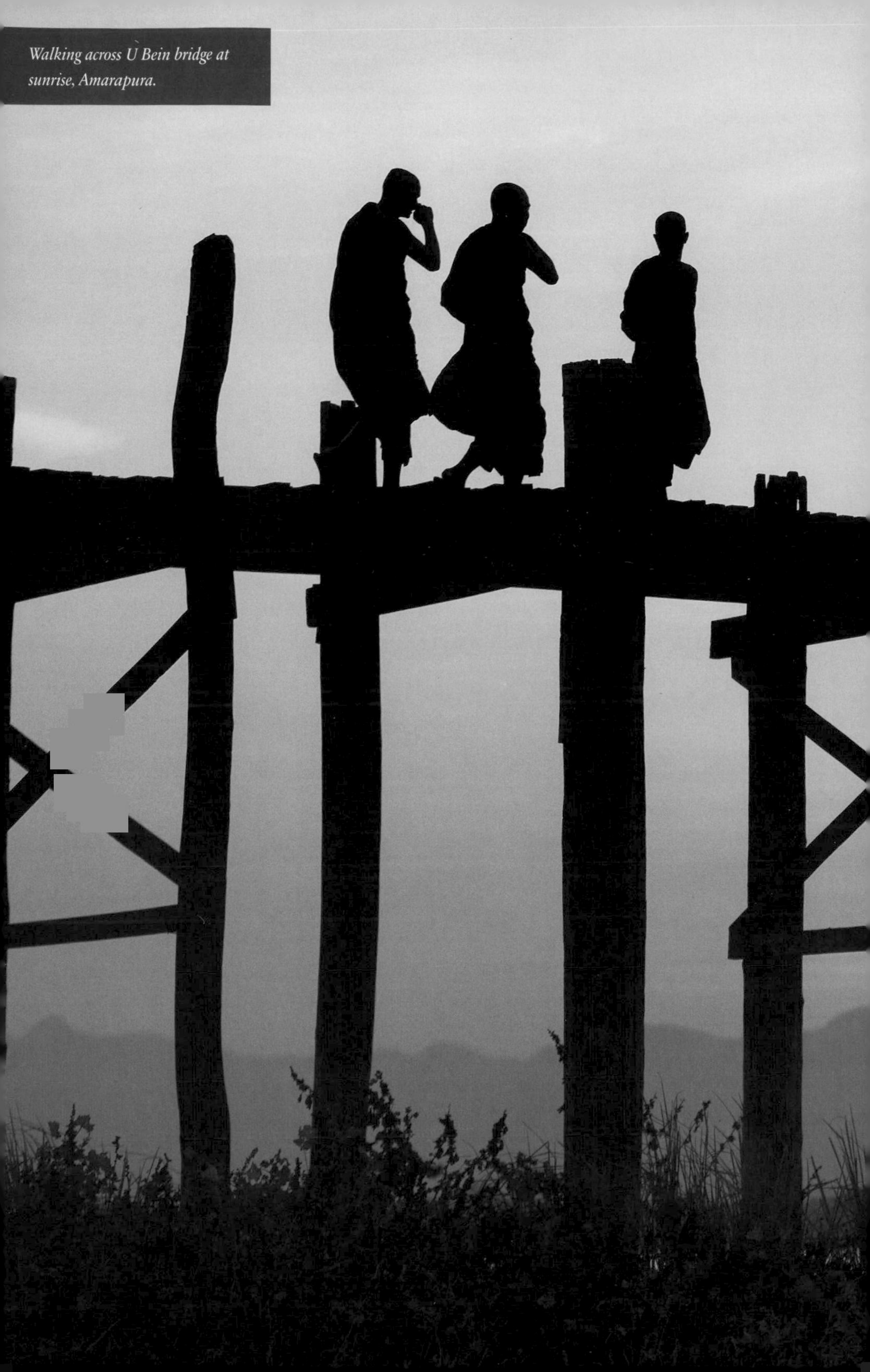

Walking across U Bein bridge at sunrise, Amarapura.

MYANMAR

With its exotic sights and pervasive Buddhist culture, visiting Myanmar (Burma) has always been a magical experience. With political changes in recent years, things look better than ever.

A teak carving detail on Shwe In bin Kyaung, Mandalay.

The essence of Myanmar lies in its atmosphere, its varied scents and colour, its ambience recalling past ages. Until very recently it suffered a brutal military regime that savagely oppressed the population. Thankfully in 2010, human rights activist Aung San Suu Kyi was released from indefinite house arrest. In 2012 she and 43 other members of her party were elected to seats in the Burmese parliament. Aung San Suu Kyi has encouraged tourism to help stimulate the economy and bring international ideals of democracy and freedom to the country. Investment is flooding into the country and with it, countries like the USA have re-opened local embassies as well.

Today, the country's name remains contentious. In 1989, the Burmese authorities implemented a series of name changes replacing colonial names with equivalents closer to actual Burmese usage. The most important change was to the name of the country, officially changed from the 'Union of Burma' to the 'Union of Myanmar'. The same is true with 'Rangoon', which became 'Yangon', a name given to the city as far back as 1755 by Alaung-paya when he captured and renamed the city of Dagon, while the Irrawaddy River is now the Ayeyarwady. In this book we use the new names, with the old names in parentheses in the first reference of each chapter. The name of the country, thus, is referred to chiefly as Myanmar, however the language Burmese, since this is derived from the internationally accepted term 'Tibeto-Burman'.

Canoeing around Nampam village, Inle lake region.

Political issues aside, Myanmar is a truly spectacular destination. From the sublime pagodas and colonial buildings of Yangon (Rangoon) north to the otherworldly palaces and temples of Mandalay, and the fabulous ruins of Bagan (Pagan) – where one can marvel at more than 2,200 stone buildings built during the First Burmese Empire – a spellbinding experience awaits the adventurous traveller.

DECISIVE DATES

The Burmese dynasties

1057 AD
Anawrahta founds first Burmese empire.

1287
Fall of first Burmese empire following Mongol invasion.

1364
Inwa (Ava) founded as capital.

1519
Portuguese establish trade station at Mottama.

Depiction of the ancient city of Mien as seen by Marco Polo.

1531
Second Burmese Empire established.

1635
Burma capital is moved to Inwa. British, French and Dutch develop trade with Burma.

1752
Mon conquer Inwa, ending the Second Burmese Empire.

1755
Alaungpaya founds Third Burmese Empire at Shwebo.

1785
King Bodawapaya conquers Rakhaing (Arakan).

Colonial period to World War II

1824–6
First Anglo-Burmese war; under Treaty of Yandabo, Britain gains Rakhaing and Tanintharyi (Tenasserim).

1852
Second Anglo-Burmese war; Britain annexes Yangon (Rangoon) and Southern Burma.

Mrauk-U, or Arrakan, in the Portuguese settlement of Daingri-pet, 1676.

1861
King Mindon (1853–78) transfers his court to Mandalay.

1886
Britain annexes all of Burma.

1937
Burma is separated from India.

1942–5
The Japanese invade and occupy Burma for four years.

Independence and military rule

1948
Burma regains independence as Union of Burma.

1962
Military coup brings General Ne Win to power; Burma Socialist Programme Party founded.

1964
All legal political parties and organisations except BSPP are banned.

1967
Anti-Chinese riots in Yangon.

1971
First BSPP Congress is held and the Twenty-Year Plan announced.

1974
New constitution becomes effective, creating the Socialist Republic of the Union of Burma.

1979
Burma withdraws from Non-Aligned Movement.

1987
UN General Assembly approves Least Developed Nation status for Burma.

1988
Major demonstrations at Yangon University campuses. Martial law is declared in Yangon. Five days later general strike and demonstrations in Yangon; the army kills many demonstrators.

SLORC takes power

1988
On 18 September, the military takes power in a coup. State Law and Order Restoration Council (SLORC). Aung San Suu Kyi founds National League for Democracy (NLD).

1989
The name of Burma is changed to Myanmar.

1990
While Aung San Suu Kyi is confined under house arrest, general elections are held and the NLD gains over 80 seats in the Assembly.

1991
SLORC refuses to recognise election results. Daw Aung San Suu Kyi is awarded Nobel Peace Prize.

1992
The UN Human Rights Commission condemns Myanmar for serious rights violations. Saw Maung is succeeded by Than Shwe as Prime Minister.

1993
The largest rebel group, Kachin Independence Organisation (KIO), as well as 14 other insurgent groups, signs a cease-fire agreement with the government.

1997
SLORC is renamed State Peace and Development Council (SPDC). Myanmar is admitted to the Association of Southeast Asian Nations (ASEAN).

2002
General Ne Win, accused of plotting to overthrow the military, dies after a long illness.

2004
The SPDC reconvenes a national convention to write a new constitution.

2005
The capital is moved from Yangon to Naypyidaw.

2007
Peaceful protests led by the monks and known as the 'Saffron revolution' are harshly suppressed. Aung San Suu Kyi remains under house arrest.

2008
On 3 May, Cyclone Nargis ravages the Ayeyarwady Delta, killing an estimated 200,000 people. The military junta refuses international aid.

2010
National elections are held as part of a raft of constitutional reforms. Further reforms see a wind down of press censorship and the release of hundreds of political prisoners – among them NLD leader, Aung San Suu Kyi.

2012
Aung San Suu Kyi is one of 44 NLD representatives elected to parliament. Tourist numbers increase rapidly as the tourism boycott is lifted. US President Barack Obama visits.

2012–2013
Riots and increased tension between Muslims and Buddhists. President Thein Sein visits Washington and Britain.

A crowd watches Aung San Suu Kyi speak in Yangon.

To visit Kakkiu pagoda you need to be accompanied by a guide.

PEOPLE AND CULTURE

Myanmar's population is a diverse collection of
people, their origins found in the cultures of
ancient China and Thailand.

The Burmese name for the country,
Myanmar, implies that the nation is a
federation of many peoples. But it is an
uneasy federation. 'Burma Proper' – as it was
called by the British – was the chief settlement
area of the Bamar (Burman) majority, encircled
by 'Outer Burma', the separate ethnic minority states of the Chin, Kachin, Shan, Kayin or
Karen, Kayah (Red Karen/Karenni), Mon and
Rakhaing (Arakanese). Through the centuries,
there has been mistrust, antagonism, and frequent wars among the various groups, and the
situation is no different today.

The current administrative divisions were
built into Burma's 1948 constitution, which was
based on a model devised by the British. During the colonial era, the British established the
distinction between Burma Proper and Outer
Burma. Burma Proper was placed under the
direct rule of British India, but the minorities
were left with much greater autonomy under
indirect rule. At the time, nearly 250 separate
languages and dialects were spoken.

While the Bamar were denied a place in the
colonial army, the British heavily depended on
the fighting skills of the various minorities.
The racial enmity between the Bamars and the
minorities festered just beneath the surface
until independence was granted in 1948. Since
that time, there has been a succession of violent
domestic confrontations.

No fewer than 67 separate indigenous racial
groups have been identified in Burma, not
including the various Indians, Chinese and others who make the country their home. In fact,
the Burmese authorities currently recognise no
fewer than 135 minorities, but this is difficult
to verify and likely to be another part of the
military policy of divide and rule.

Relaxing at a street-side café in downtown Yangon.

The earliest inhabitants

Man has inhabited the area now known as
Burma since prehistory, long before the ancestors of the modern Burmese moved southwards
from central Asia and Tibet. These early inhabitants eventually moved on towards what is
now Indonesia. Anthropologists believe that
the indigenous people of the Andaman Islands
in the Bay of Bengal may be direct descendants.

Three separate migrations were historically
important in Burma's development. The first
to arrive were the Mon-Khmer people from the
arid plains of Central Asia, and it is not difficult
to imagine their motivation. Anyone who has
seen the mountains of golden rice piled high
at harvest time will understand why the first

Mon-Khmer kingdom was called Suvannabhumi, or the Golden Land.

They were followed by the Tibeto-Burmans, who pushed the Mon-Khmers further to the south and east, away from the middle reaches of the Ayeyarwady (Irrawaddy) River. First the Pyu, then the Bamar, moved down the valleys of the Ayeyarwady and Sittoung (Sittang) rivers, establishing their magnificent empires at Thayekhittaya (Sri Ksetra) and Bagan (Pagan).

Between the 12th and 14th centuries, the Tai (known today in Myanmar as Shan), a Sino-Tibetan race, began moving south from Yun-

The bride at a Pa O wedding ceremony.

nan down the river valleys. When they tried to force the Bamar out of the Ayeyarwady Valley, centuries of warfare ensued.

Bamar and Mon

There are about 38 million Bamar in Burma today, constituting over two-thirds of the population. They are the major landholders, and dominate the government. As such, they attract a great deal of interracial hostility from other groups.

Most of the cultural forms described subsequently are broadly representative of the Bamar, who typically live in thatched dwellings and work as rice farmers. Perhaps their greatest distinguishing trademark is a pale

yellow powder, made from *thanaka* bark, which Bamar women apply to their faces as protection against the sun.

The Buddhist Mon, long since displaced by the Bamar, live mainly around the cities of Mawlamyaing (Moulmein) and Bago (Pegu). In 1995, after decades of armed resistance, they signed a cease-fire agreement with the Burmese army. Today, the Mon – who number around 1.5 million – are largely assimilated into mainstream Burmese culture, although they continue to use their own language and have retained their own sanctioned state within the Burmese union.

Padaung and Wa

Among the smaller minority groups belonging to the Mon-Khmer language family are the Padaung and the Wa. Both groups have gained a certain fame – or notoriety – that far exceeds their meagre numbers.

There are only about 10,000 Padaung, all of whom live in the vicinity of Loikaw, capital of Kayah State. Their 'giraffe women' were publicised by various ethnographers of the 19th and 20th centuries. Despite the illusion, the women's necks have not actually been elongated at all – the brass coils worn around their necks have pushed down their collarbones and ribs. In recent years, significant numbers have moved to Thailand where they live in hilltribe 'tourist villages'.

The Wa are the notorious frontier inhabitants of Myanmar's northeast, mostly in Shan state. About 350,000 live in remote areas on both sides of the border with China. Until the 1940s,

THE FIGHTING KACHIN

Kachin State in the north of Myanmar is a real hotchpotch of hill tribes. Throughout this large, mountainous district, Jinghpaw (Kachin), Shan and Bamar share space with Maru, Lashi, Azi, Lisu, Rawang, and other groups. The label Kachin is sometimes indiscriminately applied to all inhabitants of this state, but the only true Kachin are the Jinghpaw. Animism is a part of daily life. The Kachins are famous warriors – even the Japanese failed to conquer them, and the Kachin Independence Organisation (KIO), though tentatively in a ceasefire, remain the greatest threat to the Burmese army.

Many Shan, facing military persecution, have fled to neighbouring Thailand where they are easily absorbed in the ethnically kindred Tai population. The Burmese junta is encouraging Burman settlement of traditionally Shan lands.

there was little known about them, except that they were head-hunters who offered human skulls as sacrifices to their gods.

Shan

Shan. Siam. Assam. All three geographical names have the same root meaning, an indication of the widespread migration and settlement area of this race. At just over nine percent of the population, Myanmar's 3.9 million Shan, or Tai Yai as they call themselves, are mostly Buddhists who make their homes in valleys and on high plains. Living at an average altitude of 1,000 metres (3,300ft) above sea level, the Shans are Burma's leading producers of fruits and vegetables and, over the centuries, they have developed sophisticated irrigation systems in the river valleys. After the Shan State, the next largest concentration is in Kachin State, but they can also be found throughout much of Myanmar.

Shan are recognisable by the turbans worn by men and married women. Men usually dress in baggy, dark-blue trousers rather than in Bamar-style *longyi*. Girls wear trousers and blouses until the age of 14, at which time they don colourful dresses. As they get older, their costumes grow less colourful until, at about the age of 40, the women start to wear sober black clothing for the rest of their lives.

Kayin and Kayah

The Kayin or Karen people belong linguistically to the Tibeto-Burman-speaking majority of Myanmar, numbering 4.1 million. Although they have their own separate administrative division, only about one-third of the population lives there. The Karen National Liberation Army (KNLA) is still fighting the Burmese government, as they have been since 1949. The movement split in 1994, with a Buddhist faction calling a ceasefire, while the Christian contingent fights on.

The Kayah, also known as Red Karen or Karenni, have the smallest state in Myanmar in terms of area as well as population. Virtually all members of this ethnic group – about 80,000 – reside here. The Kayah are primarily hill people, making their living by dry cultivation of rice, millet and vegetables.

Rakhaing and Chin

The Rakhaing (Arakanese), who are also known as Rakhine, inhabit Rakhaing State and constitute about 4 percent of the population. Although closely related to the Bamar, the latter have had their hands full dealing with this coastal race over the past two centuries. The

A local sits outside his house in Twante, Delta Region.

Rakhaing are about 75 percent Buddhist and 25 percent Muslim, with the two groups having little to do with each other. The Burmese military junta systematically persecute the latter group in an apparent effort to force them to migrate to Bangladesh.

The Chin, and related Naga people, make up about 3 percent of Myanmar's population. They live in the far northwest, spilling over the border into India and Bangladesh. Traditionally animist, most Chin have converted to Christianity, having been evangelised by American and Australian missionaries.

Slash-and-burn agriculture has for centuries furnished land for dry-rice growing, though the resulting soil erosion has depleted the amount of cultivable land to less than that required to sustain the population in recent decades. Some Chin along the banks of the Kaladan River, to the north of the ruined former Arakan capital of Mrauk-U, also practise subsistence fishing alongside settled farming. Among these, and throughout the jungle region to the north, senior women have elaborately tattooed faces, though the custom is rapidly dying out.

Armed insurgent groups, under the umbrella leadership of the Chin National Army (CAN), have been active in the Chin

natural event that occurs only once every 50 or so years. The fruit produced by the bamboo causes a spike in the rodent population, but when the feast is over the rats and mice target local grain stocks. Famine ensued, forcing still greater numbers or refugees across the border.

Culture and society

Myanmar's decades as a pariah state have ensured that it ranks today among the most staunchly traditional nations in Asia. And it's not just the peripheral, remote and mountainous regions where picturesque, antiquated

Catching up on local news in downtown Yangon.

heartland since Independence in 1948, but the fighting intensified following the 1988 uprising. The minority has been persecuted by the Burmese army ever since. Chin State is officially the poorest in the country, with the least infrastructure: 70 percent of its population live below the poverty line and 40 percent live without adequate food. As a consequence, and to flee the violence perpetrated by the *tatmadaw*, hundreds of thousands of Chin have fled across the Indian frontier to neighbouring Mizoram – a cause of political controversy between the two countries.

The ongoing problem of food shortages in Chin State reached crisis proportions in 2006, after the region's bamboo forest flowered – a

traditions still hold sway. Even in the cities, adherence to traditional values remains to the fore – something you'll notice from the minute you step off the plane. Traditional dress is ubiquitous, and the Burmese are remarkably polite and deferential towards their elders and strangers. Conventions of hospitality remain strong, as do the beliefs and practices of Theravada Buddhism, fervent adherence to which is a fact of daily life in a country where monks queue in the street each morning to accept alms from lay people and the terraces of huge gilded pagodas throng from sunset to sunrise with pilgrims and worshippers.

Because they comprise by far the largest and most dominant cultural group in Myanmar, the following account refers principally to the Bamar and Mon, the overwhelming majority of whom are Buddhists.

Dress

The Burmese emphasise their national identity through the clothes they wear. Most evident is the *longyi*, introduced by immigrant families from southern India. Similar to the Malaysian sarong, it consists of a kilt-like piece of cloth worn from the waist to the ankle. Together with the *eingyi*, a transparent blouse that is worn with a round-collared, long-sleeved

The ceremony itself is considered *lokiya*, or 'earthly', in the Buddhist tradition, and as such is not officiated over by a monk or abbot, although to gain merit, monks may well attend the betrothal dinner or wedding reception. Instead, a Brahmin priest presides over the ritual, which begins with the blowing of a conch shell as the couple have the palms of their hands bound together in cloth and placed in a silver bowl – the Burmese for marriage is '*let htat*' or 'join palms'. Sanskrit verses are intoned by the Brahmin, who then raises the couple's hands and unties them, to more

Shopping at Nampam market, Inle lake region.

jacket, the *longyi* still takes precedence over Western-style garments.

Marriage

By and large, and unlike their Indian cousins across the Andaman Sea, Burmese choose their own life partners. Traditions of romantic love are strong. Couples meet, court and decide to marry themselves, albeit in a style that appears very old-fashioned and demure to Western eyes. Should the parents disapprove of the match there is little they can do about it. Parental opposition to any marriage in Myanmar will typically result in an elopement, followed by a gradual rehabilitation of the couple if the marriage proves a success.

blasts from the conch shell. Afterwards, there will be entertainment and speeches, and with more affluent families, perhaps a reception dinner at a smart hotel.

Traditional dress is worn throughout by the participants and those attending, even among more sophisticated urbanites – though with wealthier families the bride's dress tends to be an extravagant modern designer twist on the traditional *htamein* featuring a wealth of embroidery, pearls, sequins and even on some occasions gold.

Burmese get married expecting it to be for life; comparatively few marriages end in divorce, but those that do, see their common property divided equally.

RELIGION

Religion is a defining element in Burmese life. Buddhism permeates the everyday lives of Myanmar's people, placing great emphasis on individual achievement.

I t has often been said that Myanmar is the most profoundly Buddhist country in the world. That may well be true. But the brand of Buddhism practised in this isolated land is unique on the face of the Earth.

Burmese Buddhism, theoretically, is Theravada or Hinayana Buddhism, that sect of Buddhism adhering most closely to the Buddha's original teaching, and which is the dominant form throughout Southeast Asia. It was preceded in Burma, however, by the animistic beliefs of the hill tribes and by the Hindu-Brahmanism of early traders, which has had a profound effect on the ongoing local cosmological concepts.

Burmese cosmology

Strictly speaking, Burmese cosmology is Buddhist cosmology, but it has been shaped by around three millennia of influences from other cultures, particularly that of the Brahmans. According to the Burmese, the Eurasian continent, Jambudvipa, is the southernmost of four islands situated at the cardinal points surrounding Mount Meru, the centre of the world. This southern island is the only place where future Buddhas can be born.

There are considered to be a total of 31 planes of existence on, above, and below Mount Meru. They can be divided into three main groups: the 11 planes of *Kama-Loka*, the realm of the sensuous world; the 16 planes of *Rupa-Loka*, the realm of subtle material matter; and finally, the four planes of *Arupa-Loka*, the realm of formlessness.

The Realm of the nats

King Anawrahta, founder of the First Burmese Empire, devoted his attention to simplifying

A nun praying at U Min Thonze Pagoda, Sagaing.

spiritual beliefs. When he introduced Theravada Buddhism into Upper Burma as the national religion, he was unable to eliminate certain animistic beliefs of his people, the most persistent of which was the belief in *nats* – a collection of deities including spirits of trees, rivers, ancestors, snakes, and especially the spirits of people who have met a violent or tragic death. *Nats* appreciate a peaceful life, and can wreak destructive vengeance on those who annoy them. Anawratha decided to limit their influence by decreeing that there was not an endless number of *nat* deities. Instead he came up with the number 36, to which a 37th, borrowed from the Indian Brahmanic tradition, was added. This was Thagyamin, the guardian *nat* of Buddhism, who was declared head of the *nat* pantheon.

Thagyamin aside, the oldest and most powerful *nats* are the Mahagiri Nats, spirits of a brother and sister who suffered untimely deaths at the hand of King Thinlikyaung (344–387 AD). According to *The Glass Palace Chronicle* of Mandalay, their spirits entered into a *saga* tree that floated down the Ayeyarwady (Irrawaddy) to Bagan (Pagan), where local craftsmen made images of the brother and sister – 'Lord of the Great Mountain' and 'Lady Golden Face' – and installed them on Mount Popa, an extinct volcano southeast of Bagan, which became the spiritual home of the *nats*.

Theravada Buddhism

Theravada Buddhism is recognised as the principal religion of about 80 percent of all Burmese people. While there are significant numbers of Hindus, Muslims, Christians and animists (especially among the northern hill tribes), it is safe to say that over 99 percent of the Bamar (Burman), Mon, Shan and Palaung are Theravadins.

Meditating inside Botataung pagoda, Yangon.

THREE JEWELS, FOUR NOBLE TRUTHS AND THE EIGHT-FOLD PATH

As there is no true form of worship in the Theravada style of Buddhism, the only crucial ritual to which both monks and laity submit themselves is the recitation – three times a day – of the 'Three Jewels', or the *Triratna*:

'I take refuge in the Buddha. I take refuge in the Dhamma. I take refuge in the Sangha'.

The formula of the Three Jewels offers solace and security. These are needed for strength, if one understands the "Four Noble Truths" expounded upon by Gautama Buddha in his first sermon:

Life always has in it the element of suffering
The cause of suffering is desire

In order to end the suffering, give up desire and give up attachment

The way to this goal is the Noble Eight-fold Path

The Noble Eight-fold Path consists of right view, right intent, right speech, right conduct, right means of livelihood, right endeavour, right mindfulness, and right meditation. This 'path' is normally divided into three areas:

View and intent are matters of wisdom.

Speech, conduct or action, and livelihood are matters of morality.

Endeavour, mindfulness, and meditation are matters resulting from true mental discipline.

The Buddha denied the existence of a soul. There is no permanence, he explained, for that which one perceives to be 'self'. Rather, one's essence is forever changing. The idea of rebirth, therefore, is a complicated philosophical question within the structure of Buddhism. When a Buddhist (or any person, for that matter) is reincarnated, it is neither the person nor the soul that is actually reborn. Rather, it is the sum of one's *karma*, the balance of good and evil deeds. One is reborn as a result of prior existence. A popular metaphor used to explain this transition is that of a candle. Were a person to light one candle from the flame of another, then extinguish the first, it could not be said that the new flame was the same as the previous one. Rather, in fact, its existence would be due to that of the previous flame.

The Noble Eight-fold Path, therefore, does not lead to salvation in the Judeo-Christian sense. By pursuing matters of wisdom, morality and mental discipline, one can hope to make the transition into *nirvana*, which can perhaps best be defined as extinction of suffering, cessation of desire. It is not heaven, nor is it annihilation. It is simply a quality of existence.

The monk

There are no priests in Theravada Buddhism. But the faithful still need a model to follow on the path to salvation, and the monks provide this. In Myanmar, there are about 800,000 monks. Most of these are students and novices who put on the monk's orange robe only temporarily; nearly all male Burmese devote a period – from a few weeks to several years – in their lifetime to the monkhood. There are three fundamental rules to which the monk must subscribe. First, the renunciation of all possessions, except eight items: three robes, a razor for shaving, a needle for sewing, a strainer (to ensure that no living thing is swallowed), a belt, and an alms bowl. Second, a vow to injure no living thing and to offend no one. Finally, the vow of complete sexual celibacy.

The monk must make his livelihood by seeking alms, setting out two hours before dawn and going door to door. The food received is the monk's only meal of the day. Beyond this, monks should avoid alcohol and other intoxicating subjects, rise at dawn when it is possible to distinguish the lines on one's palms by the growing light, refrain from eating from midday until the next dawn, and practise meditation.

A young Burmese begins his novitiate at around the age of nine. Most have left the monkhood before their 20th birthday. Those who are fully ordained devote their lives to meditation, the study of the Pali scriptures, and the instruction of the laity. Nuns are much fewer in number than monks, and are generally restricted to women who have already raised families and become grandmothers, so that their religious duties do not interfere with normal domestic life.

Young monks at Kaba Aye pagoda, Yangon.

THE BUDDHIST SCHISM

The division between the two main strands of Buddhism occurred in 235BC when King Ashoka convened the Third Buddhist Synod at Pataliputra, India. The Buddhist elders (Theravada means 'the way of the elders') held tight to their beliefs. They were opposed by a group that sought to understand the personality of the historical Buddha, and its relationship to human, as opposed to purely individual salvation. This Mahayana or 'Greater Vehicle' school established itself in Tibet, China, Korea, Mongolia, Japan and Vietnam. The Theravada school thrived in Sri Lanka, Burma, Thailand, Laos and Cambodia.

Responsible tourism

After more than two decades, foreign visitors are no longer being asked to boycott visiting Myanmar on ethical grounds, but challenges still exist.

In 2010, after the military government embarked on a process of democratic reform in Myanmar, Aung San Suu Kyi's National League for Democracy (the NLD) declared an end to the country's long-standing tourism boycott. Foreigners had been discouraged from visiting the country on the grounds that their presence legitimised and generated income for the repressive regime of Myanmar and its cronies – while thousands of political prisoners languished in jail, and ethnic minorities such as the Karen, Kachin and Chin were subject to torture, forced labour and other forms of abuse perpetrated by the Burmese army (Tatmadaw).

Things have moved on rapidly since the NLD's announcement. Peace accords have been signed with most of the rebel groups, tourism is booming as never before and the country is well on the way to becoming a democracy, with its own fully elected parliament.

However, the NLD has remained somewhat ambivalent about tourism, maintaining a stance against large tour groups, and advising visitors to avoid hotels owned by or connected to high-ranking members of the junta – even though tax revenue from such enterprises is nowadays benefiting a government of which the NLD is a part.

Ethical practice

So is it now really ethical to visit Myanmar? The answer is 'more so than in previous decades', but with some caveats.

Basically, it is impossible to make sure none of your cash ends up in the back pockets of unscrupulous middle men and entrepreneurs connected with shadier corridors of power. However, this is also true of visiting neighbouring countries ruled by corrupt regimes; particularly Communist Vietnam. But you can, by following some simple principles, ensure your presence in Myanmar, or neighbouring Laos, Cambodia and Vietnam for that matter, is as much of a force for good as possible. The following are based on recommendations formulated by the British NGO, Tourism Concern (tourismconcern.org).

Travel independently rather than as part of a large organised tour, using locally owned accommodation wherever possible.

If you do book a tour, avoid large foreign-owned operators in favour of smaller, independently run ones with a clear policy on benefiting local economies.

Quiz your holiday company on its stance regarding ownership of the hotels they use. In compiling accommodation recommendations, we consulted the most up-to-date blacklist compiled by the Paris-based pressure group, Info Birmanie (info-birmanie.org), an organisation with close connections to Aung San Suu Kyi and the NLD. Blacklisted hotels have been excluded from our listings, except where

Try some genuinely local delicacies, like these crickets at Bogyoke market in Yangon.

they are the only options in any given place, in which case their connection with the junta or its associates is flagged.

Spread your money around as widely as possible. Patronise different taxi drivers, eat in family-run restaurants and buy souvenirs from local shops rather than the boutiques back at your hotel.

Interact at every opportunity with Burmese people you meet – though avoid at all costs discussing politics or any subject likely to incriminate them in the eyes of the government.

Rather than giving money to individuals, make donations to projects such as schools, orphanages and clinics, though it is best to do some prior research and ensure your money will be used responsibly.

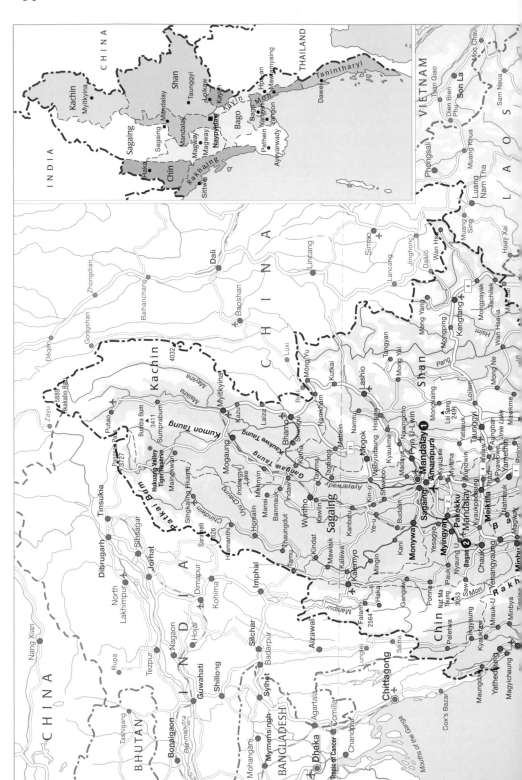

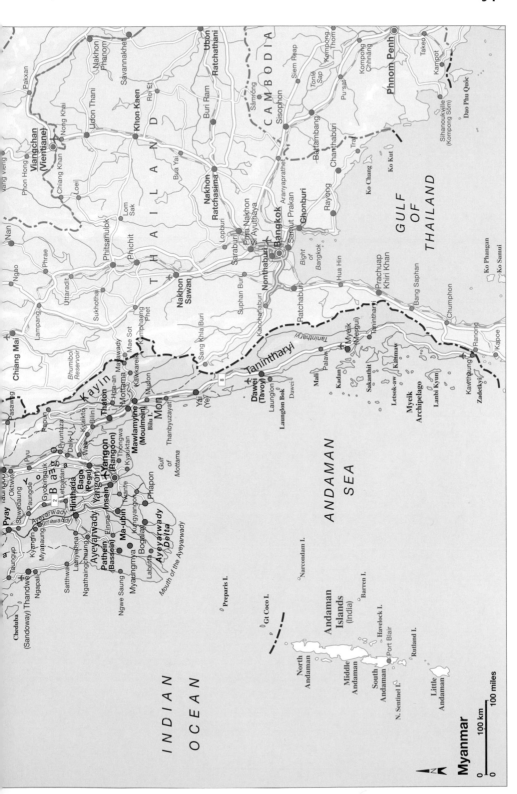

Myanmar

0   100 km
0   100 miles

N

INDIAN
OCEAN

ANDAMAN
SEA

GULF
OF
THAILAND

THAILAND

CAMBODIA

Andaman
Islands
(India)

North
Andaman

Middle
Andaman

South
Andaman

Little
Andaman

N. Sentinel I.
Port Blair
Rutland I.
Havelock I.
Barren I.
Gt Coco I.
Preparis I.
Narcondam I.

Myeik
Archipelago

Tanintharyi

Mon

Kayin

Ayeyarwady
Delta

B a g o

Viangchan
(Vientiane)

Chiang Mai

Bangkok

Nonthaburi

Phnom Penh

Khon Kaen

Nakhon
Ratchasima

Nakhon
Sawan

Dawei
(Tavoy)

Myeik
(Mergui)

Yangon
(Rangoon)

Bago
(Pegu)

Mawlamyine
(Moulmein)

Thaton

Pathein
(Bassein)

Pyay

Hinthada

Ma-ubin

Insein

Ubon
Ratchathani

Chonburi

Cheduba
(Sandoway) Thandwe

The amazing golden stupa of the Shwedagon.

YANGON (RANGOON)

Kipling had ogled, Theroux has prophesied.
Myanmar's former capital of Yangon, or Rangoon,
continues to evoke lyricism from those who venture
among its streets of 'dispossessed princes'.

I t's been more than 100 years since Kipling was mesmerised by the glistening golden stupa of the Shwedagon Pagoda as he first set eyes on the city of Yangon (Rangoon). Today, the pagoda continues to dominate the city's landscape, a perfect symbol of a country in which Buddhism pervades every aspect of life.

But while the Shwedagon Pagoda may dominate Yangon, it is far from the whole show. If you look beyond the ageing British colonial architecture, you will find an oddly cosmopolitan city of 19th-century charm, with quiet, tree-lined avenues and a people that are known to be gracious and fun-loving. The downtown area around Sule Pagoda may be sprouting a few high-rise buildings, but overall the face of the city has preserved a good deal of the ambience present when the British left in 1948.

Water on three sides

Yangon is surrounded on three sides by water. The Hlaing River flows down its west flank, while to the east is Pazundaung Creek; the two converge to form the Yangon River, flanking the south of the city.

The first accounts of "Dagon, the town with the Golden Pagoda" were recorded by European travellers in the 16th century. In 1586, an English

merchant, Ralph Fitch, described Shwedagon as "the fairest place, as I suppose, that is in the world", although it was the nearby town of Syriam, across the Bago and Hlaing rivers from Dagon, that was the most important European trading colony and Burma's main port well into the 18th century.

King Alaungpaya founded Yangon in 1755 when he captured Dagon from the Mon. He called the settlement Yangon, or 'End of Strife', which the British later altered to Rangoon. With the destruction of Syriam the following year after

Main Attractions

Sule Pagoda
Strand Hotel
Bogyoke Aung San Market
National Museum
Shwedagon Pagoda

Embarking on the boat to Dalah (Delta Region), in Downtown Yangon.

it was captured from the Mon, Yangon assumed its commercial pre-eminence. After the British conquered the town in 1824 during the First Anglo-Burmese War, its importance as a trade port flourished. But fire devastated the town in 1841 – and 11 years later it was again almost completely destroyed in the Second Anglo-Burmese War.

Exploring Yangon

The old heritage district downtown is compact enough to explore on foot, albeit with frequent heat-beating pit stops in teahouses and cafés along the way. Motorbikes and scooters are not permitted in this area, making it a lot quieter and more relaxing for pedestrians than other cities such as Mandalay. However, quite a few of Yangon's sights lie further afield and are best reached by taxi. Cabs, identifiable by the signs on their roofs, come in a variety of shapes and sizes, but offer great value for money, with few trips across town costing more than K2,000–2,500 ($3–4). Moreover, the drivers themselves are considerably more courteous and honest than their counterparts in

Sule pagoda seen from the sky bar on the top of the Sakura tower.

other Asian cities. That said, few speak fluent English, so it can help if you have the name of your destination written in Burmese.

The Sule Pagoda

In the downtown area is the city's commercial centre amidst the mildewing grey brick government offices erected by the British, and the high-rise hotels built by Singaporean investors. And it is here, especially in the markets, that the true colours of Yangon's diverse population can be seen.

If the Shwedagon is the soul of Yangon, then surely the **Sule Pagoda** Ⓐ is its heart. For centuries it has been the focus of much of the social and religious activity of the city, although much of the current structure only dates from the 19th century (the *chedi* dates to the 15th century). The British centred the urban area around the pagoda when they structured their Victorian street-grid system in the mid-19th century. Today, the 48-metre (157ft) pagoda remains among the taller structures in the city centre.

The ancient origins of the Sule

Pagoda are bound up in the mythical prehistory of the country. Perhaps the most credible tale is that of two monks who were sent from India as missionaries to Thaton around 230BC. After some hesitation, the king of Thaton gave them permission to construct a shrine at the foot of Singuttara Hill. Within it the monks preserved one of the Buddha's hairs, which they had carried from India.

The pagoda's octagonal structure, which is consistent up to the bell and inverted bowl, clearly indicates its Brahman-Buddhist heritage. During the first centuries of the Christian era, when the influence of Indian merchants and settlers was especially strong, astrology blended with *nat* worship and Buddhist doctrine to create the unique Burmese brand of Buddhism. The Sule Pagoda was at the heart of this early religion, and even today, it remains a magnet for astrologers and fortune-tellers.

Colonial remnants

On the northeast corner of Sule Pagoda Road and Maha Bandoola Street, facing Sule Pagoda, is the **Yangon City Hall B**. Built by the British, it is a massive stone structure worth a glance for its colonial architecture with Burmese ornamentation. There is a traditional Burmese peacock seal high over the entrance.

At the southeast corner of the intersection is **Maha Bandoola Garden** (open daily; charge), named after a Burmese general of the First Anglo-Burmese War and centred on the **Independence Monument C**, a 46-metre (150ft) obelisk surrounded by five smaller 9-metre (30ft) pillars. The monument represents Burma's five former semi-autonomous states – Shan, Kachin, Kayin (Karen), Kayah and Chin – in union with their more numerous Bamar (Burman) brothers. Facing the square on the east side stands the Queen-Anne-style **Supreme Court**, dating from 1911, and the similarly grand **High Court** building.

On Strand Road is the famous **Strand Hotel D**, positively dripping in opulent colonial-era luxury. Before its substantial and expensive renovation in the mid-1990s, most of the formerly mosquito-infested rooms were cooled by electric paddle fans and serviced by dribbling water pipes. It's worth stepping into the teak-furnished lounge for a cup of tea or bottle of cold beer.

Heading east on Strand Road for several blocks, you'll come to the **Botataung Pagoda E**. It is said that when eight Indian monks carried some relics of the Buddha here more than 2,000 years ago, 1,000 military officers (*botataung*) formed a guard of honour at the place where the rebuilt pagoda stands today.

The markets

West of the Sule Pagoda are Yangon's main street markets. Before World War II, most of the inhabitants of the city were Indian or Chinese, and their influence is still reflected in this jam-packed district. Take a stroll through **Chinatown** stretching from Shwedagon Pagoda Road, west over 24th, Bo Yawe,

The Buddha statue inside Botataung pagoda.

The red-brick high court and the Indepenence statue, Mahabandoola Gardens.

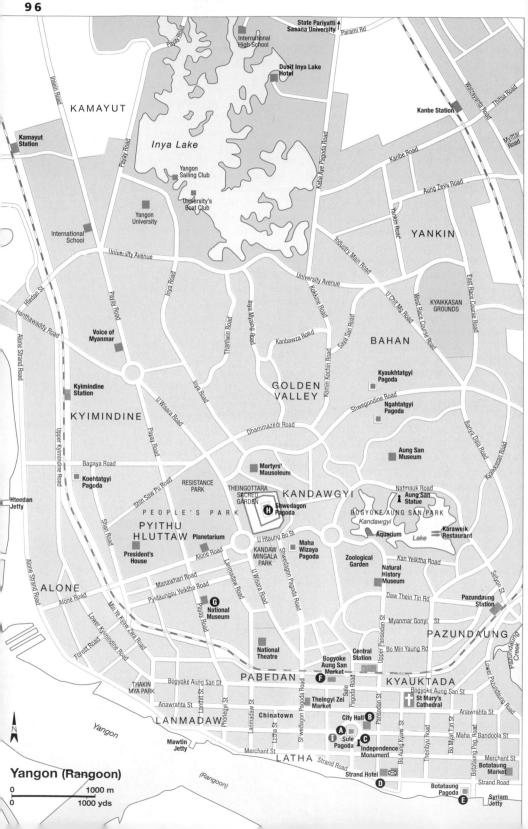

Yangon (Rangoon)

KAMAYUT

Kamayut
Station

Inya Lake

International
High School

State Pariyatti
Sasana University

Dusit Inya Lake
Hotel

Parami Rd

Kanbe Station

Payay Road

Insein Road

Yangon
Sailing Club

University's
Boat Club

Yangon University

International
School

Kaba Aye Pagoda Road

Kanbe Road

Aung Zeya Road

Yankin Road

Industry Main Road

University Avenue

YANKIN

Waizayanta Road

Thitsa Road

Myittar Road

University Avenue

Kokine Road

U Chit Mg Road

West Race Course Road

East Race Course Road

KYAIKKASAN
GROUNDS

Hledan St

Hanthawaddy Road

Alone Strand Road

Voice of
Myanmar

Payay Road

Inya Road

Thanlwin Road

Inya Myaing Road

Kanbawza Road

Komin Kochin Road

Saya San Road

BAHAN

Kyaukhtatgyi
Pagoda

GOLDEN
VALLEY

Shwegondine Road

Ngahtatgyi
Pagoda

Banya Dala Road

Kyaikkasan Road

Kyimindine
Station

KYIMINDINE

U Wisara Road

Payay Road

Dhammazedi Road

Aung San
Museum

Upper Kyimindine Road

Bagaya Road

Koehtatgyi
Pagoda

Shin Saw Pu Road

RESISTANCE
PARK

Martyrs'
Mausoleum

THEINGOTTARA
SACRED
GARDEN

Shwedagon
Pagoda

KANDAWGYI

Natmauk Road

Aung San
Statue

Hteedan
Jetty

Shan Road

PEOPLE'S PARK

PYITHU
HLUTTAW

Planetarium

President's
House

Alone Road

U Htaung Bo St

KANDAW
MINGALA
PARK

Maha
Wizaya
Pagoda

BOGYOKE AUNG SAN PARK

Kandawgyi
Lake

Aquarium

Karaweik
Restaurant

ALONE

Alone Strand Road

Alone Road

Manawhari Road

Pyidaungsu Yeiktha Road

Lanmadaw Road

Shwedagon Pagoda Road

U Wisara Road

Kan Yeiktha Road

Daw Thein Tin Rd

Zoological
Garden

Natural
History
Museum

Sein Yon St

Pazundaung
Station

Min Ye Kyaw Zwa Road

Lower Kyimindine Road

Forest Road

G
National
Museum

Payay Road

National Theatre

PAZUNDAUNG

Myanmar Gonyi St

Upper Pansodan St

Bo Min Yaung Rd

Lower Pazundaung Road

Pazundaung Road

THAKIN
MYA PARK

Bogyoke Aung San St

PABEDAN

Bogyoke
Aung San
Market

F

Central
Station

KYAUKTADA

Bogyoke Aung San St

St Mary's
Cathedral

Anawrahta St

Anawrahta St

Phonegyi St

Lanthit St

Lanmadaw St

Latha St

Shwedagon Pagoda Road

Theingyi Zei
Market

Pansodan St

Bo Aung Kyaw St

Theinbyu Road

Bo Myat Tin St

Maha Bandoola Pag. Road

Bandoola Road

Merchant St

Botataung
Market

LANMADAW

Chinatown

City Hall

B

Sule
Pagoda

A

i

Mawtin
Jetty

Merchant St

LATHA

Independence
Monument

C

Strand Road

Strand Road

D
Strand Hotel

Yangon

(Rangoon)

Botataung
Pagoda

E

Syriam
Jetty

N

Yangon (Rangoon)

0 — 1000 m

0 — 1000 yds

Latha and Sint Oh Dan roads. Here the cracked sidewalks are piled high with all manner of goods – bamboo baskets, religious images, calligraphy, peanut candy, melon seeds, flowers, caged songbirds, tropical fish for aquariums and live crabs. In the evening these streets turn into a rambling outdoor restaurant, with stalls offering delicious soups, curries and other local dishes.

A few blocks back towards Sule Pagoda, the aroma of curry powder and other ground spices emanates from the Indian Quarter. **Theingyi Zei** (Indian Market) offers mounds of red chillies and cinnamon bark, boxes of tropical fruits such as mangosteen and durian, dried fish and seafoods, medicinal herbs, bottled concoctions and local snacks. The market is at the side of a Hindu temple on Anawrahta Street.

The largest and most interesting of Yangon's bazaars, however, is the **Bogyoke Aung San Market** 🟥 (formerly the Scott Market) to the north of the Indian and Chinese quarters at the corner of Sule Pagoda Road and Bogyoke Aung San Street. Stalls sell a wonderful range of Burmese handicrafts, a wide variety of textiles and craft objects, woodcarvings, lacquerware, dolls, musical instruments, colourful *longyis*, Shan bags and wickerware. It's also a good place to shop for jade and gems, with nearly the entire ground floor taken up by ruby sellers. Opposite the Bogyoke Market, the New Bogyoke Market specialises in imported textiles, household appliances and medicines.

The National Museum

The **National Museum** 🟥 (Mon–Fri 10am–4pm; charge) is in a neighbourhood filled with foreign missions. The showpiece is the Lion's Throne, upon which King Thibaw once sat at Mandalay Palace. After the Third Anglo-Burmese War in 1886, the throne and 52 other pieces of royal regalia were carted off by the British. Some items were left behind in the Indian Museum in Calcutta; others were kept in the Victoria and Albert Museum in London. They were returned to Burma as a gesture of goodwill in 1964 after Ne Win's state visit to Britain. The throne is 8 metres (27ft) high and is inlaid with gold and lacquer work. It is a particularly striking example of the Burmese art of woodcarving. Among the other Mandalay Regalia, as they are known, are gem-studded swords, jewellery and serving dishes. Also in the archaeological section of the museum are artefacts from Burma's early history in Beikthano, Thayekhittaya (Sri Ksetra) and Bagan (Pagan).

Shwedagon Pagoda

One of the most spectacular sights anywhere in Asia, the glorious bell-shaped stupa of the **Shwedagon Pagoda** 🟥 (daily 4am–9pm; charge, tickets are not sold to foreigners before 6am) soars nearly 100 metres (330ft) above Singuttara Hill. It is plated with a total of 8,688 solid-gold slabs – said to contain more gold than the vaults of the Bank of England. The tip of the stupa is set with 5,448 diamonds and 2,317 rubies, sapphires and topaz. A huge emerald sits in the middle to catch the first

TIP

Although most Burmese are hungry to discuss politics and to learn what the outside world thinks of the situation in their country, it is important to never raise the subject of politics, the military or Aung San Suu Kyi within earshot, or even sight, of a policeman or soldier. Be tactful – it isn't you who will get into trouble, but those you talk to.

Jewellery for sale at Bogyoke Aung San Market.

The Shwedagon at dusk, seen from the Northern exit.

and last rays of the sun. All of this is mounted upon a 10-metre (33ft) -high umbrella (*hti*), built upon seven gold-plated bars and decorated with 1,500 gold and silver bells. More than 100 other buildings, including smaller stupas, pavilions and administrative halls, surround the central stupa.

While the origins of the Shwedagon are shrouded in legend, it was definitely well-established when Bagan dominated Burma in the 11th century. Queen Shinsawbu, who ruled in the 15th century, is revered today for giving the pagoda its present shape and form.

Standing before the stupa is humbling. The octagonal base is ringed with 64 smaller stupas and an extensive marble platform, which is meticulously swept by the pious every day at dawn. Early morning is the best time to visit, as visitors must remove their shoes and socks, and the marble soon heats up to fierce temperatures which can make walking on it a painful experience by noon. This platform plays a prominent role in the Shwedagon Festival, celebrated on the full moon day of Tabaung (March) every year.

Parks and lakes

Yangon boasts more than a dozen public parks and gardens, and locals take great pleasure in spending the hot hours of the day resting in them, preferably beside a lake, in the shade of mature trees. Just east of the Shwedagon Pagoda, the northern shore of **Kandawgyi** (Royal) **Lake** is given over to **Bogyoke Aung San Park**, dedicated to the country's most famous martyr, and whose children's playgrounds and picnic areas are popular attractions with young families.

The park's best-known sight is the surreal **Karaweik Restaurant I**, on the eastern shore. Constructed in the early 1970s, the floating structure replicates a *pyi-gyi-mun*, or royal barge, such as those that Burma's kings and queens would traditionally have used on ceremonial occasions. With its double bow depicting the mythological *karaweik*, a water bird from Indian prehistory, and a multi-tiered pagoda on top, the restaurant is made of brick and concrete and anchored to the lake bottom. Its equally sumptuous interior contains some striking lacquerwork marble and

mother-of-pearl. In the evenings, starting at 6.30pm, popular buffet dinners (K20,000/US$25 per head) feature a three-hour culture show including music, classical dance and puppetry.

Inya Lake and around

Continuing through the winding residential streets north of the Shwedagon, past the 'Yangon modern' stucco houses built for Westerners in the colonial era, you'll arrive at enormous **Inya Lake**. As well as the Yangon University campus, the lush area surrounding it holds some of the city's most prized real estate and exclusive neighbourhoods, including the British-era home of NLD leader, Aung San Suu Kyi, whose tall, barbed-wire-covered gates are invariably patrolled by a gaggle of photographers and journalists. Next to the university, the 15-hectare (37-acre) lakeside park is the most popular place in the city for romantic trysts – images of couples schmoozing on the grassy verges are a cliché of Burmese movies and popular song videos.

The southwest corner of the lake, by contrast, is tainted with much darker associations. During the civil unrest of 1988, an estimated 283 students were beaten to death or drowned by military police on the shore – an event dubbed 'the White Bridge Massacre'. A further 3,000 people are thought to have lost their lives in the brutal crackdown that ensued.

With its prize exhibits now moved to a display in the new Burmese capital, Naypyidaw, the government-run **Gems Museum**, at 66 Kaba Aye Pagoda Road (Tues–Sun 9am–5pm; charge), just north of Inya Lake, is a lacklustre affair despite some impressive sapphires and star rubies, as well as a whole floor of jewellery emporia where you can purchase objects fashioned from Burmese jade and precious stones.

Around Yangon

In addition to the pottery town of Twante on the Ayeyarwady Delta, a couple of other destinations across the Bago River offer escape from the crowds and noise of Yangon. Foremost among them is the port of **Thanlyin**, overlooked by a particularly wonderful hilltop pagoda.

Ornate Karawik restaurant, Kandawgyi Lake.

Courtyard in Mahamuni Paya.

MANDALAY

The city of Mandalay, made famous in Rudyard Kipling's verse, is the religious and cultural centre of upper Myanmar, and surrounded by magnificent temples and pagodas.

ounded as recently as the mid-19th century (although several Buddhist sites and nearby centres are far older), the capital of Upper Myanmar is a young city – and a relatively modern, industrial and dusty one at that. Nonetheless, **Mandalay ❶**, can be a magical place. It was the country's last royal capital, and remains a notable Buddhist centre. Hundreds of pagodas dot the surrounding landscape, ranged around the hills over the Ayeyarwady (Irrawaddy) River, and the warmth and vitality of its people is legendary.

Located 620km (400 miles) north of Yangon, this northern centre is only 80 metres (260ft) above sea level. It sprawls across the dry plains of the upper Ayeyarwady River, its scenic beauty and historical tragedy inextricably linked. There is the indestructible Mandalay Hill with its kilometre-long covered stairways and remarkable pagodas towering above the ruins of the Royal Palace, King Mindon's 'Golden City' of ancient prophecy. In the middle of the city is Zegyo Market, centre of trade for all the people of Upper Myanmar who can be seen in their colourful national costumes. Skilled artisans and craftsmen are found here, working their age-old wonders with gold and silver, marble and chisel, thread and loom. The Ayeyarwady flows by

Shwe In bin Kyaung.

with its bustling wharves and flotillas of rice-laden boats.

Mandalay was founded in 1857 by King Mindon to coincide with an ancient Buddhist prophecy. The 'Golden City' was formally completed in 1859, and Mindon then shifted his government and some 150,000 people from nearby Amarapura, dismantling then rebuilding most of the previous palace to help create the new capital.

The dream of Mandalay was short-lived, however. In November 1885, King Thibaw handed the town

over to the British army and went into exile with his queen. Mandalay soon became just another outpost of British colonialism, albeit one crowned with richly furnished palace buildings.

The palace structures were almost universally built of teak, and this was to prove their demise. In March 1945, British troops shelled the stronghold, at the time defended by a handful of Japanese and Burmese soldiers. By the time the siege had ended, the interior of the Golden City was in ashes. The walls and the moat were all that remained intact before part of the palace was reconstructed.

Centre of the world

Mindon had built his **Royal Palace** Ⓐ (daily 7.30am–4.30pm; charge) on the model of Brahman-Buddhist cosmology to represent the centre of the world, the fabled Mount Meru. The palace formed a perfect square, with the outer walls facing the four cardinal directions, while the 12 gates, three on each side, are marked with the signs of the zodiac. In the exact centre of the

palace was the throne room, called the Lion's Room. The Royal Palace with the Lion's Room and the *pyathat* have been rebuilt.

These days the renovated palace shares the grounds of **Mandalay Fort** (Mon–Fri 8am–6pm) with the army. The grounds and a museum of Mandalay history are open to the public. A little to the west is a scale model of the ancient palace created by archaeologists, illustrating the location of all main and secondary buildings within the old palace walls, which gives a good idea of the 'centre of the world' concept. King Mindon's mausoleum is also in the palace grounds.

Mandalay Hill

You might start a visit to Mandalay by climbing the famous **Mandalay Hill** Ⓑ (daily 8am–5pm; charge), which rises 240 metres (790ft) above the surrounding countryside and offers grand views. The slopes are scaled via covered stairways, which contain small temples at regular intervals. There are 1,729 steps to the top, but the walk is not particularly difficult. About halfway up the hill, you'll encounter the first large temple, said to contain three of Buddha's bones.

About two-thirds of the way to the top of the hill stands a gold-plated statue of the Shweyattaw Buddha. His outstretched hand points to the place where the Royal Palace was built. This stance is unique; in all other Buddha images anywhere else in the world, Gautama is in one of the *mudra* positions. The statue was erected before King Mindon laid the first stone of his Golden City and symbolises Gautama Buddha's prophecy.

On the way up the steps, there is also a statue of a woman kneeling in front of the Buddha, offering up her two severed breasts. According to legend, Sanda Moke Khit was an ogress, but she was so impressed by the Buddha's teachings that she decided to devote the rest of her life to following the Enlightened One. As a sign of

Feeding fish in Mandalay Palace's moat.

humility, she cut off her breasts. The Buddha smiled as he accepted the gift, and the ogress's brother asked why he did so. He replied that Sanda Moke Khit had collected so many merits that in a future life she would be reborn as Min Done (Mindon), king of Mandalay.

At the base of Mandalay Hill's southeast stairway, surrounded by a high wall, is Mindon's **Kuthodaw Pagoda ●** (daily 8am–5pm; charge). Its central structure, the 30-metre (100ft) -high Maha Lawka Marazein Pagoda, was erected in 1857 and modelled on the Shwezigon Pagoda in Nyaung U, near Bagan (Pagan). Sometimes called the 'world's largest book', it was created by a team of 2,400 monks who required almost six months to recite the text. The canons were recorded on the marble slabs by devoted Buddhist scholars, and the letters were originally veneered with gold leaf.

Close to the Kuthodaw are other important pagodas and monasteries. Not far from the south staircase is the **Kyauktawgyi Pagoda ●** (daily 8am–5pm; charge). Begun in 1853, the original plan was to model this after the Ananda Temple at Bagan, but a revolt in 1866 hampered this and other projects. The building was eventually completed in 1878. The main point of interest here is a huge Buddha figure carved out of a single block of marble from the Sagyin quarry. This undertaking was of ancient Egyptian proportions: 10,000 men required 13 days to transport the rock from the Ayeyarwady to the pagoda site. The statue was finally dedicated in 1865, with 20 figures on each side of the image representing the Buddha's 80 disciples. A painting of King Mindon is also contained within the pagoda.

The **Sandamuni Pagoda ●** (daily 8am–5pm; charge) was built on the site where King Mindon located his provisional palace during construction of the Mandalay Palace. There are two monasteries located south of the Kuthodaw Pagoda, not far to the east of the palace moat. The **Shwe Nandaw Kyaung ●** (daily 8am–5pm; charge), at one time part of the royal

FACT

The makers of oiled bamboo paper live on 37th Road. This kind of paper, which is placed between layers of gold leaf, is produced by a remarkable three-year process of soaking, beating flat and drying of bamboo.

Monks walk through Kuthodaw Paya's covered walkways.

Mandalay

0 — 1000 m
0 — 1000 yds
N

Ayeyarwady (Irrawaddy)

Shwetachaung

Madaya

GOLF COURSE

Shweyattaw Buddha

MANDALAY HILL **B**

9th
10th
11th

76th
73rd

YADANABON ZOO

Kyauktawgyi Pagoda **D**

10th

Kuthodaw Pagoda **C**

Sandamuni Pagoda **E**

12th

Atumashi Kyaung **G** **F**

Shwe Nandaw Kyaung

North Moat

Lay Thein Gate

14th
15th
16th
17th
18th

82nd
81st
83rd

Mandalay Palace

NANDAWUN PARK

Shwe Nandaw Cultural Museum **A**

Arlawie Kyae Mhon Gate

MYAINGHAYWUN PARK

Royal Palace

On Htate Gate (East Gate Entrance)

16th
17th
19th

64th
63rd
62nd

School of Fine Arts, Music and Drama

Inwa
Moat
West Moat
East Moat

19th
21st

Shwe Pan Myaing Pagoda

Buffalo Point

Pinya

22nd (C)
23rd
24th
25th

89th
88th
87th

Shwekyimyint Pagoda **K**

Mandalay Cultural Museum **L**

Sacred Heart Cathedral

Independence Monument

Mingalar Bridge

23rd

South Moat

City Hall

26th (B)
27th
28th
29th

Clock Tower
Zegyo Market **M**

Bayintaung

Eindawya Pagoda **J**

26th
27th
28th
29th

70th

i

Marionette Theatre

Mingun Ferry

Setkyathiha Pagoda

30th
31st

Market

Central Station **i**

30th
31st
32nd

69th
68th
67th
66th
65th

32nd

78th
77th
76th
75th
74th
73rd
72nd
71st

86th
85th
84th
82nd
81st
80th
79th

33rd
34th

Judson Baptist

Father Lafon's Church

33rd

Yangyiaung

35th (A)

Bagan Ferry

Shwe In Bin Kyaung **I**

Yan Gyi Aung Bridge

Shwe Hninsi Gold Leaf Workshop

35th

36th

Ngwe Ta

Yay Ni

Pyin-U-Lwin

38th

38th

69th
66th
65th
64th
63rd
62nd

Thinga yazar
Chaung

39th
40th

Moustache Brothers

Yangon

41st
42nd

82nd

Chan Mya Bridge

Maha Muni (Great Sage) Pagoda **H**

Shwetachaung

Sagaing

Mandalay Environs

Yenatha

Thonze

On-ma-thi

Sadaung

Madaya

Kyabin

Lamaing

Hsipaw, Lashio

3

Sagaing

Mu

Ayeyarwady (Irrawaddy)

Taungbyon

31

M a n d a l a y

Wetwun

Peik Chin Myaung

Mingun

Nyaungbintho

Q

Kaungmudaw Pagoda

Ondaw

Mandalay

N
Amarapura

Pyin U-Lwin (Maymyo)

Zegôn

Sagaing

Lake Taungthaman

Ngazun

Inwa (Ava)

P

O U Bein Bridge

Myitnge

Palek

Lema

Kyaukse

Myitnge

1

0 — 10 km
0 — 10 miles

palace, is the only building from Mindon's Golden City that has survived the ravages of the 19th century.

Beside the Shwe Nandaw lie the remains of the **Atumashi Kyaung**  **G** (daily 8am–5pm; charge), which means 'Incomparable Monastery'. An 1890 fire destroyed the monastery, taking with it four historic sets of the Tipitaka (Buddhist scriptures). This extraordinary masonry-and-teak monastery has now been restored according to the original plan.

Maha Muni Pagoda

The most important religious structure in Mandalay is the **Maha Muni (Great Sage) Pagoda** **H** (daily 8am–5pm; charge), also called the Rakhaing (Arakan) Pagoda or Payagyi Pagoda. Located about 3km (2 miles) south of the city centre on the road to Amarapura, it was built in 1784 by King Bodawpaya and then reconstructed after a fire a century later.

The Maha Muni Buddha is almost 4 metres (13ft) high and is coated with layers of gold leaf several centimetres thick. Except during the rainy season, when the Buddha's body is cloaked with robes, you can watch the Buddhist faithful pasting on the thin gold leaf.

There are four other Buddhist buildings in the vicinity of downtown Mandalay that are definitely worth visiting. Fortunately, the city's grid street plan makes them easy to find. Heading north from the Maha Muni Pagoda, one first encounters the **Shwe In Bin Kyaung** **I**. This monastery, situated to the south of 35th Road, contains very fine 13th-century woodcarvings. At 31st Road and 85th Street stands the **Setkyathiha Pagoda,** rebuilt after being badly damaged in World War II.

Proceeding northward leads to the **Eindawya Pagoda** **J** at 27th Road and 89th Street. The pagoda houses a Buddha figure made of chalcedony (a form of quartz), carried to Burma in 1839 from Bodhgaya, the place in

India where Gautama attained enlightenment. The pagoda was built in early 1847 by King Pagan Min. Today it has been covered with gold leaf. The oldest pagoda in the city is the **Shwekyimyint Pagoda** **K**, on 24th Road between 82nd and 83rd streets. Erected in 1167 by Prince Minshinsaw, the exiled son of King Alaungsithu of Bagan, it houses a Buddha image consecrated by the prince himself.

A couple of blocks from the Shwe Kyi Myint, at 24th Road and West Moat Road, is the **Mandalay Cultural Museum** **L** (Tue–Sun 10am–4pm; charge). Its collection extends across many eras of Burmese history. One of its most interesting pictures shows King Thibaw and Queen Supyalat on the eve of their exile to British India in 1885.

Market centre of the north

For the Chin of the west, the Kachin of the north, and the Shans of the east, Mandalay is the primary market for goods. The **Zegyo Market** **M**, located on the west side of the

Working at a marble Buddha workshop.

The Maha Muni Buddha at Mandalay.

Teak carving details at Shwenandaw.

Mingun Paya.

city centre, on 84th Street between 26th and 28th roads, is Mandalay's most important bazaar. In 1903 the Italian Count Caldrari, first secretary of the Mandalay municipal government, had the Zegyo Market laid out around the Diamond Jubilee Clock, recently erected in honour of Queen Victoria's 60-year reign. Rebuilt as a new concrete structure in the 1990s, the market still offers visitors a fine opportunity to see Myanmar's ethnic minorities in their national costumes, and at the same time gives a glimpse of daily Burmese life.

Craftsmen of the south

In the southern part of Mandalay, especially in the precincts of the Maha Muni Pagoda, are the artists' and craftsmen's quarters. This is where you can watch as Burmese men pursue their trade in religious sculpture, using the same skills and methods as their forefathers – Buddha images in all postures, lotus-blossom pedestals, or even the occasional Virgin Mary, a reminder of the city's small Christian population.

Around Mandalay

The area around Mandalay is full of things to see. Just 11km (7 miles) south of the city – easily reached by taxi or bicycle – is the former royal capital of **Amarapura** – built by Bodawpaya in 1782. Nothing remains of its former **Royal Palace,** but the four pagodas that once marked the corners of the city wall can still be seen, as can two stone buildings – the treasury and the old watchtower. The graves of Bodawpaya and Bagyidaw are also here.

U Bein's Bridge is a remarkable 1.2km (0.75-mile) structure made of teak, which leads across shallow Taungthaman Lake to the eponymous village. In the southern part of Amarapura sits the well-preserved Patodawgyi Pagoda, built by King Bagyidaw in 1820. A bell-shaped stupa, it stands on five terraces covered with Jataka reliefs. There is an inscription stone nearby that tells the story of the construction of the pagoda. Amarapura is home to one of the largest monasteries in Myanmar, with up to 1,200 monks (during the

A HILL STATION RETREAT

Those who are nostalgic for the atmosphere of British colonial times, and others just seeking to escape the dusty misery of Mandalay's hot season, should visit Pyin U-Lwin (Maymyo) in the foothills of the Shan Plateau at an altitude of 1,070 metres (3,510ft). A two-and-a-half-hour drive by jeep northeast of Mandalay winds into the hills, from where there are breathtaking views of the Mandalay plain. The rambling town itself is a lovely collection of old country houses and tree-lined streets, botanical gardens and a golf course. The temperature is much cooler than on the plains, and if you stay at Candacraig, a former 'chummery' where bachelor employees of the colonial government and teak companies once lodged, roaring log fires are lit each evening during the cold season.

Buddhist lent) contributing to the pervasively religious atmosphere.

The town is well known in Myanmar for its weaving industry – cotton and silk are woven into Myanmar's loveliest festive clothing. A second industry is bronze casting. Cymbals, gongs and images of the Buddha are made here out of a special alloy of bronze and lead. The famous statue of Bogyoke Aung San, which stands at the entrance to Aung San Park in Yangon, was cast here.

Whereas Amarapura was left largely to the mercy of the elements, **Sagaing ⓟ** remains very much alive, and is considered to be the principal Buddhist centre in Myanmar. The city reverberates with the echoes of cymbals, gongs and pagoda bells. Devout families bring their young sons to undergo the *shin pyu* ceremony and thereby join the community of the faithful. In the hills and in the many-fingered valleys of the west bank of the Ayeyarwady are some 600 monasteries, as well as numerous temples, stupas and caves dedicated to the memory of the Gautama Buddha.

About 5,000 monks live in this arcadian landscape laced with endless stairways and colonnades. There are numerous interesting pagodas and temples to visit around the town, including the **Htupayon Pagoda** and **Aungmyelawka Pagoda.**

At the northern end of the chain of hills flanking Sagaing, resting on the banks of the Ayeyarwady, is the village of **Mingun ⓠ**, home of the largest intact bell in the world and an unfinished pagoda sometimes described as the biggest pile of bricks on earth. Sharp eyes can spot it from Mandalay Hill, although it lies more than 10km (6 miles) to the northwest.

Unlike Amarapura, Mingun was not a royal city but it is significant in its own right and has many interesting sights. The village is only accessible by river; boats leave Mandalay daily and take about an hour to make the trip. Behind the ferry pier is the famous **Mingun Bell**. It weighs 87 tons, stands 3.7 metres (more than 12ft) high, and is 5 metres (16.5ft) wide at its mouth.

Monks looking out at the view from Sun U Ponya Shin pagoda.

BAGAN

One of Asia's most venerable wonders and home of the temple of omniscience, Bagan is an ancient and deserted city, full of awe-inspiring pagodas.

Buddha statue inside Sulamani temple.

In many respects **Bagan ❷** (Pagan) has changed very little in the past century. It remains the way Sir James Scott saw it, as "Burma's deserted capital on the Irrawaddy, thickly studded with pagodas of all sizes and shapes". It was – and still is – a veritable elephants' graveyard of medieval Burmese culture. There are few sights on earth so striking as the view across the plain of Bagan, one ancient red-brick pagoda after another rising above the flat land on the dusty eastern shore of greatest river in Myanmar.

Between the time of Anawrahta's conquest of Thaton in 1057 and the conquest of Bagan by Kublai Khan's forces in 1287, some 13,000 temples, pagodas, *kyaung* and other religious structures were built on this vast plain. After seven long centuries, just over 2,200 of these remain standing.

There has been a settlement in the region of Bagan since early in the 2nd century AD, when Thamuddarit, a Pyu king, led his followers here. King Pyinbya erected the city walls in 849, but it was left to King Anawrahta, 42nd ruler of the Bagan dynasty, to usher in the city's age of glory.

The main centre on the plain today is at **Nyaung U**, about 5km (3 miles) to the north of the walled village of Bagan. There are a few important monuments in the immediate vicinity of Nyaung U, notably the Shwezigon Pagoda, and a few others to the south of Bagan village near Myinkaba. Picturesque Bagan village, once situated around the main temples, was relocated in a controversial military operation in 1990 to clear the principal temple quarter of local inhabitants. **New Bagan**, as it is called, was built some 8km (5 miles) south of its original site, close to the village of Thiripyitsaya.

Bagan monuments

All visitors to the **Bagan Archaeological Zone** (daily Tue–Sun 9.30am–3.30pm) – which encompasses most of the temple and stupa ruins of note – must pay a US$10 entry charge, which is valid for one week.

Many travellers begin their exploration of the ancient ruins at the **Ananda Temple Ⓐ**, just to the east of the old city wall. This impressive whitewashed edifice dominates the view as one approaches Bagan from the north. Considered the apogee of Mon architecture, it was completed in 1091. King Kyanzittha, successor of Anawrahta, is said to have been so awe-struck by its unique style that he personally executed the architect by Brahman ritual to assure that the temple could not be duplicated, thereby sealing its uniqueness. Some of the statues in the temple are actually copies, as temple thieves destroyed the originals. The desecration of temples has been a serious problem in Bagan for a very long time. As far back as mid-16th century, Thohanbwa, Shan King of Inwa (Ava), gave impetus to the temple robbers when he said, "Burma pagodas have nothing to do with religion. They are simply treasure chambers."

The most important time of year at the Ananda Temple is January, when an exuberant festival is held to raise money for the upkeep of the temple. This is a joyous spectacle, and the corridors and vestibules of the temple, normally lined with small stalls, are especially lively.

A standing Buddha – Kassapa – at Ananda.

Temple of omniscience

Thatbyinnyu Temple Ⓑ dominates the centre of Bagan, about 500 metres/yds to the southwest of the Ananda. Known as the 'temple of omniscience', it is the tallest building in Bagan at 61 metres (201ft). The construction of this temple introduced the idea of placing a smaller 'hollow' cube on top of a larger Bamar-style structure, whereas the previous Mon-style temples were of one storey. The centre of the lower cube is solid, serving as a foundation for the upper temple, which houses an eastward-looking Buddha figure.

A short distance north of the Thatbyinnyu is the **Thandawgya Ⓒ**, a huge seated Buddha figure. Six metres (20ft) tall, it was erected by Narathihapate in 1284. The Buddha's hands

Ananda temple and surrounding temples.

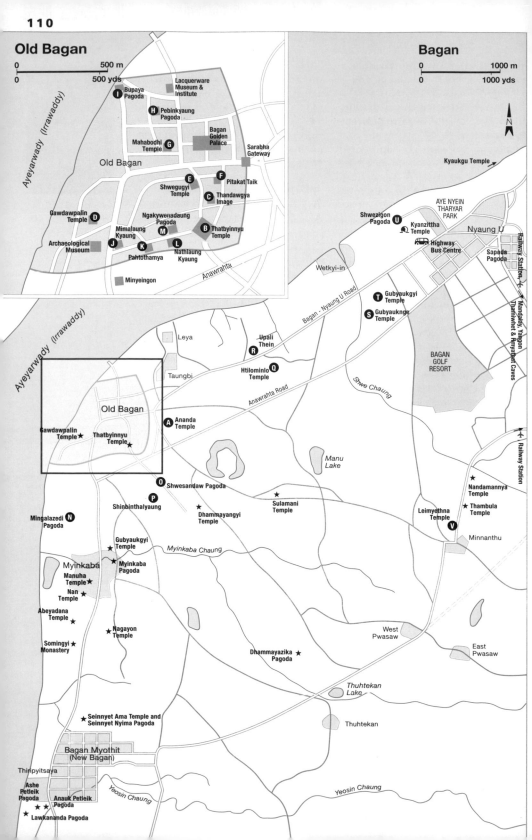

Old Bagan

0	500 m
0	500 yds

Lacquerware Museum & Institute

I Bupaya Pagoda

Ayeyarwady (Irrawaddy)

H Pebinkyaung Pagoda

Bagan Golden Palace

G Mahabodhi Temple

Old Bagan

Sarabha Gateway

E Shwegugyi Temple

F Pitakat Taik

C Thandawgya Image

Gawdawpalin Temple **D**

Ngakywenadaung Pagoda

M Mimalaung Kyaung

B Thatbyinnyu Temple

Archaeological Museum

J

K Pahtothamya

L Nathlaung Kyaung

Anawrahta

Minyeingon

Bagan

0	1000 m
0	1000 yds

N

Kyaukgu Temple

AYE NYEIN THARYAR PARK

Shwezigon Pagoda **U**

Kyanzittha Temple

Nyaung U

Highway Bus Centre

Railway Station, Mandalay, Yangon, Thanlwhet & Pyinyathet Caves

Sapada Pagoda

Bagan - Nyaung U Road

Wetkyi-in

T Gubyaukgyi Temple

S Gubyauknge Temple

BAGAN GOLF RESORT

Leya

R Upali Thein

Q Htilominlo Temple

Taungbi

Anawrahta Road

Shwe Chaung

Railway Station

Ayeyarwady (Irrawaddy)

Old Bagan

Gawdawpalin Temple ★

Thatbyinnyu Temple ★

A Ananda Temple

Manu Lake

Nandamannya Temple ★

O Shwesandaw Pagoda

Leimyethna Temple ★

Thambula Temple ★

P Shinbinthalyaung

Sulamani Temple ★

V

Mingalazedi Pagoda **N**

Dhammayangyi Temple ★

Minnanthu

Myinkaba Chaung

Gubyaukgyi Temple ★

Myinkaba

Myinkaba Pagoda ★

Manuha Temple ★

Nan Temple ★

West Pwasaw

East Pwasaw

Abeyadana Temple ★

Nagayon Temple ★

Somingyi Monastery ★

Dhammayazika Pagoda ★

Thuhtekan Lake

Seinnyet Ama Temple and Seinnyet Nyima Pagoda ★

Thuhtekan

Bagan Myothit (New Bagan)

Thiripyitsaya

Ashe Petleik Pagoda ★

Anauk Petleik Pagoda ★

Yeosin Chaung

Yeosin Chaung

Lawkananda Pagoda ★

are in the *bhumisparsa* mudra, signifying the moment of enlightenment.

Close to the bank of the Ayeyarwady River is the 12th-century **Gawdawpalin Temple ⓓ**, built by King Narapatisithu in Bamar style to resemble the Thatbyinnyu Temple. This impressive building suffered more than any other monument in the 1975 earthquake. Just south of the temple is a museum containing displays of Bagan's varied architecture, iconography and religious history.

The oldest of the Bamar-style temples, the **Shwegugyi Temple ⓔ** is a short distance up the road toward Nyaung U. King Alaungsithu had it built in 1131, and it took just seven months to raise, according to the temple history inscribed on two stone slabs within.

One of the few secular buildings in Bagan that has been preserved over the centuries is the **Pitaka Taik ⓕ**, King Anawrahta's library, close to the Shwegugyi Temple. Across the main road is the **Mahabodhi Temple ⓖ**. This temple is an exact replica of a structure of the same name in India's Bihar State, built in AD 500 at the site where the Buddha achieved enlightenment. The pyramid-like shape of the temple tower is a kind that was highly favoured during India's Gupta period, and it is quite different from the standard bell-shaped monuments in the rest of Myanmar.

Pebinkyaung Pagoda

A short distance north of Bagan's Mahabodhi is the **Pebinkyaung Pagoda ⓗ**, most notable for its conical Sinhalese-style stupa. The stupa contains relics mounted on top of the bell-shaped main structure in a square-based relic chamber. The construction of this pagoda in the 12th century confirms that close ties existed between Burma and Sri Lanka.

A few steps from the Pebingyaung on the banks of the Ayeyarwady is the **Bupaya Pagoda ⓘ**. According to tradition, the pagoda was built by the third king of Bagan, Pyusawti (ad 162–243) but it was more likely constructed in the 19th century. As the original Bagan Pagoda, this edifice became the basic model for all pagodas built after

Entrance to Dhammayazika pagoda.

Stairs leading up to the Shwesandaw Pagoda.

The Bupaya Pagoda is located on a prime site overlooking the river.

A horse and cart waits outside Mingalazedi.

it. It has a bulbous shape, similar in some ways to the Tibetan *chorten*, and is built on rows of crenellated walls overlooking the river. Because of the way it stands out on the banks, it is used as a navigation aid by boats. On the pagoda grounds, beneath a pavilion with a nine-gabled roof, is an altar to Mondaing, *nat* of storms.

The **Mimalaung Kyaung Temple J**, near the old city's south gate, was erected in 1174. The small, square temple is characterised by multiple roofs and a tall spiral pagoda that stands on a 4-metre (13ft) -high plinth intended to protect it from destruction by fire and floods.

Just to the east of this temple is the **Pahtothamya Temple K**, dating from before Anawrahta's reign. King Taungthugyi (931–64), also known as Nyaung U Sawrahan, is said to have built the temple to look like those at Thaton. No temple ruins have ever been unearthed at Thaton to allow comparison, however, and the architectural style of this temple has been proven to be that of the 11th century.

To the east is the **Nathlaung Kyaung Temple L**, a perfect example of the religious tolerance that prevailed in Bagan during the so-called Era of the Temple Builders. It is thought that it was constructed by Taungthugyi in 931 – more than a century before Theravada Buddhism was introduced from Thaton – and was dedicated to the Hindu god Vishnu. Immediately to the north, the **Ngakywenadaung Pagoda M** is much like the Pahtothamya Temple attributed to King Taungthugyi in the 10th century. A bulbous structure on a circular base, it stands 13 metres (43ft) high.

A short distance south of walled Bagan is the **Mingalazedi Pagoda N**, the last of the great stupas erected during the Era of the Temple Builders. Six years in construction, it represents the pinnacle of Bamar pagoda architecture. The terraces are adorned with large terracotta tiles depicting scenes from the *Jataka*.

About halfway between the temple and the walled Bagan centre are the **Shwesandaw Pagoda O** and the **Shinbinthalyaung P**, which houses a reclining Buddha. One of only three religious structures Anawrahta

built in Bagan, the Shwesandaw was erected in 1057 upon his victorious return from Thaton. Its stupa enshrines some hairs of the Buddha sent to Anawrahta by the king of Bago. The long, flat building within the walls of the Shwesandaw enclosure contains the Shinbinthalyaung Reclining Buddha, over 18 metres (60ft) in length. Created in the 11th century, this Buddha lies with its head facing south to denote a sleeping Buddha (only a dying Buddha's head would point north).

The last Bamar-style temple built in Bagan, the **Htilominlo Temple Q**, is about 1.5km (1 mile) northeast of Bagan proper on the road to Nyaung U. King Nantaungmya had this building constructed in 1211 at the place where he was chosen to be king. Four Buddha figures placed on the ground and four more figures on the first floor face the cardinal points. Some of the old murals can still be discerned, as can a number of the friezes. Several old horoscopes, painted to protect the building from damage, can be found on the walls.

To Nyaung U and beyond

Approximately 1.5km (1 mile) down the road from Bagan proper, towards the regional centre of Nyaung U and almost directly opposite the Htilominlo Temple, lies the **Upali Thein R** or Hall of Ordination. Named after the monk Upali, it was erected in the first half of the 13th century. The Upali Thein was renovated during the reign of the Konbaung dynasty in the late 1700s; during the renovation, its walls and ceilings were decorated with beautiful frescoes representing the 28 previous Buddhas, as well as scenes from the life of Gautama. Sadly, the plaster came off the walls during the 1975 earthquake, and most of the fresco work was destroyed.

Near the village of Wetkyi-in are the **Gubyauknge Temple S** notable for the fine stucco work on its exterior walls, and the **Gubyaukgyi Temple T** a short distance further east. The Gubyaukgyi dates from the early 13th century, and it has a pyramidal spire very similar to that of the Mahabodhi. Inside are some of Bagan's finest frescoes of the *Jataka* tales.

TIP

Bicycles are readily available for hire, but remember to wear a hat, long sleeves and trousers, especially in the hot season, as the plain around Bagan gets baking hot – regularly exceeding 40°C (104°F). Alternatively, hiring a pony and trap is a pleasant, reasonably priced and memorable experience.

Feeding pigeons outside Shwezigon Pagoda, Nyaung U.

A short distance west of Nyaung U village is the **Kyanzittha Cave**, a cave temple that served as monks' lodgings. Although its name points to Kyanzittha as its creator, it probably dates from Anawrahta's reign. The long, dark corridors are embellished with frescoes from the 11th–13th centuries; some of the later paintings even depict the Mongols who briefly occupied Bagan after 1287.

The **Shwezigon Pagoda**  a short walk north of the cave temple, is the prototype for all Burmese stupas built after the rule of Anawrahta. It was built as the most important reliquary shrine in Bagan, a centre of prayer and reflection for the new Theravada faith that Anawrahta was establishing in Bagan.

Cave temples

There are several cave temples to the east of Nyaung U. Just 1km (0.62 miles) to the southeast of the town are the caves at **Thamiwhet** and **Hmyathat**, formed by the excavation of hillsides during the 12th and 13th centuries. Their purpose was to give monks a cool place to live and meditate, a refuge from the scorching heat of central Burma.

About 3km (2 miles) upstream from Nyaung U, standing on the ledge of a cliff overlooking the Ayeyarwady, is the **Kyaukgu Temple**. The structure could be described as an ideal cave temple – the manner in which it is built into the hillside gives the impression that a small stupa stands on top of the temple, when it actually rests on a pillar. The Kyaukgu's ground floor dates from the 11th century.

Minnanthu temples

The village of Minnanthu is located about 5km (3 miles) southeast of Bagan proper. There are a large number of temple ruins in the vicinity, but few of major significance. One of the largest is the **Sulamani Temple**, not in Minnanthu itself but about halfway between the village and Bagan. Immediately to the north of the village is the **Lemyethna Temple**  built by Naratheinhka's minister-in-chief, and a short distance to the north, the **Thambula Temple**, which dates from 1255.

Cycling, a popular way to visit the temples, near Dhammayangyi temple.

A KING'S ATONEMENT

Despite his brief tenure as monarch, King Narathu (1167–70) is remembered as the founder of Bagan's largest shrine, the **Dhammayangyi Temple**. Consumed with guilt and deeply concerned about his karma for future lives after having murdered his father, Narathu built the Dhammayangyi to atone for his misdeeds. Narathu himself was later assassinated by an Indian suicide squad dispatched by the father of one of his wives, whom he had executed because he disliked her Hindu rituals. Today the temple is the best-preserved temple in Bagan. The temple is over a kilometre to the southeast of the city walls towards Minnanthu.

Aung San Suu Kyi

Also known by her supporters as 'The Lady', Aung San Suu Kyi has come to be seen both in Myanmar and abroad as a symbol of implacable but peaceful resistance to military oppression.

Born in 1945, Aung San Suu Kyi is the daughter of the late Burmese nationalist leader, General Aung San, whose resistance to British colonial rule culminated in independence in 1948. After attending school in Yangon, Suu Kyi lived in India before going to Britain for her higher education. There she met and married her late husband, Michael Aris, an Oxford University professor specialising in Tibetan Studies. Aris accepted that his wife's destiny might ultimately lie in Myanmar. "Before we were married I promised my wife that I would never stand between her and her country," he said.

Political prisoner

Suu Kyi first came to prominence when she returned home in August 1988 to visit her ailing mother. She became the leader of a burgeoning pro-democracy movement in the aftermath of the brutal repression of the uprising. Inspired by the non-violent campaign of Mahatma Gandhi, Suu Kyi organised rallies and travelled the country, calling for peaceful democratic reforms and free elections. The movement quickly grew into a political party, the National League for Democracy (NLD), which went on to win 51 percent of the national vote and 81 percent of seats in parliament, by which time she had already been under house arrest for a year. The military regime, however, refused to relinquish power and stepped up intensified repression of the NLD.

Aung San Suu Kyi spent 15 of the next 21 years under house arrest, restricted in her movements and slandered by the pro-government media as a political opportunist and even a 'genocidal prostitute'. This last unlikely phrase derived from the military regime's obsession with her marriage to Michael Aris, who died of prostate cancer in Oxford in 1999 at the age of 53. Throughout Aris's final illness, the Yangon authorities denied him permission to visit Myanmar. Fearing that she would not be allowed to re-enter the country, however, Suu Kyi declined the option of leaving and remained separated from her husband and two sons at the time of his death.

A new era

Finally, decades of international pressure and sanctions bore fruit on 13 November 2010, when the woman regarded by most of the world as Myanmar's leader-in-waiting was released 'for good conduct' from her Yangon home. The end of her detention came only six days after a widely criticised national election.

For most of the following year, the NLD leader campaigned for her party in the run-up to a key by-election in which her party won 43 of the 45 seats it was allowed to contest. In its wake, Aung San Suu Kyi took her seat in the Pyithu Hluttaw, the lower house of Myanmar's parliament, for the first time, and met with US Secretary of State, Hillary Clinton. The event signalled the start of what most impartial observers hope will be Myanmar's full democratic rehabilitation. Indeed, President Thein Sein went so far as to say in September 2013 that he would accept the opposition leader Aung San Suu Kyi as president, if she were eventually elected. The next general election is due by November 2015.

Myanmar pro-democracy leader Aung San Suu Kyi.

Monk at the Phapheng Falls near the Cambodian border.

LAOS

Laos is a fascinating and rewarding country to visit. Definitively off the beaten track, it has retained its culture and charm, traditional village life, wild forests and beautiful countryside.

Market stall in Luang Prabang.

One of southeast Asia's least-known countries, Laos is an ancient land with a surprisingly sophisticated culture; at the same time, it is simple, easy-going and a great deal of fun to visit. From the 14th century to the 16th century, during the Kingdom of Lan Xang or 'One Million Elephants', Lao civilization reached its golden age, and many of the country's religious and cultural traditions date from this period. Subsequently Lan Xang went into decline, and the Lao people found themselves dominated by their more powerful neighbours, Thailand and Vietnam.

Throughout the centuries the country remained distinctively Lao, however – a society dominated by lowland, wet-rice growing Buddhists closely related to the neighbouring Thai. Yet in the mountains almost 50 percent of the population is still made up of widely varying minority groups, each with its own distinctive and colourful traditions, clothing and worldview.

A visit to Laos is, in many ways, a trip back into the past. Cultural links with neighbouring Thailand are immediately apparent in the saffron robes of the Buddhist monks, the similarities in temple architecture and the speech of the people – yet Laos is more like the Thailand of 35 years ago. Although it opened up to tour-

Vang Vieng.

ism more than 20 years ago, there is still little of the rampant commercialism and vibrant entertainment industry that characterises its neighbour. The waters of the Mekong River that form the boundary between the two countries may flow past both Lao and Thai banks at the same rate, but the flow of life in the two countries proceeds at two entirely different speeds.

There is another side to Laos, too, which further enriches an already sophisticated culture. At least in terms of architecture and cuisine, Laos has benefited from its long association with its other neighbours and from influences from France. Lao food is delicious, but one is also able to eat in Chinese and Vietnamese restaurants, as well as enjoy excellent coffee, fresh baguettes, croissants and French home cooking.

DECISIVE DATES

The Siamese army during the Haw wars in 1875.

The Mists of Time

3000 BC–AD 1000

Laos is settled by Austro-Tai-speaking peoples.

The 'Kingdom of a Million Elephants'

1353

Fa Ngum founds the Kingdom of Lan Xang. He makes Theravada Buddhism the state religion.

1421–1520

Lan Xang suffers a hundred years of petty wars and rivalries.

1520

King Phothisarat comes to the throne and reunifies the kingdom, moving the capital to Vientiane.

1637–94

King Sulinya Vongse presides over the Golden Age of Lan Xang from his capital at Vientiane.

1700

After the death of Sulinya Vongse, the kingdom of Lan Xang begins to break up.

Fragmentation and decline

1778

The Siamese absorb southern Laos.

1826–8

Chao Anuvong of Vientiane attempts to re-establish Lao independence but is defeated. In 1828, Vientiane is comprehensively sacked by the invading Siamese.

1885

Laos, as far south as Vientiane, is plundered by bands of Yunnanese Chinese known as Haw in the Haw Wars.

The colonial interlude

1893–1907

Unequal colonial treaties forced on Siam lead to French control over all Lao territories east of the Mekong.

1900–39

French colonial policy continues traditional Vietnamese policies east of the Mekong. In Laos, as in Cambodia, Vietnamese settlement is encouraged. Laos remains a colonial backwater, of little economic value.

1939–45

World War II ends in Laos with a brief Japanese-inspired declaration of independence, followed by the return of the French.

1947

Laos becomes a constitutional monarchy, still under French tutelage.

1950–1

The United States and the United Kingdom recognise Laos as part of the French Union. The pro-communist Pathet Lao rejects this development and forms a government of national resistance.

Laos and the Indochina Wars

1952

The Pathet Lao begins a low-scale insurgency in the northeast of the country.

1953

France withdraws, leaving an independent Laos divided between Royalist forces in Vientiane and the leftist Pathet Lao.

1955

Laos is admitted to the United Nations.

1957

Prince Souvanna Phouma leads a coalition government in Vientiane.

1963

The Communist government of North Vietnam begins extensive use of the Ho Chi

King Sisavang Vong ruled from 1904 until 1959.

Minh Trail in Laos. Covert US military activities begin.

1973

US troops withdraw from Vietnam, and the CIA 'Secret War' in Laos is wound down.

1975

After the Communist victory in Vietnam, the Lao People's Democratic Republic is established.

The development of modern Laos

1977

Treaty of friendship and co-operation signed between Laos and Vietnam.

1975–89

Rigid socialist policies introduced; most of the country's intelligentsia and urban middle classes flee. Communist attempts to weaken the popularity of Buddhism do not work. Former King Savang Vatthana and other members of the royal family die in prison camps. Disaffection grows as poverty increases.

1992

Death of Lao president Kaysone Phomvihane. Nouhak Phoumsavanh succeeds him.

1992

A slow start is made in restoring individual liberties; the country begins opening up to tourism.

1994

The 'Friendship Bridge' opens across the Mekong, linking Laos and Thailand.

1997

Laos is admitted to the Association of Southeast Asian Nations (ASEAN).

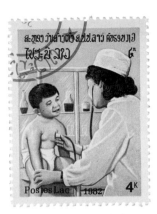

Socialist healthcare highlighted on a postage stamp.

1998

Khamtay Siphandone becomes president.

1999

Laos moves cautiously closer to Thailand as Vietnamese influence diminishes.

2003

Gradual transition to market economy continues.

2006

Choummaly Sayasone becomes president in June.

2009

Rail link with Thailand opened over the Mekong at Nong Kai.

2011

A new stock market opens in Vientiane. Choummaly Sayasone elected for a further five-year term by parliament.

2012

Hillary Clinton becomes the first US secretary of state to visit Laos for 57 years. Laos approves plans to build a massive dam at Xayaburi, on the lower Mekong river, despite international protest.

PEOPLE AND CULTURE

The population of Laos is a broad ethnic mix, the product of an uneasy history, but past hostilities are giving way to mutual co-operation.

With around 6.2 million inhabitants, Laos has one of the lowest population densities in Asia – just over 22 people per sq km (9 per sq mile). Outside of a handful of relatively large towns in the Mekong Valley, most Lao – around 85 percent – live in rural areas.

Lao Loum, Lao Theung, Lao Soung

Around 50 percent of the population are ethnically Lao, the rest being divided between numerous tribal groups, although the methods of classification for these are varied and frequently in disagreement. The Lao government divides the population into three main ethnic categories, ostensibly according to the altitude at which they live: Lao Loum (lowland), Lao Theung (lower mountain) and Lao Soung (higher mountain). Some 50–60 percent of the population are Lao Loum, 20–30 percent are Lao Theung and 10–20 percent Lao Soung.

In general, the Lao Loum live in the Mekong River Valley, subsist on wet-rice cultivation and practise Theravada Buddhism. These are the people of the Mekong Valley lowlands who predominate in the provinces of Luang Prabang, Vientiane, Tha Kaek, Savannakhet and Pakse, and who have traditionally controlled Lao government and society. The Lao Loum are closely related to the Lao-speaking inhabitants of neighbouring northeastern Thailand and, slightly more distantly, to the central Thai or Siamese. The distinction between Lao and Thai is rather indistinct and something of a new (and politically motivated) phenomenon. Certainly the two groups are part of the same family, something both sides will happily accept – yet the Lao can be irritated by the rather arrogant

Mien child in northwest Laos.

and frequently stated Thai contention that the Lao are their 'little brothers'.

Next there are the Lao Theung, or 'approaching the top of the mountain Lao', a loose affiliation of mostly Mon-Khmer-speaking people who live at moderate altitudes and are generally animists rather than Buddhists. Formerly known to the ruling Lao Loum by the pejorative term *kha*, or slave, this group constitutes a further 15–20 percent of the population, and makes up by far the most economically disadvantaged section of Lao society.

Finally, on the distant mountaintops live – as might be expected – the Lao Soung, or 'High Lao', people whose communities are at altitudes of more than 1,000 metres (3,200ft)

It's common in Laos for shows to be put on of Lao Loum, Lao Theung and Lao Soung women dancing together in harmony in their diverse ethnic clothing. In reality, all the dancers are usually Lao Loum lowlanders.

above sea level. Representatives of this group are also to be found in northern Thailand, northwestern Vietnam and southern China, and include Hmong and Mien, together with smaller numbers of Akha, Lisu and Lahu.

overwhelmingly engaged in business. Viets also make up an influential portion of the traders and small business owners in Laos – not to mention the continuing Vietnamese military presence in some provinces. Both groups are largely urban based, the Chinese more in the north of the country and in Vientiane, the ethnic Viets in the Mekong Valley towns like Tha Khaek and Savannakhet. The Vietnamese, in particular, settled in Laos during colonial times, and were employed by the French authorities as teachers and civil servants and at lower levels of administration.

Celebrating the Lao New Year in Luang Prabang.

The Lao Soung have traditionally relied on the cultivation of dry rice and opium. An estimated 20 percent of these upland dwellers comprise Tai-speaking minority groups such as the Tai Dam (Black Tai), Tai Daeng (Red Tai) and Tai Khao (White Tai), all ethnic Tai sub-groups. All these groups are closely related to the Lao Loum.

Vietnamese and Chinese

Laos is also home to sizeable Vietnamese (Viet Kieu) and Chinese (Hua Chiao) communities. In the past decade Hua Chiao have increased markedly, as overland Chinese from Yunnan and Guangdong have migrated to Vientiane and other cities, where they are

Relations between Lao and Viet have not always run smoothly. In terms of their traditions the two peoples live on opposite sides of the great cultural fault line that divides mainland Southeast Asia into Indic and Sinitic zones.

The hostility of the Lao to the Vietnamese on an ethnic basis has perhaps dulled over the years, yet the failure of Vietnam's socialist economic system has inevitably affected Lao thinking; Thailand, whose economy for decades far outperformed that of Vietnam, is now generally regarded as a better model for economic (but not social) development for the Lao PDR, even though post-1986 economic reform Vietnam is now catching up fast.

In the past decade, the sheer number of incoming Chinese, coupled with their relative wealth and political influence, has made the local population suspicious of and even hostile to further Chinese immigration.

Thai migration

The other important immigrant community is the Thai – though it's difficult to know quite where new Thai migration begins and old Lao re-immigration ends. This is because of the almost identical linguistic and ethnic character of the lowland Lao and the people of Northeast

An Akha woman.

Thailand, who also quite happily call themselves 'Lao'. They are, in fact, one and the same people. Thai immigrants from Bangkok are easier to identify, as they speak Central Thai rather than Lao. They, too, are appearing in increasing numbers, especially in the main towns of Laos, where their longer acquaintance with capitalism, business savvy and access to capital all combine to give them a distinct business advantage. As with the ethnic Chinese, this leads to a degree of suspicion and even envy on the part of the Lao – but the fact remains that Lao and Thai are ethnic and cultural kin, speaking almost identical languages, and practising Theravada Buddhism, so hostility levels to the Thai incomers is lower. The Thais are seen as 'city slickers' and 'wide boys', but the

> *Still deeply suspicious of outside influences, authorities restrict marriages between Lao nationals and overseas visitors. Foreigners require special permission, and a reference from their embassy, before they can wed a Lao citizen.*

Chinese are considered to pose a more significant threat to the Lao identity in the long term.

The economy

Laos remains one of Asia's poorest countries, its economy heavily propped up by extensive foreign aid, which currently accounts for 25–30 percent of the annual budget, down from around 50 percent in the late 1990s. Important exports include wood, wood products and electricity, and the country is rich in minerals; tin and gypsum are the most important, but copper, gold, iron and zinc are also present. As yet these natural resources remain largely untapped, although several companies are engaged in oil exploration. Secondary manufacturing industry is slowly developing, with some clothing now being exported, but investment is needed in education to increase the skills of the workforce before more sophisticated manufacturing concerns move in. Some basic products are already produced in local factories, helping to keep imports low.

When the current government took control in 1975 it implemented a brief, disastrous programme of nationalisation and collectivisation of agriculture. In 1979 it abruptly reversed course, and embarked on a process of reform in agriculture, monetary policy and commodity pricing. Laos now has a liberal foreign investment code – at least on paper – that allows 100 percent foreign ownership for government-approved projects. Thailand, the USA and Australia now top the list of foreign investors.

Yet the overall picture is of an under-developed economy. Eighty-five percent of the population work in agriculture, fishing and forestry, and 10 percent in the armed forces or the civil service. Industry is almost non-existent. Annual per capita income hovers just below US$400. The Asian economic crisis of the late 1990s, particularly the currency woes in Thailand, sent the Lao kip into free-fall. Civil servant salaries did not keep pace with the resulting inflation, and were rendered almost worthless. Today the authorities in Vientiane are hopeful, though the current economic slowdown, particularly exhibited in neighbouring Vietnam, is cause for some concern.

The currency, while not convertible outside the country, has been allowed to float according to market forces. However, in a sign of continuing economic and fiscal weakness, the US dollar and Thai baht are generally preferred to the local currency.

The best hope for future economic growth seems to lie in the many hydro-electric projects under discussion or development – despite the environmental concerns surrounding them – as well as Lao's considerable forestry and mining potential. Thai, American, French, Australian and Lao companies have poured money into these developments, secure in the knowledge that the regional market for electricity, particularly in Thailand and Vietnam, will continue to grow rapidly.

The road network throughout the country is being upgraded so as to provide improved infrastructure for economic development. New highways and bridges have been – or are being – built to link Laos to its neighbours and create new economic crossroads for the country. With improved communications, investors are looking to develop southern towns, especially those on the Thai border and the cross-country routes to Vietnam. China is very active in the transport development stakes, and plans have been confirmed for the construction of a road (and possibly rail) bridge across the Mekong at Huay Xay in the northwest, linking China with Thailand across Lao territory. The costs of the new bridge are to be borne equally by China and Thailand.

Education

Almost all Lao men spend at least a part of their youth studying at the local *wat*, or Buddhist temple. For Lao boys in rural areas, the *wat* might offer the only chance to obtain an education and to work their way up in society.

After the Communists took control in 1975 there was a marked decline in the quality of public education. While the number of schools expanded rapidly, the limited facilities served as little more than centres for political indoctrination. Lack of funding for buildings and books, and a serious lack of qualified teachers (most

of the educated population fled after 1975), plague the system to this day.

During the Cold War, Laos' best students completed their education abroad, usually in Eastern Bloc countries. Most of these Lao later struggled to replace whatever internationally-irrelevant language they learnt overseas with English. Today, however, English is spoken to a significant degree in tourist areas. Lao students generally want to learn English and Chinese. The second language is Thai, however, especially in urban areas – an indication of the local power and influence of the Thai economy and media.

Cycling to school in the Mekong lowlands.

TOURISM'S INFLUENCE

Tourism is, inevitably, having an impact on Lao society – and not all of it good. The Lao leadership has kept an eye on the impact of tourism on Thailand, not least in terms of public morals. Vientiane wants the foreign exchange that international tourism brings, but not the narcotics or sex trade. Still more disturbing has been the emergence of child sex tourism in Cambodia to the south. The Lao authorities initially tried to control tourism by attempting to limit visitors to 'luxury tour groups, but this did not work. Laos is a near-perfect destination for budget tourists, however, and this is the fastest expanding sector.

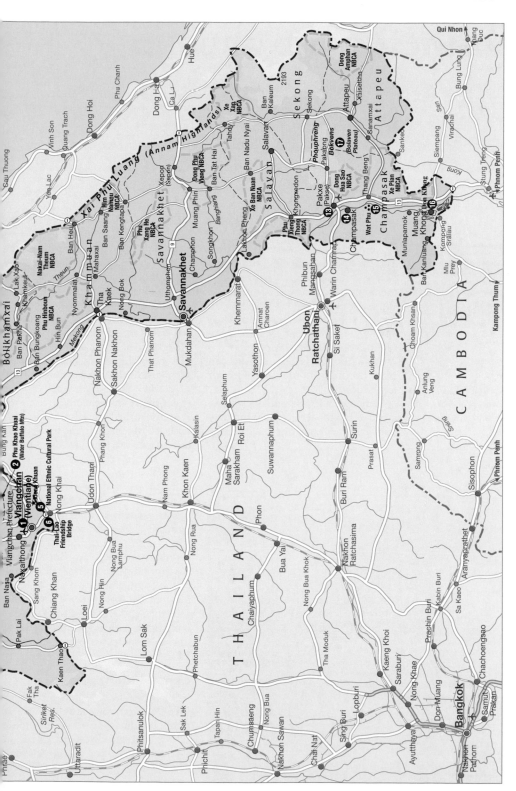

VIENTIANE AND AROUND

One the world's more obscure capital cities, Vientiane is low-rise and low-key, and compact enough to negotiate on foot. Nearby sights include the Buddha Park and the fast-developing resort of Vang Vieng.

Main Attractions

Lao National Museum
Mekong Riverfront
Talat Sao Market
That Luang
Vang Vieng
National Ethnic Cultural Park

Vientiane's Patuxai (Victory Gate) is loosely based on the Arc de Triomphe.

Lethargic and crescent-shaped, **Vientiane**  (Viangchan) reclines on the left bank of the Mekong River. Midway between the Chinese and Cambodian borders with Laos, and between Hanoi and Bangkok, it is not without foreign influences. Not as frantic as other Asian capitals, its traffic is light, and one can cross the main boulevards without fear of death.

In the mid-1500s, Vientiane was the fortified capital of the Lan Xang kingdom, ruled by Setthathirat. Within the city were a palace and two *wat*, or temples: That Luang and Wat Phra Kaew, then home for the venerable Emerald Buddha, originally from the Chiang Rai area and now in Bangkok within a *wat* of the same name. The royal city was called the City of Sandalwood, or Vieng Chan, a name still used today.

The Emerald Buddha remained in Vientiane for over two centuries, until 1778, when the Thai army, led by General Chakri (see page 30), retrieved it and returned the diminutive jade statue to the Thais. In the early 1800s, the Siamese sacked Vientiane again; most of the city was completely destroyed.

By the turn of the 21st century hardly any commercial establishments existed, as the ruling Pathet Lao had closed the country to tourism in 1975, preserving the Laotian capital in a time warp. Today, Vientiane is home to around 10 percent of the country's population of half a million. The downtown disctricts are walkable, and cheap transport to outlying sights such as That Luang is easy to find. Bicycles are useful, appropriate and cheap to rent.

Central Vientiane

As Vientiane has no central plaza, **Nam Phu Ⓐ**, a water-fountain circle on Thanon Setthathirat, is used for a reference as it is strategically placed among an assortment of travel agencies, airline

offices, bakeries, restaurants, *tuk-tuk* stands, guesthouses and hotels.

To the north of Nam Phu is the **Lao National Museum B** (daily 8am–noon and 1–4pm; charge), set on Thanon Samsenthai, one of the city's two main east–west arteries. Built in 1925, this elegant structure was the French governor's residence, and was used by the Lao government as an administrative building. The museum's permanent exhibition provides a selective history of Laos' struggle for independence, leaving out major details such as the heavy Vietnamese involvement in the 'revolution. But it is filled with interesting artefacts from the war. Just north is the **National Stadium**, and to the east is the **Lao Plaza Hotel** (www.laoplazahotel.com), one of the grandest in Laos.

A couple of minutes' walk south of Nam Phu is the **Mekong River**, one of those classically mighty rivers that lures travellers like moths to light. A dike parallels the Mekong for several kilometres, and almost all of it is walkable. A small road, Quai Fa Ngum, parallels river and dike, actually the old town wall that once provided a line of defence against both enemies and flooding of the Mekong. Part of Quai Fa Ngum near the central downtown area is lined with renovated buildings, and between the road and river are numerous but simple outdoor cafés on stilts, popular meeting places for both locals and foreigners. The river itself, especially when it is low, is a time capsule – naked children swim, grandmothers spin silk under houses, women on verandas nurse babies, and husbands sip *lao-lao* and talk.

East of Nam Phu is the **Presidential Palace C** (Haw Kham), once the royal palace and today closed to the public. Adjacent is **Haw Pha Kaew D** (daily 8am–noon and 1–4pm; charge), the royal temple of King Setthathirat, who built it in 1565 to house the Emerald Buddha. Destroyed by the Thais in 1827, the *wat* was rebuilt after World War II and contains a gilded throne, Khmer Buddhist stelae and bronze frog drums belonging to the royal family.

On the northern side of Thanon Setthathirat is **Wat Si Saket E** (daily 8am–noon and 1–4pm; charge), built

Performances of the dance drama known as Phra Lak Ram, based on the Indian epic Ramayana, are staged in Vientiane and Luang Prabang. Graceful dancers perform to classical music that is similar to the Thai classical music tradition.

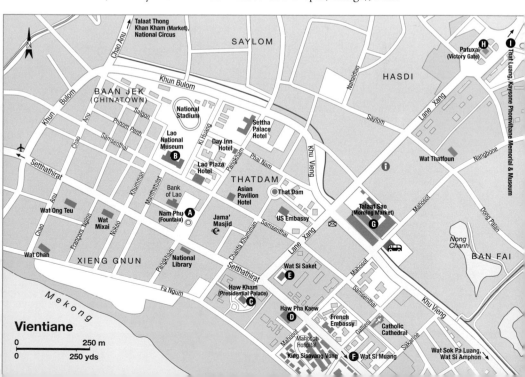

Chillies at the Km52 market north of Vientiane.

The Presidential Palace, Vientiane.

in 1818. Established as a monastery, the *wat* is perhaps the only structure the Thais left standing in 1827. The interior walls surrounding its central *sim* are filled with small niches containing more than 2,000 miniature silver and ceramic Buddha images, dating from the 16th to 19th centuries.

Further east is **Wat Si Muang** (daily; free), the most active temple in Vientiane because it houses the village pillar, or *lak muang*, the cornerstone that houses the city's protective deity. The legend goes that at the temple's dedication a virgin was sacrificed at the bottom of the posthole before the pillar was dropped in, as a harbinger of good luck to the capital's citizens.

From the Presidential Palace, a major boulevard, Lan Xang, heads northeast past **Talat Sao** ● (daily 6am–6pm), the country's best market, to the rather overwhelming **Monument Anousavari** ●, officially **Patuxai** (Victory Gate). Finished in 1969 in memory of the war dead prior to the Communist takeover of Laos, it has panoramic views (Mon–Fri 8am–4.30pm, Sat–Sun until 5pm; charge).

Past Patuxai and on high ground 3km (2 miles) from downtown sits stately 16th-century **That Luang** ● (daily 8am–noon and 1–4pm; charge). Inside this glittering national symbol lies a relic of the Buddha, a breastbone. Representing a miniature Mount Meru, the mythical peak, and some 45 metres (150ft) tall, it is painted gold and dazzles year-round. Flanked on two sides by smaller temples, it sees scant monastic activity, except on holidays such as the annual That Luang festival. During this event people come from miles around and the whole hilltop assumes a carnival air, climaxing after two weeks in a fireworks display second to none in all Laos.

Beyond Vientiane

There is plenty to do in a day using Vientiane as a hub. The most exotic day-trip, perhaps, is to **Phu Khao Khuai** ● (Water Buffalo Mountain), a pine-forested plateau surrounded by 2,000-metre (5,500ft) peaks. Here, nature rules. Butterflies, big as an open hand, dart and hover among blossoms hidden in high grass everywhere. One

of the country's National Biodiversity Conservation Areas, it is said to be full of local wildlife, including elephants, black bears, tigers and clouded leopards. The second most exotic day-trip is to the waterfall at **Taat Leuk**.

Another possible day trip is to **Ban Thalet** and the lake at **Nam Ngum ❸**. Small restaurants overlook the blue-green water, dotted with picturesque islands, one or two of which offer guesthouses.

Further north, close to the midway point between Vientiane (156km/116 miles south) and Luang Prabang (168km/105 miles north), the tiny settlement of **Vang Vieng ❹** is a great place to break on the journey in either direction. Once a backpacker party town, the government dramatically cleaned Vang Vieng up in 2012, removing the drug dealers, bars and illegal businesses that were destroying the town. Set by the banks of the Nam Song, amid a startlingly beautiful natural terrain of limestone karsts, Vang Vieng is a relatively inexpensive, relaxed destination. It is Laos' most popular adventure destination, with tubing and kayaking on the river, caving in the surrounding hills, and climbing on the precipitous limestone karst faces. Other popular activities include mountain biking, trekking, rafting and freshwater swimming in the Nam Song River. The many caves around Vang Vieng are often spectacular, vast and filled with wildlife of all kinds from swiftlets and bats to centipedes and blind fish.

South of the city centre, Tha Deua Road runs alongside the Mekong and leads to the **National Ethnic Cultural Park ❺** (daily 8am–6pm; charge), at Km18 (about 2km before the Friendship Bridge). Built in 1994, the park has mock houses in the style of the Lao Loum, Lao Theung and Lao Soung ethnic groups. The concrete structures are not at all authentic, but the place gives you some idea of the way in which the current government is attempting to combine the diverse ethnic groups of Laos into a unified

Lao people. The park also includes a small zoo – with a few very depressed specimens – and life-size replicas of dinosaurs. The riverside restaurants along the Mekong are the main attraction for Vientiane families, who often spend a day here at weekends.

Beyond the National Ethnic Cultural Park, still on Tha Deua Road, is the **Thai-Lao Friendship Bridge ❻**. Completed in 1994 and funded by the Australian government, it was the first bridge to link the two countries across the Mekong, and a railway line has recently been added. Some 1,240 metres (0.77-miles) long, it connects Nong Khai in Thailand to Vientiane, and is symbolic of the opening of Laos to outside influences. A second bridge was built near Savannakhet in 2006, and construction began in 2009 on a third between Thakek and Nakhon Phanom 100km (62 miles) further north.

Still further along Tha Deua Road, 3km (2 miles) east of the bridge, is the odd yet interesting **Xieng Khuan**, or Buddha Park (daily 8am–6pm; charge), which has a bizarre collection of Buddhist and Hindu sculptures.

Sculptures at Xieng Khuan (Buddha Park).

Monks collecting alms – small portions of glutinous rice – in their begging bowls.

LUANG PRABANG AND AROUND

The temples and culture of Luang Prabang, former royal capital of Laos, have been so well preserved that the city is now a World Heritage Site. There are numerous places of interest nearby, while further east is the mysterious Plain of Jars.

Main Attractions
Royal Palace Museum
Mount Phu Si
Wat Xieng Thong
Pak Ou Caves
Plain of Jars

With its splendid natural setting amid forested hills at the confluence of the Mekong and the Nam Khan rivers, and a long, illustrious history as a royal capital, **Luang Prabang ❼** (Louangphabang) is one of the most intriguing, magical and romantic cities in Asia. Added to Unesco's World Heritage List in 1995, the city is filled with fine old temples and its quiet streets lined with handsome colonial buildings.

For centuries before the city was founded, the river valleys of this part of central Laos played host to various Thai-Lao principalities. In 1353 King Fa Ngum consolidated the first Lao Kingdom, Lan Xang (see page 122), on the site of present-day Luang Prabang. At the time, the city was known as Xawa, possibly a local form of Java, but it was soon renamed Meuang Xieng Thong (Gold City District). A little later, the Khmer sovereign gave Fa Ngum a Sinhalese Buddha image called Pha Bang, from which the city's modern name derives.

Two centuries later, King Phothisarat moved the capital of Lan Xang to Vientiane, but Luang Prabang nonetheless remained the royal heart of the kingdom. After the collapse of Lan Xang in 1694, an independent kingdom was established in Luang Prabang, which co-existed with kingdoms based in Vientiane

and Champasak further south. Kings ruled Luang Prabang until the Pathet Lao officially dissolved the monarchy in 1975. The last king and queen were imprisoned in a cave in the northeast of the country, where they died in the early 1980s. Today Luang Prabang is increasingly a destination for pricey boutiques and travellers on a bigger budget, though deals can still be had.

The Royal Palace Museum

In the centre of the city, between Mt Phu Si and the Mekong, is the **Royal**

The city is surrounded by forested hills.

Serving noodles in a Luang Prabang street market.

Palace Museum A (Haw Kham; Thanon Sisavangvong; daily 8–11am and 1.30–4pm; charge), which offers an insight into regional history. The Palace was constructed from 1904 as the residence of King Sisavang Vong, and is a pleasing mix of classical Lao and French styles, cruciform in layout and mounted on a multi-tiered platform. In a room at the front of the building is the museum's prize, the famed Pha Bang Buddha image after which the city is named. The 83cm (32-inch)-tall image, in the attitude of Abhayamudra, or 'dispelling fear', is almost pure gold. Legend says that it originated in Sri Lanka in the 1st century AD; it was presented to the Khmers, who gave it to King Fa Ngum. The Siamese twice seized the image before finally returning it to Laos in 1867.

The Pha Bang Buddha shares a room with several beautifully embroidered silk screens and engraved elephant tusks, while the rest of the museum houses a fairly substantial collection of regalia, portraits, diplomatic gifts, art treasures, friezes, murals and mosaics.

In the southeastern area of the same compound is the **Royal Ballet Theatre**, formerly a palace building. Performances by local dancers are scheduled every Monday, Wednesday, Friday and Saturday at 6pm, and include a

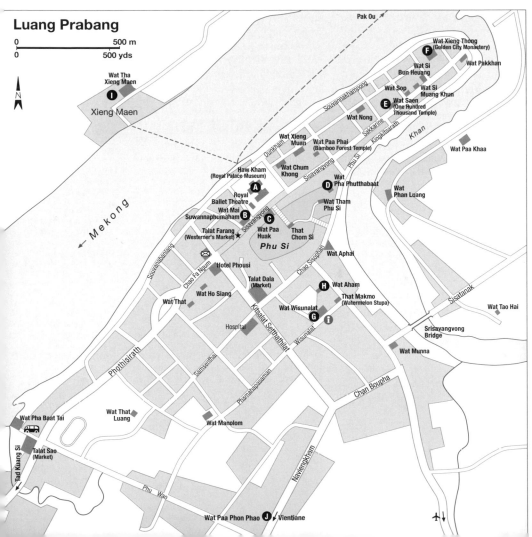

Luang Prabang

0 ———— 500 m
0 ———— 500 yds

N

Mekong

Pak Ou

Wat Tha Xieng Maen **I**

Xieng Maen

Wat Xieng Thong (Golden City Monastery) **F**

Wat Pakkhan

Wat Si Bun Heuang

Wat Sop Wat Si Muang Khun

Souvannakhampong

Wat Saen (One Hundred Thousand Temple) **E**

Wat Nong

Sakkarine

Kingkitsarath

Khan

Dungkham

Wat Xieng Muan

Wat Paa Phai (Bamboo Forest Temple)

Wat Paa Khaa

Sisavangvong

Haw Kham (Royal Palace Museum)

Wat Chum Khong

Wat Pha Phutthabaat **D**

Phu Si

Wat Phan Luang

Royal Ballet Theatre **A**

Wat Mai Suwannaphumaham **B**

Sisavangvong

Wat Tham Phu Si

Talat Farang (Westerner's Market)

Wat Paa Huak **C**

That Chom Si

Phu Si

Wat Aphai

Souvanabanlang

Chao Fa Ngum

Hotel Phousi

Talat Dala (Market)

Chao Sisophan

Wat That

Wat Ho Siang

Wat Aham **H**

That Makmo (Watermelon Stupa)

Wat Tao Hai

Sisatanak

Hospital

Kitsalat Setthathilat

Wat Wisunalat

G **i**

Wisunalat

Srisavangvong Bridge

Wat Munna

Phothisirath

Samsenthai

Phamahapasaman

Chan Bougha

Wat Pha Baat Tai

Wat That Luang

Wat Manolom

Naviengkham

Talat Sao (Market)

Tad Kuang Si

Phu Wao

Wat Paa Phon Phao **J** Vientiane

traditional ballet performance of an extract from *Phra Lak Phra Ram* (the Lao version of the Indian epic *Ramayana*). Tickets are available at the door on the evenings of the performances.

To the southwest of the Royal Palace, is **Wat Mai Suwannaphumaham** Ⓑ (Thanon Sisavangvong; daily 8am–5pm; charge). Dating from the early 19th century, this temple was once the residence of the Sangkhalat, the supreme patriarch of Buddhism in Laos. The *sim* is wooden, with a five-tiered roof in classic Luang Prabang style (see page 71). The main attraction is the gilded walls of the front verandah, the designs of which recount scenes from the *Ramayana* and the Buddha's penultimate incarnation. For the first half of the 20th century the Pha Bang was housed inside, and it is still put on display here during the Lao New Year celebrations.

Mount Phu Si

On the other side of Thanon Sisavangvong rises **Mount Phu Si**, the rocky 100-metre (330ft) hill that dominates the centre of Luang Prabang. At its foot

stands **Wat Paa Huak** Ⓒ (daily 6.30am–6.30pm; charge), which features well preserved 19th-century murals showing Mekong scenes. From this temple, 328 steps wind up the forested slopes to the 24-metre (79ft) **That Chom Si** on the summit, which has an impressive gilded stupa in classical Lao form, as well as a rusting anti-aircraft gun. There are magnificent views across the ancient city, best at sunset, with the Mekong and Nam Khan Rivers encircling the historic Unesco-protected peninsula that lies at the heart of old Luang Prabang.

The path continues down the other side of Phu Si to **Wat Tham Phu Si**, a cave shrine housing a Buddha image of wide girth, in the style known locally as *Pha Kachai*. Close by the main road is **Wat Pha Phutthabaat** Ⓓ (free), a temple containing a 3-metre (10ft) Buddha footprint dating from the late 14th century.

Along the peninsula

Heading northeast along Thanon Sisavangvong from the foot of Phu Si towards the confluence of the Nam Khan and the Mekong, you pass a string

The Royal Palace Museum, Luang Prabang.

SHOP

Every afternoon and evening, between about 4pm and 10.30pm, the southwest part of Sisavangvong Road and its extension towards Chao Fa Ngum set up shop as Luang Prabang's 'night market', also styled Talaat Farang or the 'Westerners' Market' by the locals. This is *the* place to go to buy local handicrafts of all kinds, from Hmong woven clothing, through Lao lanterns and paintings, to just about anything. IRestaurants and food stands line both sides of the market and many upscale venues sit at the far end.

Wat Xieng Thong.

of glittering temples interspersed with evocative colonial buildings. On the left, **Wat Paa Phai** (Bamboo Forest Temple; daily; free) is noteworthy for its 100-year-old fresco and carved wooden facade depicting secular Lao scenes. Further along the street, also on the left, is **Wat Saen E** (One Hundred Thousand Temple; daily; free), whose name commemorates the sizeable donation with which it was constructed. This temple is different in style to most others in Luang Prabang, and the trained eye will immediately identify it as central-Thai influenced. The *sim* was originally constructed in 1718 but was restored twice in the 20th century.

Wat Xieng Thong

Luang Prabang's most renowned temple, **Wat Xieng Thong F** (Golden City Monastery; Thanon Sakkarine; daily 6am–6pm; charge) lies on the banks of the Mekong, close to the peninsula's tip. The waterside location recalls the importance of river transport in Laos. The temple was built in 1560 by King Setthathirat (1548–71) and was patronised by the monarchy

right up until 1975. The low sweeping roofs epitomise the classic Luang Prabang style. Inside the *sim*, the eight thick supporting pillars, richly stencilled in gold, guide the eye to the serene golden Buddha images at the rear, and upwards to the roof which is covered in *dhamma* wheels. On the outside of the *sim*, at the back, is an elaborate mosaic of the Tree of Life set against a deep red background. Throughout, the combination of splendid gold and deep red gives this temple a captivatingly regal atmosphere.

Adjacent to the *sim* is a smaller building, dubbed by the French *La Chapelle Rouge*. The 'chapel' contains a unique reclining Buddha figure that employs Lao proportions, especially the robe curling outwards at the ankles, and the graceful position of the hand supporting the head. This figure was displayed at the Paris exhibition in 1931, but happily returned to Luang Prabang in 1964 after several decades in Vientiane. The chapel itself is exquisitely decorated. On the outside of the rear wall is a mosaic showing rural Lao village life, executed in the 1950s in celebration of

two-and-a-half millennia since the Buddha's attainment of Nirvana.

Also in the Xieng Thong compound are various monks' quarters, reliquary stupas and a boat shelter. Close to the east gate is a building housing the royal funeral carriage; the interior decoration is only half-finished, as work ceased after the communist victory in 1975.

It is a very pleasant stroll back towards the Royal Palace along the Mekong. Little appears to have changed in the past 30 years, nor is it likely to under the present Unesco conditions. Boutique restaurants and hotels have largely replaced the scruffy old sticky-rice places, but the buildings generally remain the same.

Southeast of Phu Si

Back in the vicinity of Mount Phu Si, another temple of note is **Wat Wisunalat** Ⓖ (Wat Vixoun; Thanon Wisunalat; daily 6.30am–5pm; voluntary donation). Built by King Wisunalat (1501–20) between 1512 and 1513, this is the oldest temple in the city still in use. The *sim*, rebuilt a decade after the original wooden structure was destroyed by fire in 1887, is unique in style, with a front roof sloping down over the terrace. Sketches by Louis Delaporte of the original building exist from the 1860s, and confirm what a later visitor wrote: '[Vat] Visunalat is shaped like a boat, the same shape that Orientals give to their coffins. The wooden walls are sculpted with extreme refinement and delicacy.' Though the wood has gone, the builders who performed the restoration attempted to capture the shapes of the original wood in the stucco work. Inside is an impressive collection of Buddhist sculpture.

In the temple grounds is That Pathum, or Lotus Stupa, which is affectionately referred to as **That Makmo**, or Watermelon Stupa, and is just as distinctive as the temple itself. The stupa is over 30 metres (100ft) high, and was constructed in 1503–4, at which time it was filled with small, precious Buddha images. Many

of these were stolen by Chin Haw marauders from Yunnan in the 19th century – the rest are now safely on display in the Royal Palace Museum.

Next to Wat Wisunalat is the peaceful **Wat Aham** Ⓗ (daily 6.30am–5pm; voluntary donation), formerly – before Wat Mai took the honour – the residence of the supreme patriarch of Buddhism in Laos. The temple's red facade combines with striking green *yak* temple guardians and mildewed stupas to provide an atmosphere of extreme tranquillity. The temple rarely has many visitors, other than those quietly making offerings at an important shrine at the base of the two large old pipal trees.

Outside town

Across the Mekong from Luang Prabang, in Xieng Maen District, are no fewer than four more temples set in beautiful surroundings. Boats depart from the pier behind the Royal Palace, or you can charter a vessel from the pier 500 metres/yds further north. **Wat Tham Xieng Maen** Ⓘ is situated in a 100-metre (330ft) -deep cave. This is generally kept locked, but the keys are

Temple detail.

That Makmo, the watermelon stupa.

Talat Dara market in the heart of Luang Prabang.

Buddhas in the Pak Ou Caves.

held at nearby Wat Long Khun, the former retreat of kings awaiting their coronation. A small donation is requested for access to the cave temple.

Close to the southern edge of the city is a forest retreat, **Wat Paa Phon Phao** ❼, with a three-floor pagoda (daily 8–10am and 1–4.30pm; voluntary donation) complete with an external terrace near the top that affords excellent views of the surrounding countryside. The *chedi* is a popular destination for locals and visitors alike.

Further out, about 4km (2.5 miles) beyond the airport, is the Tai Lü village of **Ban Phanom** ❽, renowned as a silk- and cotton-weaving village. At weekends a small market is set up for those interested in seeing the full range of fabrics produced (although villagers will show off their wares at other times). All weaving and dyeing is done by hand using traditional techniques, a fascinating process to watch. In the vicinity, a few kilometres along the river, is the tomb of Henri Mouhot, the French explorer who took the credit for 'discovering' Angkor Wat in 1860. He died of malaria in Luang Prabang

in 1861, though his tomb was not rediscovered until 1990.

A two-hour (by long-tail boat), 25km (15-mile) journey upriver from Luang Prabang is the confluence of the Mekong and the Nam Ou. Opposite the mouth of the Nam Ou, in the side of a large limestone cliff, are the **Pak Ou caves** ❾ (daily; charge). Legend maintains that King Setthathirat discovered these two caves in the 16th century, and they have been venerated ever since. Both caves are full of Buddha images, some of venerable age. The lower of the two caves, Tham Ting, is easily accessible from the river. The upper cave, Tham Phum, is reached by a staircase, and is considerably deeper, requiring a torch for full exploration. There is a pleasant shelter between the two caves, an ideal spot for a picnic lunch.

On the way to Pak Ou, boats will stop by request at **Ban Xang Hai** ❿ (Jar-Maker Village), named after the village's former main industry. Jars still abound, but they are made elsewhere, and the village devotes itself to producing *lao-lao*, the local moonshine ricewine. Archaeologists digging around the village have unearthed jars dating back more than 2,000 years. Opposite, at Ban Thin Hong, close to Pak Ou village, recent excavations have uncovered even earlier artefacts – tools, pottery and fabrics – around 8,000 years old. As yet, the site hasn't been developed as a tourist attraction.

Several waterfalls in the vicinity of Luang Prabang make for attractive half-day or day excursions, perhaps combined with stops in some rural villages along the way. About 30km (20 miles) south of the town are the multi-tiered **Kuang Si Waterfalls**, replete with beguiling limestone formations and crystal-clear pools. Food vendors keep most of the local visitors at the lower level of the falls. Up a trail to the left of the lower cascade is a second fall with a quieter pool that makes for good swimming. The trail continues to the top of the falls, though after rain it can be dangerously slippy.

Taat Sae ⓫ falls, also south of town, are closer to the city (15km/9 miles away), and hence more crowded at weekends. The falls here have more pools and shorter drops. They can be reached by boat from the delightful village of Ban Aen on the Nam Khan.

East to the Plain of Jars

The **Plain of Jars ⓬**, around 10 hours by bus from Luang Prabang, is one of the country's top attractions. Huge stone jar-shaped vessels are scattered over a dozen locations on the lonely plateau around Phonsavan. Various key questions remain unanswered about these fascinating and mysterious ancient megaliths. Who constructed them? When did they build them, and why?

Three major sites are easily accessible from Phonsavan, and have been cleared of unexploded American bombs (UXO), although it's still best to stay on the main paths. **Site 1** or **Thong Hai Hin** (Stone Jar Plain) is located 15km (9 miles) southwest of Phonsavan (daily; charge). This site has the biggest collection of jars, numbering over 250, and also the largest jar, which according to local lore is the victory cup of the legendary Lao king Khun Jeuam, who is said to have liberated the local people from an oppressive ruler. On nearby hillsides are odd bottle-shaped excavations; the locals use these as bird traps. Although the site is impressive, the presence of a nearby Lao air force base and buildings erected for the visit of Thailand's crown prince a while back detract from the overall atmosphere.

Another jar site, known locally as **Hai Hin Phu Salato** (daily; charge), or **Site 2**, is located 25km (16 miles) south of Phonsavan. Here about 100 jars are spread across two adjacent hillsides.

The most attractive site is a further 10km (6 miles) south from Site 2, and is called **Hai Hin Laat Khai** (daily; charge), or Site 3. Here about 150 jars are located on top of a small hill from which one can enjoy great views of the surrounding plains and the farming community of Ban Sieng Dee, set on an adjacent hillside. This Lao village, another 2km (1.25-mile) walk from the jar site, has a small Buddhist temple and visitors are welcome.

TIP

If you plan to visit only Site 1 on the Plain of Jars, a jumbo (motorised trishaw) chartered in Phonsavan will suffice, but hardier transport such as a jeep is recommended for visiting all three sites. Any of the hotels or travel agencies in Phonsavan can make the necessary arrangements. Hmong villages are located in the vicinity of Phonsavan and can be included in the itinerary.

The Plain of Jars.

SOUTHERN LAOS

River towns, temples, idyllic waterfalls, quiet villages and captivating landscapes are just some of the attractions of the southern Lao regions, reached by scenic boat trips along the Mekong.

Main Attractions
Pakse
Wat Phu, Champasak
Si Phan Don islands
Khon Phapheng Falls
Bolaven Plateau

Wat Luang, Pakse.

Southern Laos offers a wealth of attractions in close proximity. Travellers seeking ancient history and culture will want to linger at the Khmer temple of Wat Phu, while the Si Phan Don (Four Thousand Islands) region in the far south will appeal to anyone who appreciates scenic beauty and tranquil rural life. Of the main urban centres, Pakse still has sufficient Vietnamese and Chinese residents to feel distinctly Indochinese, while Champasak still carries the unexpected air of a former tiny Lao royal principality. The temperate Bolaven Plateau is home to a number of Mon-Khmer minorities and offers superlative natural beauty.

Pakse and environs

The town of **Pakse** ⑬ (Pakxe) is home to many ethnic Chinese and Vietnamese, and has a livelier ambience than elsewhere in the country. The impressive compound of **Wat Luang** (daily; free) close to the Don River is hard to miss. The **Champasak Palace Hotel** (www.champasakpalacehotel.com) is 500 metres/yds east on busy Route 13. Construction of this edifice began in 1968; it was to become the residence of the last Prince of Champasak. After serving as a venue for Communist Party congresses it was converted into a hotel in the 1990s and immediately became the place to stay in Pakse. It is a fascinating mix of regal splendour and communist austerity. Directly east of the Champasak Palace Hotel lies **Wat Tham Fai** (daily; free), which due to its sprawling grounds is the site of many temple fairs. Beyond lies the **Champasak Historical Heritage Museum** (daily 8–11.30am and 1.30–4pm; charge). Currently something of a cultural mishmash, the museum nevertheless has some beautiful pieces on the ground floor.

An interesting excursion is to cross the Don River and visit **San Jao Suk Se** (daily; free), a truly idyllic temple with lovely views across the Mekong back to Pakse.

Champasak and Wat Phu

There are regular buses and *songthaews* heading south to **Champasak** (Ban Wat Thong), the starting-point for a visit to Wat Phu and nearby sights of historical interest. Alternatively you can take a boat: depending upon your budget – and your pain threshold – there are a variety of options available for the 30km (19-mile) cruise down the Mekong.

Sleepy **Champasak** ⑭ once served as the administrative centre for the southern region, and was the residence of Champasak's royal family. The town is pleasant enough, but the main reason to come here is to visit the magnificent site of **Wat Phu** ⑮ (www.vatphou-champassak.com; daily 8am–4.30pm museum and until 6pm for the temple; charge), 9km (5.5 miles) to the south, which is one of the highlights of a trip to Laos. The site, beneath the mountain of Phu Pasak, was sacred to the Khmers from the 6th century onwards. Most of the buildings were the work of a pre-Angkorean Khmer civilisation in the 9th century; later the Theravada Buddhist Kingdom of Lan Xang converted the Hindu temples into Buddhist shrines. Although it lacks the grandeur of Angkor, Wat Phu nonetheless exudes a notable presence.

Wat Phu is famous for its *boun* (festival), which takes place in January or February. During the three-day event the site is filled with pilgrims and makes a fascinating spectacle.

The far south

After the historical and cultural focus of Wat Phu, the islands of **Si Phan Don** are a natural attraction, offering scenic beauty and a glimpse into rural life. The Mekong River is at its widest in Laos here, close to the Cambodian boder: during the rainy season it is up to 12km (7.4 miles) across, and when the waters recede many small islands emerge. It is from this phenomenon that the Si Phan Don region takes its name, meaning 'four thousand islands'. One of the larger islands is **Don Khong** ⑯, accessed by bus or boat (www.vatphou.

com) from Champasak. There is appealing accommodation in restored French villas in the main town, Muang Khong, and some charming restaurants.

Just 15km (9 miles) south of Muang Khong, on the small island of Don Khon, are the impressive **Li Phi Falls** (daily; charge). A unique attraction is the endangered **Irrawaddy dolphin**, which can be seen off the southern tip of the island. On the mainland south of Ban Nakasang are the **Khon Phapheng** (Phapheng Falls; daily; charge), the largest series of waterfalls on the lower Mekong. The falls are a dramatic sight, and are best viewed from a pavilion located above them – three separate cascades merge at this spot.

East of Pakse and Champasak, the lush **Bolaven Plateau** ⑰ is known for its minority peoples, waterfalls and beautiful scenery. At an average altitude of 1,200 metres (4,000ft) the area is suitable for the cultivation of temperate crops. The French introduced the production of high-quality coffee; production declined during the Vietnam War but is now experiencing a major renaissance.

The Buddhist Magha Puja festival (often called the Boun Makha Busa) is held at Wat Phu in January or February.

Harvesting rice in the Mekong Valley.

FESTIVALS

Religion gives the festivals in the region their flavour – but there are many reasons to celebrate.

The festivals of Southeast Asia are diverse and rich. Many are based on religion, and since this is such a diverse region, various places benefit from their multi-cultural inheritance, ensuring that festivals take place throughout the year.

There are other reasons to celebrate. The remaining royalty still enjoy a degree of pomp and power. In December the Royal Guard in Bangkok, splendidly attired in colourful coats and outrageous hats, troop their colours for the Thai royal family, while in Brunei the Sultan's birthday in July is celebrated across the country with various events, starting with morning prayers devoted to him. In Cambodia, the king's birthday often coincides with the big water festival (Bon Om Tuk) at the end of October or early November. King Norodom Sihamoni also shows he is a man of the people, if not of the soil, when he gets behind an ox to participate in Royal Ploughing Day (Bon Choa Preah Nengkal) in Phnom Penh in May.

Elsewhere, parade-filled days celebrate the cessation of hostilities, independence from colonial rulers and the founding of republics. In Vietnam, the last day of April commemorates the 1975 surrender of South Vietnam to the North. Lao National Day (2 December) recalls the overthrowing of the monarchy, also in 1975, while in Cambodia, National Day celebrates the end of the Khmer Rouge regime. The National Day Parade in Singapore on 9 August marks the anniversary of formal separation from Malaysia in 1965. Indonesia celebrates the start of its fight for independence from the Dutch on 17 August.

The lunar New Year – any time between mid-January and mid-February – is marked by Chinese communities throughout the region with fireworks and firecrackers; in Vietnam it is called the Tet festival.

Parade to Wat Xieng Thong for the New Year Festival, Luang Prabang.

The Buddhist New Year is celebrated each April in Thailand, Laos, Cambodia and Burma with a deluge of water. Everybody gets soaked during the festivities that can last four or five days

A participant at the colourful Thaipusam festival at Batu Caves in Malaysia.

Villagers celebrate a purification ceremony on the beach in Bali, Indonesia.

BALI: FESTIVAL CAPITAL OF SOUTHEAST ASIA

Bali is undoubtedly the festival capital of Southeast Asia, if not the world. Nearly 90 percent of the island's population are Hindu-Buddhists and temple festivals, with offerings, dancing, eating and sometimes cockfighting, can be seen throughout the year. But events are not always easy to determine as they follow three different calendars: the Saka solar-lunar calendar of 354 days, the Pawukon (or Wuku) calendar with a cycle of 210 days, and the Western calendar. New Year in the Saka calendar (March or April) is extremely loud as people make as much noise as possible to ward off evil spirits, while monster effigies called *ogoh ogoh* are paraded and burnt. The most important Pawukon festival is Galungan, an island-wide five-day festival when ancestral souls visit their descendants. Pigs are slaughtered for offerings, temples are festooned with decorations and ritual feasting takes place. Other spectacles include the International Kite Festival in Sanur in July, which sends messages to the Hindu gods to bring a full harvest.

'lypast celebrates Singapore National Day.

w racing festival in An Giang, Vietnam.

The Loi Krathong Sai, or Lantern Festival, celebrated every year in the north of Thailand, around the end of October. Revellers release hot-air lanterns into the night sky, after making wishes.

The Mekong River is the lifeblood of Cambodia.

*Timeless beauty in the countryside
south of Phnom Penh.*

Novice monks at Angkor.

CAMBODIA

After its brutal period under the Khmer Rouge,
Cambodia is now emerging as a beguiling destination.
The magnificent ruins of Angkor are without equal,
while the buzzing capital city makes an enjoyable base.

Traditional masked dance.

Avisit to Cambodia is a special experience. Once the largest city in the world, with over one million inhabitants, Angkor dominates the country's past and present, and is already making an invaluable commercial contribution to its future. Even after several visits one struggles to come to terms with the immensity of its scale; it is as though all the treasures of the Valley of the Nile were assembled in a single place. There is nowhere else like it on the face of the earth.

Of course Cambodia is more than just Angkor. There is Phnom Penh, once an exquisite hybrid of Cambodian and French architecture and – despite the destruction of the war years and depopulation by the Khmer Rouge – destined to become so again. Like Laos, Cambodia has retained many of the beneficial aspects of French colonialism, and there can be few more romantic settings in which to sample French *haute cuisine* and sip a glass of wine than by the Chatomuk, or Quatre Bras, where the Mekong, Bassac and Sap Rivers come together.

Stone Buddha.

There are also many wonderful temples, hundreds of years old and still buried in the forests, waiting to be discovered. Some are not yet accessible, but each year clearance and restoration work is pressed forward, so that in the not-too-distant future Cambodia is destined to become one of the region's major tourist destinations.

Finally there is the Cambodian coast, once the weekend retreat of French colonial officials and the Cambodian elite, but which suffered badly under the puritanical Khmer Rouge regime. Now the coastal resort of Kep is being rebuilt, while the beaches of Sihanoukville are being developed into a tourist playground. Offshore, the warm waters of the Gulf of Thailand are studded with some entrancingly beautiful tropical islands. Meanwhile in the remote and inaccessible Cardamom Mountains and elsewhere, national parks are being established, so Cambodia also looks set to develop as a major wildlife destination in the years to come.

DECISIVE DATES

Earliest times

100 BC–AD 500

Establishment of a flourishing trading state called Funan in the Mekong Delta.

500–700

A proto-Khmer state, known as Chen La, is established inland from Funan near the confluence of the Mekong and Sap rivers.

The greatness of Angkor

802–50

Reign of Jayavarman II, who proclaims himself a god-king and begins the great work of moving the capital to Roluos near Angkor.

889–908

Yasovarman I moves the capital to Angkor.

1113–50

Surayavarman II begins the construction of Angkor Wat.

1177

The Chams sack Angkor.

1181–1219

Jayavarman VII constructs the Bayon at Angkor Thom.

1352–1430

The Siamese Kingdom of Ayutthaya sacks and pillages Angkor four times, taking away the court regalia and many prisoners.

Division and decline

1432

King Ponhea Yat abandons Angkor. Subsequently Lovek, to the north of Phnom Penh, becomes the capital.

1618–1866

The capital is moved to Udong, north of Phnom Penh.

The French in Cambodia

1863

The French force King Norodom to sign a treaty making Cambodia a French protectorate.

1866

A new capital is established at Phnom Penh.

Early 20th-century engraving of Angkor Wat.

1904

King Norodom dies and is succeeded by King Sisowath, who reigns until 1927.

1941

Thailand invades northwestern Cambodia.

1942

Norodom Sihanouk becomes king.

Independence and the Indochina Wars

1945

King Sihanouk declares Cambodian independence with Japanese support.

1953

Cambodia gains full independence from France under King Sihanouk.

1954

At the Geneva Conference, France formally confirms its withdrawal from Cambodia.

1955

Sihanouk abdicates but retains real power for himself.

1965

Vietnam War escalates; Communist forces seek sanctuary in Cambodia.

1967

Pol Pot's group of Cambodian Communists – dubbed 'Khmer Rouge' by Sihanouk – launch an insurgency in the northwest.

1969

US B-52 bombardment of Vietnamese sanctuaries in Cambodia begins.

Bas-reliefs at Angkor Wat.

1970
A coup is launched by right-wing General Lon Nol. Sihanouk takes refuge in Beijing.

The Zero years
1975
Khmer Rouge take Phnom Penh on 17 April; cities are immediately evacuated, and the country is cut off from the outside world. Brutal persecution of Buddhism.

1976
Large-scale starvation occurs in the northwest as hundreds of thousands of urban dwellers are deported there.

1978
Refusal to negotiate with Vietnam over burgeoning border war.

1979
Vietnamese troops invade and overthrow Pol Pot regime. People's Republic of Cambodia established.

Cambodia reborn
1979–88
Up to 100,000 Vietnamese forces are stationed in Cambodia to prevent a DK resurgence.

1989
Vietnamese forces start to withdraw.

1991
Prince Sihanouk returns to Phnom Penh.

1993
General elections are held, supervised by the United Nations. Coalition government of Prince Norodom Ranariddh's FUNCINPEC Party and Hun Sen's People's Party.

1996
Khmer Rouge forces split; Ieng Sary defects to the government in return for an amnesty.

1998
Pol Pot dies in mysterious circumstances and the Khmer Rouge finally disintegrates.

1999
Cambodia joins ASEAN.

2003
Anti-Thai riots break out in Phnom Penh.

2004
Hun Sen is re-elected by parliament. King Sihanouk

Norodom Sihanouk in 1983.

abdicates and his son, Norodom Sihamoni, succeeds him.

2005
UN approves a war crimes tribunal to try surviving Khmer Rouge leaders.

2007
UN-backed genocide trials begin.

2008
Hun Sen's ruling Cambodian People's Party retains power in elections.

2009
Former S21 commander Duch is the first former Khmer Rouge leader to stand trial; tensions flare with Thailand over the border area at Preah Vihear.

2010
Comrade Duch is found guilty of crimes against humanity and given a 35-year prison sentence.

2011
Three most senior surviving Khmer Rouge members go on trial on charges of genocide and crimes against humanity.

2012
Former king, Norodom Sihanouk, dies at 89. Tensions with Thailand ease over Preah Vihear.

2013
Opposition leader Sam Rainsy returns from exile. Ruling party of premier Hun Sen claims victory in parliamentary elections, opposition alleges widespread irregularities. Large demonstrations held in Phnom Penh, with minor, sporadic violence.

Most Cambodians are Theravada Buddhists.

PEOPLE AND CULTURE

Ethnic Khmers dominate, but Cambodia's population of 12 million also includes minority groups, including large numbers of Vietnamese.

Under the murderous Khmer Rouge the Cambodian people suffered trauma on a mass-scale. Apart from the horrors they witnessed and endured, the Khmer Rouge eliminated the educated, skilled and wealthy classes – the foundation needed to lift society from the wrecked, third-world cataclysm where it was left. The Maoists moved the entire urban population into the countryside to develop an agrarian pseudo-society fuelled by slavery, torture and starvation. When it inevitably collapsed there was an uneducated, desperate population remaining, struggling to emerge from so much death and destruction.

After more than three decades, Cambodians have made a remarkable recovery, though the emotional scars will last a lifetime for those that endured the Khmer Rouge, and for many of their children. Indeed, much of Cambodia's population has been born after those bleak years and did not experience the suffering themselves. Today's generation exhibits a pride in their country and all things Angkor, and wishes to leave the painful past of the Khmer Rouge behind.

A trishaw on the streets of Phnom Penh.

The Khmers

Ethnic Khmer, Cambodia's predominant indigenous people, make up more than 90 percent of the country's 12 million population. They are among the longest-established of settled agricultural peoples in Southeast Asia, all speaking variants of the same Khmer language, which is a part of the larger Mon-Khmer linguistic group.

Khmers tend to think of themselves as a single people, the dominant ethnic group of Cambodia, the founders of the Khmer Empire and builders of Angkor Wat. This is by-and-large correct, but it is also something of a simplification, constructed on a nationalist desire to emphasise Khmer unity in the face of external challenges, particularly from Vietnam. Certainly the Khmer can be considered a single entity, but they may also be further subdivided into the majority Cambodian Khmer, and two smaller groups: the Khmer Krom or 'Lower Khmer' of 'Lower Cambodia' – that is, the Mekong delta, which now forms part of Vietnam, and the Khon Suay or Surin Khmers of eastern Thailand.

Little is known of their precise origins. It is thought that Khmer-speaking peoples arrived at least three thousand years ago, probably from the north, possibly displaced by expanding waves of Sino-Tibetan and Sino-Tai groups

A citizen of Cambodia is generally referred to as a 'Cambodian' regardless of ethnicity or linguistic background. This includes ethnic Vietnamese, Chinese or Thai immigrants. To be a Khmer, however, is to identify with the country's predominant ethnic group.

(themselves under pressure from the expanding Han Chinese population to the north).

Khmers remain the dominant political and cultural force of the Cambodian population,

independent estimates suggest there are between 500,000 and 1 million. They tend to live in the big cities, where they work as restaurateurs or in other small businesses, or make a living as fishermen along the Mekong and Sap rivers.

The Cham

A second distinctive minority in Cambodian society is the Cham Muslims, one of the oldest, but nowadays least considered, peoples of Indochina. There are some 400,000–500,000 Chams in Cambodia, despite their having been

Cambodians are relatively poor by regional standards.

although their economic influence is far less, on a per capita basis, than that of the ethnic Chinese and Vietnamese. Most are Theravada Buddhists, although Christianity made a small number of converts during the 20th century.

The Vietnamese

The largest national minority in Cambodia is the Viet Kieu or migrant Vietnamese. Because traditionally little love has been lost between Khmer and Viet, there is a tendency on the part of the Cambodian authorities to underestimate the number of Vietnamese in the country. According to figures published by the Cambodian government, there are just 100,000 Vietnamese residents, but

particularly targeted for extermination by the Khmer Rouge in the 1970s.

Chams are inheritors of a proud tradition that stretches back some 2,000 years: Champa was the first Indianised kingdom in Indochina, its founding predating both Chen La (6th century AD) and the first major expansion of the Vietnamese south from Tonkin (mid-10th century). At the peak of their power, about 12 centuries ago, the Chams controlled rich and fertile lands stretching from north of Hue, in central Annam, to the Mekong Delta in Cochin China, as well as regions of Cambodia and Laos. I. Their kingdom rivalled that of Angkor. In Cambodia the name of an eastern province and its capital, Kompong Cham, are a reminder of their presence.

In 1820 the Cham king and many subjects fled to Cambodia rather than submit to the Vietnamese. Most Chams moved up the Mekong, into territories that now constitute the Cambodian heartland. They settled north and east of Phnom Penh, notably in the province and town of Kompong Cham, and along the shores of the Tonlé Sap. Here they became well known and relatively prosperous through their skills as fishermen. During the 18th and 19th centuries Sunni Islam spread widely among the Cambodian Chams.

The Khmer Rouge persecuted the Cham community. All mosques were either demolished or turned over to secular purposes for use as ammunition stores and Khmer Rouge barracks. Tens of thousands of Chams were murdered, like their Khmer compatriots, only proportionately in much higher numbers. By the time Vietnamese armed forces swept across the frontier in December 1978, between a half and two-thirds of the Cham community had been murdered, starved to death or driven out of the country.

The Ethnic Chinese

Most of Cambodia's Hua Chiao, or Overseas Chinese, trace their origins to the southern coastal provinces of Hainan, Guangdong and Fujian. Estimates of their overall numbers vary from 300,000 to 500,000. In recent years a new wave of Chinese migration to Cambodia has got under way, and the presence of both Taiwanese and Malaysian Chinese in business circles is marked. The Chinese are almost exclusively urban, and, since they intermarry readily with urban Khmers, are not Muslim like the Chams, and are not disliked and feared like the Vietnamese; Chinese ethnicity is more readily subsumed within Khmer society. It is also interesting to note that fully 80 percent of the top Khmer Rouge leadership, including Pol Pot and Nuon Chea, were Sino-Khmers. Intermarriage between Khmers and Chinese is common and widespread, especially in urban areas.

The Khmer Loeu

Ethnic minorities in Cambodia include the Khmer Loeu or Upland Khmer – hill tribes of Mondulkiri and Ratanakiri, such as the Kuy, Mnong, Brao, Tapuon and Jarai, as well as the Pear and Saoch of the southwest. Collectively they probably number no more than 80,000.

Some of these groups fared comparatively well under the Khmer Rouge, who perceived them as 'pure', unpolluted by capitalism and an urban environment, even models of primitive Communism (see box below).

Other minorities

Three smaller groups fared less well under the Khmer Rouge – the Thai, Lao and Shan. Faced with vicious discrimination in 1976–9, those Thais who were not killed fled to neighbouring Thailand. Surviving Lao also fled in droves. The Shan – a few thousand were long-term residents

The kramaa head scarf is worn by Khmers.

PREFERENTIAL TREATMENT

In 1968, shortly after the Khmer Rouge embarked on an armed struggle, its leadership began operations in regions inhabited by non-Khmer upland minorities. Traditionally looked down on by Khmers, the KR valued them for their knowledge of the jungle, survival skills and prowess as hunters. They were also 'poor and blank': in Maoist terms, ideal vessels for indoctrination. When KR forces rolled into Phnom Penh in 1975, the presence of AK-47-bearing 'savages' in the midst of the victorious Communist forces shocked the city dwellers. As Dith Pran wrote: 'They seemed to be from the jungle, or a different world.'

of Pailin, where they worked as gem miners – were even less fortunate, and seem to have been wiped out entirely.

Finally, mention should be made of the South Asians, a few hundred of whom live in the larger cities like Phnom Penh and Battambang, working chiefly as small businessmen and traders.

Economy and industry

The Cambodian economy was twice virtually destroyed in recent decades, first when the Khmer Rouge entered Phnom Penh in 1975, and again with the 1989 withdrawal of the Viet-

Khmer farmer.

namese and the collapse of the Soviet Union, a major source of aid. Today, with Phnom Penh's move away from communist ideology to market economics, the situation has improved, but the long-term development of the economy still remains a huge challenge, and prospects aren't helped by the fact that corruption is so well entrenched. Cambodia joined ASEAN in 1999, and opened itself up to global markets in 2005 when it joined the WTO.

By far the largest sources of foreign revenue are wood exports and foreign aid, neither of which is sustainable in the long term. Another significant area of revenue, also of dubious long-term soundness, derives from the shipment of gold and cigarettes from other Asian countries to Vietnam, where tariffs are significantly higher. Other than timber and gemstones, also a source of income, Cambodia has few natural resources. Rubber used to be a major export, with the Soviet Union purchasing almost the entire annual production, but has become less important in recent years. The garment industry, however, is relatively robust and has developed some encouraging export trade.

Various proposals have been made, mainly for the establishment of hydroelectric facilities. So far nothing has come of these proposals, but they have brought to light the serious risks to Cambodia posed by similar projects upstream in Laos and China. As Cambodia is so dependent on the annual rise in the waters of the Mekong and Tonlé Sap and the fertile deposits this brings, any change in the flow of the river could potentially have disastrous effects on agriculture. The possibility of a decline in numbers and species of fish in the lake and river is also of concern.

The Cambodian government continues to work with bilateral and multilateral donors, including the World Bank and IMF, to resolve the country's many pressing needs. The major challenge in the short to medium term is to adapt the economic environment to the country's demographic imbalance – more than 50 percent of the population are 20 years or younger. Cambodia is gradually starting to attract foreign investment – mainly Thai and Malaysian – in the services sector. With the tourist industry growing stronger by the year (there were more than 2 million visitors in 2007), there is potential for major expansion. Unfortunately, as a result of the lack of regulation in the country, much of this investment seems to be concentrated on casinos and the seedy side of the entertainment scene.

As in neighbouring Laos, heavy investment is needed in education, basic infrastructure and telecommunications before Cambodia will start to look more attractive to foreign investors.

For the foreseeable future, tourism may be Cambodia's greatest chance of securing sustainable foreign exchange. Tourist numbers have risen encouragingly, with Angkor being one of the world's most marketable assets. As the clearing of land mines continues, and facilities for tourist accommodation and transport improve, there is no reason why this valuable resource should not be developed responsibly and successfully.

Pol Pot

The man who was to become one of the most reviled in history was born into a relatively prosperous family.

The Khmer Rouge leader Pol Pot, known to his followers as 'Brother No. 1', was born in 1928 in the village of Prek Sbauv, near the provincial capital of Kompong Thom, some 140km (88 miles) north of Phnom Penh. He was the eighth of nine children of well-to-do farmers and was named Saloth Sar. In common with most revolutionary communist leaders, Saloth Sar was neither a peasant nor a proletarian; his family enjoyed close relations with the royal court in Phnom Penh.

In 1934 Saloth Sar was sent to live with his relatives at court. During this time he spent several months as a novice monk at Vat Bottum Vaddei, a monastery near the palace that was favoured by the royal family, and studied the Buddhist scriptures and Khmer language. Later he learnt French and studied at Russei Keo Technical College in Phnom Penh. Although not an outstanding student, he was chosen as one of a group sent for further education in Paris. Here he came into contact with Cambodian nationalists, including Ieng Sary, who would become one of his key associates.

In 1952, having returned to Cambodia without any qualifications but with a newly acquired and keen sense of nationalism, he joined the Indo-Chinese Communist Party which was dominated by the Vietnamese. Although secretly nurturing an intense hatred for all things Vietnamese, Saloth Sar rose steadily through the ranks and became General Secretary of the (still clandestine) Cambodian Communist Party in 1962.

Soon after that Saloth Sar and his close colleagues disappeared into the jungled hills of Ratanakiri Province, where they began building the Communist guerrilla faction that King Sihanouk dubbed the 'Khmer Rouge'. During the subsequent years of civil war Saloth Sar used his increasingly powerful position to eliminate Hanoi-trained or pro-Vietnamese cadres – building, in essence, a movement which, though nominally internationalist, was deeply xenophobic, anti-urban and above all hostile to Vietnam.

Seizing power

In 1975 – Year Zero – the Khmer Rouge seized power and established the Democratic Kampuchea regime, but still Saloth Sar, now hiding behind the pseudonym 'Pol Pot', remained out of the limelight. Between 1975 and his overthrow in 1979 he gradually eliminated all those whom he saw as a potential threat to his personal power – not to mention more than two million ordinary Cambodians who were murdered, worked to death or died of starvation.

Overthrown by the Vietnamese in 1979, Pol Pot and his followers took to the jungles where, for almost 20 years, their numbers dwindled through desertion, disease and military attrition. Pol Pot was eventually arrested by his few remaining comrades, and either died or was killed near Anlong

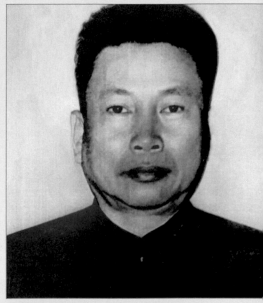

A portrait of Pol Pot in 1977.

Veng in 1998. In retrospect it is difficult to see what inner demons drove Saloth Sar to develop into the paranoid political monster Pol Pot. Certainly his elder brother, Loth Suong, who survived the Zero Years, was unable to explain it, commenting with obvious bewilderment that Pol Pot was 'a lovely child'.

Pol Pot never lived to face justice through the courts, nor did his chief military commander Ta Mok and foreign minister Ieng Sary, who each died in prison in Phnom Penh in 2006 and 2013, respectively. However, a few Khmer Rouge leaders, namely Brother No 2 Nuon Chea, Ieng Thirith, Khieu Samphan and Duch, survive in prison. Duch was convicted in 2010 but the other three still await trial.

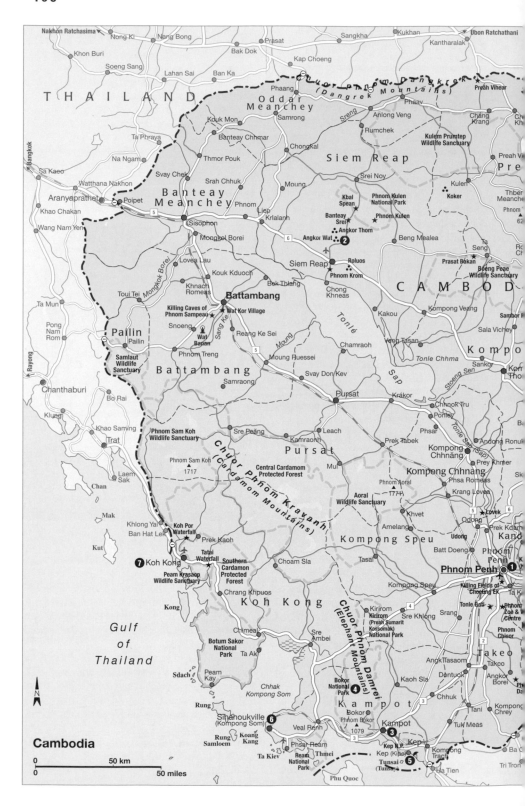

Cambodia

PHNOM PENH

Phnom Penh's fortunes have risen and fallen with Cambodia's turbulent history, but the future looks bright: new shops, hotels and restaurants are moving in as the tourist industry expands.

Main Attractions
Royal Palace
Silver Pagoda
National Musuem
Old Market (Psar Chaa)
Wat Phnom
Tuol Sleng

Street life in Phnom Penh.

Phnom Penh , the Cambodian capital, is an attractive riverside city of broad boulevards and numerous sights. Once rather shabby and run-down owing to the long years of war and four years of Khmer Rouge abandonment, the future now looks bright, with new shopping centres, luxury residence complexes, enormous hotels and fine-dining restaurants opening. Most of the important attractions are on or within walking distance of the Phnom Penh riverside, and this area also contains many of the best restaurants and cafés.

Once a Funan-era settlement, the city was re-founded in the 1430s, with the decline of Angkor and the shift of power eastwards. The legend relates how a woman named Penh found four images of the Buddha on the shores of the Mekong River, and subsequently built a temple on the tallest hill in the area in which to keep them. The city that later grew up around the hill became known as Phnom Penh, or 'Penh's Hill'.

In 1772, now a major centre of commerce, Phnom Penh was completely destroyed by the Thais. The city was soon rebuilt but grew little until 1863, when the French took control. A relatively prosperous period ensued. Growth continued until the Khmer Rouge arrived in 1975, forcing the urban dwellers into the countryside and leaving the city virtually abandoned. The city recovered very slowly

The Royal Palace

A good place to start a tour of Phnom Penh, the extensive grounds of the **Royal Palace** Ⓐ (daily 8–11am and 2–4.30pm; charge) are off Sothearos Boulevard, immediately to the south of the National Museum. The palace was built in 1866 in Khmer style with French assistance. It functioned as the official residence of King Norodom Sihanouk from the time of his return to the capital in 1991, followed by his son, King Norodom Sihamoni, who ascended to the throne in 2004.

The public entrance to the palace is opposite the now-closed, colonial-style Renakse Hotel, to the east of the palace grounds. Certain areas within the complex, including the king's residential quarters, are not open to the general public, but much of the rest of the site is accessible. Just beyond the entrance gate stands the **Chan Chaya Pavilion**, formerly used by Cambodian monarchs to review parades and for performances of classical Khmer dancing. Nowadays dance performances are regularly presented at the nearby Cambodiana Hotel.

Dominating the centre of the larger, northern section of the royal compound is the **Royal Throne Hall**. This was built as recently as 1917 in the Khmer style, the architect self-consciously borrowing extensively from the Bayon at Angkor. Inside the Throne Hall, the walls are painted with murals from the *Reamker*, the Khmer version of the *Ramayana*. As well as coronations, the Throne Hall is used for important constitutional events and, on occasion, for the acceptance of ambassadorial credentials.

To the right (northwest) of the Throne Hall stands the restricted **Royal Residence Compound** of the king, while to the left are several structures of interest. These include the **Royal Treasury**, the **Royal Banqueting Hall** and the **Napoleon III Pavilion**. The pavilion, which was renovated by French volunteers using French money, was originally given by Emperor Napoleon III to his wife, Empress Eugénie. In the 1870s, she had it dismantled and sent across the seas to Phnom Penh as a gift for King Norodom.

The Silver Pagoda

Leaving the main northern compound of the palace by a clearly marked gateway in the southeastern corner, proceed along a narrow south-westerly route that leads to the North Gate of the celebrated **Silver Pagoda**

compound. Commissioned by King Norodom in 1892, and then extensively rebuilt by Sihanouk in 1962, the floor of the pagoda is lined with more than 5,000 silver tiles weighing more than 1kg each, or 5 tonnes in total. Rather disappointingly, a thick carpet protects almost the entire floor, except for a small area, so the scale of the grandeur is not so obvious.

The pagoda is also known as **Wat Preah Keo**, or 'Temple of the Emerald Buddha'. It houses the sacred symbol of the nation, the Emerald Buddha, which dates from the 17th century and is made of crystal. There is also a much larger Buddha figure here, comprised of a total of 90kg (198lbs) of pure gold, encrusted with 9,584 diamonds, the largest of which is 25 carats. Photography within the building is forbidden.

National Museum of Cambodia

Continuing northwards from the Royal Palace on Sothearos Boulevard you will soon come to a public green, behind which is the **National**

Lemon grass and galangal root, two Cambodian culinary staples.

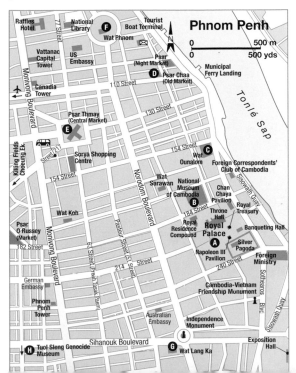

A performance by RUFA students.

The National Museum.

Museum of Cambodia ⓑ (227 Kbal Thnal, Preah Norodom Boulevard; tel: 023-217 643; www.cambodiamuseum.info; daily 8am–5pm; charge; no photography allowed, except in the courtyard). The museum, housed in a red pavilion opened in 1917, holds a wonderful collection of Khmer art, including some of the finest pieces in existence. As you enter, buy a copy of the museum guidebook, *Khmer Art in Stone*, which identifies and discusses the most important exhibits, including a 6th-century statue of Vishnu, a 9th-century statue of Shiva and the famous sculpted head of Jayavarman VII in meditative pose. Particularly impressive is a damaged bust of a reclining Vishnu, which was once part of a massive bronze statue found at the Occidental Mebon Temple in Angkor.

Wat Ounalom

The headquarters of the Cambodian Buddhist *sangha* and Phnom Penh's most important temple, **Wat Ounalom** ⓒ stands northwest of the **Foreign Correspondents' Club of Cambodia** (FCCC) and the Royal Palace. Founded in 1443, this extensive temple suffered badly at the hands of the Khmer Rouge, but is fast recovering. Unfortunately the once-extensive library of the Buddhist Institute, also housed here, will take many years to replace.

To the west of the main temple stands a *stupa* said to contain an eyebrow hair of the Buddha. Within the temple are several archaic Buddha figures, smashed to pieces by the Khmer Rouge but since reassembled. Also on display is a statue of Samdech Huot Tat, head of the *sangha* when Pol Pot came to power and subsequently killed. The statue was recovered from the nearby Mekong and reinstalled after the collapse of Democratic Kampuchea.

On leaving the temple, turn right (south) along Sisowath Quay, the road that runs along the Sap River. This is a delightful area of small riverside cafés and restaurants, where it is possible to experience the international affluence of the new Cambodia. It is a good place to stop for Italian coffee and French pastries, or a burrito and gelato. Alternatively, the FCCC is a popular, if somewhat touristy, night spot and offers unsurpassed views across the Sap and Mekong rivers from its well-appointed second-floor restaurant.

Markets and shops

The *Psar Chaa*, or **Old Market** ⓓ, located near the riverfront at the junction of Streets 108 and 13, is a densely packed locale offering a wide selection of souvenirs, books, clothing, jewellery, dry goods, street food and fresh produce. Unlike some of the markets, it stays open late into the evening. A tidy, modern night market is held in the square across the street, facing the river, and is now a favourite spot for weekend souvenir shopping.

A short distance to the southwest, at the commercial heart of Phnom Penh, is the extraordinary *Psar Thmay*, literally 'New Market', but generally known in English as **Central Market** ⓔ. Built in 1937 during the French colonial period, it is Art Deco in

style and painted bright ochre. The design is cruciform, with four wings dominated by a central dome, and the overall effect has been likened to a Babylonian ziggurat. In and around the four wings almost anything you can think of is for sale, including electronic equipment, DVD, clothing, watches, bags and suitcases, and a wide variety of dried and fresh foodstuffs. There are many gold and silver shops beneath the central dome, which sell skilfully crafted jewellery as well as Khmer *krama* scarves, antiques, pseudo-antiques and other souvenirs. In 2009, Central Market was renovated – with new stalls, wider aisles and fresh paint, it is much cleaner, more orderly and safer. Within view of the Central Market is **Sorya**, Cambodia's premier shopping centre, and the best place in Cambodia for Western imported cloth, electronics and household items, as well as fast-food chains.

The best market for souvenir bargains and discounted, locally manufactured designer clothing is *Psar Tuol Tom Pong*, otherwise known as the **Russian Market** because of the many Russians who shopped here in the 1980s. It is located in the southern part of town, beyond Mao Tse Toung Boulevard (also known as Issarak Street) at the junction of Streets 163 and 432. Despite its unprepossessing appearance from the outside, this is a great place to shop for genuine and imitation antiquities, Buddha figures, silk clothing, silver jewellery and ornaments, gems and old banknotes from previous regimes.

Interestingly, the notes for sale include those of the Khmer Rouge, which had currency printed in China but then had a change of mind; in a radical frenzy, it outlawed money altogether, blew up the central bank and ultimately never issued any notes to the public. The Khmer Rouge money is readily recognised by both its pristine condition – it was never circulated – and the warlike themes on the notes: look for rocket-toting guerrillas, howitzers, machine-guns and fierce-faced Khmer Rouge girl-soldiers.

Head deeper inside to find the full selection and the best bargains. Outdoors, on the rear side, you can also

Street vendor, Phnom Penh.

find an ample selection of delicious street food. The market and S21 are often visited together.

Wat Phnom

Built on a small mound in the north of the city not far from the banks of the Sap River, **Wat Phnom** ❶ (daily; charge) is perhaps the most important temple in Phnom Penh, and from it the capital takes its name. According to legend, around six centuries ago a Cambodian woman called Penh found some Buddha figures washed up on the bank of the Sap. Being both rich and pious, she had a temple constructed to house them on top of a nearby hill – in fact a mound just 27 metres (88ft) high, but for all that the highest natural point in the vicinity – hence 'Phnom Penh' ('the hill of Penh').

Wat Phnom is eclectic, to say the least. Although dedicated to Theravada Buddhism, it also houses (to the north of the *vihara*) a shrine to Preah Chau, who is especially revered by the Vietnamese community, while on the table in front are representations

of Confucius and two Chinese sages. Finally, to the left of the central altar is an eight-armed statue of the Hindu deity Vishnu. The large stupa to the west of the *vihara* contains the ashes of King Ponhea Yat (1405–67).

To the north and east of Wat Phnom, along Street 94 and Street 47 (also known as Vithei France), lie the colonial buildings of the old **French Quarter**. Should you wish to explore it, leave Wat Phnom by the main eastern stairway and walk due east to the Sap River, noting en route the colonial-style Post Office building, usually resplendent with large portraits of Cambodian royalty. At the river turn left onto Sisowath Quay and then take the next left turn down onto Street 47. Walk north along Street 47 to the roundabout, turn south down Monivong Boulevard, past the French Embassy (on the right) and the British Embassy (on the left), and then turn east by the railway station along Street 106. This route takes you past many examples of French colonial-style architecture.

South of the Royal Palace

As you walk south along Sothearos Boulevard from the palace you will pass an extensive park accommodating the **Cambodia-Vietnam Monument**, dedicated to the supposedly unbreakable friendship that links the two peoples: of course the reality is somewhat different.

Southwest of the nearby Independence Monument is **Wat Lang Ka** ❻ (daily; free), a flourishing example of the revival of Buddhism in Cambodia. Saffron-robed monks abound, while newly painted murals from the *jataka* (Buddha life-cycles) gleam from the restored *vihara* walls.

The Sisowath Quay offers views over the junction of the Sap and Mekong rivers, but to understand the unique confluence of waters at Phnom Penh properly you should also see the Bassac River – best viewed from the Monivong Bridge, south of the city

The Independence Monument.

centre. The confluence of the rivers, known in Khmer as **Chatomuk** or 'four faces', is remarkable for a unique phenomenon: the reversal, from May to October, of the Sap River, which more than doubles the size of the Tonlé Sap lake in central Cambodia. Then, in mid-October, as the level of the Mekong diminishes, the flow of the Sap is again reversed, carrying the surplus waters of the Tonlé Sap southwards to the Mekong and Bassac deltas. The time in October when the waters return to their normal course is celebrated as *Bon Om Tuk*, one of Cambodia's most important festivals.

Reminders of genocide

A visit to the former Tuol Sleng Prison (S21), now **Tuol Sleng Genocide Museum Ⓗ** (daily 7.30am–5.30pm; charge) is not for the faint-hearted. Here, during Pol Pot's years in power, around 20,000 people were interrogated under torture and subsequently murdered, generally together with their families.

The former prison – once a school – is a chilling sight; the pictures of many of those killed stare out at the visitor in black and white from the museum walls, and primitive instruments of torture and execution are on display. Former classrooms were divided up into tiny cells, and everywhere there are crude shackles and cuffs. Initially those executed here were people the Khmer Rouge perceived as 'class enemies' and supporters of the former regime, but soon the Communist regime began to consume itself in a frenzy of paranoia. By the time Tuol Sleng was liberated, in 1979, nearly all those suffering torture and execution were Khmer Rouge officials who had fallen from grace. Only now are some of those responsible being brought to justice – see panel below.

About 12km (7 miles) southwest of the town is the infamous **Killing Fields of Choeung Ek** (www.killing fieldsmuseum.com; daily 8am–5.30pm; charge), where victims of the Khmer Rouge were executed and buried in mass graves. Many of these graves have now been exhumed, and a stupa-shaped mausoleum has been erected in the victims' memory.

FACT

'Land grabs' by developers in new districts around Phnom Penh began receiving international attention in 2008. Neighbourhoods that were once undesirable slums are now hot real estate as the city modernises. Poor families are often squatters with no legal deeds to their property, with little power to negotiate compensation for forced eviction. Some families who receive offers of compensation initially refuse, misguidedly holding out for a 'better offer' that never comes.

National Museum, Phnom Penh.

BRINGING THE KHMER ROUGE TO TRIAL

Nearly thirty years after the Khmer Rouge devastated Cambodia, a few of the senior cadres are finally being brought to trial at 'The Extraordinary Chambers in the Courts of Cambodia' (www.eccc.gov.kh). Despite overwhelming public desire for them to proceed, the trials have not been without controversy. The original $60 million budget for three years was increased to $170 million for five years, but international funding was placed on hold when accusations of corruption within the court system surfaced. Many have suggested that the high price tag would be better spent on social programs in this impoverished country, while others argue that justice and closure for the victims is worth any cost.

Prosecutors would like to bring more than the initial five defendants to trial, but the government has restricted the scope of the trial. So many former Khmer Rouge officers run the present government – including Prime Minister Hun Sen himself – that the government fears a trial of larger scope would destabilise the country. Certainly, there are former Khmer Rouge officers, guilty of heinous crimes, freely going about their business at all levels of Cambodian society.

In 2010, commander Duch, who oversaw S21, was sentenced to 35 years in prison, which was later increased to a life sentence. Three others await trial from prison: Brother No 2 Nuon Chea, Ieng Thirith, and Khieu Samphan.

Entering South Gate at Angkor Thom.

ANGKOR

This ancient capital of the Khmer kingdom is the cultural and spiritual heart of Cambodia. Although monumental in scale, it offers intimate glimpses into lives lived in a distant past.

Angkor is one of the wonders of the world. Perhaps nowhere else on earth, save the Nile Valley in Egypt, are the relics of antiquity found on so monumental a scale. Dating from the golden years of the Khmer civilisation between around AD 800 and 1400, it is a unique repository of incredible craftsmanship on a staggering scale.

Angkor Wat ② itself refers to just one part of the rambling complex. Angkor Thom, to the north of Angkor Wat, encompasses many fine temples and palaces, including the Bayon, Preah Khan and Ta Prohm. Roluos, to the southeast of both Angkor Wat and Angkor Thom, are the earliest surviving Khmer relics in the entire Angkor area, predating Angkor Wat by about 200 years. Most visitors generally take either two or three days to explore the site, but one could easily spend longer.

The entrance to the main site is just 5km (3 miles) north of Siem Reap. The road leads past the **Angkor National Museum** (www.angkornationalmuseum. com; daily 8.30am–6.30pm; charge), to a tollbooth. Buy your visitor's pass or have your pass inspected here before you proceed on your tour.

About 1km (0.6 miles) beyond the tollbooth, the road reaches the south side of Angkor Wat, and you will catch your first sight of the famous monument. For the moment, however, it is probably better to drive past

The famous five towers of Angkor Wat.

Angkor Wat by the west road and visit the city of Angkor Thom, as the former should be visited in the later afternoon when the complex is best illuminated by the sun.

Angkor Thom and the Bayon

Angkor Thom ⒶA or 'Great City' encompasses a huge, square area of land enclosed within an 8 metre (26ft) high defensive wall and outer moats approximately 100 metres (330ft) wide. Each side of the wall is

Main Attractions
The Bayon, Angkor Thom
Angkor Wat
Preah Khan
Ta Prohm
Roluos

TIP

The Angkor complex (all areas) is open daily from 5.30am until 6.30pm. A day ticket costs US$20. Multiple-entry tickets, which require one passport photograph, are available for 3 days ($40) or 7 days ($60).

about 3km (2 miles) long, and it has been suggested that, at the height of its wealth and power, the city may have supported as many as 1 million people. The founder and architect was the Buddhist King Jayavarman VII (1181–1220).

There are five gateways into Angkor Thom, each approached by a causeway built across the moat. As you approach from the south the view of the forti-fications is impressive. The causeway is flanked by 108 large stone figures, 54 gods on the left and an equivalent number of demons on the right. In the distance, at the far end of the cause-way, the southern gateway bears four huge enigmatic faces facing in the cardinal directions.

Passing through this prodigious gateway, the road continues north-wards for around 1.5km (1 mile) to reach the **Bayon**, at the centre of Ang-kor Thom. Always a favourite with vis-itors, it is possibly the most celebrated structure after Angkor Wat itself.

The Bayon is thought to represent a symbolic temple mountain and rises on three levels, the first of which bears eight cruciform gateways. These are linked by galleries that contain some of the most remarkable bas reliefs at Angkor; they combine numerous domestic and everyday scenes with historical details of battles won and lost by the Khmers. The domestic scenes, many of which are in smaller bas reliefs below the main war scenes, show fascinating details of daily life.

After viewing the galleries, spend some time at the third level examining the vast, mysterious faces with their sublime smiles. The central shrine, which is circular, is also at the third level, and features the faces of the *bodhisattva* Avalokitesvara.

Kings' terraces

Passing the once mighty Baphuon – a former palace that has undergone extensive restoration – and the former royal palace of Phimeanakas, you reach the celebrated **Elephant Terrace.** Also built by Jayavarman VII, this structure is over 300 metres (970ft) long, and has three main platforms and two lesser ones. The terrace was probably used by the king, the royal family,

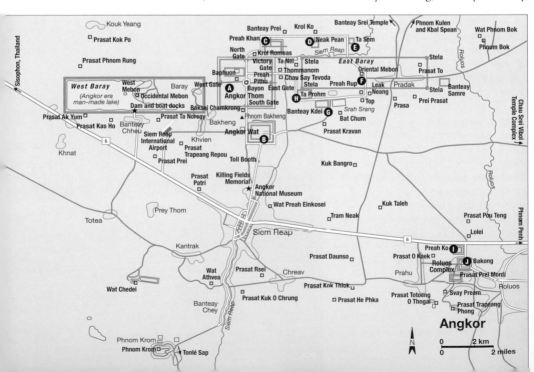

ministers and generals to review their forces, and perhaps to watch other entertainments. The whole terrace is elaborately decorated not only with the sandstone elephants that give it its name, but also with detailed tigers, lions, geese and lotus flowers.

Immediately to the north stands the **Terrace of the Leper King.** Like the Elephant Terrace, this much smaller structure dates from the late 12th century and is chiefly remarkable for its many bas reliefs.

Head southwards back to the Bayon and leave Angkor Thom by the South Gate. A few hundred metres beyond the South Gate, to the west side of the road, the hill of **Phnom Bakheng** rises 67 metres (218ft) above the surrounding plains. This is an ideal spot from which to view the distant spires of Angkor Wat at sunset (although it does get crowded). On the east side a steep and treacherous stairway (at times closed for repairs) provides a swift but difficult means of ascent. Alternatively, and much more easily, a winding path leads to the summit via the south side of the hill.

Angkor Wat

From Phnom Bakheng hill continue south to **Angkor Wat** Ⓑ. By any standards this must be the highlight of any visit to the Angkor region – the great temple is simply unsurpassed by any other monument. Construction of this masterpiece is thought to have begun during the reign of Surayavarman II (1112–52), and to have been completed some time after his death. Authorities claim that the amount of stone used in creating this massive edifice is about the same as that used in building the Great Pyramid of Cheops in Egypt, though Angkor Wat has many more exposed surfaces, nearly all of which are elaborately carved to a remarkable standard.

The sheer scale of Angkor Wat is difficult to grasp in a single visit. The area of land covered by the complex is around 210 hectares (500 acres) and it

is surrounded by a 200 metre (650ft) wide moat. Just walking to the central shrine across the moat and along the main causeway is a humbling experience. At the end, the main towers of the temple rise to an astonishing 65 metres (210ft) through three separate levels. At the third level there are five great towers – one at each corner, and the great central spire. These towers are conical, tapering to a lotus-shaped point.

Angkor Wat: first level

Proceeding along the central causeway you should enter the central sanctuary at the first level and turn right to walk round the entire gallery of bas reliefs – no small feat, as there is much to see. Near the entrance to the first gallery there is a huge stone standing figure with eight arms bearing symbols that indicate that the statue was of Vishnu. In recent times, however, a Buddha head has replaced that of Vishnu, and the statue is now much venerated by local Buddhists.

The bas reliefs of Angkor's first-level galleries are all truly remarkable, but even so some stand out.

One of the thousands of sculptures on the Bayon.

Angkor Wat's towers are 65 metres (210ft) tall.

In the West Gallery

The Battle of Kurukshetra: The southern part of the west gallery depicts a scene from the great Hindu epic, the *Mahabharata*.

The Battle of Lanka: This panel depicts a well-known scene from the *Ramayana* and must be considered one of the finest bas reliefs at Angkor Wat. It depicts a long struggle between Rama and the demon-king of the island of Lanka, Ravana.

In the South Gallery

The Army of King Surayavarman II: This splendid panel shows the victorious army in triumphal march. Surayavarman rides a great war elephant and carries a battle axe. He is shaded by 15 umbrellas and fanned by numerous servants. The main ranks of Khmer soldiers march in close order. To the west is one of the earliest representations of Thais, at this time fighting as mercenary troops for the Khmer Empire. Contrasting with the serried ranks of the Khmers, the Thais march out of step and wear long, dress-like sarongs.

The Scenes of Heaven and Hell:

Elephants are one of the recurring themes at Angkor.

The scenes on this panel, depicting the various rewards and punishments of heaven and hell, are truly terrifying. Sinners are dragged to hell by hideous devils wielding heavy clubs.

In the East Gallery

The Churning of the Ocean of Milk: This is probably the best executed and most spectacular of all the bas reliefs at Angkor. In one huge, brilliantly carved panel, 88 *asura* (devils) on the left (south side) and 92 *deva* (gods) on the right (north side) churn the ocean of milk with a giant serpent for a thousand years. Their purpose is to extract the elixir of immortality, which both covet. Overhead finely carved *apsara* sing and dance to encourage the gods and devils in their endeavour.

The Victory of Vishnu over the Demons: Vishnu, riding on a *garuda*, is engaged in mortal combat with devils.

In the North Gallery

The Victory of Krishna over Bana: In this panel Vishnu, as Krishna, rides a *garuda*. A burning walled city is the residence of Bana, the demon king. The

ANGKOR AS IT WAS INTENDED

Angkor Wat was established as a Hindu temple dedicated to the god Shiva, but it is also thought to have been envisaged as a mausoleum for Surayavarman II. Its orientation is different from that of most temples at Angkor, as the main entrance is from the west rather than the east: this is thought to be related to the association between the setting sun and death. The bas reliefs – one of the most important elements of the temple – are intended to be viewed from left to right, conforming to Hindu practice.

A Chinese envoy, Chou Ta-kuan, visited Angkor during the reign of Indravarman III (1296–1308) and left a detailed manuscript describing his experiences. Chou records: 'The walled city of Angkor was some five miles in circumference. It had five gates, with five portals. Outside the wall stretched a great moat across which massive causeways gave access to the city. The Palace stands to the north of the Golden Tower and the Bridge of Gold; starting from the gate its circumference is nearly one-and-a-half miles. The tiles of the central dwelling are of lead; other parts of the palace are covered with pottery tiles, yellow in colour... Out of the Palace rises a golden tower, to the top of which the ruler ascends nightly to sleep. By contrast, the houses of the ordinary folk were thatched with straw, for 'no one would venture to vie with the nobility'.'

garuda puts out the fire and captures Bana; then, in a spirit of mercy, Krishna kneels before Shiva and asks that the life of the demon king be spared.

The Battle between the Gods and the Demons: This finely carved panel features yet another battle scene. Here gods of the Brahmanic pantheon struggle with various devils. The gods are distinguishable by their traditional mounts and aspects: Shiva, for example, rides a sacred goose, while Vishnu has four arms and is seated on a *garuda*.

Angkor Wat: upper levels

In times past, only the king and the high priest were allowed on the top (third) gallery of Angkor Wat. The central sanctuary rises 42 metres (137ft) above the top level, bringing the overall height of the central tower to the same height as that of the cathedral of Notre Dame in Paris. The exterior of this level is rather plain, but within more than 1,500 *apsara* – celestial dancers – grace the walls. The uppermost level is once again open to the public after the installation of safer wooden stairways.

The central sanctuary and the third level of Angkor Wat are ideal places to visit at sunset. Superb views are available across the entire temple, and – perhaps for the first time – it is possible to grasp clearly the stupendous size of the entire complex. As the sun sinks, warm, golden or red rays of sunshine pierce the elaborately carved sandstone window buttresses, illuminating the very finest and best preserved *apsara* to be found anywhere at Angkor. It is truly an unforgettable experience.

Preah Khan

From Siem Reap head north past Angkor Wat, through Angkor Thom, to the North Gate. Next, turning due east, stop opposite the row of cold-drink stalls directly in front of the west entrance to **Preah Khan ⓒ**, the temple of the 'sacred sword', also founded by the Buddhist King Jayavarman VII. Built in the style of the Bayon and dedicated to Buddhism, the temple served as both a monastery and the centre of the former royal city. It has a magical quality stemming from the feeling of proximity to nature; this is

Angkor Wat's Bayon Temple.

View of ruined Khmer temples in Roluos.

A shaft of sunlight illuminates apsara figures in an inner chamber at Angkor Wat.

Banteay Kdei.

because the temple still awaits full restoration, and great trees with smothering roots still cling to the sandstone and laterite walls.

The central sanctuary of Preah Khan is cruciform, with four entrances. Look for the 'Hall of Dancers', with its finely carved rows of *apsara* that decorate the walls. If you are agile enough to clamber over (and sometimes under) the great piles of fallen stone in the northeastern section of the main sanctuary, you can visit 'the Shrine of the White Lady': an elegant figure, supposedly not an *apsara* but the wife of Jayavarman VII, tucked away in a hidden room. The shrine is still venerated, and supplicants light incense and leave offerings of money. You may need a guide to find this out-of-the-way spot.

Neak Pean

After leaving Preah Khan head eastwards along the road leading to the East Baray, the area once covered by a large reservoir. About 2.5km (1.5 miles) from Preah Khan a track leads south to the temple of **Neak Pean** , or 'the coiled serpents'. The temple, which is quite small by Angkorean standards, is set in an artificial pond 70 metres (230ft) square. This central pool is surrounded at the cardinal points by four smaller square pools set somewhat more deeply into the earth. In the centre of the main pool is a circular island bearing a stepped laterite shrine dedicated to the *bodhisattva* Avalokitesvara. Two intertwined serpents circle the base of the island and give the complex its name.

About 2km (1.25 miles) east of Neak Pean stands the tranquil and charming temple of **Ta Som** Ⓔ. It is off the beaten track, sees relatively few visitors, and as a consequence is filled with birdsong and the sound of cicadas.

In the East Baray

Located in the midst of the East Baray, the 10th-century Oriental Mebon is another example of an artificial temple mountain representing Mount Meru – one of the enduring themes of classical Khmer architecture. Close by is **Preah Rup** Ⓕ, dedicated to Shiva Climb to the top of the monument for excellent views. As you leave Preah Rup heading west, the road passes the great reservoir of Srah Srang, or 'royal bath'. In the late afternoon and evening it makes a delightful sight as buffaloes bath in its tranquil waters.

Immediately west of the landing stage a gateway in a high laterite wall gives access to **Banteay Kdei** Ⓖ, the 'citadel of the cells'. The temple was used as a Buddhist monastic complex until the mid-20th century. As a consequence it is less overgrown than some of the other outer temples, and very pleasant to stroll through.

Ta Prohm

Continue past Banteay Kdei for a distance of about 1km (0.6 miles) to reach the spectacular temple of **Ta Prohm** Ⓗ or 'ancestor of Brahma'. This very large complex was, yet again, the work of Jayavarman VII and dedicated to Buddhism. A stone stele, now removed to the Angkor National Museum, tells us quite a lot about it: for example, in its prime the temple owned 3,140 villages and was maintained by some 79,365 people including 18 high priests, 2,740 officials, 2,202 assistants and 615 dancers.

Ta Prohm is a long, low complex of buildings all on the same level, with a series of concentric galleries connected by passages that provide shade in the heat of the day. The entire complex is surrounded by a rectangular laterite wall of around 700 metres (2,270ft) in width by 1,000 metres (3,300ft) in length. What makes Ta Prohm so special is that, following an unusual archaeological decision, the jungle has been only partly cut back, so that the buildings are covered with the roots of huge banyan and kapok trees which rise high above the temple. Spectacular roots bind lintels and crack vaulted passageways, while parrots fly in the upper canopy and break the stillness with their sharp cries.

The Roluos complex

Some 11 centuries ago King Jayavarman II (802–50), remembered as the founder of the first unified Khmer state, made his capital at Hariharalaya ('the dwelling place of Hari-Hara', a deity combining the attributes of both Vishnu and Shiva). Today the Roluos complex of temples, the oldest in Angkor, marks the site of this first Angkorean capital. Roluos is located to the southeast of the other temples. There are some magnificent carvings and well-preserved stone inscriptions, and tumbledown ruins being reclaimed by the jungle.

Just to the south stands **Preah Ko** ❶, the 'sacred bull'. Built by King Indravarman I (877–89), it is somewhat off the beaten track, and as a result it is a tranquil place to visit. The main sanctuary consists of six brick towers set on a low laterite platform.

A short distance beyond Preah Ko rises the solid mass of **Bakong** ❶, a late 9th-century Hindu temple dedicated to Shiva. A thousand years ago Bakong was the central feature of Hariharalaya. It is built as a temple mountain on an artificial mound surrounded by a moat and outer enclosure walls. Bakong, which is easily the largest monument of the Roluos Group, is best entered from the east by a processional way decorated with seven-headed *naga* serpents.

TIP

Ta Prohm was used in the filming of Tomb Raider in 2000. The central courtyard features in the scene where Angelina Jolie picks a jasmine flower and is promptly dropped into a deep vault.

Ta Prohm.

CAMBODIAN SOUTH COAST

Old French beach resorts are reawakening as foreign tourists and Phnom Penh's wealthiest head back to sand and surf. All the while, the country's greatest ecological treasures are only just being discovered.

<table>
<tr><td>Main Attractions</td></tr>
<tr><td>Kampot</td></tr>
<tr><td>Bokor National Park</td></tr>
<tr><td>Sihanoukville</td></tr>
</table>

Serendipity Beach, next door to Occheuteal Beach in Sihanoukville, is home to number of comfortable resorts and bars.

The coast has been developed as a premier tourist destination, and foreign investors have joined local businessmen in developing hotels, resorts and better-quality restaurants. To be sure, there is some way to go – but for the people of Phnom Penh and for foreign travellers, trips to the coast and long hours of swimming and sunbathing by the Gulf of Thailand are back in vogue.

Kampot

Kampot ❸, the capital of the epony-mous province, is a small, relaxed town of around 39,000 people. Just 5km (3 miles) inland, by the banks of the Sanke River, there is a coastal feel to the place that adds to its rather lan-guid appeal. 'Downtown' Kampot cen-tres on a large roundabout space about 400 metres (1,300ft) east of the river. The road north from the roundabout leads out past a large covered market – a favourite with visitors from Phnom Penh, who stop off here to buy the fresh seafood for which Kampot is renowned. Of more interest to the foreign visitor, however, is the series of narrow, colon-naded streets leading west from the roundabout to the riverfront. Although in need of restoration, there are some fine examples of French architecture to be seen in this warren, as well as the best of Kampot's restaurants and hotels.

Bokor National Park

About 37km (23 miles) northwest of Kampot and located within **Bokor National Park** ❹ is the 1,079-metre (3,506ft) -high former hill station of **Bokor**. Often shrouded in mist, the hill resort was built by the French in the early 1920s, but later fell on hard times under the Communist guerrillas and the Khmer Rouge.

The ruins of the old hill station include the **Black Palace** complex King Sihanouk's former retreat, the old **Bokor Palace Hotel** and a small, aban-doned church. The area went under extensive redevelopment by a Korean investor for several years and a resort, casino and cable car are now open.

Kep

Another old, celebrated resort town is **Kep ❺** (Kipe). The 30km (20-mile) drive from Kampot can be covered by *moto*. In pre-war times the 7km (4-mile) stretch of palm-fringed beach was lined with the villas of rich Cambodians and French settlers, but then the Khmer Rouge arrived and destroyed virtually every building in town.

Today Kep is back on the tourist circuit, though much rebuilding remains to be done. Ruined villas and mansions, purchased (speculatively) by Cambodia's powerful elite for a pittance in the 1990s, dot the countryside. Although there are good hotels and restaurants here, many visitors choose to stay in Kampot, driving out to Kep for a day of sunbathing, fishing, swimming and indulging in the excellent local seafood – particularly crab.

Sihanoukville

For the foreseeable future, **Sihanoukville ❻**, also known as Kompong Som, will remain the heart of Cambodia's 'Riviera'. The resort town is packed with visitors from the capital at weekends. As the country's third-most-visited tourist destination, Sihanoukville can be crowded during the dry season. There are numerous hotels and guesthouses of all classes, with many run by expat Westerners. Sihanoukville's restaurants offer a wide choice of cuisines, and seafood is fresh and plentiful. The city also has a healthy nightlife, with countless beach bars, nightclubs and karaoke bars, and even a casino.

The main activities are, as one might expect, sunbathing and swimming. There's also good snorkelling and fishing, while diving trips are available with experienced dive instructors. In all, Sihanoukville has about 10km (6 miles) of beachfront, divided into four main beaches. These are: **Victory Beach, Independence Beach, Sokha Beach** (dominated by the Sokha hotel),

and **Ochheuteal Beach**; the most popular and divided into two sections: Serendipity Beach and Otres Beach.

Koh Kong

The coast to the west of Sihanoukville is almost completely undeveloped. A journey overland to the isolated but beautiful province of Koh Kong requires a long drive on National Highway 48.

Koh Kong ❼ – confusingly the name of the province, the provincial capital *and* an offshore island – is a fast-developing coastal resort designed especially to appeal to visitors from neighbouring Thailand. It is also a convenient point for entering or leaving Cambodia by land. Koh Kong's other claim to fame is as a base for ecotourism. The nearby **Koh Kong Conservation Corridor** encompasses the **Cardamom Mountains**, **Peam Krasaop Wildlife Sanctuary**, **Koh Por** and **Tatai waterfalls**, **Koh Kong Island**, **Southern and Central Cardamoms Protected Forests**, and a portion of **Botum Sakor National Park**. All of these sights present endless outdoor activities and opportunities to see endangered species.

Old French villa, Kep.

Kep Beach, Kep.

ANCIENT ARTEFACTS

Influenced by diverse religious and artistic currents, Southeast Asia's ancient cultures have bequeathed a magnificent array of treasures.

Since early times, the cultural traditions of the Southeast Asian lands have blended with those of China and – especially – India, as traders came to exploit the rich supply of gold and spices. The gradual infusion of the powerful Hindu-Buddhist cultural traditions of India through *vaisyas* (merchants) and brahmans (religious men) resulted in the so-called 'Indianisation' of much of the region. Other areas, such as northern Vietnam, were under Chinese influence and remained outside of the Indic sphere, while the islands of the Philippines were largely removed from both.

The artistic culture of the Indianised kingdoms was innovative and extraordinary, but it should be remembered that the themes and designs spreading east and south from the subcontinent only provided a base for the indigenous people to develop their own artistic styles. It is their genius that is reflected in the artefacts and superlative architecture created at remarkable sites such as Angkor, Bagan and Borobudur.

On occasion, the influence may well have flowed in the other direction. Fourth-century BC bronzeware found in Ban Chiang, in northeast Thailand, indicates that this form of metallurgical technology was probably transferred from Thailand to China, not the other way round. This find is significant to the on-going debate over whether the region was a centre of innovation rather than merely a receptacle for outside influences.

Detail on Prambanan temple, near Jogja, central Java.

A Buddha figure is embraced by the roots of a tree at a Thai temple.

Stone carving at Borobudur.

Borobudur in central Java.

THE PLUNDERING OF BOROBUDUR

Borobudur is one of the most impressive monuments ever created. It was built around AD 800 when the Sailendra dynasty of central Java was at the height of its artistic and military power, taking 75 years to complete. It probably fell into neglect by about AD 1000. It was completely overgrown and suffering from earthquake damage when a military engineer serving under Thomas Stamford Raffles rediscovered it in 1814.

In the years that followed, Borobudur was uncovered to the elements and to people, enduring almost a century of decay, plunder and abuse, during which thousands of stones were "borrowed" by people living nearby. Scores of priceless sculptures ended up as garden decorations in the homes of the rich and powerful. Typical of the attitude of Dutch officials at the time was the presentation, in 1896, of eight cart-loads of Borobudur souvenirs to visiting King Chulalongkorn of Thailand, including 30 relief panels and five Buddha statues. Many of these and other irreplaceable works of Indo-Javanese art ended up in private collections, residing now in private museums worldwide, a process replicated region-wide.

...e of the enigmatic faces at Angkor Thom, dating from the ...h century.

Abeyadana temple details, Bagan Archaeologiacal zone, Myanmar.

Cambodia is a rich repository of ancient art, with noteworthy relics scattered around the country. This Buddhist figure at Wat Nokor Bayon near Kompong Cham dates from the 11th century.

Sheltering from the sun in central Vietnam.

At Hue's citadel gate.

VIETNAM

In the past few decades, Vietnam has managed to overcome its painful legacy of war and economic and political isolation. It is now one of Southeast Asia's most exciting and rewarding destinations.

Harvesting radishes near Dalat.

About the size of Germany or Arizona, Vietnam offers a wonderful experience for visitors, even if the country's infrastructure can still at times test the average traveller's patience. This is truly one of those destinations where the inconveniences pale beside the remarkable, and where the beauty of the landscape, people and culture seduce all. It is no wonder that over the last decade Vietnam has become one of the fastest-growing tourism destinations in the region.

Northern Vietnam is anchored by Hanoi, an ancient city established nearly 1,000 years ago. This political capital clings to the rhetoric of a Communist system while at the same time embracing a government-controlled capitalism. The restored villas and façades of the French colonial era give the city an ambience not found elsewhere in Asia. Nearby is the remarkable beauty of island-studded Halong Bay.

Uncle Ho at the Ho Chi Minh Museum.

To the south, following the historical movement of the Viet people, is a chain of coastal provinces washed by the South China Sea. In the old imperial city of Hue, an overwhelming sense of the past pervades its older streets. The beautiful old coastal town of Hoi An, and the atmospheric ruins of My Son, are close by. The antiquities don't end here. In these lands of the ancient kingdom of Champa – extending south to Nha Trang and Mui Ne, today popular seaside resorts – are decaying sanctuaries, temples and towers that testify to the conquest by the Viet people from the north. Inland, the cool climate and lovely scenery of Dalat is another major draw.

Then there is Ho Chi Minh City. Often still called Saigon, it maintains its long-time image as a commercial hub and bustling city of people. Where Hanoi is quiet, Ho Chi Minh City screams. Where Hue has a subtle and refined beauty, Ho Chi Minh City grabs you by the lapels and shakes. If Hanoi is a city of earth tones, Ho Chi Minh City is neon, all lit up in gaudy lights.

DECISIVE DATES

Earliest history

1st millennium BC
Bronze Age. Dong Son culture flourishes in the Red River basin and Tonkin coast.

258 BC
Kingdom of Au Lac.

208 BC
Kingdom of Nam Viet.

Chinese control

AD 39–42
Trung sisters lead an unsuccessful rebellion against the Chinese. Viet people are placed under Chinese rule.

542–4
Ly Bon leads an uprising against China.

545–938
Vietnam languishes under periodic Chinese rule.

Dynasties

939–1009
A succession of three short dynasties: Ngo, Dinh and Tien Le.

1010–1225
Hanoi established as Thang Long by Ly Thai To.

1225–1400
Further consolidation under Tran dynasty.

1400–28
Ho dynasty.

1428–1527
Le dynasty.

1471
Le dynasty takes over the southern Champa territory.

1527–92
Short-lived Mac dynasty.

1672
The country is divided by rival Trinh and Nguyen lords.

1771–92
Tay Son Rebellion.

1802–1945
Nguyen dynasty.

Colonial rule

1861
French capture Saigon and within six years take over southern Vietnam.

1883–1907
Various anti-French movements are crushed.

1919
Ho Chi Minh presents an anti-colonial petition at the Versailles Conference.

1926
Emperor Bao Dai ascends the throne.

1930
Ho Chi Minh rallies several communist groups; becomes founder of Indochinese Communist Party.

1942–3
Ho Chi Minh imprisoned in China. He is released and recognised as the chief of the Viet Minh.

1945
Japan overthrows the French and renders Vietnam 'independent' but under Japanese 'protection'.

Statue of Emperor Bao Dai in Phan Thiet.

Japanese surrender to the Allies a few months later, and the Viet Minh takes over the country. Ho Chi Minh declares Vietnam's independence while Emperor Bao Dai abdicates.

1946
Hostilities against French begin after the latter try to reclaim Vietnam.

1951
Ho Chi Minh consolidates Viet Minh and announces the formation of the Workers' Party.

Division and the Vietnam War

1954
French are defeated at Dien Bien Phu. Geneva Accord divides Vietnam at 17th parallel. Democratic South Vietnam is led by Ngo Dinh Diem; North Vietnam under the communist Ho Chi Minh.

1955
Escalation of hostilities between North and South Vietnam. Direct US aid to South Vietnam begins.

Vietnam suffered extensive bombing in the war with America.

The modern era

1995
Diplomatic ties are restored with the US, and a US embassy opens in Hanoi. Vietnam is admitted to the Association of Southeast Asian Nations (ASEAN).

1997
Asian economic crisis; investors leave Vietnam.

2000
Bill Clinton becomes the first US president to visit Vietnam since the war.

2001
The US and Vietnam enter a trade agreement. Foreign investment picks up.

2007
Vietnam joins the WTO.

2008
The economy suffers as food prices skyrocket. Inflation hits 25 percent. The government begins a media clampdown.

2009
Vietnam cracks down on online social media, imprisons bloggers, blocks Facebook.

2010
Tensions with China rise over South China Sea territorial dispute.

2012
American human rights activist Nguyen Quoc Quan arrested and imprisoned. In June, Vietnam becomes the world's largest exporter of coffee.

2013
Vietnam makes it a crime to discuss current events via online social media.

1959
North Vietnam infiltrates South Vietnam via the Ho Chi Minh Trail through parts of Laos and Cambodia.

1960
North Vietnam forms the National Liberation Front (NLF) in the war against the south. Its counterpart communist movement in South Vietnam is dubbed Viet Cong.

1963
Ngo Dinh Diem is overthrown and assassinated.

1964
North Vietnam sends North Vietnamese Army (NVA) troops to reinforce the Viet Cong.

1965
US bomb military targets in North Vietnam. First US ground combat troops land in Vietnam at Danang.

1968
The Viet Cong launch the Tet Offensive, the turning point in the Vietnam War. The US embassy in Saigon is raided. Peace talks begin in Paris.

1969
Ho Chi Minh dies, aged 79.

1973
Paris Peace Agreement ends hostilities. Last US troops depart from Vietnam in March.

1975
In April, North Vietnamese troops enter Saigon. The South Vietnamese government surrenders. Saigon is renamed Ho Chi Minh City.

Reunification

1976
Vietnam is officially reunified as a communist country.

1976–85
A period of severe economic hardship. Millions of refugees, or 'boat people', flee, facing persecution by the new government.

1977
Vietnam admitted to the UN.

1978–9
Vietnam signs friendship treaty with the Soviet Union. Hostilities with Cambodia and China.

1986
Programme of socio-economic renovation called *doi moi* is launched.

1990
Diplomatic relations established with the EU.

1994
US lifts the trade embargo.

PEOPLE AND CULTURE

Vietnam today is trying to balance rapid economic and population growth rates with a proudly traditional culture – all this under the watchful eye of a Communist government.

Some 3,000 years ago in the foothills and valleys of the Red River Delta, a distinctive culture emerged that can be traced to the people who now call themselves Vietnamese. This is where, in the 7th century BC, the kingdom of Van Lang came into being. This tiny kingdom is considered the cradle of Vietnamese culture, and the Hung kings the forefathers of the Vietnamese people.

Studies on the earliest origins of the Vietnamese show that the people who first settled in the region most likely came from China and the high plateaux of Central Asia as well as islands in the South Pacific. Vietnam can thus be considered the proverbial melting pot into which the major Asiatic and Oceanic migrations converged.

The main racial groups

Almost 87 percent of Vietnam's 86 million-strong population lists its ethnicity as Kinh (or Viet) – the commonly accepted term for its main indigenous race – but in reality, most Vietnamese have evolved from a mixture of races and ethnicities over thousands of years. That mixture is the result of repeated invasions, particularly from China or into Champa, along with continual migrations within Vietnam itself, most commonly from north to south. As a result, the dominant Viet population shares the country with distinct ethnic minority groups – the hill tribes of the northern and

A tribal woman in Sapa in the far north.

central highlands, and tiny pockets of Cham and Khmer people in the south, whose kingdoms were vanquished by Vietnamese armies from the north.

The ethnic Cham people primarily inhabit the Phan Rang and Phan Thiet regions and the Mekong Delta. Today they only number around 100,000, but the Champa kingdom was once home to a powerful culture that lasted for several centuries. Ethnic Khmers, who are part of the same stock as Cambodians, number around 900,000, most of whom live in the Mekong Delta area.

Minority groups have been among the last to reap the rewards of Vietnam's new-found prosperity – with one exception. Ethnic Chinese,

> With 72 percent of its people under the age of 35, Vietnam has one of the youngest populations in the world, a powerful engine for driving the country's growth.

ostracised as recently as the late 1970s, have not only benefited from but, in many ways, fuelled the country's economic growth. This is particularly pronounced in Ho Chi Minh City, the country's main economic hub. Most of Vietnam's 1.7 million Chinese, known as *Hoa*, have adopted Vietnamese citizenship. Many are shopkeepers and businesspeople who settled in Ho Chi Minh City's Cholon district.

Village and family bonds

Much of Vietnamese culture has been heavily influenced by the Chinese, from where

A hilltribe woman (montagnard) in Dalat.

administrators and teachers imported religion, philosophy and a written language, the *chu han*. Vietnamese society is deeply influenced by Confucian principles: children are taught the importance of *hieu* (filial piety) and respecting one's elders was once enshrined by the law. The family in turn is duty-bound to pay homage to its ancestors. A traditional family home would typically have as many as three generations under the one roof: grandparents, parents, married sons with wives and children, and unmarried children. In the event that one member needed money for an investment or for university studies, the entire family would chip in to help.

Traditionally, having a boy in the family was a 'must' as the eldest son would assume the duties of his father as head of the family when the latter died. Women were generally brought up for domestic duties, and were less educated than men. Despite growing affluence and gender equality today, especially in urban areas, there is a still a clear preference for boys, as witnessed by the number of sex-selective abortions.

But change is in the air as Vietnamese receive better education and travel overseas for leisure. All this has spurred a desire for personal independence and individualism among younger Vietnamese. Increasingly, young married couples are buying apartments and moving out of the family home. The youthful population increasingly dominates Vietnamese society, despite the collective control of the state and that of older generations

---

VIETNAMESE NAMES

All Vietnamese names follow a simple structure: family name, middle name and given name. When a Vietnamese hands you a business card you should address the person with the name on the far right. A man named Nguyen Manh Hung, for example, should be addressed as Hung.

There are roughly 140 Vietnamese family names in use today. The most common is Nguyen, which was also the name of the last royal dynasty. Other royal surnames still in use today include Tran, Trinh and Le. While a person with one of these family names may be a descendant of that royal family, the name was probably acquired to show loyalty to the monarch in power, or taken on as a mark of respect when a new dynasty rose to power.

Only around 30 of the 140 or so family names used in Vietnam are actually of Vietnamese origin. For the most part, family names are of Chinese (Khong, Luu, Truong, Lu, Lam), Cambodian (Thach, Kim, Danh, Son), or ethnic minority (Linh, Giap, Ma, Deo) origins.

The most common Vietnamese middle names are Van for men and Thi for women. The middle name is also used to indicate a person's generation, or the separate branches of a big family, or a person's position within the family – for instance, Ba is for the first son of the first wife, Manh for the first son of the second wife and Trong for a second son. In recent times, the Vietnamese have adopted more meaningful middle names.

raised on Confucian principles during less privileged times.

Language and society

The country shares one common tongue, a blend of several languages – ancient and modern – that has evolved through Vietnam's contact with other cultures. Its roots, while still debated, come from a mixture of the Austro-Asiatic, Austronesian and Sino-Tibetan language families.

Nonetheless, the distinct dialects spoken in Vietnam reveal strong regional identities.

> *Vietnamese can come across as quite blunt; being called beo (fat) can be a well-intentioned remark that someone's just looking well and happy rather than overweight.*

items in particular are recognisably French – *ca phe* (café), *pho mat* (fromage), *ga to* (gâteau) and *bia* (bière).

Over the course of its recent history, Vietnam has had close ties with France, the Soviet Union and other Eastern European countries.

Exercising at Tao Dan Park in Ho Chi Minh City.

Often, northerners and southerners confess they cannot understand each other. Some letters of the alphabet are pronounced differently, and regional vocabularies contain different words. Even the syntax is altered. In addition to Vietnamese, the country's many ethnic minorities often speak their own distinct languages and dialects. In the Mekong Delta, for example, so many people speak the Khmer language of Cambodia that local television broadcasts Khmer-language shows.

Thousands of words in contemporary Vietnamese – as much as 70 percent of the language – are derived from Chinese. There is a touch of French too, with words that entered the lexicon during the colonial period. Several food

As a result, older generations who may have studied abroad or worked closely with foreigners might speak French, Russian or possibly German, rather than English. But times have changed, and these days English is the language of choice for most of the younger Vietnamese. Children in the more urban areas learn English at school and at private language schools. Their confidence with the language and easy interaction with foreigners are noticeable. Teenagers listen to English songs and watch Hollywood movies on DVD, and everyday speech and online chats are liberally sprinkled with English words and slang.

But whatever language they use, no subject is taboo. So at your very first encounter with a Vietnamese, you are likely to be asked where you're from, whether you are married, how much you earn, what car you drive, and so on, in whatever fractured English the speaker can muster. This curiosity should not be misinterpreted as nosiness. There is a genuine fascination with foreigners, especially in the less visited areas of Vietnam.

Sex and marriage

Marriages were once seen as a form of business transaction between two families. Spouses were screened and then selected by parents

A village chief plays a traditional wind instrument in the highlands near Dalat.

and other senior family members rather than by the prospective partners. These days, it's more common for couples to court each other before the wedding, though family approval is still part of the process.

Whatever the case, even today the wife is expected to move to the husband's house upon marriage. This is a stressful and daunting prospect for any young bride as she is expected to please the whole family and follow the rules of the house.

Vietnam is still a very traditional country, though not necessarily a prudish one. Pre-marital sex is taboo for the older, more conservative generations, but there are signs that attitudes are changing rapidly. Internet chat rooms, websites, blogs and columns in the state-run media have become forums for young people to discuss subjects like love, sex and sexual orientation. In the past few years there has been an upsurge in short stories or novels written by female writers on female sexuality.

Socialising

Vietnamese people of all ages love to *di choi* (go out to play). This means going out to have fun, hanging out with friends at a bar or café, sing karaoke songs, etc. When Vietnamese *di choi*, it's often a case of the more the merrier. Whether it's celebrating a birthday or a job promotion, they will usually invite all their friends and partners/spouses out for a meal. Vietnamese typically drink with a meal, so local restaurants are often filled with boisterous drinkers shouting 'Tram phan tram' (literally 100 percent) before downing a glass of beer or shot of *ruou* (rice liquor).

It's customary for the person who extended the invitation to pick up the tab. In fact, Vietnamese rarely split the bill, even if it isn't a special occasion. Friends are forever trying to grab the bill in cafés and restaurants or surreptitiously bribing the waiter in an attempt to be presented with the bill first.

Street life

Living in cramped houses filled with extended three-generation families means that life often spills onto the streets. Itinerant vendors on bicycles and on foot, streetside barbers, shoeshine boys, not to mention the constant and chaotic flow of traffic, will assail your senses. Even in quieter residential areas, families often gather in the lanes to gossip with neighbours or buy fruit from passing vendors.

With more cars, motorbikes and people than ever before, Vietnam's major cities suffer from chronic congestion, leading the government to impose restrictions on street activity. Street vendors, shopkeepers and food

While Vietnam doesn't have a reputation for sex tourism like Thailand or Cambodia, prostitution is more widespread than it appears. Often, karaoke bars and massage parlours serve as fronts for illicit activities.

stalls are perpetually playing hide and seek with local police and district authorities who will confiscate goods – plastic stools, baskets, whatever – if these items are deemed to be blocking traffic or pushing pedestrians onto the road.

Competitive spirit

The Vietnamese love for sports is apparent in every town and city. When dawn breaks, t'ai chi practitioners get into action in town centres. At dusk, thousands of makeshift streetside badminton courts suddenly appear in Hanoi and

in positions of authority. Even teachers frequently receive 'gifts' from parents in the hope their child might receive extra attention at school. When accidents occur, traffic policemen will skip the paperwork and issue a verbal warning in return for an outright bribe.

The government is trying to root out corruption, but it's an uphill task given the fact that it is so deeply ingrained. In the past, Vietnamese would have blamed the war for the country's poverty; these days, corruption is often cited as the main reason for any perceived ills.

Buffalo riders.

The new face of Vietnam.

Ho Chi Minh City. Tennis and golf are now the sports of choice for the well-heeled, but football is by the far the most popular working-class sport. Vietnamese men both play (and watch) the game with great enthusiasm. It's not uncommon for men to stay up all night to watch European football matches being screened from the other side of the world on TV – and then going to work the next day bleary-eyed.

Under the table

Corruption is an entrenched part of Vietnamese society. Palms are often greased to skip bureaucratic hurdles, win contracts and invite preferential treatment from people

KEEP SMILING

Vietnamese often smile when embarrassed, confused or when they're being scolded by an older person or their boss, or when they don't understand what a foreigner is asking. If you lose your temper and this happens, it doesn't mean they are not taking the situation seriously, but rather that he or she is embarrassed for you. To make your feelings known, be firm, but don't lose your cool – that only makes things worse. Likewise, when a traffic accident is averted, Vietnamese often crack into a wide smile, especially if you're a foreigner. It means 'I'm sorry!' or perhaps 'Aren't we lucky nothing serious happened!'

ARTS, CRAFTS AND LITERATURE

The Vietnamese are among the world's most literate
and poetic people but, after decades of neglect, their
traditional performing arts must now compete with
more modern forms of entertainment.

Vietnam has a long history of artistic endeavour, in fine arts, crafts, music and literature. The first flourishing of the arts occurred during the Dong Son period in the first millennium BC. The Chinese influence has been pervasive, although the culture of the Cham kingdom was far closer to that of India.

Music

The ancient Dong Son bronze drums, which depict dancers performing to the accompaniment of musical instruments, testify to the importance of music and dance traditions in Vietnam since its early days. For a long time, however, musical performance was largely confined to religious ceremonies and only relatively recently became part of the cultural landscape in a broader sense.

Generally Vietnamese music falls into two basic categories: *dieu bac*, the northern mode which exhibits more of a Chinese influence, and *dieu nam*, southern mode, featuring the slower tempo and sentimentality of ancient Cham culture.

Folk music takes the form of tunes sung by villagers illustrating their life in the countryside. There are several broad categories: lullabies, known as *hat ru* in the north, *ru em* in the centre and *au o* in the south; work songs or *ho*; and mushy love songs, known as *ly*.

Perhaps the most important catalyst in the development of contemporary Vietnamese folk entertainment was the appearance of the call-and-response dialogue song, a genre found widely throughout Southeast Asia. This developed into various forms, including the unique Red River Delta form known as *quan ho*, a complex and technically demanding style of romantic folk singing. *Quan ho* has close links

A folk music and dance performance in Hoi An.

to the custom of *ket cha* (establishing friendship between villages) in which male and female singers, accompanied by a small music ensemble, perform songs interspersed with improvised repartee.

Various *quan ho* festivals are held throughout the north after the Tet festival, the largest and most important being the Hoi Lim Quan Ho festival in Bac Ninh province.

One traditional Vietnamese folk art undergoing something of a revival today is *ca tru*, often described as sung poetry, but the accompanying music is an integral part of the performance. A group usually consists of three performers. The singer, always a woman, plays the *phach*, an instrument made of wood or bamboo beaten with two wooden sticks. A musician called *kep* accompanies the singer on the *dan day*, a long-necked lute. There is also a drummer, *trong chau*, who moves with the rhythm of the singer or the songs.

Traditionally, before enjoying the music at a communal house, private home or inn, guests would purchase a stack of bamboo cards. These cards were given to the singers in appreciation of the performance, each singer receiving payment in proportion to the number of cards received.

Despite the establishment of an independent Viet kingdom in the 10th century, succes-

Theatre

Today's theatrical varieties – *cheo*, *hat tuong* and *cai luong*, are a blend of court theatre and folk performances with some foreign influences.

Cheo is as old as the Vietnamese nation itself and has been depicted on the engravings of Bronze Age drums and urns. Although it hails from the north of the country, it is promoted today as a national art form. The dramas provide a framework within which the players improvise; the troupe is judged according to its ability to vary and reinvent a familiar theme. The musicians play drums, gongs, rattles,

Learning classical dance in Hanoi.

sive rulers continued to mimic the courtly traditions of their powerful Chinese neighbour. Confucian music and dance traditions were increasingly appropriated from the Chinese imperial court. Court music was also influenced by the music of the old Hindu kingdom of Champa.

In the early 20th century, the royal court at Hue became increasingly Westernised and, during the reign of French-educated Bao Dai (1926–45), the last of the Nguyen kings, traditional royal music and dances were rarely performed. Since the late 1980s, court music has been revived in the old imperial capital by the Thua Thien Hue Provincial Traditional Arts Company and the Hue Royal Palace Arts Troupe.

VIETNAMESE CRAFTS

Two of the best known Vietnamese crafts are pottery and lacquerware. The combination of skilled potting, fine finishing and glazing, as well as free and calligraphic embellishing, are all features typical of the Vietnamese ceramic tradition. Lacquered wood objects have been found in tombs dating from the 3rd century AD. Today, lacquerware *(son mai)* – including paintings and screens – is fast becoming a major export item. The tradition of Vietnamese villages specialising in certain crafts has survived into the present day. Craft villages near Hanoi are the best known: Van Phuc for silk, Dong Ho for woodcuts and Bat Trang for pottery.

stringed instruments and a flute. Many of the country's professional *cheo* companies have been obliged to diversify their activities into more commercial forms of entertainment in order to survive.

Unlike *cheo*, which is uniquely Vietnamese, *hat tuong* arrived from China (in the 13th century), with distinctly Chinese make-up, ceremonial costumes, masks, stylised gestures, percussion and wind-instrument music, and the emphasis on heroic and noble themes. The action, always dramatic, is guided by Confucian moral virtues and concepts.

Water puppet theatre, Hanoi.

Cai luong, a far more recent arrival on the theatre scene, interprets classical Chinese stories in a more accessible style. Influenced by the European stage, it has evolved into its present spoken-drama form, abandoning the cumbersome epic style in favour of shorter acts, emotional and psychological play. Whilst audiences for most traditional Vietnamese theatre genres have declined over the years, *cai luong* has retained its appeal by appropriating elements from contemporary culture.

Fine arts

After decades of obscurity and isolation, Vietnamese artists have started to make inroads into the international arena. Sold in galleries and exhibited in museums worldwide, Vietnamese paintings are routinely featured in auctions of Southeast Asian art at Christie's and Sotheby's.

While China, Japan and Korea share long painting histories, Vietnam's artistic tradition emerged entirely from the 19th-century French colonial influences. Prior to this time, local artistic achievements had been restricted to decorative arts for religious and communal purposes, with only a limited output of paintings, coloured embossments and silk portraits.

New opportunities for creative achievement arose during the colonial period, with painting becoming the most developed artistic expression. Through this Western influx, a unique French-Vietnamese amalgamation of cultures emerged. In 1925, under the initiative of the French painter Victor Tardieu, the Ecole des Beaux-Arts de l'Indochine (EBAI) was founded in Hanoi. The establishment was responsible for creating the 'first generation' of Vietnamese masters.

WATER PUPPETS

The annual flooding of the Red River lowlands inspired a form of entertainment that is found only in Vietnam, namely water puppetry *(mua roi nuoc)*. The flooded paddies were, of course, the perfect platform in which to conceal both the puppeteer and the long bamboo poles used to control the puppet. Gradually, these theatrical events would have transferred to the small ponds and lakes beside the communal houses found in a typical 11th-century Vietnamese village.

Today, the puppeteers still perform in a chest-deep pool of water but behind a curtain on stage. The water is kept deliberately murky so as to obscure the poles and mechanics used to control the puppets, which are protected from the elements by a layer of lacquer.

As its origins and themes hark back to farming communities in feudal times, water puppetry is not merely enjoyable theatre, but also a living portrait of Vietnamese culture. A performance will consist of 12 to 18 acts, each telling a mythological story about Vietnam and its history, while a small ensemble of traditional musicians and cheo singers provide background music. Characters can be heroic, legendary or mythical, but most are ordinary peasants with plot lines that tend to be action-oriented.

Not all of its artists shared the same vision or produced the same style of painting, but each shared a desire to champion European modernism while remaining true to their Vietnamese spirit and heritage. Through their innovative use of traditional materials and their depiction of domestic themes in warm colours, all of these artists can be accredited with freeing Vietnamese painting from its colonial academism.

Despite the terrible effects of decades of war, isolation and censorship on this nascent art community, these philosophies survived – although it was not until 1986, when *doi moi* (economic 'renovation') began, that the artistic climate throughout the country began to flourish once again. Today, most Vietnamese painters have their roots, in some way, in the traditional European school of painting.

A new generation of artists is emerging, who enjoy more freedom and international recognition than ever before. Artists are also working in more diversified mediums. You can find experimental performance art, video and installations as well as neo-traditionalists who paint nudes, calligraphy and Chinese-style scrolls.

Both Hanoi and Ho Chi Minh City are awash with highly commercialised art that has flooded the tourist market. With fine Vietnamese art selling for six-figure sums or more in international art circles compared to the paltry US$200 or so it used to fetch two decades ago, it's not surprising that a rash of mediocre Vietnamese artists are trying to cash in on its popularity. The sheer number of art shops can be overwhelming for first-time visitors with no prior knowledge of the local art scene.

The literary scene

Classical Vietnamese literature has been fed by the country's seemingly endless wealth of oral storytelling traditions. Nearly every Vietnamese reads and remembers the Tale of Kieu, a 3,254-verse story written over 200 years ago by one of Vietnam's most respected writers, Nguyen Du, and considered by some as the cultural window to the soul of the Vietnamese people.

During the early half of the 20th century, the Romanised Vietnamese script called *quoc ngu* grew popular. As the literary traditions of France and the rest of Europe became more accessible, Vietnamese literature was enriched with new ideas of Western thought and culture. One of the finest Vietnamese novels of this era is *Dumb Luck*, a brilliant satire on modernisation in Vietnam during the late colonial era. Written by Vu Trong Phung and first published in 1936, it follows the absurd and unexpected rise within colonial society of a street-smart vagabond named Red-Haired Xuan. The novel still has relevance today.

After 1975, Communist Party cadres controlled publishing; even today, government censors must approve writings before publication. In the 1980s authors and poets often used analogy and parody to evade censorship and publish stories that would send ripples of amusement

Weaving silk.

and scandal through the reading public. Some authors chose not to skirt around the issue. Contemporary writer Duong Thu Huong's anti-establishment novels have been banned in Vietnam and she was even placed under house arrest.

Despite interest in Vietnamese literature, the lack of English-language translations limits readership. Wayne Karlin, a Vietnam veteran and author, has translated numerous modern works in recent years. Together with Ho Anh Thai, one of the country's most acclaimed authors, he edited the short-story anthology *Love After War*, which features the work of several leading contemporary writers. Their stories reveal the relationships and concerns of everyday life, and the erosion of life in modern Vietnam.

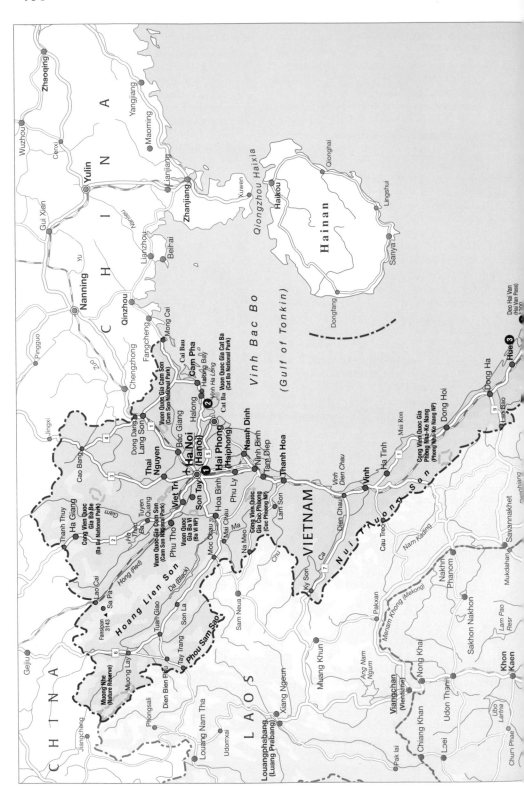

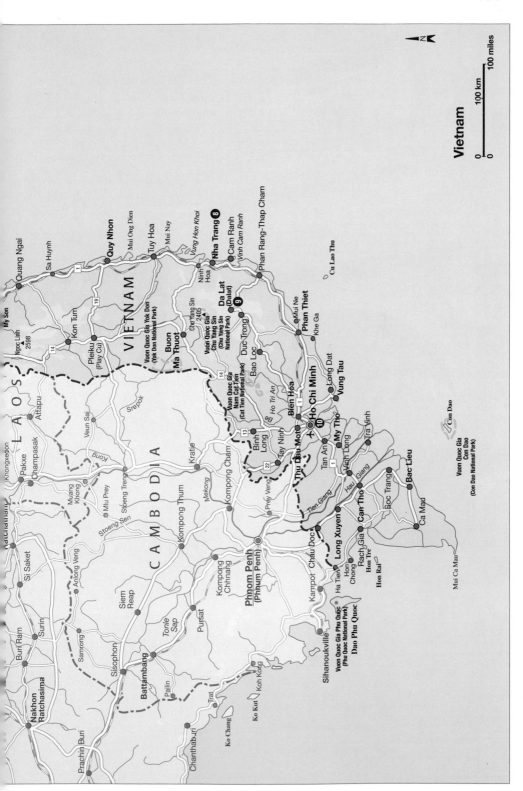

Vietnam

0 — 100 km
0 — 100 miles

N

L A O S

My Son
Ngoc Linh
2598
Quang Ngai
Sa Huynh
Kon Tum
Pleiku
(Play Cu)
14
19
1
Quy Nhon
Mui Ong Dien
Tuy Hoa
Mui Nay
Vung Hon Khoi
V I E T N A M
Chu Yang Sin
2405
Buon Ma Thuot
Vuon Quoc Gia Yok Don
(Yok Don National Park)
Vuon Quoc Gia Chu Yang Sin
(Chu Yang Sin National Park)
Ninh Hoa
Nha Trang ❽
Cam Ranh
Vinh Cam Ranh
Phan Rang-Thap Cham
Da Lat (Dalat) ❾
Duc Trong
Bao Loc
Cu Lao Thu
Mui Ne
Phan Thiet
Khe Ga

Attapu
Veun Sai
Srepok
14
Vuon Quoc Gia Nam Cat Tien
(Cat Tien National Park)
Kong
Kratie
Kompong Cham
13
Binh Long
Ho Tri An
Da
Bien Hoa
1
Ho Chi Minh
Long Dat
Vung Tau

Pakxe
Champasak
Muang Khong
Stoeng Sen
Stoeng Treng
C A M B O D I A
Mlu Prey
Kompong Thum
Mekong
Prey Veng
Kompong Cham
22
Tay Ninh
Tan An
❿
Thu Dau Mot
My Tho
Tra Vinh
Vinh Long
Hau Giang
Long Tau

Khongxedon
Si Saket
Surin
Buri Ram
Nakhon Ratchasima
Prachin Buri
Sisophon
Siem Reap
Tonle Sap
Pursat
Kompong Chhnang
Phnom Penh (Phum Penh)
Kampot
Chau Doc
Tien Giang
Long Xuyen
Can Tho
Rach Gia
Soc Trang
Bac Lieu
Ca Mau
Mui Ca Mau

Samrong
Battambang
Pailin
Trat
Ko Chang
Ko Kut
Koh Kong
Sihanoukville
Ha Tien
Hon Chong
Hon Rai
Hon Tre
Vuon Quoc Gia Phu Quoc
(Phu Quoc National Park)
Dao Phu Quoc
Con Dao
Vuon Quoc Gia Con Dao
(Con Dao National Park)

Chanthaburi

HANOI AND HALONG BAY

Vietnam's attractive capital retains an ambience in architecture and layout that recalls the earlier French years. To the east is Halong Bay, one of the region's top scenic attractions.

Today, with a population of nearly 6.6 million, **Hanoi ❶**, the political and cultural capital of Vietnam, extends more than 3,346 sq km (1,291 sq miles) in size. New buildings in the city centre around Hoan Kiem Lake are restricted to six floors, which leaves Hanoi's original character very much intact, preserved in its traditional pagodas and temples, colonial architecture, tree-lined streets and lakes. The soul of this ancient Thang Long city rests in the old town centre, which dates from the 15th century.

Downtown Hanoi comprises four districts: Hoan Kiem (Restored Sword), Hai Ba Trung (Two Trung Sisters), Dong Da (where King Quang Trung defeated the Manchu invasion in 1789) and Ba Dinh. In 2008, Hanoi absorbed neighbouring Ha Tay Province and several other districts, growing nearly 4 times in size. Now many towns are considered part of the greater city, which is surrounded by numerous lakes and mountains.

Central Hanoi is accessible from the north by three bridges: Long Bien, Chuong Duong and Thang Long, a modern span changing into a four-lane highway to Noi Bai Airport. The 1,682-metre (5,520ft) -long Long Bien Bridge was built by the French architect Gustave Eiffel and opened in 1902 by Governor-General Doumer, after whom it was originally named. It

suffered some damage from American bombing during the Vietnam War, but it was continually repaired. Until 1983, all northbound road and rail traffic passed over it. These days, it is reserved for cyclists, pedestrians and trains.

Around Hoan Kiem lake

In the very heart of the old town of Hanoi lies **Ho Hoan Kiem Ⓐ**, or Lake of the Restored Sword. Legend has it that in the 15th century, King Le Thai To was given a magic sword by a tortoise that lived in the lake. He used the

Main Attractions

Museum of the Vietnamese Revolution
Ba Da Pagoda
Dong Xuan market
Vietnam Fine Arts Museum
Ho Chi Minh Mausoleum
White Silk Lake
Halong Bay

Old quarter street scene.

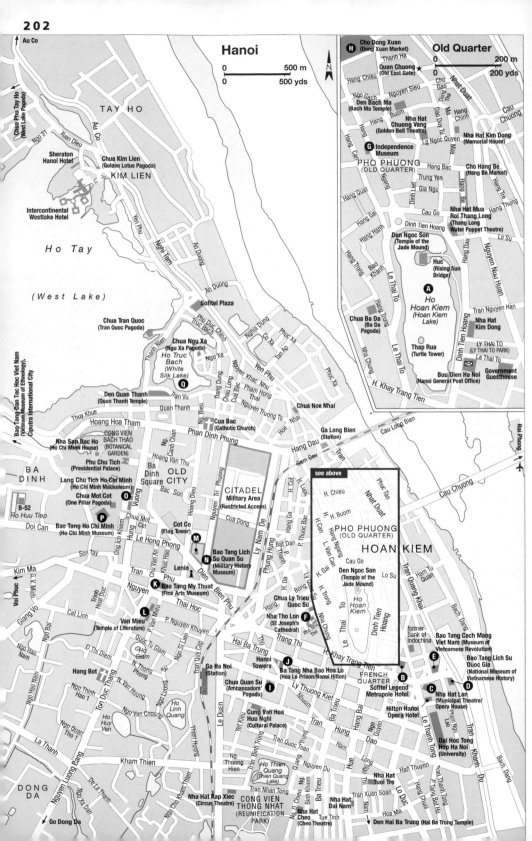

Hanoi

0 — 500 m
0 — 500 yds

N

Old Quarter

0 — 200 m
0 — 200 yds

Au Co

TAY HO

Chua Phu Tay Ho
(West Lake Pagoda)

Sheraton
Hanoi Hotel

Chua Kim Lien
(Golden Lotus Pagoda)

KIM LIEN

Intercontinental
Westlake Hotel

Ho Tay

(West Lake)

Chua Tran Quoc
(Tran Quoc Pagoda)

Sofitel Plaza

Chua Ngu Xa
(Ngu Xa Pagoda)

Ho Truc
Bach
(White
Silk Lake)

Q

Den Quan Thanh
(Quan Thanh Temple)

Bao Tang Dan Toc Hoc Viet Nam
(Vietnam Museum of Ethnology),
Ciputra International City

Cua Bac
(Catholic Church)

Chua Noe Nhai

Ga Long Bien
(Station)

Nha San Bac Ho
(Ho Chi Minh House)

CONG VIEN
BACH THAO
(BOTANICAL
GARDEN)

Phan Dinh Phung

Hang Dau

Phu Chu Tich
(Presidential Palace)

BA
DINH

Ba
Dinh
Square

OLD
CITY

Lang Chu Tich Ho Chi Minh
(Ho Chi Minh Mausoleum)

O

Chua Mot Cot
(One Pillar Pagoda)

CITADEL
Military Area
(Restricted Access)

B-52
Ho Huu Tiep

Cot Co
(Flag Tower)

M

see above

PHO PHUONG
(OLD QUARTER)

HOAN KIEM

Den Ngoc Son
(Temple of the
Jade Mound)

Bao Tang Ho Chi Minh
(Ho Chi Minh Museum)

P

Bao Tang Lich
Su Quan Su
(Military History
Museum)

N

Lenin

Cau Go

Ho
Hoan
Kiem

K

Bao Tang My Thuat
(Fine Arts Museum)

Van Mieu
(Temple of Literature)

L

Chua Ly Trieu
Quoc Su

Nha Tho Lon
(St Joseph's
Cathedral)

F

Hang Bot

Ga Ha Noi
(Station)

Hanoi
Towers

J

Ba Tang Nha Bao Hoa Lo
(Hoa Lo Prison/Hanoi Hilton)

FRENCH
QUARTER

B

former
Bank of
Indochina

E

Bao Tang Cach Mang
Viet Nam (Museum of
Vietnamese Revolution)

Bao Tang Lich Su
Quoc Gia
(National Museum of
Vietnamese History)

Chua Quan Su
(Ambassadors'
Pagoda)

I

Sofitel Legend
Metropole Hotel

C

Nha Hat Lon
(Municipal Theatre/
Opera House)

Hilton Hanoi
Opera Hotel

Cung Van Hoa
Huu Nghi
(Cultural Palace)

Dai Hoc Tong
Hop Ha Noi
(University)

DONG
DA

Go Dong Da

Nha Hat Rap Xiec
(Circus Theatre)

CONG VIEN
THONG NHAT
(REUNIFICATION
PARK)

Nha Hat
Cheo
(Cheo Theatre)

Nha Hat
Dai Nam

Ho Thien
Quang
(Thien Quang Lake)

Nha Hat
Tuoi Tre

Den Hai Ba Trung (Hai Ba Trung Temple)

Old Quarter (inset)

Cho Dong Xuan
(Dong Xuan Market)

H

Quan Chuong
(Old East Gate)

Den Bach Ma
(Bach Ma Temple)

Nha Hat
Chuong Vang
(Golden Bell Theatre)

Nha Hat Kim Dong
(Memorial House)

Independence
Museum

G

PHO PHUONG
(OLD QUARTER)

Cho Hang Be
(Hang Be Market)

Nha Hat Mua
Roi Thang Long
(Thang Long
Water Puppet Theatre)

Den Ngoc Son
(Temple of the
Jade Mound)

Huc
(Rising Sun
Bridge)

A

Ho
Hoan Kiem
(Hoan Kiem
Lake)

Chua Ba Da
(Ba Da
Pagoda)

Thap Rua
(Turtle Tower)

Nha Hat
Kim Dong

LY THAI TO
(LY THAI TO PARK)

Buu Dien Ha Noi
(Hanoi General Post Office)

Government
Guesthouse

sword to drive the Chinese from the country, but later the tortoise is said to have snatched the sword from his hand and disappeared into the lake. Near its middle is a small, 18th-century tower, Thap Rua, or Tortoise Tower.

To the east of Hoan Kiem Lake, behind the main Post Office on Ly Thai To Street, is the Government Guest House, a compound with a hotel in the back and an ornate French colonial building, painted yellow with green trim, in front. It was once the palace of the French governor of Tonkin. Today, Vietnamese officials meet visiting foreign dignitaries here.

Across the street is the venerable **Sofitel Legend Metropole Hotel** **B**, built in 1901 during the French colonial era and still one of the city's premier hotels. Not far from the Metropole, and dating from the same time, is one of Hanoi's most famous landmarks, the **Opera House** **C** (Nha Hat Lon; also known as the Municipal Theatre). The ornate building is a small-scale replica of the Palais Garnier in Paris.

Nearby, the **National Museum of Vietnamese History** **D** (Bao Tang Lich Su Vietnam; www.baotanglichsu.vn; Tue–Sun 8–11.30am and 1.30–4.30pm; charge) is housed in a hybrid-Indochinese style building. Exhibits displayed here cover Vietnam's fascinating and complex history. The **Museum of the Vietnamese Revolution** **E** (Bao Tang Cach Mang; Tue–Sun 8–11.45am and 1.30–4.15pm; charge) on Tong Dan Street documents the struggles of the Vietnamese people from ancient times up until 1975.

On the west side of the lake is **Nha Tho Street** (Church Street). Once the property of the Catholic Diocese, it is now a trendy shopping area. Facing it at the end of the street is **St Joseph's Cathedral** **F** (Nha Tho Lon; daily 5am–10pm, free), consecrated on Christmas night in 1886.

A narrow passageway next to 5 Nha Tho, leads to the **Ba Da Pagoda** (Chua Ba Da; daily 8am–5pm, free). This charming pagoda was built in the 15th century following the discovery of a stone statue of a woman during the construction of the Thang Long citadel. The statue, which was thought to have magical powers, disappeared and has been replaced by a wooden replica.

On Ly Quoc Su Street, to the right of the cathedral, is the small **Ly Trieu Quoc Su Pagoda** (Chua Ly Trieu Quoc Su), also known as the Pagoda of Confucius (Chua Kong). It contains some attractive wooden statues. The **Bach Ma Temple** on Hang Buom Street dates all the way back to the 9th century, although it was reconstructed in the 18th and 19th centuries.

The **Independence Museum** **G** (Mon–Sat 8am–4pm) is housed within a small building on Hang Ngang Street, which was once a secret meeting place for communist revolutionaries. Ho Chi Minh wrote Vietnam's declaration of independence here in 1945, borrowing liberally from America's own declaration.

The area around busy **Dong Xuan Market** **H** in the northern part of the so-called Old Quarter rewards

Lucky red lanterns are sold at Tet, the Vietnamese New Year.

Peaceful Hoan Kiem Lake.

TIP

Most Hanoi businesses and shops close every day for an hour or two over lunch. In the summer months, Hanoians tend to start their day around 5am, and retreat indoors once the heat sets in. Government offices close at 4.30pm and are shut on Sunday

exploration on foot. The market is a good place to find cheap clothing and kitchenware, and in the surrounding streets farmers squat on the pavement selling their produce to passers-by. Southeast of the market, at **87 Ma May Street**, is a restored 19-century antique house (daily 8.30am–5.30pm; charge).

Southwest of the lake, several blocks away on Quan Su Street, is **Ambassadors' Pagoda ❶** (Chua Quan Su; daily 8am–5pm; free). In the 17th century, the site was a house that accommodated visiting foreign ambassadors and envoys from other Buddhist countries. Two blocks away was the infamous **Hoa Lo Prison ❶** (Tue–Sun 8–11.30am, 1–4.30pm; charge), dubbed the 'Hanoi Hilton' by American prisoners. The main gate and front portion of the prison have been preserved as a museum. Across the street is the Hanoi People's Court. To the south of the prison and the Quan Su pagoda is a small, lovely lake, **Ho Thien Quang**, where visitors can rent paddle boats. Across the street is an entrance to **Reunification Park**, and to its right, Hanoi's circus.

Street games outside St Joseph's Cathedral.

The old French quarter

West from the centre of town is the old French quarter, now the diplomatic area of Hanoi. Here, the old villas house foreign embassies and government offices on quiet, tree-lined streets. The **Vietnam Fine Arts Museum ❶** (Bao Tang My Thuat; www.vnfineartsmuseum.org.vn; Tue–Sun 8.30am–5pm; charge), at 66 Nguyen Thai Hoc Street, features an extensive collection of artefacts. Exhibits cover some of Vietnam's ethnic minorities and history. On display are beautiful wooden statues of Buddha from the 18th century, Dong Son bronze drums and other Vietnamese art, both ancient and contemporary.

Nearby, across the street, is the **Temple of Literature ❶** (Van Mieu; Tue–Sun 8.30–11.30am and 1.30–4.30pm; charge). Built in 1070 under the reign of King Ly Thai Tong, the temple is dedicated to Confucius. In 1076, it was combined with 'The School of the Elite of the Nation' (Quoc Tu Giam), Vietnam's first national university. The large temple enclosure is divided into five walled courtyards. After passing through the temple gate and the first two courtyards,

one arrives at the Pavilion of the Constellation of Literature (Khue Van Cac), where the men of letters used to recite their poems. Through the Great Wall Gate (Dai Thanh Mon), an open courtyard surrounds a large central pool known as the Well of Heavenly Clarity (Thien Quang Tinh).

To the north nearby, on Dien Bien Phu Street, is one of the symbols of Hanoi, **Cot Co ⓜ**, the flag tower. Built in 1812 under the Nguyen dynasty as part of the Hanoi Citadel, the hexagonal 33.4-metre (110ft) now houses the military. Portions of the restored and excavated citadel may at times be open for visitors. Next to it, **Vietnam Military History Museum ⓝ** (Bao Tang Lich Su Quan Su; www.btlsqsvn.org.vn; Tue–Thur, Sat–Sun 8–11.30am, 1–4.30pm; charge) chronicles Vietnam's battles for independence and unification against the French and American patrons of the former South Vietnam. Across the street is a small, triangular-shaped park with a statue of Lenin. About 100 metres (328ft) past the flag tower, right on Hoang Dieu Street is a small archaeological dig and the original city gates. Across the street at No. 30, shrouded by trees, is the home of General Vo Nguyen Giap, who in 2009 celebrated his 99th birthday here.

Excavations at 18 Hoang Dieu to construct government buildings have unearthed an astounding range of artefacts from Hanoi's past. Across the street is **Ladies Pagoda** (Di Tich Hau Lau). At the corner of Hoang Dieu and Phan Dinh Phung is the North Gate (Bac Mon). From the tower above the gate you can look into the military grounds.

One block west of Hang Dieu looms the imposing and impressive structure of **Ho Chi Minh Mausoleum ⓞ** (Lang Chu Tich Ho Chi Minh; Tue–Thur, Sat–Sun 8–11am; charge), in Ba Dinh Square. Ho's embalmed corpse lies in a glass casket in this monumental tomb – contrary to his wish to be cremated. It was from this square that Ho Chi Minh read his declaration of independence

speech on 2 September 1945. Nearby is the unique **One Pillar Pagoda** (Chua Mot Cot). Built in 1049 under the Ly dynasty, this beautiful wooden pagoda rests on a single stone pillar rising out of a lotus pool. The small Dien Huu Pagoda shares this lovely setting.

Behind the park with the pagodas is the **Ho Chi Minh Museum ⓟ** (Bao Tang Ho Chi Minh; Tue–Thur and Sat 8–11.30am and 2–6pm; charge). A massive concrete structure, the museum contains some rather bizarre exhibits, but it presents a thorough history of Ho's life.

Ho Truc Bach

From Ba Dinh Square, where the National Assembly building is located across from the mausoleum, and where there is a war memorial, head north towards **White Silk Lake ⓠ** (Ho Truc Bach). This was the ancient site of Lord Trinh's summer palace, which became a harem where he detained his wayward concubines. This lake derives its name from the fine white silk the concubines were forced to weave for the princesses of ancient Vietnam.

In Hanoi's Fine Arts Museum.

The Ho Chi Minh Mausoleum.

Figures in one of the city's many Mahayana Buddhist temples.

Villas, hotels and restaurants have now sprung up around the lake.

Nearby, the ornate temple of **Quan Thanh** (Den Quan Thanh; daily 8am–5pm; free) beside the lake was built during the Ly dynasty (1010–1225). It houses a huge bronze bell and an enormous, four-ton bronze statue of Tran Vu, guardian deity of the north, to whom the temple is dedicated.

Halong Bay

No trip to northern Vietnam would be complete without a trip to Quang Ninh Province, 165km (100 miles) from Hanoi. This province shares a border with China in the north, and harbours one of the wonders of the world, with perhaps the most stunning scenery in Vietnam at **Halong Bay ❷** (Vinh Ha Long). The bay's tranquil beauty encompasses 1,500 sq km (560 sq miles) dotted with well over 3,000 limestone islands, many of them unnamed. Bizarre rock sculptures jutting dramatically from the sea and numerous grottoes have created an enchanted, timeless world, immortalised in the 1992 French film,

Indochine; Halong Bay has been twice designated a Unesco World Heritage Site: first in 1994 for its natural scenic beauty, and again in 2000 for its great biological interest.

Halong Bay's awesome scenery looks the stuff of legends – which it is. Ha Long means 'Descending Dragon,' originating from the myth that a celestial dragon once flung herself headlong into the sea, her swishing tail digging deep valleys and crevices in the mainland. As she descended into the sea, these filled with water, creating the bay. According to another legend, the Jade Emperor ordered a dragon to halt an invasion by sea from the north. The dragon spewed out jade and jewels which upon hitting the sea turned into wondrous islands and karst formations, creating a natural fortress against enemy ships. The dragon was so enchanted by her creations that she decided to stay in the bay. To this day, local fishermen claim to see the shape of a dragon-like creature in the waters.

Throughout history, Halong Bay was the downfall of many marauding invaders. General Ngo Quyen defeated Chinese forces in 938 by embedding hundreds of iron tipped stakes in the Bach Dang River, then luring the fleet upstream in high tide. He then attacked as the tide turned, driving the Chinese downstream and onto the exposed stakes. Incredibly, four centuries later, in 1288, Kublai Khan fell for the same ruse, this time masterminded by General Tran Hung Dao.

Islands and grottoes

Geologists believe that the karst outcrops were formed by a giant limestone sea bed, eroding until only pinnacles remained behind. Locals named them after the shapes they resemble: teapot, toad, elephant's foot, etc. Over the centuries, elements within the rock slowly dissolved by rain formed hundreds of bizarre-shaped grottoes; several of them may be visited.

Boats usually visit a couple of caves en route. Best known is found on

Tourist vessels on Halong Bay.

the island nearest to Ha Long City – **Grotto of Wooden Stakes** (Hang Dau Go), where General Tran Hung Dao amassed hundreds of stakes prior to his 1288 victory. On the same island, **Grotto of the Heavenly Palace** (Hang Thien Cung) has some impressive stalactites and stalagmites, as does **Surprise Grotto** (Hang Sung Sot) on an island further south. **Hang Hanh** is a tunnel cave that extends for 2km (1.5 miles) – access by sampan is strictly regulated by tides. **Three Tunnel Lake** (Ho Ba Ham), a shallow lagoon surrounded by limestone walls on **Dau Bo Island**, can only be reached by navigating three low tunnels at low tide.

Cat Ba Island, the largest in Halong Bay at 354 sq km (136 sq miles), has a spectacular, rugged landscape – forested limestone peaks, offshore coral reefs, coastal mangrove and freshwater swamps, lakes and waterfalls. Almost half the island and adjacent waters are a national park, with diverse flora and fauna. You can trek through here, cruise through **Lan Ha Bay** or Halong Bay itself. Although the island is dotted

with a few villages, Cat Ba town is the main settlement – some boats dock in the fishing harbour, where mini-hotels and basic tourist services are located. Although tourism is increasing, Cat Ba is still a fishing community.

Many tourist boats spend one or two nights here, or visit the national park. Despite Cat Ba Island being overrun in the summer with numerous tourist boats in the vicinity, Halong Bay is still a peaceful spot. Several tour companies now sail further east into **Bai Tu Long Bay** in search of more solitude. Bai Tu Long's little-frequented islands, such as **Quan Lan Island** – with sweeping deserted beaches and welcoming fishing communities – are well worth a visit..

A boat trip on the bay is best organised from Hanoi, where numerous tour companies (see page 207) offer a variety of tours to suit every interest and budget. These range from one-day trips with a four-hour cruise, to five-day adventures including luxurious onboard accommodation. Kayaking trips have become an ideal way to see the smaller grottoes and bays.

Cat Co Beach 1 on Cat Ba Island.

SAILING ON HALONG BAY

The only way to appreciate Halong Bay is by boat, and every single Hanoi tour operator arranges one- to four-day tours of this premier attraction. Pointless efforts have been made by the government to regulate the boats and ticketing systems. Booking a tour with an agency in Hanoi is perhaps more convenient than attempting to arrange anything on the bay. Boats depart from Bai Chay, which lies some 165km (102 miles) east of Hanoi by road. For those with limited time, there are one-day tours with roughly four hours cruising, but this is not worthwhile given the three-hour road journey to Bai Chay.

Most tour operators use standard engine-powered wooden boats with dormitory-style cabins. Luxury junk boats, with top-notch dining, large sundecks and en-suite cabins, are also available. **Handspan** (tel: 04-933 2375–7; www.handspan.com) operates the most economical trips on board its comfortable Dragon's Pearl junk with 18 cabins. **Buffalo Tours** (tel: 04-828 0702; www.buffalotours. com) operates the mid-priced Jewel of the Bay luxury junk with five cabins. **Emeraude Classic Cruises** (tel: 04-934 0888; www. emeraude-cruises.com) runs the most expensive luxury cruises on a replica paddle steamer.

Kayaking trips often involve one or two nights on one of the islands. All boats depart daily from Bai Chay in Ha Long City.

CENTRAL VIETNAM

From the imperial capital of Hue to the charm of Hoi An, the central segment of Vietnam also encompasses some beautiful sandy beaches, fabulous Cham ruins and, to the south, the highland resort of Dalat.

Main Attractions

The Imperial City, Hue
Royal tombs
Hai Van pass
China Beach, Danang
Old Quarter, Hoi An
My Son temples
Nha Trang
Dalat

The mountain resort of Dalat.

The ancient imperial city of the Nguyen kings, **Hue ❸** is located 12km (7 miles) from the coast, midway between Hanoi and Ho Chi Minh City on a narrow stretch of land in Thua Thien Hue Province. The first ethnic Vietnamese noble to reach Hue was Lord Nguyen Hoang (1524–1613), in the spring of 1601. He found a particularly good location in the former Champa kingdom to build a capital and erected the Phu Xuan Citadel.

Nguyen Hoang also built the **Celestial Lady Pagoda** (Chua Thien Mu), which remains intact on the left bank of the Perfume River, said to be named after a type of fragrant plant that grows near its origins. The seven tiers of the temple's octagonal tower each represent a different reincarnation of Buddha. The main temple, Dai Hung, is in an attractive garden of ornamental shrubs and trees.

Nguyen Hoang was the first in an uninterrupted succession of 10 feudal lords to rule over the area of Hue until 1802. That year, after quelling the Tay Son uprising, the 10th Nguyen lord proclaimed himself Emperor Gia Long and founded the Nguyen dynasty, which would last for 143 years, until 1945. But just 33 years into the dynasty's reign, the French invaded Hue. A quick succession of emperors graced the throne. The anti-French demonstrations and strikes of the colonial era were followed by the Japanese occupation in 1940 and the abdication of Bao Dai, the last Nguyen emperor, in August 1945.

The relative peace that reigned after 1954, when Hue became part of South Vietnam (following the country's division into two parts), was shattered under Ngo Dinh Diem's regime. Repressive anti-Buddhist propaganda sparked off a series of demonstrations and protest suicides by Buddhist monks in 1963.

Always an important cultural, intellectual and historical city, Hue remains one of Vietnam's main attractions. The charm of this timeless old city lies not

only in its historical and architectural value, but also in the natural beauty of its location along the banks of the Perfume River.

The Imperial City, Hue

The **Imperial City** (Dai Noi; daily 7am–5.30pm; charge) of Hue is made up of three walled enclosures. The Hoang Thanh (Yellow Enclosure) and the Tu Cam Thanh (Forbidden Purple City) are enclosed within the Kinh Thanh (exterior enclosure). Stone, bricks and earth were used to build the exterior wall, which measured 8 metres (26ft) high and 20 metres (65ft) thick, built during the reign of Emperor Gia Long. The Yellow Enclosure is the middle wall enclosing the imperial city and its palaces, temples and flower gardens. Through the Ngo Mon (Noon Gate), walk across the Golden Water Bridge, which at one time was reserved for the emperor. It leads to the **Palace of Supreme Harmony** (Dien Thai Hoa), the most important palace in the imperial city. Here, the emperor received local dignitaries and foreign diplomats, and the royal court also organised important ceremonies here. Built in 1805 during Gia Long's reign, the palace was renovated first by Min Mang in 1834 and later by Khai Dinh in 1924. Today it stands in excellent condition, its ceilings and beams decorated in red lacquer and gold inlay.

The temples within the enclosure are dedicated to various lords: the temple of **Trieu Mieu** to Nguyen Kim; the **Thai Mieu** to Nguyen Hoang and his successors; the **Phung Tien** temple to the emperors of the reigning dynasty; and the **Hung Mieu** to Nguyen Phuc Lan, emperor Gia Long's father. **The Mieu** is well-preserved – dedicated to the sovereigns of the Nguyen dynasty, it houses the shrines of seven Nguyen emperors plus monuments to the revolutionary emperors Han Nghi, Thanh Thai and Duy Tan, added in 1959.

In front of the temple, completely undamaged, is the magnificent **Pavilion of Splendour** (Hien Lam Cac), with the nine dynastic urns, known as Cuu Dinh, lined up before it. The **Dien Tho** palace, built by emperor Gia Long in 1804, served as the Queen Mother's residence. Beyond the Palace of Supreme Harmony, the **Forbidden Purple City** (Tu Cam Thanh) was reserved solely for the emperor and the royal family. This area was extensively damaged during the Tet Offensive of 1968, but has undergone dubious renovations. The main building in the enclosure is the **Palace of Celestial Perfection** (Can Thanh). The other once-grand palace, Can Chanh, was where the emperor used to receive dignitaries. Sadly, it is now in ruins.

Another world lies beyond the walls of the citadel, which is surrounded in the south and east by Hue's commercial area. This is confined mainly to the area around the arched Trang Tien Bridge, which spans the Perfume River, and the Gia Hoi Bridge. Both bridges lend their names to the areas surrounding them. Located in Phu Cat, with its mainly Chinese and Minh Huong (Vietnamese-Chinese)

Weather-beaten stone statues line the courtyards of the Imperial City.

Huyen Khong Cave in the Marble Mountains.

China Beach, famous for its white sand, pounding surf and as the landing site for US Marines in 1965.

population, is the lively **Dong Ba Market** (much of which is now a shopping centre), which has been around since the beginning of the 20th century.

The **Hue Historical and Revolutionary Museum** (Bao Tang Tong Hop; Tue–Sun 7.30–11am, 1.30–5pm; free) was opened in 1975 and showcases archaeological artefacts from the Champa and Sa Huynh epochs in the central building. To the left and right are museums of the first (French) and second (American) Indochina wars. Missiles, tanks and other weaponry guard the courtyard.

Southeast of Trang Tien Bridge is the **Royal Antiquities Museum** (Cunh An Dinh; daily 7am–5pm; charge) at 150 Nguyen Hue Street, which occupies the former private residence of Emperor Khai Dinh.

Royal tombs and pagodas

Unlike the other dynasties, the Nguyen did not bury its deceased in their native village (Gia Mieu, in Thanh Hoa Province). Instead, their imperial tombs lie scattered on the hillsides on either side of the Perfume

The Khai Dinh Tomb outside Hue.

River to the south of Hue. Although the dynasty had 13 kings, only seven of them reigned until their deaths, and it is these who are laid to rest in this valley of kings. The tombs are just a short distance from the city and can be reached by bicycle, by taxi or, in some cases, by boat.

Minh Mang's Tomb (all tombs open daily 8am–5pm; charge) is located at the point where the Ta Trach and Huu Trach tributaries of the Perfume River meet. Begun a year before his death, in 1840, it was finished by his successor Thieu Tri in 1843. The setting is at its best in mid-March, when the Trung Minh and Tan Nguyet lakes blossom with a mass of beautiful lotus flowers.

Tu Duc's Tomb, 8km (5 miles) southwest of Hue, built in 1864–7, can be accessed by a pleasant cycle ride through pine forests and lush hills. **Thieu Tri's Tomb** is nearby. Thieu Tri, Minh Mang's son, was the third Nguyen emperor from 1841 to 1847.

Khai Dinh's Tomb (daily 8am– 5pm; charge) is completely different from any of the other Nguyen tombs.

If anything, it resembles a European castle, its architecture a blend of the oriental and occidental. A grandiose dragon staircase leads up to the first courtyard, from where further stairs lead to a courtyard lined with stone statues of elephants, horses, civil and military mandarins.

Gia Long's Tomb (daily, 8am–5pm; charge), 16km (10 miles) from Hue on a hillside, is somewhat inaccessible by road. However, a more pleasant way to reach the tomb is by boat. The tomb, began in 1814, was completed a year after the emperor's death in 1820.

Danang

The 110km (68-mile) route from Hue to Danang, via the 1,200-metre (4,000ft) **Hai Van pass** ❹, is one of the most spectacular in Vietnam. The 3.5 hour drive (by private car only) on Highway A1 follows a vertiginous route up, down and around mountains that hug the coast.

A highlight of **Danang** ❺, Vietnam's fourth-largest city, is the **Museum of Cham Sculpture** (Bao Tang Dieu Khac Champa; daily 8am–5pm; charge). It has the world's largest display of artefacts from the Cham people, whose temples can be seen not far away at My Son (see page 212).

Several bridges connect Danang over the Han River with the beach. **China Beach** is the name given by American servicemen to the beautiful 30km (19-mile) stretch of white-sand beach: this was where US marines first landed in 1965.

For nearly three decades following the war, much of the beach remained deserted. But not any more. Investors have bought up tracts of prime beachfront. Several upmarket hotels, such as the Furama Resort, are now well-established, and more are always on the way.

Montgomerie Links (www.montgomerielinks.com) 18-hole golf course, between Non Nuoc and An Bang beaches, sits across the street from the many beach resorts. Designed by and named after the Scottish golf ace Colin Montgomerie, there are several luxury villas on site.

About 11km (7 miles) south of Danang stand five large hills known as the **Marble Mountains** (Ngu Hanh Son). Each hill is named after one of the five Taoist elements. Their caves were once used by Cham people and now shelter altars dedicated to the Buddha, various bodhisattvas and local deities. The highest cave, **Huyen Khong**, has a small tunnel that leads to the very top of the hill, where there is a lookout with views of the sea and the countryside.

Hoi An

Located 25km (15 miles) southeast of Danang on the banks of the Thu Bon River is the ancient town of **Hoi An** ❻, It was once a seaport for the ancient Champa kingdom. Today it is a relaxed town of around 120,000, 10 percent of whom live in the **Old Quarter**, a Unesco World Heritage Site that has become a showpiece for tourists. Unfortunately many of Hoi An's monuments are threatened by annual floods (mainly in October and

Linh Ung Pagoda, Danang.

A market in Hoi An.

TIP

Note: the route to My Son is quite far and winds through the countryside, so it's better to book a tour in Hoi An or Danang. Seeing all the temples requires a significant amount of walking, so be sure to wear comfortable shoes and a hat.

A Hoi An restaurant.

November) when the water spills over the river banks and submerges streets in up to 3 metres (10ft) of water, causing serious damage.

Many of the Old Quarter's older homes, with their wooden beams, carved doors and airy, open rooms, have been turned into souvenir shops masquerading as museums. While it's certainly the old architecture that draws the tourist buses, there's no denying that shopping is the new heart and soul of Hoi An. Bespoke tailor shops are found everywhere, and its not uncommon to see tourists lugging entire suitcases filled with newly tailored suits and dresses. In fact, some worry that the very thing that makes Hoi An attractive – its quiet charm and peaceful atmosphere – is being ruined. Nearly all the buildings in the Old Town have been turned into shops or restaurants, and about 80 percent of the residents now directly derive their income from tourism.

An admission ticket (sold by various tourist offices around the perimeter of the Old Town) gains you entry to one each of four museums, four old houses, three assembly halls, the Handicraft Workshop (with traditional music performance) and either the Japanese Bridge or the Quan Cong Temple. The complicated system is designed so that you need to purchase a total of four tickets to see everything – something people rarely do. Most sites are open daily from 7am–6pm. Although many of the old Hoi An homes have been restored over the years, they retain their original wooden framework, distinctive crab-shell ceilings, carved doors and windows, and decorative stuccos. Many of the houses also contain rare antiques from China, Japan and France, as well as Vietnam.

Just 5km (3 miles) from Hoi An is the broad silvery expanse of **Cua Dai Beach**. This is where to find Nam Hai, Vietnam's most exclusive hotel. There are also a number of elegant villas on this palm-fringed shore.

My Son

My Son ❼ (daily 7am–4.30pm; charge), tucked under the green slopes of Cat's Tooth Mountain (Nui Rang Meo) some 50km (31 miles) from Hoi

An, is the site of Vietnam's most important Cham monuments. It was declared a Unesco World Heritage Site in 1999 and is one of the most atmospheric locations anywhere in the country, with crumbling ruins set in a verdant jungle. Chosen as a religious sanctuary by King Bhadravarman I in the 4th century, many temples (*kalan*) were built in this area. Most were dedicated to kings and Brahman divinities, especially the god Shiva, considered the creator and defender of the Champa kingdom.

According to legend, the Cham towers were ingeniously constructed from raw bricks and fired in a giant 'bonfire'. Research has shown the bricks were actually bonded using a vegetable resin (*dau rai*), allowing them to withstand the onslaught of time and the elements, but not, however, the Vietnam War. In 1969, American B-52s bombed the temples, where the Viet Cong had established a base and mined the valley. Many ancient buildings were damaged or completely destroyed.

There are 11 designated temple groups in My Son, and there are likely to be other groups of ruins that are either unpublicised or undiscovered. As you walk among these ancient structures, imagine them humming with monks' incantations. At the height of the Champa kingdom, only a handful of attendants would have resided here, leaving the area a place of quiet mysticism for the gods to live in.

Nha Trang

Beaches. Nightlife. Diving. These three words encapsulate the experience of **Nha Trang** ❽ for most travellers. Vietnam's favourite party town has many hidden charms, however, for those who delve deeper and explore its museums, aquariums and rich ethnic culture. Nha Trang is serviced by daily flights from Hanoi, Danang and Ho Chi Minh City, placing an idyllic beach holiday within easy reach when these big cities start to grate.

With a population of about 392,000, it has grown from a relatively

run-down little beach town to an internationally recognised holiday destination and the fifth-largest city in Vietnam. Nha Trang is developing rapidly and each year the buildings climb higher and spread further down the beach. The Russians have also colonized the town, now with regular direct flights from cities like Vladivostok. Nha Trang has a stunning location, bordered by mountains on one side and a beautiful stretch of beach on the other. There are always visitors basking away in the warm sun. Cool breezes blow through popular beach spots fronted by bars and restaurants, such as the famous Sailing Club and Louisiane Brewhouse. Upmarket resorts like the plush Evason Ana Mandara shield their patrons from the persistent hawkers selling fruit, barbecued seafood and sunglasses.

But there is also a lot to see. On a hill above the Cai River, at the city's northern entrance, stand the majestic towers of the famous Cham sanctuary and temple **Po Nagar** (daily 8am–6pm; charge). The 25-metre (82ft) main tower is dedicated to the Cham

Cham ruins deep in the jungle at My Son.

Diving in, near Nha Trang.

Dalat is well known for its fresh produce. There are numerous markets, and an abundance of cheap and delicious street food.

Domaine de Marie Convent in Dalat is an example of colonial architecture.

goddess Po Yan Inu Nagar (worshipped by local Buddhists as the goddess Thien Y Ana), the 'Holy Mother' of the Champa kingdom, and considered to be Shiva's female form.

Opposite the Po Nagar Cham towers is a picturesque fishing village called **Xom Bom**. Although the settlement is being chipped away by new resorts moving in, it occupies a remarkable natural harbour punctuated by small islets and boulders. From either Xom Bong Bridge or Tran Phu Bridge, you can watch the blue and red fishing boats returning with their fresh catches; early mornings are best.

Some of Nha Trang's most interesting French colonial architecture and crumbling 19th-century Chinese houses can be seen around **Dam Market** (Cho Dam), near the Cai River. This former Chinese quarter is truly the most underrated part of town. Nha Trang's busy market sees surprisingly few foreign tourists, and is a welcome contrast to the rest of the modernised city – and a great place to snack on local foods.

Dalat

Some five or six hours (205km/127 miles) from Nha Trang, at an altitude of 1,500 metres (4,920ft), is the bracing cool mountain town of **Dalat ❾**. The large open spaces, picturesque waterfalls, colonial architecture and incredibly fresh produce provide respite for those wishing to escape the heat and humidity of Ho Chi Minh City and the lowlands of southern Vietnam. It is easy to see why the colonial French, who developed it as a hill station and sanatorium, were so enamoured of Dalat and why it was the favourite getaway for the last emperor, Bao Dai.

These days the city has a population of around 209,000, but it has retained its laid back charms. With many gardens and lakes, it is a wonderful place to explore on foot – although you run the risk of getting thoroughly lost in the narrow streets that wrap around the hill.

For those seeking culture and exotic adventures, Dalat is also the gateway to the central highlands area where hill-tribe villages abound. The 'garden city' lies in an agricultural region that

produces fruit and vegetables in abundance, and makes red and white wine. Annual temperatures range between a comfortable 16°C (61°F) and 24°C (75°F), making Dalat Vietnam's most popular fair-weather retreat and its top honeymoon destination. The dry-weather months run from December to April, while the wet season is from May to November.

The hill resort was built around the grand **Langbian Palace Hotel** in the early years of the 20th century, a historic hotel that was renovated and reopened as the Sofitel Dalat Palace (now simply, the Dalat Palace) in 1995. The **Hôtel du Parc**, diagonally opposite, followed in 1932. Both hotels have changed management and branding several times over the years.

Dalat's **Central Market** (Cho Da Lat; daily 6am–10pm) is one of the largest in the country, and one of the city's principal attractions. Set in a deep hollow of a hillside and surrounded by rows of cafés and shops selling wine and candied fruit, the current market was built in 1960s. On Saturdays and Sundays from 7–10pm, the streets surrounding the market are closed to vehicles and a carnival-like atmosphere ensues with an influx of pedestrians, souvenir and clothing pedlars, and more food vendors.

Xuan Huong Lake (Ho Xuan Huong) extends through the heart of the town. On the northern banks of the lake, a golf course built for the last emperor, Bao Dai, has been supplanted and expanded into the Dalat Palace Golf Club (www.vietnamgolfresorts.com). The 18-hole championship course is a sister club to the Ocean Dunes Golf Club in Phan Thiet.

The **Summer Palace of Bao Dai** (Biet Dien Quoc Truong; daily 7.30–11am and 1.30–4pm; charge) is tucked under pine trees on a hill in Trieu Viet Vuong Street. This Art Deco-influenced abode of Vietnam's last emperor was built in 1938. Also referred to as Dinh III, this is one of three palaces (neither Dinh I and Dinh II is currently open to the public) belonging to Bao Dai. It's said that tunnels connect all three so that the emperor could secretly visit his mistresses in each one.

The Elephant Falls is located in verdant countryside outside Dalat.

EVER-EVOLVING MUI NE

In 1995, when it was declared to be the best spot in Vietnam to view the solar eclipse, Mui Ne Beach caught the attention of resort developers looking for fresh territory to stake out. Within a few years, this obscure little fishing community nestled in a coconut grove had morphed into the premier beach-resort capital of Vietnam. Then in 2004, when the Boxing Day Tsunami struck Southeast Asia, it initiated another turning point for Vietnam: the Russian invasion. Scores of Russian tourists who used to vacation in Thailand suddenly came to Vietnam instead. Henceforth, Mui Ne has become a favourite spot of Russian tourists in particular. Activities on offer include kiteboarding, as well as simple sunbathing and bar-hopping.

Neon-lit Ben Thanh Market.

HO CHI MINH CITY

Once known as Saigon – and still called so by many residents – and former capital of South Vietnam, Ho Chi Minh City is the entrepreneurial heart of the country and centre of Vietnamese pop-culture.

Built on the site of an ancient Khmer city, the area now covered by sprawling **Ho Chi Minh City** ⓾ (HCMC; Thanh Pho Ho Chi Minh) was, until the 17th century, a thinly populated malarial backwater of forests, swamps and lakes. Yet thanks to a strategic riverside location close to the coast, it became an important trading centre in the following century. ""

In the 19th century, southern Vietnam continued to prosper. In 1859, the French captured Saigon and it became the capital of the French colony of Cochinchina a couple of years later. The French filled in the ancient canals, drained marshlands, built roads, laid out streets and quarters, and planted trees. The city developed rapidly, acquiring something of the character of a French provincial town, served by two steam-powered trams.

After the division of the country in 1954 into North Vietnam and South Vietnam, Saigon became the capital of the Republic of South Vietnam, a status maintained until the city fell to the Communists in April of 1975.

The revolutionary authorities renamed it Ho Chi Minh City, after the founder of the modern Vietnamese state. Ho Chi Minh was, of course, anathema to supporters of the

Ho Chi Minh City is one of the region's most polluted cities.

southern regime that lost the war. To many of its 7 million inhabitants, the city remains Saigon.

Downtown Saigon

Some 50km (30 miles) inland from the coast, Vietnam's largest city and river port sprawls across an area of 2,000 sq km (760 sq miles) on the banks of the Saigon River. The French presence remains in this southern city, lingering not only in the minds of the older generation but physically in the legacy of colonial architecture, and in

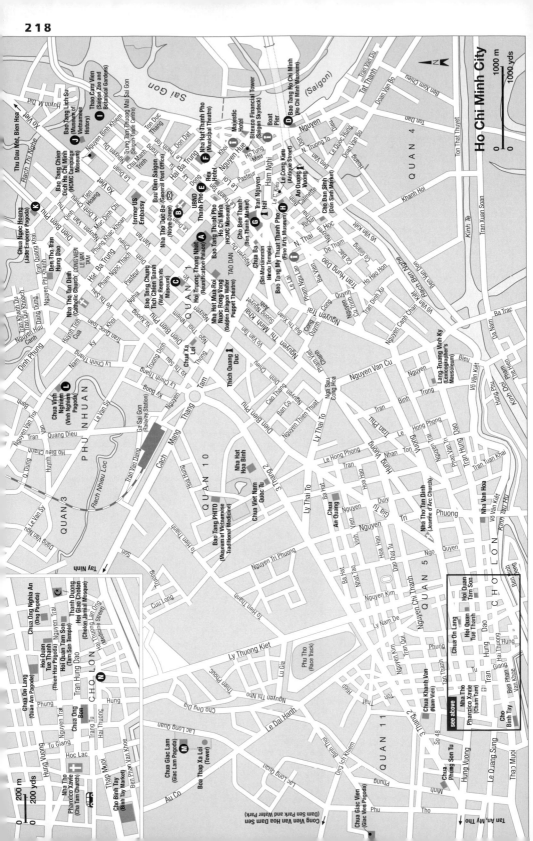

the long, tree-lined avenues, streets and highways they left behind.

Prominently located in the city's District (Quan) 1 is a building that symbolises – to the Communists – the decadence of the Saigon regime. The former Presidential Palace of South Vietnam is now called **Reunification Palace** Ⓐ (Hoi Truong Thong Nhat; www.dinhdoclap.gov.vn; daily 7.30–11am, 1–4pm; charge includes guide). Surrounded by extensive gardens, this large and modern edifice rests on the site of the former French governor's residence, the Norodom Palace, which dated back to 1868. After the Geneva Agreement put an end to French occupation, the new president of South Vietnam, Ngo Dinh Diem, installed himself in the palace and called it Independence Palace. In 1962, the palace was bombed by two South Vietnamese air force officers and a new building was erected to replace the damaged structure. The present building was designed by Ngo Viet Thu, a Paris-trained Vietnamese architect, and completed in 1966.

The left wing of the palace was damaged by another renegade South Vietnamese pilot in early 1975, and before the month was out, on 30 April, tanks from the Communist forces crashed through the palace's front wrought-iron gates and overthrew the South Vietnamese government – the tanks are now displayed on the front lawn.

Today, the former palace can be visited as a museum, with everything left much as it was in April 1975 when South Vietnam ceased to exist. The ground floor includes the banquet room, the state chamber, and the cabinet room, which was used for daily military briefings during the period leading up to the overthrow of the South Vietnamese government. Behind the palace is Cong Vien Van Hao Park, a nice and shady green spot. In front, Le Duan is bordered by a large park shaded with trees.

Further down Le Duan is the **Cathedral of Notre Dame** Ⓑ (Nha Tho Duc Ba; daily 7am–10pm), with two bell towers, standing in the square across from the post office. Construction of this cathedral began in 1877, and it was consecrated in 1880. A statue of the Virgin Mary in front of the cathedral, looks down Dong Khoi Street.

Across the street, the main **Post Office** (Buu Dien Saigon; daily 7am–10pm) at 2 Cong Xa Paris, with its gingerbread facade, has been repainted and repaired but retains its old tile floors, wooden writing tables and benches, and a map of Saigon in 1892.

The former War Crimes Exhibition, now the **War Remnants Museum** Ⓒ (Bao Tang Chung Tich Chien Tranh; daily 7.30am–noon and 1.30–5pm; charge) occupies the former U.S. Information Agency building on Vo Van Tan Street, near the Reunification Palace. Among items on display here are American tanks, infantry weapons, photographs of war atrocities committed by the Americans, and the original French guillotine brought to Vietnam in the 20th century, which saw a lot of use during the colonial period. Graphic pictures

Ho Chi Minh City's Cathedral of Notre Dame.

The Post Office is also a tourist attraction.

of deformed children illustrate the effects of chemical defoliants such as Agent Orange. Although a visit here is likely to be distressing, it is a sobering reminder of the human cost of war and is obligatory for many visitors.

The **Ho Chi Minh City Museum**  (Bao Tang Thanh Pho Ho Chi Minh; Tue–Sun 7.30–11.30am and 1.30–5pm; charge), one block east from the Reunification Palace on Ly Tu Trong Street, is found in a white neoclassical structure once known as Gia Long Palace. The walls of the former ballrooms of this colonial edifice are now hung with pictures of the war, and there are displays of the flat-bottomed boats in which Viet Cong soldiers hid guns.

A network of reinforced concrete bunkers stretching all the way to the Reunification Palace lies beneath the building. Within this underground network were living areas and a meeting hall. It was here that President Diem and his brother hid in the early 1960s just before they fled to a church in Cholon, where they were captured and subsequently shot.

The Ho Chi Minh City Fine Arts Museum.

If the Reunification Palace is a symbol of the former South Vietnam regime, then the **City Hall** Ⓔ (UBND Thanh Pho), at the top of Nguyen Hue Street, is the symbol of the French colonial era. It was finished in 1908 after almost 16 years of ferment over its style and situation. Its ornate facade and equally ornate interior, complete with crystal chandeliers and wall-size murals, is now the headquarters of the Ho Chi Minh City People's Committee. Illuminated at night, the building is a lure for insect-hungry geckos.

Across the street is the **Rex Hotel**, (Khach San Rex; www.rexhotelvietnam. com), originally a French garage, it opened as a government hotel in 1976. Its fifth-floor Rooftop Garden Restaurant and Bar has great views. Nearby is a plaza with a statue of Ho Chi Minh posing as 'every child's Uncle Ho'. The plaza is crowded on weekend nights.

Nguyen Hue is a broad boulevard lined with fancy hotels and upscale restaurants. This area of town buzzes with energy, especially at night. At the corner of Le Loi, there is another plaza with a fountain that is crowded

SAIGON: WHAT'S IN A NAME?

When the newly formed Socialist Republic of Vietnam compelled Saigon to take the name of Ho Chi Minh City in 1976, it was like rubbing salt into the wounds of its inhabitants. Today, many locals still defiantly refer to their city as Saigon as a matter of principle (and prefer to call themselves Saigonese). At the very least, people use the name Saigon for downtown District 1, one of the first sectors of the city to be built and the original French Quarter. Although great measures have been taken – even to this day – to wipe away the Saigon name in most official capacities (some publications, for example, are not allowed to use the Saigon title), it is still, confusingly, allowed to be used in some forms: notably, the river winding its way around the city remains Saigon River, the main city newspaper is the *Saigon Times* and the city's state-owned tour company is Saigontourism. Place names like Saigon Zoo, Port of Saigon and Saigon Railway Station are still in use, and the three-letter ticket code for the city's Tan Son Nhat International Airport is SGN. No wonder visitors get confused. Similarly, the government has renewed bans on tourist signs written in English as well as place-names that mention China (such as 'China Beach' and the 'South China Sea').

with a carnival-like atmosphere into the evenings. Near the end of Le Loi is the **Municipal Theatre** ⑥ (Nha Hat Thanh Pho), which faces Dong Khoi Street between the Caravelle and the Continental hotels. The theatre was built in 1899 for opera, but was used as the fortress headquarters of the South Vietnam National Assembly. These days, it serves its original purpose, with occasional classical music and dance performances: well worth experiencing for the sense of occasion and as the only opportunity to see inside.

South of Downtown

At the junction of Ham Nghi, Le Loi and Tran Hung Dao boulevards, in the centre of town, is the busy **Ben Thanh Market** ⑥ (Cho Ben Thanh; daily 6.30am–6.30pm). The market covers over 11,000 sq metres (120,000 sq ft) and was opened in 1914. Here is an amazing collection of produce, meat, foods, cell phones, flowers, cameras, calculators, fans, jeans, counterfeit brands, leather bags, and all manner of souvenirs. Outside the market, the streets become a popular evening food spot for seafood and local fare.

Not far from the Ben Thanh Market, down Duc Chinh Street, is the **Ho Chi Minh City Fine Arts Museum** ⑥ (Bao Tang My Thuat Thanh Pho Ho Chi Minh; Tue–Sun 9am–5pm; charge). Housed in a grand colonial-era building, the collection of ancient and contemporary Vietnamese arts is small and disappointing.

The **Mariamman Hindu Temple**, three blocks from the Ben Thanh Market and on Truong Dinh Street, was built at the end of the 19th century and caters to the city's small population of Hindu Tamils.

North of Downtown

At the end of Le Duan, the **Saigon Zoo and Botanical Gardens** ⑥ (Thao Cam Vien; www.saigonzoo.net) provides a welcome alternative to the noisy chaos of the streets and constitutes the most peaceful place in Ho Chi Minh City. The attractive gardens were established in 1864 by two Frenchmen – one a botanist, the other a veterinarian – as one of the first projects the

Snake and scorpion wine at Ben Thanh Market.

A statue of the city's namesake outside City Hall.

Detail at Giac Lam Pagoda.

The Jade Emperor Pagoda.

French embarked upon after they established their new colony. It has some 800 specimens from 120 species as well as 2,000 trees. Animal feeding times are usually 3–5pm and there are elephant shows at weekends.

The **Museum of Vietnamese History** (Bao Tang Lich Su; Tue–Sun 8–11.30am and 1.30–5pm; charge), located to the left of the entrance of the botanical gardens, is an excellent museum for those suffering from war fatigue, inside a building built by the French in 1927. The museum documents the evolution of Vietnam's cultures, from the Dong Son Bronze Age through to the Funan, Chams and Khmers. A small attached outdoor theatre, **Saigon Water Puppets** (Mua Roi Nuoc; Tue–Sun) gives half-hourly performances.

To the right of the entrance is the Den Hung, a temple dedicated to the ancestors of Hung Vuong, founding king of Vietnam.

The Sino-Vietnamese **Jade Emperor Pagoda** (Chua Ngoc Hoang; daily 8am–5pm; free), at 73 Mai Thi Luu, dates from 1909. It was built by Cantonese Buddhists and is one of the city's most colourful pagodas. The elaborately-robed and Daoist Jade Emperor surveys the main sanctuary. Just to his left is the triple-headed, 18-armed statue of Phat Mau Chau De, mother of the Buddhas of the Middle, North, East, West and South. A door off to the left of the Jade Emperor's chamber leads to the Hall of Ten Hells, where carved wooden panels portray, in no uncertain detail, the fate that awaits those sentenced to the torments found in the 10 regions of hell.

The Buddhist **Vinh Nghiem Pagoda** (Chua Vinh Nghiem; daily 8am–5pm; free) at 339 Nguyen Van Troi, District 3, is the largest of the pagodas in the city. Built with aid from the Japanese Friendship Association, this Japanese-style pagoda was begun in 1964 and finished in 1973. The temple's screen and large bell were made in Japan. The bell, a gift from Japanese Buddhists, was presented during the Vietnam War as the embodiment of a prayer for an early end to the conflict. The large three-storey funeral tower behind the main temple holds

ceramic burial urns containing ashes of the dead.

The **Giac Lam Pagoda**  (Chua Giac Lam; daily 8am–6pm; free) on the western outskirts of the city and thought to be the city's oldest, dates to the end of the 17th century. Carved wooden pillars within the main building bear gilded inscriptions in old Vietnamese *nom* characters, which have also been used on the red tablets that record the biographies of the monks of previous generations, whose portraits adorn the left wall. The pagoda houses many beautifully carved jackwood statues.

Cholon

Ho Chi Minh City's Chinatown, **Cholon** , was formerly a separate city, but it is now in Ho Chi Minh City's District 5, spilling into Districts 6, 10 and 11, thanks to the outward growth of the suburbs. Cholon remains a thriving commercial centre in its own right. With a population of over 1 million Hoa – Vietnamese of Chinese origin – Cholon has come a long way since 1864, when it was home to just

6,000 Chinese (mostly shopkeepers or traders), 200 Indians and 40,000 Vietnamese. Some historical shop houses and colonial buildings are now being demolished or have fallen into disrepair, and the once-atmospheric canal is being developed, though the smell can be overpowering. Nonetheless, Cholon is still a fascinating and authentic commercial and residential area.

Two temples can be visited on Nguyen Trai Street, near Cholon. At number 710 is the richly-decorated Chua **Thien Hau**, (Heavenly Lady Pagoda; daily 8am–5pm; free), more commonly known as Chua Ba (Women's Pagoda). Dedicated to the Goddess Protector of Sailors, it was built by Cantonese Buddhists at the end of the 18th century. As one would expect, the temple is mainly frequented by women. One altar is dedicated to the protection of women and newborn babies, another to childless mothers. The smaller **Ha Chuong Pagoda** (Chua Ha Chuong), at number 802, contains several wooden sculptures and statues, including a statue of the god of happiness and an altar for sterile women.

Typical buildings in Cholon.

The legacy of war

The war may be over, but its aftermath is omnipresent. From rusty bullets for sale in shops to the politics of international relations, the war's impact can still be felt.

In the years following the war with the US, Vietnam survived largely in isolation from the West. From 1975 until 1994 it was illegal for US firms to trade with Vietnam, with the only form of help coming from Soviet quarters, up until the late 1980s. But by the early 1990s, relations with America were thawing and in 1995 formal diplomatic relations were restored by the then US president Bill Clinton. In 2000 Clinton became the first US head of state to visit the country since the war, which played a large part in normalising relations. A raft of trade deals has since been signed that has catapulted Vietnam's economy forwards, and by the end of 2011 bilateral trade

Tourist on the firing range at Cu Chi Tunnels.

would reach US$20 billion, a 10 percent rise on 2010's figures.

In addition to economics, it is in both the US's and Vietnam's strategic interests to remain close, even if only to help keep rival China in check. Nonetheless, while Vietnam values its relationship with the US for financial reasons, it walks a fine line as it must be careful not to allow its growing US links to damage its ties with China. Vietnam therefore views a relationship with the US as a useful buffer against any Chinese aggression, while paradoxically looking to repair relations with China. This delicate balancing act, amid US calls for improved human rights, has placed limits on how far the relationship with the USA can progress.

Interest in the war

Nonetheless, despite the healthy trade relations and Vietnam's welcoming attitude to tourists – be they American, British or French – it would be a mistake to think that all is forgotten and forgiven. The war is still within living memory of many Vietnamese and Americans, and there are scars on both sides that will take generations to heal. Still, most Vietnamese have few qualms about discussing the war and tourists should not consider it a taboo subject. Indeed, it would be virtually impossible to visit Vietnam and not have a conversation about the country's recent history.

The war has an influence on nearly everyone. Its effects on the physical landscape around the DMZ are clear, from the devastating impact of Agent Orange on local fields to the still-visible bomb craters and, more significantly, the thousands of landmines that may still lie undiscovered. For some, the war remnants offer an entrepreneurial edge as they sell fake war medals and memorabilia to tourists – and some war sites (notably the Cu Chi Tunnels near Ho Chi Minh City) are full-scale tourist attractions.

Interest in the war is inevitable and Vietnam does its best to oblige, even toning down some of the jingoistic propaganda. A case in point is the museum in Ho Chi Minh City originally known as 'The House for Displaying War Crimes of American Imperialism and the Puppet Government'. This was later changed to the slightly less inflammatory 'Museum of American War Crimes' and today it's known far more euphemistically as the War Remnants Museum.

Another factor is the inevitable change as the country develops and new generations grow up. Younger citizens seem happy to embrace Western ideals. Many are now pushing traditional boundaries in terms of lifestyle choices, while the number of English-language schools is proof of how important the tourist industry has become. Maybe the biggest post-war change has come in terms of attitudes to the West. Ask Vietnamese teenagers whom they most admire today and they are more likely to name an English Premier League footballer than Uncle Ho (Chi Minh).

The war in literature and film

Among the numerous books on the war, several stand out. *A Bright Shining Lie* by Neil Sheehan (Pimlico, 1998) tells of the journalist's conversations with Lt Col John Paul Vann, who was so appalled by the incompetence of the South Vietnamese and US generals that he started briefing reporters on what was really happening. *Dispatches* by Michael Herr (Picador, 1991) details the hundreds of notes that Herr, a former journalist, amassed after front-line reporting in Vietnam. The result is a part-fictitious, part-factual narrative that brilliantly captures the swirling, horrific mess of war. Robert Timburg's *The Nightingale's Song* (Simon &

Schuster, 1995) looks at the experiences of several notable veterans, including author Oliver Stone and US politician John McCain, while *Born on the Fourth of July* (2005, Akashic) details the memoirs of Ron Kovic, who was paralysed by a bullet. The book was later made into a movie of the same name. *Vietnam: Rising Dragon* by Bill Hayton (Yale University Press, 2010) gives a comprehensive overview of contemporary Vietnamese history.

Perhaps the ultimate Vietnam war movie is actually based on a book about Africa. *Apocalypse Now* is Francis Ford Coppola's seminal film, and is heavily influenced by Joseph Conrad's Heart of Darkness. Marlon Brando plays Kurtz, a colonel who has lost his mind due to the horrors of war. *Full Metal Jacket*, director Stanley Kubrick's tale of a teenage recruit who ends up in Hue during the 1968 Tet Offensive, is a powerful and brutally blunt, no-holds-barred vision of war. Kubrick's film tells the story from a soldier's perspective, as does *Platoon*, another violent and gripping tale. *Hamburger Hill* is based on the 101st Airborne Division's disastrous assault on the heavily fortified hill' deep within the jungle.

My Lai Massacre exhibit at the War Remnants Museum in Ho Chi Minh City.

A FEAST OF FRUITS

There is a sizeable range of fruits in Southeast Asia, many of which may be unfamiliar. As well as bananas and pineapples, there are brilliantly coloured and strangely shaped varieties for the adventurous.

In Asia, afternoon snacks usually involve an incredible variety of fruits. For visitors who are in need of a boost, fruit can be a great source of refreshment and energy. Traditional fruit sellers have glass-fronted carts stacked with blocks of ice and peeled pieces of seasonal fruits. Choose a selection of what you want to eat and the vendor will pop it into a bag for you along with a toothpick for spearing the slices. Some fruits, like pineapple, are eaten with a little salt and ground chilli, a twist of which is supplied separately. Don't be afraid of this combination – the natural sweetness of the pineapple is enhanced by this bitter condiment, surprisingly enough.

One of the best ways to cool down is to drink a delicious fruit juice. Another favourite drink is fruit juice blended with ice, what Westerners might call a fruit 'smoothie'. You can have syrup mixed in to sweeten your juice or add salt (as the Thais do) to bring out the flavour of the fruit.

People either love or hate durian. Ask any visitor to those Southeast Asian countries where durians are popular (nearly all) to recall the first time they came across it and they will describe, in detail, its 'perfume'. To most foreigners the durian's odour is repugnant, but in Asia the fruit commands the utmost respect, even if most hotels prohibit them in hotel rooms.

The hairy rambutan (rambut means hair in Malay) is a close relative of the lychee, and its translucent, sweet flesh has a similar taste. There is a technique to squeezing it open to avoid squirting yourself with its juices.

Dragon fruit, also known as pitaya fruit, has a refreshing, light sweet taste. Native to Central America, it is grown throughout the region, most notably in Vietnam.

The only way to enter the great durian debate is to try it for yourself. If you can't face eating the fruit *au naturel* there is durian cake, ice-cream and chewing gum.

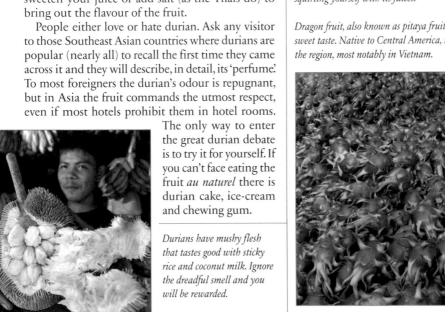

Durians have mushy flesh that tastes good with sticky rice and coconut milk. Ignore the dreadful smell and you will be rewarded.

Farming by the Mekong River in Northeast Thailand.

THAILAND'S GROWING CONCERN

Farming and fishing have always been at the centre of Thai life. Despite rapid industrialisation, this is still the case. Thailand is self-sufficient in food, and agribusiness is an important pillar of the Thai economy, accounting for nearly a quarter of GDP and making Thailand Asia's main net food exporter. Thailand is also the world's leading exporter of canned pineapple and has large overseas markets in canned logans and rambutans.

Fruit production is expected to increase as available land and labour resources dwindle and farmers switch from producing staple crops, such as rice and cassava, to cash crops like soya beans, fruits, sugar cane and rubber. Large fruit farmers are starting to process their products before they reach the consumer, and many are now applying for loans to invest in equipment to dry and freeze their produce. Although some of this produce will be sold to Thailand's neighbours, much of it will end up in the snack food departments of Japanese supermarkets – Japanese businesses have already set up factories in Thailand to process fruits, vegetables and nuts for their home market.

…ake fruit, as found in Bali, are the size of a fig and resemble …lic cloves when peeled. The taste is generally sweet and acidic.

…marillos, sometimes known as tree tomatoes for their …pearance, for sale by the roadside in Ubud, Bali.

Custard apples and mangoes for sale, downtown Yangon, Myanmar.

Crossing the FRIM canopy walkway in Selangor, near Kuala Lumpur.

A rainy night in the urban metropolis of Kuala Lumpur.

Walking at sunset in Penang.

MALAYSIA

One of Southeast Asia's most progressive
countries, Malaysia is a fascinating ensemble of
different cultures and awe-inspiring nature.

*A traditionally dressed
Kadazan dancer, Kota
Kinabalu.*

Situated in the equatorial heart of Southeast Asia, Malaysia is home to a polyglot and multi-ethnic people who have guided their country to prosperity and stability. Malays and indigenous tribes make up over half the population, while the sizeable numbers of Chinese, Indians and others also form part of the cultural and ethnic spectrum that is 'Malaysian'. Meanwhile, about 30 percent of the forested land and the surrounding seas of this richly endowed nation are protected repositories of the world's most precious biodiversity.

Peninsular Malaysia accounts for 40 percent of the land area and 70 percent of the population. Separated from the peninsula by the South China Sea – and in many ways almost like another country – are the East Malaysian states of Sabah and Sarawak. These are on the island of Borneo, which Malaysia shares with Indonesia.

Since independence from the British in 1957, the country has faced a series of economic and political pitfalls and triumphs. Perhaps the biggest achievement is a complete transformation of the economy from commodity dependence to a broad manufacturing base. The government is promoting service sectors such as trade, finance and tourism, whilst at the same time attempting to balance economic growth with environmental sustainability and unity among the country's different ethnic groups.

*Roof detail on Khoo Kongsi in
George Town, Penang.*

Kuala Lumpur possesses some of the world's most striking buildings, as well as traffic jams to rival Manhattan's. But the past, in the form of pre-war shophouses and elaborate festivals, sits comfortably within this modernity. The island of Penang maintains old-fashioned elegance in its 18th-century capital, George Town, a Unesco World Heritage Site. Across the sea, Sarawak and Sabah are breathtaking in both their natural grandeur and the ancient rainforest-based traditions of their numerous indigenous peoples.

DECISIVE DATES

Early centuries

300 BC
Advent of Bronze and Iron Age cultures in Malaysia.

200 BC
Trading contacts established with India and China.

AD 500–800
Development of Hindu-Buddhist culture.

1402
Foundation of Malacca maritime empire by Sumatran prince.

1445
Malacca adopts Islam, becomes a sultanate, controls world trade.

The colonial period

1511
Portuguese colonise Malacca.

1641
Dutch take Malacca from the Portuguese.

1786
British occupy Penang.

1824
Malacca ceded to the British in exchange for Indonesia.

1826
British limit Thai influence on the peninsula and establish Straits Settlements comprising Malacca, Penang and Singapore.

1840s
The importance of tin increases; British bring in Chinese tin miners.

1841
English trader James Brooke established as Rajah of Sarawak.

Sultan Abu Bakar of Johor in the early 20th century.

1874–1909
British intervene and control the peninsula.

1894
Beginings of local resistance against colonialists in North Borneo.

1920–41
Malay nationalism, opposing British rule, begins to surface.

Malaya, Merdeka, Malaysia

1941–45
Japanese conquest and occupation.

1945
British reoccupy Malaysia.

1946
The Malayan Union, introduced to simplify administration, is opposed by Malay political party UMNO (the United Malay National Organisation); Sarawak and British North Borneo (Sabah) become Crown colonies.

A carved stone wall at A' Famosa fort in Melaka (formerly Malacca).

1948
Federation of Malaya, with 11 states, replaces Malayan Union. Communist insurgency results in a state of emergency declared.

1955
Ethnic-based Alliance Party wins first local elections.

1956
Tunku Abdul Rahman leads a delegation to London to negotiate for independence.

1957
Malaya becomes independent; Tunku is first Prime Minister.

1960
The state of emergency ends.

Post-independence
1963
Creation of Malaysia, comprising Malaya, Singapore, North Borneo and Sarawak.

1963–6
Confrontation with Indonesia.

1965
Singapore leaves Federation.

1969
Politically-motivated civil unrest between Malays and Chinese in the wake of the general elections on 13 May.

1970
New Economic Policy (NEP), established to encourage a fairer distribution of wealth among the races.

The Mahathir era
1981
Malaysia's most influential and powerful prime minister,

Dr Mahathir Mohamad, takes office.

1983–8
Mahathir strips power from sultans, the hereditary rulers; ends judiciary's independence; arrests opposition members and restricts the media.

1988–97
Malaysia experiences double-digit GDP growth, with large-scale industrialisation and ambitious enterprises such as the national car project, Proton, the launch of first satellite and the building of new administrative capital, Putrajaya.

1997
Petronas Twin Towers completed, then the world's tallest buildings. Asian financial crisis slows growth, currency control laws are imposed.

1998
A political crisis is provoked by the arrest of Mahathir's successor, popular deputy prime minister Anwar Ibrahim, on charges of sodomy and corruption.

2003
Mahathir retires and Abdullah Ahmad Badawi is appointed Prime Minister.

2004
Barisan wins elections by a landslide.

Political tsunami
2007
Large street demonstrations show public dissatisfaction with Barisan's administration and policies.

Prime Minister Dato' Sri Mohd Najib Tun Razak.

2008
Elections see the Anwar-led Pakatan Rakyat, win four states and dent Barisan's Parliamentary majority for the first time since independence.

2009
Badawi pressured to step down. Mohd Najib Abdul Razak takes over, shadowed by controversy. Anwar on trial again for sodomy.

2010
Religious tensions increase surrounding Islamic fundamentalism. Three Malay women flogged under Sharia law for extramarital sex.

2011
Police use water cannon and tear gas to disperse thousands of protestors demanding election reform.

2010
Anwar Ibrahim acquitted on sodomy charges.

2013
Malaysian troops clash with Filipino separatists. Thirty people killed.

A Malay fisherman with his boat on the peninsula's east coast.

PEOPLE AND CULTURE

Malaysian multiculturalism is evident in everything from skin tones and speech to festivals and a Dionysian offering of culinary choices.

The cultural diversity of Malaysia has been a long time in the making. It can trace its origins back to the first century AD, when the Malay archipelago became an important link in the developing trading network between Africa and China. The resulting influx of peoples began a process of cultural hybridisation and heterogeneity that has resulted in a colourful, multicultural society.

Today, while Malaysian cultural and societal values are well established – particularly in religion and marriage – borrowings and adaptations are commonplace and creative, influencing daily life from food to dress, social mores to customs, and language to worldview. Malaysians call this *rojak*, after a popular mixed fruit desert – a mixture that is decried by some, celebrated by others, but unavoidable when cultural boundaries are so porous. Therefore, the categorisation of Malaysia's ethnic groups is only a starting point for understanding Malaysian society.

Barbequeing fish at a streetside market in Kota Kinabalu.

Indigenous people

Malaysia's indigenous people encompass a wide variety of ethnic groups and languages. In common with minority groups elsewhere in the world they struggle with land rights issues and identity concerns due to the pressures to conform and integrate into mainstream society.

Peninsular Malaysia's indigenous people are called *orang asli*, which in Malay means 'original people'. As they make up less than 0.4 percent of the population, and tend to live on the margins of society, many Malaysians have never encountered them. There are 18 groups, classified into three main groups – Negrito, Senoi and Aboriginal Malay. The *orang asli* do not

see themselves as homogenous, but, they have banded under this common identity to fight for their rights. Most live on the fringes of, or in urban areas; only a fraction retain their fully traditional lifestyles.

The **Negritos** are the oldest people in Malaysia, having lived in the peninsula's northeast and northwest for at least 25,000 years. Thought to be linked to the Vietnamese Palaeolithic Age people, they are originally nomads. The **Senoi** settled in the middle of the peninsula around 2000 BC. Traditionally farmers, they are the most integrated into mainstream society. In the south are the agrarian **Aboriginal Malays** who arrived about 3,000 years ago; some intermarriage with the island people resulted in a degree of resemblance to, and assimilation with, the majority Malays.

Sabah and Sarawak

The Bornean states of Sabah and Sarawak have an even more diverse indigenous population. Referred to as 'natives', they actually form the majority of the people in East Malaysia, and enjoy strong political representation.

About 60 percent of Sabahans are indigenous, speaking around half of the languages of Malaysia. Of the 39 groups, the largest is the **Kadazandusun**, who live in northwestern and

An orang asli woman.

central Sabah, mainly in urban areas. Mount Kinabalu is their spiritual resting place and their biggest festival is the Kaamatan or Harvest Festival.

The **Murut**, the 'hill people' of northeastern Sabah, were purportedly the last group to give up head-hunting. Most of the coastal-dwellers are made up from the **Bajau** and **Malayic** families, traditionally skilful fishermen and boatmen.

Sarawak is home to 29 ethnic groups, the largest of which is the **Iban**, who migrated from Kalimantan, and so are related to the Borneon Dayaks. Traditionally longhouse dwellers and rice-planters, the Gawai Harvest Festival is their most important cultural celebration.

> *Notwithstanding the ubiquity of jeans and T-shirts, common Malaysian apparel includes the female baju kurung top and sarong. Fridays see Malay men wear baju melayu, complete with a short sarong.*

The **Bidayuh** live in the greater Kuching area while the interior-dwellers are the **Orang Ulu**, the most skilful handicraft-makers and artists in the land. The **Melanau** are coastal folk, famed as sago planters and fishing folk; they have a stronghold on politics in Sarawak. The **Lun Bawang** and **Kelabit** are highland dwellers, while the **Penan** are the arguably Borneo's most famous ethnic group, thanks to international media exposure on the logging of their forest homes.

Malays

The *Melayu* people arrived in the Malay archipelago some 3,000–5,000 years ago from southern China and Taiwan. Over the years they intermarried and assimilated with other groups – Chinese, Indians, Arabs and Thais. Today their ancestors make up the Malay, Indonesian and Filipino communities.

In Malaysia, Malay culture and language show strong Javanese, Sumatran, Siamese and, especially, Indian influence. Linguistically, Malay is Austronesian, but some vocabulary has been absorbed from a slew of other languages, including Arabic, Sanskrit, Tamil, Portuguese, Dutch, Chinese and English.

Making up nearly half the population, a Malay is actually defined in Malaysia's Federal Constitution as one who practises Islam and Malay culture, speaks the Malay language, and whose ancestors are Malays. Malays therefore comprise ethnic backgrounds as diverse as indigenous people in Sabah to Indians in Penang.

Traditionally an agrarian people, many responded to Malaysia's industrialisation in the 1960s by leaving their *kampung* (village) lifestyles for modern, urban living. Today, Malays are a dominant presence in government and key sectors of the economy. The Malay-based UMNO political party has led the government since independence. In daily life, Malay customs are observed, and Islam is key. The main festival is Hari Raya Aidilfitri at the end of the Ramadan fasting month.

Indians

Indian traders arrived in northern Kedah in the first century AD, leaving a lasting influence on Malay culture and language. However, most of today's Malaysian Indians are the descendants of 19th-century indentured workers imported from South Asia by the British to work on the plantations and to a lesser degree, in the civil service.

The majority are Tamil, with smaller numbers of Punjabis, Telugus, Sikhs and Sri Lankans. Largely Hindu, other religions practised include Christianity, Sikhism and Buddhism. Indian Muslims are classified as Malay or mainly in urban areas. Like the Indians, the Chinese presence in Malaysia goes back a long way, linked with maritime trade that began over 1,500 years ago.

Also in common with the Indians, most of today's Malaysian Chinese are descendants of indentured labourers imported by the British in the 19th and 20th centuries. Originally from South China, they worked the peninsula's tin mines, and eventually set up businesses and plantations throughout what would become Malaysia. By the time of independence in 1957, they largely controlled

There is a sizeable Hindu population of Indian descent in Malaysia.

bumiputra. Indians make up Malaysia's largest number of professionals per capita, notably doctors and lawyers. Many also run their own businesses.

Indian culture is a rich and colourful part of Malaysian life: clothing such as *kurtha* tops and the *salwar-khameez* trouser suits are popular, Hindi movies have a huge fanbase, Hindu temples and celebrations such as Thaipusam and Deepavali enrich the collective consciousness, while nothing beats ethnic divide-bridging like banana-leaf curries and Indian tea *(teh tarik)*.

Chinese

The Chinese community makes up around 24 percent of the country's population, living

MALAYSIAN ENGLISH, LAH

Listening to Malaysians speak English can be bewildering. You could get East Coast American or Received Pronunciation or staccato unintelligibility – sometimes from the same person. A British colonial legacy, English is linked to status and education, the language of commerce and science. In cities, it is an emergent *lingua franca* levelling out ethnic differences. There are richly colourful varieties. Grammar is often simplified; for example, '*Came from where?*' translates to 'Where did you just come from?' Malaysian English's most famous inflection, '*lah*', is a filler used to cajole, tease, or signify impatience or firmness.

the economy. The Chinese share of the economic pie has declined a little since then, but they still make up the majority of the middle- and upper-income classes. Comprising three main dialect groups, Cantonese, Hokkien and Hakka, the Chinese are mainly Taoist/Buddhists, or Christian, and their main festival is the Chinese New Year.

The 15th-century Chinese migrants who settled in the Malay peninsula's ports and adopted Malay customs and/or married locals, came to be known as Peranakan, 'local-born', or *Baba-Nonyas*. Aspects of their culture are

Eating on Petaling Street in Kuala Lumpur's Chinatown.

manifest in language (infused with Malay and Thai words), dress (particularly the Malay-influenced sarong *kebaya*), food (strong curries and spicy salads) and architecture (largely Chinese with colonial influences).

Eurasians and other communities

There are small communities of Malaysians of mixed Asian and European ancestry, mainly Portuguese, Dutch and English. Eurasian communities were established in Melaka during the Portuguese colonial period in the 16th–17th centuries. The community there still speaks a distinct form of Portuguese called Kristang. Another sizeable Eurasian community is in Penang, formed by 18th century Thai-Portuguese

migrants. While a minority, the Eurasians played a key role in education and the local establishment of Catholicism.

There are many other smaller communities, and Malaysia's ethnic composition continues to become increasingly more and more complex with the new migrant labourers on which the country has been heavily dependent since the 1970s. Tourists may encounter a Bangladeshi waiter, an Indonesian room cleaner, a German hotel manager, and a Nepali Gurkha security guard.

The state and race

Malaysians live in harmony, but politics is racially prejudiced. The ruling coalition comprises race-based political parties who use ethnic categorisation for colonial-type divide-and-rule purposes. Yet, for tourists, the state projects a perfect-harmony utopia, encapsulated by Tourism Malaysia's tagline, *Malaysia Truly Asia*.

When Malaysia's administration is threatened, its rhetoric darkens with warnings of a scenario of a society on the brink of tribal blood-shedding, particularly by invoking the 'May 13 Incident'. Colonial-era inequalities were not addressed fully at Malaysia's independence and came to haunt the country in this incident.

On 13 May 1969, the ruling alliance led by a Malay political party lost many seats to a largely Chinese-based opposition party. Motivated by political firebrands, civil unrest broke out between the two ethnic groups. The New Economic Policy came in the aftermath to address ethnic and economic inequality and to eradicate poverty by developing the economy. A key element of the Policy were affirmative action rights for Malays.

Political and institutional racism has been a problem, but worse since the ruling coalition suffered historic losses during the 2008 general elections; alarming tactics have been deployed to ratchet up racial tension.

On the whole, though, the society enjoys its multiculturalism, and people are proud to be Malaysian. Moreover, having sought to attain developed nation status, a 2009 poll saw the economy topping concerns, rather than racial and unity issues. Affluence and the continued pursuit of material gains tend to level out differences.

A Peranakan townhouse

The double-storey Peranakan townhouses of the Straits Settlements were always much longer than their entrances suggested. During the Dutch era, property owners were taxed based on the frontage width, so to reduce tax, shrewd owners built longer houses.

The front of the house is so decorative, it is like a heady visual perfume: brightly coloured tiles, elaborate doors, wooden shutters and large gold Chinese characters on the signboard. It is distinctly oriental, but the plaster motifs look Western and the whole is unified. This is the Peranakan townhouse.

Described as Chinese Palladian, the architectural style of these buildings of the Malaysian Straits Chinese is a unique meld of Victorian, Chinese and Malay. Lining the streets of Melaka's Old Town, they are also found in Penang's back-streets and in selected nooks of Singapore. But the Melaka buildings are among the oldest town-houses in the country, dating back to the 17th century. Those along Jalan Tun Tan Cheng Lock are particularly elaborate because they were status symbols for their affluent owners.

The houses have two sets of doors. The main wooden doors, with their intricately carved panels, are left open during the day to let air in. The second outer set are swinging half-doors based on the Malay *pintu pagar* (literally, fence door). On either side are large square windows with vertical bars and sometimes shutters. Above the windows are air vents, which are sometimes decorated.

The centrepiece of the main or reception hall is usually an altar, large and beautifully carved. More likely than not, the deity among the candles and burning joss sticks would be the white-robed Kwan Yin, goddess of mercy. Twin arched entrances lead to the sitting room. The main furniture would usually be made of imported blackwood inlaid with mother-of-pearl and marble. These pieces were often set against the walls, from where portraits of ancestors in gilded frames peered down.

Behind the sitting room is the dining room and, right at the back, the huge kitchen. In between would be one or more courtyards or air wells to let light into the otherwise dark house. The courtyards serve as indoor gardens with potted plants, a fountain, and a well or large ornate jar filled with water, and were always lower than the rest of the ground floor, with drain holes so that the house wouldn't be flooded during a downpour.

The bedrooms sit upstairs at the top of a wooden staircase with balusters. The rooms and bathrooms are capacious and carry through the elements of carved lacquered wood, embroidery, and porcelain.

Visiting a townhouse

Many of these houses are being restored for commercial purposes. In the process, however, numer-

Peranakan architecture in the Baba Nyonya Heritage Museum.

ous traditional tradesmen have been evicted, and the quality of the restoration work compromised for a fast buck. The best preserved are probably the Chan family-owned Baba Nyonya Heritage Museum, which straddles two adjoining townhouses and the Puri Hotel on Jalan Tun Tan Cheng Lock. Others have been converted into hotels, restaurants or tourist trinket shops.

The Chan family has converted the third town-house, once living quarters for their servants, into a café downstairs and a cosy six-bedroom guest-house upstairs. Although not as ornately decorated as the museum next door, Café1511 (www.cafe 1511.com) still retains the same architectural elements, giving guests a Peranakan living experience but with modern touches.

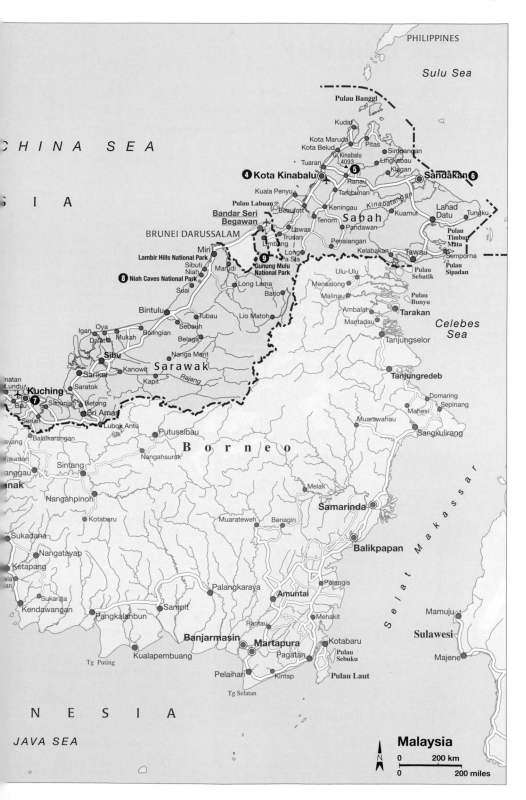

PHILIPPINES

Sulu Sea

C H I N A   S E A

S I A

Pulau Banggi

Kudat

Kota Maruda
Kota Belud   Pitas   Simpangan
Tuaran   Lingkabau
G. Kinabalu   Klagan
4093
❹ Kota Kinabalu   **❺**   **Sandakan ❻**
Ranau
Kuala Penyu   Tambunan
Pulau Labuan   Kinabatangan   Lahad
Beaufort   Keningau   Kuamut   Datu   Tungku
Bandar Seri   Tenom   **S a b a h**
Begawan   Lawas   Pandawan   Pulau
BRUNEI DARUSSALAM   Trusan   Pensiangan   Kelabakan   Timbun
Limbang   Tawau   Mata
Miri   Long   Semporna
Lambir Hills National Park   Pa Sia   Ulu-Ulu   Pulau
Sibuti   **❾**   Sebatik   Sipadan
Niah   **Gunung Mulu**
❽ Niah Caves National Park   Marudi   **National Park**   Mensalong
Suai   Long Lama   Malinau   Pulau
Bintulu   Bakjo   Bunyu
Tubau   Lio Matoh   Ambalat   **Tarakan**
Igan   Oya   Sebauh   Mantadau   *Celebes*
Dalat   Mukah   Belaga   Tanjungselor   *Sea*
Sibu   Balingian   Nanga Merit
Sarikei   Kanowit   **S a r a w a k**
Saratok   Kapit   Rajang   **Tanjungredeb**
Kuching   Simunjan   Betong   Domaring
Bau   **❼**   Mahesi   Sepinang
Serian   **Sri Aman**   Muarawahau   Sangkulirang
Balaikarangan   Lubok Antu
ayang   Putussibau

jauman   Nangahsurak   B o r n e o

anggau
nak   Sintang   Melak

Nangahpinoh
Kotabaru   Muarateweh   Benagin   **Samarinda**

Sukadana
Nangatayap   **Balikpapan**

Ketapang   Palangkaraya   Patangis
an   **Amuntai**
Sukaraja   Sampit   Mehakit   Mamuju
Kendawangan   Pangkalanbun   Rantau

Banjarmasin   Kotabaru   **Sulawesi**
Kualapembuang   **Martapura**   Pulau
Tg Puting   Pagatan   Sebuku   Majene
Pelaihari   **Pulau Laut**
Kintap

S e l a t   M a k a s s a r

Tg Selatan

N E S I A

JAVA SEA   **Malaysia**

N   0   200 km
0   200 miles

KUALA LUMPUR

A mining outpost just a century ago and now the capital of Malaysia with a population of over 7 million, KL is one of the major centres of Southeast Asia.

Bangunan Sultan Abdul Samad.

n the 1850s, **Kuala Lumpur ❶** was little more than a representation of what its name means in Malay: 'muddy river mouth'. At that time, a group of tin prospectors, financed by the local chief, journeyed upriver to the confluence of the less-than-crystal-clear waters of the Klang and Gombak rivers. The discovery of tin led to British rule and determined the city's role as an administrative centre.

More than five decades after independence, any lingering colonialism has been wrung out of Kuala Lumpur – or 'KL' as it is popularly known. Here, more than anywhere else in the country, national aspirations towards a globalised identity have helped to create a contemporary, wired and international city, the legislative and financial capital of Malaysia.

Towers of steel and glass dominate the cityscape, traffic is a nightmare and a robust consumer culture much in evidence. Still, older traditions are maintained in a variety of ways, from the crumbling old mosques and temples to the consulting of spiritual mediums and dining in roadside eateries.

Colonial city centre

West of the confluence of the Gombak and Klang rivers, you will come to the old city centre with its 19th-century Mughal-style administrative buildings, the hub of British colonial rule. Now under the management of the Ministry of Information, Communication and Culture, these are clustered around **Dataran Merdeka ❹** (Independence Square), a grass-covered area anchored at the southern end by a large flagpole.

The most imposing of the buildings is the **Bangunan Sultan Abdul Samad** (Sultan Abdul Samad Building), the colonial administrative centre. Stretching for some 137 metres (450ft) along Jalan Raja, it was the first to be built in the Mughal style, and is a study in symmetry. Its centrepiece is a clock tower that Malaysians gather

around to hear herald in the first day of each New Year.

To the left of this building across the river is a trio of buildings exhibiting the hybrid Orientalist style: the **Old Supreme Court** in the back, with four pepper-pot turrets, the **Old Town Hall**, and adjoining it on the left, the former **Federated Malay States (FMS) Survey Office**, which trails down Jalan Tun Perak. The latter two buildings feature Gothic elements and large Mughal-inspired domes over porches.

Across Dataran Merdeka is the mock-Tudor **Royal Selangor Club**, a members-only social club that was the centre of British colonial life. To the right of the Bangunan Sultan Abdul Samad, and linked to it by a bridge, are more Mughal-style buildings, the **Old General Post Office**, with its leaf-shaped pediments, and across the road, the red-and-white banded **former FMS Railway headquarters**.

The Mughal style of architecture was also applied to the **Masjid Jamek** (Jamek Mosque), which can be viewed from behind the Bangunan Sultan Abdul Samad. Sitting at the confluence of the Gombak and Klang rivers, this was the principal Muslim centre for prayer in the city until the opening of the National Mosque after independence. It is not open to non-Muslims.

Down the road from the Dataran Merdeka is the towering white **Kompleks Dayabumi**, a modern tower block that boasts beautiful Islamic filigree latticework. This complex hosts the Pejabat Pos Besar (General Post Office). Further south, the old **Stesen Keretapi Kuala Lumpur ⑧** (Old KL Railway Station) has been defunct since 2001, but to arrive by rail here was once a fantastic experience, as turrets, spires, minarets and arches greeted the eye in every direction. Inside, the design is that of many large Victorian railway stations in England.

The **Bangunan ktm Berhad** (Railway Administration Building), headquarters of Malaysian Railways, lies opposite. It features a pastiche of architectural elements, from Mughal-style minarets to large Gothic-style windows and ancient Greek columns.

Kompleks Dayabumi.

Lively street restaurants around Jalan Alor.

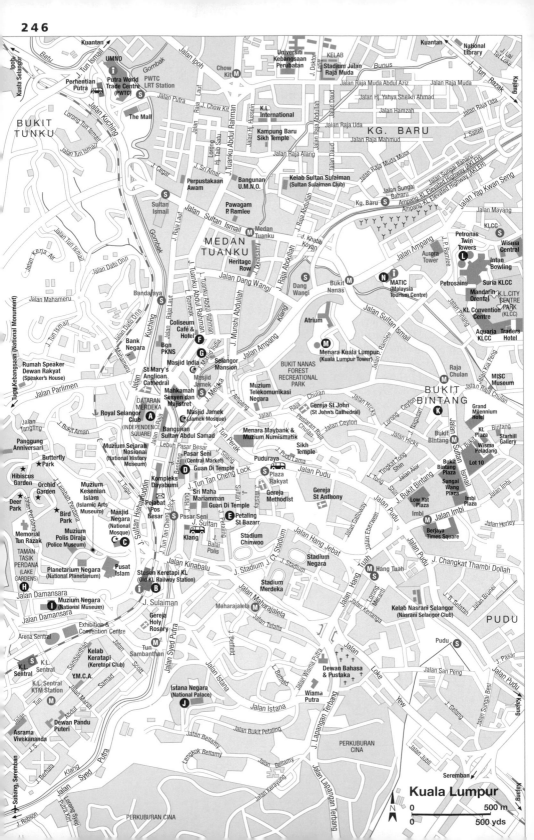

Up the road from this Victorian enclave is the **Masjid Negara** ⓒ (National Mosque; tel: 03-2693 7784; Sun–Thur 9am–12.30pm, 3–4pm and 5.30–6.30pm, Fri closed in the morning). Completed in 1965, the jagged star-like roof represents the 13 states of Malaysia and the five pillars of Islam. On the roof are 48 smaller domes, their design and number inspired by the great mosque in Mecca. Its Grand Hall can accommodate 8,000 worshippers.

Petaling Street and Jalan TAR

On the other side of the river from the Kompleks Dayabumi is **Pasar Seni** ⓓ (Central Market; www.centralmarket. com.my; tel: 03-2031 0399; daily 10am–10pm). A former fruit-and-vegetable market, this Art Deco restoration showpiece is now one of the city's most popular tourist stops, with souvenir shops purveying everything from batik scarves to portraits done on the spot. Its Annexe showcases everything from traditional *wayang kulit* (shadow puppet) performances to cutting-edge theatre and art exhibitions.

To the southeast is the city's most famous street bazaar (daily 10am–11pm). Known as **Petaling Street** ⓔ, it lines Jalan Petaling and Jalan Hang Lekir. It is most famous for pirated versions of branded goods, from handbags and jeans to watches. Rather a tourist trap, bargaining hard can still result in good buys.

Around this area are several temples worth exploring: close to the Central Market is **Sin Sze Si Ya Temple**, which honours the architect of KL, Yap Ah Loy; and the ornate South Indian **Sri Maha Mariamman Temple**. South of Petaling Street is the **Chan Shee Shue Yen Clan Association**, famous for its intricate friezes.

North of Dataran Merdeka lies another area of interesting shops. The main road here is **Jalan Tuanku Abdul Rahman**, named after the first king of Malaysia and one of the city's longest

roads. It is now at the centre of the garment district. At Nos 98–100, are the colonial institutions of the **Coliseum Cinema**, built in the 1920s, and the **Coliseum Café and Hotel** ⓕ (daily 8am–10pm). The bar at the latter once drew out-of-town Somerset Maugham planter types, who sought solace from the tropics in drink and company there. Now rather seedy, the cafe still serves a decent ribeye and baked crabmeat.

Parallel to this road is **Jalan Masjid India** ⓖ, a thriving commercial area of shops, restaurants and hotels. An eye-popping array of Indian silks and glittering handmade jewellery is displayed in the many shops, as well as Indonesian batik.

Lake Gardens

The best-known and most popular of KL's parks is **Taman Tasik Perdana** ⓗ or the Lake Gardens (daily 24 hours; free), comprising 104 hectares (257 acres) of undulating green with magnificent trees and flowering plants as well as several attractions. In the relative cool of the early mornings, it is full of joggers and senior citizens

Out and about on Petaling Street in Chinatown.

Guard on horseback at the Istana Negara.

Kuala Lumpur's contrast between old and new.

performing t'ai chi routines. It is also a great place to watch KL families at play. At the heart of the gardens is the lake, Tasik Perdana.

Within the Lake Gardens the **Bird Park** (daily 9am–6pm; charge), **Butterfly Park** (daily 9am–6pm; charge) and **Deer Park** (daily 10am–noon, 2–6pm, Fri 10am–noon, 3–6pm, Sat–Sun 10am–6pm; free) house local and foreign species in forested enclosures. Flora enthusiasts should not miss the **Hibiscus Garden**, **Orchid Garden**, **Conservatory** and **Herbal Garden** (daily 9am–6pm; Mon–Fri free, Sat–Sun charge). The **National Planetarium** is not very good, but has a delightful garden dotted with replicas of ancient observatories (free).

Islamic Arts Museum

Do not miss the excellent **Muzium Kesenian Islam Malaysia** (Islamic Arts Museum Malaysia; www.iamm.org.my; daily 10am–6pm; charge), to the east of the park. Within the beautifully designed repository of Islamic artefacts, an interesting exhibit comprises intricate architectural models of famous monuments and structures of the Islamic world. The museum also hosts notable temporary exhibitions.

Opposite the Lake Gardens across Jalan Parlimen is the **Tugu Kebangsaan** (National Monument; daily 24 hours; free), erected to commemorate those who died in the struggle against the Communist insurgency of 1948–60. At the edge of the gardens, on an incline on Jalan Damansara and facing Jalan Travers, is the **Muzium Negara** ❶ (National Museum; www.jmm.gov.my; daily 9am–6pm; charge). The exhibits are slightly disappointing, although the neo-traditional exterior is impressive, inspired by local Malay architecture and featuring two massive batik murals depicting nationhood.

Head east along Jalan Istana to reach the **Istana Negara** ❶ (National Palace), the official residence of the king. Once the townhouse of a wealthy Chinese businessman, the palace is off-limits, but get there on the hour to photograph Royal Guard horsemen – dressed in British uniforms – change shifts. The Royal Guard foot soldiers dress in Malay regalia.

MUGHAL ARCHITECTURE

Mughal-style architecture was brought to Malaysia by two colonial architects, A.C. Norman and A.B. Hubback. Both men had spent some time in India, and they deemed that a British fantasy pastiche of 16th- and 17th-century Indian design would best suit a predominantly Muslim country. Amidst a cacophony of domes, minarets and arches, the architects added classical Greek and Gothic elements such as columns, colonnades and pointed arches. In designing these edifices, the goals were multifarious: the buildings had to be of a stature befitting a colonial capital, sow confidence in Chinese investors to set up their businesses here, reflect the Islamic mores of the land and take into account the humid, tropical climate.

Bukit Bintang

The fulcrum of modern consumer life in KL is **Bukit Bintang** Ⓚ, an area of shops, restaurants, and hotels to suit every budget. You will find a number of large shopping malls in this area: Sungai Wang Plaza and the adjacent Bukit Bintang Plaza offer more than 500 shops, including some of the most affordable, trendy clothing options in KL; Imbi Plaza and Plaza Low Yat concentrate on computers and software; higher-end shoppers would appreciate the mammoth Pavilion Kuala Lumpur, the luxury Starhill Gallery and Lot 10.

Petronas Twin Towers

The city's most striking landmark is also the world's tallest twin building: the 452-metre (1,483ft) -tall **Petronas Twin Towers** Ⓛ, whose identical towers are linked midway up by a skybridge. The towers reach a numerically auspicious 88 storeys above the traffic-congested streets and house the contemporary Suria KLCC shopping mall, an excellent concert hall and thousands of offices. Visitors can ascend to the towers' **Skybridge** (daily 9am–7pm, closed Fri 1–2pm; one visitor may collect five tickets, limited to 1,000 visitors per day; free), but for a better view of the city, try the nearby **Menara Kuala Lumpur** Ⓜ (KL Tower; www.menarakl.com. my; daily 9.30am–9.30pm; charge), a 421-metre (1,380ft) telecom tower, one of the highest such structures in the world. At its base is a lovely tropical forest park deserving of a wander; free tours are conducted by Tower staff.

Linking these two high-rise monsters, historic Jalan Ampang presents a very different aspect of urban architecture – a row of early 20th century tin miners' mansions that uniquely combine Eastern and Western design elements. The best preserved is the **Malaysia Tourism Centre** Ⓝ (MTC; www.mtc.gov.my; tourist info desk daily 8am–10pm). Built in 1935 by a wealthy Chinese tin mogul and rubber planter, it was refurbished in the late 1980s. Traditional performances are held daily at the **Mini Auditorium** (Mon, Tue, Thur, Sat 3–5pm; charge).

In the Lake Gardens.

萬佛光明燈吉祥法會

萬福

PENANG AND LANGKAWI

The handsome architecture of George Town, wonderful beaches and some of the country's best food make Penang irresistible.

With the outstanding architectural and multicultural heritage of its capital, George Town, and a range of beautiful tropical beaches, the island of Penang is high on the list of tourist priorities. It has one of Southeast Asia's greatest diversity of communities, faiths, cultures and languages, and one of the largest collections of 19th- and 20th-century vernacular buildings.

Once under the dominion of the Sultan of Kedah, Penang was largely deserted until the British arrived in the late 18th century. To encourage trade and commerce, the colonial administrators made the island a free port. This strategy worked well, and in eight years the population increased to 8,000, comprising a diverse grouping of immigrants – Chinese, Indians and Bugis (from Sulawesi in Indonesia), among others.

George Town

George Town ②, named by the British after King George III, grew into a fascinating, buzzing amalgamation of places of worship, clan associations, traditional trade shops and bazaars. That much of this has survived into the present day is largely down to a 1948 Rent Control Act, which put a ceiling on rentals. When that Act was repealed at the turn of the 21st century, conservationists led by the

Penang Heritage Trust and the Consumers' Association of Penang – thankfully backed by the government – pushed hard to gain Unesco World Heritage status and save the city from indiscriminate redevelopment.

Maps of George Town are plentiful, so it is easy and fun to hotfoot it or take a trishaw round the maze-like streets. Alternatively, join one of the numerous guided tours (www.pht.org.my). Wherever you go, do sample the lip-smacking delights of the local cuisine: from Indian-Muslim curry and Malay grilled

Main Attractions

Fort Cornwallis
Cheong Fatt Tze Mansion
Khoo Kongsi
Masjid Melayu
Han Jiang Ancestral Temple
Pinang Peranakan Mansion
Kek Lok Si
Batu Feringghi
Penang National Park

Typical George Town architecture.

seafood, to Chinese *hokkien mee* (prawn noodle soup). Much of the best food is found at unfashionable roadside stalls and cramped coffee shops in the old parts of George Town, especially along Gurney Drive and Jalan Burma.

Fort Cornwallis

Fort Cornwallis Ⓐ (Mon–Sat 9am–7pm; charge) was the first major structure in George Town, built using convict labour. Named after the British governor of Bengal, the old fort today houses cells, a gunpowder magazine and a history gallery.

Adjacent to the fort is the **Padang Kota Lama**, the town green, along whose seaside length stretches the **Esplanade** (Jalan Tun Syed Sheh Barakhbah); the latter is popular with locals who enjoy the evening breeze. Handsome 19th century colonial buildings stand at one end of the Padang, serving as government offices. At the other end, near the entrance to Fort Cornwallis, traffic circles the **Clock Tower Ⓑ**, presented to Penang by a rich Chinese *towkay* in commemoration of Queen Victoria's Diamond Jubilee.

The dignified **St George's Church Ⓒ**, built in 1818 on nearby Lebuh Farquhar, is the oldest Anglican church in Southeast Asia, having survived World War II intact. At the **Penang Museum and Art Gallery Ⓓ** (Sat–Thur 9am–5pm; free), on the other side of the street, visitors can peer into a 19th-century Chinese bridal chamber and admire 19th-century landscape paintings of Penang. Further west along the waterfront is the stark white **Eastern and Oriental Hotel Ⓔ** (www.e-o-hotel.com), established in the late 19th century. With a charming sea frontage and atmospheric pre-war bar, this is one of Asia's grand hotels.

Blue Mansion

Perpendicular to the hotel is the start of **Jalan Penang** (better known as Penang Road), the main shopping street ending at the landmark **Komtar**, Penang's tallest building (currently under redevelopment); at the bottom of komtar is the main bus station. Walk through the nightlife area of Upper Penang Road to get to Lebuh Leith and the **Cheong Fatt Tze Mansion Ⓕ** (Blue Mansion;

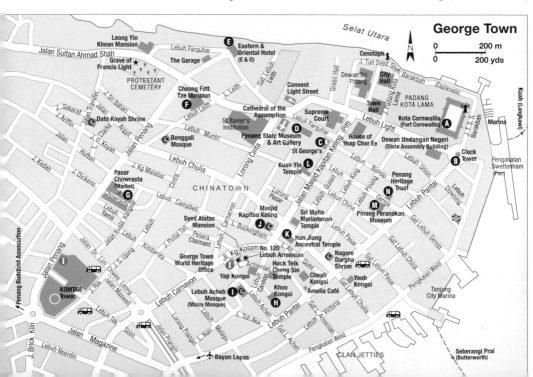

George Town

www.cheongfatttzemansion.com; guided tours daily 11am, 1.30pm and 3pm; charge). Owned by China's Consul in Penang in the late 19th century, the mansion is a marvel of Chinese geomantic *feng shui* architectural elements and one of the first award-winning restoration projects in Penang.

Take a stroll through **Pasar Chowrasta G** (Chowrasta Market), between Lebuh Campbell and Jalan Chowrasta. A wet market with the customary wet market odours, it has a section facing Penang Road that offers the Penang specialities of local biscuits and preserved nutmeg and mango. On Lebuh Tamil is the row of *nasi kandar* (mixed curry rice) stalls whose food is reputed to be the best in the country.

Typical Malaysian institutions are the *pasar minggu* or *pasar malam*, the weekly market or night market. These are temporary affairs that spring up in the street or an open space in the evenings or at weekends. Bargains range from tiny trinkets to cheap batik sarongs and plastic slippers.

Khoo Kongsi

Many of the Chinese immigrants arriving in Malaysia 100 years ago fell under the 'protection' and control of one of the clan associations, whose functions were not unlike those of medieval European guilds. The ancestral halls of these clan associations – such as the Khoo, Ong, Tan and Cheah – are called *kongsi* and are scattered all over town. The most impressive is the clan hall built by the **Khoo Kongsi H** (www.khookongsi.com.my; daily 9am–5pm; charge) whose entrance is on Lebuh Carnarvon. Completed in 1901 and designed to capture the splendour of an imperial palace, it has a seven-tiered pavilion, 'dragon' pillars and hand-painted walls engraved with the Khoo rose emblem. The original design was so ambitious that conservative Khoo clansmen cautioned against it, lest the emperor of China be offended. A century later, the clanhouse was fully restored by traditional craftsmen.

Nearby in Lebuh Acheh, is an Arab/Achenese enclave established by a rich merchant who built the important Arabic monument, the **Lebuh Acheh Mosque I** (Malay Mosque). The 1808 mosque incorporates Achehnese, Anglo-Indian and Chinese elements and is surrounded by 19th-century Arab houses. The area was once nicknamed the Second Jeddah because it was a gathering point for Mecca-bound pilgrims from all over the Malay islands, prior to sailing to the Arab peninsula.

Masjid Kapitan Keling

Heading up Jalan Masjid Kapitan Keling towards the Padang, look out for the Mughal-style **Masjid Kapitan Keling J**, built in 1800 and the state's oldest mosque. Originally a simple structure, it was redesigned by British architects who had their own idea of what qualified as Muslim architecture.

Opposite is the **Han Jiang Ancestral Temple K** (daily 9am–6pm; free), a Chinese teochew temple built in 1870, whose simple facade belies ornately decorated interiors. Another award-winning restoration project; note the

Elaborate roof detail on Khoo Kongsi.

Floor tiles at a Baba-Nonya house.

pierced woodcarvings of characters in Teochew Opera and Chinese legends.

Further along Jalan Masjid Kapitan Keling, past the massive elaborate gateway of the South Indian Sri Mariammam Temple, is the **Kuan Yin Temple ⓛ** (daily 9am–6pm; free), Penang's oldest Chinese temple and its most crowded. A Buddhist deity who refused to enter Nirvana as long as there was injustice on earth, Kuan Yin typically personifies mercy, and is one of the most popular deities in the traditional Chinese pantheon of gods and goddesses.

Penang's unique Baba-Nonya heritage (see box) is on display at the eclectic Straits-style **Pinang Peranakan Mansion ⓜ** (www.pinangperanakanmansion.com.my; bookings only; tel: 04-264 2929; daily 9.30am–5pm) at 29 Church Street. Owned by a former clan leader, it houses over 1,000 artefacts. Opposite is the **Penang Heritage Trust ⓝ** (www.pht.org.my; 26 Lebuh Gereja; tel: 04-264 2631; Mon–Fri 9am–5pm, Sat 9am–1pm), located in a restored shop house typical of the 1860s. Get information and book heritage tours here.

Char koay teow, a local dish with prawns and flat rice noodles.

Buddhist temples and botanical gardens

The variety of Buddhist worship in Penang is so striking as to make sightseeing a new experience in every temple. On Lorong Burma, one can enter the gigantic meditation hall at **Wat Chayamangkalaram** (daily 6am–5.30pm; free) and find a workman polishing the left cheek of the 32-metre (100ft) -long Reclining Buddha, among the largest statues of its kind in the world. Opposite the Wat is the **Dharmikarama Burmese Buddhist Temple** (daily 5am–6pm; free), which houses an 8.3-metre (27ft) -tall Standing Buddha.

High above the bustle of George Town on an auspicious hilltop at **Ayer Hitam**, a few kilometres from downtown, looms the **Kek Lok Si** (daily 9am–6pm). This temple, dating from 1890, is one of the largest and most important Buddhist temple complexes in Southeast Asia. Attractions include large statues of the Heavenly Kings, a Laughing Buddha, and a bronze statue of Kwan Yin that is visible from afar. Both the Kwan Yin deck and a seven-storey pagoda afford great views.

BABA-NONYA CULTURE

It is impossible to tell who is Baba-Nonya in a crowd, but the culture of this sizeable Penang community, also known as Peranakan (local-born) Chinese, is manifest most obviously in its cuisine – a delightful, piquant blend of Malay and Chinese cooking. Don't miss sampling the Nonya *kuih* or cakes. Traditional female clothing is also distinct and draws from Malay, Chinese and Western influences. The recent revival of the delicate embroidered voile Nonya *kebaya*, paired with a batik sarong, has saved this unique dress style from obscurity. Meanwhile, as you walk George Town's streets, look out for shop houses that contain aspects of Peranakan architecture in the form of colourful tiles on walls or floors, and highly ornamental doors and windows.

The **Penang Botanical Gardens** (daily 5am–8pm; free) are situated about 3km (2 miles) northeast of Penang Hill. This mature and beautifully cultivated showcase of tropical plants from all over the country was established in 1884 as a nursery for the 'planting of colonial products'.

Batu Maung, a fishing village on the southeastern tip of the island about 3km (2 miles) from the Bayan Lepas Airport, houses a shrine marking the sacred 85cm (33-inch) footprint in stone, believed to be that of Admiral Cheng Ho, the 'Chinese Columbus'. On **Pulau Langkawi** (see page 255) is a similar footprint said to belong to the admiral. The two are believed to be a pair and anyone who lights joss sticks and places them in the urns beside the footprint will have good luck and great fortune.

Batu Feringghi

Although the waters are not as clear as on the eastern coast of the Malay peninsula, the beaches of Penang north of George Town are still quite seductive for their seascapes and sea breeze. Of these, **Batu Feringghi** is the liveliest, with hotels, eateries, cheap batik beachwear, souvenirs and a lively *pasar malam* (night market) that starts up at 7pm.

About 20 minutes north at **Teluk Bahang** is the **Tropical Spice Garden** (www.tropicalspicegarden.com; daily 9am–6pm, last admission 5.30pm; guided tours daily 9am–5pm; charge), with more than 500 specimens of flora from all over the tropical world and a great little café. Further along the same road is the **Penang Butterfly Farm** (www.butterflyinsect.com; Mon–Fri 9am–5.30pm, Sat–Sun and public holidays 9am–6pm; charge), home to thousands of butterflies and other tropical insects.

For the real thing, an easy two-hour trail winds through the **Penang National Park** (tel: 04-881 3530; daily 8am–6pm; free; register at the office for an entry permit), from Teluk Bahang, ending at Monkey Beach. Before you set off, arrange a boat to take you back.

Langkawi

A beautiful limestone cliff and forest archipelago of some 100 islands, **Langkawi** ❸ – 100km (60 miles) to the north of Penang – has white sandy beaches and an abundance of beautiful scenery. Pantai Cenang and Pantai Tengah, in the southwest, are the most popular beaches, lined with accommodation, restaurants and souvenir shops.

In the northwest are the pretty beach of **Burau Bay** and the seven-step **Telaga Tujuh** (Seven Wells) waterfall, while the Langkawi Cable Car (Mon–Tue, Thur 10am–6pm, Wed noon–6pm, Fri–Sun 9.30am–6.30pm, closes at 5pm during Ramadhan; charge) brings you to the top of the 708-metre (2,320ft)-high Gunung Machincang for magnificent views of the surrounding forest and the Andaman Sea. The northern beaches house luxury resorts.

Other activities on offer include a limestone mangrove swamp tour in the Kilim Nature Park, island-hopping to enjoy marvellous deserted beaches; and snorkelling or diving in the clear waters at Pulau Payar.

FACT

Travellers arriving by ferry will be greeted by a giant statue of the Brahminy Kite, a common bird of prey after which some say Langkawi is named, *lang* being Malay for eagle. The kite feeds on fish and small mammals; some tour agencies have taken to the unhealthy activity of feeding them to attract tourists, which makes them dependent on humans and encourages the spread of disease.

Snorkelling off Langkawi.

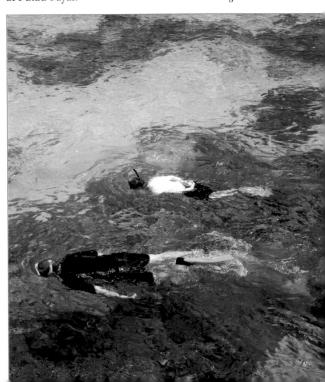

SABAH AND SARAWAK

Forming the northern part of the large island of Borneo, these Malaysian outposts offer pristine jungles, some of the world's best diving and the lofty mountain of Gunung Kinabalu.

Main Attractions

Sabah State Museum
   and Heritage Village
Kinabalu Park
Sepilok Orang-utan
   Rehabilitation Centre
Kinabatangan River
Diving at Pulau Sipadan
Kuching Waterfront
Sarawak Museum
Niah Caves National Park
Gunung Mulu National
   Park

Mount Kinabalu and its foothills.

The Malaysian states of Sabah and Sarawak cover the northern section of the world's third-largest island, Borneo, which Malaysia shares with Indonesia. Although their population accounts for just 22 percent of the country's total, the land area is larger than the other 11 states combined. The pace of life is relaxed compared to that of peninsular Malaysia.

Formerly one of the world's largest intact rainforests, harbouring unique fauna and indigenous tribes, Borneo's ecosystems have suffered considerably in the past decades, first with extensive logging for timber and oil palm plantations, and in the late 1990s by extensive and highly destructive fires that burned out of control for months at a time. These fires, more often than not on the Indonesian side and lit by farmers seeking to clear land, clouded the air across the entire region.

Nonetheless, with global pressure on environmental conservation and the rise of nature tourism as a key foreign exchange-earner, protected areas are being consolidated and increasingly well managed. Facilities and guides are generally good.

Sabah: Kota Kinabalu

The capital of Sabah, **Kota Kinabalu ❹**, is a sprawling, relaxed town on the west coast of the state. Within the past two decades, a slew of development has transformed KK, as it is commonly called, with the likes of the hotel and marina complex of **Sutera Harbour** and the mall-and-hotel development of **1Borneo**, 7km (4 miles) north of the city centre. The seafront has been smartened up with a paved Esplanade and the Waterfront dining and clubbing centre.

It is possible to experience some of its old charm by visiting its markets – the fresh produce **Central Market** on the seafront, the souvenir **Handicraft Market** next door and the truly local **Tamu Penampang**, a little way out of the city centre.

Spend a few hours at the **Sabah**

State Museum and Heritage Village (daily 9am–5pm; charge), 4km (2.5 miles) from the city centre. Designed in the longhouse style of the Rungus and Murut tribes, the museum has a wealth of historical, archaeological, and natural history exhibits. Visit the striking collection of 10 life-size traditional houses set in the museum gardens, each depicting the architecture of a different ethnic group. The complex also has a science centre and an art gallery.

South of town, off the road leading to the airport, is the famous beach at **Tanjung Aru**. The sea here is clear, the sand is clean and the coastal food stalls and restaurants offer delicious local seafood. Offshore is the **Tunku Abdul Rahman Park** (www.sabahparks.org.my; daily 8.30am–5pm; charge), a group of pretty islands 20 minutes by boat from KK, terrific for sunbathing, snorkelling and diving.

Mount Kinabalu

Home to one of the greatest concentrations of plant species in the world, **Gunung Kinabalu ❺**, at 4,093 metres (13,428ft), is Southeast Asia's highest peak outside of New Guinea. Two well-laid paths with steps and rails help climbers ascend and descend the mountain in just two days (taking in a sunrise, too). Accommodation is available both at the park headquarters and on the mountain slopes.

The headquarters of the Unesco World Heritage listed **Kinabalu Park** (www.sabahparks.org.my; daily 7am–10pm; charge), are on the mountain slopes close to the main trail to the summit. After trekking, soak yourself in the Poring Hot Springs near the headquarters; it also has a tropical garden and a canopy walkway.

Sandakan

Sandakan ❻ is most famous for the **Sepilok Orang-Utan Rehabilitation Centre** (www.orangutan-appeal.org.uk; Sat–Thur 9am–noon, 2–4pm, Fri 9–11am, 2–4pm; feeding times 10am and 3pm; charge), a 20-minute drive westward from town. The centre helps orang-utans who have lived in captivity or been orphaned to adjust gradually for a return to the wild.

WHERE

For a great and free bird's eye view of Kota Kinabalu and its outlying isles, head to **Signal Hill**, the highest point in the city. There is an observatory platform there (daily 8am–midnight); the night view is quite lovely.

Orang-utans are some of Borneo's most famous inhabitants.

DIVE PARADISE

The waters off Semporna (southeastern Sabah) are a haven for scuba diving. The most famous spot is **Pulau Sipadan**, Malaysia's only true oceanic island rising up 600 metres (2,000ft) from the seabed. With turtles galore, giant shoals of swirling barracuda and other wonders, the marine life of Sipadan has been hailed by both the Worldwide Fund for Nature and the late Jacques Cousteau as among the best in the world. All resort operations have been relocated to preserve this world-class diving spot, and many are now in **Pulau Mabul**, itself renowned for muck-diving. Other island dive destinations in this area are **Mataking** and **Kapalai**. Elsewhere, Layang-Layang is well known for deep-sea species such as hammerhead shoals, while Labuan offers exciting wreck-diving.

Sandakan is also the jump-off to the three islands within the confines of the **Turtle Island Park**. Large numbers of green and hawksbill turtles come here to lay eggs nearly every night of the year, but the best time to watch is between July and October. Since the laying and hatching occur under the cover of darkness, it is well worth staying a night here (www.sabahparks.org.my; charge).

Another excursion that can be undertaken from Sandakan is a cruise up the mighty **Kinabatangan River**. After crossing Sandakan Bay, the first stage of the journey is dominated by mangrove swamps and twisting waterways. The Kinabatangan and its tributaries are famed as the home of the long-nosed, pot-bellied proboscis monkey, but a host of wildlife can be seen here, including Bornean pygmy elephants, 10 species of primates and eight species of hornbills.

Sarawak: Kuching

The name of Sarawak still evokes romance rather than reality. White Rajahs and Borneo headhunters ring more nostalgic bells than the reality of the 20th-century oil boom, Kuala Lumpur's interest in developing and modernising the state, and the logging disputes of recent decades. Nonetheless, defined as it is by large rivers and with the majority of the land under forest cover (including almost 30 gazetted protected areas), the call of the wild is irresistible.

Sarawak's charming 19th-century capital city, **Kuching** ❼, is spread out on both banks of the Sungai Sarawak, which a leisurely river cruise will help visitors appreciate. A stroll along the paved 1km (0.6-mile) -long **Waterfront** is also enjoyable. On the Waterfront's western section, look across the river to admire the 1870-built Astana, the stately home of Charles Brooke, Sarawak's second White Rajah; it is now the Governor's residence.

On this side of the river and built around the same time, is Kuching's **old courthouse**, with a clock tower in front of it. Once the administrative centre of the Brookes, it now houses the **Sarawak Tourism Complex** (tel: 082-410 944; www.sarawaktourism.com) and **National Parks Booking Office** (tel:

Dragonboats on Kuching's waterfront.

082-248 088). Both are open Mon–Fri 8am–6pm, Sat and Sun 9am–3pm. The General Post Office, with its Corinthian columns, is more decorative. Meanwhile, the Square Tower started life as a prison in 1879, and ended up as a dance hall.

Walk eastwards past the **Main Bazaar**'s beautifully preserved 19th-century Chinese shophouses to visit the **Chinese History Museum** (Sat–Thur 9am–6pm; free), an insightful historical documentation of the Chinese in Sarawak, and the busy, ornate century-old Taoist **Tua Pek Kong** temple (free).

On both sides of Jalan Tun Haji Openg is the marvellous **Sarawak Museum** (www.museum.sarawak.gov.my; tel: 082-244 232; daily 9am–6pm; free). Alfred Russel Wallace, the illustrious 19th-century naturalist, spent many years in Borneo and became a particular friend of Rajah Charles Brooke. With Wallace's encouragement, Brooke built the museum to house a permanent exhibition of native arts and crafts, as well as specimens from Wallace's extensive collection.

Sarawak Cultural Village and parks

Beach lovers and golfers head for **Damai Beach**, just 30 minutes by road from downtown Kuching. Nearby is the popular **Sarawak Cultural Village** (www.scv.com.my; daily 9am–5.15pm; charge), which spreads across 6 hectares (15 acres) of jungle at the foot of Santubong Mountain. The entrance fee is a bit steep, but the site features beautifully constructed dwellings of six main ethnic groups, as well as a cultural show twice a day. The annual Rainforest World Music Festival (www.rainforestmusic-borneo.com), which takes place here, is worth a visit.

Nature enthusiasts will want to consider exploring the rainforest close to Kuching. Sarawak Forestry has excellent information on its website (www.sarawakforestry.com): the **Matang Wildlife Centre**, which has an orang-utan rehabilitation programme, sits within the palm-rich **Kubah National Park;**

Bako National Park, accessible only by boat, is fascinating for panoramic coasts and diverse ecosystems; while the world's largest flower, the Rafflesia, is the star attraction of the **Gunung Gading National Park.**

Miri's parks

Other magnificent natural encounters can be experienced from the birthplace of Malaysia's oil industry, **Miri**, northward and near the Brunei border. The **Niah Caves National Park** ❽ (www.sarawakforestry.com; headquarters open daily 8am–12.30pm, 1.30–5.15pm; charge) is one of Malaysia's most important archaeological sites, and famous for its Palaeolithic paintings.

Twenty minutes by plane from Miri is the Unesco World Heritage Site of **Gunung Mulu National Park** ❾ (www.mulupark.com; charge), an inland expanse of diverse terrain and vegetation with unique cave systems and limestone features, including the spectacular Pinnacles, as well as some of the most magnificent landscapes in the land. Accommodation ranges from simple lodges to a deluxe resort.

TIP

Traditional longhouse stays provide unparalleled insights to local life, even in spruced up guesthouses: Iban homestays are available at **Batang Ai** close to Kuching, Melanau homestays in **Mukah**, near Sibu, Orang Ulu homestays in **Kapit**, and Kelabit homestays in the **Bario** highlands.

A cultural village dance performance in traditional dress.

SOUTHEAST ASIAN WILDLIFE

The natural habitats of Southeast Asia, on land and at sea, are some of the richest on earth, home to a remarkable range of animal life.

Compared with East Africa or India, relatively few visitors to Southeast Asia take the time to explore the region's national parks and wildlife reserves. Yet there is a great deal to see, and not just in the more renowned hotspots such as Borneo or Komodo.

The tropical rainforests of Malaysia and parts of Indonesia are some of the oldest on the planet. Wildlife includes orang-utans, numerous species of monkey and smaller primates such as the tarsier and slow loris. Dwindling populations of forest elephants, tigers, leopards, wild dogs and sun bears can also be seen. One of the most unusual animals is the Malayan tapir, a distant cousin of the elephant. Even more scarce are two sub-species of rhinoceros – the Javan and Sumatran; the former is thought to be the world's rarest large mammal.

Further north in Thailand, Myanmar, Laos, Cambodia and Vietnam the equatorial jungles gradually give way to monsoon forest, where the species are adapted to more pronounced wet and dry seasons.

The Mekong River runs through the region and, with more than 1,200 known species of fish, it is one of the richest aquatic systems for biodiversity on the planet. A few river dolphins survive in southern Laos and Cambodia. The Philippines and the islands of Indonesia east of Bali have long been isolated from the rest of the continent, and this is reflected in their wildlife.

Spectacular birdlife includes giant hornbills, found in equatorial forests from Malaysia to Papua.

Tarsiers are nocturnal primates indigenous to the forests of the Philippines, Sarawak and parts of Indonesia. They are among the smallest primates, and have the largest eyes relative to body size

Native to the Bornean and Sumatran rainforests, orang-utans are the only 'great apes' found outside of Africa. Numbers have diminished to the point that these beautiful creatures are classified as highly vulnerable.

A hornbill in Kota Kinabalu's wildlife park.

Crocodiles are plentiful in rivers and coastal areas throughout the region.

EXPLORING THE WILDS

The distinguished naturalist Alfred Russel Wallace (1823–1913), best known for his work on the theory of evolution, spent a great deal of time exploring the Malaysian and Indonesian forests. He divided the Indonesian archipelago into two zoological areas, separated by what is known as the Wallace Line, which runs between Kalimantan/Sulawesi and Bali/Lombok: the western half lies within the main Asian zone, whereas the eastern islands are grouped together with Australasia.

A century after his death, new species are still being discovered on a regular basis in the far-flung jungles of Indonesia, notably in the remarkable high-altitude forests of central New Guinea.

For visitors keen on seeing Southeast Asian wildlife for themselves, the leading national parks in the region include Taman Negara in peninsular Malaysia, which protects one of the largest areas of ancient rainforest on earth; Khao Yai National Park, relatively close to – but a world away from – Bangkok; Kirirom in the Cardamon Mountains of southern Cambodia; the Cuc Phuong Reserve in the Annamite Mountains of Vietnam, and Komodo, Tanjung Puting and Lore Lindu in Indonesia.

...utheast Asia is home to three sub-species of wild elephant. ...ke all forest animals, they are threatened by ongoing habitat ...s due to logging, slash-and-burn agriculture, urban ...velopment and pollution.

...easuring up to 3 metres (10ft) in length, the Komodo dragon ...the world's largest reptile. They are found on Komodo and ...ighbouring Rinca islands in Indonesia.

Numerous species of monkey are found in Southeast Asia.

Brunei's Sultan Hassanal Bolkiah inspects his royal guard of honour.

The Jame'Asr Hassanal Bolkiah Mosque, lit up at night.

BRUNEI

**A tiny sultanate close to the equator on Borneo's
north coast, oil-rich Brunei intrigues with its wealth,
Islamic culture and densely forested interior.**

*Kampong Ayer, a village
on stilts.*

Ruled by an absolute monarch who is also among the world's richest men, the Sultanate of Brunei (officially Brunei Darussalam) is a peaceful, modern nation whose identity revolves around respect for Malay culture, Islam and the monarchy, known as MIB or *Melayu Islam Beraja*. Its head of state, Haji Hassanal Bolkiah Mu'izzaddin Waddaulah is the 29th ruler in a long-surviving dynasty as well as the country's prime minister, defence minister and finance minister.

Once a Borneo-wide trading empire, the sultanate was saved from losing all its land to Sarawak by British protection, gaining independence only in 1984. Today it is geographically one of the world's smallest nations, twice the size of Luxembourg or the American state of Rhode Island. But thanks to oil, which was discovered in the early 20th century, Brunei's gross domestic product exceeds US $17 billion per year. The government has no foreign debt, and treasury reserves are immense.

*Boy in traditional Brunei
costume.*

Bruneians have all benefited from their oil wealth. The population of about 412,000 enjoys one of the highest per capita incomes in Asia. Nearly a quarter of the government budget is spent on education and social services, and Brunei has more than 95 percent literacy among its young people. Many tropical diseases have been completely eliminated. Life expectancy is high and infant mortality is low. Crime is virtually non-existent.

Islam is the official religion and is strictly observed. This is manifested in the dominance of mosques and the banning of the sale of alcohol. Culturally, Islamic mores are strongly upheld by the majority Malay population. But there are also large minorities of Chinese and indigenous peoples, who freely practise their faiths. Meanwhile, foreigners from Southeast Asia and Europe make up a fifth of Brunei's residents.

Tourist infrastructure is not as well developed as its neighbours, but Brunei is warmly welcoming and especially keen to capitalise on being part of the biodiversity treasure trove that is Borneo. Thanks to remarkable conservation policies, its pristine primary rainforests are surprisingly accessible and well worth visiting.

BANDAR SERI BEGAWAN AND BEYOND

Eschewing mass tourism, Brunei is unapologetically true to itself. The opulent mosques and pervasive sense of wealth combine with earthy river life and lush forests to create an eclectic mix.

Main Attractions

Sultan Omar Ali
 Saifuddien Mosque
Royal Regalia Building
Open market
Kampong Ayer
Jame' Asr Hassanal
 Bolkiah Mosque
Brunei Museum
Ulu Temburong National
 Park

*Water taxis at the
Yayasan shopping
centre.*

With only 200,000 people, **Bandar Seri Begawan ❶** feels more like a small town than a capital city. It takes no more than 15 minutes to walk from one side of the centre to the other. It comprised entirely water villages until 1906 when the British started building infrastructure on land. Today's BSB (as it is commonly known) is largely the result of two key periods of modernisation in the 1950s and 1980–90s. The city has one of the highest living standards in the world. Most activities in the city seem to revolve around shopping, dining and parties…or else shopping, dining and Islam.

The **Sultan Omar Ali Saifuddien Mosque** (SOAS Mosque; Sat–Wed 9am–noon, 2–3pm, 5–6pm; free) dominates the downtown skyline. Built in 1958 by the previous sultan, its Arabic architecture features numerous arches, towers, columns, onion domes and minarets. The great golden dome rises to a height of 50 metres (170ft), towering above the adjoining lagoon with a replica of a 16th-century royal barge.

Royal Regalia Building

North of the mosque at the junction of Jalan Stoney and Jalan Sultan is the impressive **Royal Regalia Building** (Sun–Thur 9am–5pm, Fri 9–11.30am, 2.30–5pm, Sat 9.45am–5pm; free). On view inside are chariots and ceremonial armoury. Do not miss the replica of the ceremonial hall of the Sultan's palace. Next door is the **Brunei History Centre**, a research facility that traces the country's history and the genealogy of the Sultan.

Across Jalan Sultan is the Lapau (Royal Ceremonial Hall), which is used for important state occasions. Heading south to the waterfront, you will see a Taoist temple at the junction of Jalan Elizabeth Dua and Jalan Sungai Kianggeh. The half-century-old Hokkien-style **Siong Hong Kong Keng** (daily 7am–7pm) is the oldest temple in BSB. It is busiest during the eighth lunar month, when Chinese opera is staged.

Next door is the **Bangunan Persatuan Guru-Guru Melayu Brunei**, (Mon–Thur 7.45am–12.15pm, 1.30–4.30pm; free), whose 17th floor offers views across the city; permission to enter is required from the security guard, unless you are with a tour guide.

On the other side of Jalan Sungai Kianggeh is the atmospheric *tamu* or **open market** (daily 6am–6pm), at its most animated on Friday and Sunday mornings, when locals haggle over fresh produce from land and sea. Turning right along Jalan MacArthur leads to the waterfront. On the right is the Yayasan **Sultan Haji Hassanal Bolkiah**, the largest shopping centre downtown. It affords a camera-friendly vista of the SOAS Mosque.

Kampong Ayer

From the waterfront, take a water taxi (24 hours; B$1) across Sungai Brunei (Brunei River) to **Kampong Ayer**, the traditional part of the capital. Dating back to the 16th century, the world's largest water village comprises over 40,000 structures and is home to one-tenth the population of BSB.

Hire a water taxi to get around the village (negotiate the price before getting into the boat), heading first to the **Kampong Ayer Tourism Centre and Gallery** (Sun–Thur 9.45am–5pm, Fri 9–11.30am, 2.30–5pm, Sat 9.45am–5pm), and subsequently, getting off at any jetty to walk around. Villagers are hospitable and you might even get invited home for tea. Kampong Ayer can also be accessed on foot on a bridge behind the SOAS Mosque.

Time this tour to end at sunset so that you can continue up Sungai Brunei to **Damuan** to view the mangrove-dwelling proboscis monkeys feed. Big-bellied and pendulous-nosed, these unusual primates can be found only on Borneo. Because they and their mangrove habitat are protected in Brunei, they are amazingly accessible here, so close to the city.

This boat route to Damuan also offers the best view of **Istana Nurul Iman**, the 1,788-room home of the Sultan. Part of the world's largest residential palace is open to the public but only during Hari

TIP

Tour operators run a night safari on the Sungai Brunei river to spot crocodiles and other nocturnal creatures, as well as taking in Kampong Ayer's night lights.

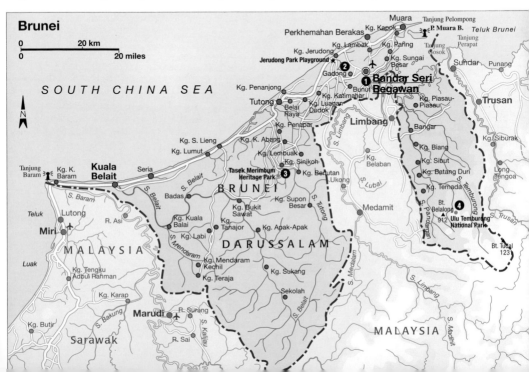

Raya Aidilfitri, when visitors can meet the royal family and enjoy a buffet meal.

Gadong

Back on the mainland, head west to **Gadong ②**. This is the location of Brunei's largest mosque, the opulent Masjid Jame', officially, the **Jame' Asr Hassanal Bolkiah Mosque** (Sat–Wed, 9am–noon, 2–3pm, 5–6pm; free). Built in 1994 to commemorate the Sultan's 25th year in power, the mosque has four main minarets, all elaborately ornamented, 29 golden domes, crystal chandeliers, Italian marble and beautifully landscaped and fountained gardens.

Gadong is also home to **The Mall**, Brunei's largest shopping centre, and the unmissable *pasar malam* (daily 6pm–midnight), a bustling food and produce market serving some of the best food in town.

Kota Batu

Northeast of BSB is the old capital of Kota Batu. At the **Arts and Handicraft Centre** (Sat–Thur 8am–5pm, Fri 8–11.30am, 2–5pm; free) on Jalan Residency, young artisans make

A rainforest village on a way to Ulu Temburong National Park.

silverware, brassware, baskets and brocade. Two specialties are miniature cannons and *keris*, the Malay dagger. Its restaurant is notable for tasty local buffets enjoyed over a fine view of Kampong Ayer.

Five km (3 miles) east of BSB is the **Brunei Museum** (Sun-Thu 9.30am–5pm, Fri 9–11.30am & 2.30–4.30pm; free), with galleries showcasing natural history, traditional culture, archaeology and 13th-century treasures salvaged from shipwrecks. Its Islamic gallery has a collection of gilded Korans, pottery, weapons and textiles from the Sultan's private collection.

For those with time, a path leads from the museum to the **Archaeological Park**, which houses two serene royal mausoleums and an archaeological museum (under construction), while a drive down the hill goes to the **Malay Technology Museum** (Sun-Thur 9.30am–5pm, Fri 9–11.30am, 2.30–4.30pm, free), which showcases traditional crafts and technology. Otherwise, head on to experience living culture at **Kampong Sungai Matan** (bookings tel: 889 3061), a fishing

village where villagers can demonstrate traditional seafood processing and visitors can try their luck casting large nets.

The **Jerudong Park Playground**, about 25km (15 miles) from BSB, has improved over the last few years but isn't as popular as it was in its early days. Instead, catch colourful tropical sunsets (5.30–6pm) over the Laut Cina Selatan (South China Sea) at **Jerudong Beach** or over non-alcoholic cocktails at the **Pantai Restaurant** of the premier Empire Hotel and Country Club (www.theempirehotel.com; Mon–Sat 6.30–10.30pm).

Rainforest bounty

With two-thirds of its land laudably protected by conservation laws, Brunei's tropical rainforests are pristine and can be easily accessed in a day trip from the city. Nonetheless, other than in recreation parks, infrastructure and interpretation are lacking – which means you will have to depend on tour operators.

The **Tasek Merimbun Heritage Park ❸**, home to Brunei's largest lake, is 40 minutes' drive west of BSB. Growing around the lake is swamp forest vegetation, with large swathes of sedges up to 2 metres (7ft) tall. There are three easy-walking trails, picnic spots and an Information Centre (Sun–Thur 9am–5pm, Fri 9–11.30am, 2.30–5pm, Sat 9.45am–5pm; free) with a great view of the lake.

Huge mangrove trees are found on **Pulau Selirong**, a 2,570-hectare (6,350-acre) island at the mouth of Sungai Brunei some 45 minutes from BSB. A 2km (1.2-mile) wooden walkway brings visitors close to immense stilt roots. Look out for flying foxes and squirrels.

Ulu Temburong

The jewel in Brunei's rainforest crown is the 50,000-hectare (120,000-acre) **Ulu Temburong National Park ❹**. Protecting lush mixed dipterocarp forest, its top attraction is a wobbly-knee-inducing canopy walkway, which elevates visitors 45 metres (148ft) above the forest floor. Getting there is an adventure in itself, with boat rides between nipa palm-lined banks followed by an ride through small rapids. Spend the rest of the time swimming, kayaking, jungle-trekking and exploring waterfalls.

The indigenous people of Brunei, including the Kedayans and the Iban, comprise around 3.5 percent of the population.

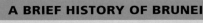

A BRIEF HISTORY OF BRUNEI

Local inhabitants engaged in trade with China and other parts of mainland Asia as early as the 6th century AD. During the 10th century, they came under the Buddhist kingdom of Srivijaya and later, the Hindu Majapahit Empire. By the 14th century, Brunei was a powerful seafaring state with a sultan based in Batu on the Brunei River, and an Islamic cultural tradition that has endured to this day.

During Brunei's golden age under the charismatic Bolkiah, the remnants of Ferdinand Magellan's fleet weighed anchor in Brunei in 1521 as the first Europeans to visit the sultanate. In the century that followed, other Spanish, Portuguese and Dutch traders eroded Brunei's trading power, but Brunei remained independent until the 19th century.

Then, British trader James Brooke became Rajah of Sarawak, but spent much of his energy chipping away at the power of the sultanate. To preserve his nation from being completely swallowed up by Sarawak, the sultan asked for British protection in 1888. Oil was discovered in 1929 and 30 years later, the nation achieved internal self-rule, although Britain continued to administer its foreign affairs and defence. In 1963, despite intense pressure, Brunei refused to become part of the Federation of Malaysia. Soon after, the 21-year-old Sandhurst-educated Prince Muda Hassanal Bolkiah became Sultan. Sovereignty was achieved in 1984.

Lian Shan Shuang Lin Temple in Singapore.

SINGAPORE

Often derided by budget travellers as sanitised and boring, Singapore offers respite from the exhausting travails encountered elsewhere in the region. But there is much to enjoy here: the food is superb, the shopping unmatched, and the districts of Little India and Chinatown animated and colourful.

Shopping in Little India.

Minutes after landing at the stunningly efficient Changi Airport, the visitor is whisked down a highway lined with tropical palms and bougainvillaea, and mile after mile of housing blocks, with probably the highest rate of home ownership in the world. Offshore, ships from all over the globe wait their turn in the world's busiest container port.

On a map of nearly any scale, the island of Singapore is just a 699-sq-km (267-sq-mile) -dot at the southern tip of the Malay Peninsula. One of Asia's most successful economies has gone far beyond what Sir Stamford Raffles, its founder, envisioned when he bought the island from its Malay ruler in 1819 and set up as a trading post. From a sleepy village, Singapore grew rapidly, drawing immigrants from China, India, Europe and neighbouring Malaya and Indonesia.

Singapore has a population of 5.31 million, of whom nearly 75 percent are Singapore residents. The non-resident population includes a sizeable number of expat employees of multinational corporations as well as unskilled labourers. In deference to the original settlers, Malay is the national language, but the *lingua franca* is English. Nearly every Singaporean is bilingual. English, Chinese, Malay and Tamil are official languages.

Singapore's skyline at night during the Grand Prix.

For most who visit Singapore, and for many who live there, it's all about dining and shopping. Singapore prides itself as perhaps the greatest food destination in Southeast Asia. Its mix of refined Chinese, Malaysian, and Indian cuisines – as well as imports from other traditions throughout the region – is indeed renowned. The cultures that support these cuisines are readily visible in the city's vibrant Chinatown and Little India.

Asian and Western culture and values meet and mix in this cosmopolitan city. But Confucian precepts still temper ideals of personal freedom. Society and public discourse are kept on a tight rein, with fines for jaywalking, littering and other social misdemeanours. The result, however, is an uncommonly clean and efficient city, with probably the cleanest streets outside Switzerland.

DECISIVE DATES

The early years

2nd century AD

Sabara, a trading emporium, is identified in Ptolemy's *Geographic Huphegesis* as being at the southern tip of the 'Golden Chersonese', possibly Singapore.

1200s

Settlement called Temasek reported on Singapore Island.

1300s

A settlement called Singapura is founded.

14th–18th centuries

Siam seizes the small island but shows little practical interest in it. In the 17th century, Singapore is settled by about 100 sea nomads. In the last years of the 18th century, the British open a trading post at nearby Malacca.

British colonial rule

1819

Sir Stamford Raffles arrives.

Sir Stamford Raffles.

Posing amidst rubber trees.

1823

Raffles issues regulations outlawing gambling and slavery.

1824

The British agree to withdraw from Indonesia, in return for which the Dutch recognise British rights over Singapore. The Sultan cedes Singapore in perpetuity to the British.

1826

The trading stations at Penang, Malacca and Singapore are named the Straits Settlements, under the control of British India.

1839

First ship built in Singapore is launched.

1851

Straits Settlements placed directly under the rule of the Governor-General of India.

late 1800s

The Suez Canal opens and the number of ships calling in at Singapore increases. Malaysia and Singapore develop into the world's main rubber producers.

1911

Population grows to 250,000 and the census records 48 races on the island, speaking 54 languages.

1923

Singapore is linked to Malaysia by a causeway.

1941

Japan invades Malaysia. Singapore is bombed on 8 December.

1942

British troops surrender Singapore to Japan.

1945

Japanese rule ends.

Independence and federation

1948

Emergency declared in June. Malayan Democratic Union dissolved.

1951
Legislative Council Election. Singapore formally proclaimed a city with a royal charter.

1955
Rendel Commission granted by the British leads to elections and David Marshall becomes chief minister. The Labour Front have a majority, but the PAP (People's Action Party) forms a powerful opposition.

1956
PAP Central Executive Committee election; Communists decline to run. Chinese riots; leftist PAP leaders arrested.

1958
A constitutional agreement for partial independence for Singapore is signed in London.

1959
PAP wins general election. Lee Kuan Yew becomes the country's first Prime Minister and Singapore is declared a state.

1963
The people of Malaya, Sarawak, North Borneo (now Sabah) and Singapore vote to form the Federation of Malaysia.

1964
PAP wins only one seat in Malaysian general election. Communal riots.

The Republic of Singapore

1965
Singapore leaves the Federation of Malaysia and becomes an independent sovereign nation, joining the United Nations and the Commonwealth.

1967
Singapore, Malaysia, Thailand, Indonesia, the Philippines and Brunei form a political and economic union, ASEAN (Association of Southeast Asian Nations).

1974
Japanese Red Army and Popular Front for the Liberation of Palestine terrorists take hostages at Shell Oil refinery.

1981
In a by-election, J.B. Jeyaretnam of the Workers' Party wins the first seat to be held by a member of an opposition party.

1984
PAP loses two of 79 seats in general election, its first loss of a seat in a general election since 1964.

1996
As a result of a decision by the OECD, Singapore is no longer considered a 'developing nation'.

1999
The economy makes a rapid recovery following the 1997 Asian crisis.

2001
The economy takes a tumble in the face of the US and global economic slowdown.

2003
Outbreak of Severe Acute Respiratory Syndrome (SARS) quickly controlled.

2004
Lee Hsien Loong takes over as prime minister. Goh Chok Tong continues as senior minister and Lee Kuan Yew, minister mentor.

2005
The green light is given to legalise casino gambling.

2007
Singapore Airlines the national carrier takes delivery of the first Airbus 380 superjumbo jet.

2009
Singapore appears to emerge from its worst recession on record.

2013
Singapore demands urgent action from Indonesia when forest fires create hazardous air pollution over the state.

Singapore's Marina Bay Sands casino, part of the massive development completed in 2010.

PEOPLE AND CULTURE

The island of Singapore is a proverbial melting pot of cultures, and it is this diversity that gives the famously disciplined city-state its distinctive character.

Singapore's population consists of three main groups – Chinese, Malays and Indians – as well as numerous minorities. Today, the Chinese make up about 75 percent of the resident population. When Sir Stamford Raffles hoisted a Union Jack ashore and founded modern Singapore in 1819, Chinese planters, pirates, fishermen and traders were already established on the island. Five years after the colony was established, Singapore had 3,000 Chinese and more were arriving weekly.

The term 'Straits Chinese' refers to Chinese immigrants who began settling in the Malay Peninsula and Riau islands more than 400 years ago in order to take advantage of the rich trade along the Straits of Malacca. Straits Chinese culture is often called by a different name, Peranakan, and the people themselves are sometimes called Babas and Nonyas.

A hybrid Straits Chinese culture evolved over the centuries, with its own distinct language, architecture, cuisine and clothing. Their *lingua franca* is Malay, but an idiosyncratic version of Malay. Peranakan food is unique in its lavish

Young Singaporeans partying during the Grand Prix.

> Ever since early settlers borrowed the Sanskrit words Singha Pura (Lion City) in the naming of the island, Singaporean society has continued to draw heavily from the Indian subcontinent.

use of spices and shrimp paste for cooking and can be readily found all over the island. Katong on the eastern part of the island is a characterful Peranakan enclave noted particularly for its string of popular Straits Chinese restaurants and boutiques selling Peranakan artefacts.

Shortly after Raffles founded British Singapore in 1819, junks started bringing waves of immigrants from coastal areas of southern and eastern China. Some of the largest groups comprised Hokkien Chinese from southern Fujian province. These hardy Chinese were usually traders and businessmen, largely the roots of today's Hokkien population that account for two-fifths of the Chinese in Singapore. Other Chinese came in large numbers, speaking distinct dialects, cooking different foods and engaged in other work. They took on the back-breaking jobs that no one else wanted to do.

Today's Singapore has a curious mixture of the new and old Chinese, broadly labelled

'English-educated' or 'Chinese-educated'. The latter tend more towards Chinese chauvinism and strong links to their heritage, responding more slowly to the new Singaporean identity. They sometimes look upon English-educated Chinese with shades of the contempt that their great ancestors held for barbarians not of the Middle Kingdom. The English-educated frequently perceive them, in return, as being conservative and unprogressive. Increasingly, though, with China emerging as an economic powerhouse, younger Chinese Singaporeans who are effectively bilingual in both English and Mandarin comfortably traverse Western and Chinese cultures.

The Malays

Like the Chinese and Indians, Singapore's Malays are largely descendants of immigrants, although their arrival most certainly predates that of the other races. Today they make up 14 percent of Singapore's resident population.

Despite Singapore's Chinese influence, its Malay origins are enshrined in the symbolic trappings of statehood – the national anthem is sung in Malay, the national language is Malay and the island's first president after independence was a Malay.

Historically, the Malay community, which is almost entirely Muslim, has been socio-economically weaker than the Chinese and Indians. This is partly because of its rural roots and partly due to Malay education, which closely follows a religious syllabus and has a reputation of lagging behind the English school system. The government, aware of these problems, set up a self-help organisation called Mendaki to promote the progress of the Malay community. Today, Malay youths are successfully entering the mainstream, slowly improving the negative perceptions attached to their community. Having imbibed the government's ambitious approach, a good number have merged into the landscape as professionals and entrepreneurs.

The Indians

The aroma of incense and freshly pounded spices floats over several square kilometres of Little India. Sixty percent of Singapore's Indians are Tamils, from the eastern part of southern India, and approximately 20 percent Malayalis Hindus from Kerala state on the other side of the subcontinent. The rest are Bengalis, Punjabis, and others; among whom one finds a colourful mixture of Hindus, Buddhists, Christians, Sikhs and Parsis. A minority of just 9 percent of Singapore's population, Indians nevertheless influence every aspect of life.

Much of the classical Indian culture has survived in Singapore, from old-style recipes to dance, art and literature. The casual traveller wanting a three-day taste of India might well find the taxi fare to Little India a better investment than a plane ticket to India.

Marking Diwali at Sri Veeramakaliamman Temple.

EURASIANS AND OTHER GROUPS

Now comprising less than 2 percent of the population, the Eurasians are some of Singapore's earliest residents. Most trace their roots back to colonial times, when the Portuguese, Dutch and English married local women. These days, Singapore plays host to a significant number of expat foreigners, many of whom have acquired permanent residency status. Most work in white-collar professions, primarily the IT and finance industries. Also in the local workforce are Chinese, Filipinos, Indonesians, Thai, Burmese, Sri Lankans and South Indians, often employed in construction, as well as women who work as live-in domestic maids.

The city-state's skyline at night.

SINGAPORE

Straddling the equator, tropical Singapore offers the very best of everything in urban Southeast Asia, from shopping and dining to entertainment and pampering.

Almost 200 years after Raffles first set foot in Singapore, the island is still governed from the colonial nucleus he established along the bank of the Singapore River. As well as being the hub of government, the old colonial district is also the location of Singapore's most famous landmark. Nearly everyone who comes to Singapore ends up at **Raffles Hotel Ⓐ** at one point or another – usually to try the world famous Singapore Sling, a cocktail invented at Raffles in 1915 at the Long Bar. Opened in 1887 by the Sarkies brothers, Raffles has seen its fair share of kings and queens, presidents and prime ministers, movie actors and lions of literature, as well as millions of ordinary people who are attracted to this paragon of tropical elegance and style.

Towering beside the hotel is a silver monolith called **Raffles City Ⓑ** (www.rafflescity.com.sg), one of the island's largest retail, office and hotel complexes and a busy hub of the Mass Rapid Transit (MRT) network. Next door is **Swissôtel The Stamford**, one of the world's tallest hotels, with panoramic views offered from its penthouse restaurant at the top. Across the street from Raffles City is **Chijmes Ⓒ**, a former Catholic convent and church dating back to 1860, but now restored into a pleasant hub of restaurants, bars and boutiques.

Raffles Hotel.

To the south across Stamford Road is the graceful spire of **St Andrew's Cathedral Ⓓ** (Mon–Fri 9am–5pm, Sat 9am–1pm, Sun 9am–1,30pm; guided tours Mon–Fri 10.30am–noon, 2.30–4pm). Built by Indian convict labour, it owes its sparkling white surface to a plaster made of egg white, egg shell, lime, sugar, coconut husk and water. The cathedral, in the style of an early Gothic abbey, was consecrated in 1862.

East of Raffles City across Beach Road is the **War Memorial Park Ⓔ**, dedicated to civilians who suffered

and died at the hands of the Japanese during World War II. On the opposite side of the park are two huge developments on reclaimed land that was once part of the sea. One is a massive convention, hotel and shopping development, called **Suntec City** and the other is **Marina Square**, a huge mall with hundreds of shops.

A world-class arts centre

South of Marina Square along Marina Bay is the prickly hedgehog-like outline of **The Esplanade – Theatres on the Bay** ❻ (www.esplanade.com), a S$600-million performing arts centre that opened in 2002 with grandiose dreams of establishing itself as a cultural landmark akin to Australia's Sydney Opera House. Housing a concert hall, theatre, an open-air amphitheatre, practice studios, outdoor spaces for informal performances and sculpted gardens, its distinctive facade of sharp-edged metal sunshades has been likened to the thorny shell of the *durian* fruit. From this vantage point are expansive views of

The striking Esplanade – Theatres on the Bay building.

Singapore's CBD skyline with the statue of the water-spewing **Merlion** in the distance, the half-fish, half-lion creature that is associated with Singapore's mythical past.

Across Esplanade Drive is **Esplanade Park** ❼, with its tree-lined **Queen Elizabeth Walk**, formerly a seafront promenade where colonial-day Europeans spent their leisure time strolling or playing cricket. West of the park across Connaught Drive is an expanse of green called the **Padang** ❽ ('field' in Malay), previously a frequent venue of Singapore's annual National Day celebrations on 9 August. Flanking the Padang are two of Singapore's oldest leisure clubs, **Singapore Recreation Club** (1883) and the **Singapore Cricket Club** (1852) – the former newly rebuilt on its original site.

Facing the Padang is **City Hall** ❾, completed in 1929 with a facade of Greek columns and a grand staircase. It was on these steps that Lord Louis Mountbatten accepted the surrender of Singapore by the Japanese General Itagaki on 12 September 1945. Lee

Kuan Yew declared Singapore's independence from Britain on the same spot in 1963. Next door is the former **Supreme Court**, built in 1927 with its stout Corinthian columns and green dome. Across Parliament Place is **The Arts House** (www.theartshouse.com.sg), a performing arts centre housed in an 1820s-structure, formerly the old Parliament House. The new **Parliament House**, completed in 1999, is next door, while the colonial structure to the east is **Victoria Concert Hall and Theatre** ❶, built in the 1880s to commemorate Queen Victoria's Diamond Jubilee and now a venue for opera, ballet and classical music. An 1887 bronze statue of Stamford Raffles graces the front of the theatre, a replica of which is found at the **Raffles' Landing Site** ❿ along the edge of the Singapore River. This is claimed to be the very spot where the founder of modern Singapore stepped ashore on 28 January 1819.

To its left is the stately **Asian Civilisations Museum** ❶ (www.acm.org.sg; Sat–Thur 10am–7pm, Fri 10am–9pm; charge), a beautiful restored neoclassical building that dates back to 1854 and formerly used as government offices. The museum displays a fine collection on the civilisations of East, Southeast, South and West Asia.

From here, cross the 1910 **Cavenagh Bridge** to get to Singapore's former General Post Office. This grand Palladian-style building has been restored to its current glory as the five-star **Fullerton Hotel** ❿ (www.fullerton1hotel.com). Originally built in 1928 and named after Robert Fullerton, the first governor of the Straits Settlements, the building is a wonderful example of the neoclassical style that once dominated the district. For a study in architectural contrast, take the underpass beneath the Fullerton Hotel to the glass-and-steel **One Fullerton** structure, a restaurant and nightlife hub by the waterfront. There are swanky restaurants and bars, most with floor-to-ceiling windows offering magnificent views of **Marina Bay** and **Marina Bay Sands** (www.marinabaysands.com), a 2,600-room resort offering Las Vegas-style gaming. The large luxury property

Raffles' Landing Site and surrounding skyscrapers.

Singapore City

0   500 m

0   500 yds

is one of two 'Integrated Resorts' in Singapore, designated as such, in part, to put a better face on their controversial casino centrepieces.

On the other side of the Singapore River is **Boat Quay** , an area of historic interest that has become something of a tourist trap. Dozens of Victorian-era shophouses have been restored and transformed into bars and restaurants with alfresco riverside seating.

The core of 'Singapore Inc' runs along the waterfront from south of Boat Quay to Keppel Road. The commercial area once centred on **Raffles Place** , which has been transformed into an open-air plaza with an MRT station below. Singapore's tallest skyscrapers are centred here: **OUB Centre, OUB Plaza** and **Republic Plaza**, all of which reach a height of 280 metres (920ft), the maximum allowed by civil aviation rules.

Chinatown

It may seem strange to have a **Chinatown** in a place that's over 75 percent Chinese, but this can be traced back to Raffles, who subdivided his new town into various districts in the early 1820s.

The heart of Chinatown is an area off South Bridge Road that embraces Pagoda, Temple and Trengganu streets. Begin your exploration in Pagoda Street, where the **Chinatown Heritage Centre** (www.singaporechinatown.com.sg; Mon–Thur 9am–8pm, last entry 7pm; charge) is located in the conservation shophouse at No. 48. It showcases the area's cultural heritage and includes a re-creation of the cramped living conditions of early residents.

In the evenings, Pagoda, Trengganu and Sago streets are closed to traffic and transformed into the lively **Chinatown Night Market** (Sun–Thur 5–11pm, Fri–Sat 5pm–1am). With over 200 stalls selling both traditional Chinese goods like calligraphy, masks and lanterns as well as contemporary items including jewellery and accessories, the market deserves a leisurely trawl. Another good place to shop in the neighbourhood is **Chinatown Point**, at the corner of New Bridge Road and

Chinatown's colourful night market is a great place to soak up the atmosphere and find a few bargains.

Playing draughts in Chinatown.

Cross Street, with its shops selling arts, crafts, souvenirs and antiques.

It is worthwhile stopping by the **Buddha Tooth Relic Temple** (daily 7am–7pm), on South Bridge Road, for the magnificent relic chamber – if not to gawk at the Tang dynasty-inspired architecture. On level two are a tranquil teahouse and bookstore with a good collection of Buddhism books and music.

One of the most curious things about Chinatown is that it harbours some of the island's most interesting Hindu and Muslim shrines. Towering above the shophouses are the brightly painted figures adorning the *gopuram* (tower) at the entrance of the **Sri Mariamman Temple** (daily 5.30am–9pm) on South Bridge Road, the oldest Hindu shrine in Singapore. Brightly clad devotees perform *pujas* amid gaudy statues and vivid ceiling frescoes. Built in the 1820s, this is the site of Thimiti – the fire-walking festival – when the faithful work themselves into a trance and walk over burning embers to fulfil their vows to the goddess Droba-Devi. A block

away is the **Jamae Chulia Mosque** (daily 5.30am–9.30pm), with its pagoda-like minarets rarely seen in mosque architecture and reflecting strong Chinese influence.

Telok Ayer Street once ran along the waterfront, but today the road is blocked from the sea by a wall of gleaming skyscrapers. It was here that seafarers and immigrants from China's Fujian Province set up a joss house in gratitude for their safe arrival after their long sea voyage from China in the early 1820s.

The little joss house eventually became **Thian Hock Keng Temple** (daily 7.30am–5.30pm), the Temple of Heavenly Happiness dedicated to Ma Chu Po, Goddess of the Sea, who reputedly has the power to calm the ocean waters and rescues those in danger of drowning.

Further along the road is **Nagore Durgha Shrine**, also called Masjid Chulia. Currently closed for renovations, the mosque, built by Muslims from southern India in 1830, is another example of the ethnic and religious variety in Chinatown.

The exterior of the Peranakan Museum.

Upstream along the Singapore River, **Clarke Quay** **Q** – bounded by River Valley Road, Tan Tye Place and North Boat Quay – is lined with restored 19th-century warehouses now home to dining and nightlife establishments. To the north is historic **Fort Canning Park** **R**. Once known as Bukit Larangan (Forbidden Hill), in the early years of Singapore's history, this strategic location was the site of grand palaces protected by walls and swamps. In 1860, the British built a fort atop the hill, from where dawn, noon and dusk were announced each day by way of cannon fire.

At the base of the hill, at the junction of Coleman and Hill streets, is the **Armenian Church** **S** (daily 9am–6pm), also called St Gregory the Illuminator. Built in 1835, this exquisite church is the oldest in Singapore, and a cemetery in the grounds serves as a tribute to some eminent Singaporeans, among them Agnes Joaquim (1864–99), after whom Singapore's national flower, Vanda Miss Joaquim, is named. At No. 62 Hill Street is

another architectural gem of a building, the old red-and-white **Central Fire Station** **T**, headquarters of the Singapore Fire Brigade, which was completed in 1909. On the ground level is the **Civil Defence Heritage Gallery** (Tue–Sun 10am–5pm) where a gleaming red fire engine from 1905 takes pride of place.

Down Hill Street and left into Armenian Street is the **Peranakan Museum** (www.peranakanmuseum.sg; Sat–Thur 10am–7pm, Fri 10am–9pm; charge), noted for its comprehensive collection of Straits Chinese artefacts. Around the corner on Stamford Road is the **National Museum of Singapore** (www.nationalmuseum.sg; daily 10am–8pm; charge, free admission from 6.30pm). The museum has reinvented itself as a venue in which to learn about history with interactive displays and lifestyle programmes. Look out for the permanent exhibitions at the Singapore History and Singapore Living Galleries. Also in various galleries are 11 national treasures, from the Singapore Stone, a rock with inscriptions dating back to the

Singapore is a mixture of different architectural influences, reflecting its cultural diversity.

Sri Veeramakali-amman Temple.

10th century, to 14th-century Majapahit gold ornaments.

At nearby Bras Basah Road is the **Singapore Art Museum** (www.singart.com; Mon–Sun 10am–7pm, Fri until 9pm; charge, Fri 6–9pm free), with rotating exhibits covering Singaporean, Asian and Western artists. The museum houses the world's largest collection of contemporary Southeast Asian art.

Orchard Road and environs

The de facto heart of modern Singapore is **Orchard Road**, which begins just north of the Raffles Hotel area. Plaza Singapura and Park Mall are the first of the big shopping centres that have given this thoroughfare its international reputation.

Near Plaza Singapura is the **Istana** , the official workplace and expansive residence of Singapore's president. The palace and its lavish garden are strictly off-limits to the public, except on National Day and certain public holidays, when the gates are thrown open to curious sightseers. The Istana was built in 1869 on the grounds of an old nutmeg plantation, and it served as the residence of the British governor until independence.

Northwards on Orchard Road are the famous shopping malls that inspired one commentator to call Singapore the world's largest shopping centre with immigration controls. Near the Centrepoint mall is the charming **Peranakan Place** , a complex of six Peranakan-style terrace houses that have been transformed into a commercial hub of restaurants and bars. Take a walk behind the houses to **Emerald Hill**, where there are some lovely old restored homes that once belonged to wealthy Peranakan families.

Little India

A walk down Scotts Road leads to **Newton Circus Hawker Centre** , where you can sample Singapore's famed cuisine. Not far from here is **Serangoon Road**, where the visitor is plunged into a replica of the Indian subcontinent, with undulating music punctuated by car horns and bicycle bells, women drifting gracefully along

Inside a Kampung Glam fabric shop.

in vivid *saris* and the pungent aromas of spices. This is **Little India** 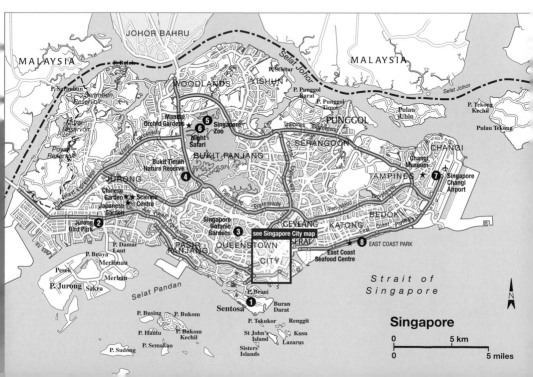, a marvellously colourful and atmospheric part of the city. It is filled with interesting religious sights – not just Hindu temples, but shrines representing the entire spectrum of Singapore's various faiths. Tucked away on Dunlop Street is the lovely old **Abdul Gafoor Mosque** (daily 9am–6pm), with an entrance elaborately decorated in carvings and Arabic calligraphy.

Hindus congregate at the **Sri Veeramakaliamman Temple** (daily 5.30am–noon, 4–9pm), dedicated to Kali, Shiva's consort, who epitomises the struggle against evil. She is shown ripping a hapless victim apart. Kali's sons – Ganesh, the elephant god, and Murugan, the child god – are depicted with her at the side of the temple. Further up Serangoon Road, the great *gopuram* (tower) of the **Sri Srinivasa Perumal Temple** (daily 7am–noon, 6–9pm) is visible, showing the different incarnations of Vishnu. The annual Thaipusam procession sets off from here. Devotees, their tongues, cheeks and bodies pierced by metal

skewers supporting *kavadi* (cage-like constructions decorated with wire and peacock feathers) make their way to the **Sri Thandayuthapani Temple** (better known as Chettiar Temple) in Tank Road. This is done in gratitude or supplication to Lord Murugan.

Race Course Road may have lost its horses, but the street is now renowned for its South Indian 'banana-leaf' curry restaurants. Down the street are a few Chinese temples. **Leong San See Temple** (daily 5.30am–6pm), dedicated to Kuan Yin, is richly carved and ornately decorated. At the back is a spacious courtyard and numerous ancestral tablets. Over the road is the stunning **Sakya Muni Buddha Gaya Temple**, also known as the Temple of 1,000 Lights (daily 8am–4.30pm), where a 15-metre (50ft) -high Buddha sits in a halo of light, atop a base depicting scenes from the life of Prince Siddharta Gautama.

At the very heart of the nearby Beach Road district is **Kampung Gelam**, site of Istana Kampung Gelam, the old royal palace built in the early 1840s by Sultan Ali Iskandar Shah. Arab traders

Singapore

– together with Bugis from Sulawesi, Javanese, Sumatrans, Malays and people from the Riau islands – eventually settled in the area, transforming Kampung Glam into a commercial hub, especially the stretch along Arab Street, which still draws those looking for fabric and basketware. The **Malay Heritage Centre** (www.malayheritage. org.sg; Tue–Sun 10am–6pm; charge) in the compound has interesting displays tracing the history and heritage of the Malays. Dominating the neighbourhood is the golden bulk of **Sultan Mosque ❷** (Sat–Thur 9am–1pm, 2–4pm, Fri 2.30–4pm), the largest mosque in Singapore and where the *muezzin* calls the faithful to prayer five times a day – the women to their enclave located upstairs, the men to the mosque's main prayer hall.

Sentosa and the West Coast

Immersed in the city and its shopping centres, it's easy to forget that there is another, less built-up side to Singapore – so take the opportunity to enjoy a little island hopping. The most accessible island is **Sentosa ❶** (www.sentosa.com.sg; charge), which has become a major resort and recreation area, after its previous life as a military base. A cable car stretches from **Mount Faber** to Sentosa, or you can reach the island via MRT from HarbourFront station at **VivoCity** on Telok Blangah Road, followed by a bus or Sentosa Express ride. It is also a pleasant 15-minute walk across a boardwalk. Its name may mean 'Island of Tranquillity', but Sentosa is now dominated by one of Singapore's two 'integrated' casino resorts, the Resorts World Sentosa (www. rwsentosa.com), a Universal Studios theme park and a Marine Life Park featuring the world's largest oceanarium. Still, on a quiet weekday, it is possible to relax on its fine sandy beaches and soak up the sun.

Plants and wildlife

Western Singapore embraces both industrial areas such as Jurong and Tuas and a major recreation zone that has some of Singapore's largest green spaces and theme parks, such as the

Spotting wildlife on a Singapore Zoo Night Safari.

Jurong Bird Park ❷ (www.birdpark. com.sg; daily 8.30am–6pm; charge), the world's largest bird park. Scarlet ibis welcome visitors at the entrance of this 20.2-hectare (50-acre) park, also home to 8,000 birds of 600 species.

The lovely **Botanic Gardens** ❸ (www.sbg.org.sg; daily 5am–midnight; free) near Tanglin Road have been in bloom for over a century, although its lineage can be traced back to the 1820s, when Sir Stamford Raffles planted an experimental garden on Fort Canning Hill. Its orchid gardens are not to be missed. For less-manicured flora and fauna, six jungle trails weave throughout the **Bukit Timah Nature Reserve** ❹ (daily 6am–7pm; free), about 12km (8 miles) from the city centre. The thick tropical vegetation resembles the entire scenery of Singapore when Raffles first arrived. This 163-hectare (403-acre) park has a rich collection of local wildlife, including long-tailed macaque monkeys, flying lemurs, tropical squirrels, pangolins and brilliant forest birds.

The **Singapore Zoo** ❺ (www.zoo. com.sg; daily 8.30am–6pm; charge) at Mandai Lake Road, is one of the best zoos in the world and has the finest wildlife collection in Southeast Asia. The place bills itself as an 'open zoo' – few of the animals are in cages or behind bars. It is home to 2,500 specimens from 315 species, of which 16 percent are endangered. For a different perspective, consider the **Night Safari** ❻ (www.nightsafari.com.sg; daily 7.30pm–midnight; charge), where nocturnal animals can be observed outside under special lighting.

East Coast

Visitors have their first experience of Singapore en route to the city from **Changi Airport** ❼ along the east coast, with sandy beaches on one side of the coastal highway, and luxury condominium blocks on the other. The east coast is packed on weekends as Singaporeans escape to the beach, but during the week it is very quiet. **East Coast Park** ❽ stretches for more than 15km (9 miles) along the coast between Marina Bay and the airport, fringed with casuarinas, coconut palms and flowering trees.

Quiet sands at Palawan Beach on Sentosa

SINGAPORE HAWKER FOOD

A visit to the city-state is incomplete without a meal at one of its food centres, where an astonishing variety of dishes is cooked on the spot.

The hawker centre offers multi-ethnic Singapore cooking at its best. Whether it's a simple dish of noodles for S$3 or a S$20 three-course meal of barbecued fish, chilli prawns and fried vegetables with rice, the cost is a fraction of what you would pay for a similar meal in a restaurant. Prices apart, the experience is unique, and a pleasant reminder of your stay in this food-crazy city. When celebrity chef Anthony Bourdain visited Singapore, he proclaimed, 'I love the hawker centres. The whole style of casual eating here is sensational.'

For the uninitiated, here's how you order a meal at a hawker centre. If there's a group of you, have one person sit at a table to *chope* (meaning reserve in local parlance) seats for the rest of the party. Don't be surprised if you see seats with bags or packets of tissue paper on them; it's a sign that they have been taken. The others, having noted the table number, should order their food and tell the stall owner the table number they are seated at, unless of course it's a self-service operation. If you're on your own, you can share a table with strangers. As you savour your meal, you will realise why dedicated gourmets will head for their favourite food stall at every opportunity.

Satay vendor at Lau Pa Sat Festival Market in the Central Business District.

Plate-sized and bright-red crabs smothered in a piquant chilli and tomato sauce is a typical Singapore dish that you'll find at hawker stalls that specialise in seafood. The dish isn't as fiercely spicy as it looks, but if you're not feeling particularly adventurous, order black pepper crabs instead, which are just as delicious.

Queuing for food at the Tekka Centre.

Tucking in at Glutton's Bay.

CHANGING TIMES FOR THE HAWKERS

In the old days, there was no such thing as a hawker centre. Instead, the roving hawker was a familiar fixture in the neighbourhood. The sound of an ice-cream bell, or the clacking of a bamboo stick against a wooden block, or the chant of the *mua chee* man selling sticky nougat-like candy, would send children – and their parents – scrambling from their homes into the streets to buy their favourite snack. The fare on offer was amazing, from bread and bowls of steaming noodle soups to peanuts and *poh piah* (spring rolls).

Then came the roadside hawkers, who set up their makeshift stalls on the streets after dark, when parking lots were emptied of cars and replaced by wooden tables and stools, and pushcarts which doubled as mobile kitchens. By 1987, thanks to urbanisation and an official obsession with cleanliness, the last of the roadside hawkers were cleared. The only places where you can find roadside hawkers today are Chinatown's Smith Street and Glutton's Bay at The Esplanade. These sanitised recreations of yesteryear do their best to resemble the city's once bustling and colourful street life.

...ood centre at Geylang sells a large range of dishes. Most ...ablishments include photographs of each dish for ease of ...ntification.

...si briyani is a hugely popular dish at hawker centres.

Cha kuay teow is made from wok-fried flat rice noodles (kway teow) and yellow noodles (mee) with garlic and bean sprouts and various other ingredients including fish cakes or fresh shrimps.

One of many stunning beaches in
the Indonesian archipelago.

Borobudur Temple at sunrise,
Yogyakarta.

Leaving offerings at the Pura Tirtha Empul spring.

INDONESIA

An immense nation extending across one-eighth of the world's circumference, Indonesia is Asia's most diverse country and a rising star, both politically and economically.

Batik scarves for sale in Ubud's market.

The immense archipelago of tropical islands that make up modern Indonesia encompasses a mind-boggling range of peoples, cultures and societies, past and present – from ancient Hindu-Javanese temples to Bali's modern luxury resorts, the stone-age tribes of the Papuan highlands to the immense metropolis that is Jakarta. The country's motto, *Bhinneka Tunggallka*, or Unity in Diversity, is no mere slogan. The population of nearly 220 million people is derived from 300 ethnic groups who speak over 250 (some sources say as many as 500) distinct languages.

Almost 90 percent of the people are Muslims, with a significant Christian population. There are also smaller numbers of Hindus and Buddhists. In most cases, particularly in the rural areas, these beliefs are augmented by indigenous, centuries-old animistic traditions. The fourth-most populous nation on Earth, Indonesia straddles two geographically defined racial groups, the Asians to the west and the Melanesians in the east. Over the centuries, commerce and trade has brought Indians, Arabs and European settlers.

Sundanese wayang golek (wooden puppets).

In the years since the dictator Soeharto's fall in 1998, Indonesia has proved that democracy can indeed work within a primarily Muslim population. Both Middle Eastern and Western nations now view Indonesia as a reliable voice that can bridge gaps, and thanks to the competent leadership of Susilo Bambang Yudhoyono, the country's stature in ASEAN has risen substantially.

Today's Indonesia is Asia's third-fastest growing economy, and appears to be weathering the global downturn better than most. It is respected for its strong record in fighting terrorism and corruption, and reforms to its police force and military have been monumental. The relatively young democracy still has a lot of work to do, not least to improve its environmental record as huge areas of rainforest continue to be felled, but according to analysts, it's time for the world to change its perception of Indonesia.

DECISIVE DATES

Prehistory

1.7 million years ago
Java Man (Homo erectus) lives in Java.

250,000 years ago
Solo Man, the evolutionary descendent of Homo erectus, inhabits Java.

40,000 years ago
Fossil records of modern humans (Homo sapiens) found in Indonesia.

5000 BC
Austronesian peoples begin moving into Indonesia from the Philippines.

Indianised kingdoms

AD 400
Hindu kingdoms emerge.

850
Sanjaya and rival Buddhist Sailendran (Syailendran) dynasties merge through marriage. Sanjaya seizes control of central Java. The

Sailendrans flee to Srivijaya in southern Sumatra.

860–1080
The golden age of Srivijaya.

Singasari and Majapahit

13th century
Ken Arok founds Singasari dynasty; Mongol invasion joins Wijaya in civil war in Singasari. First-known Muslim kingdom, Majapahit.

1389
Majapahit's decline begins.

15th century
Majapahit and Kediri are conquered by the new Islamic state, Demak, on Java's north coast. The entire Hindu-Javanese aristocracy moves to Bali.

Early 16th century
Two Islamic sultanates in Java are established: Banten and Cirebon.

An early 18th-century Dutch map from a time when only the north coastal ports of Java were well known to the Dutch.

Dutch colonial years

Early 17th century
Senopati founds second Mataram kingdom; Dutch ships arrive. Both contest the sovereignty of Java.

1602–19
The Dutch form the United Dutch East Indies Company (VOC) and establish trading posts in Banten and Jayakarta (Jakarta), later renaming it Batavia.

1613–71
Mataram expands rapidly and attacks Batavia, enraging the Dutch. Its capital is shifted to Kartasura, west of Surakarta.

1740–55
A major conflict originates in Batavia. Mataram is split into two major courts: Surakarta and Yogyakarta.

1767–77
The VOC fights a bitter campaign to conquer eastern Java, resulting in the demise of the last Hinduised kingdom in Java.

1799–1800
The VOC is dissolved and the Dutch assume control.

Resistance and repression

1811–7
Brief period of English rule under Thomas Stamford Raffles. Raffles pens History of Java.

1825–30
Diponegoro leads the Java War against the Dutch.

A 19th-century portrait of a Dayak man.

Raffles deposes him; he dies in exile.

1830–50

The Dutch introduce a tax payable by labour or land use known as the 'Cultivation System'; severe famines occur, 250,000 people die.

National awakening

1908–30

Indonesians attending Dutch schools begin to form regional student organisations; new national consciousness takes shape. Turbulent period of organised rebellions.

1927

Sukarno tries to unite all citizens. He is imprisoned and later exiled.

World War II and independence

1942–4

Japanese invade Indonesia and promise independence.

1945

Japan surrenders. Sukarno and Muhammad Hatta declare Indonesia's independence. The Dutch resume control; war for independence breaks out.

1949

The Dutch acknowledge Indonesia's independence under pressure from the United Nations.

Sukarno and Soeharto years

1960–3

Sukarno dissolves parliament; his anti-colonial sentiments become more militant.

1965

After a failed Communist coup, the Chinese are the focus of anti-Communist attacks.

1966

Sukarno signs over powers to his protégé, Soeharto, who takes over presidency. Until 1998, Soeharto is 're-elected' six times.

1997

The rupiah crashes, banks collapse and foreign debt surges during the Asian economic crisis.

1998

Soeharto is forced to resign amid mass student uprising; vice-president B.J. Habibie takes over as Indonesia's third president.

Sukarno on his trip to Washington DC.

Contemporary Indonesia

1999

Indonesia's first democratic elections in 40 years are held; Abdurrahman Wahid becomes the country's fourth president.

2002

Bali bombings by Muslim extremists kills 202 people, mainly tourists.

2004

First direct presidential election is held; Susilo Bambang Yudhoyono is elected.

2005

Aceh peace accord signed, ending nearly 30 years of fighting in Nanggroe Aceh Darussalam.

2009

Government increases crackdown on Muslim extremists and terrorists.

2012

Bomb-maker Umar Patek sentenced to 20 years in prison for his role in the 2002 Bali attacks. The sentencing brings an end to a 10-year investigation.

PEOPLE AND CULTURE

Indonesia is the world's fourth-most populous nation, encompassing an astonishing range of peoples and cultures.

The complexity and diversity of peoples, languages, customs and cultures found in the Indonesian archipelago is truly astounding. Living here are 300 distinct ethnic groups, each with its own cultural identity, who together speak a total of more than 250 (some sources say up to 500) mutually unintelligible languages, but all sharing the official Bahasa Indonesia as a common tongue.

Migratory theories

The physical differences of people from one end of the archipelago to the other – in pigmentation, stature and physiognomy – are easily recognisable. To explain this range of racial types, scholars once postulated a theory of wave migrations. According to this theory, various Indonesian groups arrived from the Asian mainland in a series of discrete but massive migratory waves, each separated by a period of several centuries.

The first wave of migrants, it was thought, were the dark-skinned, wiry-haired negritos – people of pygmy stature who today inhabit remote forest enclaves on the Malay peninsula, in the Andaman Islands north of Sumatra, and on several of the Philippine islands. It was suggested that the negritos somehow migrated the length of the Eurasian continent, from Africa, eons ago.

The second wave, too, were thought to have arrived from Africa or perhaps India. These peoples were dubbed the Australoids, and are the Melanesian inhabitants of New Guinea, including Papua (Irian Jaya) and Australia. The third wave, proto-Malays, were thought to have migrated from China by way of Indochina.

The last wave, the deutero-Malays, were related to and closely resembled the Chinese.

Balinese locals.

These peoples today inhabit the plains and coastal regions of all the major islands, and many developed large hierarchical kingdoms, attaining a level of pre-modern civilisation comparable to the most advanced societies elsewhere in the world.

The 1891 discovery of *Homo erectus* (Java Man) fossils in Indonesia – million-year-old remains of one of our earliest ancestors – brought a new understanding of the distant past. It now appeared that the so-called negrito and Australoid people, with their darker skin pigmentation, actually evolved partially or wholly in the tropical rainforests of Southeast Asia, just as the light-skinned Malays evolved in the cold temperate regions of east and central Asia. During the last Ice Ages, when land bridges linked the major islands of the Sunda shelf to the mainland, these peoples circulated freely and even crossed the oceans, populating Australia by about 50,000 years ago.

The wave theory of coordinated, coherent mass movements seems unlikely for a number of reasons. In a fragmented region like the Indonesia archipelago, village and tribal groups were constantly on the move, at least in historic times, dissolving and absorbing each other as they went. Many anthropologists now suggest

> Great linguistic diversity – such as that found across Indonesia – is generally interpreted by anthropologists as an indication that an area has been settled and stable for a long period.

bush knife, to clear a forest plot. Traditionally, by carefully timing the burn immediately to precede the onset of rains, the farmer simultaneously fertilises and weeds the land. While these semi-nomadic farmers now comprise less than a tenth of Indonesia's total population,

Making pottery in Lombok.

Muslim schoolgirls in northern Bali.

that it is more realistic, therefore, to imagine a situation in which small groups of hunters, gatherers and cultivators percolated into the region relatively slowly, absorbing and replacing the original inhabitants over a period of many millennia.

Cultural distinctions

One important distinction when considering Indonesia's people focuses on the two main agricultural patterns: *ladang* and *sawah*. *Ladang* agriculture, also referred to by the Old English word *swidden* and by the descriptive expression slash-and-burn, is practised in forested areas, generally outside of Java and Bali. The *ladang* farmer utilises fire as a tool, along with axe and

they are scattered throughout more than two-thirds of the nation's land area.

Most rural Indonesians, by contrast, inhabit the narrow plains and coastal regions of the major islands, where the principal farming method is *sawah*, or wet-rice paddy cultivation. In fact, 60 percent of Indonesia's population of 237 million live on Java and Bali, which between them comprise only 7 percent of Indonesia's land. On Java, population densities can be as high as 2,000 people per sq km (5,000 per sq mile) – some of the world's highest concentrations of humanity – motivating past governments to relocate Javanese and Balinese to less-populated provinces (this 'transmigration' continues, but in a more restricted manner).

Sawah cultivation is a labour-intensive form of agriculture that can be successfully practised only under the special conditions of rich soil and adequate water, but one that seems capable of producing seemingly limitless quantities of food. The farmers who plant wet-rice paddies actually reshape their environment over a period of many generations, clearing the land, terracing, levelling and diking the plots, and constructing elaborate irrigation systems. As a result, this system has both required and rewarded a high degree of social cooperation. Particularly in Java and

A long-eared Dayak man in east Kalimantan. Kenyah Dayak ceremonies are held at longhouses on Sundays.

Bali, populous villages have long been linked with towns – economically and culturally – through a hierarchically defined framework that has coordinated labour to maintain the fragile irrigation works. The food surpluses produced by these villages has historically permitted a degree of urban opulence.

As might be expected, the *sawah* societies of Java and Bali are strikingly different from the *ladang* communities of the outer islands. The Javanese, for example, put great emphasis on cooperation and social attitudes. Village deliberations are concluded not by majority or autocratic rule, but by a consensus of elders or esteemed individuals. *Rukun*, or harmony, is the

primary goal, achieved through knowing one's place within society.

City folks

Sharply contrasting with Indonesia's primarily subsistence farmers and fishermen are the urbanites. Jakarta, a sprawling metropolis of around 10 million people, is the country's economic and political hub. Luxury apartment complexes, upscale shopping malls, restaurants serving every imaginable cuisine, and jobs with international corporations beckon young professionals, who seemingly quickly adapt to life

A woman in traditional costume in Sulawesi.

in 'modern' Indonesia. Sophisticated urbanites frequent trendy nightclubs, and spend their wages on the latest electronics and other consumer goods. Although Jakarta is the country's largest city by far, similar scenes can be seen in other sizeable urban areas, such as Surabaya, Makassar, Balikpapan and Medan.

Smaller cities, such as Yogyakarta (Jogja) and Bandung bustle with university life and attract the brightest of Indonesia's youth, who dress in jeans and carry backpacks. These Indonesians bear a great similarity to college students worldwide.

In Bali, where a substantial proportion of the population is involved in the tourism industry, many citizens have a higher degree of sophistication than is seen in villages. Tour guides speak a multitude of foreign languages, and hotel and restaurant staff are every bit as comfortable conversing with foreigners as their counterparts elsewhere on the planet.

But regardless of how worldly they appear to be, when most Indonesians *pulang kampung* (go home to their villages), they instantly revert to the customs from where they grew up. For many, local languages and dialects are still spoken at home; the houses they grew up in may have dirt floors and no running water or electricity; or they may be called upon by their families to help in the fields or perform a ceremony.

To glimpse just how deeply their rural traditions are embedded, one only needs to witness what has been called one of the world's largest mass migrations – as Muslims either *pulang kampung* at the end of Ramadan, visit the Erau festival in eastern Kalimantan, a thanksgiving celebration of Dayak arts and cultures, or follow a procession to Jogja's neaby Parangtritis beach where offerings are made to the South Sea Goddess. While not as widely known as Bali's cremations and temple ceremonies, traditional rituals are held throughout the country and are widely attended by both city folk and villagers.

Time, balance and harmony

A favourite expression in Indonesia is *jam karet*, which translates, literally, as 'rubber time'. Rarely does a social event or a meeting start exactly at the appointed hour; time can be stretched to suit the occasion. Another universal trait is the

respect and deference shown to superiors and elders, with distinct speech levels used according to the status of the person in some of Indonesia's languages.

To lose face, to be made ashamed (*malu*), is something to be avoided at all costs, and for this reason many Indonesians often suggest that something can be done when they know it cannot. A local may often give wrong directions – or ticket prices or information – rather than say they don't know. When doing business, it can be rather difficult to figure out whether or not you've been misinformed.

Villagers celebrate a festival on the beach, Bali.

OTHER CULTURES

'Unity in Diversity' is Indonesia's national creed. The Balinese are arguably its most famous citizens, and the Javanese comprise the largest majority by far, but did you know…

Other than the majority Javanese, Java is also home to the gentle Badui and Sundanese in the west; the Betawi in Jakarta; and the quick-tempered Madurese and Hindu Tenggerese in the east.

Sumatra's ethnic groups include the staunchly Muslim Acehnese and one of the world's largest matrilineal groups, the Minangkabau, with the primarily Christian former-cannibal Bataks tucked between the two areas.

In Lombok, the predominantly Muslim Sasaks are divided into two groups: the Wetu Telu and Wetu Lima.

Western Flores is the home of the Manggarai. Eastern Flores is known for its fine, hand-woven *ikat* cloths and houses Indonesia's largest Catholic seminary.

Many of the people in Indonesia's remote Nusa Tenggara islands still practise animism.

The Torajans in Sulawesi hold elaborate funeral ceremonies, lasting up to five days. Sulawesi also includes the seafaring Bugis and Makassarese.

In the villages of the Baliem Valley, Papua, many men still wear traditional *koteka* (penis gourds), and bare-breasted women wear skirts woven from orchid fibres.

INDONESIAN TEXTILES

Although batik is Indonesia's most famous textile, its wide variety of traditional hand-woven cloths is admired throughout the world.

Batik is one of the most prominent expressions of cultural identity in Indonesia. Nowhere in the world has the art of batik evolved into such high standards, fine-tuned over the centuries under the patronage of the Javanese royal courts. Today, the making and wearing of batik remains a source of national pride. It is the formal attire of both Jakarta urbanites and simple villagers.

In Central Java and Bali, hand-woven striped and checked textiles are known as *lurik* and *keling* respectively, and remain ritually important. Each motif is defined by a specific palette and organisation of stripes. *Ikat* cloths are created using a resist-dye technique; sections of threads are tied, untied, and retied as each dye colour is applied. Once the desired colours have been achieved, traditional weavers use a backstrap loom to weave the cloth. Warp *ikat*, with the lengthwise threads tied and dyed to form a motif, is found across eastern Indonesia, Kalimantan and Sulawesi, while weft *ikat*, with the crosswise threads forming the motif, is made in Bali and Sumatra. If gold or silver threads are woven into the cloth as a supplementary thread across the warp or the weft, it is called *songket*. *Songket* is found in Bali, Lombok, Sumbawa and Sumatra. Today, batik, *lurik*, *ikat* and *songket* appear in the fashions of some of Indonesia's most popular designers.

Songket weaving in Lombok.

Modern Indonesians mix cloth from regions other than their own, for example a songket sh. from Bali, Lombok, Sumbaw. or Sumatra with a hip and he. cloth from Java.

Batik shirts for sale at 'Batik Keris' shop, Yogyakarta.

Traditional methods of batik making are painstaking.

INDONESIAN BATIK

In 2009, UNESCO added Indonesian batik to its Cultural Heritage list, honouring its symbolism and deep philosophy. Most treasured is batik *tulis*, which is painstakingly hand-drawn with wax in a resist-dye technique, boiled and dyed many times to achieve the desired motifs and colours. *Cap* (pronounced 'chap') batik is also hand-made, using copper stamps fashioned by artisans. Today textiles called 'batik' are also machine-printed and produced by silk-screening processes. They are less expensive, but every Indonesian knows they are not the real thing.

Although the use of synthetic dyes and machine-spun threads speeds up production, thus reducing costs, modern cloths can never replace the treasure of exquisite traditional weavings using hand-spun threads and natural dyes.

...ditional weaving is a thriving cottage industry, with great ...ounts of cloth woven in bright colours.

...e detailed pattern on a finished cloth.

Gunung Bromo and Gunung
Semeru (erupting) in eastern Java.

JAVA

Although it covers only 6 percent of Indonesia's land area, Java is by far the nation's most populous island and its political and economic centre.

Java has much to offer to the intrepid traveller, from rich and complex ancient cultures and cool mountain retreats to magnificent volcanoes. The countryside is a mix of densely populated lowlands carpeted in verdant rice fields, and upland areas with mixed agriculture, fewer people and a few remaining areas of forest. Of Indonesia's six Unesco World Heritage Sites, four are here: Borobudur, Prambanan and Sangiran – the Java Man site – all in central Java, and Ujung Kulon National Park in western Java.

This is Indonesia's powerhouse. The most populated island (with 125 million, around 52 percent of the Indonesian total), it is the location of the country's largest city – Jakarta, the centre of government and the country's commercial hub.

The Javanese constitute about two-thirds of the island's total population and originate from the fertile plains of the centre and east, plus much of the island's northern coast. In the Jakarta area the native tribe is the Betawi, while in western Java, the inhabitants are mainly Sundanese, except for a small pocket of Badui who still adhere to age-old traditions. Madura and the adjoining east coastal region are home to the Madurese people, while near Gunung Bromo is the island's last enclave of Hindus, the Tenggerese.

Traffic headed into modern Jakarta.

The trading ports of the northern coast also harbour Chinese, Arabs and a scattering of Europeans, as well as people from other Indonesian islands.

Jakarta

Capital of the world's fourth-most populous nation and home to more than 9 million Indonesians (not counting sub-district populations – the entire urban area, known as Jabotabek, has a population of around 23 million), **Jakarta** ❶ is a metropolis that verges on the chaotic. Every

Main Attractions

Jakarta
Bandung
Semarang
Yogyakarta (Jogja)
Borobudur
Surakarta (Solo)
Surabaya
Gunung Bromo

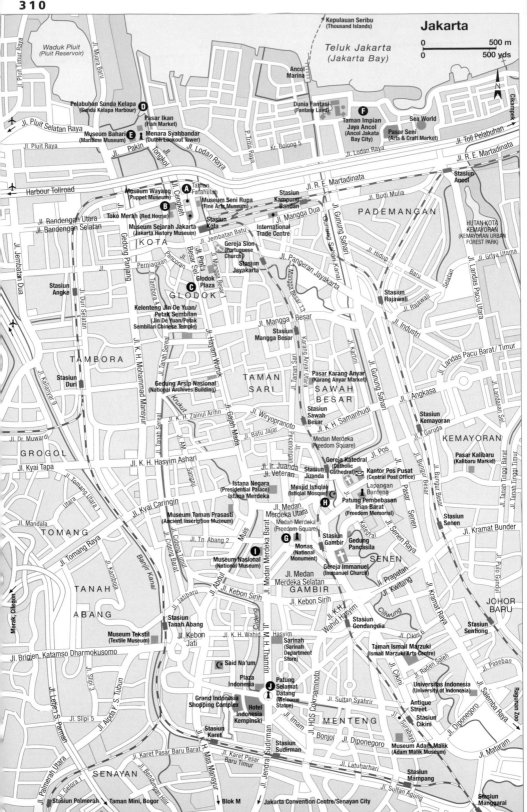

Jakarta

day, thousands of vehicles crowd into the busy Thamrin-Sudirman corridor during rush hour, causing traffic jams that can last several hours. Throughout Jakarta, shopping and entertainment areas such as the busy Glodok and Blok M throb with neon signs and modern malls with luxury-brand boutiques, hypermarkets, entertainment centres, restaurants and international five-star hotels. In Kemang, a middle-class suburb in the south, expatriates and Indonesians frequent trendy eateries, while in the north, Kelapa Gading is home to many wealthy families.

Much of Jakarta today is hardly recognisable from two decades ago, yet there are other parts of the city that seem frozen in time. In some residential districts, large houses stand alongside *kampung* (village) dwellings imparting something of a rustic atmosphere.

Old Batavia

Following the demolition of the old city in the early 19th century (see page 309), only the town square area survived. Very different to the rest of downtown, it has been gradually restored and renamed **Taman Fatahillah Ⓐ**. Many surrounding colonial edifices have been converted into museums. The area is currently experiencing something of a regeneration, with **Café Batavia** offering an eclectic combination of decor and cuisine. Historical walking tours can be arranged through the **Bank Mandiri Museum** (Jalan Lapangan Stasiun No. 1; Tue–Sun 9am–4pm; charge). The **Museum Wayang Ⓑ** (Puppet Museum; Tue–Sun 9am–3pm; charge) on the western side of the square, displays puppets and *topeng* (masks) from all over Indonesia.

Jakarta's Chinatown, **Glodok Ⓒ**, is adjacent to Taman Fatahillah and is primarily known for its electronics shops. In 2000, the 35-year ban against the public use of Chinese characters was lifted, and today Glodok is the site of festive *Imlek* (Chinese Lunar New Year) celebrations.

To the north lies the old spice trading centre, **Sunda Kelapa Harbour Ⓓ**, with a mile-long wharf in use since 1817. Early morning is the best time

Jakarta History Museum.

A BRIEF HISTORY

In 1618, the architect of the Dutch empire in the East Indies, Jan Pieterszoon Coen, ordered construction of a new town: Batavia, modelled on Amsterdam. Starting out as a modest, walled town, it prospered, then declined as corruption, decreasing market prices and frequent epidemics of malaria, cholera and typhoid took their toll. In the early 19th century, the old city was demolished to be replaced by a better-planned version, around today's Medan Merdeka (Freedom Square). During the Japanese occupation of World War II, Batavia was renamed Jakarta (Djakarta), and transformed into a city of more than 1 million. The rapid development continued following independence from the Dutch in 1949, and since then it has been the unrivalled political and economic centre of Indonesia.

FACT

The Dutch East India Company (Vereenigde Oost-Indische Compagnie or VOC) was formed in 1602, two years after its English counterpart, allowing Dutch merchants to join forces to maximise profits from trade with the Indonesian islands (the East Indies). The Company was empowered to negotiate treaties, raise armies, build fortresses and wage war to further Dutch interests. As with the English in India, its activities eventually resulted in the establishment of a formal empire under government control.

The National Museum.

to walk among the ships' prows and gangways and watch the unloading of cargo from the majestic wooden *pinisi* schooners built by the seafaring Bugis people of South Sulawesi.

The area around Sunda Kelapa is rich in history, and the best way to survey it is on foot. Near the river stands a 19th-century **Lookout Tower** (Uitkik), constructed by the Dutch on the site of the original customs house (Pabean) of Jayakarta. This is where traders once rendered their gifts and tribute to the local ruler in return for the privilege of trading here.

Behind the tower stands a long, two-storey structure dating from Dutch East India Company times (see margin, left), now the **Museum Bahari ⓔ** (Maritime Museum; Jalan Pasar Ikan No. 1; Tue–Fri 9am–3pm, Sat–Sun 9am–2pm; charge). This former warehouse was erected by the Dutch in 1652 and was used for many years to store coffee, tea and Indian cloth. Inside are displays of traditional sailing craft from all corners of the Indonesian archipelago, as well as some old maps and photographs

of Batavia. Down a narrow lane and around a corner behind the museum lies **Pasar Ikan**, the fish market, beyond which are numerous stalls selling nautical gear.

Further east along the waterfront is a giant seaside recreation area called **Ancol Jakarta Bay City ⓕ** (www. ancol.com; daily 24 hours; charge). Once swampland, it now features beachfront hotels, swimming pools, a golf course, bowling alley and a crafts market. There are also several theme parks inside, including **Sea World** (daily 9am–6pm; charge) and **Dunia Fantasi** (daily 9am–6pm; charge), an amusement park complete with roller coasters and a Ferris wheel. Thousands of Indonesians converge here on the weekends and holidays.

Central Jakarta

A circumnavigation of central Jakarta begins at the top of **Monas** (National Monument; Tue–Sun 9am–4pm; charge), a 137-metre (450ft)-tall marble obelisk set in the centre of **Medan Merdeka ⓖ** (Freedom Square), sporting a 14-metre (45ft) bronze flame

sheathed in 33kg (73lbs) of gold. A high-speed elevator rises to the observation deck, where on a (very rare) clear day there is a mesmerising 360-degree view of Jakarta. There is a museum in the basement, with dioramas that show the history of Indonesia's struggle for independence from the Dutch.

East of Medan Merdeka is the imposing white marble **Mesjid Istiqlal**  (Sat–Thur except prayer times and holy days), with its massive dome and rakish minarets, on Jalan Veteran. It was built on the former site of the Dutch Benteng (Fort) Noordwijk. During the Ramadan fasting period, the mosques are filled to capacity.

On the west side of Medan Merdeka lies one of Indonesia's great cultural treasures, the excellent **National Museum** (www.museumnasional.or.id; Tue–Thur and Sun 8.30am–2.30pm, Fri 8.30–11.30am, Sat 8.30am–1.30pm; charge). Opened in 1868 by the Batavian Society for Arts and Sciences – founded 90 years earlier as the first scholarly organisation in colonial

Asia – the museum houses priceless collections of antiquities, books and ethnographic artefacts acquired by the Dutch during the 19th and early 20th centuries. It is best to allow several hours to explore this treasure trove.

Hail a cab and cruise west across the wealthy Menteng residential area to the **Welcome Statue** , a busy roundabout with a statue of two waving youths and a fountain. Jalan Thamrin, lined with shopping malls and office buildings, runs north and south here, turning into Jalan Sudirman a few blocks south. At the roundabout is the **Hotel Indonesia Kempinski** (www.kempinski.com), attached to a mega multi-storey shopping and entertainment complex. Across the street is the ritzy Grand Hyatt perched atop one of Jakarta's many upmarket malls, **Plaza Indonesia** (www.plazaindonesia.com).

Adjacent to the Sultan Hotel is the **Jakarta Convention Center** (www.jcc.co.id). Everything from art exhibits and cultural events to rock concerts is held here. Further south on Jalan Sudirman, behind the Senayan sports field, venue for national soccer

Jakarta's Welcome Statue.

Monas towers over Medan Merdeka.

Working at a tea plantation.

South Jakarta

Heading south about 15km (9 miles) from the centre of the city is the **Ragunan Zoo** (daily 7am–6pm; charge), set in a tropical park. There are over 3,000 animals, most of which are indigenous to Indonesia, including Komodo dragons, orang-utans and Sumatran tigers.

Just off the super highway leading south to Bogor is a theme park, **Taman Mini-Indonesia Indah** (Beautiful Indonesia-in-Miniature Park; www.tamanmini.com; Mon–Sun 8am–5pm; charge). There are pavilions representing Indonesia's provinces, constructed using authentic materials and workmanship to showcase the architecture of each province. Inside are displays of handicrafts, traditional costumes, musical instruments and artefacts indigenous to the regions. All are clustered around a lake containing islands that make up a three-dimensional relief map of the Indonesian archipelago. It is a good place to familiarise

matches, are five more upscale shopping malls, including the **Senayan City** (www.senayancity.com).

yourself with Indonesia's remarkable ethnic variety.

Other attractions on site include a bird park, orchid garden, IMAX cinema, cable-car ride, transport museum, oil and gas museum, stamp museum, swimming pool, and the splendid **Museum Indonesia** (tel: 021-840 9246; Tue–Sun 8am–5pm; charge), a three-storey Balinese palace filled with Indonesia's cultural arts. The **Museum Purna Bhakti Pertiwi** (Presidential Palace Museum; tel: 021-840 1687; Tue–Sun 8am–5pm; charge) established by the late First Lady Ibu Tien Soeharto is a showcase for the family's private collection of antiques, art and many diplomatic gifts.

Beyond Jakarta: western Java

Western Java may be roughly divided into two distinct regions: the Parahyangan (Abode of the Gods), an area of volcanic highlands centred around the provincial capital, Bandung; and the northern coastal plain. The coast is much more mixed, having absorbed a multitude of immigrants

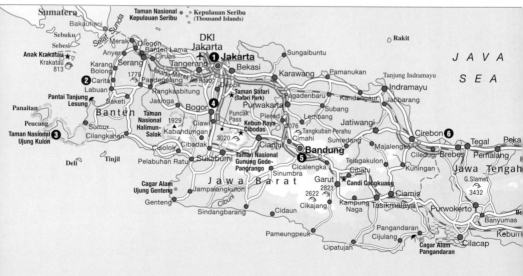

and influences via its trading ports for many centuries.

For a quick getaway from Jakarta, visit the sandy and secluded west coast beaches. **Anyer** and **Carita** ❷ are weekend retreats for Jakartans, with swimming, sailing and diving plus numerous dining and accommodation options. This palm-fringed coast is famous for its views of the volcanic **Krakatau** islands. On the southwestern tip of Java is **Ujung Kulon National Park** ❸, the last refuge for the highly endangered Javan rhinoceros (see page 261).

Bogor ❹, 'Rainy City', is situated in the hills just 48km (30 miles) south of Jakarta, and accessed in 40 minutes via toll highway. A former resort from the Dutch era, it lies between Mount Salak and Mount Gede-Pangrango at a modest altitude of around 200 metres (650ft). The **Bogor Botanical Garden** is located in the heart of the city and has a collection of hundreds of species of tropical plants. The **Presidential Palace** is inside the botanical garden. The gong factory and wooden-puppet maker are well worth exploring.

Also easy to reach from Jakarta via a toll road (2 hours), the highland city (altitude 750 metres/2,460ft) of **Bandung** ❺ offers a cool alternative to the coastal heat. Despite the proliferation of modern buildings, there is still an abundance of Dutch colonial, Art Deco architecture to see, including the magnificent **Gedung Sate**, a skewer-shaped building of impressive Indo-European architecture. You can also browse factory outlet shops along Jalan Cihampelas and check out the famed 'Java Man' at the Geological Museum on Jalan Diponegoro. The impressive volcano, **Tangkuban Perahu**, is just 30 minutes to the north; cars can drive all the way up to the crater.

The north coast

Java's northern coastal ports were once the busiest and richest towns on the island. In **Cirebon** ❻, the **Keraton Kasepuhan** (Palace of the Elder Brother), built in 1678, sits on the site of the 15th-century Pakungwati palace of Cirebon's earlier Hindu rulers. Just next to the palace stands the

A Muslim man at prayer.

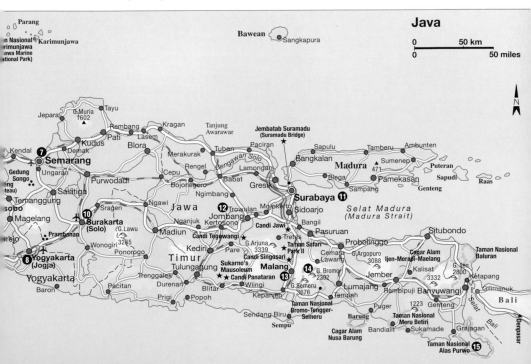

The Keris dagger Is a distinctive Indonesian item.

Transport in Yogyakarta.

Grand Mosque, or Masjid Agung, constructed around 1500. Cirebon is known for its unique batik featuring Chinese-inspired patterns such as *mega mendung* (meaning 'cloudy sky').

About 310km (195 miles) to the east, **Semarang ❼** is wedged into a narrow coastal plain between the sea and steeply rising foothills. Known during old Islamic times for its skilled shipwrights, today it is the commercial hub and provincial capital of Central Java. Relics of the past bear witness to the presence of a large population of Dutch traders and officials, and a generous sprinkling of affluent Chinese merchants.

Gereja Blenduk, the old Dutch church on Jalan Suprapto downtown, with its copper-clad dome and Greek cross floor plan, was consecrated in 1753 and stands at the centre of the town's 18th-century European commercial district. The most interesting area, however, is **Pecinan** (Chinatown), a grid of narrow lanes tucked away in the centre of the city, reached by walking due south from the old church along Jalan Suari to Jalan Pekojan. Here, some old townhouses retain the distinctive Nanyang style of elaborately carved doors and shutters.

Yogyakarta (Jogja) and around

The green crescent of fertile rice lands that blankets Gunung Merapi's southern flanks – with historic Yogyakarta as its focal point – is today inhabited by over 11 million Javanese, with at least 3 million urban residents. Rural population densities here soar above 1,000 people per sq km (2,500 per sq mile), and in some areas, a square kilometre feeds an astounding 2,000 people with labour-intensive farming.

Although it was founded only in 1755, sprawling **Yogyakarta ❽** (locally called Jogja; www.jogjapages.com) is situated at the very core of an ancient region known as Mataram, site of the first great central-Javanese empires. From the 8th until the early 10th centuries, this fertile plain was ruled by a succession of Indianised kings – the builders of Borobudur, Prambanan and dozens of other elaborate stone monuments. In about AD 900, however,

these rulers suddenly and inexplicably shifted their capital to eastern Java, and for more than six centuries thereafter, Mataram was deserted.

Modern-day Jogja is a vibrant town and the heart of traditional Javanese culture. Its exceptional universities attract young people from throughout the archipelago and abroad, and its renowned fine arts academy is home to aspiring arts students.

The Keraton

The first stop for all visitors to Jogja is the **Keraton** (Kraton), the Sultan's Palace (tours Sat–Thur 8am–2pm, Fri 8–11am; charge), a 200-year-old palace complex that stands at the very heart of the city. According to traditional cosmological beliefs, the Keraton is literally the 'navel' or central 'spike' of the universe, anchoring the temporal world and communicating with the mystical realm of powerful deities. In this scheme of things, the Keraton is both the capital of the kingdom and the hub of the cosmos.

It houses not only the present Sultan, Hamengkubuwono X, and his family, but also the powerful dynastic regalia (*pusaka*), private meditation and ceremonial chambers, a magnificent throne hall, several audience and performance pavilions, a mosque, a vast royal garden, two great gateways, several courtyards, stables, barracks, an armaments foundry and two parade grounds planted with sacred banyan trees. All of this is in a carefully conceived complex of walled compounds, narrow lanes and massive gateways, and bounded by a fortified outer wall measuring 2km (1.5 miles) on each side. The Sultan still commands great respect from the local people although his only legal power is as the Governor of the Special Province of Yogyakarta.

Construction began in 1755 and continued for almost 40 years. Today, only the innermost compound is considered part of the Keraton proper, while the maze of lanes and lesser compounds, the mosque and the two vast squares have been integrated into the city. Long sections of the outermost walls still stand, however, and many if not most of the residences inside are still owned and occupied by descendants of members of the court.

There is much else to see within the Keraton, including the **Batik Museum** (daily 10.30am–noon; free), the **Kereta Museum** (same hours; charge) and various cultural performances including gamelan and poetry (daily 9 or 10am–noon).

Behind and just west of the Keraton stand the ruins of the opulent and architecturally ingenious royal pleasure garden, **Taman Sari** (daily 9am–3pm; charge). Dutch representatives to the Sultan's court marvelled at its construction: a large artificial lake (long since replaced by houses), underground and underwater passageways, meditational retreats, a series of sunken bathing pools, and an imposing two-storey mansion of European design. Sadly, only the crumbling remains of its walls remain.

TIP

There are as many as 75,000 artisans in the Jogja area hand-crafting fine art and souvenirs from products ranging from natural fibres to silver, stone to leather. While many visitors head for Jalan Malioboro to shop, bolder travellers will be rewarded with the sights and experiences of visiting the villages where these items are made, some as near as 30 minutes to 1 hour away from the city centre. Ask at your accommodation for locations, or visit www. jogjapages.com.

In Taman Sari.

The father of the current Sultan of Jogja was revered across Indonesia for his efforts in securing independence from the Dutch. When Indonesia became a republic, all the sultans across the country relinquished their powers to the new central government. Many, however, retained local prestige, which is particularly pronounced in the case of Hamengkubuwono, the current Sultan of Jogja. He has also continued his father's patronage of Javanese arts and traditions.

Borobudur temple.

Main street, Jogja

Jogja's main thoroughfare, **Jalan Malioboro**, begins directly in front of the royal audience pavilion, at the front of the palace, and ends at a phallic *lingga* some 2km (1.5 miles) to the north, a shrine dedicated to the local guardian spirit, Kyai Jaga. It was laid out by Hamengkubuwono I as a ceremonial boulevard for colourful state processions, and also as a symbolic meridian along which to orient his domain. Today, Jalan Malioboro is a busy avenue lined with shops and souvenir stalls, teeming with vehicles, horse-drawn carriages and pedicabs; it is primarily a shopping district, but also an area of historical and cultural interest. Begin at the north town square (*alun-alun utara*) and stroll up this latter-day processional, stopping first at the **Sono Budoyo Museum** (Tue–Thur 9am–2pm, Fri 8–11am, Sat 8am–1pm; charge) on the northwestern side of the square. It was opened in 1935 by the Java Institute, a cultural foundation of wealthy Javanese and Dutch art patrons, and today houses important collections of prehistoric artefacts, Hindu-Buddhist bronzes, *wayang* puppets, dance costumes and traditional Javanese weapons.

Proceed northward from the square through the main gates and out across Jogja's main intersection. Immediately ahead on the right stands the old Dutch garrison, **Benteng Budaya** (Fort Vredeburgh; Tue–Thur 8.30am–2pm, Fri 8.30–11am, Sat–Sun 8.30am–noon; charge), now a cultural centre, hosting art exhibitions and performances. Opposite it on the left stands the former Dutch Resident's mansion. Used during the post-war independence struggle as the presidential palace, it is now the State Guest House. Farther along on the right, past the fort, is the huge enclosed central market, **Pasar Beringharjo**, a rabbit warren of small stalls frequented by housewives and souvenir shoppers.

Jogja also has some other not-to-be-missed art galleries and museums, including **Affandi Museum** (Jalan Laksda Adi Sucipto No. 167; www.affandi.org; daily 9am-4pm; charge), with the work of Jogja's most famous artist; and **Cemeti Art House** (Jalan D.I. Panjaitan

No. 41; www.cemetiarthouse.com; free) and **Jogja Gallery** (Jalan Pekapalan No. 7, Alun-Alun Utara; charge), both specialising in contemporary art.

Borobudur

A leisurely one-hour drive from Jogja leads to the steps of fabled **Borobudur** ❾ (www.borobudurpark.com; daily 7am–6pm; charge; multilingual licensed guides available), 40km (25 miles) northwest of Jogja. This huge stupa, the world's largest Buddhist monument, was built during the Sailendra dynasty, between AD 778 and 856, around 300 years before Angkor Wat. Yet, within little more than a century of its completion, Borobudur and all of central Java were abandoned. At about this time, neighbouring Gunung Merapi erupted violently, and some theorised that volcanic ash from that eruption concealed Borobudur for centuries.

It is estimated that 30,000 stonecutters and sculptors, 15,000 carriers and thousands more masons worked for 20 to 75 years to build this astonishing monument. Seen from the air, Borobudur forms a mandala, a representation of the cosmos. Seen from a distance on the ground, it is a stupa or reliquary, a model of the cosmos in three vertical parts: a square base supporting a hemispheric body and a crowning spire. As one approaches along the traditional pilgrimage route from the east and then ascends the terraced monument, circumambulating each terrace clockwise in succession, every relief and carving contributes to the whole.

About 100km (60 miles) northeast of Borobudur, the heights of the volcanic **Dieng Plateau** are home to the oldest temples in central Java, dating back to the late 7th century. Eight temples named after the heroes of the Hindu *Mahabharata* epic stand amid brightly coloured sulphur springs and bubbling geothermal mudholes.

East of Jogja is a volcanic plain littered with ancient ruins. Because these *candi* (temples) are considered by locals to be royal mausoleums, the region is known as the Valley of the Kings. In the centre, 17km (10 miles) from Jogja, lies the **Prambanan temple complex** (daily 7am–6pm; charge). Completed around AD 56 to commemorate an important

Carvings at the Prambanan temple complex.

Javanese tourists at Borobudur temple.

military victory, it was deserted within a few years and eventually collapsed. The original restoration of the central temple began in 1937 and was finally completed in 1953. Further restoration continues today.

Surakarta (Solo)

The quiet, old court city, **Surakarta** ❿ (more commonly known as **Solo**), lies just an hour east of Jogja by car. At the southern end of the city's main street, Jalan Slamet Riyadi, is the pedestrian-friendly 'Solo City Walk'. From here, many tourist attractions are accessible by foot or tram. One of the main attractions is a functioning 18th-century palace, **Keraton Kasunanan** (Sat–Thur 8.30am–2pm; charge) constructed between 1743 and 1746 on the banks of the mighty Bengawan Solo River. The **Keraton Museum** was established in 1963 and contains ancient Hindu-Javanese bronzes, traditional weapons, and coaches dating back to the 1740s. Dance rehearsals at the Keraton take place in the front pavilion within the palace, Bangsal Smorokoto, every Sunday at 10am.

In the Arab quarter bazaar at Surabaya.

About 1km (0.6 miles) northwest of the main palace is **Puro Mangkunegaran** (Sat–Fri 8.30am–2pm, Sun 9am–1pm; charge), established by another branch of the royal family in 1866. The *pendopo* (pavilion) is the largest in central Java and has four gamelan orchestras. Weekly music and dance rehearsals are held here every Wednesday at 10am. The museum houses the private collections of Mangkunegara IV: dance ornaments, *topeng* (masks), jewellery, ancient Javanese and Chinese coins, bronze figures, and a superb set of ceremonial *keris* blades.

Performances of *wayang orang*, a folk version of the courtly dance-dramas, are held nightly at **Taman Hilburan Rakyat (THR) Sriwedari** at no. 275. Jalan Slamet Riyadi. Just west of the Keraton is **Pasar Klewer**, where visitors can browse and bargain for souvenirs and Solo batiks. Also of interest is **Triwindu Antiques Market** on Jalan Diponegoro, a feast of memorabilia for flea market lovers. Buyers beware: not all 'antiques' on display are what they seem.

NATURE AT ITS FINEST

The Jogja region is bounded by forest-covered hills, volcanoes and plantations to the north and by the Indian Ocean to the south. Its location lends itself to almost every outdoor pastime imaginable. Enquire about adventure tours and outdoor activities at your accommodation or travel agent.

Most of the southern beaches have lava sand and rough seas. The most famous is **Parangtritis**, a black-sand stretch where ceremonies are held to appease Ratu Kidul, the goddess of the south sea, who is said to beckon people to her underwater castle. At **Kukup**, with white sand and a swimming lagoon, fishermen sell their daily catch, which can be cooked to customers' specifications on the spot.

Some 22km (14 miles) southeast of Jogja, the limestone hills of **Gunung Kidul**, with its many subterranean chambers, are a delight for cavers. To the north of town, the highly volatile 2,910-metre (9,550ft) **Gunung Merapi** (Fire Mountain) constantly belches lava and steam, but hikes up the mountain are possible and popular. Treks beginning from **Kaliurang**, a hill town 25km (16 miles) north of Jogja, leave in the pre-dawn hours and reach the upper slopes in time for glimpses of the glowing lava at sunrise. Treks are also possible from **Ratu Boko** temple near Prambanan.

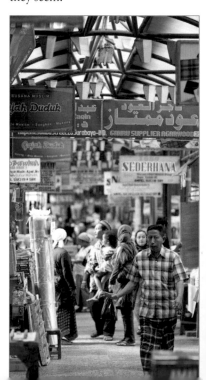

For batik aficionados, the museum at **House of Danar Hadi** (216–263 Jalan Slamet Riyadi) showcases a 10,000 piece private collection of antique batiks. At day's end, rest your weary feet at **Gladag Langen Bogan** (from 6pm; street musicians perform on Sat) on Jalan Mayor, packed with vendors of Solo speciality foods.

Surabaya and eastern Java

With over 400 years of colourful history, **Surabaya** ⓫, East Java's provincial capital, was the largest and most important seaport in the archipelago until the turn of the 20th century. Today, the port ranks second after Jakarta's Tanjung Priok.

In the centre of the town is the wonderfully refurbished **Hotel Majapahit** (www.hotel-majapahit.com), built nearly a century ago in the tradition of the Strand in Yangon, Burma, and Raffles Hotel in Singapore. It is worth visiting for its combination of colonial elegance and Art Deco trimmings.

On Jalan Selompretan stands Surabaya's oldest Chinese shrine, the 18th-century **Hok An Kiong Temple**, built entirely of wood by native Chinese craftsmen. Chinatown is also known for **Kya-Kya**, a street pedestrianised at night, with hawker stalls and open-air dining. Near the Kali Mas canal on Jalan Kalisosok is the **House of Sampoerna** (6 Taman Sampoerna; www.houseofsampoerna.museum; daily 9am–10pm; free), a restored Dutch building housing a museum, gift shop and café. Visitors can see the rolling, cutting, packing and wrapping of *kretek* (clove cigarettes). Nearby is **Sunan Ampel**, the lively Arab quarters with shops selling Muslim clothes, prayer beads and other wares.

The delightful mountain resort **Tretes**, 55km (35 miles) south of Surabaya, is an excellent base for exploration of eastern Java's ancient Majapahit monuments at **Trowulan** ⓬.

Malang ⓭ is another pleasant highland town, a 2-hour drive south of Surabaya. In the vicinity are three temples, **Candi Singosari, Candi Jago** and **Candi Panataran**. The latter is East Java's only sizeable temple complex, built between AD 1197 and 1454.

The steep slopes of the active volcanoes of eastern Java have been the home of the primarily Hindu Tenggerese people for several centuries. In the twelfth month of the Tenggerese calendar, the colourful Kasada festival takes place. Villagers bring offerings to the holy volcano, Bromo, asking their god for protection and blessings. **Gunung Bromo** ⓮ itself is a squat volcanic cone inside a gigantic caldera. Trekkers ascend the mountain on foot or horseback (arrange at your accommodation) in the early morning hours to position themselves on the volcanic lip at dawn. The light of the rising sun illuminates the fog-filled caldera, and on clear mornings, the cone of **Gunung Semeru**, Java's highest point – and an active volcano – looms to the south.

On the southern coast of the **Alas Purwo National Park** ⓯ is one of the world's most extreme surfing areas, **G-Land. Gunung Ijen**, also within the Alas Purwo National Park, has a haunting sulphuric crater lake.

Artefacts at Trowulan's museum.

Merapi volcano at sunrise.

Preparing for a temple festival at the holy complex of Pura Besakih.

BALI

Bali is a high priority for most visitors to the region. Intense commercialisation has changed the southern part of the island, but elsewhere the magical ambience remains.

Bali is, first and foremost, a masterpiece of nature, a stunningly beautiful tropical island formed by an east-to-west range of volcanoes rising out of the deep blue sea, fringed by sandy beaches and enriched with fertile soil. And the Balinese have done much to turn these natural blessings to their advantage. All but the steepest land has been painstakingly terraced over the centuries with rice paddies that hug the volcanic slopes like steps. The land repays these efforts with abundant harvests, which in turn give the people time and energy to devote to their renowned cultural pursuits, the arts and religious obligations.

Abundant harvests are attributed to the goddess of rice and fertility, Dewi Sri. Her symbol is the *cili*, two triangles connected in the form of a shapely woman. Divine spirits dwell in the lofty mountains; dark and inimitable forces lurk in the seas. The human's rightful place is the middle ground between these two extremes, and each home, village and kingdom in Bali, has traditionally been aligned along this mountain–sea axis.

Isolation and confrontation

Bali was settled and civilised relatively early, as evidenced by stone megaliths scattered about the island. Around a thousand years ago, it became a vassal

of the great Hindu empires of eastern Java. Yet Balinese culture developed a sophisticated persona all its own. Bali was united in 1550 under an independent ruler and for two generations experienced a cultural golden age in which an elaborate ceremonial life, and also the arts, flourished.

Due to their traditional fear of the sea and suspicion of foreigners, the Balinese lived in virtual isolation from the rest of the world until the early 20th century, despite Dutch attempts to control the island.

Main Attractions

Nusa Dua
Kuta
Pura Tanah Lot
Sanur
Pura Taman Ayun, Mengwi
Ubud
Pura Besakih
Candidasa

Young surfer at Kuta.

EAT

The best-known Balinese dish is spit-roasted suckling pig, known as *guling celeng*, or by its Indonesian name, *babi guling*. Stuffed with herbs and spices, the skin is basted with turmeric juice before the piglet is roasted over glowing charcoal.

Throughout the 1800s, the Dutch, under the guise of seeking treaties of friendship and commerce, attempted to establish sovereignty over the island. Their incursions culminated in horrific mass suicides (*puputan*) in 1906, in which Balinese kings and courtiers threw themselves on *keris* daggers, or ran headlong into Dutch gunfire rather than face the humiliation of surrender. In the end, the Dutch failed in their bid to conquer Bali. Throughout their invasions, traditions of dance, music, painting, sculpture, poetry, drama and architecture were nonetheless refined and elaborated, ostensibly for the benefit of Bali's numerous gods. Since those days, Bali has been adept in absorbing influences from the outside, while retaining, if not strengthening, its cultural touchstones.

Southern Bali

As the focus for Bali's tourism, commerce and government, the south is by far the busiest region. But don't be deceived by the area's development. The temple festivals here are legendary for the intensity of their trance dances and the earthiness of their rituals. Denpasar's palace ceremonies rank among the most regal on the island, and major hotels host highly professional dance performances nightly. During Nyepi (Hindu Day of Silence), thousands of villagers, arrayed in their ceremonial finery, flood the southern shores of Kuta bearing offerings of food for the *melis* purification rites.

South of the **Ngurah Rai International Airport**, a bulbous peninsula fans out to form **Bukit Badung ❶**. The western and southern shorelines are rimmed with sharp, jutting cliffs, and until the early 1990s there was nothing but scarcely populated dry land. These days, **Bukit** (as the peninsula is generally known) is home to luxury resorts, villas and Bali's largest golf course. It is also the site of the region's most illustrious temple, **Pura Luhur Uluwatu ❷**, or Temple Above the Headstone (daily daylight hours; charge). The ocean 300 metres (1,000ft) below the temple's cliff-top perch is favoured by extreme surfers.

Surfing is big business in Bali.

Nusa Dua ❸, an extensive planned-resort area on the northeastern coast of Bukit Badung, has superb beaches that give way to **Benoa**'s mangroves. Benoa Harbour, lined with higher-end hotels and watersports operations, is the island's busiest seaport and accommodates fishing boats, inter-island ships and catamarans taking tourists to nearby **Nusa Lembongan** and **Penida** for diving.

Kuta and around

Whereas Nusa Dua caters to more upmarket visitors, **Kuta** ❹ is a kind of cluttered, traffic-packed tinseltown with a cosmopolitan feel, especially during peak season (Aug–Sept and Dec–Jan). The resort – and Bali's tourist industry – was shattered by the horrific bombs of 2002 and 2005, and while in some ways those events have changed it forever, Kuta remains a major tourist hub.

Its natural attractions are a broad beach, pounding surf and sunsets. Away from the beach, Kuta is packed with pubs, bars, restaurants, boutiques, surf shops, and inexpensive hotels. The built-up area merges north into the more sedate **Legian**, while still further north is decidedly hip **Seminyak**, which, like Kuta and Legian, has a wide sandy beach and thundering surf but without the crowds. There are a handful of upmarket hotels and a large number of good restaurants and bars. Past the Oberoi Bali hotel is the small but key temple **Pura Dalem Petitenget**, the Temple of the Awesome Box (daily daylight hours; donation). Many ceremonies are held at this temple, named after the box of betel-chewing ingredients left behind by the Javanese Hindu priest Dang Hyang Nirartha. The main road continues to **Kerobokan** and then west to **Canggu**, a black-sand beach.

The road from Canggu ends at **Pura Tanah Lot** ❺, or Temple of the Land in the Sea (daily daylight hours; charge). Perched on a large rock just offshore, it was founded by Dang Hyang Nirartha, the 16th-century Brahman sage considered to be the ancestor of Balinese high priests. To the northwest of the temple is an open

TIP

For insight into Balinese performing arts, visitors can observe dance and music classes in progress at ISSI, Jalan Nusa Indah in Denpasar.

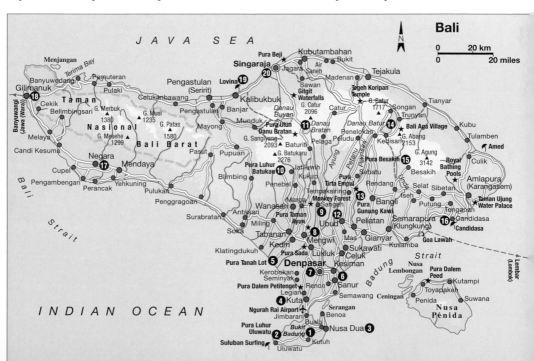

Selling flowers for offerings at Pasar Badung, Denpasar.

stage where regular *Ramayana* and *kecak* dance performances are held right after visitors enjoy the famous sunset backdrop over the temple.

Over on the eastern coast is **Sanur** ❻, a relatively quiet cluster of hotels and restaurants, with a good beach and water-sports facilities. Of interest is **Museum Le Mayeur** (daily except Wed 8am–4pm, Fri 8am–1pm; charge) on the beach north of the Inna Grand Bali Beach Hotel. It exhibits the works of the Belgian painter Jean Le Mayeur de Mepres (1880–1958), who moved to Bali in 1932. All of his paintings depict his wife, Ni Polok, a renowned *legong* dancer.

Denpasar

Denpasar ❼ is the capital of Bali province. Its main square was the scene of the horrific mass suicide in 1906, when almost the entire royal house of Denpasar rushed headlong into blazing Dutch guns. Successive governments have erected monuments commemorating the event. East of the square stands the town's main temple, **Pura Jagatnatha** (daily daylight hours; donation), with a figurine of Tintya, the almighty godhead, glinting from high on the temple's central shrine. The **Museum Negeri Propinsi Bali** (also called Museum Bali; Tue–Sun 8am–5pm; charge) next door houses a fine collection of artefacts and examples of Balinese craftsmanship. In the centre of town is **Pasar Badung**, a four-storey building housing the island's largest traditional market.

Central Bali

North of Denpasar, Ubud is the most popular point outside southern Bali. It is the island's artistic heart and can be the hub for excursions to the east, north and west.

One of the most important temples between Denpasar and Ubud is **Pura Sada** (daily daylight hours; donation) in **Kapal**. Dating from the 12th century, it has 64 stone seats resembling megalithic ancestral shrines that are believed to commemorate loyal warriors who fell in battle. Just down the road, **Tabanan**, with its breathaking terraced rice fields, is an ideal place

for all-terrain vehicle and four-wheel-drive adventures, as well as cycling and trekking. Past Kapal, a turn-off toward the mountains leads to **Mengwi** ⑧, a few kilometres north of Kapal. In 1634, the Raja of Mengwi built a magnificent garden temple, **Pura Taman Ayun** (daily daylight hours; charge). The temple's spacious compound is surrounded by a moat and is adjacent to a lotus lake. In the surrounding pavilions, priests recite their Vedantic incantations.

Northeast at **Sangeh** ⑨ is one of Bali's two famed monkey forests. According to Balinese versions of the *Ramayana* epic, this is where Hanuman's army landed when the monkey king lifted the sacred mountain, Mahameru, and broke it apart in order to crush Rawana. A moss-covered temple lies deep within the jungle.

North of Tabanan is one of Bali's most venerated temples, **Pura Luhur Batukau** ⑩ (daily daylight hours; charge), on the slopes of 2,276-metre (7,467ft) Gunung Batukau. Further north at **Danau Bratan** ⑪, a lake on the road crest to the north shore and a water source for surrounding farmlands, is Pura Ulun Danu Bratan (daily daylight hours; charge), which honours Dewi Danu, goddess of the lake.

Ubud

Ubud ⑫ and its 15km (9-mile) radius form Bali's artistic epicentre. Within this area is **Sukawati**, halfway between Denpasar and Ubud, once an important kingdom and a centre for Chinese traders during the Dalem dynasty period. A phalanx of shops and a market now conceal the grand Puri Sukawati palace. **Pasar Seni Art Market** in Sukawati is the island's largest art centre offering paintings, sculptures and pretty much everything else. Further north is **Mas**, a village of master carvers. In former times, woodcarvers worked only on religious or royal projects, but now they primarily produce decorative works for export.

Artists have thrived in Ubud since the 1930s when local aristocrat Cokorda Sukawati, German painter Walter Spies and Dutch artist Rudolf Bonnet formed the Pita Maha Art Society. Many of the finest works of the early Pita Maha years are exhibited in **Museum Puri Lukisan** (www.museumpurilukisan.com; daily 9am–6pm; charge) on Jalan Raya Ubud. The **Neka Art Museum** (www.museumneka.com; Mon–Sat 9am–5pm, Sun noon–5pm; charge), west of downtown, also has a superb collection of Balinese art.

Three other great art museums have been established in Ubud. The **Agung Rai Museum of Art** (www.armabali.com; daily 9am–6pm; charge), on Jalan Pengosekan, displays works by famous artists, including the only paintings in Bali by the Javanese artist Raden Saleh. **Museum Rudana** (www.museumrudana.com; Mon–Sat 9am–5pm, Sun noon–5pm), at Jalan Cok Rai Pudak No. 44, has traditional and contemporary Balinese art, and the **Blanco Renaissance Museum** (www.blancomuseum.com; daily 9am–5pm;

TIP

The monkeys that inhabit the forests near Ubud are very tourist-savvy and expect remuneration in the form of bananas and peanuts for their antics.

Carving religious works from stone in Ubud.

Puppet for sale in Tenganan, which retains its own culture.

Pura Besakih, or the 'Mother temple'.

charge) in Campuan, established by the late Spanish-born artist Don Antonio Blanco and his Balinese wife Ni Ronji, features the artist's drawings and paintings.

Pura Penataran Sasih (Lunar Governance), in **Pejeng**, east of Ubud, contains Indonesia's most important Bronze Age antiquity: the 2,000-year-old Moon of Pejeng drum. Shaped like an hourglass, beautifully etched, and over 3 metres (10ft) long, it is the largest drum in the world to be cast as a single piece. According to Balinese legend, it fell from the sky, but the discovery of an ancient, similarly shaped stone mould in Bali proves that sophisticated bronze-casting techniques were known here from an early time.

Pura Gunung Kawi ⑬ is a complex of stone-hewn *candi* (temples) and monks' cells reached by descending a long, steep stairway through a stone arch into a watery canyon. The Balinese refer to their religion as Agama Tirta, the religion of the waters. It is not surprising, then, that a pilgrimage to the **Pura Tirta Empul**

spring at **Tampaksiring**, 2km (1.5 miles) upstream from Gunung Kawi, is an essential part of every major Balinese ceremony and ritual.

Further north, in the old Gunung Batur crater, is **Danau Batur** ⑭. Here, **Pura Ulun Danu Batur** is one of two major *subak* (irrigation society) temples on the island. Nearby **Trunyan** village is the home of the Bali Aga, a tribe that has remained separated from modern Bali for over 600 years.

Eastern Bali

To go from southern Bali to the north and the east, take Bypass Ida Bagus Mantra, dubbed Sunset Road as it parallels the beach from Denpasar up to Kusamba, between Semarapura and Amlapura. Several kilometres after **Kusamba**, at the foot of a rocky escarpment, is the cave temple **Pura Goa Lawah** (daily 7am–6pm; charge), one of the nine great temples of Bali. About 15km (9 miles) further, a side road to the right leads to picturesque **Padangbai** harbour town, departure point for ferries to Lombok.

Pura Besakih

The mountain road north from **Semarapura** (formerly Klungkung) climbs along some of Bali's most spectacular rice terraces, passing through several villages on the way until the road ends at the island's holiest spot, **Pura Besakih** ⑮ (daily 8am–8pm; charge). With the massive **Gunung Agung** peak as their backdrop, the broad, stepped granite terraces and slender, pointed black pagodas of this 60-temple complex are a fitting residence for the gods. The first record of Besakih's existence is an inscription dating from AD 1007. From at least the 15th century – when Pura Besakih was designated as the sanctuary of the deified ancestors of the Gelgel god-kings and their very extended family – this has been the 'mother' temple for the entire island.

Candidasa and Amlapura

Candidasa ⓰ is a perfect base for exploring **Tenganan**, home to a pre-Hindu Bali Aga tribe. Located several kilometres inland in an area of lush bamboo forests and mystical banyan trees, it was never assimilated to the island's Hindu-Balinese culture, and thus it has retained its own traditions of architecture, religion, dance and music. Tenganan supplies the rest of the island with several valuable items, notably the double-*ikat geringsing* fabrics, some of which are considered to be sacred.

Twenty-five kilometres (16 miles) farther east, the road crosses a wide lava bed and enters **Amlapura**, a medium-size town formerly known as Karangasem and once the capital of Bali's 'cultured king'. **Puri Kanginan** (also called Puri Agung Karangasem; 8am–5pm; charge), the palace where the last raja was born, is an eclectic creation reflecting strong influences of his European education and of his Chinese architect, Tung.

During his tenure, the colourfully named King I Gusti Bagus Jelantik, a self-educated architect, built three royal bathing pools – the most celebrated of which is **Taman Ujung** (also called Taman Sukasada; daily 8am–5pm; charge). Victim of many earthquakes, Taman Ujung was completely refurbished in 2004 under the supervision of Unesco to its original splendour as a floating royal summerhouse.

Northern and western Bali

The drive along the southwestern coast follows a long line of black-sand beaches before arriving in the district capital of **Negara** ⓱, near the island's westernmost coast. Negara is famed for its buffalo races between July and October, introduced from eastern Java and Madura less than a century ago.

At the western extreme of Bali is **Gilimanuk** ⓲, a rather nondescript town with frequent ferries across the straits to eastern Java. Nearby is **Cekik**, headquarters for the **Taman**

Nasional Bali Barat (West Bali National Park; headquarters: Mon–Thur 7.30am–3.30pm, Fri 7.30–11am, Sat 7.30am–1pm). Trekking permits and guides (required) are available at Cekik and at the Visitor Centre in Labahan Lalang. **Menjangan Island**, in the west end of the park, offers Bali's best scuba diving.

The culture of the north is different in several ways: the language is less refined, the temple ornamentation more fanciful. The north coast is peppered with quiet villages. **Pemuteran**, an emerging resort area not far from Menjangan, is a secluded beachside destination offering snorkelling and diving excursions. **Lovina** ⓳ has countless bungalows for travellers seeking an alternative to the more developed southern part of the island.

Further on, **Singaraja** ⓴ a port city and the capital of Bali under the Dutch, has sizeable communities of Chinese and Muslims. From Penulisan, the winding road seems to drop straight out of the sky, flattening out several kilometres before **Kubutambahan** village on the coast.

Tourists set off for early-morning dolphin watching from Lovina.

OTHER ISLANDS

From the highlights of Sumatra to the amazing jungles of Kalimantan, Sulawesi and Papua, some of the world's best dive sites and the varied wonders of Nusa Tenggara, the vast sprawl of islands that make up Indonesia offer endless possibilities for intrepid travellers.

Main Attractions

Orang-Utan Centre,
  Gunung Leuser
Danau Toba
Bukittinggi
Lombok
Komodo National Park
Ikat weaving, Flores
Jungle treks, Kalimantan,
  Kalimantan
Baliem Gorge, Papua
Sorong, Papua

Get around by ferry.

The little-visited islands outside overcrowded Java and Bali are a real-life paradise for adventurers and anthropologists. It is mind-boggling how many different cultures – each with its own handicrafts, languages, architecture and rituals – can be found in a single country, and the vast majority of them are outside Indonesia's two major points of entry.

In Sumatra, ethnic groups range from the mostly Christian, once cannibalistic Batak to one of the planet's few matrilineal clans, now primarily Muslim. Kalimantan has its Dayak tribes, and in Sulawesi the Torajans still hold elaborate funeral rituals, requiring the sacrifice of hosts of buffalo and pigs. Papua (formerly called Irian Jaya) is the land of Indonesia's most remote tribes, and the eastern part of sparsely inhabited Nusa Tenggara ('Southeastern islands'), extending eastwards from Lombok to Timor, is home to hand-weaving cultures that have survived for generations in Indonesia's poorest area.

Extreme surfers have long known about the power waves, particularly off southern shores. Divers have only begun to discover various subterranean ecosystems. The islands' majestic volcanoes and mountains beg to be climbed, their caves explored, and their forests trekked. Some of the planet's rarest creatures are found in the 'Other Islands' of Indonesia. Be forewarned that travel to areas outside of major cities and towns can be slow and difficult. But, of course, it is their very remoteness that has kept old traditions alive.

Sumatra

Entering Sumatra via **Medan ❶**, **Gunung Leuser National Park** is Sumatra's prime orang-utan viewing destination. Encompassing 8,000 sq km (5,000 sq miles) of dense jungle, the Park is also home to elephants, rhinos, sun bears, tigers, and some 500 bird species. The **Bohorok Orang-Utan Rehabilitation Centre** (www. orangutans-sos.org) at Bukit Lawang has

a well-run station with a superb visitor centre and offers guided jungle treks.

The mountain heartland

To visit the heartland of the once-cannibalistic Batak, take the scenic route from Medan to **Danau Toba** ❷ (Lake Toba) via Berastagi. On the eastern shore of this, the world's largest and deepest crater lake, is **Parapat** – offering deluxe hotels, golf courses, watersports and a refreshingly brisk climate. **Samosir**, the island that dominates the lake is, at 1,000 sq km (380 sq miles), almost the size of Singapore. The carved boat-like tomb of animistic King Sidabutar and ritual statues of buffalo sacrifices are in **Tomok** on Samosir's east coast. Nearby **Ambarita** has three megalithic complexes where the fates of prisoners were once decided and prisoners were executed and eaten.

The world's largest matrilineal society, the Minangkabau culture, is reached via picturesque **Bukittinggi** ❸, some 250km (155 miles) to the south. From there, make excursions to the plains of Tanah Datar to see traditional Minangkabau architecture, with roofs turned up

to resemble the horns of a water buffalo. The area's *kain songket* (hand-woven cloths with gold or silver borders) are coveted formal wear for Jakarta ladies and are relatively expensive.

Coasts and islands

Off Sumatra's west coast is a string of ancient islands, the most-visited of which is **Nias**, known for its stone architectural styles and rituals – and world-class surfing.

Comprising estuaries, marshes and open grassland along the southeast coast, **Way Kambas National Park**, entered via **Bandar Lampung** ❹, is the best place to see wild elephants, while birdwatching is a delight. All are best observed by boat trips arranged by Park authorities. Elephant-training classes are held daily at 8am and 3pm.

Lombok to Timor

The unique Sasak culture of **Lombok** ❺ and its especially fine earthenware attract a few visitors, but the island is best known for its beaches and scenery. Lombok is part of the Lesser Sunda Islands chain. The capital is

A horse and cart in Bukittinggi.

Minangkabau architecture near Bukittinggi.

Mataram, at the southern end of the coastal tourist strip.

Senggigi's beautiful beaches, on Lombok's western coast, have good coral for snorkelling and diving, and primarily attract those who seek solace from Bali's hustle and bustle, with accommodations ranging from budget to deluxe. Kuta is famous for beautiful, deserted, white sand beaches. Southern Lombok is considered among the best in the world for surfing, and includes Desert Point at Banko Banko. Sekotong, in southwestern Lombok, is known for its numerous scuba diving locations. Volcano climbing – not for novices – and trekking for all levels are popular in **Rinjani National Park** (www.rinjaninationalpark.com). Budget-minded divers revel in the laid-back remoteness of three small islands off the northwest coast: **Gili Meno**, **Gili Air** and **Gili Trawangan**.

Sumbawa and Komodo

East of Lombok is **Sumbawa ❻**, whose port town, **Bima,** is a gateway for Komodo National Park. There is world-class surfing on the west coast

and epic waves on the southeastern coast at **Hu'u's** Lakey's beach. **Gunung Tambora** – for serious climbers only – has a gaping 2,820-metre (9,250ft) -high caldera and spectacular views.

Komodo island ❼, east of Sumbawa, is home to the world's largest reptile, *Varanus komodoensis*, the Komodo dragon. Treks begin at Loh Liang ranger station to see these remarkably large lizards in their natural habitat. Neighbouring **Rinca** (pronounced *ren-cha*) island, is more rugged and not as crowded as Komodo can be in the high season (July and August), and is a great place for trekking. Scuba diving and snorkelling in the offshore waters is some of the best in the region.

Flores, Ikat weavings and crater lakes

The Trans-Flores highway winds its way from western **Flores ❽** at **Labuhanbajo** – an entry point to Komodo National Park – to Larantuka in the east, the departure point to the Solor and Alor archipelagos.

From the west, **Ende** is the beginning of Flores' magnificent hand-woven

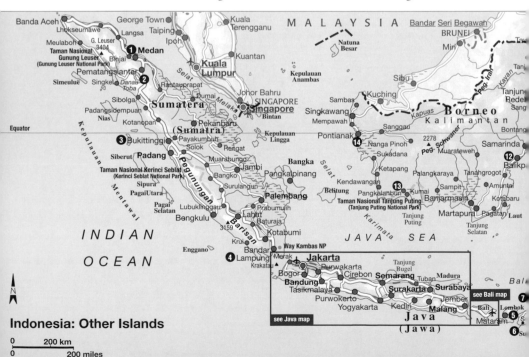

Indonesia: Other Islands

0   200 km
0   200 miles

textile cultures, while the *ikat* cloths of villages near **Maumere** sport a greater variety of colours. At Moni, visit **Gunung Kelimutu** at sunrise to see three adjacent volcanic crater lakes believed to house the spirits of sorcerers, sinners and virgins.

For hand-woven textile enthusiasts, the main attraction of the **Solor** and **Alor** ❾ islands are their primitive *ikat* weavings. Recently, Alor has established itself as a prime diving site. Between the two groups of small islands is **Lembata**, noted for its harpoon-wielding traditional whalers.

Timor and other islands

Kupang ❿, Timor, is the usual turn-around point for excursions from the west through Nusa Tenggara. **Rote** (also spelt Roti), southwest of Timor, shelters more than 18 ethnic groups and is known for its colourful *ikat* weavings and its southern beaches.

Although **Sawu** (also spelt Savu), further west, is a poor, dry island, its people, particularly the women, and their hand-woven *ikat* cloths are exquisite.

Of all the *ikat* weaving cultures in eastern Indonesia, **Sumba** ⓫ is perhaps best known. Its elaborate megalithic tombs, annual Pasola ritual battles, and mind-blowing surfing have attracted visitors for decades.

Kalimantan

Despite the well-documented efforts of the logging companies, much of Kalimantan – the Indonesian part of the huge island of Borneo – is still a remote jungle wilderness.

The principal point of entry to eastern Kalimantan is the town of **Balik-papan** ⓬, although neither it, nor **Samarinda** up the coast, hold much interest for travellers. These two towns are, however, gateways to the great **Sungai Mahakam** (Mahakam River), where several Dayak tribes live. Tour packages are the easiest way to traverse the Mahakam, and **Tenggarong**, about 2 hours away, is where cruises begin.

Muara Muntai, home to the Kutai Dayak, is the departure point for exploring the mid-Mahakam lakes region. At **Tanjung Isuy**, the most popular destination in the area, Dayak welcome rituals are frequently performed.

TIP

Oddly enough, Lombok has become host to an annual International Ballroom Dancing Championship, attracting competitors from around the globe. The mastermind is Dutch-born World Champion Marcel De Rijk, the grandson of a Javanese sultan, who has a dance studio in Senggigi. Ballroom dancing is growing rapidly in Asia.

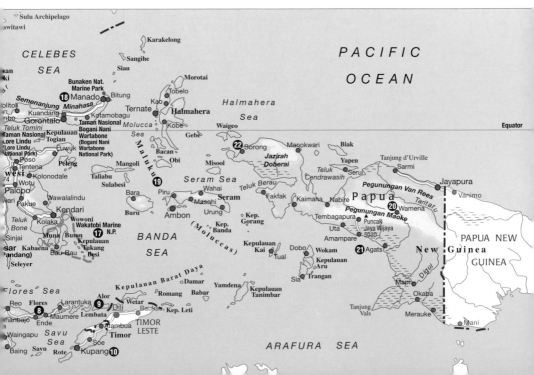

Enjoying the picture-postcard setting of Lombok.

Dance performance in East Kalimantan.

There is a rebuilt longhouse with 24 doors – the only two-storey longhouse in Kalimantan – at **Mancong** village.

Downriver from **Melak** is the **Rasi Fresh Water Dolphin Information Centre**, supplying locations for spotting freshwater dolphins in the Mahakam River. The **Kersik Luwai** orchid reserve houses 100-plus species of orchids, including the famous 'black' variety. Upriver from Melak is **Barong Tongkok**, where the nearest authentic longhouses are located.

Most visitors to Central Kalimantan come to see its orang-utans. The starting point is **Pangkalanbun** ⓭, and from there it's a 20-minute drive to **Kumai**, the entry point to **Tanjung Puting National** Park (www.orangutan.org).

The Park's highlight orang-utans can be seen at one of three outposts: **Tanjung Harapan**, **Pondok Tanggui**, and the most famous of the three, **Camp Leakey**. During feeding sessions, orang-utans that hang around near the stations are offered bananas and milk to supplement seasonal lack of food in the forest.

Local guides can be hired for treks through Tanjung Puting's peat swamp forest, where there is interesting fauna and flora. Not-to-be-missed are proboscis monkeys belly-flopping from tree to tree, hornbills and estuarine crocodiles along the riverbanks.

The coastal road heading north from **Pontianak** ⓮ to Dayak heartland passes the **Tugu Khatulistiwa** (Equator Monument). At **Kampung Saham,** a longhouse settlement of the Kendayan tribe has a beauty all its own.

Sintang is the home of some of West Kalimantan's most traditional Dayak groups. Nearby, **Gunung Kelam** (Dark Mountain) looms over the countryside, its superb sheer-walled rock a challenge to even the best of climbers. For traditional Dayak country, head up the Sungai Melawi (Melawi river).

Putussibau, the last town on the Sungai Kapuas (Kapuas river), is near traditional Kayan Dayak villages and Maloh longhouses.

Sulawesi

Makassar ⓯ is the entry point to reach **Tana Toraja**, tucked amid rugged peaks and fertile inland plateaux.

Reaching Tana Toraja from Makassar is a 10–12 hour journey by road, passing through **Pare Pare**. **Rantepao** is the centre of Torajan culture. Interspersing rice paddies with breathtaking mountain views are cave-tombs where rows of wooden effigies (*tau tau*) stare eerily from suspended balconies. The best-known gravesites are at **Londa**, **Lemo** and **Ke'te**.

Known for their elaborate funerary rituals requiring many animal sacrifices, the Torajan traditionally live in *tongkonan* houses with boat-shaped roofs and exquisitely carved panels.

To reach one of the country's most important biological refuges, **Lore Lindu National Park**, travellers must first make their way to **Palu** ⑯. The Park hosts incredibly diverse plant and animal life. Hornbills, Tonkean macaques, *maleo* fowls and butterflies abound, but more difficult to spot are Sulawesi's strangest mammals, the *anoa* (dwarf buffalo), *babirusa* (deer-pig), tarsier and cuscus.

Megalithic statues estimated between 700 and 5,000 years old dot the valleys of **Napu**, **Besoa**, and **Bada** in Lore Lindu. The statues – obviously phallic and carved with humanoid faces – are scattered throughout open fields.

South Sulawesi's most-visited area is **Wakatobi Marine National Park** ⑰, which encompasses the remote **Tukang Besi** islands, the largest of which are **Buton**, **Muna** and **Wowoni**, off the southeastern tip of Sulawesi. There is spectacular diving off the many atolls and uplifted limestone islands that string out into the deep Banda Sea. On Buton, the **Kakanawue Nature Reserve** offers a good chance to see macaques, tarsiers and hornbills.

The **Minahasa Highlands** surrounding **Manado** ⑱ are rife with clove trees, vanilla and rice fields, with coconut groves lining long sandy beaches. Panoramas include the steaming crater **Gunung Mahawu** and an impressive waterfall at **Tincep**. Visit the 'flower city', **Tomohon**, or the ancient stone sarcophagi at **Sawangan**.

Manado is also an excellent staging point for scuba-diving and snorkelling trips to **Bunaken National**

A traditional rubber plantation.

An orang-utan at Tanjung Puting National Park.

THE SPICE TRADE

Known as the Spice Islands, Maluku (The Moluccas) was zealously sought for many years before Portuguese mariners happened upon it in the 1500s. Men like Christopher Columbus, Vasco da Gama, Ferdinand Magellan and Sir Francis Drake all dreamed of finding their wealth there. In fact, one of the main incentives for Europe's Age of Discovery was the avid search for spices, easily worth their weight in gold then. Spices like cloves, nutmeg and mace were used to camouflage the taste of spoiled meat in the days before refrigeration, and for medicine. As far back as the 3rd century BC, the Chinese knew of cloves, calling them 'odoriferous nails'. By the 4th century AD, fragrant cloves had reached Europe. Yet for hundreds of years, the world's total clove production poured forth only from five little islands off the west coast of Halmahera.

While its current production of nutmeg and mace is negligible, for centuries the tiny Banda islands supplied every last ounce of both, their origin a well-kept secret by Arab traders in Venetian markets, prior to the arrival of the Portuguese. Control of the spice-producing islands assured vast fortunes, and countless lives were lost in the quest for them. But the introduction of refrigeration and British success in propagating nutmegs and cloves in Sri Lanka were to end the spice wars forever.

Dani tribals in the Wamena region.

Fishing at sunrise in southern Sulawesi.

Marine Park, one of Asia's best dive spots. The coral reefs teem with thousands of different species of colourful tropical fishes along steep drop-offs that plunge thousands of metres into the abyss. Sea turtles, sharks, pods of dolphins and dugongs make their way around the park, and there is also a World War II wreck to explore.

Maluku (The Moluccas)

Today's **Maluku**  (The Moluccas) is best known for its superb diving. With more than 3,000 species of fish and several hundred species of coral – and the tallies still rising – the incredible biodiversity surrounding the original Spice Islands attracts experienced divers to Banda, Ambon and surrounding Maluku islands. The undersea base of **Banda's** active volcano features magnificent table corals and a World War II wreck. Tiny Mandarin fish and large pelagic species abound. **Ambon's** slopes, walls and pinnacles are unrivalled with their twisting caverns teeming with life. Muck diving reveals dwarf cuttlefish, crocodile fish and octopus.

Papua

Forming the western half of the large island of New Guinea, Papua's remote cultures occasionally attract intrepid adventurers. The fertile Baliem Valley, entered through **Wamena** ⑳, is home to tribes who still used wood, flint and stone for weapons and tools until steel was introduced to them in the 1960s.

Trekking follows locally used footpaths through breathtaking landscapes. One- or two-day jaunts take hikers into the **Baliem Gorge** through sweet potato fields, along the powerful Baliem River, and into Dani villages where there are ancient mummies to see. A five-day trek will take those in good shape to Yali country, or drive to **Habcma lake** surrounded by orchid-producing high mountain forest. If energy and time permit, there's still glacier-capped **Mount Carstensz** waiting to be climbed.

The Asmat

Timika is the jump-off point for travel to **Agats** ㉑, the only town in Asmat (the land as well as the people share this name). Once feared headhunters and cannibals, the Asmat achieved acclaim in 1961 when Michael Rockefeller arrived to collect their unique primitive carvings for American museums and was never seen again.

Villages can be 'hired' for several hours to don traditional dress and perform dances. The Asmat are usually quite happy to assemble in the men's house and answer questions about their former headhunting days.

Raja Ampat diving

In addition to cultures, Papua is now attracting attention as a premier dive destination at **Raja Ampat**, which is entered through **Sorong** ㉒, on the far northwestern edge of Papua. Still largely unexplored, the area contains 1,500 atolls and countless World War II wrecks. Its species range from the smallest seahorses to the curious, flat, bottom-dwelling wobbegong shark and large numbers of rays.

Indonesia's Environmental Challenges

Its position on shifting continental plates in the Pacific Ring of Fire means that the country is prone to earthquakes, volcanic activity, landslides and tsunamis – some of Indonesia's problems cannot be overcome by man.

However, others could be more easily remedied, in theory. Indonesia faces some daunting man-made environmental challenges, including pollution and population pressure on the land, and the destruction of its tropical rainforests. The onslaught on the latter has been well documented. Illegal logging continues, with instigators remaining at large and as many as 20 million Indonesians depending on forests for their livelihoods. Depending on which NGO or governmental agency report you believe, the major contributor of Indonesia's rampant forest fires – each year destroying thousands of hectares and threatening the survival of countless species – are local farmers, pulpwood producers, or palm oil plantation developers, using slash-and-burn techniques. The resulting haze causes respiratory problems as well as major economic disruption and makes Indonesia the world's third-largest contributor of greenhouse gases.

Rising sea levels resulting from global warming are also a potential threat to Indonesia. Millions of its impoverished citizens live in low-lying coastal areas, and outlying islands may harbour rich oil and gas reserves, thus much-needed revenues. Meanwhile, pollution of the nation's waterways limits access to clean drinking water for as many as 100 million Indonesians, and flooding continues to plague major cities due to clogged sewers, rivers and overbuilding.

Indonesia's strategy

Can this developing nation rise above such tremendous challenges? Indisputably, more needs to be done, but progress is being made, particularly as many of its educated citizens join the planet's cry for change. Statistics show that forest fires and illegal logging have been reduced over the last decade or more. President Susilo Bambang Yudhoyono (familiarly known as SBY) has hosted two historic international summits on climate change in Indonesia. In 2009, he successfully negotiated a Tropical Forest Conservation debt-for-nature agreement with the US. Worth nearly US$30 million in grants over eight years, Indonesia will reduce its US debt payments in exchange for tropical forest protection and restoration. Also in 2009, SBY was instrumental in securing a consensus to the Indonesia-hosted Manado Ocean Declaration at the World Ocean Conference in Sulawesi, with the result that the connection between oceans and climate change is now on global agendas. Indonesia has established a 3.4-million-hectare (8.5-million-acre) Marine Protected Area in the Savu Sea.

There is more room for long-term, sustainable development goals that decrease poverty, increase health care and education, and protect the country's rich biodiversity simultaneously. Environmentally sound land-clearing practices would benefit millions of local farmers, while more strictly enforced laws and regulations would balance the other end. Ultimately illegal logging will need to be brought to an end alongside providing alternate sources of income for labourers in that industry. The question remains, will the government get serious enough about protecting its natural heritage in time to reverse all of the damage done?

Indonesia's forested terrain.

Mayon volcano.

THE PHILIPPINES

Spanish and American influence over four
centuries has made this intriguing
archipelago Asia's unexpected treasure.

*A paradise beach on Bohol
in the Visayas.*

They lie like lovely gems atop Asia's continental shelf in the western Pacific, these 7,107 islands with fluid names like Luzon, Mindoro, Palawan and Sulu. This tropical archipelago is a sprawl of half-drowned mountains, part of a great cordillera extending along the earthquake-prone Ring of Fire from Japan south to Indonesia.

The Philippines is the only predominantly Christian nation in Asia and has always been the odd man out. The legacy of the Spanish and Americans has been overlaid on to the far older Malay/Bornean society, and together they give the Philippines a unique, almost Latin American, flavour. Even in matters of food, it seems out of place. Instead of fiery curries or spicy grilled meats, Filipino cuisine tends to be a sedate mixture of an ascetic atoll diet, combining elements of Chinese imagination and Spanish conservatism.

Gigantic, sprawling Manila is the starting point for most journeys. The traveller leaving Europe or North America for the first time might find the megalopolis intimidating in its chaos and frantic energy. It is an old city, with a history that lingers in its architecture: Malacañang Palace, the inner city of Intramuros, the statues and boulevards.

*Crowding into one of the
Philippines' famous jeepneys.*

North of Manila are the lofty highlands of Baguio, Ifugao and beyond. These are serene lands of cascading rice terraces. Further south, surrounded by warm tropical seas, are the Visayas, an ever-changing group of islands for travellers to explore. Here lies Cebu, the gateway to the area and a booming second city of the country, and the beautiful beach resort of Boracay. Further west, Palawan is known for its remote jungles, fine beaches and superb diving.

Despite the many hardships they have endured in their checkered past, most recently the devastating effects of Typhoon Haiyan, the Filipinos have kept their equanimity, knowing that life is all about adapting to change. They are a friendly lot, as you'll discover when you experience the archipelago's many attractions, ranging from unspoilt beaches and serene countryside to exciting nightlife.

DECISIVE DATES

Early years

Pre-history

Migrants cross the land bridge from Asian mainland and settle the archipelago.

AD 900

Chinese establish coastal trading posts over the next 300 years.

Colonial intrusions

1521

Magellan lands on Cebu, claims region for Spain. Lapu Lapu (Rajah Cilapulapu), in defending the island from the Spaniards, slays Magellan, thus driving the expedition from Islands.

1543

Next Spanish expedition led by Ruy de Villalobos lands in Mindanao. He names the archipelago 'Fillapinas', after Crown Prince Felipe II.

Rise of nationalism

1896–8

Execution of the nationalist José Rizal in 1896 instigates the Philippine Revolution against Spanish colonial rule.

A scene from the 1898 revolution.

1898

The United States goes to war with Spain, and wins. Treaty between the US and Spain grants the US authority over the Philippines, along with Puerto Rico and Guam.

1899

War breaks out between the US and the Philippines. US rule continues, but scattered resistance remains throughout the decade.

1935

General Douglas MacArthur takes charge of the

The assassination of Jose Rizal is depicted at Rizal Park in Manila.

Philippines' defence against Japan.

World War II

1941

On 22 December, Japanese land on Luzon. MacArthur soon flees to Australia.

1944

MacArthur returns, with a landing in Leyte, beginning the Allied effort to retake the Philippine archipelago from the Japanese.

1945

The Allies recapture Manila, declared an 'open city' by the Allies and thus subject to unlimited bombardment. Much of the city is destroyed.

Independence

1946

Roxas defeats Osmena for presidency. On 4 July, the Philippines proclaims independence.

1965

Ferdinand Marcos defeats Macapagal in his bid for re-election to the presidency.

1972–81
Martial law imposed by Marcos, who erects monuments to himself and accumulates a vast fortune.

1983
Leading opposition leader Benigno Aquino returns to Manila from exile in the US, is assassinated on arrival at Manila airport. Circumstances point to government involvement.

1985
General Fabian C. Ver and 25 others charged with slaying Aquino, but are acquitted. Marcos announces snap election. Over a million people petition Cory Aquino, widow of the assassinated Aquino, to run against Marcos. Aquino agrees.

1986
Violence escalates before the elections, at least 30 killed on Election Day. Election rigging enrages Filipinos, and millions join in uprising against Marcos regime. On 26 February, Marcos flees. Aquino survives seven coup attempts.

1987
The MV Doña Paz passenger ferry sinks on 20 December after colliding with a tanker. More than 4,300 fatalities makes it the deadliest ferry disaster in history and the world's worst ever peace-time maritime disaster.

1989
Ferdinand Marcos dies in Hawaii.

1991
Negotiations between the United States and Philippines over US military base access in the country erode. The US military and many Americans depart. Mount Pinatubo erupts, causing one of the largest volcanic events worldwide in a century.

Revival

1992
Fidel Ramos, Aquino's defence minister and a strong ally who backed her during coup attempts, wins presidential election. Foreign investors return.

1998
Joseph Estrada is elected president.

2000
Estrada is impeached for bribery, betrayal of public trust and violation of the constitution.

2001
Estrada is ousted from office against his will and Gloria Macapagal Arroyo, his vice-president, takes over.

2004
Arroyo wins the presidential elections on 30 June and is sworn in for a six-year term.

Typhoon Haiyan wrought devastation.

2006
A state of emergency is declared on 24 February after an alleged coup attempt. The declaration is lifted less than two weeks later, but political stability in the country remains fragile.

2009
Corazon 'Cory' Aquino, the leader of the 'People Power Revolution' dies on 1 August.

2010
Benigno 'Noynoy' Aquino, son of Corazon 'Cory' Aquino, elected president.

2012
Major Philippines and Chinese naval stand-off over territory in the South China Sea. The government signs a peace plan with Moro Islamic Liberation Front, ending a 40-year conflict that has cost nearly 120,000 lives.

2013
Tropical cyclone Typhoon Haiyan strikes on 8 November, causing catastrophic destruction in the Visayas, killing over 6,000 Filipinos and injuring many more.

PEOPLE AND CULTURE

From Christian fervour to ancestral worship, and from clans to mountain tribes, the richness of Filipino culture creates one of Asia's most vibrant societies.

Filipinos are generally descended from a proto-Malay stock, preceded only by nomadic aborigines who crossed land bridges from mainland Asia before these were submerged to isolate the archipelago. Those early Philippine inhabitants intermarried into Chinese settlements and later with the Spanish during their 333-year period of colonization. Many present-day Filipinos, or *Pinoys* as they call themselves, are of mixed heritage, known as Spanish *mestizo*. It's unclear how many of these people live in the Philippines today: estimates range from 3.5 million to 36 million.

Filipinos have a justifiable reputation as one of the most hospitable people in the world. Clans are the rule of survival, and are both the main strength and source of corruption in Filipino society. They operate as custodians of common experiences (many old families religiously keep family trees), and as the memory of geographical and racial origins. Clans also act as disciplinary mechanisms, employment agencies and informal social security systems.

Conversation often starts with questions about family, a topic that allows both sides to go into detail about parents, siblings, children, and their global whereabouts. Filipinos generally know a bit about world geography as a family member has probably worked abroad. Since there are no major ongoing feuds with foreign governments (China is on the watch list from 2012, however), Filipinos harbour little suspicion toward foreign visitors, though cannot hide their pride in having thrown off colonial rule.

Direct confrontation is generally avoided. When forced to deliver a negative message, Filipinos are fond of emissaries and indirect allusions, out of respect for the sensitivity of

The Philippines is a very family-oriented country.

the other party. Strong and fixed eye contact between males is considered aggressive. Eyebrows raised with a smile are a silent 'hello' or 'yes' to a question. One might be pointed toward a direction with pursed lips. Polite language and gentle conversation are ever important, even during inevitable disputes between travellers and local merchants. If foreign guests are invited to a Filipino home, they should give special acknowledgment to elders.

The arrival of Christianity

Following the arrival of the Spanish, the majority of the population quickly converted to Christianity. The spirits of nature, and a pantheon of mythical monsters, were replaced

> *The Philippines has traditionally been one of the best-educated societies in Asia, and education – including further education, even for poor families – is highly valued.*

by (and in many cases, incorporated within) an extended Christian family. Depending on the temperamental and cultural quirks of the village or larger area, the emphasis varied between Mother, the Virgin Mary, or the Child Jesus. In the shrines and churches of

fire prevention to earthquake-proofing (especially of churches). The pre-Christian deities of rain, fertility and the entire range of human needs and concerns were also absorbed into Philippine Christianity, as the new faith developed into a fusion of Western and indigenous influences.

In the same tradition, there is hardly a Catholic home without its own shrine to the Virgin and Child, usually near the master bedroom. Just a generation ago, it was a standard practice to affix a Maria or a Jesus Maria to a Filipino child's given name.

Religious models reference the country's Catholic culture.

Luzon, where women's equality with men had long ago extended into roles of power as priestesses, Mary became the standard-bearer of Catholicism. In the Visayas of Queen Juana, where children to this day are indulged in extended childhood, the Santo Niño was king. The difference can still be seen today in the oldest churches of the country, particularly in the Tagalog provinces, and in Cagayan, Ilocos, Cebu and Panay islands.

Propaganda was part and parcel of the missionaries' strategy. Friars made sure that every important event in the lives of their flock was attributed to divine intervention. Thus Mary and Jesus (along with the various local patron saints) became the agents for everything from

WOMEN IN THE PHILIPPINES

After the Philippines was liberated from Spanish repression, the status of women improved in the early 20th century, and they eventually achieved a higher status than their counterparts in most other Asian societies. The country has had two female heads of state, Corazon Aquino and Gloria Macapagal Arroyo. Greater gender parity has spread throughout society, with women holding powerful positions in government, corporations and in the arts. The Philippines doesn't suffer from many of the ingrained gender-related problems of some other societies, either, such as a bias towards the birth of boys, and daughters are cherished as much as sons.

In the last decade, the Catholic Church has been challenged in the Philippines by the emergence of dynamic Protestant faiths, often based on the crusading fundamentalist Christian sects of the United States. Protestant 'televangelists' are now a common site on late night TV, and huge gatherings of devotees fill the parks for songs, faith healing and emotional sermons. Protestants still make up a small portion of Philippine society, but their evangelical approach is a strong attraction for some passionate Filipinos who find traditional Catholic Mass less stimulating. The Catholic

Indigenous peoples tend to inhabit the more isolated islands.

Church has responded with a Catholic sect, called El Shaddai, which mirrors many of the livelier and passionate practices of fundamentalist Protestant religions.

Ethnic and minority groups

Of the Philippine population, now just under 100 million, some 10 percent are classified as cultural or ethnic minorities. Most of these people live outside the cultural mainstream of lowland Filipino Christians. They comprise the most diverse and exotic population of the nation, with the majority, some 60 percent, made up of various Muslim groups living on the southern islands of Mindanao

and the Sulu Archipelago. These groups have waged a decades-long separatist movement that continues today, with some help in recent years from radical international Islamic organisations.

The remaining peoples, who are mostly animists, inhabit the mountain provinces of northern and central Luzon, and the highland plains, rainforests and the isolated seashores of Mindanao and Palawan. These people often live as they have for generations.

There are five major ethnic groups spread across the Cordillera highlands of northern Luzon: Ibaloi, Kankana-ey, Ifugao, Kalinga and Apayao. Other indigenous groups of northern Luzon include the Bontoc and Tingguian. These are the unconquered people of the north who have evolved robust cultures and traditions in highland seclusion, far removed from lowland colonial history. These mountain tribes live sedentary lives based upon a highly developed agricultural economy. They worship tribal ancestors or spirits of nature, and are generally suspicious of the 'intruders' from the lowlands.

Probably the best-known are the Kankana-ey, mountain people who combine American missionary teaching with their ancestral religion. The Ifugao of the eastern and central Cordillera are the master architects of the famous rice terraces (see page 362). The gold- and copper-mining Ibaloi are another group.

Considered as a whole, the Muslims of the south constitute the largest cultural minority of the Philippines. Also known as Moros and with a well-deserved reputation for being fiercely independent and combative, they are classified into five major groups: Tausug, Maranao, Maguindanao, Samal and Badjao.

Another unique cultural group, living on Basilan Island south of Zamboanga amidst the Sulu Islands, are the Yakan. They are of partial Polynesian origin, with mixed Muslim and animistic beliefs. They are the most superb textile weavers of the southern archipelago.

The non-Muslim ethnic tribes of the Mindanao highlands are the least studied of the Philippine cultural minorities, and among the most highly costumed and colourful. There are over 10 tribes living in relative isolation in the Mindanao interior, including the Tiruray, the Bagobo and the Subannon.

Diver's haven

Most of the 7,107 Philippine islands drop off quickly into the ocean. The best way to explore this extraordinary underwater world is with scuba gear.

Divers in the Philippines will swim in near perfect visibility with groupers and snappers. Some will photograph multicolored feather stars. They may float over coral gardens, past sharks (gentle ones), and around massive World War II wrecks.

Many of the islets mentioned in this guidebook beckon intrepid divers to plunge into waters that are seldom explored only for lack of amenities on land. More popular coastal magnets, such as Alona Beach, Puerto Galera, and Boracay, have grown a reputation among travellers largely, if not only, because of diving.

Clownfish and coral

Would-be divers can usually choose an instructor on arrival in a beach town and get internationally recognized certification within days. Equipment is rented on the spot. Europeans, Japanese, and Korean expat diving guides cater to fellow nationals in bigger towns. Prices of instruction can be steep, however, with some rates quoted in the hundreds of euros.

Luzon's most accessible dive area is Anilao in Batangas, a few hours' drive south of Manila. Facing severe environmental degradation 30 years ago, the locals banded together to protect their coral reefs. Healthy again, coral, clownfish, and anemones now thrive in these waters.

Across the strait from Anilao, in Puerto Galera, swifter currents encourage tremendous coral growth and ample numbers of big fish. Another hour by pump boat leads from Puerto Galera to Verde Island, where strong ocean currents attract plenty of marine life to an undersea wall.

One of the best Philippine dive sites, Apo Reef, a 34 sq km (13 sq mile) atoll-like reef in the Mindoro Strait, has suffered from dynamite fishing. But boats allow divers access to the reef's sheer walls and drop-offs, which are breeding grounds of tuna, barracuda, manta rays, and marine turtles.

Underwater wrecks

Divers can visit several World War II wrecks in Subic Bay, though visibility tends to be hazy. The famed 19th-century battleship USS New York lies in 27 meters (90ft) of water, with El Capitan, a 130-meter (430ft) -long freighter, submerged just 12 meters (40ft) below. Coron Bay, off northern Palawan's Calamian Island, also covers some of the Philippines' best wrecks accessible to divers.

Balicasag Island is Bohol's best-known dive site. One of the archipelago's finest walls is illuminated by shafts of sunlight. On Cebu Island, divers

Returning from a dive off Boracay's White Beach.

prefer Moalboal, where a 35-meter (115ft) wall drops right off the shores of Panagsama Beach and a variety of dives await in Pescador Island Marine Park.

The Sulu Sea's Tubbataha Reefs, off south Palawan, has surged in fame due to numerous glowing write-ups and a quest to stop illegal fishing. White-tip and hammerhead sharks, marine turtles, manta rays, and eagle rays are common in the open-sea area open to divers from February to June.

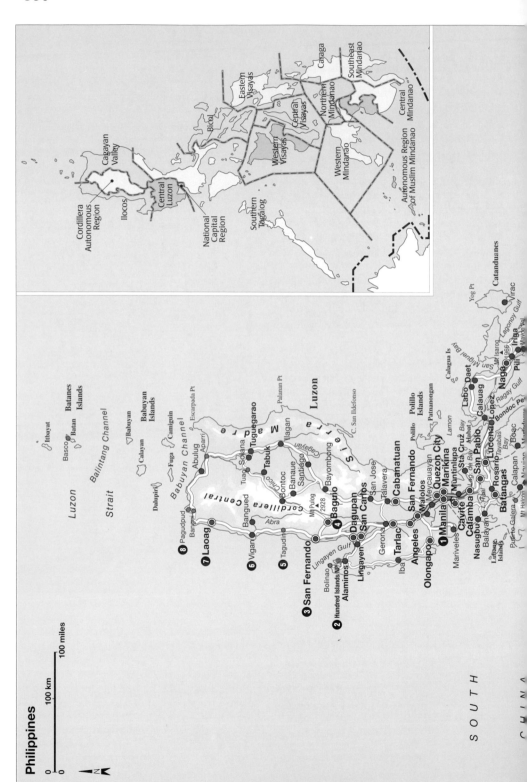

Philippines

0 100 km
0 100 miles

N

Inset map regions:
Cordillera Autonomous Region
Ilocos
Cagayan Valley
Central Luzon
National Capital Region
Southern Tagalog
Bicol
Eastern Visayas
Central Visayas
Western Visayas
Western Mindanao
Northern Mindanao
Central Mindanao
Southeast Mindanao
Caraga
Autonomous Region of Muslim Mindanao

Main map labels:

SOUTH CHINA

Luzon Strait
Balintang Channel
Babuyan Channel

Batanes Islands
Ithayat
Basco Batan
Babuyan
Calayan Babuyan Islands
Fuga Camiguin
Dalupiri

Bangui
Pagudpud
Abulug Aparri
Escarpada Pt
Solana Tuguegarao
Tuao Ilagan
Tabuk
Bontoc Santiago
Banaue
Bangued Chico
Abra
Mt Pulog 2928
Vigan
Tagudin
Cordillera Central
Palanan Pt
C. San Ildefonso

Sierra Madre
Luzon

⑧ Laoag
⑦ Vigan
⑥ San Fernando
⑤ San Carlos
④ Baguio
③ San Fernando
Dagupan
Lingayen Gulf
Bolinao
② Hundred Islands/NP
Alaminos
Lingayen
Gerona
Tarlac
Iba
Angeles
Olongapo
San Jose
Talavera
Cabanatuan
Meycauayan
Malolos
San Fernando
① Manila
Quezon City
Marikina
Mariveles
Cavite
Muntinlupa
Nasugbu
Balayan
Batangas
Calamba
Sta. Cruz
San Pablo
Lucena
Rosario
Calapan
Puerto Galera
Boac
Mt Halcon
Mindoro

Polillo Islands
Polillo
Panamongan
Calagua Is
Labo
Daet
Calauag
Lopez
Bondoc Pe
Ragay Gulf
Tayabas
Naga
Pili
Iriga
966
Mt Isarog
San Miguel Bay
Lagonoy Gulf
Virac
Catanduanes
Yog Pt

SOUTH CHINA

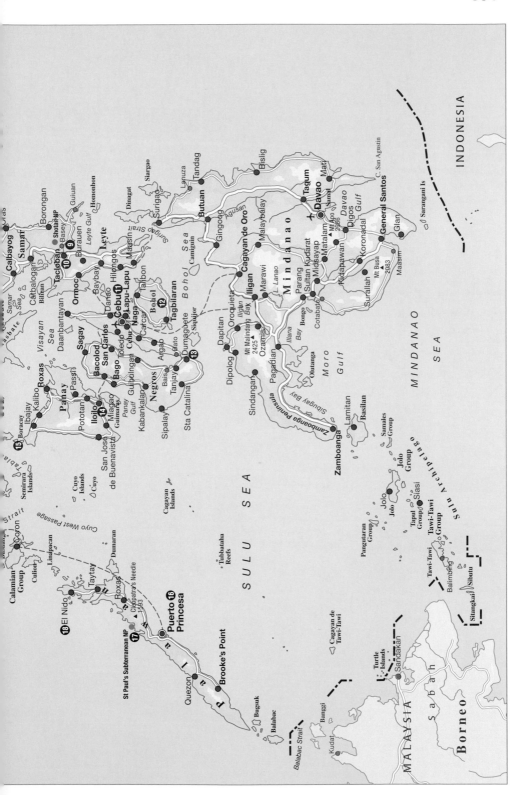

A jeepney in front of the Philippines Stock Exchange.

MANILA

Vast, chaotic, in a heady flux of never-ending motion – this is a city that does nothing in half measures.

Most visitors' first contact with the Philippines' will be through its chaotic capital. **Manila ❶** is undeniably a congested, somewhat daunting city that is not easy to get to grips with – or to get around, which leads to many negative first impressions. But for those who are willing to take the time to explore, it has a lot to offer. It can't compete with most other Asian cities when it comes to modern public transport, parks and other civic amenities, but it is undeniably rich is history – and at the same time bursting with Filipino energy and vitality.

In common with many Southeast Asian mega-cities, sprawling Metro Manila has no true city centre, but is rather a diverse collection of areas. Because it is difficult to traverse quickly, particularly during the working week, visitors should choose their hotels in proximity to the sites they want to visit.

Old Manila, including **Intramuros** and the **Ermita/Malate area** has most of the interesting historical sights, while the **Binondo/Chinatown** area presents an intense immersion in Filipino/Chinese culture. The business centre of **Makati** is home to the embassies and many top hotels and restaurants, while neighbouring **Fort Bonifacio** – which used to be a

military base but is now a booming commercial area – offers high-end retail shops, mixed with historical markers such as an impressive American military cemetery. **Ortigas** is a centre for malls and shopping, and is one of the quietest and safest neighbourhoods in the city, but has almost no nightlife after 9pm.

Intramuros

What is commonly called Metro Manila is bisected by the **Pasig River**. The Spanish conquistador Miguel

Bustling streets in Manila: the city has one of the world's highest population densities.

Manila

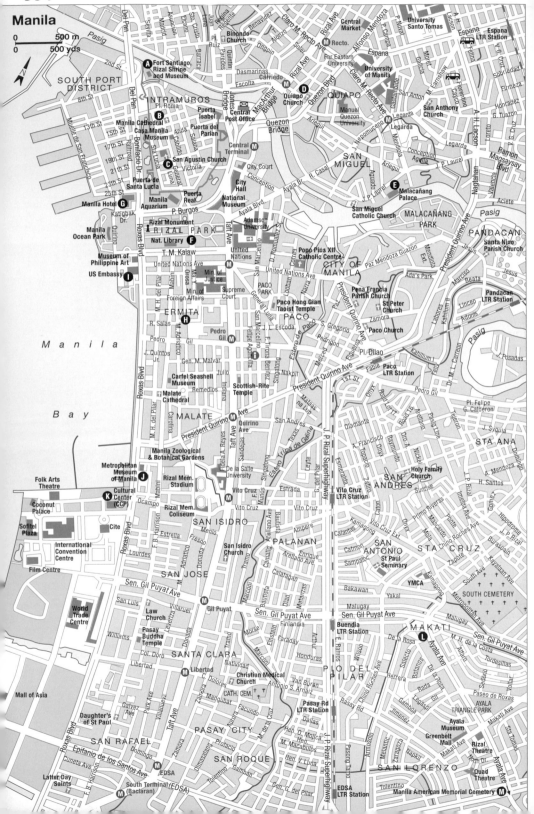

Lopez de Legazpi arrived in the area in 1571. After a battle, he took over the ruins of the ruler's fortress at the mouth of the Pasig. According to legend, the ruler, Sulayman, razed his palace in the face of his impending defeat to Legazpi. Legazpi founded Spanish Manila that same year, and began the construction of a medieval fortified town (Fort Santiago) that was to become Spain's most durable monument in Asia.

The city fortress was an expanded version of the original Fort Santiago, defended by moats and walls 10 metres (30ft) thick, equipped with well-positioned batteries. It was called **Intramuros** or 'Within the Walls'. **Fort Santiago** Ⓐ (daily 8am–6pm; charge) is situated close to where the Pasig empties into Manila Bay. On this site four centuries ago stood the bamboo fortress of Rajah Sulayman, the young warrior who ruled the palisaded city-state of about 2,000 inhabitants before losing it to Legazpi. Four gates connected Intramuros to the outlying boroughs, where lived the *indios* (as the Spaniards called the natives), *mestizos* (people of mixed blood), Chinese, Indians and other foreigners, including a number of Spanish commoners. Trade and commerce flourished to such an extent that these suburbs soon outstripped the city proper in area and population.

Though Intramuros is very different from its former state – Manila having been heavily bombed during World War II, portions of the old city have been restored, including the *Ayuntamiento* (Municipal Hall), once the grandest structure here. Part of the continuing restoration plan is to replicate eight houses to illustrate different styles of local architecture. A few are already open to the public, including the splendid **Casa Manila** (Tue–Sun 9am–6pm; charge), a restored Spanish merchant's house from the late 1800s.

From Fort Santiago, cross over to the **Manila Cathedral** Ⓑ, an imposing Romanesque structure that would not look out of place in Madrid or Seville. A plaque on its facade tells of a phoenix-like cycle that holds true for most old churches in the country – beginning in this case in 1571 – of construction and reconstruction after the repeated ravages of fire, typhoons, earthquakes and war.

Fronting the cathedral is **Plaza Roma**, where Spanish bullfighters performed in the 18th century. Colonial soldiers once drilled in the plaza, originally called Plaza de Armas. Later the Spanish rechristened it Plaza Mayor when it became the centre of government. It was also briefly known as Plaza McKinley during the American occupation at the end of World War II.

If you stand here facing Manila Cathedral, imagine the former Intramuros laid out as a rough pentagon or triangle. The perimeter measured nearly 4.5km (3 miles). Following Legazpi's blueprint for the capital, succeeding Spanish governors constructed 18 churches and chapels, convents, schools, a hospital, publishing house, university (as early as 1611),

Manila Cathedral.

Modern Manila's skyline as seen from the old Spanish fortress district of Intramuros.

palaces for the governor-general and the archbishop, soldiers' barracks, and houses for the assorted elite.

From Plaza Roma, walk down General Luna Street, past the western side of the cathedral, for four blocks to the intersection of General Luna Street and Calle Real. Here, incongruous Chinese *fu* dogs carved of granite guard the entrance to the courtyard of **San Agustin Church** **C** (daily 8am–noon, 1–6pm; charge), the only structure in Intramuros not bombed in World War II. The church facade is notable for its combination of styles – Doric lower columns and Corinthian upper columns – and the evident absence of its original left tower, victim to the violent earthquakes of 1863 and 1889. The remarkable main door is carved out of a Philippine hardwood called *molave*, and it is divided into four panels depicting Augustinian symbols and the figures of St Augustine and his mother, Santa Monica.

From San Agustin Church, there are several options. Turn right at Calle Real and explore the remainder of Intramuros until reaching Muralla Street. Here, follow the walls or pass through one of the restored gates leading back to the Pasig River, or to a plaza, **Liwasang Bonifacio**. On this busy square is a statue of the revolutionary leader Andres Bonifacio, with the **Central Post Office** just to the north.

Between these two landmarks is a system of overpasses and underpasses handling, at all hours, the great bulk of Manila's traffic. The left lane leads to Jones Bridge, the centre lane to MacArthur Bridge, and the right one to Quezon Bridge. These three bridges are the major thoroughfares across the river, leading to the half of Manila north of the Pasig.

Quiapo

The district of Quiapo lies immediately north of the Pasig. Recto Avenue is marked by a stretch of small shops selling new and second-hand schoolbooks for the university belt, an area that begins right after Recto Avenue's juncture with Quezon Boulevard. Quiapo is saturated with colleges,

Stocking up on produce at a market.

offering degrees in just about everything – education having long held a high status in Philippine society. Turning left at Quezon Boulevard leads to **Central Market**, really more of a textile emporium, and eventually to España, which leads northeast to the vast residential and governmental area of Quezon City.

Turning right at Quezon Boulevard from Recto Avenue will take you to **Quiapo Church ●**. The area beside the church is the terminal for most public road transport plying north–south routes of the metropolis. Teeming with people, it has long been considered the heart (some say the armpit) of downtown Manila. Close to where Recto Avenue becomes Mendiola Street is the **San Sabastion Church**, reputedly the only prefabricated steel church in the world.

Mendiola Street leads to **Malacañang Palace ●**, formerly the office and residence of Philippine presidents. It now houses the **Malacañang Museum** (Mon–Fri 9am–4pm by appointment made at least one week in advance; charge). Originally a country estate owned by a Spanish nobleman, Malacañang became the summer residence of Spanish governor-generals in the middle 1800s. Since Independence Day in 1946, 10 Filipino chief executives have resided here, including Ferdinand Marcos. His successor, Corazon Aquino, broke with tradition by choosing to operate from the adjacent Guest House. Joseph Estrada, in turn, installed himself in the Malacañang, and the tradition continues today.

Rizal Park

Back on the south side of the Pasig, **Rizal Park ●**, formerly known as Luneta (Little Moon, for its crescent shape), is a large rectangular field broken up into three sections, with an elevated strolling ground bounded by Roxas Boulevard and ending at the sea wall facing Manila Bay. On the harbour end is the **Manila Hotel ●** (www.manila-hotel.com.ph), once the most exclusive address in the Pacific.

In the middle of the park is the **Rizal Monument**, a memorial to the national hero (see box) and the object

Lanterns in Rizal Park.

of much wreath-laying by visiting dignitaries. Under 24-hour guard, the regular drill manoeuvres of the sentries are an attraction in themselves. Behind the monument is a series of plaques on which are inscribed Rizal's poem *Mi Ultimo Adios (My Last Farewell)* in the original Spanish and in various translations. A marble slab marks the spot where Rizal met his martyr's death by firing squad.

This central section of the park, where the Rizal Monument is located, is bordered by Roxas Boulevard to the west, T.M. Kalaw Street to the south, M. Orosa Street to the east, and Padre Burgos Street to the north. Close to the Burgos side are the Japanese and Chinese gardens, and an orchidarium, all of which charge token fees for entrance. On this side, too, is the city planetarium.

The eastern side of the park is bounded by Taft Avenue, one of the city's major thoroughfares. Burgos Street, on the park's northern side, leads past the Old Congress Building, once home to the Philippine Senate and which still houses the **National Museum** (www.nationalmuseum.gov.ph; Tue–Sun 10am–5pm; charge, free on Sundays), featuring an interesting array of paintings depicting the galleon trade, as well as other historic periods in the Philippine history. To the north is Manila City Hall, and beyond, Liwasang Bonifacio, from where the three bridges noted earlier lead to north of the Pasig River.

Ermita

From Taft Avenue, turn right at any of the perpendicular streets beginning with United Nations Avenue; this will lead to **Ermita** , an unusual district in many respects. This is the city's best-known nightlife area, overflowing with a smorgasbord of eateries, nightspots, boutiques, antique shops, handicraft and curio stalls. There are diverse music venues featuring Filipino folk singers, rock bands, and jazz groups. Here, still, another facet of the Ermita spirit may be glimpsed – the bohemian lifestyle of its younger, well-educated residents made up of artists, writers, musicians and dancers. These days Ermita can be described as gritty rather than sleazy.

Manila Bay.

Legend has it that around 1590, a Mexican hermit made the small seaside village his retreat. Four years later, an Augustinian priest founded the hermitage dedicated to Nuestra Señora de Guia, and the label *Ermita* ('hermitage') has stuck ever since. By the 19th century, the district had become an aristocratic suburb, together with the adjacent district of **Malate** further south.

Roxas Boulevard

Running parallel to Manila Bay and Ermita is Roxas Boulevard and its sea-wall fronting the bay. The wall begins where the sprawling grounds of the **US Embassy** ❶ end – it's hard to miss with the long lines of visa seekers outside. Along President Quirino Avenue on the landward side is a government complex that includes the Manila Hospital, the Central Bank of the Philippines and the **Metropolitan Museum of Manila** ❿ (www.met museum.ph; Mon–Sat 10am–5.30pm; charge). The small, well-maintained museum displays many of the works of Filipino national artists. Behind the hospital are the **Manila Zoological and Botanical Gardens** (daily 7am–6pm; charge).

Past the Navy Headquarters and on the seaward side of Roxas Boulevard is the immense **Cultural Center of the Philippines** ❿ (www.culturalcenter. gov.ph), the centrepiece of a spit of reclaimed land called CCP complex. The main building houses two theatres and two art galleries, a library and a museum with a permanent collection that includes traditional Asian musical instruments. In the northwest corner is a former Marcos guesthouse, the **Coconut Palace** (Tue–Sun 9–11.30am, 1–4.30pm; charge), built entirely of indigenous materials including coconut wood and husks. The palace hosts lavish parties for Manila's rich and famous.

Makati

From NAIA Avenue, take a short bus or taxi ride to **Makati** ❿ via Epifanio de los Santos Avenue (EDSA), Makati's main east–west boulevard and focus of the 1986 People's Power demonstrations. Makati's main north–south street, Ayala Avenue, is the financial hub of the country. On Makati Avenue is the **Ayala Museum** (www. ayalamuseum.org; Tue–Fri 9am–6pm, Sat–Sun 10am–7pm; charge). It has an outstanding archive and a permanent exhibit of dioramas portraying significant episodes in Philippine history, and detailed replicas of ships that have plied Philippine waters.

From the end of Ayala Avenue at the EDSA, cross the highway to **Forbes Park**, a swanky housing area. Forbes Park's McKinley Road leads to the Manila Polo Club and to the **Fort Bonifacio Global City** (www.fbdcorp.com) development with the **Fort Bonifacio Entertainment Center**. Nearby **Serendra** has fashionable bars, restaurants and shopping, while at the **Manila American Memorial Cemetery** ❿ (daily 6.30am–5pm), 17,000 Allied dead rest below seemingly endless rows of white crosses.

Yellow ginger (turmeric) for sale at Divisoria Market.

MANILA MALLS

Shopping malls have become a staple of life in Manila. The consumption-driven economy, fuelled by money sent home to relatives by Filipinos working overseas, has resulted in several massive shopping centres – in fact, three out of the world's 10 largest malls are in Manila. Filipinos have expanded the notion of a shopping mall to include just about every aspect of life. Medical centres, museums, and art galleries sit beside the usual food courts and retail shops.

At the Greenbelt shopping centre in Makati, some of the hottest nightclubs in the city rock into the wee hours. The Mall of Asia, which covers a whopping 407,000 sq metres (4.4 million sq ft), has an ice-skating rink and dozens of restaurants with views of the famous Manila Bay sunset. For the kids, there is a hands-on science museum and an IMAX theatre.

In the Ortigas business area of the city, three malls – Robinson's Galleria, SM Megamall and Shangri-la – sit beside each other. A simple straight walk through the three of them is an exhausting but eye-opening experience. In the SM Megamall, look for the Old Manila shop on the fourth floor. This interesting antiques and curiosity shop has old books and coins, vintage posters and post cards from the martial law days and before, and many other interesting items.

NORTH TO ILOCOS

The northwestern part of Luzon island, far beyond the congestion of Manila, is home to cool mountain highlands, beach areas to rival the southern islands, and well preserved indigenous traditions.

Main Attractions
Hundred Islands National Park
Baguio
Vigan
Paoay Church
Banaue Rice Terraces
Pagudpud

A horse-and-cart in Vigan Heritage Village.

There is a rugged symmetry to Ilocos that sets it, and its people, apart from others in the Philippines. The land of northwestern Luzon rises from the South China Sea to rocky bluffs, behind which a slim, arable strip of land is tucked under the towering Cordillera Mountains. Within this narrow confine lie the Ilocano provinces of La Union, Ilocos Sur, and Ilocos Norte.

Lingayen Gulf and Baguio

Amid the flat plains of Pangasinan, the lone over-burdened highway northward splinters into a half dozen roads, one of which leads west to **Alaminos** and the **Hundred Islands National Park ❷**. Facilities are rudimentary, but the day-long *banca* boat rides among the tiny islands in this area make it worth a visit. Bring plenty of water and items to shade you from the tropical sun.

On the other side of Lingayen Gulf sits **Agoo-Damortis National Seashore Park**, where iron deposits colour the sands almost black. The **Museo de Iloko** (Mon–Fri 9am–4.30pm; donation), in the old Presidencia of Agoo, houses artefacts of Ilocos culture.

As the highway makes its way into the rolling hills of southern Ilocos, the first province along the way is La Union, where the sea begins to glint behind the palms. There is a lively resort in the beach town of **Bauang**, where you can join American military retirees, and sun-seeking European budget travellers, for a drink at the **Bali Hai Beach Resort**'s friendly bar (www.balihai.com.ph).

Nearby **San Fernando ❸** is awash with colour on market day: loud gourd hats from up north, burnished earthenware and bright blankets line the stalls and shops. Overlooking it all is a dragon-encrusted Chinese temple. Six km (4 miles) to the north, a tiny surfing community has formed along Monalisa Beach.

Inland from La Union is the bustling mountain city of **Baguio ❹**, more or less the gateway to Luzon's highlands if coming from the Manila area. If you are travelling further north to the mountains, it is the last stop for modern amenities such as banks and hotels, shopping malls and international restaurants.

Traditionally, the main visitor's area in Baguio has been **Session Road**, a lively stretch of bookstores and coffee shops. Today, however, the huge **SM shopping centre** that sits atop the highest peak in the city draws more visitors, and though it is a mall, it is an open-air architectural achievement that is worth a visit. The converted US military base, Camp John Hay, is equipped with a golf course, picnic areas and green spaces that are lacking in the rest of the city.

Back along the coast and a few kilometres inland sits **Naguilian**, the *basi*-making capital of the Ilocos. Basi, the local Ilocano wine, is a fermented sugar-cane concoction, coloured with *duhat* bark. Have your headache pills handy if you overdo it. Not far from Baguio, the small town of **La Trinidad** allows visitors to pick their own strawberries, and offers the same northern

arts and crafts available in Baguio for a fraction of the cost.

Ilocos Sur

The narrow province of Ilocos Sur extends northwards along the coast. In some places, the Cordilleras range extends right down to water's edge. Because the land is ill-suited for agriculture, most people in Ilocos Sur have turned to trade and handicrafts, and each town in the region seems to have its own specialty. In San Esteban, there is a quarry from which mortars and grindstones are made. San Vicente, Vigan and San Ildefonso specialise in woodcarving, importing their raw material from the mountain provinces. Skilled silversmiths work in Bantay. Other towns make saddles, mats, brooms and hats. Sisal and hemp-fibre weaving are household industries everywhere.

The first town along the National Highway is **Tagudin** ❺, where a sundial built by the Spanish in 1848 sits in front of the Municipal Hall. The next, **San Esteban**, has a round stone watchtower built by the Spanish to keep a lookout for Moro pirates, and

Making the famous burnay storing jars.

Busy SM shopping centre in Baguio.

Exhibit at the Marcos Museum, Batac.

Laoag's belltower.

attractive Apatot Beach.

The small burg of **Santa Maria** is distinguished by a centuries-old church perched atop a hill, which served as a fortress during the 1896 revolution and now stands as a national landmark. Nearby are the Pinsal Falls, pools of water within rocks that resemble giant feet – the legendary footprints of the Ilocano giant, Angalo.

Vigan

A living repository of Spanish architecture and Filipino culture, **Vigan ❻** was the third Spanish city to be built in the Philippines, in 1572, following Cebu and Intramuros, in what is now Manila. The **Cathedral of St Paul**, built in 1641, is at the heart of the city, and stretching out in front of it is Plaza Salcedo, an elliptical plaza with the Salcedo Monument and a towering bell tower. Across the plaza to the west is the **Ayala Museum** (Tue–Sat 8.30–11.30am, 1.30–4.30pm; charge), also called the Burgos House, with an exhibit of dioramas depicting the Philippine revolution of 1896–8.

The most notable attractions in Vigan are the old ancestral houses in the former Mestizo District, known as **Vigan Heritage Village**, south of St Paul's along Mena Crisologo Street. Each building in the district has been lovingly preserved, and many now house antique shops, bakeries, and craft shops. Other Vigan attractions include the **Crisologo Memorial Museum** (Sun–Fri 8.30–11.30am, 1.30–4.30pm; free) on Liberation Boulevard, with its eclectic collection of art, old photographs, pottery and other memorabilia maintained in a somewhat ramshackle building. Stop at RG Potter, at the southwest end of Liberation Avenue, where the famous Ilocano jars, or *burnay*, are made for storing vinegar and basil. Walk back into the kiln area to see one of the best examples of a Chinese dragon kiln anywhere in the world.

Outside of Vigan, the church in **Bantay** features Philippine earthquake baroque with Gothic influences. Its belfry, a few metres away from the church, was used as a lookout for Moro pirates. Further north, in **Magsingal**, the Museum of Ilocano Culture and Artefacts has a collection of early trade

---

THE BANAUE RICE TERRACES

An essential trip on any visit to the Philippines is to the mountainous area of Ifugao and Mountain provinces in the centre of northern Luzon. With a cool, misty climate and well-preserved tribal traditions, it is quite different from anywhere else in the Philippines. The city of Banaue is the jumping-off point for the famous **Banaue Rice Terraces**, although these are merely the easiest to view from the city. To see the most spectacular rice terraces – verdant rice fields cut into the side of mountains – requires a certain amount of hiking but is worth the effort.

Travelling north from Banaue, the road becomes rough and narrow as the majestic views exponentially increase. Further north, at the end of a hair-raising mountain stretch, lies the pleasant town of **Sagada**. Filled with gourmet coffee houses, good restaurants, small bookshops, and at the heart of breath-taking scenery and hiking trails, it attracts Filipinos from around the rest of the country and the world, as well as a vibrant community of ex-pat foreigners and of course, visiting travellers.

The open coffins placed in caves around Sagada by the indigenous people of the area are a fascinating part of any visit. The local people have been burying their dead in caves and hanging their coffins from cliffs for centuries.

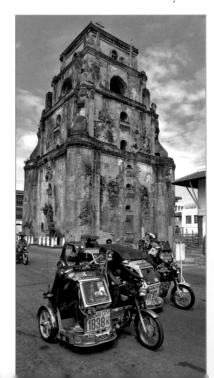

porcelains, Neolithic tools, weaponry, baskets, and old Ilocano bead wear.

Ilocos Norte

Unlike its poorer cousin to the south, Ilocos Norte is rich in timber, minerals, fisheries, and agriculture. In the small town of **Paoay** sits one of the most famous churches in Ilocos. It is a successful hybrid creation of the strong features of 'earthquake Baroque' (such as massive lateral buttresses) with an exotic Asian quality, reminiscent of Javanese temples. Built of coral blocks at the turn of the 18th century, its bell tower served as an observation post during the Philippine revolution and was later used by guerrillas during the Japanese occupation. Paoay Church has been declared a Unesco World Heritage Site. Not far from the town is Lake Paoay where loom weaving is a major activity, producing textiles with ethnic Ilocano designs.

South of **San Nicolas**, back down the National Highway in **Batac**, is the mausoleum of Ferdinand Marcos and the house in which he grew up. The **museum** (variable opening hours; charge) remembers the achievements of the longtime ruler of the country, who is still popular in his home province. Across the bridge from San Nicolas is the capital of Ilocos Norte, **Laoag** ❼. This city has become a popular tourist destination for visitors from Taiwan, less than an hour's plane ride to the north. A popular casino and international standard resort, called Fort Ilocandia, offers water sports, cultural shows and a relaxing, upscale beach area.

Further north, **Pagudpud** ❽ on Bangui Bay has been called the next great beach area in the Philippines, and is said to rival Boracay in terms of beach quality. The beaches here are beautiful, but perhaps not quite as stunning as those of their famous counterpart to the south. The facilities in Pagudpud are fairly basic, but for those who want to escape the highly developed beach areas of Boracay and Cebu, this is a quiet alternative. Saud Beach Resort is a good place to start with a cold drink to get your bearings, but plenty of other smaller resorts are in the area as well. Many of the resorts are family run, and don't yet have a website.

Trekking through northern Luzon's terraced rice fields.

Strolling on Boracay's White Beach.

THE VISAYAS

Six major islands and clusters of smaller islets together create a vista of idyllic images – the calm waters, shimmering coves, rocky coasts and palm-fringed beaches that are the Visayas.

anging like a necklace of uneven beads strung together by various geographic threads, the islands of the Visayas lend themselves to the sort of languid exploration that is perhaps more associated with the South Pacific. People from Luzon, when asked about these southern islands, generally point out the slower pace, the seductive lilt to the Visayan accent and, perhaps chauvinistically, the sensuousness of the women.

The Visayas have been described by one poetically inclined visitor as 'islands of now in a sea of yesteryear.' The six major islands and smaller islets – stretching for some 300km (200 miles) between Luzon and Mindanao – lend themselves readily to such wistful descriptions. They parade a series of idyllic images – calm waters, shimmering coves and palm-fringed beaches – while the carefree attitude of locals makes for an ideal holiday setting. On the other side of the coin, most of the islands remain rather poor and undeveloped, and the more easterly – Samar and Leyte in particular – often bear the brunt of destructive typhoons sweeping in from the Pacific, as was the case when Typhoon Haiyan struck devastatingly in late 2013.

Samar

This large island, well removed from the tourist trail, lies opposite the southeastern tip of Luzon and can easily be reached from Manila via the National Highway. First landfall is at the town of **Allen** with its nearby hot springs. The main roads wind along the northern coast to **Catarman**, capital of Northern Samar Province. Several attractive waterfalls are found in the interior of this part of the island, although reaching them requires considerable hiking.

In the southwest corner of the island is the San Juanico Bridge, the longest in the Philippines, linking

Main Attractions
Cebu City
Moalboal
Chocolate Hills, Bohol
Siquijor
Boracay

Hand-crafting guitars in Cebu, which is known for the skill.

FACT

In 1521, Ferdinand Magellan sailed up through the Canigao Channel to the island of Cebu, where he Christianised the local Rajah and 500 of his followers. A minor Rajah of Mactan – a flat, muddy island where Cebu's airport now stands – mounted a rebellion to the Rajah of Cebu and his new foreign guests. Now known as Lapu Lapu, Rajah Cilapulapu defended his island with some 2,000 warriors against 48 armour-clad Spaniards. During the battle that raged for just over an hour, Magellan was killed.

Grilling skewers of meat at a street stall in Tacloban.

Samar to the adjacent island of Leyte. Near the approach to the bridge is **Basey** , known for Sohotan Caves, Sohotan Natural Bridge, and **Sohotan National Park**. Basey is also the home of mat weavers whose designs have become popular items in the markets of Tacloban, on Leyte across the bridge.

Leyte

Tacloban ⓾, the capital of Leyte, was virtually obliterated by Typhoon Haiyan, which struck on 8 November 2013. Of the roughly 6,000 Filipinos known to have been killed in the storm, approximately 80 percent were from the Leyte towns of Tacloban, Tanauan and Palo. Little infrastructure remained intact after the typhoon, so it is important to confirm itineraries and reservations before travelling to the area.

The island has several fine beaches on its western coast, notably Agta Beach in Almeria and Banderrahan Beach in Naval. The town of **Caibiran**, on the eastern coast, has the spring-fed San Bernardo pool and the falls of Tumalistis, once claimed to have the sweetest water in the world.

From Tacloban, the National Highway follows the eastern coastline southward past Palo and **Tolosa**, the hometown of Imelda Marcos, where a visit to her former grand residence has been a highlight. Past Abuyog, the road veers west and crosses Leyte's Central Cordillera Mountains to the town of Baybay. The road then follows the western coastline to southern Leyte's provincial capital of **Maasin**.

Cebu

The oldest city in the Philippines, **Cebu** ⓫ is the commercial and education centre of the Visayas, and the hub of air and sea travel throughout the southern Philippines. It is second in commercial activity only to Manila. While the city itself suffered relatively minor damage compared with Leyte, mountainous areas just to the north were laid waste by Typhoon Haiyan's winds.

As the oldest Spanish settlement in

the country, Cebu has a rich colonial heritage. The foremost example is the refurbished **Fort San Pedro** (daily 7am–10pm; charge), a Spanish fort built in the early 1700s to repel the attacks of Muslim raiders. Housed in a chapel on Magallanes Street, located in the heart of the downtown area, is a piece of a wooden crucifix left by Magellan in 1521. On Juan Luna Street is **Santo Niño Basilica and Museum** (www.basilicasantonino. org.ph; Mon–Sun 8–11.45am and 1.30–4.45pm, Wed closed; charge), built in 1565 to house the country's oldest religious relic, the Image of the Holy Child Jesus, presented by Magellan to Queen Juana of Cebu.

The **Magellan Marker** is out in Lapu Lapu City, some 20km (12 miles) from downtown Cebu en route to Mactan Island. Erected in 1886, it marks the spot where the peripatetic Spaniard was slain on Mactan's shore. The **Lapu Lapu Monument** stands at the plaza fronting the Lapu Lapu City Hall.

Cebu is well known for its attractive, sun-drenched white beaches and dive sites. Among them are **Mactan Island**, just offshore from Cebu city, the **Olango Islands** and **Moalboal**, all of which have good facilities and accommodation, though there may still be some typhoon damage. Moalboal, on the southwest coast, is a haven for scuba-diving enthusiasts as well as budget travellers. Many come here to obtain their PADI dive certificate – this being one of the cheapest places in Asia to take the dive course.

Cebu is also known for its handcrafted guitars and ukuleles made of soft jackfruit wood. The guitar-making industry is centred in Maribago and Abuno on Mactan.

Bohol

A short flight or ferry ride southeast from Cebu is the island of **Bohol ⑫**. One of the major coconut-growing areas of the country, its many historical and natural attractions are well linked by a good road system, while the coastline is marked by picturesque coves and clean, white-sand beaches.

Most of the beaches are a short ride from **Tagbilaran** in the southwest, the provincial capital and Bohol's main port of entry (1 hour 45 minutes by ferry from Cebu). Seven km (4 miles) from Tagbilaran is Baclayon Church, built by Jesuits in 1727. Also known as the Church of La Purisima Concepcion (Immaculate Conception), it has an interesting museum housing a rich collection of religious relics, ecclesiastical vestments, and old librettos of church music in Latin on animal skins.

But what remains Bohol's most famous attraction, with which in fact the island has become synonymous, is a unique panorama in the vicinity of **Carmen**, a town 55km (34 miles) northeast of Tagbilaran in Bohol's central regions. Here, several hundred small-but-perfectly-formed hills rise some 30 metres (100ft) above the flat terrain. These are the **Chocolate Hills**, so-called for the

Trishaw transport in Bohol's capital, Tagbilaran.

Traditional boats on Bohol's Alona Beach.

confectionery-like spectacle they present at the height of the dry season (February–April), when their sparse grass cover turns dry and brown.

Negros

The large island of Negros lies west of Cebu. The capital of Negros Oriental (Eastern Negros) Province, **Dumaguete** is a small university town built around the Protestant-run Silliman University. Offshore is **Siquijor Island**, accessible by an hour's fast ferry from Dumaguete. This small, entrancingly beautiful island, has long been considered the centre of sorcery in the southern Philippines. There are some 50 *mananambal*, or folk healer-sorcerers, classified as 'white' or 'black' depending upon the nature of their abilities and intents. Siquijor's scenery and beaches are outstanding, and there is plenty of accommodation here.

Dominating the northwest shore is **Bacolod,** the capital of Negros Occidental (Western Negros) Province. Its points of interest do not extend much beyond several fine antique collections, ceramic shops, and weaving centres producing principally *hablon* fabric – a textile originally developed in Bacolod and much in vogue in the 1960s.

A few minutes' drive north is **Silay**, small and sleepy, but with several interesting old houses recalling the Castilian past. A bit further north is Victorias Milling Company, reputedly the largest sugar-cane mill and refinery in the world. Within the Vicmico compound is St Joseph the Worker's chapel noted for its psychedelic mosaic made from pop bottles depicting an angry Jesus and saints as Filipinos in native dress. It is still sometimes referred to as the Chapel of the Angry Christ.

Panay

From Bacolod, it is a two-hour ferry ride west to **Iloilo** on Panay Island. By the river's mouth is (yet another) **Fort San Pedro**, originally built in 1616 with earthworks and wooden palisades, and transformed into a stone fort in 1738. In 1937 the fort became quarters for the Philippine Army, but it has since been turned into a promenade area, popular in the early evening. The **Museo ng Iloilo** (Iloilo Museum; Mon–Fri 9am–noon and 1–5pm; charge) on Bonifacio Drive showcases prehistoric artefacts from the many burial sites excavated on Panay, including gold-leaf masks for the dead, seashell jewellery, and other ornaments worn by pre-Spanish islanders.

The district of **Molo**, 3km (2 miles) from the city centre, has a Gothic-Renaissance church completed in the 1800s and the Asilo de Molo, an orphanage where little girls hand-embroider church vestments. Panaderia de Molo (Molo Bakery), the oldest bakery in the South is a favourite. Off the northwest tip of the island is **Boracay** , the Philippines's premier resort (see page 369), famed for its white sands and well-developed tourist set-up.

The Chocolate Hills, Bohol. Bright green for much of the year, they turn chocolate brown during the dry season.

Boracay

The beautiful tropical beach resort of Boracay is the best-known destination in the Philippines.

Boracay, situated off the northwestern tip of Panay Island in the blue waters of the Sulu Sea, is an outstandingly beautiful resort island. Just 8km long by 3km wide (5 miles by 2 miles) and shaped like a slender butterfly drawn in sugar-fine white sand, this quintessential tropical paradise was first 'discovered' back in the 1960s, when beachcombers went looking for its rare *puka* shells. By the 1970s, it was on the must-see list of the more adventurous backpackers. They came in small numbers at first, staying in the *nipa* huts along White Beach for a couple of dollars a night.

But like every other magical spot – with a pristine environment and an increasing cachet amongst travellers – the word spread. By the 1980s, the adventurers had become the hordes, and boutique resorts sprang up all along White Beach. It was still difficult to reach, as it remains today, but that was part of the attraction.

Today, Boracay has moved upmarket. Since the mid-1980s, it has attracted the well-heeled of Europe, America and Asia, as well as Filipinos, who have lately begun to outnumber the foreign visitors. Boracay has become a beach scene, like Bali, Phuket or Waikiki, with performers, hawkers and merrymakers creating its own particular atmosphere.

All this has inevitably brought growing pains, with complaints about overdevelopment and pollution scares. But the area's popularity continues, and growth is unabated. Where backpackers once paid the equivalent of a few dollars for a night's accommodation, today there is a Starbucks where they could barely get a cup of coffee for that price.

Activities

Visitors can hire sailboats, kiteboards and windsurfing boards at any of the scores of rental shops that have sprung up along White Beach. There is also an array of other watersports, such as jet skiing, parasailing, snorkelling and scuba diving. Bicycles and motor scooters are available to explore the minuscule island. Thirty minutes of bike riding leads through the corn and cassava fields to fishing villages that retain their traditional feel. Yap-ak village on the northern end has interesting *puka* shells.

Getting to and staying on Boracay

Accommodation is comprehensive in terms of price and standard. There are still some basic backpacker places, though even those are wired with Wi-fi and offer gourmet coffee. Check out Dave's Straw Hat Inn for funky and affordable lodging. There is an abundance of two and three star hotels – nondescript 'cable TV and hot water' type places – at relatively competitive prices, which principally serve the domestic tourist trade. The very high end resorts, such as the Shangri-la group – have also moved in, with luxurious rooms on offer for upwards of $400 a night for a standard room. Meanwhile the eating out options are similarly diverse and cosmopolitan. Indonesian, Thai, Italian, Swiss, and even Mexican food is available along the beach.

Getting there is still an adventure. Direct flights from Manila to nearby Caticlan are often cancelled due to high winds at the small airport, but if you can get in there, it is a 15-minute boat ride to Boracay, then an odyssey of pedicabs and hiking to get to the hotels. You can also fly into Kalibo, take a 2–3 hour van ride to Caticlan, and then make the crossing.

Miles of white sand welcome you to Boracay.

PALAWAN

The long, thin island of Palawan is one of Southeast Asia's great adventure destinations, with wild forests, remote and beautiful beaches and superb diving.

Main Attractions
Tabon Caves
St Paul's Subterranean River
El Nido
Coron Bay diving

The entrance to St Paul's underground river.

O n the southwestern edge of the Philippine archipelago lies the elongated island province of Palawan, pointing towards northern Borneo – to which it was once linked.

More than anywhere else in the Philippines, this is nature in its raw state, and for the intrepid traveller it's a place that rewards exploration with stunning finds: there are magnificent stands of primary rainforest, some truly gorgeous beaches and a wealth of great diving.

Puerto Princesa and around

Puerto Princesa ⓰, the regional capital and only large town, is the hub of travel for the area, with daily flights from Manila and at least three major shipping lines making regular voyages.

It is a pleasant enough place with some good restaurants and bars, but there is not a great deal to see; most visitors will only use it as a launch-pad to the rest of the island. The most noteworthy sights are the beaches and islands of **Honda Bay** to the north of town. Boat rides in the bay, with stops for snorkelling, are offered. Beyond Honda Bay, the coast some 50km (30 miles) from the capital has excellent beaches, with the most attractive being at Tanabag.

Tabon Caves

For those interested in the obscure pre-colonial history of the Philippines, check out the **Tabon Caves**, about 155km (100 miles) southwest of Puerto Princesa. The four-hour bus ride, and half-hour boat ride, ends in a fascinating complex of some 200 caves. In this area, human remains were found and carbon-dated to 22,000–24,000 years ago, the oldest traces of humans in the Philippine archipelago. Burial jars and kitchen utensils give a rare glimpse into the ancient life the country's earliest inhabitants.

St Paul's Subterranean River

In northern Palawan lies the province's top tourist destination: the underground river in **St Paul's Subterranean National Park** ⓱ (www.puerto-undergroundriver.com). This is reached by travelling overland from Puerto Princesa to Baheli, close to the west coast, 60km (40 miles) away, and proceeding on motorised outriggers or pumpboats for another two hours. Alternatively, travellers may want to base themselves at the attractive beach resort of **Sabang**, from where the caves can be accessed via a beautiful 2–3 hour jungle walk. *Banca* trips may be arranged for delving into St Paul's cavern – a fascinating passage through a subterranean world of exquisite cathedrals with massive stalactites; icy lagoons where the eerie quiet is occasionally pierced by shrill cries of swooshing bats and striking cavewall formations.

High-powered lamps handled by the expert cave guides illuminate the attractions. It is an exhilarating experience that can range from an hour-long incursion into the half-submerged bowels of the earth to an extended exploration of two to four hours.

North to El Nido

It is possible to take a *banca* from Sabang up the west coast to the beautiful jungle-surrounded beach resort of **Port Barton**, and from there all the way up to the far north. **El Nido** ⓲, close to Palawan's northern tip, is known for its staggeringly beautiful scenery. The cliffs around are famous for their swiftlets' nests, used by the Chinese to make bird's nest soup.

The stupendous scenery has helped El Nido to develop as the most exclusive resort area in the Philippines. The **El Nido Resorts** (www.elnidoresorts.com) on Lagen Island and Miniloc Island have their own landing strip and host a loyal group of international visitors, including celebrities, at their pristine, environmentally friendly resorts. Nearby **Apulit Island** is another highly regarded resort.

For divers, northern Palawan's **Coron Bay** offers world-class wreck diving, and many dive shops and facilities. In

September 1944, US reconnaissance planes spotted 24 tiny islands in the waters off Coron that appeared to be moving. The islands – Japanese ships camouflaged in green leaves and shrubbery – were sunk by a convoy of US Navy SB2C Helldivers shortly after. The wrecks have become historical underwater landmarks.

Another unusual site in northern Palawan, off the northern tip of Busuanga Island, is the rather remarkable **Calauit National Wildlife Sanctuary** on Calauit Island. Giraffes, zebras and various gazelles were shipped here in 1977 by arrangement between President Ferdinand Marcos and an African potentate. For a while the game preserve was rumoured to be a private shooting range for presidential son 'Bongbong' Marcos.

The Conservation and Resource Management Foundation, tasked with overseeing the sanctuary, has done such a good job – despite occasional poaching by disgruntled former islanders – that the African animals have prospered to help make the island a singular destination for photo opportunities.

Travelling by boat.

The clear waters off Palawan offer exceptional diving.

BEACHES AND RESORTS

The coastlines and islands of Southeast Asia are home to some of the world's best beaches, with sun and sand to meet every taste and budget.

Southeast Asia's shorelines are well represented on any list of the world's best beaches. The region's waterfront areas are some of the world's most diverse. One beach will offer exotic charm, the next one will have an all-inclusive family resort, the next will be a psychedelic backpacker enclave, and others will cater only to the ultra-rich.

Thailand is the king of Southeast Asian sun and sand destinations, with Patong, Phuket, being the region's top beach area. Located less than an hour's flight south of Bangkok, and with direct connections to many other cities in the region, Phuket is one of the world's great beach scenes. The increasingly popular Phi Phi Islands are less crowded.

Vietnam's Nha Trang has a stunning beach, but the surrounding area is still experiencing growing pains – if you can face down the vendors, it is a great, affordable beach experience. In Malaysia, Penang and Langkawi offer world-class facilities, as does Bali, which lives up to its global reputation as not only an excellent beach area but also a destination for arts and culture. In the Philippines, Boracay is the country's most popular resort and, although it is hard to access, it has many charms.

For those who are looking for beaches off the beaten track, Southeast Asia has many. Both the Philippines and Indonesia have enough remote beaches and deserted islands to satisfy the most demanding adventurer. In Thailand, a few islands, such as Tarutao, remain pristine and unspoiled, as do Cambodia's southern beaches and islands. The most untouched area of all is southern (peninsular) Myanmar, but, for now, this remains largely out of bounds.

There are many paradise-like beaches and coves in the Philippines, such as this one on Palawan.

Beachside dining on Bohol.

Showing the tourists how it's done at Kuta, Bali.

Diving off Nha Trang, Vietnam's main hub for the sport.

DIVE GREEN

Southeast Asia is an outstanding dive destination. Not only does the region offer clear, accessible water and outstanding coral, it has (in most cases) modern, international-standard dive services at competitive prices.

Phuket in Thailand is a regional leader in diving. There are extensive, prime dive areas not far from shore, plus an abundance of dive shops competing for business. Any level of diver can enjoy themselves here.

In the Philippines, the Batangas area south of Manila is popular, as are the more remote islands of Coron and Palawan, as well as the Moalboal resort in Cebu. Further north, the World War II ships sunk in protected Subic Bay are a rare look at history preserved underwater. In Malaysia, parts of the east coast and the still-wild area of Sabah are prime dive spots, while Indonesia's utterly spectacular underwater areas are concentrated off the islands of Sulawesi and Flores. Nha Trang is the principal dive resort in Vietnam.

Forward-looking dive operators try to give something back to mother earth. Leading this effort is the Green Fins program, which has outlets in Thailand, the Philippines and Indonesia, and sets out environmentally-sound dive guidelines. The program provides a list of eco-friendly dive operators, as well as beach and coral clean-up programs.

...ailand is the king of Southeast Asian sun and sand ...stinations. The Phi Phi Islands, south of Phuket on the ...daman coast, offer stunning scenery as well as the obligatory ...ite sand and turquoise water.

...gapali beach on Myanmar's southwestern coast is the country's ...ly fully fledged beach resort, attracting luxury tour groups.

Strolling along Mui Ne beach in Vietnam.

INSIGHT GUIDES TRAVEL TIPS SOUTHEAST ASIA

Overview

Thailand

Myanmar

Laos

Cambodia

Vietnam

Malaysia

Brunei

Singapore

Indonesia

Philippines

OVERVIEW

GENERAL TIPS ON TRAVELLING IN SOUTHEAST ASIA

GETTING AROUND SOUTHEAST ASIA

By Air

Bangkok, Kuala Lumpur, Manila and Singapore are the main airline hubs. There are frequent air links between the major cities, often with a choice between full service and budget airlines. Every country has a flag carrier. Singapore Airlines is one of the region's best known, while Singaporean airline Silk Air also covers local destinations. Thai Airways is also well established, and the country's second carrier, Bangkok Airways, has developed new destinations including World Heritage Sites. Malaysia Air System (MAS) and Philippine Airlines (PAL) are well known, reliable carriers.

Several regional budget airlines are based in Singapore, including Jet Star Asia and its sister Valuair, with links to major cities in Indonesia. Another is Tiger Airways, which flies to Chiang Mai, Phuket, Hanoi, Ho Chi Minh City, Danang and Manila.

Hong Kong has a number of low-cost airlines serving the region, while neigbouring Macau is also a useful access point for low-cost flights to several Southeast Asian cities.

By Rail

Rail travel is one of the best ways to get around Southeast Asia. One exceptional trip is the train from Bangkok to Singapore, which stops at the major Malay cities and takes about 41 hours. The Eastern & Oriental Express is a luxury train based in Bangkok, which also takes the route to Singapore, and in addition goes to Chiang Mai and Vientiane in

Laos (www.orient-express.com).

In the Philippines, the Peñafrancia Express is a Japanese-built train that runs the 480km (300-mile) route from Manila to Legazpi City in 12 hours.

By Bus

Buses are generally the cheapest and easiest way to get around and, though mainly reliable, services can be slow.

Where roads are bad, it can be an uncomfortable experience, too. First-rate air-conditioned buses operate in Thailand, Malaysia, Vietnam and Singapore.

Private transport

Taxis are cheaper if they are shared, and inexpensive city transport is provided by a variety of *tuk-tuk*s and

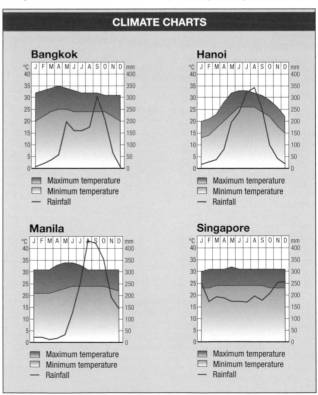

CLIMATE CHARTS

Bangkok
- Maximum temperature
- Minimum temperature
- Rainfall

Hanoi
- Maximum temperature
- Minimum temperature
- Rainfall

Manila
- Maximum temperature
- Minimum temperature
- Rainfall

Singapore
- Maximum temperature
- Minimum temperature
- Rainfall

Time Zones

GMT + 6hr 30 min: Burma
GMT + 7hr: Laos, Cambodia, Thailand, Vietnam, western Indonesia
GMT+ 8hr: Malaysia, Brunei, Singapore, central Indonesia, Philippines
GMT + 9hr: eastern Indonesia
Because the countries are near the equator, daylight remains at roughly 12 hours throughout the year (around 6am–6pm), so daylight saving time is not used.

rickshaws.
Car hire: Outside the main cities, it is best to hire a car with a driver. Note that tourists are currently not allowed to drive cars in Cambodia and Vietnam. Motorbike hire is another possibility though local licenses are required in Vietnam and Cambodia.

By Boat

Ferries are often the only way to reach the many islands in Southeast Asia, particularly in Indonesia and the Philippines, though be warned that the safety record of some of these is not impressive.
Cruise lines Star Cruises is one of the major cruise lines operating in the region (www.starcruises.com).
River cruises A number of cruise ships ply the waterways, notably the Mekong River. Pandaw River Cruises is the largest operator.

CLIMATE

Tropical conditions exist throughout Southeast Asia (see charts) where there is an average temperature of 30°C (86°F). In Indochina and most of the Philippines there is a slightly cooler, dry season (December–February), which is best for travelling. This is followed by a hot season from March to May, after which the rainy southwest monsoon arrives and continues until October. The rains are unpredictable, but generally bring downpours for a few hours each day and provide a refreshing break from the heat. In Cambodia and Laos they can be particularly destructive.

In Indonesia there are two monsoon seasons; the north monsoon from November to March and the south monsoon from May to October.

Typhoons can hit the Philippines and Vietnam from June to November.

FESTIVALS

Religion dominates the seasonal life of countries in Southeast Asia, and this is demonstrated in numerous festivals; during major events, hotels may be full, restaurants crowded and transport difficult to obtain. Many of these are moveable feasts, so check current dates. These are the main annual events, but some countries have several large populations of different practising faiths.
Chinese New Year: Singapore, Malaysia, Thailand (Jan/Feb)
Tet: Vietnam (Jan/Feb)
Buddhist New Year: Burma, Thailand, Laos, Cambodia (April)
Ramadan: Malaysia, Brunei, Indonesia (Sept)
Christmas and Easter: Philippines (Dec, Mar/April)
See page 144.

MONEY

Each country has its own currency, but the exchange rates of lesser-used currencies are not always great, so use the ATMs on arrival and try to change no more than you need.

US dollars are accepted in Cambodia, Vietnam and Laos, and may be accepted in larger cities elsewhere, getting a better rate than euros – which are also fairly widely used. Thai baht are accepted in Burma, Laos and Cambodia border towns, and Singapore dollars (legal tender in Brunei) are acceptable in many tourist areas.

BUDGETING FOR YOUR TRIP

Singapore and Brunei are the high flyers in the region, with prices matching those of Western countries. There are also many smart resorts and hotels that are picked by the likes of *Condé Nast Traveller*, which ensure your holiday will be no cheaper than many other high-end long-distance breaks.

For the rest, Southeast Asia remains primarily a budget holiday and backpackers' destination, where you can live comfortably on around US$30–40 a day; it is even possible to stay at top hotels and get by on $140–200 a day. The major expense for many will be the cost of getting to the region in the first place. Detailed budgeting for each country is described under the relevant sections in the following pages.

HEALTH

You need to drink a lot of water in the heat. Also pack plenty of sun cream. Mosquitoes are a nuisance and can carry dengue and malaria: prepare with coils and unguents, which you can buy at your destination, and sleep beneath a net. Cover up your arms and legs particularly if you are out at dawn and dusk when they are most active.

Stomach problems may occur simply though a change of water and diet, but be prepared. Check with your own doctor well in advance of travel for vaccinations, especially if you are visiting more remote areas.

Note also that towns in Southeast Asia can be very noisy: unless you are staying in a double-glazed hotel, take some earplugs with you.

FURTHER READING

A Dragon Apparent by Norman Lewis. Travels though Indochina in the waning days of the French empire.
Dispatches by Michael Herr. An extraordinary book about American soldiers in Vietnam.
Lord Jim by Joseph Conrad. An Englishman abandons ship, hides in Malaya and becomes a lord.
Krakatoa: The Day the World Exploded; August 27 1888 by Simon Winchester. The story of one of the greatest natural disasters in history.
The Malayan Trilogy by Anthony Burgess. The first novels of the English novelist, who taught in Kuala Lumpur and was fluent in Malay.
Noli Me Tangere by José P. Rizal. Filipino national hero Rizal's semi-autobiographical account of harsh life under Spanish rule.
The Map of Lost Memories by Kim Fay. A well-researched historical adventure novel focused on Cambodia.

Language

In Singapore and much of the Philippines, English is perfectly understood. It is not a *lingua franca*, but it is the main foreign language of much of the region, though in Cambodia and Vietnam French may also be useful when speaking with senior citizens. Cantonese is helpful if you happen to have it. The languages of the countries are not mutually intelligible and there are many dialects, but attempts should be made to get to grips with just a few local words.

THAILAND

TRANSPORT, ACCOMMODATION, EATING OUT, ACTIVITIES AND AN A–Z OF TRAVEL INFORMATION

FACT FILE

Situation Thailand is bordered by Malaysia to the south, Myanmar to the west, Laos across the Mekong River to the northeast and Cambodia to the east.
Area 514,000 sq km (198,455 sq miles), nearly the size of France or twice as large as England, with 2,600km (1,600 miles) of coastline.
Capital Bangkok.
Population 67 million, of whom 75 percent are Thai and 11 percent Chinese.
Time zone 7 hours ahead of Greenwich Mean Time (GMT), so New York is 12 hours, Los Angeles 15 hours and London 7 hours behind, Australia 3 hours ahead.
Currency Baht, approximately B31 to US$1.
Electricity 220 volts, with flat-pronged or round-pronged plugs.
International dialling code 66.

TRANSPORT

Getting there

By air

Bangkok is a gateway between east and west and a transport hub for Southeast Asia served by major airlines. In addition to Bangkok, Thailand has four other international airports: Chiang Mai, Chiang Rai, Phuket and Hat Yai.

Thai Airways International (THAI; www.thaiairways.com) flies to more than 70 cities worldwide. **Bangkok Airways** (www.bangkokair.com), **AirAsia** (www. airasia.com) and **Orient Thai** (www. orient-thai.com) operate routes between

Bangkok's waterways

Chao Phraya River express boats (tel: 0 2623 6143) run regular routes at 15- to 20-minute intervals along the Chao Phraya River, between Tha Nonthaburi pier in the north and Tha Wat Rajsingkorn near Krungthep Bridge in the south. The service runs from 6am to 7pm. Fares are collected on board.

Ferries also cross the river at dozens of points and are very cheap. They begin operating at 6am and stop at 10pm or later.

It is also possible to catch a long-tail taxi to many points along the Chao Phraya or the canals.

major tourism centres in Thailand and Asian cities. A direct flight (such as on British Airways, EVA Airways, Qantas and THAI) from the UK and Europe takes about 12 hours. From the west coast of the US, it takes about 18 hours (not including transit time) and involves a connection in North Asia – Japan, Korea or Taiwan. The east coast route via Europe takes about 19 hours. From Australia and New Zealand, the flight is about 9 hours.

By sea

Star Cruises (www.starcruises. com) operates luxury cruises around the Asia-Pacific. Its various cruises around Southeast Asia, set off from Singapore and call at Phuket.

By rail

Trains operated by the **State Railways of Thailand** (tel: 1690, www.railway. co.th) are clean, cheap and reliable, albeit slow. There are only three entry points into Thailand, two from Malaysia on the southern Thai border

and one to Vientiane, Laos.

A daily train, the *International Express*, leaves Butterworth, the port opposite Malaysia's Penang Island, at 11am and 2.05pm, arriving in Bangkok at 9.05am and 11.10am the following day. There are second-class cars with seats that are made into upper and lower sleeping berths at night. There are also air-conditioned first-class sleepers and dining cars. Trains leave Bangkok's Hualamphong Station daily in the early morning and mid-afternoon for the return journey to Malaysia.

By road

Malaysia provides the main road access into Thailand, with crossings near Betong and Sungai Kolok. It is possible to cross from Laos into Nong Khai via the Friendship Bridge, or by river ferry into Chiang Khong. From Cambodia, visitors can cross at Poipet into Aranyaprathet.

Getting around

On arrival

Suvarnabhumi Airport
Bangkok's international airport, **Suvarnabhumi** (tel: 0-2132 1888,

Arrive in style

The Eastern and Oriental Express (www.orient-express.com) is Asia's most exclusive travel experience. Travelling between Singapore, Kuala Lumpur and Bangkok, the 22-carriage train, with its distinctive green-and-cream livery, passes through spectacular scenery. It's expensive but classy.

www.suvarnabhumiairport.com), lies approximately 30km (19 miles) east of the capital and is linked to the city by a system of elevated highways. Road travel to most parts of Bangkok averages 45 minutes.

Limousine service
Airports of Thailand Limousines (AOT, tel: 0-2134 2323–6) operates a variety of vehicles that can take you to the city centre for about B1,000. Luxury cars like a top-end 7-series BMW will cost B2,200. Rates to Pattaya start at around B2,600, depending on the vehicle used.

THAI Airways Limousines (tel: 08-1652 4444) also operates a premium car service. Prices are similar to those charged by AOT.

Airport bus
The Airport Express bus services have closed. City bus service leave from the public transit centre. Line 555 (to Rangsit, stopping at Don Muang airport, 60 minutes, 3.30am–10pm, B23) and line 556 (to the Southern Bus Terminal, 90 minutes, 6am–9pm, B23). Both the buses and public vans with the same number drive the same route.

Taxis
Operating 24 hours daily, all taxis officially serving the airport are air-conditioned and metered. Contact the taxi counter at exits 3 or 10 on the second level. Alternatively, take the express shuttle bus to the Public Transportation Center's taxi stand.

At the arrival hall's taxi desk, a receipt will be issued, with the licence plate number of the taxi and your destination written on it in Thai. At the end of your trip, pay what is on the meter plus a B50 airport surcharge. If the driver uses the

Bangkok taxi talk

Thai taxi drivers are not renowned for their fluency in English, so it is often wise to have your destination written in Thai to hand to the driver.

Note that in Bangkok, Wireless Road, home to many embassies, a large hotel and several banks, is more commonly known by its Thai name, Thanon Witthayu. Similarly, Thanon Sathorn, a main thoroughfare divided into north and south, which runs between Lumphini Park and the river, is often referred to as Sathorn Neua (north) and Sathorn Tai (south).

Distinctively Thai features in Bangkok's Suvarnabhumi International Airport.

expressway (with your consent), toll fees also apply.

Depending on traffic, an average fare from the airport to the city centre is around B300, excluding toll fees and airport surcharge.

Don Muang Airport
In 2012 the government changed its single airport policy and is encouraging low budget carriers to use Bangkok's old Don Mueang Airport (tel: 0-2535 1111, www.donmuangairportonline.com), which was reopened for international flights. Air Asia moved its entire operation to Don Mueang late the same year. A small number of THAI domestic flights and all domestic flights operated by Orient Thai and Nok Air (www.nokair.com) were already using Don Mueang.

Chiang Mai Airport
Chiang Mai's airport is a 15-minute drive from the city centre. There is no bus service, visitors should choose between one of the following services:
Taxis: If you have not made arrangements with your hotel to pick you up, airport taxis are available for the 15–20-minute ride to the city for B100.

Phuket Airport
Travelling to Phuket Town from the airport takes about 45 minutes, while Patong Beach can be reached in around half an hour.
Taxis: Airport taxis and limousines can be hired at the arrival hall at set rates. Prices start at B200–400 for the nearby northern beaches, rising to B550–750 for other locations.
Minibus: Tickets for these 8-seaters are sold on the right-hand side

outside the airport. The fare starts from B900.
Airport bus: Tickets for the airport bus to Phuket Town or to the beaches can be bought on board or from designated booths in the arrival hall. The fare is about B90.

By air
The domestic arm of **Thai Airways International** (THAI: www.thaiairways.com) operates a network of daily flights to 12 of Thailand's major towns aboard a fleet of Boeing 777s and various Airbuses. THAI offers a 'Discover Thailand' visitor's pass, allowing three domestic flights, for around US$280 within a three-month period. Contact a TAT office for further details (see page 387).

In addition, **Bangkok Airways** (www.bangkokair.com) flies from Bangkok to several domestic destinations daily, including Sukhothai, Chiang Mai, Ko Samui and Phuket. It also connects the capital city to other cities in the region, including Phnom Penh and Siem Reap in Cambodia, Luang Prabang in Laos, and Xian in China.

Other airlines offering domestic services, often at lower fares than either THAI or Bangkok Airways, include **AirAsia** (www.airasia.com), **Nok Air** (www.nokair.com), and **Orient Thai** (www.orient-thai.com).

Note that if you are planning a trip to the tropical island of Ko Samui from Bangkok, you will save much travelling time if you go by air, a journey of less than two hours; the same trip by road and boat may take as long as 14 hours.

By rail
The State Railways of Thailand (www.railway.co.th) operates three principal

MYANMAR

LAOS

CAMBODIA

VIETNAM

MALAYSIA

BRUNEI

SINGAPORE

INDONESIA

PHILIPPINES

routes from Hualamphong Railway Station. The **northern** route passes through Ayutthaya, Phitsanulok, Lampang and terminates at Chiang Mai. The **upper northeastern** route passes through Ayutthaya, Saraburi, Nakhon Ratchasima, Khon Kaen, Udon Thani and terminates at Nong Khai, with a lower northeastern branch from Nakhon Ratchasima to Ubon Ratchathani. The eastern route goes due east from Bangkok to Aranyaprathet on the Thai–Cambodian border and also stops at Pattaya. The **southern** route crosses the Rama VI bridge and calls at Nakhon Pathom, Phetchaburi, Hua Hin and Chumphon. It branches at Hat Yai, one branch running southwest through Betong and on down the western coast of Malaysia to Singapore. The **southeastern** branch goes via Pattani and Yala to the Thai border opposite the Malaysian town of Kota Bharu.

A shorter spur line leaves **Bangkok Noi** station, in Thonburi, on the western bank of the Chao Phraya River, for Nakhon Pathom and Kanchanaburi in western Thailand. There is also a short route leaving Bangkok Noi that travels west along the rim of the Gulf of Thailand to Samut Sakhon and then on to Samut Songkhram.

Express and rapid services on the main lines offer first-class, air-conditioned or second-class, fan-cooled cars with sleeping cabins or berths and dining cars. There are also special air-conditioned express day coaches that travel to key towns along the main lines.

Reservations can be made at the station or with any travel agent within 30 days prior to departure. Tel: 0-2220 4261.

Bangkok's main stations include **Hualamphong Station:** Thanon Rama IV, tel: 0-2621 8701, (information), 0-2220 4444 / 1690 (for reservations five days or more before departure) and **Bangkok Noi (Thonburi) Station**, Thanon Arun Amarin (near Siriraj Hospital), tel: 0-2411 3100.

By road

Bus services are reliable, frequent and very affordable to most destinations in Thailand. Rest stops are regular, and in some cases refreshments are available.

Fan-cooled buses, painted orange, are the slowest since they make stops in every village along the way. For short distances, they can be an entertaining means of travel, particularly in the cool season when the fan and the open windows make the trip reasonably comfortable.

Blue air-conditioned buses are generally a faster, more comfortable way to travel. VIP buses are available on some of the longer routes; these usually have larger seats, more leg room and toilets.

Bus stations

For bus and coach journeys to destinations outside of Bangkok, the major terminals are:

Eastern, Thanon Sukhumvit, opposite Soi 63 (Soi Ekkamai), tel: 0-2391 8097. Departures for Pattaya, Rayong, Chanthaburi.

Motorcycle rental

Motorcycles can be rented in Chiang Mai, Pattaya and Phuket (just about everywhere, in fact) for economical rates. Remember that when you rent a motorcycle, you must surrender your passport for the duration.

Motorcycles range in size from 100cc to giant 750cc models. The majority are 100cc step-through bikes. Rental outlets can be found along beach roads and main roads in each town.

It is not uncommon for rental bikes to be stolen; lock them up when not in use, and only park them in areas with supervision.

Northern and Northeastern, Mo Chit Mai, Thanon Kamphaeng Phet 2, tel: 0-2936 2841 48. Departures for Ayutthaya, Lopburi, Nakhon Ratchasima, Chiang Mai.
Southern, Thanon Boromrat Chonnani, Thonburi, tel: 0-2435 1200. Departures for Nakhon Pathom, Kanchanaburi, Phuket, Surat Thani.

To reach a small town from a large one, or to get around on some of the islands, *songthaew* (meaning two rows), pick-up trucks with benches along either side of the bed, function as taxis.

Public transport

Bangkok
Taxi, Tuk-Tuk and Motorcycle: All car taxis in Bangkok are metered, air-conditioned and reliable, but the drivers' command of English is usually minimal.

Make sure your taxi driver turns on the meter before you begin your journey. The basic fare at flagfall is 35 baht, after which the fare increases in increments according to time and/or distance. Taxi drivers do not charge you an extra fee for baggage stowage or extra passengers, and tipping isn't necessary (though much appreciated).

Occasionally a driver will try to negotiate a flat fare instead of turning on his meter. Sometimes the fare quoted amounts to thievery; you will nearly always get a better rate from a metered taxi. Note that any trips made along the expressway ('highway' to some drivers) will involve an additional toll of B30–70, which you will be expected to pay. Also, most taxi drivers do not

Travelling by motorbike in the northwest of the country.

maintain a ready supply of small change; it's best not to offer anything larger than a B100 note when paying your fare.

If the English fluency of taxi drivers is limited, that of *tuk-tuk* (also called *samlor*, meaning three wheels) drivers is even less. *Tuk-tuks* are the brightly coloured three-wheeled taxis whose nickname comes from the noise made by their two-stroke engines. They are fun for short trips, but choose a taxi for longer journeys. A *tuk-tuk* driver on an open stretch of road can seldom resist racing, and the resultant journey can be a hair-raising experience. For very short trips, the fare is B30.

As the traffic situation worsens in Bangkok, so motorcycle taxis have proliferated. Passengers are required to wear helmets on the major roads, but the drivers do not always supply them. In the case of an accident, not a rare occurrence, the driver will likely not hold any insurance. In spite of the risks, this means of travel is worth trying when the streets are jammed.

Bus and minibus: Bus transport in Bangkok is very cheap but can also be equally arduous, time-consuming and confusing. Municipal and private operators all come under the charge of the **Bangkok Mass Transit Authority** (tel: 0-2246 0973, www. bmta.co.th).

With little English signage and few conductors or drivers speaking English, you need to work out in advance which bus you need.

Skytrain and MRTA: The Bangkok Transit System (BTS), or **Skytrain** (tel: 0-2617 7340, www.bts.co.th), is the perfect way to beat the city's traffic congestion. Trains arrive every three-to-five minutes, and no journey exceeds 30 minutes. Single-trip fares range between B15 and B40. Tourists may buy an unlimited ride 1-day Pass (B100) or the 30-day Adult Pass (B440: 20 rides; B600: 30 rides; B800: 40 rides).

The Skytrain consists of two lines: the **Sukhumvit Line** runs from On Nut along Thanon Sukhumvit to Siam Square, Thanon Phayathai, Victory Monument and Mo Chit. The **Silom Line** extends from Saphan Taksin through Silom's business district, Siam Square and ends at the National Stadium. The two lines cross at Siam Square.

A 20km (13-mile) underground subway system, operated by the **Metropolitan Rapid Transit Authority** (MRTA, tel: 0-2624 5200, www.bangkokmetro.co.th), opened in 2004 with 18 stations extending from Hualamphong Railway Station to Bang Sue. The line intersects the BTS Skytrain routes near the Asoke and Mo Chit Skytrain stations.

The air-conditioned trains are frequent (2–4 minutes peak, 4–6 minutes off-peak). Fares range between B16–41. Coin-sized plastic tokens are used, and tourists may buy an unlimited ride 1-day Pass (B120), 3-day Pass (B230) or stored-value Adult Card (B230).

Chiang Mai

Bus: Chiang Mai has red *songthaew* that carry passengers almost anywhere within the town for a minimum of B30 per person per trip. There are buses that run along the main streets, the fare is B20 per person.

Tuk-tuk: They charge according to distance, starting at B20. You must bargain for the price before you get in.

Samlor: These pedal trishaws charge a minimum of B30. Bargain before you board.

Phuket

Bus: Wooden buses ply regular routes from the market to the beaches. They depart every 30 minutes between 7am and 5pm between Phuket Town market and all beaches. Flag one down along the beach roads; B40 per person.

Tuk-tuk: The small cramped *tuk-tuks* function as taxis, and will go anywhere. Barter your fare before getting on. For example, Patong to Karon, B250, Patong to airport, B450. Within town, B50.

Motorcycle taxi: B40–50 per ride. A convenient, if dangerous, way to get around.

Private transport

Limousine

Most major hotels operate air-conditioned limousine services. Although the prices are at least twice those of ordinary taxis, they offer English-speaking drivers and door-to-door service.

Rental car

Thailand has a good road system with over 50,000km (31,000 miles) of paved highways. Road signs are in both Thai and English. An international driver's licence is required.

Driving on a narrow and busy road can be terrifying; right of way is generally determined by size. It is not unusual for a bus to overtake a truck even if the oncoming lane is filled with vehicles. It is little wonder that, when collisions occur, lives are often lost. In addition, many of the long-distance drivers consume pep pills and have the throttle to the floor because they are getting paid for beating schedules. Take great care if driving at night.

Avis, Hertz, Budget and numerous local agencies offer cars with and without drivers, and with insurance coverage for Bangkok and upcountry trips. A deposit is usually required except with credit cards.

In the provinces, agencies can be found in major locations such as Chiang Mai, Pattaya and Phuket. These also rent four-wheel-drive jeeps and minibuses. When renting a jeep, read the fine print carefully and be aware that you are liable for all damages to the vehicle. Ask for first-class insurance, which covers both you and the other vehicle involved in a collision.

ACCOMMODATION

Choosing a hotel

The top-end hotels in Thailand's major tourist centres are equal to the very best, anywhere in the world. Service is second to none. Indeed, most of Thailand's moderately priced lodgings rival what in Europe would be considered first-class hotels. Even the budget and inexpensive hotels in Thailand will often have a swimming pool and more than one food outlet.

Note: A resort hotel does not always have the same connotation in Thailand that it might in the West; often it means nothing more than the fact that the hotel is located in the countryside or by the beach.

Those on a tight budget will find numerous guesthouses offering clean and decent accommodation. Once of primary interest only to backpackers because of their scant facilities, many have been upgraded to include air-conditioning and en suite bathrooms. In Bangkok, these are mainly found along Thanon Khao San, Soi Ngam Duphli (off Thanon Rama IV) and Sukhumvit Soi 1–15. In Chiang Mai, guesthouses are strewn along the Ping River and in the Thanon Moon Muang area. In Pattaya and Phuket, guesthouses are much less common. In most small towns, guesthouses are generally family-run establishments, mostly found near bus and railway stations, and along main streets.

Gourmet Thai food.

Rates and bookings

Thailand has plenty of good value accommodation, but as more hotels and guesthouses upgrade to compete with boutique and design-oriented hotels, prices have begun to creep up. Hotel rates can range widely, even among the luxury hotels. Depending on the season, discounts can exceed 50 percent or more off the published rack rate. In Bangkok especially, where there is a glut of rooms, rates can often be highly discounted during non-peak periods.

During peak holiday periods (holidays, Christmas, New Year,

Chinese New Year, Songkran etc.), generally from November through April, hotels in the resorts tend to be full and prices are high. Booking early in advance is advisable. For the rest of the year, it is always worth asking for a discount. Alternatively, check online hotel sites, like Agoda (www.agoda.org) and Hotel Club (www.hotelclub.com) for better rates.

Note: Most hotels also charge a value added tax (VAT) of seven percent to the bill, and at the mid- and top-end hotels, a service charge of 10 percent as well.

EATING OUT

Thai restaurants

Thai cuisine is justly regarded as being among the best in the world. The variety of curries, desserts, fruit, soups and snacks is staggering (see page 38).

Major cities have a range of international cuisine, but elsewhere the options will be almost exclusively Thai. If you are anywhere near the coast, check out the local seafood for the giant prawns, crab and lobster. Eating out is so cheap that few Thais bother to cook at home. Roadside stalls can serve up delicious noodle soup, or *kuaytiaw*, for B30, while even at the fanciest restaurants the bill will rarely top B500 per head. Expect

to pay B250 per head on average. Service charges are sometimes included, if not a 10 per cent tip is appreciated. Most restaurants are open throughout the day, closing around 11pm.

If you have a sweet tooth, it is worth leaving room for dessert. Be sure to try mango and sticky rice and banana in coconut milk.

ACTIVITIES

The arts

Modern pop culture seems to have gained an edge over traditional Thai arts, despite government support for Thai arts and performers. Relatively little is done to attract foreign performers in the manner of, say, Hong Kong's Art Centre and the annual Hong Kong Arts Festival.

The many museums in Bangkok and in major towns around the country are devoted to preserving the past and contain some superb specimens. Exhibitions of modern art are arranged by private gallery owners, foreign cultural centres, or corporate patrons, usually banks.

Theatres

The **National Theatre** presents Thai works and, occasionally, big-name foreign ensembles like the New York Philharmonic. For more experimental works, Thai or foreign, look to the

Thailand's nightlife

Thai people love to party so there is always something to do once the sun goes down. Many Thais spend their evenings eating and drinking in large open-air restaurants. If you prefer a little more action, most towns have nightclubs where live bands perform a mix of Thai and Western songs. The scene in Bangkok and some of the resorts is more varied.

The reputation for bawdiness is still well deserved. For years, the country has been known as a centre for sex of every persuasion and interest. Times and clienteles have changed, to a degree – the American GIs of the 1960s and the German and Japanese sex tourists of the 1970s and 80s having been replaced by well-heeled tourists, usually couples. Nonetheless, there are massage parlours and karaoke bars in every Thai town, though usually catering to locals rather than tourists. The Patpong and Nana

districts in Bangkok, and nearly all of Pattaya, are still notorious for their go-go bars and raunchy stage shows.

In Phuket, 'beerbars' line the streets of Patong beach's Soi Bangla and similar areas of Karon and Kata. While Chiang Mai can't compete with Bangkok, the town has an increasing number of bars and pubs.

Bangkok

Bangkok's reputation as a centre for sex of every persuasion frequently overshadows its other night time offerings. While there has been no reduction in the number of massage parlours and bars, there has been an upsurge in other activities to meet the needs of the new breed of travellers. Jazz clubs, cool bars and chic clubs are aplenty, attracting young Thais and visitors in droves. Serious clubbers head to the area known simply as RCA for its cavernous, Western-style clubs, or

the Silom district. Most clubs now impose entrance fees – unheard of previously.

The only damper in Bangkok's nightlife scene is the intrusive Social Order Campaign introduced in 2001, which forces nightlife spots to close early and allows the police to raid bars and clubs to conduct random urine tests on patrons for drugs. Be sure to bring along your passport (even a photocopy will do) to be allowed entry at some nightspots.

Massages

'Traditional Thai Massage' and 'Ancient Thai Massage' are therapeutic massages performed according to age-old traditions. The best place for this is at Bangkok's Wat Pho. 'Special' massages are sexual. Punters pick a woman from behind a one-way mirror and spend the next hour getting a bath and whatever else they arrange.

Thailand Cultural Centre (tel: 0-2247 0028). The centre, which is a gift of the government of Japan, is located on Thanon Ratchadapisek north of central Bangkok. Its three stages present everything from pianists to puppets. See newspapers for announcements.

It is also possible to find Chinese opera being performed during festivals such as the Vegetarian Festival that takes place each September in Chinatown. Performances are normally not announced, but are an unexpected surprise one stumbles across in back alleys.

Likay, the village version of the great *lakhon* and *khon* dance/dramas of the palace, was once staple fare at temple fairs, but most of the fairs have faded away in the city and are found only in rural areas. Performances of *kae bon*, an offshoot of *khon*, can be seen at Lak Muang, where successful supplicants pay a troupe to perform for gods of the heavens and angels of the city.

Traditional puppet theatre is best represented by **Joe Louis Theatre** (Suan Lum Night Bazaar, 1875 Thanon Rama IV, tel: 0-2252 9683), which stages a *hun lakhon lek* puppet show, inspired by local folk tales and the *Ramakien*, nightly (8pm).

Built in 1933, **Sala Chalerm Krung** (66 Th. Charoen Krung, tel: 0-2222 1854, www.salachalerm krung.com) is a convenient space to hear Thai classical music, as it hosts *khon* masked drama performances every Friday and Saturday evening from 7pm.

Concerts

The Fine Arts Department offers concerts of Thai music and dance/drama at the **National Theatre** (tel: 0-2224 1342). At 2pm on Saturdays, Thai classical dance is presented at the auditorium of the **Public Relations Building** on Ratchadamnoen Klang Avenue, opposite the Royal Hotel.

Concerts of European music

Shoppers' map

Nancy Chandler's *Map of Bangkok*, available in bookstores and hotels, is an invaluable reference for shoppers. It is the best map for pointing you in the direction of the top shopping areas, restaurants and sights.

and dance are now regular events. The Bangkok Symphony Orchestra and groups from western countries give frequent concerts. *See Bangkok Post's* supplements for information.

Art galleries

The **National Gallery** is located to the north of the National Museum in Bangkok, across the approach to the Phra Pinklao Bridge at 4 Thanon Chao Fa (tel: 0-2281 2224; Wed–Sun 9am–4pm; charge). The gallery displays works by Thai artists and offers frequent film shows. Exhibitions of paintings, sculpture, ceramics, photographs and weaving are numerous.

Silpakorn University, opposite the Grand Palace on Thanon Na Phra Lan, is the country's premier fine arts college. It frequently stages exhibitions of students' work. Other promoters of Thai art and photography are the British Council, the Goethe Institut and Alliance Française.

Art galleries seem more interested in selling mass-market works than in promoting experimental art; but one, **Visual Dhamma** (44/28 Soi 21 (Soi Asoke), Thanon Sukhumvit, tel: 0-2258 5879), takes an active role in ensuring that talented artists exhibit their works. It is interested primarily in a new school of Thai art that attempts to re-interpret Buddhist themes.

Shopping

Whatever part of your budget you have allocated for shopping, double

A Sala Rim Naam dance show based on the Ramayana at the Mandarin Oriental Hotel in Bangkok.

it or regret it. The widest range of handicraft items is found in Bangkok and Chiang Mai.

Value Added Tax: Non-Thai visitors are entitled to reclaim the seven percent VAT charged on goods and services purchased from stores displaying the 'VAT Refund for Tourists' sign. Ask sales staff for details. Claims must be made before departure at any of the international airports.

What to buy

Real/fake antiques

Wood, bronze, terracotta and stone statues from across Thailand and Burma can be found in Bangkok and Chiang Mai. There are religious figures and characters from classical literature, carved wooden angels, mythical animals and more. Most fake antiques passed off as real are crafted in Chiang Mai and surrounding villages.

Export permits

The **Fine Arts Department** (tel: 0-2226 1661) prohibits the export of all Thai Buddha images, images of other deities and fragments (hands or heads) of images dating from before the 18th century.

All antiques and art objects, regardless of type or age, must be registered with the Fine Arts Department. The shop will usually do this for you. If you decide to handle it yourself, take the piece to the Fine Arts Department at the National Museum on Thanon Na Phra That, together with two postcard-sized photos of it. The export fee ranges between B50–200, depending on the antiquity of the piece.

Fake antiques do not require export permits, but airport customs officials are not art experts and may mistake it for a genuine piece. If it looks authentic, clear it at the Fine Arts Department to avoid problems later on.

Thai silk and fabrics

Silk is perhaps Thailand's best-known craft. First brought to international attention by American entrepreneur Jim Thompson, Thai silk has enjoyed enduring popularity and is on many visitors' shopping lists. Sold in a wide variety of colours, it is characterised by the tiny nubs that rise like embossings from its surface – and, of course, by its smooth silkiness.

Unlike sheer Indian silks and shiny Chinese patterned silks, Thai silk is a

THAILAND

MYANMAR

LAOS

CAMBODIA

VIETNAM

MALAYSIA

BRUNEI

SINGAPORE

INDONESIA

PHILIPPINES

thick cloth that lends itself to clothes, curtains and upholstery, but is also used to cover purses, tissue boxes and picture frames.

Mutmee is a silk from the northeast of Thailand and whose colours are sombre and muted. A form of tie-dyed cloth, it is sold both in lengths and as finished clothing or accessories.

Batik Southern Thailand is a batik centre and offers ready-made clothes and batik paintings.

Wall hangings Burmese in origin and style, *kalaga* wall hangings are popular. The figures are stuffed with *kapok* to make them stand out in relief.

Baskets

Thailand's abundant bamboo, wicker and grasses are transformed into lamps, storage boxes, tables, colourful mats, handbags, letter holders, tissue boxes and slippers. Wicker and bamboo are turned into storage lockers with brass fittings and furniture to fill the house.

Yan lipao, a thin, sturdy grass, is woven into delicate patterns to create purses and bags for formal occasions. Although expensive, the bags retain their beauty for years.

Ceramics

Best known among the distinctive Thai ceramics is the jade green celadon, which is distinguished by its finely glazed surface. Statues, lamps, ashtrays and other items are also produced in dark green, brown and cobalt blue hues.

Modelled on its Chinese cousin, blue-and-white porcelain includes

pots, lamp bases, household items and figurines. Quality varies according to the skill of the artist, and of the firing and glazing.

Bencharong (meaning five colours) describes a style of porcelain derived from 16th-century Chinese art. Normally reserved for bowls, containers and fine chinaware, its classic pattern features a small religious figure surrounded by intricate floral designs, usually green, blue, yellow, rose and black.

Decorative arts

Lacquerware comes in two styles: the gleaming gold-and-black variety normally seen on temple shutters, and the matte red type with black and/or green details, which originated in northern Thailand and Burma. The range includes ornate containers and trays, wooden figurines, woven bamboo baskets and Burmese-inspired Buddhist manuscripts. Pieces may also be bejewelled with tiny glass mosaics and gilded ornaments.

Black lacquer is also the base into which shaped bits of mother-of-pearl are pressed. Scenes from religious or classical literature are rendered on presentation trays, containers and plaques.

Gems and jewellery

Thailand is a major exporter of cut rubies and sapphires. Customers should patronise only those shops that display the trade's official emblem: a gold ring mounted with a ruby.

Thailand is now regarded as the world's leading cutter of gemstones,

the 'Bangkok cut' rapidly becoming one of the most popular. Artisans set the stones in gold and silver to create jewellery and bejewelled containers. Light green Burmese jade (jadeite) is carved into jewellery as well as into art objects.

Phuket produces international-standard, natural, cultured Mob (teardrop) and artificial pearls. Costume jewellery is a major Thai business.

Hill-tribe crafts

Northern hill tribes produce brightly-coloured needlepoint in a variety of geometric and floral patterns. These are sold as produced, or else incorporated into shirts, coats, bags, pillowcases and other items.

Hill-tribe silver work is valued less for its silver content (which is low) than for its intricate work and imagination.

Metal art objects

Silver and gold are pounded into jewellery, boxes and other decorative pieces, many set with gems. Tin, mined near Phuket, is the prime ingredient in pewterware, of which Thailand is a major producer. Items range from clocks and steins to egg cups and figurines.

A–Z

Budgeting for your trip

It's possible to survive on as little as B500 a day, but to experience all Thailand has to offer in comfort it's best to budget for B1,500–3,000 a day.

Basic accommodation can be found for B400, while B1,000 will ensure a comfortable night's sleep and anything above B3,000 will garner a more luxurious option. Look for discounts during the low season (May to October).

A budget bowl of noodles is as low as B30. Normal restaurants cost B200 a head and top-of-the-range eateries will result in a bill of B1,000 or more per head.

Large bottles of beer cost around B70, while a glass of house wine (wine isn't widely drunk) is B100 a glass. Service charges are sometimes included.

Taxis from Suvarnabhumi Airport to downtown Bangkok will cost B300 (insist that they turn the meter on). Costs to other destinations depend on distance and your negotiating skills.

Lacquerware, at Chatuchak Market, Bangkok.

Bangkok's skytrain (BTS) reaches most parts of the city for between B15–40 for a single ticket.

Climate

There are three seasons: hot, rainy and cool. But for most tourists, Thailand has only one season: hot. To make things worse, it drops only a few degrees during the night and is accompanied by round the clock humidity above 70 percent. Only air-conditioning makes Bangkok and other towns tolerable during the hot season. The countryside is cooler, but the northern regions can be hotter in March/April than Bangkok.

Hot season (Mar–mid-June), 28–38°C (82–100°F).
Rainy season (June–Oct), 24–32°C (75–90°F).
Cool season (Nov–Feb), 18–32°C (65–90°F), but with less humidity.

What to bring/wear

Lip balm and moisturisers are needed in the north during the cool season. Sunglasses, sunblock and hats are essential. Clothes should be light and loose. Open shoes (sandals during the height of the rainy season, when some Bangkok streets get flooded) and sleeveless dresses for women or short-sleeved shirts for men are appropriate. A sweatshirt or fleece is needed for nights in the north. In general, Thailand lacks the formal dress code of Hong Kong or Tokyo. Casual but neat and clean clothes are suitable for most occasions.

One exception is the clothing code for Buddhist temples and Muslim mosques. Vests and revealing attire are taboo, and improperly dressed and unkempt visitors will be turned away.

Crime and safety

Pocket-picking and bag-slashing are not uncommon on Bangkok buses. Phuket has a growing problem with petty crimes, scams and occasional violent crime in tourist areas. Keep your wallet in a front pocket and your bag in front of you at all times.

Customs regulations

The Thai government prohibits the import of drugs, dangerous chemicals, pornography, firearms and ammunition. Attempting to smuggle heroin or other hard drugs may be punishable by death.

Foreign guests are allowed to import, without tax, 200 cigarettes, and one litre of wine or spirits.

For more details, check the **Thai Customs Department** website at www.customs.go.th, or call 1164.

Embassies and consulates

Embassies in Bangkok
Australia
37 Thanon Sathorn Tai, tel: 0-2287 2680.
Canada
15th Floor, Abdulrahim Place, 990 Thanon Rama IV, Bangrak, tel: 0-2344 6300.
New Zealand
M Thai Tower, 14th Floor, All Seasons Place, 87 Thanon Witthayu, tel: 0-2254 2530.
United Kingdom
14 Wireless Road, tel: 0-2305 8333.
United States
95 Wireless Road, tel: 0-2205 4000.

Etiquette

When entering a temple be sure to step over, not on, the red step. Cover any bare arms and remove any hats and shoes. If seated, make sure the soles of your feet point away from the Buddha images. You can usually take photographs inside a temple.

In Thai culture certain parts of the body have significance. The head is the highest point, both physically and spiritually, so never touch a Thai person there. Similarly, the feet are the lowest point, so never use them to point and don't rest your feet on chairs. Showing the soles of your feet to someone is considered highly offensive.

Thais have a genuine affection for their royal family and it is a criminal offence to criticise any member of the monarchy. The national anthem is played at 8am and 6pm every day, when most Thais will stand in silent observation, and visitors should do the same.

When eating, don't expect chopsticks. Thais use knives and spoons or their right hands. 'Losing face' or causing embarrassment is deeply frowned upon, so never show anger or signs of aggression. Thais are generally conservative and do

Emergency numbers

Police. Tel: 191
Tourist Police. Tel: 1155

not engage in public expressions of affection, beyond holding hands.

Health and medical care

Malaria is still very dangerous in some regions of Thailand, mainly along the Burmese and Cambodian borders. Mosquitoes in several areas are resistant to many brands of anti-malarial drugs, so seek advice on medication from a tropical institute before your departure. Should you contract malaria, there is a network of malaria centres and hospitals throughout Thailand. The most dangerous form appears disguised as a heavy cold, so if you have flu symptoms, see a doctor at once.

Dengue fever, a mosquito-borne disease for which there is no vaccination or chemical prophylaxis, is relatively common in rural areas during the rainy season. The best prevention is the use of repellent during the daytime.

Establishments catering to foreigners are generally careful with food and drink preparation. But although Bangkok water is clean when it leaves the modern filtration plant, the pipes are less than new, so it may still be safer to drink bottled water or soft drinks.

Hospitals

First-class hotels in Bangkok, Chiang Mai and Phuket have doctors on call for medical emergencies. The hospitals in these three destinations are the equivalent of those in any major Western city. Most small towns have clinics that treat minor ailments and accidents.

Bangkok
BNH Hospital, 9/1 Thanon Convent, tel: 0-2686 2700, www.bnhhospital. com.
Bumrungrad Hospital, 33 Soi 3, Th. Sukhumvit, tel: 0-2667 1000, www.bumrungrad.com.
Thai Nakharin Hospital, 345 Thanon Bang Na Trat, tel: 0-2361 2712/2761.

Chiang Mai
Chiang Mai Maharaj Hospital, 110 Thanon Suthep, tel: 0-5322 1122/1075, www.med.cmu.ac.th.
Chiang Mai Ram Hospital, 8 Thanon Bunruangrit, tel: 0-5392 0300, www.chiangmairam.com.
McCormick Hospital, Thanon Kaew Nawarat, tel: 0-5392 1777, www.mccormick.in.th.

MYANMAR

LAOS

CAMBODIA

VIETNAM

MALAYSIA

BRUNEI

SINGAPORE

INDONESIA

PHILIPPINES

Phuket

Bangkok Phuket Hospital, 2/1 Thanon Hongyok Utit, Phuket, tel: 0-7625 4425, emergencies: ext. 1060, www.phukethospital.com.

Patong-Kathu Hospital, Thanon Sawatdirak, Patong Beach, tel: 0-7634 0444.

Phuket International Hospital, 44 Thanon Chalermprakiat, Ror 9, Phuket, tel: 0-7624 9400, emergencies: 0-7621 0936, www.phuketinternational hospital.com.

Medical clinics

For minor problems, there are numerous clinics in all major towns and cities. In Bangkok, the **British Dispensary**, at 109 Thanon Sukhumvit (between Soi 3 and 5), tel: 0-2252 9179, has British doctors on its staff.

In Chiang Mai, go to **Loi Kroh Clinic** on Thanon Loi Kroh, tel: 0-5327 1571. Most international hotels also have an on-premises clinic or doctor on call.

Internet

Internet cafés can now be found on almost every street in Bangkok, and even the least-developed provinces have Internet services.

All major hotels in Thailand offer Wi-fi, as do nearly all café outlets such as Starbucks.

Media

Press

There are two national English-language dailies, *Bangkok Post* and *The Nation*. Newsstands in major hotel gift shops carry air-freighted, and therefore expensive, editions of British, French, American, German and Italian newspapers. Newsagents on Soi 3 (Soi Nana Neua), Thanon Sukhumvit, Bangkok also offer Arabic newspapers.

In addition, check out Bangkok 101 *and The Big Chilli*, two local monthly magazines that feature interesting writing; book, film and restaurant reviews; shopping information; and a calendar of Bangkok events, including sport, health and kids' activities. Several pages in each magazine are also devoted to Phuket and Samui.

In Pattaya, the weekly *Pattaya Mail* contains local news and features, as well as information on events, special offers and new facilities and services in the area. The related *Chiangmai Mail* does the same for Chiang Mai and the north.

Money

The Thai baht is the national currency, and is divided into 100 satang. Banknote denominations include 1,000 (grey), 500 (purple), 100 (red), 50 (blue), and 20 (green). At the time of going to press, there were 31 baht to the US dollar.

There are B10 coins (brass centre with a silver rim), B5 coins (eight-sided silver pieces), B2 coins (silver), B1 coins (small silver), and two small coins of 50 and 25 satang (both are brass-coloured).

Thailand has a sophisticated banking system. Money is best imported in cash or traveller's cheques and converted into baht. There is no minimum requirement on the amount of money that must be converted. Foreign tourists may freely bring in foreign banknotes or other types of foreign exchange. For travellers leaving Thailand, the maximum amount permitted to be taken out in Thai currency without prior authorisation is B50,000.

Both cash and travellers' cheques can be changed in hundreds of bank branches; rates are more favourable for travellers' cheques than for cash. Hotels generally give poor exchange rates.

Most banks now have 24-hour ATM machines outside where cash (in baht only) can be withdrawn with credit or debit cards. Note, however, that some banks only accept ATM cards linked directly to Thai bank accounts; for those with ATM cards on the Plus or Cirrus networks who wish to withdraw funds directly from their home bank accounts, Bangkok Bank, Kasikorn Bank and Siam Commercial Bank are good bets. Occasionally an ATM card may not work at one machine – simply try another branch.

Credit cards are widely accepted throughout Bangkok and in larger cities. In smaller provincial destinations, it is better to check that plastic is accepted, and not to count on using cards.

Tipping

Tipping is not a custom in Thailand, although it is becoming more prevalent. A service charge of 10 percent is generally included in restaurant bills and is divided among the staff. A bit extra for the waitress would not go unappreciated.

Do not tip taxi or *tuk-tuk* drivers unless the traffic has been particularly bad; B10 would suffice for a journey costing over B60. Hotel bellmen and room porters are becoming used to being tipped in urban centres but will not hover with hand extended.

Opening hours

Government offices Mon–Fri 8.30am–4.30pm.

Offices Mon–Fri 8am or 8.30am–5.30pm. Some open Sat 8.30am–noon.

Banks Mon–Fri 8.30am–3.30pm, but many operate money-changing kiosks open until 8pm daily.

Shops 10am to 8–10pm.

Restaurants 11am–11pm, except for night markets, 6pm–5am.

Coffee shops Most close at midnight; some stay open 24 hours.

Postal services

Thailand has a comprehensive and reliable postal service. Major towns offer regular airmail services, as well as express courier services.

In Bangkok, the General Post Office (GPO, Thanon Charoen Krung (New Road), between Thanon Surawong and Thanon Si Phraya, tel: 0 2233 1050/9, 0 2235 2834), is open 8am–8pm during the week, and 8am–1pm on weekends and holidays. It is much easier to conduct business here in person, rather than by phone. A separate building to the right of the main GPO provides telecommunications services around the clock, including telephone, fax and Internet.

Public holidays

1 January New Year's Day
February full moon* Magha Puja
6 April Chakri Day
13–15 April Songkran (Thai New Year)
1 May Labour Day
5 May Coronation Day
May* Ploughing Ceremony
May full moon* Visakha Puja
July full moon* Asalaha Puja
July Khao Phansa
12 August Queen's Birthday
23 October Chulalongkorn Day
5 December King's Birthday
10 December Constitution Day
31 December New Year's Eve
Chinese New Year in January/February is not an official public holiday, but many businesses are closed for several days.
* Variable

Thai currency.

Branch post offices are located throughout the country, many staying open until 6pm. Post office kiosks along some of the city's busier streets sell stamps, aerograms and ship small parcels. Hotel reception desks will also send letters and postcards for no extra charge.

Courier services

A number of international courier agencies have offices in Bangkok: **DHL**, tel: 0-2631 2621, www.dhl.co.th **Fedex**, tel: 0-2229 8800, www.fedex.com/th **UPS**, tel: 0-2762 3300, www.ups.com/th

Telephones

The country code for Thailand is 66. When calling Thailand from overseas, dial the international access code, then 66 and the 8-digit number (without the preceding 0). To make an international call from Thailand, dial 001 before the country and area codes, then the telephone number. For international call assistance, dial 100.

Prepaid international phone cards (called Thaicard) of B300, B500 and B1,000 can be used to make international calls. These can be bought at post offices, shops that carry the Thaicard sign, or the office of the Communications Authority of Thailand in Bangkok, tel: 0 2104 3068; www.cattelecom.com.

Public phones

Most travellers will bring their own phone (see page 387), but there are still many coin- and card-operated telephone booths in the cities. Public phones accept coins, and phone cards for local calls in denominations of B50, B100 and B200 can be purchased at convenience stores. International calls can generally be dialled direct from anywhere in Thailand; failing that, most large cities have telephone offices at the GPO; hours are generally 7am–11pm. See also Bangkok's General Post Office, see page 386.

Mobile phones

Any number that begins with the prefix 08 is a mobile phone number. Just as for fixed-line phones, dial the prefix 0 for all calls made within Thailand but drop the zero when calling from overseas.

If you are planning to travel in Thailand for any length of time, it is more economical to buy a local SIM card with stored credit from a mobile phone shop. You will be assigned a local number and local calls to and from the phone will be at local rates.

Area codes

Thailand's former area codes have been incorporated into local phone numbers to produce 8-digit numbers throughout the country. Dial 0 when making domestic calls. If calling from overseas, drop the prefix 0. Dial 1133 for local directory assistance in English.

Tourist information

Overseas

Tourism Authority of Thailand's (www.tourismthailand.org) overseas offices can be found at the following locations:
Australia
Suite 2002, Level 20, 56 Pitt Street, Sydney, tel: 02-9247 7549.
United Kingdom
1st Floor, 17–19 Cockspur Street, Trafalgar Square, London SW1Y 5BL, tel: 0870 900 2007, www.tourism thailand.co.uk.
United States
61 Broadway, Suite 2810, NY 10006, tel: 212-432 0433; 611 North Larchmont Boulevard, 1st Floor, Los Angeles, CA, tel: 323-461 9814.

In Thailand

The **Tourism Authority of Thailand, or TAT**, (tel: 1672, www.tourismthailand.org) offers brochures, maps and videos of the country's attractions. TAT offices are often the best place to start when in a new town as staff are friendly and knowledgeable.
Bangkok
Head Office, 1600 Thanon New Phetchaburi, Makkasan, Rachathewi, tel: 0 2250 5500; 4 Thanon Ratchadamnoen Nok, tel: 0-2283 1500; Suvarnabhumi Airport Domestic Arrival Floor and International Arrival Floor, tel: 0-2134 0040.
Chiang Mai
105/1 Thanon Chiang Mai–Lamphun, tel: 0-5324 8604, 0-5324 8607.
Pattaya
609 Moo 10 Thanon Pratamnak, Banglamung, Chonburi, tel: 0-3842 8750.
Phuket
73–75 Thanon Phuket, tel: 0-7621 2213, 0-7621 1036.

Visas and passports

Travellers should check visa regulations at a Thai embassy or consulate or on the Ministry of Foreign Affairs website at www.mfa.go.th before starting their journey. All foreign nationals entering Thailand must have valid passports. At the airport, nationals from most countries will be granted a free tourist visa valid up to 30 days, provided that they have a fully paid ticket out of Thailand. Tourist visas allowing for a 60-day stay may also be issued in advance of arrival.

Visas can be extended before they expire at immigration offices in Bangkok and other cities.

Visitors wishing to leave Thailand and return before their visas expire can apply for a re-entry permit before departure. An exit visa is not required.

Immigration offices are located at:
Bangkok: 120 Moo 3, Th. Chaengwattana, Mon–Fri 8.30am–4.30pm, tel: 0-2141 9889, www.immigration.go.th.
Chiangmai: 71 Airport Road, Thanon Suthep, Amphoe Muang, tel: 0-5320 1755.
Phuket: Thanon Kalim Beach, tel: 0-7622 1905.

THAILAND
MYANMAR
LAOS
CAMBODIA
VIETNAM
MALAYSIA
BRUNEI
SINGAPORE
INDONESIA
PHILIPPINES

MYANMAR

TRANSPORT, ACCOMMODATION, EATING OUT, ACTIVITIES AND AN A–Z OF TRAVEL INFORMATION

FACT FILE

Situation Myanmar's coastline follows the Bay of Bengal from Bangladesh in the west to the Andaman Sea and the border with Thailand in the east. Inland, the country also borders India, China and Laos.

Area 676,552 sq km (261,218 sq miles).

Population 48.7 million.

Languages Burmese with indigenous minority languages.

Religion Primarily Buddhist with significant Muslim and Christian minorities.

Time zones Myanmar Standard Time is 6 hours and 30 minutes ahead of Greenwich Mean Time. If you come from Bangkok, you will have to set your watch back half-an-hour upon arrival in Yangon.

Currency Kyat (K). K750–K1,350 to US$1.

Weights and measures Myanmar has retained many of the old weights and measures in use during the British colonial period. The tin, or basket, is used to measure quantities of agricultural export goods. The kilogram equivalent differs for rice, sesame, and other goods.

1 viss (peith-tha) = 1,633g/3.6lbs
1 tical = 16.33g
1 cubit (tong) = 0.457 metres/18ins
1 span (htwa) = 0.23 metres/9ins
1 furlong = 201 metres/659ft
1 lakh = 100,000 (units)
1 crore = 100 lakh

Electricity The standard electrical current is 230-volt/50 hertz. Power cuts are frequent in rural areas.

TRANSPORT

Getting there

By air

Due to the trade embargo and sanctions imposed on Myanmar's former military government, comparatively few carriers operate to Yangon-Mingaladon, the main international airport. Those that do – listed below – route flights via their home hubs and/or through Bangkok or Kuala Lumpur, which tends to mean painfully long waits in transit. There are no direct flights from Europe or North America, most Yangon-bound passengers change planes at Bangkok or Doha. The only other point of arrival is Mandalay, with flights from Kunming in southwest China.

Air Asia, Ground Floor, Park Royal Hotel, tel: 01 251 885, www.airasia.com.
Air China, 13/23 Shwe Kanayei Housing, Narnattaw Road, tel: 01 505 024, www.airchina.com.
Air India, 127 Sule Pagoda Road, tel: 01 253 597, www.airindia.in.
Bangkok Airways, 3rd Floor, Sakura Tower 339, Bogyoke Aung San Road, tel: 01 255 122, www.bangkokair.com.
Malaysia Airlines, Central Hotel, 335–357 Bogyoke Aung San Road, Yangon, tel: 01 2410 0120, www.malaysiaairlines.com.
Myanmar Airways International, 08–02 Sakura Tower, 339 Bogyoke Aung San Road, Yangon, tel: 01 255 440, www.maiair.com.
Silk Air, Sakura Tower, 339 Bogyoke Aung San Road, Yangon, tel: 01 225 287, www.silkair.com.
Thai Airways, Sakura Tower, 339 Bogyoke Aung San Road, tel: 01 255 499.

Vietnam Airlines, 1702, Sakura Tower, 339 Bogyoke Aung San Road, tel: 0125 5066, www.vietnamairlines.com.

Overland

Now that the insurgency problems in Myanmar's border areas have abated, it is likely that some of the overland routes into the country will open to foreigners in the next few years. For the time being, however, crossing points are rare, and subject to tight restrictions.

In the far south, the port town of Kawthaung opposite the Myeik (Mergui) archipelago can be reached from Ranong in southern Thailand – but only on a short-stay visa. Further north, in Kayin State, the Thai and Burmese governments have also constructed a 'Friendship Bridge' across the Moei River between Mae Sot and Myawaddy, but so far travel is still not permitted between the two countries except on a single-day temporary visa (you have to leave your passport with the border guards). Travelling from Kunming in China's Yunnan Province, you may enter Myanmar at the Ruili–Muse border crossing, and continue on to Lashio (five hours further south) if an accredited tour operator has arranged your transport. Finally, from Chiang Rai in Thailand, you can head north into Myanmar's Shan State via the Mai-Sai–Tachilek crossing, though your stay will be limited to 15 days.

Note that these restrictions may well change in the near future and should be checked in advance of travel with a reputable agent in Thailand or China.

From the airport

On arrival at **Yangon-Mingaladon Airport**, 19km (12 miles) north of

A bus in downtown Yangon.

the downtown area, expect to be besieged by taxi drivers offering to drive you into the city. The fare is fixed at US$8. If you book a room through the hotel desk at the airport, transport into town is usually arranged free of charge. On departure, the fare from Yangon to the airport can usually be paid in local currency, and costs a couple of dollars less.

Getting around

By air

Travellers to Myanmar often avoid long and potentially uncomfortable road journeys by catching flights between Yangon and Mandalay, or to Nyaung U (for Bagan), Thandwe (Ngapali Beach), Heho (Inle Lake), Sittwe (for Mrauk U), Kengtung (Shan State), Myitkina (on the Upper Ayeyarwady River) and Putao (in the far north). A handful of carriers fly these routes daily (see page 389), and to 39 other regional airports across the country. However, none enjoys a particularly good reputation for reliability or safety. The worst is the government-run Myanmar Airlines, whose fleet of ageing Fokker F27s and Douglas DC3s has a poor accident record.

It generally works out cheaper to book your tickets through an agent in Myanmar rather than direct with the airline. You'll also be better off going to an agent to obtain Air Mandalay's good-value Discover Myanmar Pass, which buys you four flights between Yangon, Mandalay, Bagan, Heho (Inle) and Thandwe (Ngapali Beach) for US$330 (plus taxes). Domestic Airlines include:
Air Bagan, 56 Shwe Taung Gyar Street, Bahan Township, tel: 01 513 322, www.airbagan.com.
Air Kanbawza, 33–49 Corner of Bank Street & Maha Bandoola Garden Street, Kyauktada Township, tel: 01 372 977, www.airkbz.com.
Air Mandalay, 146 Dhammazedi

Road, Bahan Township, Yangon, tel: 01 525 488, www.airmandalay.com.
Asian Wings, 34(A1) Shwe Taung Gyar Street, Bahan Township, tel: 0973 135 991, www.asianwing sairways.com.
Myanmar Airways, 08–02 Sakura Tower, 339 Bogyoke Aung San Road, tel: 01 255 260, www.maiair.com.
Yangon Airways, No.166, Level 5 MMB Tower, Upper Pansodan Road, Mingalar Taung Nyunt Township, tel: 01 652 533, www.yangonair.com.

By sea

Myanmar Five Star Line (www.mfsl-shipping.com) manages the country's overseas and coastal routes with a fleet of 21 vessels, only eight of which take passengers. Of interest are the services linking Yangon with Thandwe, Kyaukpyu, Sittwe in Rakhaing and Dawei, Myeik and Kawthaung in Tanintharyi. The Yangon office is at the corner of Merchant Road and Theinbyu Street (tel: 01 295 279).

By rivers

Myanmar has more than 5,000km (3,000 miles) of navigable river. Even at the height of summer, when water levels are lowest, it's possible to travel by ferry along the Ayeyarwady all the way from the Delta to Bhamo in the north of the country, and in the monsoons you can even reach Myitkyina. Other rivers serving as major transport arteries include the Chindwin, which joins the Ayeyarwady southwest of Mandalay, and the Thandlin (Salween), in the far southeast.

On a package tour, the only kind of boat you are likely to come into contact with is a **luxury cruiser**. These vessels tend to be beautifully restored antique steamers, or else modern replicas, complete with timber-walled cabins furnished in high colonial style, with sun decks, bars and restaurants. Trips typically last from five to around 13 nights,

and include plenty of sightseeing excursions to towns and other places of interest along the way.

By bus

Long-distance public bus travel tends to be slow and tedious. Many roads are poor, vehicles are overcrowded, and in the fairly common event of a breakdown, it can be hours before mechanical assistance becomes available.

Private buses

Several companies run comfortable air-conditioned buses from Yangon's Highway Bus Centre, 3km (2 miles) northeast of the airport, just off Highway 3. Services to most destinations (including Mandalay) run overnight, with arrival times more reliable than those of the trains. There are regular stops for food and refreshments.

Air-conditioned coaches and minibuses are the most common form of travel for foreign travellers on group tours. Tickets may be booked in advance at the company's offices between Aung San Stadium and Yangon Railway Station on Kun Chan Rd.

By train

Myanmar Railways comprises 5,402km (3,357 miles) of track, with Yangon's Central Railway Station as its hub. While the main Yangon–Mandalay line is reasonably quick, clean and efficient, the same can't be said of the rest of the network. Rolling stock ranges from shabby to decrepit and long delays are frequent. That said, if you're not in a rush, travelling by rail in Myanmar has its pleasures – not least gazing out of the open windows.

There are three classes: Upper (reclining seats); First (wooden slatted seats with padded leatherette bottoms); and Ordinary (bare slatted seats). Some services between Yangon and Mandalay also have sleeper carriages – 'standard' and 'special'; the latter with compartments instead of benches. Either way, expect a noisy ride, and bring a fleece as it can get cold at night in winter.

Foreigners can purchase their tickets through Myanmar Travels & Tours or direct at the railway station (tel: 01 274 027), advisably 24 hours ahead of departure.

City/town transport

Bicycle trishaws (*sai-kaa*) or motorised three-wheelers (*thoun bein*) are the most popular means of getting around the streets of the larger cities – less

THAILAND

MYANMAR

LAOS

CAMBODIA

VIETNAM

MALAYSIA

BRUNEI

SINGAPORE

INDONESIA

PHILIPPINES

Travelling en masse near Bagan.

so in Yangon and Mandalay where taxis have taken over. Easily available and cheap, they take their passengers anywhere they want to go in the city for US$1 or less per trip. Diesel-powered auto-rickshaws (*thoun bein*) are much handier, though, if you have more ground to cover, and rarely charge more than US$1.

Taxis are ubiquitous and inexpensive in all the major cities, where they stand in ranks outside the main hotels and transport hubs. Meters rarely work, but few trips across town cost more than K3,000–4,000 (US$4–5). For longer day trips out of town, expect to pay US$50–60, depending on the age and condition of the vehicle.

Car and driver

If you are travelling independently, you will probably do most of your travelling in a rented car. In Myanmar, these come with a driver (self-drive is still virtually unknown). Tourist cars tend to be no more than two or three years old, and are air-conditioned. Expect to pay around US$100 for a maximum of 12 hours driving per day, including petrol, the driver's fee and expenses, and all toll charges.

ACCOMMODATION

Despite the decades-long tourism boycott of the country, Myanmar offers a wide choice of accommodation in all its principal tourist centres, and the number of beds looks set to soar now that the boycott is more or less at an end. During the peak season from mid-November through January, vacancies in the most popular hotels can be hard to come by.

Accommodation ranges dramatically in cost, from US$10 backpacker dives with flea-ridden mattresses and barking dogs in the yard, to glittering US$250 a night

palace hotels where you'll have rose petals scattered in your bath tub and complementary chocolates left on your luxury kingsize at fold-down time.

EATING OUT

In most of the country's market towns and cities, the standard place to eat is a small, canteen-like restaurant where traditional Burmese curries and rice are the mainstays. Prepared early each morning, the dishes – which will include a few vegetarian options as well as meat and seafood – are typically displayed on a hot plate behind a glass screen, at the back of a no-frills, brick or cement-floored cafeteria. With the help of the staff, you simply indicate which main dish you'd like and they'll plate it up and bring it to your table, along with a host of side dishes containing white rice, steamed vegetables, soup, dips, nuts, crunchy noodles, soy sauce and salt, to name but a few of the extras.

In such places, you will rarely spend more than $7–8 per head for a filling meal. Stick to lunchtimes to reduce the risk of stomach upsets (although rarely re-heated the following day, the food tends to be kept warm until the evening, by which time it may have started to turn bad).

In the evenings, rough-and-ready, Chinese-style BBQ joints – *a'gin zein* – are the most common local eating option. The meats, seafood and vegetables are displayed on skewers; you select what you want and the cook will grill it in front of you while you wait, then serve it with a selection of side dishes, and maybe a cold beer if you're lucky.

Noodle shops are another Myanmar institution. Again, they tend to offer few frills, but the food will be fresh and tasty, and very authentic.

Most Burmese teahouses also serve a range of light bites and

snacks. While out on street corners of Mandalay and Yangon, you will encounter innumerable stalls selling snacks such as samosas, Burmese pancakes – both sweet (*bein moun*) and savoury (*moun pyar thalet*) – and a range of delicious deep-fried bites served with dipping sauces. In addition, Indian and Chinese restaurants are numerous.

ACTIVITIES

The arts

The best place to experience traditional Burmese dance and music – known as *pwe* – is on the city street or pagoda grounds at festival times. If your visit does not coincide with a festival, however, there are two public theatres in Yangon and smaller establishments in Mandalay, which have various performances, including some showcasing the country's lively puppet tradition.

The National Theatre, Myoma Kyaung Lan, Yangon. Performances of *pwe* are often staged at the National Theatre, along with concerts by international artists. Check with your tour rep or staff at your hotel to find out what is on while you are in town.

Mandalay Marionettes, 66th Street, between 26th and 27th streets, Mandalay, www.mandalaymarionettes.com. Popular with backpackers and tour groups alike, delightful puppet shows take place each evening at Mandalay Marionettes from 8.30pm.

Moustache Brothers, 39th Street, between 80th and 81st streets, Mandalay. The Moustache Brothers' famous satirical show is an institution in Mandalay. A brand of traditional theatre known as a *yeint*, which combines clowning with dance and puppetry, it is staged by three moustachioed locals who were imprisoned for poking fun at the government. They are now only allowed to perform for foreigners.

Nightlife

Yangon's nightlife is the most dependably lively in Myanmar, thanks to the handful of small clubs attached to the city's five-star hotels, where a mixture of rich kids, bored expats, government cronies and movie industry movers, shakers and starlets shake their stuff on weekends, watched by tables full of restless young men. Most double as pick-up joints for sex workers, and close earlier than clubs in more developed countries. For those after a less brassy atmosphere, and who can do without expensive imported liquor, **19th Street** – a narrow back lane in the old enclave of Latha Township – is lined with beer terraces, bars and barbecue joints where both foreigners and locals hang out through the evening.

Shopping

Nearly everywhere you visit in Myanmar will have markets (*zei*) selling traditional handicrafts and other potential souvenirs, and these are great places to spend your money as you can be sure most of it will reach the local people who most need it. In addition, upscale hotels nearly all have souvenir boutiques, selling similar merchandise at inflated prices. Either way, you are most likely to have to pay with cash.

Among the well-heeled urban middle classes, however, modern air-con, multi-storey malls are the preferred places to shop. There is an ever-increasing number of them springing up in Yangon and Mandalay, though for obvious reasons – and because their prices are higher than those of similar shopping places in Bangkok and Singapore – they tend to frequented by few foreign tourists.

For sheer variety, you can't beat the country's largest shopping area, Yangon's **Bogyoke Aung San Market**, which holds around 2,000 shops under one roof, offering a massive selection of antiques, fake antiques, arts and handicrafts, in all price brackets. It opens Mon–Sat 9.30am–4.30pm.

There are also **open-air markets** across Bogyoke Aung San Street, at the corner of St John's Road and Pyay Road; and east of the Botataung Pagoda. The **Theingyi Indian Market** is just off Anawrahta Street. The biggest and oldest market in Yangon, it sells household wares, textiles and traditional medicine and herbs. The **Thirimingala Market** in Ahlone Township at the northern end of Strand Road sells fresh fruit, vegetables and meat and provides some good photo opportunities. There is also a **Chinese Market** at the corner of Mahabandoola Street and Lanmadaw Road. Separate **night markets** are open on specified streets after dark; the best ones are in Yangon's Chinese and Indian quarters.
Augustine Souvenir Shop, 23 (A) Attiyar St (Thirimingalar St) Kamayut, Yangon, tel: 01 705 969, www. augustinesouvenirshop.com. This

Myanmar's famous Moustache Brothers (now a duo since one member died).

sumptuous emporium is crammed with quality antique silverware, lacquer, woodcarving, metalwork, colonial furniture, stone figures and traditional porcelain.
Nandawun 55 Baho Road, Ahlone, Yangon, tel: 01 221 271, www. myanmarhandicrafts.com. This is the largest privately owned craft centre in Myanmar, offering a huge range of tapestries, silk, authentic tribal costume, paintings on silk and cotton, as well as woodcarving, lacquerware and other craft forms.
FMI Centre. Among the most popular of Yangon's air-con malls, and conveniently situated next to Bogyoke Aung San Market.

MANDALAY

Mandalay's **Zegyo Market** (at 84th Street, between 26th and 28th streets) opens early in the morning and remains open until dark. The **Kaingdan Market** fruit and vegetable market is found by walking a couple of blocks west from the Zegyo. The cheapest market for household goods is in Chinatown between 29th and 33rd streets. The **night market** is on 84th Street between 26th and 28th.
Sein Myint Artist, 42 Sanga University Road, tel: 02 26553. Sells gorgeous silk *kalagas* and has an interesting gallery with paintings and carvings.
Yadanapura Art Centre, RM(6), BLOG (B-3), Malikha Shopping Complex, Yadanar Road, Thingangyun Yangon, tel: 01 564316, www.yadanapura.com. This government-run enterprise has a good selection of quality handicrafts, jewellery and paintings.
Soe Moe Momento World, No.469, 84th Street near the Mayae Son Won Pagoda, Kyauk Sit Tan Road, Mandalay, tel: 02 70558. Soe Moe stocks a vast selection of traditional handicrafts, from embroidery to bronze deities – some of them made on site. The prices are nominally fixed, but you can usually negotiate discounts.

BAGAN

Most of Myanmar's best lacquerware is made in Bagan, specifically the village of New Bagan (Bagan Myothit), the residential area 8km (5 miles) south of the archaeological zone. There are literally dozens of outlets dotted around the ruins, but three dependable favourites include: Chan Tan (Main Road, Myinkaba), Ever Stand (between Old Bagan and Nyaung U); and Golden Bagan (Khyae Main Road, Old Bagan).

A–Z

Budgeting for your trip

If you are travelling on a pre-arranged tour, where all the transport and accommodation costs are covered by the price of your holiday, your main expenses are likely to be dining and shopping. If you are not fussy about your surroundings, it is easy to find a filling meal for less than US$10. Allow around US$10–15 per head for a two-course meal in a regular, mid-scale restaurant, or US$20–40 in a five-star hotel. The most upmarket establishments may cost a little more than this. Breakfasts are usually included in your hotel tariff, but it is sometimes worth checking. How much your souvenirs set you back will depend on your ability to haggle, but as a rule of thumb count on around US$10–15 for a puppet, or US$100–200 for a top-notch lacquerware bowl.

Independent travellers will also need to factor in accommodation costs: allow around US$30 for a double room in a good-standard budget hotel. Transport costs are generally quite low, particularly the buses, but any internal flights will rapidly increase your expenditure.

THAILAND
MYANMAR
LAOS
CAMBODIA
VIETNAM
MALAYSIA
BRUNEI
SINGAPORE
INDONESIA
PHILIPPINES

Climate

Like all countries in South and Southeast Asia's monsoonal region, Myanmar's year is divided into three seasons: there are regional variations, but essentially it is hot and wet from May to October, cooler and dry from November to February, and hot and dry in March and April.

The Southwest Monsoon brings rains beginning in May, which is most intense between June and August. This is a time of high humidity – especially in the coastal and delta regions – and of daily afternoon/evening showers, as winds carry the moisture in from the Indian Ocean. The central inland region is drier than other parts of the country, but is also subject to much rain during this time. Travel during the rainy season can quite often be interrupted due to flooded roads and railway lines; it is made even more difficult as this information is not always made available through the media.

In October, the rains let up. From November through to May the Northeast Monsoon brings mainly dry weather, particularly away from the south. The cool season (November–February) is the most pleasant time to visit. The average temperature along the Ayeyarwady plain, from Yangon to Mandalay, is between 21°C and 28°C (70°F and 82°F), although in the mountains in the north and east, the temperature can drop below freezing and snow can fall.

The hottest weather occurs during March and April, before the rains, with temperatures in the central plain, particularly around Bagan (Pagan), climbing as high as 45°C (113°F).

What to wear/bring

Dress in Myanmar is casual but neat. Unless you are conducting business, you won't be expected to wear a tie anywhere. Long trousers for men and a dress or long skirt for women, lightweight and appropriate to the prevailing climatic conditions, is the generally accepted mode of dress for visitors. Quick-drying clothes are a good idea for visits during the rainy season or Thingyan (the 'water festival'). There is no law against shorts or short skirts, but this type of clothing is not common in the country outside the trendy clubs of Yangon.

Essentials include insect repellent, sunblock, sunglasses and a sun hat. Also bring an adequate supply of prescription medicines – always carry them with you, as checked luggage can get lost or delayed.

Crime and Safety

Although no dependable statistics on the subject exist, most travellers will affirm that Myanmar is a safe and welcoming place to travel. Muggings and petty thefts may have increased since the decline in the country's economic fortunes over the past couple of decades, but they are still rare – and much less frequent than in more developed Asian countries. Even so, take the same precautions as you would at home: don't wander about unfamiliar parts of Yangon or Mandalay on your own at night. Keep your passport and other valuables under lock and key at all times.

In addition, it is advisable to avoid all demonstrations and large gatherings, and don't take photographs of soldiers, police, military installations or equipment.

Customs regulations

Tourists are allowed duty-free import of limited quantities of tobacco – 400 cigarettes, 100 cigars, or 250g (8oz) of pipe tobacco, as well as two litres of alcoholic beverage, and a half-litre bottle of perfume or eau de cologne and articles for personal use. Any foreign currency in excess of US$3,000 should be declared on arrival, but you won't be required to obtain clearance for valuables such as a laptop, DVD recorder, camera or mobile phone.

Items prohibited from import into Myanmar:

Counterfeit currency
Pornography
Narcotic and psychotropic substances
Toy guns and remote-control toys
Firearms
Live animals/birds

Prohibited exports

Stone-Age implements and artefacts

Fossils
Antique coins
Bronze and clay pipes
Palm leaf manuscripts and *parabaike* (folding manuscripts)
Inscribed stones and bricks
Inscribed gold and silver plates and other objects
Historical documents
Religious images and statues
Carvings or sculptures of bronze, stone, stucco and wood
Frescoes and fragments of frescoes
Burmese regalia and paraphernalia

Departure tax

A flat departure tax of US$10 is levied at check-in. Make sure you keep a nice crisp dollar bill for the purpose. In addition, travellers on domestic flights have to pay a fee of K1,000 (just over US$1).

Foreign currency

Foreigners may bring in as much foreign currency as they wish. Amounts in excess of US$2,000 or its equivalent must be declared on the Foreign Exchange Declaration Form (FED). However, the import and export of Burmese kyat is forbidden, and the export of foreign currency is limited to the amount declared upon entry.

Embassies

All foreign embassies are based in Jakarta, though many have consulates in Bali. France, Italy and the Netherlands also have consulates in Jogja.

Despite the fact that Naypyidaw is nowadays the official capital, most of the foreign embassies and consulates remain in Yangon. The major embassies in Jakarta are:
Australia, 88 Strand Road, tel: 01 251 810, www.burma.embassy.gov.au.
Singapore, 238 Dhamazedi Road, Bahan Township, tel: 01 559 001,

Street snacks for sale in downtown Yangon.

www.mfa.gov.sg.
Thailand, 437 Pyay Road, Dagon Township, tel: 01 222 784, www.thaiembassy.org/yangon.
United Kingdom, 80 Strand Road (Box 638), tel: 01 380 322, http://ukinburma.fco.gov.uk/en.
United States, 110 University Ave, Kamayut Township, tel: 01 536 509, http://burma.usembassy.gov.

Etiquette

In common with most Asian countries, the Burmese are quite formal (by Western standards) in the way they engage strangers, especially foreigners, and anyone of a different gender. You will find them painstakingly polite, considerate and gentle – and appreciative of those who respond in a similar fashion, particularly in homes and places of worship.

When introduced to people in Myanmar, it is considered good manners to call them by their full title and full name, beginning with 'U' (the equivalent of 'Mr') and 'Daw' ('Mrs', 'Ms' or 'Madam').

It is particularly difficult for a Burmese to address a Westerner only by his Christian name, even when they are close friends. Thus a Burmese would never call a friend 'Jamie', but will address him as 'Ko Jamie' or 'Maung Jamie' – similarly, Jenny would be called 'Ma Jenny'.

Health and medical care

Health officials require certification of immunisation against cholera, and against yellow fever if you arrive within nine days after leaving or transiting an affected area. Proof of smallpox vaccination is no longer required.

All visitors to Myanmar should take appropriate anti-malarial precautions before entering the country, and should continue to take medication throughout their stay. The risk is highest at altitudes below 1,000 metres (3,000ft) between May and December. Many upcountry hotels have mosquito nets, but any hole makes them worthless. Bring your own mosquito net and carry mosquito coils to burn while you sleep.

It is best to discuss your travel plans with your personal physician with regard to recommended immunisation (tetanus, hepatitis, typhoid) and the specific anti-malarial drug needed. If you require any medication, it is best to bring along a sufficient supply.

For longer stays, and if your travels should take you to outlying areas,
consider bringing your own medical kit as your specific prescription or drug may not be available.

Medical treatment
Asia Royal General Hospital, 14 Baho Street, Sanchaung Township, Yangon, tel: 01 537 296, www.asiaroyalmedical.com. One of the few hospitals in the country offering international-standard medical services.
International SOS Clinic, Dusit Inya Lake Resort, 37 Kaba Aye Pagoda Road, Yangon, tel: 01 667 879, www.internationalsos.com. Full outpatient and emergency services, delivered by a professional team of expatriate and national doctors.

Pharmacies

Yangon has several pharmacies, all with 24-hour counters. Outside Yangon, pharmacies are few and far between.
May Pharmacy, 542 Merchant Street.
AA Pharmacy, 142 Sule Pagoda Road.
Global Network, 155 Sule Pagoda Road.

Internet

Internet access is readily available in Yangon and Mandalay, and in busy tourist centres such as Bagan and Inle Lake, but much less so elsewhere (only 25 percent of Burmese have a dependable electricity connection and the cost of a computer lies well beyond the reach of most local families). Connection speeds tend to be too slow for browsing, but are generally adequate for sending and receiving emails; power surges and failures are commonplace. Wi-fi is all-but standard at most high-end hotels these days.

Note that at the time of writing, Skype and other internet voice-call providers were banned, and numerous sites blocked by the government, though following democratic reforms, such restrictions are expected to ease.

Media

Co-sponsored by the Ministry of Information and Myanmar army (Tatmadaw), the English-language edition of the government-run daily, the *New Light of Myanmar* (www.president-office.gov.mm/en/?q=media-room/newspaper), features endless reports on visits by the generals to factories, schools and religious
institutions. Foreign news comes from agencies such as Reuters, via the government censors.

The Myanmar Times (mmtimes.com) is marginally more open and eclectic, but still stops short of being critical of the government. Like every other publication in Myanmar, it has to submit to pre-publication censorship imposed by the Press Scrutiny and Registration Division, whose Draconian rule explains why the country has so few dailies (the Ministry cannot process any more overnight).

The International Herald Tribune and other international newspapers are sometimes available at hotel newsstands, along with weekly news magazines. If you are desperate for reading material, used magazines can be purchased inexpensively from street vendors.

Myanmar broadcasts three free-to-air channels, all of them run by the government. The MRTV-4 channel hosts global sports, news and documentary channels, including National Geographic, BBC World, CNN, ESPN and Fox Movies.

Money

Myanmar's official currency is the *kyat* (pronounced 'chat'), which comes in denominations of K1, K5, K10, K20, K50, K100, K200, K500, K1,000 and K5,000. For foreign visitors, however, the US dollar serves as an alternative. Most hotels and travel agents charge in dollars, and you'll also need them for air and rail tickets, and to pay admission charges for major sights. For just about everything else – including souvenir shopping, bus travel and meals in independently run restaurants – you'll use *kyat*.

Either way, expect to have to carry large bundles of cash. With a few exceptions, nowhere accepts credit or debit cards, or travellers' cheques. And there are as yet no ATMs from which to draw local currency.

Over the past decade, the official rate of exchange has wavered between K5.75 and K7 to the dollar. However, no one pays any attention to this, not even banks and exchange counters at airports, where rates are over 100 times more than the official government rate (between K750 and K1,350 for US$1).

Dollar bills also have to be in **perfect condition**, and ideally issued no earlier than 2008. Again, check when you first purchase them back home that they are all mint, or something close to it. The higher

THAILAND

MYANMAR

LAOS

CAMBODIA

VIETNAM

MALAYSIA

BRUNEI

SINGAPORE

INDONESIA

PHILIPPINES

denomination the bill, the better the exchange rate.

Service charge and tax

International-standard hotels levy a government tax and a service charge of 10 percent each; some restaurants impose a 10 percent government tax only. Rumours were circulating in late 2012 that these rates will soon be hiked to 20 or 30 percent, which will add dramatically to the cost of a holiday in Myanmar.

An additional departure tax of US$10 is levied on all domestic flights; it has to be paid in cash when you check in.

Tipping

Tipping isn't as yet the norm in Myanmar, and not expected, though this is bound to change as tourism becomes more widespread. That said, a small consideration of K100 at monasteries and remote religious sites will always be welcome.

Opening hours

Business hours for all government offices (including post offices) are Mon–Fri 9.30am–4.30pm, Sat 9.30am–12.30pm. Shops open between 8am and 6pm. Restaurants open at 8–9am, depending on whether they offer breakfast, and close at around 9pm.

In Yangon, the main government travel agent and tourist information service, **Myanmar Travels & Tours**, opens 8am–8pm seven days a week.

Postal services

The Yangon General Post Office (tel: 01 285 499) is located on Strand Road at the corner of Bo Aung Gyaw Street and is open 7.30am–6pm Monday to Friday. All other post offices are open Monday to Friday 9.30am–4.30pm, and Saturday 9.30am–12.30pm. They are closed Sunday and public holidays.

The only exception is the Mingaladon (Yangon) Airport mail sorting office. It is open round-the-clock daily, including Sunday and holidays, for receipt and dispatch of foreign mail. Ordinary letters and postcards will be accepted here at any time. Registered letters can be taken at the airport postal counter only during normal government working hours.

For larger parcels, DHL is a faster and more reliable method of posting – though a far from cheap one. The main DHL office in Myanmar is at 7A Kaba Aye Pagoda Rd in Yangon (open

Mon–Sat 8am–6pm; tel: 01 664 423; www.fastforward.dhl.com).

Telephones

The country code for Myanmar is 95, the code for Yangon is 1 (01 when dialling in the country) and 2 (02) for Mandalay. Myanmar has direct satellite links to seven countries: Japan, Hong Kong, Singapore, Thailand, India, UK and Australia. Siemens of Germany has installed additional satellite communication lines that have brought telecommunication connections up to Western standards.

When dialling from outside the country omit the 0 in the area code. IDD (International Direct Dialling) is easily available in major Yangon and Mandalay hotels and at kiosks; costs are based on US$ rates plus a service fee. From the smaller towns it may be possible to call Yangon, but not overseas.

The Central Telegraph Office (tel: 01 281 133), located one block east of the Sule Pagoda on Mahabandoola Street, is open Monday to Saturday 8am to 9pm, and Sunday and public holidays from 8am to 8pm.

Mobile phones

There is no international GSM roaming facility for mobile phones in Myanmar. Phones brought in from outside the country may officially be subject to temporary confiscation at the airport, to be returned upon departure (though in practice this rarely, if ever, occurs). You can, however, purchase local Burmese SIM cards and top-up card for around US$20 and use these to make national or international calls and texts.

Tourist information

The only official source of tourist information is Myanmar Travels & Tours (MTT), whose head office at 118 Mahabandoola Garden St (tel: 01 371 286, www.myanmartravelsandtours.com) is the best place to arrange permits for the more off-track parts of the country open to visitors. They also book airline and rail tickets, but offer little in the way of useful, practical information beyond handing out town plans and leaflets. MTT maintains no offices abroad.

Travel to certain areas requires hiring the services of an approved tour operator. Other areas are strictly off-limits. The 'official list' (viewable on the MTT website) distinguishes between areas open to individuals and those restricted to package tours.

Public holidays

All offices are closed on the following days:
4 January Independence Day
12 February Union Day
2 March Peasants' Day
27 March Resistance (Tatmadaw) Day commemorates the World War II struggle against Japan
1 May Workers'/May Day
19 July Martyrs' Day is a memorial to the country's founding father, Aung San, and seven other leaders of the pre-independence interim government who were all assassinated on that day in 1947

Visas and passports

Visitors to Myanmar of all nationalities must present a passport valid for a minimum of six months after the proposed date of entry, and a tourist visa obtained in advance at one of the country's overseas embassies or consulates.

An entry visa for tourists (EVT) is valid for a maximum of 28 days and entitles you to enter the country only via an international airport, not overland.

Applications procedures, processing times and costs vary from country to country but appear in full on the relevant Myanmar embassy website. Anyone listing a media job can expect a prolonged wait and should consider declaring a suitably vague alternative, such as 'consultant' or 'teacher'.

Note that children above seven years of age, even when included on their parents' passport, must have their own visas.

At the time of writing, business visas for most foreign nationals were available on arrival – check on the embassy or consulate websites prior to departure.

Websites

Myanmar Himalaya Trekking & Culture: www.myanmar-explore. com
Myanmar Shalom: www.myanmar shalom.com
Inspiration Myanmar: www. inspirationmyanmar.com
Putao Trekking House: www.putao trekkinghouse.com
Heritage Travels & Tours: www. myanmarheritagetravel.com
Myanmar Elite Tours: www.myanmar elitetours.com
Travelfish: www.travelfish.org

LAOS

TRANSPORT, ACCOMMODATION, EATING OUT, ACTIVITIES AND AN A–Z OF TRAVEL INFORMATION

FACT FILE

Situation Laos is a landlocked nation bordered by China to the north, Myanmar (Burma) to the northwest, Thailand to the west, Vietnam to the east, and Cambodia to the south.
Area approximately 236,800 sq km (91,400 sq miles), dominated by the Mekong River, the 12th-longest river in the world.
Population 6.6 million.
Language Lao.
Religion Theravada Buddhism.
Time zone 7 hours ahead of Greenwich Mean Time (GMT).
Currency kip (but US$ widely used). Approx 7,900 to US$1.
Electricity 220 volts at 50Hz, using two-prong flat or round sockets – adaptors available in Vientiane.
International dialling code 856.

TRANSPORT

Getting there

By air
There are three international airports in Laos: **Wattay International Airport** in Vientiane, **Luang Prabang International Airport** in the old capital, and **Pakse International Airport** in Champasak Province. Vientiane is served by international flights from Thailand (Bangkok and Chiang Mai), Vietnam (Ho Chi Minh City and Hanoi), Cambodia (Phnom Penh and Siem Reap), China (Kunming) and Taiwan (Taipei). Most visitors travel via Bangkok, from which there are daily connections to Vientiane and Luang Prabang. It is

also possible to fly to Luang Prabang from Chiang Mai.

To save money on flying into Laos, one option is to fly from Bangkok to the northeastern Thai town of Udon Thani (for onward travel by road to Vientiane), or to Ubon Ratchathani (for onward travel by road to Pakse in southern Laos).

Lao Airlines (tel: 021-212 051/54, www.laoairlines.com), the national carrier, provides regular services between Vientiane and regional destinations. Departure taxes are now included in the ticket price.

By land
There are at present 17 international border checkpoints with Laos. You can obtain a 30-day tourist visa-on-arrival (VOA) at these checkpoints, unless otherwise indicated. As visa regulations may change without prior notice, check with a Lao embassy or consulate, or with a reliable travel agent, before travelling.

Since 2009 it has been possible to take a train from Nongkhai in Thailand, across the Friendship Bridge to Thanaleng, 13km (8 miles) from Vientiane.

From Thailand
Nongkhai/Vientiane (Friendship Bridge)
Huay Kon/Muang Ngeun
Mukdahan/Savannakhet
Chiang Khong/Huay Xai
Chong Mek/Vang Tao
Nakhon Phanom/Tha Kaek
Nakasing/Nam Hong (no VOA)
Beung Kan/Paksan (no VOA)

From Vietnam
Sop Houn/Tay Trang
Nam Xoi/Na Maew (no VOA)
Nam Can/Nam Khan in Xieng Cau

Treo/Nam Phao
Na Phao/Chalo
Lao Bao/Dansavanh
Bo Y/Ngoc Hoi (no VOA).
From China
Mengla/Boten

From Cambodia
Voen Kham/Si Phan Don (no VOA)

Getting around

By air
Lao Airlines flies to several domestic destinations, and its service is improving, though schedules still tend to be irregular – dependent on demand and the weather. It is not uncommon for flights to be cancelled or delayed. Visitors are advised to confirm their flight reservation prior to travelling even if they have a confirmed ticket, and to arrive at the airport early. All domestic tickets must be purchased using US dollars. Thai baht and other major Western currencies are sometimes accepted, but the exchange rate is not favourable. Kip is not accepted.

The most popular routes are Vientiane–Luang Prabang, Vientiane–Pakse, and Vientiane–Xieng Khuang. The major routes are served by the newer, more reliable and comfortable ATR-725 planes, while smaller Chinese-built aircraft usually serves the less popular routes.

Departure taxes are now included in the ticket prices for passengers flying a domestic route.

By boat
It is only possible to take reliable transport up and down the **Mekong River** in the north of Laos. Options in the south change from time to time.

THAILAND
MYANMAR
LAOS
CAMBODIA
VIETNAM
MALAYSIA
BRUNEI
SINGAPORE
INDONESIA
PHILIPPINES

Check with a travel agent for up-to-date information.

There are speedboats on the upper reaches of the Mekong that travel from Luang Prabang to northern Thailand, and even to the Chinese border. Bookings can be made in northern Thailand and Luang Prabang. Slow boats travel the rest of the Mekong from Luang Prabang southward to the Cambodian border.

The beautiful Nam Ou River, which flows into the Mekong near Luang Prabang, is navigable most of the year as far north as Hat Sa and is considered one of the best river cruises in Laos.

By road

Most of the many roads are now in acceptable condition. However rural roads are quite poor in places. Interprovincial transport by bus and truck is widely available, which makes it possible to visit at least part of every province.

Regular buses, many of them air-conditioned, supply the main national highways. For more remote routes, pick-ups or trucks converted into passenger vehicles by the addition of two long wooden benches in the back (all of which are known as *songthaew*) are the most common forms of road transport.

Public transport

For short trips in towns, stick to *tuk-tuks* and jumbos. The city bus system in Vientiane runs only between the centre of the city and outlying villages. Car taxis in Vientiane can be found in front of major hotels, the Morning Market and at the airport – always agree on the price before you set out.

Private transport

Perhaps the best way to get around any town in Laos is to hire a bicycle,

or, for more ambitious day trips, a motorcycle. Bicycles can be hired for the day from restaurants and guesthouses in towns throughout Laos, and small motorcycles can be hired from dealers in Vientiane, Luang Prabang and Savannakhet. Cars, pick-ups and 4WD vehicles are available for hire from private operators in Vientiane.

Asia Vehicle Rental (Europcar), 354 Samsenthai Road, Vientiane, tel: 021-217 493, www.europ carlaos.com

ACCOMMODATION

Choosing a hotel

The hotel and guesthouse standards in Laos, especially in the larger towns, have improved tremendously over the years, though there are still relatively few luxury hotels, and these are mainly located in Vientiane and Luang Prabang. Smaller, 'boutique' hotels and spas are springing up in many locations, however, and especially in Luang Prabang where the old town's Unesco-protected status prohibits the building of multi-storey structures that would change the former royal capital's character. Some of the most interesting places to stay include former royal palaces or villas, like Villa Santi in Luang Prabang and the Champasak Palace Hotel in Pakse. Elsewhere, former French colonial buildings are being similarly restored to function as boutique hotels or superior quality guesthouses, in the Mekong Valley towns like Savannakhet and Tha Khaek, as well as in Luang Prabang and the capital, Vientiane.

Away from the capital and the other three or four large towns,

it is a different matter. Most accommodation is adequate and improving, but aimed at a backpacker or budget-traveller clientele, since wealthy business people have little need to visit or stay in Attapeu, Phonsavan or Udomxai. The upside to this is that accommodation away from the main centres in Laos is really very reasonably priced, whether at mid-range or cheaper budget establishments.

Except in large, first-class hotels in Vientiane and at a few other locations, service can be slow but is always friendly. Many hoteliers (and indeed restaurateurs) tend to employ simple country folk as staff because they are inexpensive and cheerful – though they are also often not too familiar with things like calculators and computers, let alone English language. Booking ahead online is often easier than by telephone if you don't speak Lao (or Thai), but this still remains uncertain.

There are no truly outstanding websites for accommodation in Laos. Those that exist are often out of date and still display last year's information, or information from five years ago. Perhaps the best is www.agoda.com.

EATING OUT

Restaurants in Laos

Lao food is quite simple, making use of the country's abundant fresh vegetables, freshwater fish, chicken, duck, pork and beef. The staple of the Lao diet is sticky rice, which is used as a tool to eat most food by hand. One of the most common Lao dishes is *laap*, a 'salad' made from minced meat, chicken or fish, mixed with lime juice, mint leaves and other spices.

Thai, Chinese and Vietnamese food are common in Laos, a testimony to the political and cultural influences of the three surrounding powers.

The most popular beverage in Laos is the domestically produced Beer Lao. Coffee, grown in the fertile Bolaven Plateau in the south of the country, is some of the best in the world. It is usually served in a glass, mixed with both sugar and sweetened condensed milk. Fresh fruit juice – lemon, orange, coconut and sugar cane, among others – is served in outdoor stalls throughout Vientiane and other cities, and fruit shakes are widely available.

A simple local dish with rice.

Truck bus near Pakse.

Where to eat

Both Vientiane and Luang Prabang have a good selection of Lao and French restaurants, with the occasional Thai, Chinese and Vietnamese place thrown in. There are also a few good Indian restaurants, as well as places serving Lao food that has been sanitised (or at least toned down) for foreigners. Backpacker destinations such as Vang Vieng and Si Phan Don are well attuned to the tastes of their particular clientele, and it is easy enough to get Thai-Lao food or Western backpacker fare. Elsewhere in Laos it is another matter altogether, and dining choices are generally limited to noodle stalls, small rice-and-curry restaurants, and the occasional large Chinese establishment. One good thing about truck stops is that they tend to remain open quite late at night, indeed until their clientele has shut down for the night. Restaurants away from the major towns and backpacker areas close early – it may be difficult to get anything to eat after about 9pm. Even in Luang Prabang things close quite early, and most restaurants and eateries will be closed by 10.30pm, with a few bars lingering on to nearer midnight.

ACTIVITIES

The arts

Cultural performances

Lao classical music and dance began to re-emerge in the 1990s after being largely suppressed by the Communist regime, which considered them to be a link with the non-socialist past. Folk dances and music fared better since they were considered indigenously Lao, rather than the foreign-influenced classical traditions. Performances of the dance drama known as *Phra Lak Phra Ram*, based on the Indian epic *Ramayana* are now again being staged, accompanied by classical music that is rather similar to the Thai classical music tradition.

Since Luang Prabang is the former capital of royal Laos, it is not surprising that the traditions are best kept here. Cultural performances are held within the Royal Palace (National Museum) compound at the Royal Ballet Theatre on Mondays, Wednesdays, Fridays and Saturdays at 6pm. The performance includes Lao classical and folk dances and music, as well as traditional ballet enactments of episodes from *Phra Lak Phra Ram*. For information, call Mr Chandra at tel: 020-5597 1400, or 071-253 70545.

In Vientiane, you can catch these performances at major hotels and the Lao National Theatre on Manthatulat Road. The latter has a nightly traditional dance and music performance, tel: 021-242 978. Lane Xang Hotel features a good nightly traditional dance show at its restaurant, while Dok Champa Restaurant at the Lao Plaza Hotel offers Lao classical music and dance performance at dinnertime from Monday to Friday.

Nightlife

Laos is not famed for its wild nightlife. In fact, outside of Vientiane and Luang Prabang, it is non-existent. The government has played a role in this, seeing such venues as bars and nightclubs to be corrupt Western influences. The authorities have little tolerance for prostitution, and law prohibits sexual relationships between a Lao citizen and a foreigner who are not married.

Of cultural interest is the misnamed Lao 'disco', which in fact has live music and a variety of dance styles including *lam wong*, a traditional Lao group folk dance, as well as ballroom dancing. Hotels in Vientiane have Western-style discos with the latest high-volume Thai and Western favourites and are frequented by the young elite and some foreigners. A less frenetic option for an evening on the town is the pub scene. These pubs cater to foreigners with well-stocked bars, relaxing music and great atmosphere.

Shopping

A number of shops featuring Lao textiles, woodcarvings, jewellery and traditional handicrafts have sprung up on the streets of downtown Vientiane. Upmarket boutiques selling home furnishings and interior designs cater to tourists and expats alike. The Morning Market on Lan Xang Avenue is certainly the best place to check for any of these items; it is open all day, and sells almost anything you could possibly want.

A–Z

Budgeting for your trip

Laos remains a relatively inexpensive country, though of course it is possible to spend more if you stay in the most expensive hotels and dine in the most expensive restaurants. Essentially, budget travellers should allow US$20–30 a day – less away from Vientiane and the other main towns. Mid-range costs are around US$40–80 a day, while top end, including a self-drive car, will cost in the region of US$100–200 per day.

Climate

Laos has a tropical monsoon climate. During the summer months, moisture-laden air blows inland from the Indian Ocean and is known as the southwest monsoon, bringing the rainy season.

The rainy season lasts from around May or June to October and it can be as hot and sticky as a bowl of hot, sticky rice. This is followed by a cooler

THAILAND

MYANMAR

LAOS

CAMBODIA

VIETNAM

MALAYSIA

BRUNEI

SINGAPORE

INDONESIA

PHILIPPINES

dry season until February, and a hot and dry period in March and April. The average temperature is 28°C (82°F), but in April it can reach 38°C (100°F). In the mountains, temperatures are cold from December to around February, dropping to 15°C (59°F) or even lower. Relative humidity is fairly high, ranging from 90 percent down to 50 percent.

Rainfall varies according to region. The highest amount – 3,700mm (146in) annually – was recorded on the Bolaven Plateau in Champasak Province of Laos. Vientiane receives about 1,700mm (67in) annually, and Luang Prabang about 1,360mm (53in).

What to bring/wear

The Lao are very conservative when it comes to dress, and expect foreign visitors to respect this custom. Women visitors should avoid clothing that bares the thighs, shoulders or breasts; long trousers, walking shorts and skirts are acceptable, while tank tops, short skirts and running shorts are not. Dress conservatively when making a visit to a temple or government office.

Whatever the season, bring lightweight cotton clothing and a light jacket or pullover for cool nights in December and January.

Customs regulations

The duty-free allowance for each visitor is one litre of spirits, two litres of wine and 200 cigarettes, 50 cigars or 250g of tobacco.

Antique cultural items such as Buddha images cannot be exported. Officially, purchases of silver or copper items are subject to customs duty – based on their weight.

Embassies

Australia
Km 4, Thadeua Road, Ban Wat Nak, tel: 021-353 800, www.laos.embassy.gov.au
United States
19 Rue Bartholomie, That Dam Road, tel: 021-267 000, www.usembassy.gov
There is no British consular representation in Laos: the Australian embassy handles routine matters; passport replacements are dealt with in Bangkok.

Etiquette

The people of Laos are extremely polite and well mannered. Remember that local standards and expectations

of efficiency and procedure can be very different from Western perceptions – be patient.

The traditional form of greeting is the *nop*: one's palms are placed together in a position of praying, at chest level, but not touching the body. The higher the hands, the greater the respect. This is accompanied by a slight bow to show respect. The *nop* is a greeting, thanks, expression of regret and goodbye.

As elsewhere in Southeast Asia, the head is thought to be the most sacred part of the body, the soles of the feet the lowliest.

Dress: Visitors should dress modestly, especially near and in pagodas, temples and public places. Shorts should not be worn when visiting pagodas and temples, and all footwear must be taken off when entering them.

Public displays of anger or discontent are considered a weakness and will garner no respect. Similarly, most traditional Asian customs also apply in Laos, including:
Don't touch people, including children, on the head.
Don't point your foot at a person.
Buddha images are sacred objects and Buddhists treat them with the utmost respect.

Health and medical care

Tap water is unsafe for drinking, but purified bottled water is available everywhere. You should also avoid unpeeled fruit, salads and uncooked vegetables.

Malaria and Dengue is prevalent in Laos, and if planning to travel outside the main cities, you should take precautionary measures.

It is essential to arrange vaccinations and private medical insurance before departure.

Medical treatment

Standards of healthcare are generally pretty dire by Western standards. But the following reasonable facilities are available in emergencies:
International Clinic, Mahosot Hospital, Setthathirat Road, tel: 021-214 022, open daily 24 hours.
Australian Embassy Clinic, Thadeua Road, tel: 021 353 840, open Mon, Tue, Thur, Fri 8.30am–noon and 2–5pm, and Wed 8.30am–noon, US$50 per consultation.

Internet

Internet cafés and Wi-fi are found all over town in Vientiane, Luang Prabang

Emergency numbers

Police Tel: 191
Fire Tel: 190
Ambulance Tel: 195

and Vang Vieng, which receive the highest numbers of travellers, and connections are very good. Costs are also low in these major towns because of stiff competition, and can be as cheap as 100 kip per minute (about US$0.10). In many of the other provinces, Internet facilities are becoming increasingly available and reliable, but costs are higher in places in which only one or two shops offer Internet-based services. Visual Internet telephony and PC-to-phone services are also well supported. In addition, stored-value pay-as-you-use Internet cards, for use with landlines, can be purchased from Lao Telecom branches and at some Internet cafés and retail outlets.

Media

The *Bangkok Post* and *The Nation* are both good Thai newspapers in English and are sold in many shops and most hotels. International English-language newspapers, such as the *International Herald Tribune*, *Asian Wall Street Journal* and the *Financial Times* are often available in major hotels.

The Lao government produces two newspapers for the expat community in Vientiane: the English-language *Vientiane Times* (www.vientianetimes.org.la) and the French-language *Le Rénovateur* (www.lerenovateur.org.la).

Money

The official currency, the kip, comes in 100,000, 50,000, 20,000, 10,000, 5,000, 2,000, 1,000 and 500 notes. There are no coins. The kip is not convertible outside Laos.

Most major currencies, as well as travellers' cheques in US dollars, pounds sterling, and often euros, can be exchanged at banks and moneychangers in major towns. Credit cards are accepted at more and more hotels, restaurants and shops in Vientiane and Luang Prabang, where a 5–10 percent service charge is sometimes added to the bill. Cash advances can also be obtained on a Visa/MasterCard in Vientiane and Luang Prabang. There are a few ATMs in Vientiane and Luang Prabang, but other cities do not have them as yet – an indicator of Laos's sleepiness and isolation.

Tipping

Tipping is not expected in Laos, except at a few upmarket restaurants in Vientiane and Luang Prabang, where you might leave 10 percent if a service charge has not already been added to your bill. Taxi and *tuk-tuk* drivers also do not expect to be tipped, unless the trip was unusually difficult or much longer than originally expected.

Opening hours

Normal working hours are Monday to Friday 8am–noon and 1–4pm. Travel agencies and airline offices open Saturday morning, but not post offices or government offices. Almost all businesses are closed on Sunday.

Postal services

The **General Post Office** (GPO) is on the corner of Thanon Khou Vieng and Lan Xang Avenue. It offers postal services and public telephones for local, national and international calls. There is no mail delivery service in Laos; mail is collected from the boxes at the GPO. For urgent or important mail and packages, most expats use the **Express Mail Service (EMS)**.

Incoming parcels and packets must be inspected by a Customs

Public holidays

The following days are observed as official public holidays. The public holidays associated with the beginning and the end of the Buddhist fasting period are movable lunar dates:
1 January New Year's Day
6 January Pathet Lao Day
20 January Army Day
14 February Chinese and Vietnamese New Year
8 March International Women's Day
22 March People's Party Day
13, 14, 15 April Pi Mai Lao (Lao New Year)
28 April Vesak Day (Buddha Day)
1 May Labour Day
1 June Children's Day
June/July Khao Pansa (Buddhist fasting period begins)
13 August Lao Issara (Free Laos Day)
September/October Bouk Ok Pansa (End of Buddhist fasting period)
12 October Liberation Day
2 December Lao National Day

official. All mail should use the official title of the country: Lao PDR, in preference to Laos.

Telephones

Until 1990, Laos was connected with the world, except Thailand and the USSR, by only one phone line – only one incoming or outgoing international call could be placed at a time. Things have moved on since then, with all major towns linked by phone and International Direct Dialling (IDD) widely available, providing a reliable service to more than 150 destinations worldwide.

International calls can be made from Lao Telecom offices (usually operator-assisted), at post offices, or from public phones with IDD facility. For the last you will need to purchase a phone card, available at post and telecommunication offices and many shops throughout the country. Fax services are also available at most Lao Telecom offices and many post offices. Many other places, such as hotels and guesthouses, also have phone, fax and email facilities.

To call long distance within the country, dial 0 first, then the provincial area code and number. For international calls, dial 00, the country code, then the area code and number. Mobile phone numbers in Laos normally begin with the prefix 020.

Mobile phones

Mobile phone coverage is surprisingly good throughout the country. In addition to Lao Telecom (Laotel; Call Centre tel: 101), a handful of other local service providers also offer mobile phone services, including Enterprise of Telecommunications Lao (ETL). Visitors with gsm-enabled mobile phones can buy a starter kit from ETL (www.etllao.com) for US$5, which consists of a SIM card with a local phone number and about 20,000 kip (about US$2) worth of stored value, from which international and local calls and text messages can be made. The credit can be topped up at any outlet bearing the 'Tango' sign.

Tourist information

Lao National Tourism Authority
Lan Xang Avenue, tel: 021-212 248, 212 251, www.tourismlaos.org
This government-run tourism office can provide some good information about tours in the country. It is also

cooperating with local tour operators in providing ecotourism tours in the country. See also www.ecotourismlaos.com for more Internet resources.
Dielthelm Travel
www.diethelmtravel.com
Reputable agent with many years of experience in the region. Has offices in the following locations:
Vientiane
Namphu Circle, tel: 021-213 833
Luang Prabang
47/2 Sisavangvong Road, tel: 071-212 277

Visas and passports

A tourist visa is required to visit Laos, except for citizens of Brunei, Cambodia, Malaysia, the Philippines, Singapore, Thailand and Vietnam. Thirty-day single-entry tourist visas are issued on arrival at Wattay International Airport in Vientiane, Luang Prabang International Airport, Pakse International Airport, and at some international border checkpoints. You will need one passport photo and between US$30 and US$45 (visa fees vary depending on what passport you are holding) for the visa application. There is an 'overtime' charge of US$1 for entry after 4pm and on weekends. Alternatively, 30-day tourist visas and 30-day business visas can be obtained in advance of your trip at a Lao embassy or consulate, or at travel agencies in any major city in Asia.

Extension of stay

Visa extensions can be obtained from the Lao Immigration Office at the Ministry of Interior in Vientiane, opposite Talat Sao (Morning Market), tel: 021-212 529. The cost is US$2 per day up to a maximum of 30 days. Alternatively, tour agencies, guesthouses and some cafés can also arrange visa extensions for a small fee. Overstaying your visa will cost US$10 for each day.

Websites

Lao Embassy in the US: Current information on visa regulations, with links to government departments and affiliated organisations. www.laoembassy.com
Vientiane Times: Ministry of Information and Culture's English-language newspaper. www.vientianetimes.org.la
Travelfish: Well-written and up-to-date write-ups on Laos and its 18 provinces. www.travelfish.org

CAMBODIA

TRANSPORT, ACCOMMODATION, EATING OUT, ACTIVITIES AND AN A–Z OF TRAVEL INFORMATION

FACT FILE

Situation Cambodia lies on the Gulf of Thailand, between Thailand to the west, Vietnam to the east and Laos to the north.
Area about 181,035 sq km (69,900 sq miles).
Population 14.9 million.
Language Khmer.
Religions Buddhism, Cham Islam, Christianity.
Time zone 7 hours ahead of Greenwich Mean Time (GMT).
Currency riel (but US$ widely used). Approx 4,100 to US$1.
Weights and measures Metric.
Electricity 220 volts at 50Hz, using two flat or round-pin plugs (adaptors available at major markets in Phnom Penh). It is a good idea to bring along a torch with you, as temporary power outages are quite common.

TRANSPORT

Getting there

By air
Many international visitors arrive by air at the **Phnom Penh International Airport** or at **Siem Reap–Angkor International Airport**. For more information, call the airport information hotline, tel: 023-890 890, or look up www.cambodia-airports.com.

By land
There are several points of entry into Cambodia by road. From Thailand, the most popular points of entry are at Poipet/Aranyaprathet, Cham Yeam/Hat Lek and O'Smach/Chong Jom.

The crossing at Preah Vihear is often closed. From Vietnam, you can enter at Bavet/Svay Rieng, Prek Chak/Xa Xia, Phnom Den/Tinh Bien, O Yadaw/Le Tanh, Trapaeng Thlong/Xa Mat, Trapaeng Sre/Loc Ninh, Banteay Chakrey/Khanh Binh and Kham Sam Nor/Kandal. From Laos, the single entry point is Dom Kralor/Stung Treng.

The situation sometimes changes, so check with your consulate or travel agent before travelling. Cambodian border guards are notorious for running scams and overcharging, so it's a good idea to bring yourself up to date on recent border regulations before you cross.

Getting around

On arrival
Phnom Penh International Airport
The airport is 10km (6 miles) from the centre of Phnom Penh and the journey into town takes around 20 minutes. The average fare to Phnom Penh centre is about US$10 by taxi or US$5 by moto.

Siem Reap–Angkor International Airport
The airport is located about 8km (5 miles) from town. The journey by taxi or moto will take 10–15 minutes. Most hotels and some of the better guesthouses provide airport transfers for guests.

By air
Air Asia (www.airasia.com), **Bangkok Airways** (www.bangkokair.com) and **Jetstar Airways** (www.jetstar.com) serve Siem Reap and Phnom Penh. Flights to Sihanoukville are seldom. Routes and timetables change frequently; check www.cambodia-airports.com. For foreigners, a domestic airport tax of US$6 is included in the ticket price.

By boat
Air-conditioned boats ply between Phnom Penh and Siem Reap. The journey takes around 6 hours and usually begins at 7am.

With the improvement of the roads between the two cities, however, this mode of transport is fast losing its

Passing the Independence Monument in Phnom Penh.

Raffles Hotel in Phnom Penh.

popularity to air-conditioned buses, which are cheaper, more comfortable and far quicker.

By road

Several air-conditioned bus services run between Phnom Penh and various destinations, including Siem Reap, Sihanoukville, Kampot/Kep, Battambang, Rattanakiri, Koh Kong, Kratie and Poipet. The road to Sihanoukville is the best in the country. Many bus services depart from the bus terminal near the Central Market.

Public transport

Motorcycle taxis, or 'motos' can be found all over the country. The drivers are recognisable by the fact that they wear head-protection of some sort (helmets are required for the driver, not the passenger). Many moto drivers speak some English. Expect to pay US$1 for a short journey, and US$2 for longer ones. Always agree the fare beforehand. Motos normally wait outside the airport, and this can be a viable way into town if you arrive alone. The fare is usually US$5.

In Phnom Penh and Angkor *tuk-tuk* has replaced the 'cyclo' or pedicab. *Tuk-tuks* are large, four-wheel covered wagons that are pulled by motorbikes. They can carry up to four passengers and are more popular with tourists than motos.

Air-conditioned taxis are readily available at the airports. Within Phnom Penh city, they may be difficult to locate quickly. In Siem Reap, there are plenty of taxis ready and willing to take you around the temples at Angkor. At the time of writing they charge at least US$60 for a full day in and around Angkor and Siem Reap. You may have to pay up to US$100 to visit the temples further afield.

An option for long-distance travel is the share-taxi. These vehicles ply between Phnom Penh and all the major towns. Vehicles can take up to

six or seven passengers, so it is not always comfortable, although it is certainly a cheap way to get around. Freelance taxi drivers can be arranged via your hotel or guesthouse.

Private transport

Tourists are not allowed to drive their own cars in Phnom Penh and Siem Reap, and must hire a driver. Motorcycle rental is allowed in most of Cambodia, but not in Siem Reap and Angkor. In Sihanoukville, car and motorcycle rentals are occasionally problematic due to the daily whims of local police. The car and motorcycle rental regulations change from time to time, so it is necessary to plan ahead of travel. Police – particularly in Siem Reap – demand foreigners possess a Cambodian license to drive a motorcycle. If stopped, they will insist on a 'fine' of a few dollars.

By train

Passenger rail services are being renovated but their future schedules and development remains uncertain and precarious. Traditionally train travel in Cambodia was neither comfortable nor convenient, though this may change.

ACCOMMODATION

Choosing a hotel

Luxury accommodation in Cambodia is limited to a few major centres: Phnom Penh, Siem Reap and Sihanoukville. These days Phnom Penh offers a fine choice of luxury accommodation at very reasonable prices, considering the amenities on offer. Mid-level accommodation can be found in abundance in all major towns and is usually quite comfortable. At the lower end, guesthouses are common, and some of them are excellent. Compared with

what was available a decade ago, the general situation in Cambodia has improved tremendously. Above the US$15 level all rooms will be air-conditioned and normally have satellite television and a refrigerator. Hot water is usually available in mid-level and luxury accommodation. Under US$15 usually gets you a cold shower and ceiling fan with a television.

Booking ahead is a good idea, particularly in Phnom Penh and Siem Reap, as well Sihanoukville during high season (roughly October to March). It is best to book directly through the hotel rather than a tour office. Tour offices will mark up the price considerably. Moto and *tuk-tuk* drivers can drive you around and help you find accommodation when you first arrive. However, be aware that they receive a commission from the hotel, which may be added to the price of the room. Beware of taxi drivers at the airport who try to tell you that your chosen hotel is already full, under renovation or full of prostitutes. This will rarely, if ever, be true. It is common for taxi drivers to pull a bait-and-switch, taking you to the wrong hotel (one where they collect a commission). If this happens, hold your ground (unless the other hotel looks like a better deal), and don't pay the difference in the fare to take you to the correct hotel.

EATING OUT

What to eat

Cambodian food is similar in form to Thai and Vietnamese, though the flavour is milder, lacking a heavy reliance on chilli. The main national staple is, of course, rice, but French colonial influence has dictated that the Cambodians eat more bread than any other Southeast Asian country. Because of the country's incredible richness in waterways, freshwater fish and prawns are especially popular. Fresh seafood is also available from the Gulf of Thailand. Beef, pork, chicken, duck and other poultry are widely available. Soup is served as an accompaniment to nearly every meal.

Visitors upcountry will generally find themselves limited to Cambodian cuisine or to the ubiquitous baguette and pâté. In towns of any size Chinese food will also be available. In the west of the country Thai food is widespread, and in the east, Vietnamese influence is similarly common.

THAILAND
MYANMAR
LAOS
CAMBODIA
VIETNAM
MALAYSIA
BRUNEI
SINGAPORE
INDONESIA
PHILIPPINES

Cambodia overflows with fruit; among the most popular and widespread fruits are mango, coconut, rambutan, durian, mangosteen, starfruit, pineapple, watermelon and a wide variety of bananas.

Where to eat

Eating 'locally', as in Laos, is a little more challenging in Cambodia than Vietnam or Thailand. Cambodians are adventurous eaters, and dishes or snacks made with unusual creatures and internal organs are common on the street. Markets are the cheapest place to grab a hot meal or a take-away snack. They are busiest – and have the best variety early in the morning and around dinner time. Cafés with foreign coffee and free Wi-fi are popular in the big cities. Many serve good food, but portions are generally small and on the pricey side. Truck stops are a great place to pick up pre-packaged snacks, ice cream and soft drinks. Most travellers will stick to the wide variety of tourist restaurants and bars, however.

ACTIVITIES

The arts

Cultural performances

Classical *apsara* dance performances truly bring life to the Angkor experience, as they directly portray the celestial maidens depicted in the bas-reliefs of the temples. They can be seen at the Chatomuk Theatre near the Royal Palace in central Phnom Penh, as well as at major (expensive) hotels in the capital and at Siem Reap.

Another interesting dance genre is called *tontay*, which portrays *Reamker*, a Cambodian version of the Indian epic, the *Ramayana*. Performances are held at various hotels and restaurants in both Phnom Penh and Siem Reap.

Nightlife

The Cambodian nightlife scene is rather diverse. From the colonial elegance of the Elephant Bar at Le Royal Hotel to incredibly tawdry karaoke dens, there is certainly something for everybody. The substantial expatriate population has led to the establishment of quite a few Western-style bars in Siem Reap and Phnom Penh. Some are couple-friendly, but the majority of the nighttime venues cater to the needs of the single male, with the services of paid dance partners and hostesses in abundance.

Phnom Penh and Sihanoukville are not always safe after dark, and more than a few of the patrons of the wilder nightclubs and discos are both armed and intoxicated. When travelling late at night anywhere in these cities, be sure to use a car, or at the very least hire a reliable moto driver for the night, to avoid the attentions of muggers. The best part of Phnom Penh for night revelry is along the Sap River at Sisowath Quay. There are a variety of low-key nightspots and the area is safer than most. Street 51 (Pasteur Street, otherwise known as 'The Strip') between Streets 174 and 154 is also popular.

Shopping

Phnom Penh

The capital, along with Siem Reap, is the best place to shop. It has several large markets, shopping malls, art galleries and numerous boutiques offering all manner of souvenirs, including hand-woven textiles, high-quality silks, handicrafts, clothing and furniture, art, paintings and artefacts, books and small gift items such as T-shirts or postcards. Of course, pirated CDs, DVDs and used books are also widely available. In fact Phnom Penh has a much better selection of foreign bookstores than Laos and Vietnam combined.

A popular souvenir item is the distinctively chequered scarf, *krama*, which Cambodians typically wear around their head and necks as protection against the sun. Another good souvenir is the traditional handmade silver betel containers shaped like animals – small and easy to pack and carry.

For silk products, browse **Psar Tuol Tom Pong** (Russian Market) and other boutiques, for example Couleurs d'Asie (19 Street 360), Jasmine (73 Street 240) and Kambuja (165 Street 110).

Apart from the many traditional markets, such as **Central Market** (Psar Thmay) and **Psar Tuol Tom Pong**, of special interest to the visitor are **Street 178** and **Street 240** in the Royal Palace and National Museum area. Street 178, nicknamed 'Art Street' by the locals, is home to various local art galleries, souvenir shops, boutiques and restaurants. The shorter stretch of Street 240 between Norodom Boulevard and Street 19 is lined with boutiques, bars, restaurants, travel agencies and bookshops.

In addition to commercial boutiques for art, paintings and prints, and clothing, there are also non-profit shops selling good-quality handicrafts and textiles to benefit disadvantaged Cambodians. Among the latter are Rajana (Psar Tuol Tom Pong and 170 Street 450), Tabitha (Street 51), Reyum (47 Street 178, www.reyum.org); and Colours of Cambodia (373 Sisowath Quay).

Books (fiction and non-fiction), periodicals, maps and travel guides can be found in Monument Books (111 Norodom Boulevard), D's Books (two locations at 7 Street 178 and 79 Street 240) or Bohr's Books (5 Sothearos Boulevard).

Siem Reap

In Siem Reap, visitors head for the **Old Market** (Psar Chas), which has an excellent range of souvenirs. Most are similar to those found in the capital city, but some items are unique to the Siem Reap area. There are also numerous art galleries, boutiques and other shops selling pricier souvenirs in the Old Market area.

One item that is commonly sold is 'temple rubbing', which is paper that has been moulded over a piece of bas-relief (most likely a reproduction) so that it bears the impression of the carving. Other popular souvenir purchases include silver work, handicrafts, and stone and wood-carvings.

For silk products, visit **Artisans d'Angkor** at the National Silk Centre (16km/10 miles west of town, tel: 063-963 330, www.artisansdangkor.com), where you can buy silk and, if you are interested, view the entire production process at the silk farm.

In general, be very careful when buying gems, as fake and low-quality stone scams are not uncommon. Also note that the purchase, and export of any authentic antiquities from Angkor is strictly forbidden.

A–Z

Budgeting for your trip

Cambodia is the most expensive country in Indochina. The price difference between Cambodia and both Laos and Vietnam is partly due to Cambodia's reliance on the US dollar, and because so many products are imported. Also, the substantial numbers of foreign NGO workers and businesspeople living in Cambodia for the past three decades have contributed to inflation. Food and drink, transportation, internet access, medications and supplies are more expensive here, but accommodation tends to be cheaper.

Climate

In common with other Southeast Asian countries, Cambodia's climate is based on the annual monsoon cycle. Between May and October the southwest monsoon carries heavy daily rainfall, usually for a few hours in the late afternoon. The northwest monsoon, between November and March, brings somewhat cooler temperatures and lower rainfall. The coolest months are between November and January, though even then temperatures rarely fall below 20°C (68°F). The driest months are January and February, when there is little or no rainfall, and the wettest months are usually September and October. The best time to visit is certainly during the cool season; April, which can be furnace-like, is best avoided.

What to wear/bring

Clothes should be light and loose, preferably cotton. Open shoes and sleeveless dresses for women or short-sleeved shirts for men are appropriate, but visitors should abide by local ideas of modesty when visiting pagodas, temples and official places. A sweater or sweatshirt is needed for nights. Lip balm and moisturisers are needed just about anytime, as are sunblock, sunglasses and hats. Tampons and sanitary towels can be difficult to obtain in smaller towns.

Customs regulations

You are allowed to import 200 cigarettes and one litre of alcohol duty-free into Cambodia. It is illegal to take antiquities out of the country.

Embassies

Australia/Canada
11 Street 254, Phnom Penh, tel: 023-213 470, www.cambodia.embassy.gov.au

Emergency numbers

Police Tel: 117 or 023-924 484
Fire Tel: 118 or 023-786 693
Ambulance Tel: 119 or 023-724 891

United Kingdom
27–29 Street 75, Phnom Penh, tel: 023-427 124, http://ukincambodia.fco.gov.uk
United States
1 Street 96, Phnom Penh, tel: 023-728 000, http://cambodia.us embassy.gov

Etiquette

The traditional Cambodian greeting is the *sampiah*, with hands brought together in front of the face, as if to pray. The higher one raises one's hands and the lower one makes an accompanying bow, the more respect is shown.

Always smile and never lose your temper, otherwise you will lose face and embarrass those around you.

Health and medical care

Tap water is unsafe for drinking, but purified bottled water is available everywhere in Cambodia.

Malarial mosquitoes are widespread in the countryside, but as long as you are staying close to the tourist areas, the risk is greatly reduced. Nonetheless it is worth taking precautions: use repellent and coils, and sleep beneath a net. Cover up your arms and legs particularly if you are out at dawn and dusk when the mosquitoes are most active.

As the standard of healthcare is relatively low, it is essential to arrange vaccinations and private medical insurance (preferably covering evacuation in an emergency) before departure.

Medical treatment

Good hospitals are rare in Cambodia, and only a limited range of medicines is available. For major ailments it would be best to go to Bangkok or Singapore.
Calmette Hospital, 3 Monivong Boulevard, Phnom Penh, tel: 023-723 840.
International Dental Clinic, 193 Street 208, tel: 023-212 909/016-553 366.
International SOS **Medical and Dental Clinic**, 161 Street 51, tel: 023-216 911 / 012-816 911, www.internationalsos.com.
Sen Sok International University Hospital, 91–96 Street 1986, Phnom Penh, tel: 023-883 712.

Internet

There are now several internet providers in Cambodia, including

most mobile phone service providers, such as Metfone, MobiTel, Mfone, Beeline and Hello. Most restaurants, bars and cafés now offer free Wi-fi, but the speeds are much slower than in neighbouring Vietnam.

Media

There is a variety of English publications available in Cambodia. The *Phnom Penh Post* (www.phnompenhpost.com) is a tabloid newspaper, printed daily, which sticks fairly solidly with events within the country. The *Cambodia Daily* is available every day and will keep you up-to-date with world events. The *Bangkok Post* and the *International Herald Tribune* are flown in daily from Thailand.

There is a series of free monthly English-language magazines by *Canby Publications* (www.canbypublications.com) that contain thorough listings of most of the hotels, restaurants and all the local events that might interest a visitor. There are numerous expat magazines as well, of which *Asia Life: Phnom Penh* (www.asialifecambodia.com), like its Ho Chi Minh City version, is perhaps the best known.

Money

The Cambodian currency is called the riel, although the Cambodian economy is really based on the US dollar. Transactions of more than 4,000 riel usually involve American currency. Cambodian riel comes in denominations of 100,000, 50,000, 20,000, 10,000, 5,000, 2,000, 1,000, 500, 200 and 100. The import and export of riel is prohibited.

At the time of writing, US$1 was about 4,100 riel. Most locals are accustomed to rounding the rate down to 4,000 riel during transactions. It is a good idea to have plenty of small-denomination US dollars, as they are far easier to change than larger notes. It is also useful to carry some small riel notes (500 and 1,000) for minor purchases. All major currencies can be changed at the airports and upmarket hotels. Gold shops also act as moneychangers (for cash exchange only) and are found around the markets in town.

Travellers' cheques and credit cards

Travellers' cheques can be cashed in tourist areas such as Phnom Penh, Siem Reap and Sihanoukville, but they remain difficult to change elsewhere. US dollar cheques are preferable.

THAILAND

MYANMAR

LAOS

CAMBODIA

VIETNAM

MALAYSIA

BRUNEI

SINGAPORE

INDONESIA

PHILIPPINES

Credit cards have also become more widely accepted. Most good hotels, restaurants and boutiques will accept Visa, JCB, MasterCard, and sometimes AMEX. Cash advances on cards are possible in some banks in Phnom Penh, Siem Reap, Battambang and Sihanoukville. Most businesses charge a three percent fee for credit card usage.

Tipping

Tipping is not a traditional part of Khmer culture, but it is becoming expected in tourist venues, and with wages being so low it is certainly appreciated. If you feel you have been well treated, a small token of your gratitude (10 percent) would not be out of place. Hotels and top restaurants will have already added a service charge to your bill.

Opening hours

Banks are normally open Mon–Fri, 8.30am–3.30pm. Government offices and official bodies open Mon–Sat, 7.30–11.30am and 2–5.30pm. Post offices open Mon–Sat, 7am–7pm. Banks, administrative offices and museums are closed on all public holidays and occasionally on religious festivals. Shops and supermarkets are usually open for longer hours. However, Cambodians tend to go home early. It is safest to always assume shops and offices (even very busy ones) will close 30 minutes to 1 hour earlier than posted.

Postal services

The main post office in Phnom Penh is located east of Wat Phnom on Street 13, tel: 023-426 832.

A number of international courier agencies are in Phnom Penh:
DHL, tel: 023-427 726

Visas are required for most nationalities.

Fedex, tel: 023-216 708
TNT, tel: 023-424 022

Telephones

For international calls, dial the IDD access code 001 or 007, followed by the country code, then the area/network code and number. For calls within a province, simply dial the six-digit subscriber number. To call a number in another province, dial the provincial area code with the initial 0, followed by the subscriber number.

If calling from overseas, dial Cambodia's country code 855, followed by area/network code (omitting the initial 0) and the number you want.

Public phones

Many public phone booths take phonecards, which can be purchased at post offices and good hotels.

Mobile phones

A most economical way of using your own GSM-enabled mobile phone in Cambodia is to purchase a local SIM card from Metfone, MobiTel, Mfone, Beeline and Hello. Mobile phone numbers begin with the prefix 012, 011, 015, 016, 018 or 092.

Mobile phones are offered for rent at the airport. Countless shops selling new and inexpensive, used phones are in every town.

Tourist information

Ministry of Tourism

Cambodia's tourist office is at 262 Monivong Boulevard in Phnom Penh (tel: 855-23 216 66; www.tourismcambodia.com). The MOT has a useful website (www.mot.gov.kh) with travel information. Use it as a resource and deal with travel agents directly.

Public holidays

1 January International New Year's Day
7 January Victory Over
8 March International Women's Day
13–16 April Khmer New Year
1 May International Workers' Day
8 May International Children's Day
13–15 May The King's Birthday
18 June The Queen Mother's Birthday
24 September Constitution Day
29 October Coronation Day
31 October The King Father's Birthday
9 November Independence Day
10 December International Human Rights Day

Dielthelm Travel (65 Street 240, Phnom Penh, tel: 023-219 151, www.diethelmtravel.com) is a reputable agent with many years of experience in the region.

Visas and passports

Your passport should be valid for at least 6 months. An entry visa is also required for citizens of all countries except Malaysia, the Philippines, Singapore, Vietnam and Laos. Single-entry Cambodian tourist visas, valid for 30 days, are issued on arrival at Phnom Penh International Airport and Siem Reap–Angkor International Airport. For details, look up the Cambodian Immigration Department website (www.cambodia-immigration.com). Tourist e-visas are also available for entry to the two airports. Apply online at http://evisa.mfaic.gov.kh.

Tourist visas can be extended only once, for 30 days, at the Dept for Foreigners (Pochentong Road, tel: 012-581 558, email: visa_info@online.com.kh). Guesthouses and travel agencies in Phnom Penh will also handle visa extensions for a nominal fee. The fine for overstaying is US$5 per day. However, business visas, which cost only $5 more than a $25 tourist visa, can be extended indefinitely.

Websites

The following websites provide useful travel information on travel in Cambodia:
Khmer440: www.khmer440.com
Canby Publications Cambodia Guides: www.canbypublications.com
Andy Brouwer's Cambodia Tales: www.andybrouwer.co.uk

VIETNAM

TRANSPORT, ACCOMMODATION, EATING OUT, ACTIVITIES AND AN A–Z OF TRAVEL INFORMATION

FACT FILE

Situation A thin 1,600km (1,000-mile) strip extending from China down to the Gulf of Thailand.
Area 329,556 sq km (127,242 sq miles).
Population 88.8 million.
Language Vietnamese.
Religion Buddhism with Confucian/Taoist influences, Christianity.
Time zone 7 hours ahead of Greenwich Mean Time (GMT).
Currency Dong (pronounced *dome*). Approx 21,000 to US$1.
Weights and measures Metric.
Electricity Mainly 220 volts. Protect your electronic equipment against power surges.

TRANSPORT

Getting there

By air

The easiest way to get to Vietnam is by air. Hanoi's **Noi Bai Airport** is served by direct flights from Bangkok, Beijing, Berlin, Dubai, Frankfurt, Guangzhou, Hong Kong, Kuala Lumpur, Kunming, Moscow, Paris, Phnom Penh, Seoul, Siem Reap, Singapore, Sydney, Taipei, Tokyo, Vientiane and Vladivostok.

Ho Chi Minh City's **Tan Son Nhat Airport** is connected via international flights to Bangkok, Beijing, Busan, Dubai, Frankfurt, Guangzhou, Hong Kong, Kaohsiung, Kuala Lumpur, Macau, Manila, Melbourne, Moscow, Nagoya, Osaka, Paris, Phnom Penh, Seoul, Singapore, Sydney, Taipei, Tokyo, Vienna, Vientiane, Vladivostok and Zurich.

There are also direct flights to Danang from Bangkok, Hong Kong and Singapore.

All plane tickets now include departure taxes.

By sea

Cruise ships sometimes make stops in Ho Chi Minh City, Halong Bay and Hai Phong and Danang as part of South China Sea cruises, but there is no regular service. Anyone considering arriving by sea on a freighter or private vessel should contact the Hanoi immigration office directly to receive authorisation. It is possible to take a ferry from Cambodia at Vinh Xuong (30km north of Chau Doc) border crossing in the Mekong Delta to Vietnam. There is also a ferry from Ha Long City to Beihai in China.

By road

It is possible to enter Vietnam from China (and vice versa) at Dong Da (near Lang Son) and Lao Cai (by road and rail), and Mong Cai (by road only) border crossings.

It's easy to cross from Laos to Hue or Vinh by the Lao Bao border crossing. It is also possible to enter from Vientiane via Cau Treo and travel on to Hanoi. Frequent minibuses service the Moc Bai border crossing from Ho Chi Minh City to Phnom Penh, Cambodia. Travellers can also enter via Vinh Xuong, about 30km (18 miles) north of Chau Doc. Several other crossings have opened with Laos and Cambodia but they are not advisable for anyone but experienced travellers due to remoteness and potential hassles from officials. If possible, it is always best to keep to the main roads and crossings.

Getting around

By air

Flying is by far the best way to travel if you intend only to visit a few cities in Vietnam. A Vietnam Airlines flight from Hanoi to Ho Chi Minh City costs under US$200, whereas the train for the same distance, if you figure in meals for two days, is roughly the same price. Scheduled **Vietnam Airlines** flights (www.vietnamairlines.com) from Ho Chi Minh City serve Buon Me Thuot, Da Lat, Danang, Hai Phong, Hanoi, Hue, Nha Trang, Phu Quoc, Pleiku, Qui Nhon and Rach Gia. From Hanoi there are scheduled flights to Danang, Ho Chi Minh City, Hue, Vinh and Nha Trang.

The major problem with flying is finding space during the busy season before and after Tet.

You can use credit cards to buy airline tickets in Hanoi and Ho Chi Minh City, but in other cities you may be asked to pay cash.

Vietnam Airlines' **Hanoi** office is located at 1 Quang Trung Street, tel: 04-832 0320, and the **Ho Chi Minh City** office at 116 Nguyen Hue, District 1, tel: 08-832 0320.

By rail

Train travel, operated by **Vietnam Railways** (www.vr.com.vn or a better site is www.seat61.com) in Vietnam, is slow. The fastest Hanoi–Ho Chi Minh City express train, known as the Reunification Express, covers 1,730km (1,073 miles) in 30 hours, so if you need to get somewhere fast forget about the train. However, if you want to soak in the Vietnamese countryside, the train has a lot to offer, including mountain passes, ocean views, tunnels, French-era

THAILAND

MYANMAR

LAOS

CAMBODIA

VIETNAM

MALAYSIA

BRUNEI

SINGAPORE

INDONESIA

PHILIPPINES

bridges, and an opportunity to get to know the Vietnamese up close and personal. However, there have been burglaries on board so make sure you secure your bags properly.

There are five express trains every day and berths are reserved fast, so try to make reservations two days in advance. There are also local train services on the Hanoi–Ho Chi Minh City line that serves coastal cities. Lines also run from Hanoi West to Pho Lu, East to Hai Phong and North to Lang Son.

In **Ho Chi Minh City**, the train station is at 1 Nguyen Thong Street, tel: 08-823 0105 (ticket sales daily 7.15–11am and 1–3pm). Book at least 2–3 days in advance for sleepers. The private joint-venture **Golden Trains** (tel: 08-3825 7636, www.golden-train.com, daily 8am–8pm), operates upscale trains in the south with good services.

In **Hanoi**, go to 120 Le Duan Street, tel: 04-825 3949 (ticket sales daily 7.30–11.30am and 1.30–3.30pm).

By road

In Hanoi and Ho Chi Minh City it is possible to hire good cars and minivans to go on day trips or week-long excursions. Hiring a driver and vehicle is good value if your travelling party is large enough to spread the cost. Self-drive is not advised.

Modern air-conditioned tour buses travel between all the major towns and cities. Competition among tour companies is fierce and these buses are good value if you don't mind herds of tourists. Local buses are slow and often break down.

City transport

Bicycle
In the cities the best way to get around is by bicycle or *cyclo* (trishaw).

Evening in the heart of Hanoi.

Bicycles can be rented for as little as US$1 or US$2 per day from tourist cafés in Hanoi and Ho Chi Minh City. If you have a mechanical problem or a tire puncture, don't worry as there are stands set up on practically every street corner where most repairs will cost a few thousand dong.

No trip to Vietnam is complete without a ride in a cyclo. Vietnam has thousands of waiting cyclo drivers who can be hired by the kilometre or the hour. Expect to pay at least 50,000 dong for a short ride or 200,000 dong for an hour. It is essential to bargain with cyclo drivers. As a rule, halve their first offer and work up.

Motorcycle taxi
A faster way to get around town in Hanoi and Ho Chi Minh City is a motorcycle taxi, called a *xe om* (pron. *say ome*) or Honda *om*, which literally means 'hugging taxi' as passengers grab on to the driver's waist. Fares are actually much cheaper than on cyclos, and of course the ride is quicker. Some of the drivers navigate the roads badly, however, so be careful. If a driver seems unsafe, tell him to stop, get off and pay him, then find another driver. Buy a helmet if you decide to use motorcycle taxis. They're available in the markets. Some women travellers have reported problems with *xe om* drivers getting too friendly; be especially careful late at night.

Taxi
Taxis in Hanoi and Ho Chi Minh City are generally comfortable, with meters and air-conditioning, and are generally reasonably priced.

In **Ho Chi Minh City**, **Vinataxis**, tel: 08-3811 1111 and **Airport Taxis**, tel: 08-3844 6448, provide an efficient metered service. Taxis are seldom found outside these two

cities, but old jalopy-style cars are available for hire as taxis in many areas.

Bus
In Hanoi and HCMC there are city buses with defined routes and schedules. Bus maps are difficult to find but signs on the front of the buses are accurate. For 5,000 to 10,000 dong they are another Asian experience, and who knows what you will find on your trip or where you'll end up.

ACCOMMODATION

Choosing a hotel

Hotel development in Vietnam is flourishing and visitors are spoilt for choice. International chains, with service standards and prices to match, can be found in all the major cities, but there is also plenty of choice in the budget lodgings category, where a room can go for about US$10 a night.

Hotel staff are generally friendly and helpful, and adequate English is spoken in the major tourism and business centres. In more remote areas, communication in English can be a real problem. State-run hotels tend to have indifferent staff and low standards of service, which is a real pity because some of Hanoi and HCMC's most atmospheric historic hotels are state-run enterprises.

Mini hotels and homestays

If you are on a tight budget, try the so-called 'guesthouses', i.e. small, often family-run hotels with fairly modern (but modest) facilities. These abound in Hanoi and HCMC, but are also increasingly common these days in the popular resort towns.

There are also smaller family-run guesthouses that offer homestay accommodation. These are mainly found in the Mekong Delta area and offer a more personal touch (you may even be invited to have dinner with the family). In the northern highlands, a stay in a hill-tribe community can be booked with a specialist travel agency.

Rates and bookings

When booking your accommodation, always check the hotel website first to see what are the best rates on offer. If it is a smaller outfit without

a website, call directly to ask for the best rates. Hotel-booking websites should be your next port of call; these companies can sometimes get you better rates because of the volume of business they bring in.

During the school holidays (June to August) the beaches get very crowded, and during the annual Tet festival (in late January or early- to mid-February) buses and trains are packed to the rafters with domestic travellers. On those days that the lunar calendar indicates as auspicious for weddings, you'll also find many honeymooners flocking to Dalat. Hotel rates also spike during the Christmas and New Year periods. If you are making a trip during any of these times, it would be a good idea to book ahead.

Note that all hotel guests must be registered with the local police. This could mean leaving your passport with the reception for the entire duration of the stay or just overnight. In Hanoi and HCMC, the practice is either to make a photocopy or to record details from your passport and landing card. It is always handy to have a spare photocopy of your passport.

EATING OUT

What to eat

Generally, meals consist of a meat or fish dish, stir-fried vegetables and a bowl of soup (canh). A long coastline means that fish is always on the menu, and fish sauce finds its way onto every table. Other dipping sauces on the table include soy sauce and salt moistened with lime juice. There is no real post-dinner dessert culture.

The national dish is *pho* (pronounced *fuh*), noodle soup that can be eaten for breakfast or as a late-night snack, though many people eat it at lunch and dinner, too. A hot, aromatic broth is poured over noodles, then spices and herbs are added and topped either with slivers of beef (*bo*) or chicken (*ga*).

The most celebrated dish in Ho Chi Minh City is *bánh xèo*, sizzling crêpes pan-fried with pork slivers, shrimps and bean sprouts, folded over and cooked to a crispy golden brown.

A Hanoi favourite is *bun cha*, charcoal grilled pork meatballs served in a broth, accompanied by cold noodles.

Hue's cuisine is regarded as the food of emperors and its delicacies

Tet: Vietnam's New Year

Tet Nguyen Dan is the most important festival on the Vietnamese calendar. It takes place late January or early February, on the day of the full moon between the winter solstice and the spring equinox, and lasts three days. It is a time of hope, when relatives gather to celebrate new beginnings and to honour ancestral spirits.

Houses are given a good spring cleaning and decorated with flowers.

Parades and government-sponsored fireworks displays occur in parks and over Hoan Kiem and West Lakes. Excellent celebratory cakes are for sale, and families hold feasts.

During the Tet holidays, the whole of the country closes down, and transportation and hotels get booked up well in advance for the weeks before and afterwards. Don't plan spontaneous travel at this time of year.

include *banh khoai*, a rice-flour, egg and taro-based pancake, pan-fried with a filling of bean sprouts, pork and shrimp, then topped with *nuoc leo*, a local peanut sauce.

The Vietnamese can be extremely adventurous with their food, and dog, snake and turtle may find their way onto menus.

Where to eat

Street kitchens are the place to try out Vietnamese food. They offer some of the best and most authentic dishes as well as a chance to rub shoulders with new friends. The locals love to snack, and these eateries, which can be either just stalls with small stools to sit on, or eating houses that spill over the pavement, are easily tracked down, with their smouldering cauldrons, flaming barbecues and piles of fruit, There is no better place to get acquainted with the flavours of the country.

Because street food is also fantastically good value, everyone eats out. If you are going for a meal, try to arrive at a street kitchen by noon for lunch and between six and seven for dinner, as food can run out early. The same applies to upscale restaurants, as they tend to close around 10–11pm. Ho Chi Minh City is the country's culinary capital.

Hanoi has a good range of restaurants, mainly in the Hoan Kiem district. Many of the more sophisticated are Indochinese style in elegant and atmospheric former French villas.

ACTIVITIES

The arts

The main centres for the arts are Hanoi and, to a lesser degree, Ho Chi Minh City. Outside of these two cites, the pickings are generally slim.

Hanoians have a universally abiding love for the arts, and that love is reflected in the city's numerous venues for traditional art forms. But apart from the enduringly popular water puppet performances, visitors will have difficulty appreciating some of its more esoteric art forms as most are targeted at local audiences. HCMC is less exciting as a centre for the arts. Traditional music, dance and theatre are in decline, and the city's youth is more besotted with Western art forms and culture.

Nightlife

In a country where people habitually rise by 5am, it is little surprise that a drink at 9.30pm may be construed as a late night out. In the big cities, where incomes are rising and foreign influences felt, this attitude has all but disappeared as a rash of bars and clubs are making their presence felt.

Note: legal drinks licensing in Vietnam is only valid until midnight. Therefore any place of entertainment that stays open later is at the mercy of the enforcement authorities, making Vietnam's nightlife scene a constantly shifting one.

Hanoi

There are few glitzy clubs or bars as Hanoi's 'morality police' are notorious for shutting down any venue that becomes too popular or stays open too late at night. However, there are a few tried-and-tested venues that do their best to serve the city's late night crowd.

Depending on the mood of the police and the scheduling of official Party gatherings, even these places can occasionally find themselves forced to shut their doors at midnight or refrain from opening at all.

Ho Chi Minh City

During the Vietnam War, Saigon was legendary for its notorious bars

THAILAND

MYANMAR

LAOS

CAMBODIA

VIETNAM

MALAYSIA

BRUNEI

SINGAPORE

INDONESIA

PHILIPPINES

and clubs catering to American GIs. Until today, HCMC has never quite recaptured that heady wartime spirit – a long-running, police-enforced midnight curfew for bars and some clubs has proved effective.

As the main commercial hub of Vietnam, HCMC has many hip, cosmopolitan bars that keep the burgeoning ranks of expats, business travellers, tourists and moneyed locals happy. Although HCMC's clubbing scene lags behind other major Asian cities, its club and bar scene is getting better every day. The scene is extremely fickle, however, with clubs opening, closing and losing favour on a regular basis.

The official midnight curfew has exceptions, and closing times fluctuate; those in the backpacker area (around Pham Ngo Lao and De Tham streets) seem to stay open until much later. Note: practically all bars and clubs are located in District 1.

Shopping

What to buy

There is a wide variety of traditional Vietnamese handicrafts, including embroidery, lacquerware, silk paintings, pottery, mother-of-pearl inlay, ceramics, precious wood, jade, bamboo and wickerware, baskets, sculpture, wood, marble/bone carvings, jewellery, engraving, silk and brocade.

You may like to add a *non la*, the famous Vietnamese conical hat and an *ao dai*, the traditional costume worn by Vietnamese women, to your wardrobe. Green pith helmets, worn by soldiers during the war and by cyclo drivers and labourers today, are sold.

Strong laws and heavy taxation have discouraged the sale of antiquities and export is strictly controlled. A reputable dealer will obtain export papers and ship your purchase with little trouble. Copies of bronze Buddhas, old porcelain, wood statuettes and objects used by hill tribes and numerous cults are for sale in many city shops.

The general rule is that if there's no price tag, the price can be negotiated. In higher-end shops, items will have fixed prices.

Ho Chi Minh City

HCMC is fast emerging as a key Asian shopping and design hub. Although still a source of mass-produced cheap goods, Vietnam's undisputed shopping capital offers stylish, home-grown stores selling contemporary stuff at down-to-earth prices. Local talent and HCMC-based international designers create exceptional home accessories, furniture, lighting, modern art and clothing, though the shopping scene is still dominated by Vietnam's centuries-old traditional crafts.

Ceramics

Authentique, 6 Dong Khoi St, tel: 08-3823 8811. Piles of delicate ceramics in many styles, colours and sizes, some displayed warehouse-style in baskets. Everything from sake pots and espresso cups to large vases.

Home Decor, Furniture and Gifts

Saigon Kitsch, G/F, 43 Ton That Thiep St, tel: 08-3821 8019. This kooky, brightly coloured store has an equally kitsch collection of home wares, many with Vietnamese propaganda-art themes.

Embroidery and Needlework

Vietnam Quilts, 26/1 Le Thanh Ton St, tel: 08-3825 1441, www.vietnam-quilts.org. This non-profit community development organisation offers on-going employment for women in impoverished southern areas through the sales of lovely handmade cotton bed quilts. Custom-made quilts available.

Fashion

Ipa-Nima, 85 Pasteur St, tel: 08-3824 2701, www.ipa-nima.com. Flamboyant, coquettish and vintage high-end handbags (all locally made) created by a Vietnam-based Hong Konger designer-founder.

Zen Plaza, 54–56 Nguyen Trai St, tel: 08-3925 0339. A compact, multi-level shopping plaza aimed at locals. The lower floors specialise in home-grown designer fashions. Fresh, original and affordable Vietnamese fashions – mainly in small sizes.

Lacquer

Appeal, 41 Ton That Thiep St, tel: 08-3821 3614, www.christianduc. fr. Minuscule upscale store retailing high-quality crushed-eggshell lacquer pieces – furniture, lighting and home decor – in striking designs by Vietnamese French designers.

Silk

Khai Silk, 107 Dong Khoi St, tel: 08-3829 1146, www.khaisilkcorp. com. Vietnam's most exclusive silk boutique chain retails luxurious silk accessories, including ties, kimonos, embroidered scarves, lingerie, brocade shawls and bed quilts.

Souvenirs

Souvenirs like buffalo-horn servers, marble stone boxes, ceramic tea sets, silk lanterns and more are sold at the countless souvenir stores along Dong Khoi and Le Loi streets, plus around the backpacker area of De Tham and Pham Ngo Lao streets.

For one-stop souvenir blitzes, try Ben Thanh Market, intersection of Ham Nghi, Le Loi and Tran Hung Dao streets. The city's best-known covered market sells piles of cheap and cheerful souvenirs and handicrafts (like lacquerware, ceramics, coffee beans, T-shirts, conical hats and more) in a relatively compact ground-floor area. Bargaining is optional. Saigon Tax Trade Centre at 135 Nguyen Hue St, the two upper floors of this open-plan, hybrid market-mall sell a huge selection of slightly better-quality souvenirs and handicrafts than Ben Thanh at slightly higher prices, but with less hassle and in air-con comfort.

Ho Chi Minh's Market

The city's central market is **Ben Thanh Market**, at the intersection of Ham Nghi, Le Loi, Tran Hung Dao and Le Thanh Ton Streets. Just about everything is for sale here, from fruits, vegetables, rice and meats to electronics, clothes, household goods, and flowers. Not for the squeamish, there is a fascinating fish/meat section, where you may catch a glimpse of live frogs hanging by the leg and other delicacies. There are also some small food stalls selling soup and rice dishes.

Hanoi

For those with money to burn and space in their suitcases, Hanoi can be a shopper's paradise. Exquisite silks, colourful lacquerware, gems, silver and hand-tailored clothing can all be found at reasonable prices within the city centre.

In the **Old Quarter**, Hang Gai (Silk Street) has a clutch of top-notch silk shops, while south on trendy Nha Tho Street, clothing, handbags and home-decor items abound.

Throughout the Old Quarter, shops flog all manner of water puppets, scarves, fake war mementoes, and lacquer and wood Tin Tin posters.

In the city's bright, air-conditioned malls, shops selling brand-name electronics, clothing and cosmetics do a booming business thanks to a new generation of affluent

Ho Chi Minh City has a large number of modish bars.

Vietnamese consumers. But for tourists, aside from revelling in the cool air or escaping a sudden downpour, there's little reason to linger in these places.

Antiques
For the best 'antique' repros, the small shops along Hang Gai and Hang Bong in the Old Quarter are a good source, as is Nghi Tam Street in Tay Ho District. Whereas Hang Gai and Hang Bong shops deal in tourist items, the ones along Nghi Tam specialise in pricier high-quality cast-iron statues, stone Buddhas and other fascinating bric-a-brac.

Silk
Khai Silk, 96 Hang Gai St, Hoan Kiem District, tel: 04-3825 4237; 121 Nguyen Thai Hoc St, Ba Dinh District, tel: 04-3823 3508; and 56 Ly Thai To St, Hoan Kiem District, tel: 04-3934 8968 (inside Metropole Hotel), www.khaisilkcorp.com. The Khai Silk empire – which includes numerous restaurants, a resort, and shops all over the country – is the brainchild of Hoang Khai, whose skill with silk and tailoring is unmatched.

Gems and jewellery
Hang Bac (Gold Street) is home to many of Hanoi's gold and gold jewellery dealers. These small street-side shops generally have their wares displayed in glass cabinets, mainly thick gold chains, jade and Buddha pendants, and some silver. Few shop owners speak English as they serve a primarily Vietnamese clientele.

Handicrafts and home decor
Craftlink, 43 Van Mieu St, Ba Dinh District, tel: 04-3843 7710, www.craftlink.com.vn. This not-for-profit organisation/shop provides a place where ethnic minority people can sell their crafts and clothing at fair rates.

Pick up some beautiful jewellery, embroidery and small souvenirs with the knowledge that your money is going back into the community.

Shopping centres
Hanoi Towers, 49 Hai Ba Trung Street, Hoan Kiem District. Nothing flash. Only one floor of shopping, which includes a grocery store, a clothing store and some home-decor shops.

Vincom City Towers, 191 Ba Trieu Street, Hai Ba Trung District. This large shopping mall has multiple floors of shopping (Western clothing, electrical appliances, cosmetics), as well as Hanoi's first and only multiplex cinema on the sixth floor. Popular with Hanoi's upper classes.

A–Z

Budgeting for your trip
Accommodation in Vietnam can be cheap, but in Hanoi, Saigon and popular beach resorts it is getting pricey. Well-appointed guesthouses in the cities at around US$15–20 per night will include air-conditioning, TV, fridge, hot water, up to two beds, and perhaps Wi-fi. Mid-range beach hotels will cost between US$20 and US$50. Service improves as the price rises to US$100.

Street food meals cost between US$1 and US$2. Mid-range Vietnamese and backpacker restaurants will charge US$3–4 per dish. A typical restaurant catering to tourists will cost US$6–10 for three courses and drinks. There are few truly high-end restaurants outside of Ho Chi Minh City and Hanoi, where top tables can run in excess of US$25 per person.

Budget travellers can realistically get by with US$25 per day. A mid-range budget is about US$40–50

per day. Beyond that, the sky is the limit.

Vietnamese commonly charge different rates for foreigners and Viet Kieu (overseas Vietnamese) than locals. This was once mandated in government-run establishments, but has largely been abolished. Still, most Vietnamese see foreigners as an opportunity to make extra profit and continue the practice in most contexts. One should generally assume that a quoted price, especially when shopping, is at least double the normal rate and bargain the price down.

It is not uncommon for restaurants to have an expensive English menu and a cheaper Vietnamese one.

Climate
Vietnam has a monsoon climate. The south's dry season runs from December to May, with rains May to November. Temperatures rarely fall below 20°C (68°F). The centre is cooler. Along the coast, the 'dry' season is March to August, but can be fairly wet. The north's dry season is October to December. The summer months tend to be hot and sticky, with temperatures up to 40°C (104°F). Hanoi's average is 30°C (86°F).

What to bring/wear
The main thing to consider is the weather, as it can be freezing cold in the mountainous north and at the same time hot and humid on the Central Coast. If you are travelling in the north or the Central Highlands during the winter months definitely bring jeans and a warm coat or sweater. It seems that it is always raining somewhere in Vietnam, so bring lightweight rain gear. Sunblock, sunglasses and hat are also essential.

In the hot months, dress cool but conservatively. Many Vietnamese cannot understand why foreigners insist on wearing shorts and sleeveless tops when they have the money to dress well. For them, appearance is very important, so if you are dealing with an official of any rank make sure you are dressed appropriately.

Imported pharmaceutical drugs are widely available in Hanoi and Ho Chi Minh City, but it is best to bring a small supply of medicine to cope with diarrhoea, dysentery, eye infections, insect bites, fungal infections, and the common cold.

In Hanoi and Ho Chi Minh City, don't worry about running out of

THAILAND

MYANMAR

LAOS

CAMBODIA

VIETNAM

MALAYSIA

BRUNEI

SINGAPORE

INDONESIA

PHILIPPINES

something; you will probably find it in the supermarkets *(sieu thi)*.

Customs regulations

When you arrive you have to fill in a form declaring your valuables, including cameras and video cameras. You keep a photocopy of this form to show to Customs on your departure, so it's worth declaring as much as you can just in case you lose your luggage or Customs question anything as you leave. Visitors are allowed to import 400 cigarettes and 1.5 litres of alcohol duty free.

Export of anything of 'cultural or historical significance' is forbidden. So if you buy antiques you must apply for an export licence, and if you want to take any fakes home it's worth getting them cleared as fakes by the ministry so there is no hassle at Customs.

Embassies and consulates

Australia
Hanoi: 8 Dao Tan St, Ba Dinh District, tel: 04-3831 7755.
Ho Chi Minh City: 5B Ton Duc Thang St, District 1, tel: 08-3829 6035.
www.vietnam.embassy.gov.au
Canada
Hanoi: 31 Hung Vuong, tel: 04-3734 5000.
Ho Chi Minh City: 235 Dong Khoi St, District 1, tel: 08-3827 9899.
www.vietnam.gc.ca
New Zealand
Hanoi: 63 Ly Thai To St, tel: 04-3824 1481.
Ho Chi Minh City: 235 Dong Khoi St, District 1, tel: 08-3822 6907.
www.nzembassy.com
United Kingdom
Hanoi: 31 Hai Ba Trung St, tel: 04-3936 0500.
Ho Chi Minh City: 25 Le Duan St, District 1, tel: 08-3829 8433.
www.uk-vietnam.org
United States
Hanoi: 7 Lang Ha St, tel: 04-3831 4590.
Ho Chi Minh City: 4 Le Duan St, District 1, tel: 08-3822 9433.
www.vietnam.usembassy.gov

Etiquette

Arguing in a loud and aggressive manner will get you nowhere fast in Vietnam. Complaining about bad service in an international-standard hotel is fine, but will fall on deaf ears at a humble guesthouse. The very notion of service is alien to the majority of the Vietnamese, and vociferous complaining doesn't help. On the other hand, a smile can go a long way, open doors and win favours. The Vietnamese prefer a cooperative approach.

As with many other parts of Asia, Confucian attitudes remain strong, and seniority demands respect whatever the circumstances. The eldest male member of any group is invariably 'in charge'. At any party it is the eldest who is served first, gets to eat first and generally dictates the course of events.

Health and medical care

For travellers coming from Africa, the only vaccination required is for yellow fever. Immunisation against hepatitis (A and B), Japanese encephalitis and tetanus are strongly urged. It is a good idea to consult a doctor a month to six weeks before departing to leave enough time to get the injections.

Malaria (and Dengue) is widespread in Vietnam, especially in the Central Highlands and the Mekong Delta. The best protection is prevention. Always sleep under a mosquito net when visiting rural areas, use a strong repellent and wear long sleeves and trousers from dusk to dawn. Mosquitoes in several areas are resistant to many brands of anti-malaria drugs, so seek advice on medication from a tropical institute before you leave.

Do not drink tap water unless it has been boiled and avoid ice in drinks, especially in the country. Imported bottled water is available in most cities, but beware of bottles that are refilled with tap water.

Caution should be taken when eating, because food is often not prepared in sanitary conditions. Doctors advise abstaining from shellfish, especially shrimps. Fruit and vegetables should be peeled before eating; cooking them is a better idea. Avoid mayonnaise and raw eggs, raw vegetables like the herbs and lettuce served with *pho*, the noodle soup, and spring rolls. Eat in restaurants that are crowded. Because most places do not have refrigeration, eat at places where you know food will not be spoilt – if it is crowded, it is a good sign.

Should you have an accident or an emergency health problem in Vietnam, you may want to consider evacuation to Singapore or Bangkok for treatment. Vietnam has no shortage of well-trained doctors, but hospital services and supplies are

Emergency numbers

Fire Tel: 114
Information Tel: 1080
Medical aid Tel: 115
Police Tel: 13

in very short supply. It is essential to take out private medical insurance before you leave.

Hospitals and clinics

Hanoi
Hanoi French Hospital, 1 Phuong Mai St, Dong Da District, tel: 04-3577 1100, www.hfh.com.vn. A full service hospital that caters to French nationals and wealthy Vietnamese. The health-care services are expensive and of acceptable standards.
International SOS Clinic, 31 Hai Ba Trung St, Hoan Kiem District, tel: 04-3934 0666, www.internationalsos. com. The most expensive clinic in Hanoi. Staffed with international doctors and nurses. Refers patients abroad to Bangkok or Singapore for hospital treatments.
Vietnam-Korea Friendship Clinic, 12 Chu Van An St, Ba Dinh District, tel: 04-3843 7231. Excellent Korean-run clinic that is both affordable and clean. Has new facilities, and patients can choose either a Korean or Vietnamese doctor.

Ho Chi Minh City
Columbia Saigon, 8 Alexandre de Rhodes St, tel: 08-3829 8520, www.columbiaasia.com. Good reputation with international doctors and emergency evacuation.
HCMC Family Medical Practice, Diamond Plaza, 34 Le Duan St, tel: 08-3822 7848, www.vietnam medicalpractice.com. International doctors offering vaccinations, dental services and emergency evacuation.
International SOS Clinic, 65 Nguyen Du St, tel: 08-3829 8424, www.internationalsos.com. The top choice in the city has international doctors and 24-hour emergency services. Refers patients abroad to Bangkok or Singapore for hospital treatments.

Internet

Internet cafés with computer terminals are quickly losing popularity with the rapid proliferation of free Wi-fi, and the fact that most hotels have one or two computers with free access to the Internet

THAILAND

MYANMAR

LAOS

CAMBODIA

VIETNAM

MALAYSIA

BRUNEI

SINGAPORE

INDONESIA

PHILIPPINES

for their guests. Most Vietnamese cafés with indoor seating have free Wi-fi, as do many bars, restaurants and hotels that serve foreigners. Be aware that the government has banned online discussions of anything but personal information and blocks many blogs, political and news sites, as well as Facebook.

Media

All Vietnamese media must undergo a lengthy government censorship and approval process before they go public. But government-run newspapers have begun criticising corruption and some government policies.

Foreign newspapers and magazines can be purchased in larger bookstores in downtown HCMC and Hanoi, as well as some upscale hotels (although they aren't always current). Street vendors in tourist areas often sell second-hand copies too.

Vietnam has several English-language government-run newspapers, including *Viet Nam News* (www.vietnamnews.vn), *Vietnam Investment Review* (www.vir.com.vn), Thanh Nien (www.thanhniennews.com), *Vietnam Economic Times* (www.vneconomy.vn) – with a weekly supplement *The Guide* – and *Tui Tre* (www.tuoitrenews.vn).

Vietnam Pathfinder (www.pathfinder.com.vn) and *Vietnam Discovery* are free government publications for tourists. Also recommended is *The Word* (www.wordhcmc.com), an independent tourism and lifestyle magazine published by an expat in Vietnam. It is available free every month.

Voice of Vietnam (www.vov.org.vn) is the official government radio station. Two stations transmit English-language programmes on a variety of subjects several times a day on FM radio.

Most hotels, restaurants, bars and cafés now have cable or satellite television with access to Australia Network, Star TV, Discovery: Travel & Living, HBO, Cartoon Network, MTV Asia and more. In 2013 the government re-initiated attempts to censor foreign news such as CNN and BBC. As such these networks are not always available.

Money

The dong (pronounced *dome*) currently circulates in bank notes of 500,000, 100,000, 50,000, 20,000, 10,000 and banknotes and coins of 5,000, 2,000 and 1,000

Dong or dollars?

Although the government issued a decree that all transactions be conducted in Vietnamese dong, in reality the country still uses a dual-currency system. That is, most purchases can be made in US dollars as well as Vietnamese dong. However, often shops, restaurants and taxi drivers insist on a lower exchange rate when using dollars – such as 18,000 dong to US$1 instead of the current rate of exchange (about 21,000 dong to US$1). To avoid haggling, it is better to carry some Vietnamese dong with you.

denominations. The 200- and 100-dong banknotes are disappearing from use. The larger notes are made of polymer plastic ensuring a longer lifespan and fewer copies. Care should be taken when exchanging money or receiving change. The 20,000 dong notes and 5,000 notes (both widely used) are the same size and colour (blue) and easily confused.

All transactions are supposed to be conducted in Vietnamese dong; in practice, a dual-currency system exists. That is, most purchases can be made in US dollars as well as dong.

Vietnamese have an obsession with unblemished US dollars and larger dong notes. They will often refuse notes with tears or handwriting on them, although they can usually be turned in at banks. Counterfeiting of US notes $5 and higher, as well as VND100,000 and higher, is very common. Most of it actually comes through the government banks.

Credit cards and changing money

Major credit cards are accepted. Sometimes a high commission – three percent is standard – is charged when using them, however. Cash advances can be collected from major credit cards (again with the three percent commission) from major banks, including Vietcombank. ATMs can be found in all major cities.

Changing money on the street is never a good idea. Hotels, travel agencies, restaurants and cafés will also exchange dollars at bank rates. It is also possible to change dollars at almost any jewellery or gold shop; sometimes the rate is slightly higher than the bank rate. Look for a shop with the sign *Vang* (gold). Be prepared to be offered two exchange rates: one

One other potential problem is the quality of the notes. Although Vietnamese dong notes are often ripped, faded and crumpled, Vietnamese are reluctant to accept US dollars that are not crisp and new. Before taking US dollars from a bank, you should inspect them to make sure they have no stray marks or tears, or appear old.

Note: the Vietnamese currency is not convertible so you cannot legally bring in or take out dong as a foreigner. In practice though, it's no problem.

for denominations of 50 and 100 US dollars, and a lower rate for smaller denominations.

US dollar travellers' cheques are accepted in most banks and in major hotels, but not in shops and not in smaller hotels or any restaurants. Major credit cards are accepted at upscale hotels, restaurants, shops and many tour offices.

When you arrive in Vietnam, the Customs form requires you to note currency brought into the country if it is worth more than 3,000 US dollars.

Tipping and bargaining

Tipping is not traditional, although small gratuities are always welcome and it is becoming increasingly expected in venues that cater mostly to foreign tourists. But bargaining is usual (except in department stores and large hotels and restaurants). The impoverished Vietnamese see tourists as fair game for making a dong or two but remember you're probably haggling over a few cents.

Opening hours

Offices and public services generally open Monday to Friday from around 7.30 or 8am and close for lunch at around 11.30pm or noon, opening again around 1.30 or 2pm until 4.30 or 5pm.

Banks Monday to Friday 8am to 4pm in Hanoi and Ho Chi Minh City. Banks close for lunch in other cities from 11.30am to 1pm.

Shops are open from 8.30am until late in the evening seven days a week. **Food markets** generally close around 5pm.

Postal services

Post offices are open every day 7am–8pm. Every city, town and village has one of some sort, and the domestic service is remarkably reliable and fast (unlike for overseas mail). Within the country, mail reaches its destination within three days, sometimes faster. There is also an express mail service for overnight delivery.

Post offices are located at:
Hanoi 75 Pho Dinh Tien Hoang St, tel: 04-3825 7036 (domestic), 04-3825 2030 (international).
Ho Chi Minh City 2 Cong Xa Paris, tel: 08-3829 6555.
Hue 8 Hoang Hoa Tham St, tel: 054-382 3468.

Courier services

A number of international courier agencies have offices in Victnam:
DHL, tel: 04-3775 4438 (Hanoi), 08-3844 6203 (HCMC)
Fedex, tel: 04-719 8787 (Hanoi), 08-8119 055 (HCMC)
UPS, tel: 04-514 2888 (Hanoi), 08-997 2888 (HCMC)

Telephones

Vietnam upgraded its phone systems in October 2008 by adding an additional digit (which can be any number between 2 and 6) after the area code to all landline phone numbers.

Voice Over Internet Protocol is the standard method of placing overseas calls from Vietnam. Calls can be made in any Internet café, or via any telephone by first dialling 17100, followed by the country code and number. Rates average US$0.50 a minute.

Mobile phones

Local mobile phone numbers were not affected in the past telephone upgrade and still retain their 10 digits, starting with the prefix 09 (the most common being 090, 091, 095

and 098, with more added from time to time).

Most mobile phone users from overseas who have signed up for roaming with their service providers back home will be able to hook up with the GSM 900 or 1800 network that Vietnam uses. The exceptions are users from Japan and North America (unless they have a tri-band phone). It's best to check with your service provider. Alternatively, cheap phones using prepaid cards can be purchased in Vietnam for a few hundred thousand dong, along with a local number for an additional VND75,000. These prepaid cards are available at Vina-phone and Mobiphone shops, post offices, or any shop that sells mobile phones.

Tourist information

Vietnam's tourism industry lags behind other Asian countries (and for some travellers this may be a good thing). The official representative for Vietnam's tourism – domestically as well as overseas – comes under the purview of the government-operated Vietnam National Administration of Tourism (VNAT; www.vietnamtourism.com). However, it is more involved in the construction of new hotels and infrastructure development than in providing tourist services. State-run 'tourist offices' under the VNAT are merely tour agents out to make money and are not geared towards meeting the requirements of most travellers. For tours, car hire and travel-related information, you are better off with privately run travel and transport agencies.

Visas and passports

Nationals of 46 countries (at the time of press) are exempt from

The most important holiday is Tet, or Lunar New Year (late January/early February). It usually lasts for four days although the preparations begin weeks before, and the effects are felt for weeks after.

Other public holidays include:
1 January New Year's Day
10th day of the 3rd lunar month Hung Kings Day
30 April Liberation of Saigon
1 May International Labour Day
2 September National Day

visas when visiting Vietnam. Check the Vietnamese Ministry of Foreign Affairs website at www.mofa.gov.vn.

Vietnam increasingly restricts visas by price and duration. Most travellers apply for a one-month, single-entry tourist visa that costs a minimum US$45 (depending upon where you arrange it). Multiple-entry tourist visas up to six months in duration start at around US$180 and may only be available from Cambodia.

The easy way of getting a visa is to use the travel agent from whom you buy your air ticket.

Many travellers who stop over in Bangkok apply for visas there. Travel agents in Bangkok offer attractive round-trip flight and visa packages. The best place to acquire visas however, is Phnom Penh, where travel agencies can arrange to have both multiple-entry business and normal tourist visas issued in as little as 24 hours – depending upon how much you are willing to pay.

Websites

Vietnam National Administration of Tourism: www.vietnamtourism.com
Ministry of Foreign Affairs: www.mofa.gov.vn/en
Rusty Compass: www.rustycompass.com
The Word Hanoi: www.wordhanoi.com
Fish Egg Tree: www.fisheggtree.com
Regional Government & Tourist Sites:
Dalat: www.dalattourist.com.vn
Halong Bay: www.halong.org.vn
Hanoi: www.hanoi.gov.vn
Reviews of Hanoi's shops, restaurants and hotels along with classifieds:
www.newhanoian.com
Ho Chi Minh City: http://tourism.hochiminhcity.gov.vn
Mui Ne Beach: www.muinebeach.net

Hang Gai (Silk Street) in Hanoi.

MALAYSIA

TRANSPORT, ACCOMMODATION, EATING OUT, ACTIVITIES AND AN A–Z OF TRAVEL INFORMATION

FACT FILE

Situation Malaysia is divided into two: peninsular Malaysia extends southwards from Thailand to Singapore; East Malaysia (Sabah and Sarawak) covers the northern part of the island of Borneo.
Area 329,000 sq km (127,000 sq miles).
Capital Kuala Lumpur.
Population 29 million, comprising Malays, Chinese, Indians, indigenous groups and others. 21 million people live on the peninsula, with the rest in Sabah and Sarawak. Kuala Lumpur has around 2 million inhabitants.
Languages Bahasa Malaysia (Malay – official), Mandarin and Chinese dialects, Tamil and other Indian languages, indigenous languages, English is widely spoken.
Religion Islam, Buddhism, Taoism, Hinduism, Christianity, animism.
Time zone 8 hours ahead of Greenwich Mean Time (GMT). New York is 13 hours behind, Australia two hours ahead.
Currency Ringgit (RM). Approx 3.2 to US$1.
Weights and measures Metric
Electricity 220–40V, 50 cycles, using three square-pin plugs.
International dialling code 60

TRANSPORT

Getting there

By air

Malaysia is connected to international destinations by about 40 airlines.
Kuala Lumpur International Airport, or KLIA (tel: 03-03-8777 8888, www.

klia.com.my), located in Sepang 70km (43 miles) from the city centre, is the key gateway to the country.

Penang International Airport (www.penangairport.com, tel: 04-643 4411) is linked by direct international flights from several Asian cities, including Hong Kong, Bangkok and Singapore, while Langkawi (tel: 04-955 1311), Kuching (tel: 082-454 242) and Kota Kinabalu (tel: 088-238 555) airports are served by direct international flights from Singapore and other Asian destinations.

Malaysia Airlines (MAS), the national carrier (tel: 03-7843 3000, toll-free within Malaysia 1300-883 000, www.malaysiaairlines.com), flies from over 100 international and domestic destinations. Its low-cost arm, Firefly (tel: 03-7845 4543, www. fireflyz.com.my, daily 8am–9pm) has smaller planes servicing local and regional destinations.

Local budget airline **AirAsia** (24-hour call centre tel: 03-8775 4000, toll-free within Malaysia 1300-889 933, www.airasia.com) offers cheap fares online for both domestic and Asian destinations. Its long-haul subsidiary flies to Australia, London and China.

Note that there are several airports in Kuala Lumpur. Malaysia Airlines and international flights depart from KLIA while AirAsia flights (both domestic and international), Cebu Pacific and Tiger Airways depart from the Low Cost Carrier Terminal (LCC-T; tel: 03-8777 6777, http://lcct. klia.com.my), located about 20km (12 miles) from KLIA. Feeder buses running at 15-minute intervals link the two terminals.

Firefly operates from another airport, the Sultan Abdul Aziz Airport

in Subang (tel: 03-7845 3245), which is just on KL's outskirts.

By rail

Train services only operate within Peninsular Malaysia. The National Railways, or KTMB (tel: 03-2267 1200, www.ktmb.com.my) trains are clean, cheap and reliable. Trains are air-conditioned, and there are first- and second-class coaches, economy class options on some trains and bunks on the night trains. Railroads link Kuala Lumpur with Thailand in the north; Singapore in the south; and the east coast of the peninsula. The rail terminal in KL is KL Sentral.

If you are travelling from Thailand to KL, change trains in Hat Yai (southern Thailand) or Butterworth (northern Peninsular Malaysia). The express journey from Hat Yai takes about 20 hours and starts at RM48. To get to Langkawi, get off at Alor Setar or Arau and take a taxi to the ferry terminal to the island. To get to Penang island, catch a taxi, bus or ferry from Butterworth. A less-travelled route is via the east coast through the Thai town of Sungai Golok and the town of Rantau Panjang in Kelantan, from where you can take a bus or taxi to the Pasir Mas train station.

The train journey from Singapore's Woodlands Train Checkpoint to Kuala Lumpur takes eight hours and costs RM70 (first class). The express journey takes about 20 hours and costs RM150 (first class).

By road

From Singapore: The peninsula is linked to Singapore by two causeways: the **Johor–Singapore Causeway** from Woodlands (Singapore) to Johor Bahru, and the **Second Link** from Tuas (Singapore)

THAILAND
MYANMAR
LAOS
CAMBODIA
VIETNAM
MALAYSIA
BRUNEI
SINGAPORE
INDONESIA
PHILIPPINES

to Tanjung Kupang. From these two points, you can connect to the North–South Expressway, which runs along the west coast.

In Singapore, buses to Peninsular Malaysia depart from Beach Road (outside Golden Mile Complex), Lavender Street and Queen Street. The bus journey to Kuala Lumpur takes about five to six hours and costs RM80–100. **Pudu Sentral** is the main bus terminal for the cheaper bus services in Kuala Lumpur. Several of the pricier operators depart and terminate at various places in both cities. These include **Aeroline** (tel: 03-6258 8800, Singapore tel: 65-6733 7010, www.aeroline.com.my; departs from Harbourfront Centre and terminates at Corus Hotel on Jalan Ampang and in Petaling Jaya); **First Coach** (tel: 03-2287 3311, Singapore tel: 65-6822 2111, www.firstcoach. com.my; departs from Novena or The Plaza and terminates at Bangsar or Bandar Utama); **Nice Executive Coach** (tel: 03-2272 1586, www. nice-coaches.com.my, departs from Mackenzie Road and terminates at the old railway station); **Odyssey** (tel: 1300-888 121, Singapore 1800-639 7739, www.odysseynow. com.my, departs from Balestier Plaza and terminates at Mont Kiara); and **Transnasional** (tel: 1300-888 582, Singapore tel: 65-6294 7035, www.transnasional.com.my, departs Lavender Street and terminates at the Terminal Bersepadu Selatan, Bandar Tasik Selatan).

These companies use the more expensive VIP or Executive (24-seater) express coaches, which have comfortable reclining seats, drinks and meals on board. Cheaper non-express coaches make several stops on the way, including a 30-minute meal stop.

To get to Johor's Senai Airport from Singapore, passengers can catch the yellow **Causeway Link Express** coaches from Singapore's Kranji MRT Station to City Lounge in Johor Bahru, then transfer to the white **Causeway Link Express** coaches to Senai Airport. The total cost is about RM9. For more information, visit www. senaiairport.com.

If you opt for long-distance taxis, take SBS Transit bus 160 or 170, SMRT bus 950 or the Malaysian-operated Causeway Link buses to Johor Bahru and catch a taxi from there.

From Thailand: The North–South Expressway ends in **Bukit Kayu Hitam** (Kedah), the main border crossing between Malaysia and Thailand. Other border crossings are at **Padang Besar** (Perlis) and **Rantau Panjang** (Kelantan). Buses and taxis serve these points.

Buses from Thailand travel along the peninsula's west coast from Hat Yai. The journey to Kuala Lumpur takes about nine hours and costs RM50–65. Many buses from Hat Yai, Bangkok and Phuket also terminate in Penang, from where you can take a local express bus. The east coast

route is via Sungai Kolok (Thailand) and Kota Bharu.

Sarawak

A road goes from Pontianak in Kalimantan, Indonesia, to Kuching. This route (10 hours) is serviced by regular buses. Miri is joined by a long coastal road to Brunei's capital, Bandar Seri Begawan.

Getting around

On arrival

Buses and taxis operate from airports in Malaysia. Many airports, including Kuala Lumpur, Penang, Kuching and Kota Kinabalu, have taxi desks where you purchase a coupon; the price is fixed. KLIA is also linked by the very fast KLIA Ekspres train (daily 5am–midnight, tel: 03-2267 8000) to the Central Air Terminal (CAT) within the KL Sentral transport hub in the capital. If you are flying with Malaysia Airlines, Cathay Pacific or Royal Brunei, you may check in at the CAT. The KL Sentral transport hub also uses a coupon system. Elsewhere, enquire about fares at the information desk.

By air

Malaysia Airlines (tel: 03-7846 3000, toll-free within Malaysia 1300-883 000, www.malaysiaairlines.com), runs an extensive network of airways over the entire nation. In Kuala Lumpur, all MAS domestic flights operate out of KLIA.

Air Asia (tel: 03-2171 9222, www.airasia.com) offers low-fare flights throughout Malaysia, with hubs in Johor Baru, Kuching and Kota Kinabalu. The airline operates out of the LCC-T and from Terminal 2 at Kota Kinabalu International Airport.

Firefly (tel: 03-7845 4543, daily 8am–9pm, www.fireflyz.com. my) services 10 local destinations while Berjaya Air (tel: 03-2119 6616, www.berjaya-air.com, Mon–Fri 8am–7pm) flies to Langkawi, Tioman, Redang and Pangkor islands. Both airlines use small planes and operate from the Sultan Abdul Aziz (Subang) Airport in KL. Berjaya Air also offers flights from Singapore to Redang and Tioman.

By Rail

Train services, available only in Peninsular Malaysia, are operated by the **National Railways**, or **KTMB** (tel: 03-2267 1200, www.ktmb.com.my). Express services stop only at major towns; the others stop everywhere.

Water transport

Around the peninsula, boats are the chief means of travel to the islands and in parts of the interiors. Regular ferries service the islands of Pangkor (7am–8.30pm), Penang (6am–midnight) and Langkawi (7am–7pm). Ferries service Langkawi (Kuah Jetty) from Kuala Perlis between 7am and 7pm (45 minutes), tel: 04-985 2690; from Kuala Kedah between 7am and 7pm (one and a half hours), tel: 04-762 6295; and twice a day from Penang at 8.15am (three hours) via Pulau Payar and at 8.30am. During the monsoon months of July to September, seas can be choppy, and services may be cancelled.

From the Lumut Ferry Terminal, there are ferries to Pulau Pangkor, Pulau Sembilan and Pulau Jarak. There are also ferry services to Belawan, a town in Medan,

Indonesia. For more information, contact Tourism Jetty Centre at tel: 05-680 4000.

Boats out to islands on the east coast generally do not follow schedules, and in the monsoon season (November to February), services may stop altogether. Note that the sea can be choppy just before and after the monsoon period and services may be cancelled.

In the northeast, services begin between 8.30 and 9am and stop between 2.30pm and 2am. Other than during public and school holidays, it is generally fine to arrive on the Perhentian islands (from Kuala Besut) and Kapas (from Marang) without having booked your accommodation, but it is safer to pre-book accommodation, and therefore boats, at Redang and Tenggol (from Merang and Kuala Dungun respectively).

The west coast rail line goes from Singapore through Kuala Lumpur to Butterworth (Penang) and joins Thailand at Padang Besar, Kedah. The Ekspres Rakyat departs every morning from Singapore to Butterworth and vice versa. Ekspres Sinaran Pagi is the other morning service and links KL and Butterworth.

The night express trains are the Senandung Malam sleepers servicing KL–Singapore and KL–Butterworth, and Senandung Langkawi servicing KL–Hat Yai.

The east coast line branches off at Gemas in Johor, heads through the central forests and emerges at Tumpat in Kelantan, close to the Thai border. Only a few trains – the Ekspres Timuran Singapore–Tumpat and Ekspres Wau KL–Tumpat (via Gemas) take this route.

Public transport

Taxi

Taxis remain one of the most popular and cheap means of transport. You can hail them by the roadside, from taxi stands, or book them by phone, in which case, mileage is calculated from where the vehicle is hired.

Although most taxis in the main towns are fitted with meters, not all drivers use them, especially during peak periods (the start and end of the work day); drivers in Kuala Lumpur are especially notorious for ripping off tourists. Make sure that your driver is willing to use his meter, or negotiate a charge at the beginning of the journey.

There is a surcharge for a telephone booking, more than two passengers, luggage, traffic jams and toll charges. Trips between midnight and 6am will have a 50 percent surcharge.

From most airports and railway stations, taxi fares are fixed and you should prepay at the taxi counter. Reliable call taxi services in KL are **Comfort Taxi** (tel: 03-2692 2525), **Public Cab** (tel: 03-2095 3399) and **Sunlight Radio Taxi** (tel: 03-9057 1111) and in Penang, Georgetown

Railpass

For foreign tourists (except Singaporeans), KTMB offers a **Visit Malaysia Rail Pass** for travel over a period of 5, 10 or 15 days on KTMB services in Peninsular Malaysia (and Singapore). For information, contact KTMB (tel: 03-2267 1200, www.ktmb.com.my).

Taxi (tel: 04-229 5788) and Sunshine (tel: 04-642 5961).

Bus

Three types of buses operate in Malaysia: the non-air-conditioned buses that travel between the states, the non-air-conditioned buses that provide services within each state, and the air-conditioned express buses connecting major towns in Malaysia. Only express buses adhere to the schedule; others are frequent from 9am to 6pm. Buses within towns and cities usually charge fares according to distance covered.

Travelling by bus is definitely not for the faint-hearted. Except for interstate services, timetables are a mystery to most, and listings of the stops or final destinations of each route are equally elusive, save for the signs carried on the front of each individual vehicle. The exceptions are KL's RapidKL (tel: 03-7885 2585, www.rapidkl.com.my) and Penang's RapidPenang (tel: 04-238 1313, www.rapidpg.com.my) bus company, which has information and routes online. However, drivers play daredevil in attempting to meet their quotas, irrespective of traffic laws and other road users.

In KL, north- and southbound services are found at the **Puduraya Bus Station** (tel: 03-2070 0145) on Jalan Pudu; coaches to the east coast depart from the **Putra Bus Station** (opposite the Putra World Trade Centre); and the interior destinations such as Kuala Lipis are serviced from the **Pekeliling Bus Station** (tel: 03-442 1256) on Jalan Pekeliling. Some southbound buses leave from Hentian **Duta** (tel: 03-4041 4642) on Jalan Duta.

In Penang, interstate buses depart from the Sungai Nibong Express Bus Terminal near the Penang Bridge. Kuching interstate buses leave from the 3½-mile Kuching Bus Terminal on Jalan Penrissen. In Kota Kinabalu, interstate buses heading south leave from the terminal near Bandaran Berjaya while northern and eastern bound buses leave from the Kota Kinabalu North Bus Terminal; alternatively, take a van or minibus.

Train

Kuala Lumpur has excellent rail services that should be used to avoid traffic jams. These include the KTM Komuter, run by KTMB, which services greater KL and the Klang Valley; the Light Rail transport (LRT), which services the old city centre and Petaling Jaya, and the Monorail,

which covers the west and northern parts of KL.

Boat

River transport is an important – and interesting – means of getting around Sarawak. The Kuching to Sibu Express departs from the Pending jetty; you can change here to go to Kapit. Express boats also take you from Miri to the Mulu National Park. In Sabah, boats are an alternative route to Kinabatangan from Sandakan.

Private transport

Car rental

Having your own transport gives you the freedom to explore places off the beaten track at your leisure. Peninsular Malaysia has an excellent network of trunk roads and a dual-carriageway on the west coast. Driving is also enjoyable in Sabah and Sarawak, but you need a sturdy vehicle or even a four-wheel drive, and plenty of time. Visitors need an international driving licence.

But beware that normally friendly Malaysian drivers can be speed maniacs and bullies, especially in towns – the bigger the vehicle, the more so. Give way. Motorcyclists can also shoot out of nowhere or hog the road.

Cars are usually for rent on an unlimited mileage basis. Weekly rates are also available. The Automobile Association of Malaysia (AAM) is the national motoring organisation and has offices in most states. It has a breakdown service, tel: 03-2161 0808.

The big car rental firms are listed here. Most have branches in the main towns throughout Malaysia. **Avis Rent A Car**, tel: 1800-882 847, www.avis.com.my. **Hertz Rent A Car**, tel: 1800-883 086, www.hertz-malaysia.com. **Pacific Rent A Car**, tel: 03-2287 4118/9, www.iprac.com.

ACCOMMODATION

Choosing a hotel

Malaysia offers an abundance of accommodation options. There are international brands, home-grown chains, resort-themed and boutique establishments, serviced apartments as well as simple resthouses and backpacker hostels. With plenty of choices around, accommodation – even at the higher end of the scale – remains remarkably affordable.

Hotels are rated 1 to 5 stars according to international criteria such as size, facilities, number of staff and safety. For details, visit the Malaysian Association of Hotels website (www.hotels.org.my).

Always enquire about packages, which may include a buffet or local breakfast and sometimes tours and entrance fees to attractions, with the room. If you stay more than one night, you can try bargaining for better rates. Most hotels are fine with triple-share. Hotels are required to display nett rates (including the 10 percent service and 5 percent government taxes).

At the lowest end are dormitories at RM30–40 depending on location and whether the room is air-conditioned or fan-cooled. There are also higher-end 'flashpacker' outfits, and beachside Malay village-style chalets; these go from RM80 to more than RM150 and are sometimes equipped with TV, air conditioning and hot showers.

Mid-range hotels (RM300) come in traditional hotel blocks or chalets, and are popular with locals. The higher-end ones generally have full room facilities and services while the top hotel chains and resorts come complete with the usual full room facilities and services, spas and gourmet restaurants (rooms are RM300–500; rooms in luxury hotels can be upwards of RM800). Another option in the medium to upper range are serviced apartments.

Book in advance for stays over long weekends, Malaysian and Singaporean school holidays, public holidays – particularly Chinese New Year and Hari Raya Puasa, the Formula 1 Grand Prix period – and the super-peak months of July and August when Arab tourists flock to the country. There is usually a surcharge during these periods too. Internet rates are usually lower than walk-in or call-in rates.

Kuala Lumpur's budget hotels are mainly located in the Petaling Street and Bukit Bintang areas, while the medium-class and luxury accommodation is in the business and shopping areas along Jalan Sultan Ismail, Jalan Bukit Bintang and the Kuala Lumpur City Centre.

In **Georgetown**, some of the gorgeous pre-war buildings serve as 'nostalgia' and boutique hotels. The bigger hotels cater to the business sector, while budget and backpackers' accommodation is along Lebuh Leith and Lebuh Chulia. Beach accommodation is plentiful in Batu Ferringhi.

Kuching's accommodation is mostly east of the Waterfront along Jalan Tunku Abdul Rahman and Jalan Ban Hock. **Miri** has a lot of budget accommodation sprinkled throughout the city, with higher-end hotels and resorts being more recent additions. **Kota Kinabalu**'s five-star facilities are by the coast, while its budget and medium-cost accommodation is downtown.

Parks generally offer basic chalet-type accommodation, some run by the Forestry or Wildlife Department, but there are increasingly luxury options available. Likewise, islands have a range available.

Open-air *pasar malam* (night markets) are great for soaking up the local atmosphere and finding bargain-price items, including clothes (which you try on in the open), shoes, trinkets, CDs, DVDs (often pirated) and household items. You can usually buy fresh produce, including fruit, and delicious local street food and snacks. The traders are itinerant, so check locations in the local press or at your hotel.

EATING OUT

Malaysia's food is among the tastiest and most diverse in the world, drawing from the great Asian culinary traditions of China and India, as well as the Malay spice island that once fuelled global trade. On top of that are numerous regional variations, unique concoctions such as Nonya cuisine, as well as contemporary options. At the same time, international food is readily available, especially in Kuala Lumpur.

Malay cooking uses a slew of spices, with the classic dish being the rice and chilli breakfast favourite, *nasi lemak*. Nonya cuisine is an intriguing blend of Chinese and Malay cuisines, and is best enjoyed in Melaka and Penang. Cantonese, Hokkien and Hakka variations make up the Chinese cuisine palette, while Indian food ranges from the South Indian banana leaf meals to the popular Indian-Muslim rice and curries.

The best local food is often served in hawker stalls, sold on the streets or in coffee shops, although sometimes you can get authentic preparations in restaurants. All of Malaysia's medium- and top-class hotels have decent restaurants, with some of the nation's best found in five-star hotels. Hotels at the very top of the range will probably have at least one Western outlet. Note that large restaurants charge a 10 percent government tax and five percent service tax, and prices are higher in Sabah and Sarawak.

Hotels also usually offer high tea on weekends, and their coffee houses serve buffet breakfast, lunch and sometimes dinner. Fast food such as McDonald's, KFC and Burger King are everywhere, likewise coffee house chains like Starbucks and local varieties like Coffeebean and Ipoh Old Town Whitecoffee.

Boarding in Kota Kinabalu.

A traditional longhouse in Sarawak.

Breakfast is usually served 6–10.30am, lunch 11.30am–2.30pm, and dinner 6.30–11pm. Some street stalls open until early morning, and some Indian-Muslim eateries 24 hours. Local coffee and tea pack a punch, and may be too sweet for unsuspecting drinkers as they are sometimes served with condensed milk and sugar, so specify otherwise.

Alcohol is expensive in Malaysia compared to some other Asian destinations. While it is forbidden for Muslims, it is freely available in non-Muslim eateries and supermarkets. It is however not as freely available in the conservative Islamic states of Terengganu, Kelantan and Kedah.

ACTIVITIES

The arts

Museums

Traditional museums in Malaysia are still mainly government-run, but there are an increasing number of government-funded and private museums catering to specialised subjects. Some of these subjects are of historical and cultural significance, such as the Islamic Arts Museum in Kuala Lumpur, Baba Nyonya Heritage Museum in Melaka and Gopeng Museum in Perak. Others are collections of general interest such as the National Automobile Museum (Sepang, tel: 03-8787 4759)

and Penang Toy Museum, which is especially fun for children (next to Copthorne Orchid Hotel, Tanjung Bungah, mobile tel: 012-460 2096).

Most museums are open 9am–6pm daily, except for Fridays when they are closed between noon–2.30pm. Admission is free or at a nominal fee. Tours are rare, and information is usually in English and Bahasa Malaysia. Permission to view archives not on display can be obtained by consulting the curator, **Department of Museums**, tel: 03-2267-1000, www.jmm.gov.my.

Art galleries

Malaysian artwork covers an infinitesimal range of topics and styles, from nostalgia for the traditional way of life, to abstract political pieces and pop art as well as batik painting, which was born in Malaysia.

Most artists are homegrown; some have gained significant international exposure, and many more are emerging. Exhibitions by overseas artists, including regional talent, can also be found. KL has the most vibrant art scene, followed by Penang, with numerous exhibition spaces. Art spaces are as diverse, from the **National Art Gallery** at 2 Jalan Temerloh, off Jalan Tun Razak (www. artgallery.gov.my, tel: 03-4025 4990, daily 10am–6pm; free), which houses more than 2,500 pieces of artwork the country deems Malaysian from the 1930s to the present time; to the cutting-edge experimental Annexe in Central Market (tel: 03-2070 1137).

Theatre and music

Theatre and dance groups are most active in Kuala Lumpur and Penang, with notable intercultural works that engage both Asian and Western forms to showcase traditional aspects of Malaysian life in startling ways. The main theatre venues in KL are the Kuala Lumpur Performing Arts Centre and Istana Budaya, and in Penang, the Dewan Sri Pinang and the Actors Studio Greenhall. Traditional performances tend to be limited to tourist venues in the state capitals.

International Western classical music acts perform at KL's Dewan Filharmonik Petronas (www.mpo. com.my), while jazz, underground music and live music acts perform in bars, clubs, hotels and some theatre spaces.

For listings and happenings, check out the newspapers and lifestyle magazines like *Timeout Kuala Lumpur* (www.timeoutkl.com), www.cinema online.com.my, or www.kakiseni.com.

Nightlife

Pubs, clubs and karaoke dens sums up the nightlife in Malaysia. The best nightlife is in the capital, and it is among the best in the region. Elsewhere, the action concentrates in hotel lounges and clubs. Other than in Kuala Lumpur, people tend not to dress up, but shorts and sandals are definite no-nos.

Live bands are popular and almost all the larger hotels have bars featuring live music, which usually begins at around 10pm. This is usually broad-appeal, middle-of-the-road music. Clubs attract DJs from all over the world, and most clubs adhere to the 21-year-old age limit (the legal drinking age in Malaysia), but there are cases where this is openly flouted.

Happy hour is usually 5.30–9pm, when drinks are at half price, which should be taken advantage of since alcohol is very expensive in Malaysia.

Nightlife in the capital tends to congregate in specific areas; the main ones are **Jalan Sultan Ismail/Jalan Ampang**, **Asian Heritage Row** around **Jalan Doraisamy**, **Bukit Bintang**, **Bangsar**, and **Sri Hartamas**.

Shopping

From international brands to handcrafted ethnic artworks, Malaysia offers variety and choice for shoppers of every budget. The best times to shop are during the annual six-week Malaysia Mega Sale Carnival that starts in July and the month-long Savings Sale beginning in November, when prices are slashed up to 70 percent. Throughout the year, sales are also held by the large department stores.

Shopping malls are found in every city and usually comprise a supermarket, department store, and smaller stores selling clothing, shoes, watches, electrical goods, computers, mobile phones, books and more. The larger ones also have tour agencies, cineplexes and video game arcades, as well as eateries, including food courts selling hawker fare, Western fast-food chains, and restaurants.

KL has the largest range of products and Langkawi has duty-free shopping, but lacks the variety of the mainland. Meanwhile, prices in Sabah and Sarawak are higher than in the peninsula.

A–Z

Budgeting for your trip

Travelling in Malaysia is relatively cheap. If you arrive at KLIA and want to go to Kuala Lumpur's city centre, the taxi fare is around RM100. If you are travelling light, you may want to catch a bus or the train (ERL) instead.

Accommodation prices generally start from RM40 a night in budget places to over RM700 a night in five-star hotels. Many hotels include breakfast with the room rate. For those who stay in three-star accommodation and are prepared to eat with the locals, expect to pay about RM300 per day for lodging, transport and meals.

National park accommodation in Sabah is more expensive than in Sarawak, where dormitory beds can cost as much as RM180.

Good food of excellent value can be found at hawker centres, coffee shops and food courts in shopping complexes, where RM7–8 can buy you a meal and a non-alcoholic drink. At the other end of the scale are fine-dining establishments where the prices reflect the quality of food and service on offer. Alcoholic drinks are expensive; expect to pay at least RM6.50 for a beer in a coffee shop and up to around RM20 in luxury hotels and nightclubs. A glass of wine costs upwards of RM25 at moderately priced restaurants where a meal for two could total over RM200.

Public transport is cheap (RM1–4) and taxi fares are moderate (RM15) within the city. Although required by law, meters are not always used, especially during peak hours. Bargaining may be required. In such cases, make sure the price is agreed on before entering the taxi. In Kuala Lumpur, there is a 50 percent surcharge for taxi trips between midnight and 6am. Car hire is reasonably priced, but parking in city centres and five-star hotels is very expensive.

Climate

Malaysia's weather is generally hot and sunny all year round, with temperatures averaging 32°C (90°F) during the day and 24°C (75°F) at night. Humidity is high at 80 percent. Temperatures in the highland areas, such as Cameron Highlands and the Kinabalu Park, are lower.

The monsoon season of April/May brings heavy rain to the west coast of Peninsular Malaysia. The east coast of the peninsula and Sabah and Sarawak experience their monsoon season between November and February. The inter-monsoon periods can also be wet. Light showers come and go, helping to relieve the heat.

Thick haze has been recurrent from July to October, especially for the Klang Valley, Sabah and Sarawak, for some years. Most of the smoke and soot is blown in by the southwest monsoon from parts of Indonesia hit by forest fires, which have been worsened by the dry weather caused by the El Niño phenomenon.

What to bring

There is very little need to worry about leaving something important

Emergency numbers

Tel: **999** (or 112 from a mobile phone) for ambulance or police.

behind when you visit Malaysia. Bring sunglasses and personal medication but toiletries, medicines, clothes, suntan lotion and straw hats are all readily available in most towns, and definitely in the large cities. In fact, the best advice is to take as little as possible so that you can travel lightly.

If you are planning to visit the highlands, a light sweater would be a good idea for the cooler evenings. If you're embarking upon the Mount Kinabalu climb, pack warmer clothing and gloves, but all these items can be found in the major cities.

Camping gear is often available for hire in national parks, but it is also in great demand; so campers should bring a lightweight tent. If you intend to go jungle trekking, make sure you bring good and light walking shoes, a light raincoat, a water bottle and water proofing for camera/video equipment (alternatively, a plastic bag will do).

Sanitary products for women are available but tampons and condoms are not easy to come by in small towns.

What to bring/wear

Light and loose clothes work best in Malaysia's climate, so pack cottons and natural fibres. Shoes should be removed before entering temples and homes, so slip-ons are handy. Shorts and T-shirts are generally acceptable, including in shopping malls. KL-ites do tend to dress up on a night out. Women should dress more conservatively when entering places of worship, and outside of cities. Topless sunbathing is a no-no.

Because of the heat and humidity, business dress in Malaysia is often casual. Standard formal office wear for men is dark trousers and a light-coloured long-sleeved shirt and tie without a jacket, but bring one in case you need it. Some women also wear skirt or trouser suits but most wear dresses and long-sleeved blouses and skirts.

Customs regulations

Import duties seldom affect the average traveller, who may bring in 225g (0.5lb) of tobacco, 50 cigars, or 200 cigarettes, and a 1-litre bottle of liquor duty-free as well as personal items.

On rare occasions, visitors may be asked to pay a deposit for temporary importation of dutiable goods (up to 30 percent of the value), which is refundable upon departure. Be sure to get an official receipt for any tax or deposit paid.

Pornography, firearms and ammunition are strictly prohibited. The export of antiques requires a licence from the Museum Department. Possession of narcotics and other illegal drugs carries the death sentence.

Embassies and consulates

Australia
6 Jalan Yap Kwan, Seng, KL, tel: 03-2146 5555, www.malaysia.embassy.gov.au
Canada
17th Floor, Menara Tan &Tan, Jalan Tun Razak, KL, tel: 03-2178 2333, www.canadainternational.gc.ca
New Zealand
Level 21 Menara IMC, Jalan Sultan Ismail, tel: 03-2078 2533, www.nzembassy.com
United Kingdom
186 Jalan Ampang, 50450 KL, tel: 03-2170 2200, www.ukinmalaysia.fco.gov.uk
United States
376 Jalan Tun Razak, 50400 KL, tel: 03-2168 5000, http://malaysia.usembassy.gov

Etiquette

Shoes must be removed before entering any place of worship. Conservative clothing is advisable and some mosques provide free robes. Certain areas are also prohibited to non-Muslims. People entering a Sikh Gurdwara must cover their hair. Be particularly sensitive about photographing worshippers in prayer.

Some Muslims do not shake hands with members of the opposite sex. A simple nod or smile will suffice. If you get what you think is a limp handshake, it is actually a Malay greeting (salam). If invited to a Malaysian home, remove your shoes before entering. Publicly kissing and fondling are generally frowned upon, especially outside cities.

Health and medical care

Travellers have little to worry about in a country where the health standards are ranked among the highest in Asia. Visitors are advised to take out private medical insurance before they leave.

Drink only boiled water. Bottled drinks are widely available. Avoid iced water from roadside stalls. Drink sufficiently to avoid dehydration; make sure you have more liquids than you would normally if you're coming from a temperate country.

Medical treatment

All large towns have hospitals with outpatient and accident and emergency services, as well as government and private clinics. Travel and health insurance, as well as documents concerning allergies to certain drugs should also be carried. Dental treatment is also easily available in the bigger towns and is of high quality.

Below are details of some general hospitals:
Kuala Lumpur, Jalan Pahang, tel: 03-2615 555, www.hkl.gov.my.
Kuching, Kuching Specialist Hospital, tel: 082-365 777.
Kota Kinabalu, (Hospital Queen Elizabeth), Jalan Penampang, tel: 089-212 111.
Langkawi, Bukit Teguh, tel: 04-966 3333.
Miri, **Miri City Medical Centre**, Jalan Hokkien, tel: 085-426 622, www.mcmcmiri.com.
Penang, **Adventist Hospital**, George Town, tel: 04-222 7200, www.pah.com.my.
Sandakan, (Hospital Duchess of Kent), KM 3.2 Jalan Utara, tel: 089-212 111.

Internet

Most hotels across the price range offer free Internet access in their common areas and increasingly in rooms. Cybercafés with broadband or Wi-fi internet access can be found everywhere, especially in tourist areas.

Media

The main daily English-language newspapers are *The New Straits Times* and *The Star*. Business papers include *The Edge* and *Business Times*. The *Malay Mail* is an afternoon tabloid with a more chatty, local slant. Sabah and Sarawak have their own papers, including *The New Sabah Times*, *Daily Express*, *Sarawak Tribune* and *Borneo Post*. Online news sites are more

Breakfast with the papers in Kuala Lumpur's Chinatown.

THAILAND

MYANMAR

LAOS

CAMBODIA

VIETNAM

MALAYSIA

BRUNEI

SINGAPORE

INDONESIA

PHILIPPINES

liberal and have a wide following; these include http://malaysiakini.com and http://themalaysianinsider.com. International newspapers such as the *International Herald Tribune* and *Wall Street Journal* can be bought at the bigger city newsstands.

Money

The ringgit (Malaysian dollar) is available in RM1, 5, 10, 20, 50 and 100 notes. There are 1, 5, 10, 20, 50 sen and RM1 coins. There are approximately 3.4 ringgit to the US dollar.

Most currencies can be exchanged for ringgit, but the popular ones are US dollars, pounds sterling, euros and Singapore dollars. Banks and licensed moneychangers offer better exchange rates than hotels and shops, where a service charge may be levied (usually 2–4 percent).

Credit cards are widely accepted in major cities. Note that some retailers add a three percent surcharge for the privilege of using plastic – so ask first before paying. Make sure that you have enough cash before you leave for smaller towns or remote areas.

Tipping

Tipping is not obligatory as bills usually include a 15 percent charge. However, tips are appreciated. Porters are usually tipped RM2–5, restaurant staff, loose change or the rounding of the bill to the nearest denomination of 10. Obviously, you may tip according to how you feel about the service quality.

Opening hours

In an Islamic nation with a colonial past, the definition of the working week varies. It runs from Monday to Friday in all states except Terengganu, Kelantan, Kedah and Perlis, which practise a half-day on Thursday and close on Friday, the usual Sunday.

The working day begins at 8am and ends at 5pm, with time off on Friday from noon to 2.30pm for Muslim prayers. Hours are shorter during the Ramadan fasting month. Most private businesses stick to the nine-to-five routine. Shops start to close at 6pm, but large supermarkets, department stores and shopping malls are open 10am–9.30pm.

Postal services

The Malaysian postal service (www.pos.com.my) is reliable and offers all

Public holidays

1 January New Year's Day
1 February Federal Territory Day (Federal Territories of Kuala Lumpur, Putrajaya and Labuan only)
5 March Ishak and Mikraj (Kedah and Negeri Sembilan only)
1 May Labour Day
29 May Dayak Day (Hari Gawai) (Sarawak only)
30–31 May Harvest Festival (Federal Territory of Labuan and Sabah only)
5 June Birthday of Yang di-Pertuan Agong (King)
31 August National Day
25 December Christmas Day
Variable public holidays that are determined by lunar calendars are Chinese New Year (Jan/Feb), Thaipusam (end Jan, for KL, Selangor, Penang, Perak, Negeri Sembilan and Johor), Deepavali (Oct/Nov), Hari Raya Aidilfitri, Hari Raya Haji and Prophet Muhammad's birthday. The different states also declare a public holiday on the birthday of their respective sultans and Yang di-Pertua (governors).

types of services, including registered mail, parcel delivery and courier services. There are post offices everywhere. These are generally open Mon–Fri 8am–5.30pm, with some opening Sat 8am–1pm.

International courier services include **DHL** (tel: 1800-888 388), **Fedex** (tel: 1800-886 363) and UPS (tel: 1800-1800-88).

Telephones

Rooms in larger hotels have phones with International Direct Dialling (IDD) facility. To call overseas, dial 00 followed by the country code, area code and phone number. The country code for Malaysia is 60. To call a Malaysian fixed-line number from abroad, dial your international access code, followed by 60 and the local area code, omitting the initial 0, then the number you want.

To make a call to a number within a state, simply dial the number without the area code. For a call to another state, dial the area code with the initial 0 and the number you want.

Public phones

Calls from a public phone cost 10 sen per three minutes, but phone booths are poorly maintained. Some

shops and restaurants offer payphone services – but charge more.

Mobile phones

Most visitors bring their own mobile phone with them, which will automatically hook up to one of Malaysia's service providers. Otherwise, prepaid local SIM cards, with which you get a local mobile number, are very affordable, starting at RM8.50 for registration and airtime.

Tourist information

In Malaysia

Tourism Malaysia (24-hour infoline within Malaysia: 1-300-88-5050, www.tourism.gov.my) has offices throughout Malaysia, including the following:
Kuala Lumpur Head Office
Head Office, 9th Floor No. 2, Tower 1, Jalan P5/6 Precinct 5, Putrajaya, tel: 03-8891 8000

Malaysia Tourist Information Centre (MTC), 109 Jalan Ampang KL, tel: 03-9235 4848
Terengganu
11 Ground and 1st Floor, Pusat Niaga Paya, Penang
Level 56, KOMTAR, Penang, tel: 04-264 3494
Johor
L3–26, Level 3, Johor Tourism, Information Centre, 2 Jalan Ayer Molek, Johor Bahru, tel: 07-222 3591
Sabah
Lot 1-0-7, Tingkat Bawah, Blok 1 Lorong Api-Api 1, Api-Api Centre, tel: 088-248 698
Sarawak
2nd Floor, Rugayah Building, Jalan Song Thian Cheok, Kuching, tel: 082-246 575

Visas and passports

Passports must be valid for at least six months at the time of entry. Check the **Immigration Department** website (www.imi.gov.my) for details about formalities and visa requirements, as conditions may change from time to time.

A social single-entry visa valid for three months can be applied for at Malaysian diplomatic missions overseas. Citizens of Commonwealth countries (except Bangladesh, Cameroon, Ghana, Mozambique, Nigeria, Pakistan and Sri Lanka) do not require a visa if their stay does not exceed a certain period. Citizens of the US, Singapore and Brunei do not need a visa.

BRUNEI

TRANSPORT, ACCOMMODATION, EATING OUT, ACTIVITIES AND AN A–Z OF TRAVEL INFORMATION

FACT FILE

Situation A small state on the North coast of the island of Borneo, entirely surrounded on the landward side by Malaysia and facing onto the South China Sea.
Area 5,770 sq km (2,228 sq miles).
Terrain Around 70 per cent of Brunei is rainforest.
Capital Bandar Seri Begawan (BSB).
Population 412,000, of whom around 66 percent are Malays and 11 percent Chinese. The rest are indigenous tribes. About 20 percent of residents are foreigners.
Languages Malay, but most people also speak English; Chinese and indigenous dialects are spoken within the respective ethnic groups.
Religion Islam is the official religion, Christianity, Buddhism and other religions are also practised.
Time zone 8 hours ahead of Greenwich Mean Time (GMT).
Currency Brunei dollar (B$), pegged to the Singapore dollar at 1:1 (or $0.80 US dollars). Both currencies can be used.
Weights and measures Metric
Electricity 220–240V, using three square-pin plugs.
International dialling code 673

TRANSPORT

Getting there

By air

Brunei International Airport in Bandar Seri Begawan is well served by regional Asian airlines. Royal Brunei Airlines (tel: 673-2241 2222, www.bruneiair.com) is connected to international hubs such as Kuala Lumpur, Singapore, Bangkok, Hong Kong, London and Dubai. It also services Australia and New Zealand. Brunei is also served by Malaysia Airlines, Air Asia, Philippine Airlines, Singapore Airlines and Thai Airways.

By sea

Ferries travel daily between Bandar Seri Begawan and Labuan, off the southwest coast of Sabah, from where you can take another ferry to Kota Kinabalu in Sabah. The ferry service operates irregularly between 7.30am and 4.40pm from the Serasa Terminal in Muara. Ferries also go from Serasa to Limbang and Lawas in Sarawak when full between 7.30am and 4.40pm. Schedules can be checked on the Tourism Brunei website: www.bruneitourism.travel.

By road

An extensive overland road network also connects Brunei to Sarawak through Miri, Limbang and Lawas and to Sabah all the way to Kota Kinabalu. The Jesselton Xpress (www.sipitangexpress.com.my) has buses departing to all these destinations at 8am daily from the Bangunan Persatuan Guru-Guru Melayu Brunei on Jalan Sungai Kianggah.

Getting around

On arrival

Brunei International Airport is about 12km (8 miles) from the centre of Bandar Seri Begawan. Normal travel time into the city is 20 minutes. Taxis cost B$20. Hotel transport is normally available if you provide the hotel with your flight number and arrival time.

Public transport

The Brunei Bus Service has six routes in Bandar with fares starting from B$11. The buses run at intervals of 30–40 minutes between 6.30am and 6pm. The bus terminal is at the Jalan Cator multi-storey car park. Buses also leave from here to other towns such as Tutong, Seria and Kuala Belait. Buses run every one and a half hours between 6.30am and 6pm. The only public transport to Bangar (Temburong district) is by water taxi.

Taxis

There are very few taxis in Brunei and these charge exorbitant rates. It is better value to arrange local transport with tour agencies.

Private transport

Car rental
Car hire agencies at the airport and the major hotels charge B$80 per day for an economy-sized sedan. Petrol is cheap. Companies include Avis (tel: 08 760642) and Hertz (tel: 872 6000).

Water transport
Water taxis operate 24 hours a day. Between the Bandar Seri Begawan waterfront and Kampong Ayer, the standard fare for a boat trip is B$1. For charter journeys, the price is negotiable, usually B$15– 20 per hour. Water taxis also service Temburong from the Jalan Residency jetty from 7.45am to 4pm; boat frequency depends on the tide.

ACCOMMODATION

There is a range of hotels, budget accommodation and serviced apartments, mostly in Bandar Seri

THAILAND

MYANMAR

LAOS

CAMBODIA

VIETNAM

MALAYSIA

BRUNEI

SINGAPORE

INDONESIA

PHILIPPINES

Begawan. All accommodation is locally managed and service levels can vary. A backpackers' favourite is the Youth Centre in the heart of BSB. The business hotel, Sheraton Utama, is the only branded property in Brunei. Families like the high-end sprawling 180-hectare (440-acre) beachside Empire Hotel and Country Club integrated resort. Homestays are still being developed and vary in quality. Accommodation in the Ulu Temburong National Park area is comfortable but not always eco-friendly, and can be expensive. For accommodation listings, go to the Brunei Tourism website (www.bruneitourism.travel).

EATING OUT

Food is generally good in Brunei, with a large selection of local and international eateries. Buffets are very popular and affordable. Traditional Bruneian fare is Malay, which is cooked with aromatic herbs and chillies as well as coconut milk, and can be spicy. Chinese and Indian food are also popular, while a good range of international fare is available. Seafood is fresh and most eateries serve halal food, which means that pork is not available so, for example – what looks like bacon is likely to be beef. Local food is sold in hawker centres, local markets, restaurants and hotels. Breakfast is generally 7–11am, lunch 11.30am–2.30pm, dinner 6.30–10pm. Note that during the fasting month of Ramadhan, Muslim and Indian eateries open only 2–7pm. Non-Muslim eateries, food courts and fast food outlets open as normal.

ACTIVITIES

Nightlife

Because alcohol is banned, there are no pubs and clubs, and therefore, getting a caffeine buzz in coffee shops is as exciting as it gets come sundown. Alternatively, wander through a *pasar malam* (night market), catch a movie at a cinema or take a night safari on Sungai Brunei (see page 267).

Shopping

What to buy

A Brunei speciality is hand-woven textiles, called *kain tenunan*. Collectibles include the gold or silver-threaded Jong Sarat and simpler

kain beragi or *kain bertabur*. Other handicrafts include Borneon baskets, silverware and brass products such as miniature cannons. One-stop shops for such souvenirs are the Arts and Handicraft Centre at Kota Batu and the Sumbangsih Mulia cooperative 10 minutes north of BSB, where you can also watch handloom weaving in action upstairs (both Sat–Thur 8am–5pm, Fri 8–11.30am, 2–5pm). Otherwise, clothes, shoes and electronic items are available in the Yayasan Sultan Haji Hassanal Bolkiah Complex, The Mall and the Hua Ho Department Store chain (all 10am–10pm). Luxury goods are tax free, but prices of goods tend to be higher than elsewhere in Southeast Asia.

A–Z

Budgeting for your trip

Brunei is relatively expensive because of the strong Brunei dollar. Rooms in budget accommodation can go for as low as B$30, mid-range hotels, B$60–80, and higher-end hotels around B$200. Street food is cheap, going as low as B$5 a meal with drinks, while a decent restaurant meal averages B$50. There is no admission fee into museums and other attractions. Taxis are very pricey but buses and water taxis are cheap. Car hire is reasonably priced and petrol cheap. Budget B$25 a day for travel within the city. Booking tour operators is almost compulsory to visit natural attractions, and they can be pricey, with a half-day tour costing between B$70–100 and a full-day tour, B$150–200. All in, a budget of B$250 a day should serve you well.

Climate

The climate is hot, humid and sunny all year round. The rainy season is from September to January. April to July is usually the driest period. Temperatures can range from as high as 32°C (90°F) in the day to 22°C (71°F) at night.

What to bring/wear

Light cotton or summer clothes are ideal and slip-on shoes because shoes are often required to be removed when entering a venue. To go inside mosques, women will be issued a robe to wear, men need only be in short-sleeved T-shirts and long trousers. There is no dress code if you do not enter the mosque building.

Customs regulations

Duty-free allowances for Brunei (for those 17 or over) are 200 cigarettes, 60 grams of tobacco, 250ml of eau de toilette and 60ml of perfume. Foreigners are allowed to bring in two bottles of wine or spirits (about 2 litres) and 12 cans of beer for their own use, which must be declared upon arrival. Narcotics, weapons and pornography are strictly forbidden. Drug trafficking carries the death penalty.

Embassies

United Kingdom
2.01 Level 2, Block D, Yayasan Sultan Haji Hassanal Bolkiah Complex, tel: 222 2231, 222 2231, www.gov.uk/government/world/brunei.
United States
Simpang 336-52-16-9, Jalan Duta (site of the Diplomatic Enclave), tel: 238-4616, http://brunei.usembassy.gov.

Etiquette

Brunei is strictly Muslim, so alcohol is not sold, but private consumption by non-Muslims is allowed. Non-Muslim tourists are allowed to bring in limited amounts of alcohol, and consume it in hotel rooms and some restaurants. The sale of pork is limited and many eateries are halal. But Brunei is hospitable to visitors and tolerates other religions. Do adhere to the following codes of conduct:
Remove shoes before entering a mosque or private home.
Never walk in front of someone at prayer nor touch the *Koran* in a mosque.
Avoid pointing or beckoning someone with your index finger. Use a clenched fist with your thumb sticking out instead.
To call someone towards you, wave your entire hand with the palm facing down.
Do not be surprised if members of the opposite sex do not shake hands; most Malays also prefer a lighter handshake than the vigorous shake that is common in the West.
If you are offered something to eat or drink, partake a little or at least touch the container in which the food is served.

Health and medical care

Brunei is a safe country from a health and hygiene point of view. While water is potable, visitors are advised to drink bottled water and to take out private medical insurance. Yellow fever inoculation is required if you have come from an infected area.

Medical treatment

Medical standards are high in Brunei and, unlike in the rest of Southeast Asia, there is no risk of malaria, dengue, cholera and small pox. RIPAS Hospital and Jerudong Park Medical Centre are comparable to the best in Borneo, and there is a nationwide network of smaller hospitals and clinics.

Media

Newspapers

Foreign magazines and newspapers are sold in Bandar Seri Begawan. English-language publications available daily are the *Brunei Times* and the *Borneo Bulletin*.

Television and radio

TV is a diet of Bruneian, Malaysian, Indonesian and international cable TV programmes. Some of Brunei's radio channels broadcast in English while some have programmes in English at specified times. Broadcasts are interspersed with the Muslim call to prayers five times daily.

Money

The Brunei dollar comes in denominations of 1, 5, 10, 50, 100, 500 and 1,000 dollar notes and 1, 5, 10, 20 and 50 cent coins. It is sometimes referred to as Ringgit, and is pegged to the Singapore dollar at the same value. Singapore dollars – even coins – and credit cards are widely accepted. Moneychangers offer about the same exchange rates as banks but have longer opening hours.

Tipping

Bruneians do not usually tip, but visitors may tip bellboys B$1 and service staff in hotels and better restaurants, as well as tour guides.

Opening hours

The overlap of Muslim custom and modern business makes opening hours a bit complicated. **Government offices** open 8.30–11.30am, 1.30–4.30pm Mon–Thur and Sat. Closed on Fri and Sun. During the Muslim fasting month of Ramadan, open 8.30am–2pm. **Private offices** follow 8am–5pm business hours weekdays and Sat. **Shops** usually open 10am–10pm.

Banks Mon–Fri 9.45am–4.30pm, Sat 9–11am.

Photography

Different museums have different rules for photography; most have lockers to store cameras. Visitors may take photos outside mosques but not inside, and not of worshippers at prayer. People are generally open to being photographed, but ask first.

Postal services

Post offices are plentiful in all areas of Brunei. The main post office is next to the Taoist temple on Jalan Sungai Kianggeh; post offices follow government opening hours.

Telephones and internet

There are plenty of public phones throughout the capital and most of them operate on calling cards such as Hello, Netkad and Payless. These cards, in B$5, B$10 and B$20 denominations, can be purchased at most stores. Prepaid calling cards for the two mobile telephone operators, DST and Bmobile, can be purchased from their respective outlets.

The AT&T international access code is 800 1111. Wi-fi is free in hotel lobbies and coffee shops, and cheap in internet cafés at 80 cents–B$1 an hour.

Tour operators

It is difficult to visit natural attractions by yourself as public transport is inadequate and slow and good road maps difficult to come by. Good operators will enhance your tour. Some also provide transport services. There are over 40 registered operators in Brunei (www.bruneitourism.travel). Among reputable ones are Mona Florafauna Tours

Public holidays

1 January New Year's Day
January/February Chinese New Year
23 February National Day
31 May Royal Brunei Armed Forces Day
15 July Sultan's birthday
25 December Christmas Day
Muslim festivals, such as Hari Raya Aidilfitri, Hari Raya Aidiladha and Prophet Muhammad's birthday, follow the Muslim calendar and thus change from year to year.

(specialists in nature-based tours; mft.brunei@gmail.com), Sunshine Borneo Tours and Travel (the largest tour operator, www.exploreborneo.com), Freme Travel Services (www.freme.com), Intrepid Tours, MegaBorneo TourPlanner (www.megaborneo.com), and Pan Bright Travel Services (www.panbright.com).

Tourist information

Abroad

Tourist information on Brunei is limited. There are no tourist offices abroad, but you can obtain brochures from Brunei's diplomatic offices in your home country:
Australia
10 Beale Crescent, Deakin, A.C.T 2600, Canberra, tel: +61 (0) 2-6285 4500, www.brunei.org.au.
Canada
395 Laurier Avenue East, Ottawa, Ontario K1N 6R4, tel: +1 613-234 5656
United Kingdom
19/20 Belgrave Square, London SW1X 8PG, tel: +44 (0) 207-581 0521, www.brunei.embassyhomepage.com.
United States
3520 International Court NW, Washington DC 20008, tel: +1 202-237 1838, www.bruneiembassy.org.

In Brunei

Brunei Tourism's information desk is at the airport, on the left as you exit customs (Sun–Thur 9.45am–5pm, Fri 9–11.30am, 2.30–5pm, Sat 9.45am–5pm). Brochures and information are also obtainable from tour operators. There is an information centre on Temburong at Bangar (daily 8am–12pm, 1–14pm). *Brunei Insider's Guide (big) Magazine* is an excellent free guide on Brunei, which is available at the airport and hotels throughout the country.

Visas and passports

US citizens can stay up to 90 days without a visa. Citizens of Canada, Indonesia, Japan, Philippines, South Korea, Switzerland and Thailand do not need a visa for a stay of up to 14 days. British, Irish, New Zealand, Singaporean, Malaysian and EU member state passport holders can stay for 30 days without visas. Australians can obtain 30-day visas on arrival. All visitors must have onward tickets and sufficient funds to support themselves while in Brunei. If you need a visa, apply to Brunei diplomatic missions overseas. See www.mofat.gov.bn.

THAILAND
MYANMAR
LAOS
CAMBODIA
VIETNAM
MALAYSIA
BRUNEI
SINGAPORE
INDONESIA
PHILIPPINES

SINGAPORE

TRANSPORT, ACCOMMODATION, EATING OUT, ACTIVITIES AND AN A–Z OF TRAVEL INFORMATION

FACT FILE

Situation Southern tip of the Malaysian peninsula on the Strait of Malacca.
Area 699 sq km (267 sq miles).
Population 5.31 million, of whom 75 percent are Chinese, 14 percent Malays, nine percent Indians and the rest other ethnic groups.
Languages Malay, English, Tamil and Mandarin are official languages.
Religions Buddhism, with Taoist elements, is practised by the majority of Chinese. The Malay population is Muslim, and Indians Hindu, Muslim or Sikh. All Eurasians and significant numbers of Chinese and Indians are Christian.
Time zone 8 hours ahead of Greenwich Mean Time (GMT).
Currency Singapore dollar (S$). Approx S$1 to US$0.80.
Weights and measures Metric
Electricity 220–240 volts, using several plug configurations, including three-prong square, two-prong flat, and two-prong round.
International dialling code 65 (no area codes).

TRANSPORT

Getting there

By air

Singapore Changi Airport is frequently rated the best in the world. The airport is so efficient that one can be in the taxi – after clearing immigration, retrieving bags and passing through customs – 15 minutes after landing.

Over 80 airlines operate more than 4,000 flights a week to **Changi Airport**'s four terminals. Terminals 1, 2 and 3 – which can handle about 5,000 passengers per hour during peak periods – are linked to each other by the Sky Train. The Budget Terminal (what would be Terminal 4) caters to low-cost flights. Passengers can travel between the Budget Terminal and Terminal 2 with a free shuttle bus service. The airport has been conceived for maximum comfort and convenience, with a wide range of services and shops – in other words, it's a great airport to wait out a delayed flight.

Transit passengers who have a minimum of five hours' layover time before catching their connecting flight can book a complimentary two-hour sightseeing tour. Bookings can be made at the Singapore Visitors Centre counters at T2 (7.30am–3.30pm) and T3 (7.30am–3pm); tours are available on a first-come-first-served basis. Free maps and city guidebooks are available at the airport. For more information on airport services, contact the **customer service helpline** (tel: 065 6595 6868, www. changiairport.com.sg).

Flying from UK and US

There are regular daily flights out of London and major European cities direct to Singapore. Flying time is between 12 and 13 hours. Many UK and European travellers heading to Australia and New Zealand often use Singapore as a transit point to break the long journey. From Singapore it is another 4.5 hours to Perth, 7.5 hours to Sydney and Melbourne, and 10 hours to Auckland.

A flight from Los Angeles or San Francisco that crosses the Pacific

Ocean, takes about 16–18 hours with a stop in Seoul, Taipei or Tokyo along the way. From New York, flight time is about 22 hours including transit time.

The national carrier, **Singapore Airlines** (www.singaporeair.com), is based at Changi Airport. Its route network, including SilkAir destinations, covers 93 destinations in 38 countries. It has non-stop flights from Los Angeles and New York to Singapore.

By sea

Arriving slowly by sea is a pleasant experience. Most visitors arrive at the **Singapore Cruise Centre** (tel: 6513 2200, www.singaporecruise.com), located at the HarbourFront Centre. The facility is also used by several regional cruise operators such as Star Cruises (www.starcruises.com) and by many large cruise liners stopping over on their long voyages from around the world.

Tanah Merah Ferry Terminal (tel: 6513 2100), located near the Changi Airport, handles boat traffic to the resorts on Indonesia's Bintan Island as well as Tanjung Pinang, its capital, and to Nongsapura, on neighbouring Batam island. Ferries to Malaysia's Sebana Cove also depart from here.

Changi Ferry Terminal (tel: 6546 8518), also near Changi Airport, handles regular ferry services to Tanjung Relungkor on Malaysia's east coast.

By rail

Visitors can also enter and leave Singapore by rail through Malaysia. Five trains a day, all operated by **Keretapi Tanah Melayu Berhad** (KTMB) (tel: 1300 88 5862 in

The MRT system is supremely efficient.

Singapore, www.ktmb.com.my), connect Singapore to Kuala Lumpur and other west coast and central Malaysian cities. A daily *International Express* Train connects Singapore to Thailand, as does the ultra-upscale **Eastern and Oriental Express** (tel: 6395 0678 in Singapore, 800-524 2420 in the US and 0845 217 0799 in UK, www.orient-express.com).

The E&O is the ultimate recreation of a bygone age of romantic Asian rail travel. Decked out in the E&O livery of cream and racing green, it carries a maximum of 132 passengers on the three-night trip from Bangkok through southern Thailand, Butterworth to Kuala Lumpur and Singapore. There are two-night journeys northward from Singapore to Bangkok and journeys within Thailand.

The KTMB Railway Station is on Keppel Road, a 20-minute walk from the Tanjong Pagar MRT station.

By road

There are good roads down the west and east coasts of Peninsular Malaysia, crossing either the Causeway at Woodlands or the Second Link in Tuas into Singapore. The Second Link is far less prone to the frequent congestion that the Woodlands checkpoint experiences.

Private air-conditioned buses run from Hatyai in Thailand and many towns in Malaysia to Singapore. The ride from Hatyai takes about 15 hours with stops for refreshments and arrives in Singapore at Golden Mile Complex along Beach Road. Call **Five Stars Tours** (tel: 6533 7011, www. fivestarsonline.com) for bus tickets to Hatyai.

Hasry (tel: 6294 9306, www. hasrytravel.com) as well as Five Stars Tours above have buses which connect Singapore to key Malaysian cities like Kuala Lumpur, Penang and Malacca. Buses arrive and leave from its Lavender Street office.

Other coach operators such as **Plusliner** (Kuala Lumpur tel: 60-3-2272 1586, Singapore tel: 6256 5755, www.plusliner.com.my) and **Aeroline** (Kuala Lumpur tel: 60-3-6258 8800, Singapore tel: 6258 8800, www.aeroline.com.my) offer the more luxurious and roomier 26- to 30-seater, executive-class coaches. These link Kuala Lumpur and other major Malaysian cities to Singapore.

Getting around

Orientation

Singapore is an easy city to get around. The hardy walker can easily cover most areas of interest such as the Singapore River area, Chinatown, Civic District, Arab Street, Little India and the Orchard Road area on foot. These and all the outlying places of attractions can be reached easily with public transport (MRT and buses) or by taxi.

On arrival

Changi Airport is linked to the city centre by the East Coast Parkway (ECP) and to the other parts of Singapore by the Pan-Island (PIE) and Tampines (TPE) expressways. There are five types of transport from the airport – taxi, car, bus, airport shuttle and MRT.

Taxi

At all four airport terminals, the taxi stands are situated on the same level as the arrival halls. A surcharge of S$3 (or S$5 from Fri 5pm to Sun) applies in addition to the fare shown on the taxi meter. There are two other surcharges, which are added to the fare where applicable: for rides between midnight and 6am and ERP (Electronic Road Pricing) tolls. The taxi trip to the city centre takes about 20–30 minutes and costs around S$25, excluding the surcharges.

Private/rented car

If you are to be picked up by a private car at Terminal 1, take the inclined travelator in the Arrival Hall to the ground level, which leads to the Passenger Crescent where a private car pick-up point is located. At Terminal 2, the car pick-up point is on the same level as the Arrival Hall. At Terminal 3, it is at basement 1. Car rental counters are located at both terminals.

Public bus

In the basements of Terminals 1, 2 and 3 are public bus depots. Buses depart between 6am and midnight daily, and information on bus routes is available at the bus stands and www.sbstransit.com.sg. Service No. 36 gets you direct into the city. You'll need the exact fare as no change is given on board. The bus stops closest to the Budget Terminal are a 15-minute walk away on Airport Boulevard. It is easier to take the free shuttle bus service to Terminal 2 to transfer to the MRT service or to either terminal for the bus service to the city.

Airport shuttle

The airport shuttle service serves all hotels in Singapore except Changi Village Hotel and hotels on Sentosa Island. Tickets at S$9 for adults and S$6 for children are available at the shuttle counters located at the terminals.

MRT

The MRT link to Changi Airport is located underground next to Terminal 2. A ride to the city centre takes about 30 minutes and costs S$1.70.

Public transport

Bus and MRT

Singapore's public transport system is fast, efficient, comprehensive, spotlessly maintained and cheap. An especially helpful source for all information about the use of buses and the MRT is the **TransitLink Guide**, which is available at most bookstores and newsstands. This booklet gives complete details of all bus and MRT routes and contains a section on public transport services to major tourist spots. Or call one of the following:
SBS Transit, tel: 1800-2255 663, www.sbstransit.com.sg
SMRT, tel: 1800-336 8900, www.smrt.com.sg

If you are going to be moving

around a lot by public transport, it is convenient to buy the **TransitLink ez-link card**, which is a stored-value card for use on the MRT and buses. The ez-link card is available from all Transit Link offices at MRT stations and bus interchanges for S$15, of which S$5 is a non-refundable deposit. To use this card, tap it on the electronic readers located at MRT turnstiles or the entrances of buses. The electronic readers will automatically deduct the maximum fare. When exiting from MRT turnstiles and buses, tap the card again against the electronic reader and the unused portion of the fare is credited back to your card. You can top up the value of your card when it runs low. One-, two- and three-day tourist passes are also available for unlimited travel on MRT and buses (tel: 6223 2282, www.transitlink. com.sg).

Taxi

Taxis are plentiful. A string of surcharges apply to the fare: 50 percent extra from midnight to 5.59am; for trips leaving the business district; during peak hours; during public holidays; for advance bookings; Electronic Road Pricing (ERP) fees; and trips from the airport. Most drivers speak or understand some English. To book a taxi, contact:
Comfort CityCab, tel: 6552 1111
SMRT Taxi, tel: 6555 8888
Premier, tel: 6363 6888

Private transport

In a bid to tackle congestion and keep down pollution, the government severely restricts city traffic. Don't bother to drive as car rentals are prohibitively expensive and the Electronic Road Pricing (ERP) system is a hassle.

ACCOMMODATION

In terms of accommodation, amenities and service standards, Singapore's top-end hotels easily compare with the best in the world. Deluxe, first-class and business-oriented hotels all have conference and business facilities, in-room computer ports, cable TV and IDD phones.

There are price categories to suit all pockets. No doubt, accommodation in Singapore is pricier than in some Southeast Asian cities, but keep an eye out for promotional rates offered by top hotels – these can go as low as 50 percent off the published rates. It's also worth surfing the web for online reservation deals. If you intend to stay longer, you might want to consider checking into a serviced apartment. Singapore's serviced apartments generally offer all the amenities of 4- to 5-star hotels, but come with the added facilities of a fully equipped kitchen and dining area, for significantly lower rates than a hotel room. Although many are available on a short-term basis, the savings really add up when you take a long-term lease.

Backpacker hostels have proliferated, a few in the city centre, but mainly on the outskirts of the city. These are generally well run and tend to attract a younger and more rowdy crowd eager to meet and socialise with fellow travellers. You might be better off in a good budget hotel if a good night's rest is all you want, not expanding your social network.

Hotel areas

Most visitors stay in the city centre, especially around the Civic District and Orchard Road areas. The former

Local listings

The STB's *Official Guide to Singapore*, *Time Out Singapore* and *WHERE Singapore* are full of relevant information. *The Straits Times'* What's On section, *8 Days* magazine and the *IS* magazine are also excellent sources.

is where you will find attractions like the Asian Civilisations Museum and Esplanade-Theatres on the Bay, as well as a thriving nightlife scene, while the latter is the city's shopping hub.

For those who want to avoid the crowds (which can get quite chaotic on weekends) and stiff prices, head for the atmospheric charm of Chinatown or Little India. Here you will find budget accommodation in small hotels occupying old-style shophouses. The East Coast area is also worth considering for its laid-back appeal, range of local food options, proximity to the beach, and generally lower rates. Even closer to sun, sand and sea is Sentosa. Hotels on this holiday island are mainly luxury resorts, so be prepared for their higher rates. Singapore's efficient transportation system, however, makes getting around a breeze, so even if you are staying in the suburbs, the city is still within easy reach.

Prices and bookings

Hotel rates are quite high, mainly because of Singapore's rise in popularity as a tourist and business destination and a corresponding shortage in rooms, mainly in the city centre.

Hotels in this section are listed according to price ranges. Rates are subject to 10 percent service charge and 7 percent GST (Goods and Service Tax).

If you arrive without prior reservations, the Hotel Reservations counters (managed by the Singapore Hotel Association) at Singapore Changi Airport's Terminals 1, 2, 3 and Budget Terminal arrival halls can help you with bookings. Payment of the first night's room charge (by cash or credit card) is required at the point of reservation. Peak seasons include the local school holidays in June and December, and Formula 1 Singapore Grand Prix in late September when occupancy levels rise. But unless there is a big convention in town or a regional crisis, you should have no problem being accommodated at the last minute.

A hotel atrium. Singapore has a wealth of upmarket options.

A Chinatown restaurant.

EATING OUT

There are few places in the world where life revolves around food like it does in Singapore. Whether served on polystyrene in a rough and ready food centre, or on bone china in a top restaurant, food is a major focus. The racial mix of Chinese, Malays and Indians, as well as an expatriate population from the world over, has led to a range of cuisines that is nothing less than incredible.

Throughout the city, the number of dining areas make it fun – or frustrating – when making a choice. Among these are Ngee Ann City (Orchard Road), with at least three floors of restaurants; Boat Quay, Clarke Quay, Robertson Quay, Empress Place and Riverside Point with rows of restaurants (all five are strung along the Singapore River); Tanjong Pagar Road and Club Street (with a number of dining spots housed in old shophouses); Far East Square in Chinatown; One Fullerton and the Esplanade Mall at Marina Bay; and Tanglin Village, a cluster of restaurants housed in old military barracks.

ACTIVITIES

The arts

Once decried as a sterile cultural desert with no soul, Singapore has transformed itself into a lively arts and entertainment city.

The performing arts scene is enlivened by such professional and amateur companies as Theatreworks (English-language theatre), Singapore Dance Theatre (ballet) and Singapore Lyric Theatre (opera), while the annual cultural calendar is headlined by the **Singapore Arts Festival** (www.singaporeartsfest.com)

in June, which is well regarded for its line-up of innovative works from around the world.

The iconic **Esplanade-Theatres on the Bay** (tel: 6828 8377, www. esplanade.com) is Singapore's main performing arts centre, a landmark that many hope will rival the Sydney Opera House. Music, theatre, dance and outdoor performances are hosted in this large complex. This is also where the noted **Singapore Symphony Orchestra** performs regularly; check www.sso.org.sg for programme updates.

Buying tickets

Tickets to performing arts events can be booked by phone, in person and online (and paid for in all cases by credit card) with **SISTIC** (tel: 6348 5555, www.sistic.com.sg) or **Ticket Booth** (tel: 6296 2929, www. ticketbooth.com.sg).

SISTIC outlets are located at 9 Raffles Boulevard (Millenia Walk), 252 North Bridge Road (Raffles City Shopping Centre) and 435 Orchard Road (Wisma Atria). Tickets.com outlets are located at 1 Kim Seng Promenade (Great World City) and 173 Tanglin Road (Tanglin Mall).

Nightlife

Singapore's days as a risqué port may be over – the opium dens and the Bugis Street transvestites are long gone – but the city's nightlife scene is alive and booming, with stylish new bars and clubs opening all the time. Recent laws have allowed dancers to get on top of bars and do their thing, and some nightspots, away from residential areas, can remain open throughout the night.

Whether you plan to rip it up on the dance floor, unwind with a glass of premium wine, down a frothy

pint or join a snaking queue of trendy young things at the newest, hottest nightspot, there are enough choices to satisfy party animals of all inclinations (and budgets).

The best time to enjoy your favourite bar is during 'Happy Hours', usually between 5 and 8 or 9pm, when prices are more affordable. At clubs, a cover charge of between S$15 and 30 will give you admission on Friday and Saturday nights and a drink.

Shopping

The downtown area is stuffed with air-conditioned malls, department stores and boutiques, and the ethnic neighbourhoods offer additional street markets and unique shops. Most shopping centres and shops are open from 10am to 9 or 9.30pm daily.

Prices for many goods in Singapore are equal to or higher than those in Western countries. One of the best times to shop is the **Great Singapore Sale** (www. greatsingaporesale.com.sg), which runs from the last week of May through June and July. There are good discounts on a wide range of goods during these eight weeks.

Tax-free shopping: Although a Goods and Services Tax (GST) of seven percent is levied on most purchases, this can be refunded if you spend a minimum of S$100 at shops participating in the **Global Blue Scheme** (tel: 6225 6238, www.globalblue.com) or the **Premier Tax Free Scheme** (tel: 1800-829 3733, www.premiertaxfree.com). At shops with the 'Tax-Free Shopping' or 'Premier Tax Free' sticker, fill in a voucher for your purchases. Before your departure, validate the voucher at the airport customs, then present it together with your purchased items at the Global Refund counter or Premier Tax Free Scheme counter for your refund.

Where to buy

Antiques and handicrafts
Shoppers for Buddhist art and antiques should check out **Lopburi Arts and Antiques** (#01-03/04, Tanglin Place, 91 Tanglin Road, tel: 6738 3834). Shipping and certificates of authenticity are provided. There is a cluster of antique shops at **Tanglin Shopping Centre** (19 Tanglin Road), including **Antiques of the Orient** (#02-40, tel: 6734 9351, www.aoto.com.sg), **Akemi Gallery** (#02-06, tel: 6735 6315),

THAILAND
MYANMAR
LAOS
CAMBODIA
VIETNAM
MALAYSIA
BRUNEI
SINGAPORE
INDONESIA
PHILIPPINES

Hassan's Carpets (#01-12, tel: 6737 5626, www.hassanscarpets.com) and **Naga Arts and Antiques** (#01-48, tel: 6235 7084).

For a warehouse-style shopping ambience, **Tan Boon Liat Building** (315 Outram Road), near Chinatown, is filled with many antique and Asian collectible shops. **Pagoda Street** and **South Bridge Road** in Chinatown are also well known for their antique stores.

Computers

Funan DigitaLife Mall (109 North Bridge Road, tel: 6336 8327) and **Sim Lim Square** (1 Rochor Canal Road, tel: 6338 3859), are two shopping centres packed with numerous computer and tech gadget stores.

Fashion and clothing

Orchard Road is Singapore's major downtown shopping strip. Among the largest shopping malls here are Ion Orchard, the iconic, bubble-like wonder noted for its collection of luxury and cutting edge fashion labels; **Ngee Ann City**, with the Japanese department store **Takashimaya**; **Paragon**, with numerous luxury boutiques; and **Centrepoint**, a long-time favourite of Singaporeans. **Far East Plaza** and **The Heeren Shops** have trendy streetwear at low prices. Two popular home-grown emporiums are **Tangs** with well-loved fashion, beauty and household sections, and **Robinsons**, Singapore's oldest department store, located at Centrepoint.

The **Civic District** is also dominated by fashion shopping malls. These include **Suntec City Mall**, **Raffles City** and and **Marina Square**.

A–Z

Budgeting for your trip

Accommodation can cost anywhere from S$20 for a bed in a dormitory with shared facilities to S$80 a room in a budget hotel to more than S$400 per night in a top-end luxury hotel.

Food is reasonable – you can eat very well at a hawker centre for S$5 – and so is public transport (S$1 to S$2 per trip on the bus or MRT). Taxi rides in Singapore are reasonably priced as well; short journeys around the city centre will cost about S$8.

If you live frugally, it is possible to survive on a budget of S$50 a day.

City tours

Various private and group tours are offered by Singapore tour companies. These can be booked directly or through hotel tour desks. Use guides licensed and trained by the Singapore Tourism Board. There are city tours, river tours, as well as specialised tours focusing on food, farming, Chinese opera and *feng shui* (Chinese geomancy). Tour operators include **Holiday Tours** (tel: 6734 7091, www.holidaytours.net) and RMG **Tours** (tel: 6220 8722, www.rmgtours.com.sg). DUCK**Tours** (tel: 6338 6877, www. ducktours.com.sg) take you from land to river as they cover key tourist sights in their amphibious half-boat, half-truck vehicles. The same company also offers **HiPPOTours**, which are city sightseeing trips on open-top double-decker buses. Visitors can hop on and off at designated stops along the way. **Journeys** (tel: 6325 1631; www.singaporewalks. com) offer the **Original Singapore Walks**, which take you to the more unusual places of interest, including fresh-produce markets, red-light districts, 'haunted' nooks and graveyards.

If, however, you intend to live it up by eating out at good restaurants and checking out the city's nightspots, be prepared to budget about S$30 for a two to three course meal (without drinks), and a similar amount for entry into the clubs (inclusive of one drink). Drinks at bars are cheaper than at clubs but the best deals are during 'Happy Hours' from about 5 to 8pm.

Climate

The average daily temperature is 27.5°C (81.5°F), often rising to around 31°C (88°F), and cooling only to around 24°C (75°F) at night. Humidity averages 84 percent.

The northeast monsoon blows from December to March, and the southwest from June to September, and wind speeds are light all year.

Spectacular thunderstorms occur frequently between the monsoons, in April to May and October to November. The average rainfall is 2,346mm (92 in) with the heaviest rains falling between November and January, and the least falling in February and July.

What to bring/wear

Light summer clothes that are easy to move in are the most practical choice for a full day out in town. For office calls, men should wear a white shirt and tie, women a smart business suit.

In the evening, only a few plush nightclubs and exclusive restaurants favour the traditional jacket and tie. Most hotels, restaurants, coffee houses and discos accept casually elegant attire. However, jeans, T-shirts, sneakers and shorts are taboo at some restaurants and discos. To avoid embarrassment, it is best to call to check an establishment's dress code in advance.

You really can travel light in Singapore, as shops are excellent and shopping is perhaps the national sport.

Customs regulations

The duty-free allowance per adult is one litre of spirits, one litre of wine or port, and one litre of beer, stout or ale. No duty-free cigarettes are allowed into Singapore although they may be purchased on the way out.

Duty-free purchases can be made both upon arrival and departure except when returning to Singapore within 48 hours. This is to prevent Singaporeans from making a day trip out of the country to stock up on duty-free goods. In addition, visitors arriving from Malaysia are not allowed duty-free concessions.

The list of prohibited items includes drugs (the penalty for even small amounts can be death); firecrackers; obscene or seditious publications, video tapes and software; reproduction of copyright publications, video tapes or discs, records or cassettes; seditious and treasonable materials; endangered wildlife or their by-products; chewing tobacco and imitation tobacco products; and chewing gum except oral dental and medicated gum.

A complete list of prohibited, restricted and dutiable goods is available from the airport's **Customs Duty Officer**, tel: 6542 7058 (Terminal 1), tel: 6546 4656 (Terminal 2), tel: 6542 0519 (Terminal 3), tel: 6546 3090 (Budget Terminal) or check the **Singapore Customs** website at: www.customs.gov.sg.

Embassies

It is best to call to confirm opening hours before visiting.

Australia
25 Napier Road, tel: 6836 4100,
www.australia.org.sg
Canada
1 George Street, #11-01, tel: 6854
5900
New Zealand
391A Orchard Road, #15-06/10,
Ngee Ann City Tower A, tel: 6235
9966, www.nzembassy.com
United Kingdom
100 Tanglin Road, tel: 6424 4200
United States
27 Napier Road, tel: 6476 9100,
http://singapore.usembassy.gov

Health and medical care

Singapore is sparklingly clean. Safe
drinking water and strict government
control of all food outlets make
this a hygienic place to visit but,
should the need arise, medical
facilities are excellent. Most of their
services are available to non-citizens
but at substantially higher rates.
For this reason, ensure that you
have arranged an adequate travel
insurance policy.

Vaccination against yellow fever is
necessary if you are arriving from a
country where the disease is endemic.
Singapore is malaria-free although
dengue fever, spread by daytime
mosquitoes, occurs occasionally
in the residential neighbourhoods.
However, there is no cause for
alarm as these are not areas usually
frequented by tourists.

Medical treatment

Singapore has the best healthcare
facilities in the region. Private clinics
are abundant; the average cost
per visit varies between S$30–55
for a general practitioner and
S$100–150 for a first consultation
by a specialist.

Government and private hospitals,
found all over the island, include:
Singapore General Hospital,
Outram Road, tel: 6222 3322, www.
sgh.com.sg
Mount Elizabeth Hospital, 3
Mount Elizabeth Road; tel: 6737
2666, http://mountelizabeth.com.sg
**KK Women's and Children's
Hospital**, 100 Bukit Timah Road, tel:
6293 4044, www.kkh.com.sg

Emergency numbers

Fire/Ambulance Tel: 995
Police Tel: 999
International Operator Tel: 104
Local Directory Enquiries Tel:
100

Internet

To get online, head to an Internet café
or public libraries for cheap Internet
access. Alternatively, sign up for
Wireless@SG, a system that provides
free wireless connection at selected
hot spots around Singapore. Visitors
will need a mobile device with Wi-fi
facility, and will have to register with
one of the three service providers:
iCELL Network (tel: 6773 4284, www.
icellnetwork.com), M1 Net (tel: 6796
0313, www.m1net.com.sg) and Singtel
(tel: 1610, www.singtel.com). Check
the Infocomm Development Authority
website www.ida.gov.sg for an updated
list of hot spots.

Media

Newspapers and magazines

The *Straits Times* (www.straitstimes.
com), *Today* (www.todayonline.
com) and *Business Times* (www.
businesstimes.com.sg) are good
English-language dailies, with the
tabloid *New Paper* (www.tnp.sg)
appearing in the afternoons. *The
Edge Singapore* is a business and
investment weekly. The *International
Herald Tribune* is available on the
day of publication. Some of the best
sources of listings and information on
events are magazines like *8 Days*, *I-S*
and *Time Out Singapore*. American,
British, Australian, European and
Asian newspapers and magazines are
available at newsstands everywhere,
and bookstores such as MPH, Times,
Kinokuniya and Borders. These
bookstores have extensive selections
of international books and media.

Money

The Singapore dollar is divided into
100 cents. Notes are in $2, $5, $10,
$20, $50, $100, $500 and $1,000
denominations, and there are $1 and
1, 5, 10, 20 and 50 cent coins. There
are no restrictions on the amount and
type of currency you can bring into
Singapore.

Travellers' cheques are probably
the best form of money to take, in US
dollars or sterling. Banks and licensed
moneychangers offer better exchange
rates than hotels. Some shops will
even accept travellers' cheques as
cash. Major credit cards are widely
accepted, and can be used to obtain
cash at banks and ATMs.

Tipping

Tipping is usually not practised in
Singapore. It is not allowed at Changi

Airport and discouraged in many
hotels and restaurants, where a 10
percent service charge is routinely
added to bills on top of the Goods
and Services Tax (GST) of seven
percent. Tour guides and drivers
do appreciate tips (5–10 percent).
Very small tips (S$1–2) can be paid
to taxi drivers, porters and hotel
housekeeping staff.

Opening hours

Offices 9am–5pm
Banks weekdays 10am–3pm,
Saturday 9.30–11am. Some also
open Sunday 11am–4pm.
Shops 10am–9pm (most open on
Sundays). Department stores usually
open until 9.30pm. Many shops and
F&B outlets in Orchard Road open
until midnight on the last Friday of
the month.

Postal services

Singapore Post (tel: 1605, www.
singpost.com) is very efficient and
mailboxes can be found near every
MRT station. An aerogramme or
airmail postcard to anywhere costs
just 50 cents. Letters weighing not
more than 20 grams to Australia
and New Zealand, North and South
America, Europe, Africa and Middle
East countries cost S$1.10. The fee
for a registered item is S$2.20 (plus
postage).

Apart from postal services,
Singapore Post provides other
services such as parcel delivery,
insurance of travellers' cheques,
local and foreign money orders and
bank drafts, philatelic sales, post-box
mail collection, and a variety of other
services.

Telephones

Most hotels rooms have phones
that allow you to make International
Direct Dial (IDD) calls. Charges are
reasonable.

Singapore's country code is
65. There are no area codes. To
call overseas from Singapore, dial
the international access code 001
followed by the country code, area
code and local telephone number.
Alternatively you can dial 013 or 019
for cheaper IDD rates, although the
lines may be weaker.

Public phones

There are three types of public pay
phones commonly found at shopping
centres and MRT stations. Coin-
operated pay phones for local calls

(increasingly rare these days), card phones using phonecards for local and IDD calls, and credit card phones for local and IDD calls.

Phone cards can be used for both local and overseas calls. Local calls cost 10 cents for every 2 to 3 minutes depending on the public phone service provider. Phone cards can be purchased from post offices and convenience stores.

Mobile phones

Only users of GSM mobile phones with global roaming service can connect automatically with Singapore's networks. If you are planning to be in Singapore for any length of time, it is more economical to buy a local SIM card from one of the three service providers: Singtel (tel: 1626), M1 (tel: 1627) and Starhub (tel: 1633). All local mobile numbers begin with an 8 or 9.

Tourist information

The Singapore Tourism Board (www. visitsingapore.com) runs a tourist information hotline: 1800-736 2000 (daily 8am–9pm). Visitor centres are at the following locations: **Singapore Changi Airport** Terminals 1, 2 and 3 arrival halls (daily 6am–2am); **junction of Cairnhill and Orchard Roads** (daily 9.30am–10.30pm); Ion Orchard level one concierge desk (daily 10am–10pm).

Tourist information offices abroad

The Singapore Tourism Board (www. visitsingapore.com) has offices in many countries.
Australia
Level 11, AWA Building, 47 York Street, Sydney, NSW 2000, tel: 61-2-9290 2888

United Kingdom
Singapore Centre, 1st Floor Carrington House, 126–130 Regent Street, London W1B 5JX, tel: 44-20-7437 0033
United States
590 Fifth Avenue, 12th Floor, New York, NY 10036, tel: 1-212-302 4861
4929 Wilshire Boulevard Suite 510, Los Angeles, CA 90010, tel: 1-323-677 0808

Visas and passports

Visitors need to satisfy the following requirements before they are allowed to enter:
Passport valid for at least six months;
Confirmed onward or return tickets;
Sufficient funds to maintain themselves during their stay in Singapore;
Visa, if applicable.
Citizens of British Commonwealth countries (except India and Pakistan), the UK, European Union, Canada and the US do not require visas. Such visitors will automatically be given a 30-day social visit pass when arriving at the airport, in the form of a stamp in their passports.

Check with a Singapore embassy or consulate if you need a visa for entry, the rules of which are regularly subject to change, or look up the **Immigration and Checkpoints Authority** (ICA) website at www.ica.gov.sg.

In addition, the visitor must hand in a completed disembarkation/embarkation card to the immigration officer. Upon immigration clearance, the disembarkation portion will be retained while the embarkation card returned to the visitor. When the visitor leaves Singapore, the embarkation portion must be handed to the immigration officer.

Public holidays

1 January New Year's Day
January/February* Chinese New Year (two days)
March/April* Good Friday
1 May Labour Day
May* Vesak Day
9 August National Day
September Hari Raya Aidilfitri
October/November* Deepavali
November Hari Raya Haji
25 December Christmas Day
On the two days of Chinese New Year many restaurants and shops are closed. Bear in mind too that over Ramadan and the Chinese New Year accommodation and transport are usually booked.
*Variable dates depending on the Chinese, Muslim, Hindu or Christian calendars. Other public holidays with variable dates are **Hari Raya Puasa** and **Hari Raya Haji**. Check exact dates with the Singapore Tourism Board (tel: 1800-736 2000, www.visit singapore.com).

Visa extensions

Your social visit pass can be extended for up to 90 days from the date of entry into Singapore by submitting the requisite form at the ICA's **Visitor Services Centre**, 4th Storey, ICA Building 10 Kallang Road, tel: 6391 6100. Forms may be downloaded directly from the ICA website at www.ica.gov.sg. Note: a local sponsor is required in order to apply for an extension of the social visit pass. The easiest way to extend your stay is to leave the country, such as to Johor Bahru across the border in Malaysia, for a day and have your passport re-stamped on entry into Singapore.

Celebrating Chinese New Year.

INDONESIA

TRANSPORT, ACCOMMODATION, EATING OUT, ACTIVITIES AND AN A–Z OF TRAVEL INFORMATION

FACT FILE

Situation Over a distance of around 5,280km (3,200 miles), the more than 17,000 Indonesian islands (less than half of which are inhabited) are spread across over 50 degrees of longitude.

Area Though the total area (sea and land) is about 2.5 times greater than Australia, the land area is just 2 million sq km (770,000 sq miles), or a quarter of the size of Australia.

Population 247 million. Java is the most densely populated island, with almost 115 million inhabitants. Over 60 percent of Indonesians live on Java and Bali, although these islands account for only 7 percent of the nation's land mass.

Languages The national language is Bahasa Indonesia, similar to Malay, but most Indonesians also speak one of over 250 local languages. (Some estimate there are as many as 500 distinct languages.)

Religion 87 percent Muslim, with small numbers of Hindus, Buddhists, Christians and Confucians.

Time zones Indonesia's considerable spread covers three time zones. Java, Sumatra and West and Central Kalimantan are on Western Indonesia Standard Time, 7 hours ahead of GMT. Bali, Lombok, East and South Kalimantan, Sulawesi, Nusa Tenggara and West Timor are on Central Indonesian Standard Time, 8 hours ahead of GMT (the same time zone as Singapore and Hong Kong). Maluku and Papua are on Eastern Indonesia Standard Time, GMT plus 9 hours.

Currency Rupiah (Rp or IDR). Approx 11,365 to US$1.

Weights and measures Metric.

Electricity Mainly 220V using rounded two-pin plugs. Small hotels operate on 25-watt bulbs, so light can be quite dim at night. Power cuts are frequent in rural areas.

TRANSPORT

Getting there

By air
Most flights arrive either at Jakarta's **Sukarno-Hatta International Airport** or Bali's **Ngurah Rai Airport.** There are now international arrivals throughout the country.

Garuda Indonesia (www.garuda-indonesia.com) is the national carrier. AirAsia (www.airasia.com) and Malaysia Airlines (www.malaysiaairlines.com) now provide international service into some cities. The international departure tax must be paid in rupiah and averages about Rp 150,000.

By sea
Occasional luxury cruise liners stop in Bali. Check with a travel agent in your home country.

Batam and Bintan islands, part of the Riau archipelago (Sumatra), are serviced by high-speed ferries that connect to Singapore.

Intercity transport
City-to-city transport is arranged through local booking offices. The easiest way to obtain schedules and tickets is to ask your hotel for assistance.

From the airport
In Jakarta, Yogyakarta (Jogja) and Bali, taxi service from the airport is coupon based and efficient. Avoid the touts and head to the clearly marked taxi desk for a ticket, then go directly to the taxi queue. Prices are fixed and taxis are air-conditioned. Drivers may or may not speak English, so it is a good idea to have your destination and address written down.

In Jakarta, DAMRI airport buses run 4am–10pm, servicing strategic stops in the city. The air-conditioned buses run every half hour between the city and the airport for a US$2–3 fare.

Getting around

By air
Indonesia's domestic airline industry is in a constant state of flux. Remote airports extend runways to accommodate larger aircraft, airports are upgraded, and new privately owned airlines are established.

In addition to **Garuda Indonesia** (www.garuda-indonesia.com), **Tiger Airlines** (www.tigerair.com) and **Merpati Nusantara** (www.merpati.co.id), smaller airlines such as Citilink (www.citilink.co.id), **Sriwijaya Air** (www.sriwijayaair.co.id) and **TransNusa Air Service** (www.transnusa.co.id) make travelling within Indonesia easier than before.

It is best to arrange all domestic flights once you are in Indonesia. Note that in remote areas, flights are not linked to computerised reservation systems, so you have to purchase tickets in the town itself rather than pre-book them from a larger city.

Reconfirm all domestic flights to make sure they are on schedule. Be sure to get a computer printout with a confirmation number.

Each airport sets its own departure tax, which averages Rp 40,000.

By sea

PELNI (Pelayaran Nasional Indonesia), the state-owned shipping company, serves about 30 ports, with each ferry accommodating 1,000–1,500 passengers in four classes. As ferries are often dangerously overloaded, travel by sea is not recommended. However, intrepid travellers can check www.pelni.co.id for schedules.

In bad weather, the seas can be quite rough, particularly between Sumatra and Java, between Bali and Lombok, and around Komodo. Travel by sea between Lombok and Timor is not advised in January and February.

By bus

Buses are the mainstay of local transport in Indonesia. Generally, there are three classes. Top are luxury, air-conditioned buses, called *eksekutif* (executive)-class buses, with TVs and toilets. They often travel from town to town during the night when roads are less congested. On Java and Bali, *eksekutif*-class air-conditioned mini-buses and vans travel during the day, for example from Jakarta to Bandung, to serve commuters and tourists.

Bottom-grade (and very cheap, called *ekonomi*) full-sized buses or mini buses transport locals from village to village. Most offer standard routes but stop everywhere, are packed and stuffy.

In between, *ekspres* (express) buses cover longer distances. Some are a little better than *ekonomi*,

Jakarta traffic at dusk.

others are air-conditioned and can be booked ahead.

By train

There is an adequate train service in Java, a more limited one in Sumatra, but it's virtually non-existent elsewhere.

In Java, the railway extends from the west (which connects with ferries to Sumatra) and to the east (which connects with ferries to Bali). Visitors usually ask for *eksekutif*-class seats, which are far more comfortable than *ekonomi* ones. However, for long trips (such as from Jakarta to Jogja), tickets on a domestic no-frills airline can be about the same price, and the travel time is greatly reduced.

City/town transport

Be prepared for delays any time you travel in Indonesia, as roads are always crowded during the day.

Taxi

Taxis are ubiquitous in cities, and the good ones are metered and air-conditioned. If a driver refuses to turn the meter on, get out and get another taxi. Not all drivers speak English, so having your destination and address written down could be helpful.

Taxis can also be hired for the day for touring or to go from one city to another. Some have rates by the hour or distance; others may want to negotiate the fare. Ask to see the rate schedule first before agreeing on a price.

Rental car

Self-driving in Indonesia is dangerous; roads can be narrow and are always overcrowded. Motorcycles weave in and out of traffic, men pushing carts suddenly appear, and dogs and chickens frequently stray onto the roads. If a collision occurs, you are responsible for all costs, which could be endless. In addition, you need an international driving licence or tourist driving permit before hiring a car.

Bookings can be made at hotels or at the airport with either local or international car rental companies. If you do decide to self-drive, practise defensive driving diligently.

A better option is to hire a car with a driver. Negotiate better rates if you are booking a vehicle for a week or longer, but note that you are responsible for the driver's food and lodging, and for the petrol.

You can ask for an English-speaking driver. If none is available, you can hire a guide for a nominal extra cost. Guides in Jakarta, Jogja and Bali speak several foreign languages, so you can request the language you prefer. If you stop for a meal or snack, it is expected that you also treat the driver and guide. Tips for good service are always appreciated.

Public minibus/bus

Navigating Jakarta is now easier than ever via its new Transjakarta busway (www.rutebusway.com), which comprises eight corridors of bus-only lanes connecting all points to downtown Jakarta. Buses are air-conditioned and clean but are usually crowded during rush hours.

Minibuses (collectively known as *bemo* in Bali and *angkot* in Java) are inexpensive. Almost every *bemo* on the road in Bali may be hired by the trip or by the day. Just tell the driver where you want to go and then agree on a price. However, don't expect them to speak English.

Motorcycle

Motorcycles are readily available for rent in Jogja and Bali. They are very cheap and a great way to get around, as long as you take care. Always check the tyres and brakes before you rent. Note that Indonesian law requires that every driver and passenger wear a helmet.

ACCOMMODATION

In the major business centres and tourist areas, hotels range from five-

Legong performers, Bali.

to one-star and below, catering to every budget and taste. Apart from the international five-star chains such as Hyatt, Four Seasons, and Ritz Carlton, there are also high-quality local chains and boutique properties. In Bali, in addition to a mind-boggling choice of exquisite luxury resorts – including three award-winning Aman properties where the super-rich (and often famous) hide out – the options also include private villas. Often owned by wealthy foreigners and Indonesians, these can be leased on a daily or weekly basis, and can be anything from a one-bedroom beachside cottage to an exclusive eight-bedroom luxury villa with every conceivable comfort, including swimming pool and staff.

In more remote regions, anticipate only the basics and take heart that you can delight in Indonesian hospitality. Like the international hotel star-rating system, Indonesia has *melati* ratings for accommodations below the one-star level; the more amenities they offer, the higher the *melati* rating. Many are clean and comfortable. At the budget end is the humble *losmen* (homestay), often only a room with or without en suite toilet and a fan.

Bargains can sometimes be found outside of the high season (June–August, Christmas, New Year, and Ramadan), with even the fanciest rooms going at reduced rates.

EATING OUT

Rice, coconut, peanuts, soya beans and hot chilli peppers are the five pillars of Indonesian cuisine, and it is almost impossible to find a meal

that does not include one or more of them.

The staple foodstuff is rice, although in the drier eastern islands, it's corn, sago, cassava or sweet potatoes. Nearly every menu offers dishes prefixed with the word *nasi*, meaning they come with rice. *Mi* (noodles), made from rice or wheat flour, are also popular. Fermented soya bean sauces, *kecap asin* (salty) and *kecap manis* (sweet) are important flavouring agents used with gusto in almost every dish. *Sambal*, a spicy mixture of chilli paste, onions and shallots, is essential at every meal.

Dishes range from very spicy meat, fish and vegetables to those that are quite sweet. Available almost everywhere are *nasi* or *mi goreng* (fried rice or noodles with vegetables and sometimes meat), *sate* or *satay* (grilled meat on skewers served with peanut sauce), and *gado-gado* (cold, steamed vegetables served with a peanut sauce). Vegetables are largely grown in home gardens and include tender tapioca, papaya and soya bean leaves, *kangkung* (water spinach) and *bayam* (Asian spinach). Desserts are generally seasonal fruits – bananas *(pisang)*, papayas, mangoes *(mangga)*, and pineapples *(nanas)*. On special occasions, sweet, steamed cakes in a variety of colours are made of sticky rice with coconut milk, palm sugar, grated coconut or sweetened mung beans.

In the main tourist centres, many restaurants cater to visitors and serve a wide variety of cuisines. Chinese and Padang (West Sumatra) restaurants, the latter being famous for generous doses of fiery hot chillies, are found in almost every

town. Bottled drinking water can be purchased everywhere.

While the local beer, Bintang, is reasonably priced, imported beers, cocktails and wine (only available in larger cities) are expensive and can equal the price of a meal.

ACTIVITIES

The arts

In addition to traditional performing arts exhibition spaces, Indonesia's larger towns and cities have a surprisingly large number of alternative venues. Whether sponsored by foreign institutions or private establishments, their mission is cultural exchange. They offer art exhibitions, theatre, music, films, readings and other events by both local and international artists. Many offer free admission or charge only a small fee. Check for events and opening times upon arrival.

Jakarta

Taman Ismail Marzuki, or TIM (Jalan Cikini Raya No. 73, tel: 021-3193 7325) hosts a variety of Indonesian performances, theatre productions, visiting dance and music performances, art and films.

Museum Wayang (Jalan Pintu Besar Utara No. 27, tel: 021-692 9560) has traditional *wayang kulit* shadow puppet shows every Sunday at 10am (free). **Gedung Kesenian** (Jalan Gedung Kesenian, tel: 021-380 8283) is a restored Dutch Schouwburg playhouse and offers dance and musical performances.

Other venues include: **Centre Cultural Francais** (Jalan Salemba Raya No. 25, tel: 021-390 8585, www.institutfrancais-indonesia.com); **Erasmus Huis** (Jalan H.R. Rasuna Said Kav S-3, Kuningan, tel: 021-524 1069); and **Goethe Institut** (Jalan Sam Ratulangi No. 9–15, tel: 021-2355 0208, www.goethe.de).

Yogyakarta (Jogja)

Gamelan

Javanese-Mataram-style gamelan compositions are played every Monday and Tuesday 10am–noon at the Bangsai Sri Manganti *pendopo* (pavilion) at the **Keraton**.

Wayang Kulit

Wayang kulit (shadow puppet theatre) is truly the most influential Javanese art form, the one that has traditionally provided the Javanese with a framework through which to see the world and themselves. Traditional performances are always at night, beginning at 9pm and ending at dawn. However, most have been shortened for tourist enjoyment.

Venues for *wayang kulit* include: the Bangsai Sri Manganti *pendopo* (pavilion) at the **Keraton**, every Saturday 9.30am–1pm; **Sasana Hinggil**, South Palace Square (Alun Alun Selatan), every second Saturday of the month 9pm–5.30am; and **Sono Budoyo Museum**, Jalan Trikora No. 6, Tue–Thur 9am–2pm, Fri 8–11am, Sat 8am–1pm.

Javanese dance
The most wonderful time to experience Javanese dance is on a moonlit evening at **Prambanan Temple**. Visit www.borobudurpark. co.id for schedules. May–October performances are held on an open-air stage, November–April in the **Trimurti Theatre Prambanan**.

Every Thursday 10am–noon, the **Keraton** offers court dances at the Bangsal Srimanganti *pendopo* (pavilion). **Purawisata Open Theatre** (Jalan Brigjen Katamso, www. purawisatajogja.com) has nightly *Ramayana* performances 8–9.30pm. The introduction to the performance and characters is in English. Most hotels offer transport.

Bali
Beneath the exuberance of Balinese dance-dramas lie motions presented in a highly stylised form. Each gesture has a name that describes its action; for example a sidestep may be named after the way a raven jumps.

Indonesia has numerous world-class surfing sites.

Bali's most famous dance is arguably the *kecak*, which gets its name from the rhythmic chanting of the chorus, scores of men and boys who encourage the main performers. The classical *legong* dance is performed by young girls wearing elaborate costumes and headdresses.

Balinese dances accompanied by gamelan orchestras are presented at major hotels all over the island, and attending them sustains the many teachers and students who keep the dance tradition alive. Village performances – enjoyed by the local people as much as by tourists – help to support entire communities.

Dance venues and times change frequently; enquire about schedules at your hotel. In Ubud, visit the Tourist Information office, Jalan Raya Ubud (the main road), where you can also purchase tickets.

Other cities and islands
Throughout the year in all villages, towns and cities, events are held to commemorate religious, cultural or national events. In most cases, visitors are warmly welcomed. These celebrations often include local folk dances and are always accompanied by traditional foods and high spirits, an outstanding way to get a glimpse of 'real' Indonesians. Enquire at your hotel to determine if any special events are being held in the area during your visit.

Nightlife
Although Indonesia is known to have the world's largest Muslim population, young and trendy

Jakartans frequent a plethora of multimillion-dollar nightclubs: **Dragonfly, Blowfish** and **Buddha Bar** (now called Bataviasche Kunstkring – the name of the historic building it inhabits – out of respect to local Buddhists), to name a few. Backpackers often visit less modish pubs and bars around **Jalan Jaksa**, near downtown. The action rocks on until the wee hours except during Ramadan, when independent drinking establishments may close early.

Heavily dependent on making tourists happy, southern Bali offers a full range of night spots from the down and dirty beachside **Double Six**, which closes at 3am, to the elegant **KuDeTa** on Jl. Laksmana. Both are in Seminyak; both are eternally popular.

Hotels and resorts in tourist centres usually have well-stocked bars, most with live entertainment, especially on weekends. Elsewhere, nightlife trends come and go. In other large cities, ask around for the current favourite. In smaller towns you may have to settle for the local karaoke hang-out; while in most villages you'll be lucky if you can find a beer. In Java, ask if a *wayang kulit* (shadow puppet play) is being performed, which will continue all night long – alcohol-free, of course.

Shopping

Jakarta

Handicrafts
Pasar Raya (Blok M) and **Sarinah** (Jalan Thamrin) are the best one-stop shops for Indonesian products: baskets, leather goods, paintings, carvings, and batik.

Antiques
Cony Art (Jalan Melawai Raya No. 189E, tel: 021-720 2844) has antique ceramic collections. **Djody** (Jalan Kebon Sirih Timur Dalam), is especially well respected.

The 'antique' market on **Jalan Surabaya** has numerous stalls selling porcelain, puppets, brass and silver. Most of it has been made to look old.

Others
Kemang's main road, Jalan Kemang Raya, is filled with small shops selling everything from English-language books to art, scattered amongst great cafés.

Intricate batik for sale in Jogja.

Yogyakarta (Jogja)

Batik
Bima Sakti Batik Collective, Giriloyo village, near Kota Gede, is a whole village of batik makers.

Some of the best batik studios in Jogja are: **Bixa Batik Studio** (Pengok PJKA GK 1/7/43F; tel: 0274-546 545), known for its natural dyes; **Winotosastro Batik** (Jalan Tirtodipuran), for high-quality batiks; and **Brahma Tirta Sari** (Banguntapan, tel: 0274-377 881; www.brahmatirtasari.org), for traditional batik motifs in colourful contemporary designs.

Handicrafts
For a wide array of locally made handicrafts in one location, visit **Titon Handicraft** (Jalan Minggiran MJI/1627, Dukuh (Ring Road Selatan), daily 8.30am–4.30pm, tel: 0274-378 476, 371 105).

Pasar Seni Gabusan Bantul (Jalan Parangtritis Km 9.5, Bantul; tel: 0274-367 959, 788 2049) is a large, modern marketplace set up to display the works of craftsmen from the area, including pottery, batik, natural products, stone carvings, home furnishings and much more.

Silver and gold
Kota Gede, south of Jogja, is best known for its silver shops, but also produces gold jewellery. Local shoppers recommend the small shops located along both sides of Jalan Monodorakan, Kota Gede's main street.

Bali

Paintings
The artists' centre is **Ubud**, where there has been an explosion of new galleries featuring local and foreign artists. In addition to the galleries, on **Monkey Forest Road** and **Jalan Hanuman** there are many shops selling fine art as well as local whimsical art.

Jewellery
Several foreign jewellery producers are based on the island and combine the skills of Balinese master smiths with international designs. Two are: **Treasures** (Ary's Warung on Ubud's main road, tel: 0361-976 697; www.dekco. com), specialising in 18–22 karat gold; and **Gemala** (Jalan Raya Pengosekan, Ubud; tel: 0361-976 084; www.gemalabalisilver.com), offering silver and gold jewellery with semi-precious gems.

Antiques, furniture and reproductions
Be careful when buying antiques: there is no guarantee of the actual age of the items. The antique shops adjacent to Kerta Gosa in **Semarapura** house Chinese porcelain pieces, antique jewellery and weavings. On the main streets of **Singaraja** are a few of the best antique shops in Bali.

There are innumerable furniture shops in Kuta, Legian, Seminyak, Kerobokan and Sanur selling 'antiques', reproductions and garden furniture.

Ceramics
Jenggala Keramik in Jimbaran has tea sets, vases and dinnerware. In Sanur, **Pesamuan Studio** has outlets at One World Gallery on Jalan Hanoman in Ubud, Made's Warung 2 on Jalan Raya Seminyak, and at its factory at Jalan Pungutan No. 25, Sanur.

Other cities and islands
Handicrafts, textiles (see page 306) and furniture made by Indonesian artisans are exported to all corners of the globe. Visiting the villages where these items are made gives visitors a different angle on the Indonesian way of life. Prices are generally cheaper in villages than in city shops, and by buying locally you are supporting local craftsmen.

Many small villages in Nusa Tenggara (the eastern islands) are renowned for their exquisite hand-woven *ikat* textiles. Polite bargaining is expected after an interlude of getting to know the weaver, which adds an extra dimension to owning the cloth.

Enquire at your hotel which products are hand-made locally, and they will be happy to help you arrange a visit to those villages.

A–Z

Budgeting for your trip
In Jakarta and Bali, accommodation can cost per night from US$15 in budget establishments to US$40 for a standard room and all the way up to thousands of dollars for villas and fancy resorts. Rates are highest June–August, Christmas, New Year, and Ramadan. Simple Indonesian food can be had for as little as US$2.50 almost anywhere, a moderately priced meal for around US$6 (without drinks), and the sky is the limit for fine dining, averaging US$30–40. Prices are similar in all major cities. In smaller towns, dining and accommodation choices are fewer, and prices are cheaper.

Wine, cocktails and imported beers are available only in larger cities, and prices (usually expensive) fluctuate with availability. The local beer, Bir Bintang, is available most places and costs about US$2–3 for a large bottle.

Taxis and other public transportation are relatively inexpensive, but note that airfares to remote islands can be surprisingly high (ie from Bali to Sorong, Papua

THAILAND

MYANMAR

LAOS

CAMBODIA

VIETNAM

MALAYSIA

BRUNEI

SINGAPORE

INDONESIA

PHILIPPINES

runs about US$450 return). Check for no-frills airline fares in-country, as some of them do not offer online booking.

Climate

All of the archipelago's islands lie within the tropical zone, and the surrounding seas have a homogenising effect on temperatures and humidity. Consequently, local factors like topography, altitude and rainfall produce more variation in climate than latitude or season. Mean temperatures at sea level vary by only a few degrees throughout the region (28–33°C/82–91°F). In the mountains, however, the temperature decreases about 1°C (2°F) for every 200 metres (650ft) of altitude, which makes for a cool, pleasant climate in upland towns like Java's Bandung or the hills north of Jogja and Bali's Ubud.

Much of the archipelago also lies within the equatorial ever-wet zone, where no month passes without several inches of rainfall. The northeast monsoon means that many western islands receive drenching precipitation for part of each day between November and April, and the tropical sun and the oceans combine to produce continuously high humidity (between 75 and 100 percent). The eastern islands, however, receive little rainfall throughout the year.

The southeast monsoon tends to counteract this generally high humidity by blowing hot, dry air up from over the Australian landmass between May and October.

What to bring/wear

Light, loose clothing is the most practical. Shorts and scanty tops should be reserved for the beach, as Muslim Indonesians expect a high standard of modesty. Casual and smart-casual clothes are acceptable for nearly every occasion.

Essentials are insect repellent, sunblock, sunglasses and a sun hat. Also bring an adequate supply of prescription medicines and always hand carry them, as checked luggage can get lost or delayed.

Crime and safety

Take heed!

Possession of narcotics is a serious crime in Indonesia. Prosecution can mean a long prison term – perhaps even death – and/or huge fines.

Trouble spots

Although Indonesia is largely a safe country for travellers, contact your own ministry of foreign affairs to keep yourself informed of the current situation in trouble spots such as Poso (Central Sulawesi), West Papua and Maluku (the Moluccas).

Customs regulations

Each adult is permitted to bring a maximum of 2 litres of alcoholic beverages, 200 cigarettes, 50 cigars, or 100 grammes of tobacco, and a reasonable quantity of perfume. Photographic equipment and computers must be declared and are admitted, provided they are taken out on departure. Prohibited from entry are the following: narcotics, arms and ammunition, TVs, radios and cassette recorders, pornography and fresh fruit. All movie films and video cassettes must be deposited for review by the Film Censor Board. There is no restriction on import and export of foreign currencies and travellers' cheques; however import or export of Indonesian currency exceeding Rp 5 million is prohibited.

Embassies

All foreign embassies are based in Jakarta, though many have consulates in Bali. France, Italy and the Netherlands also have consulates in Jogja. The major embassies in Jakarta are:

Australia
Jalan H.R. Rasuna Said, Kav 15–16, tel: 021-2550 5555, www.indonesia.embassy.gov.au.

Canada
Jalan Jend Sudirman Kav. 29, 6th floor World Trade Center, tel: 021-2550 7800, www.canadainternational.gc.ca.

New Zealand: Sentral Senayan 2, Floor 10, Jl. Asia Afrika, No. 8, tel: 2995 5800, www.nzembassy.com/indonesia.

Singapore: Jl. H.R. Rasuna Said, Kav. X-4, No. 2, Kuningan, tel: 2995 0400, www.mfa.gov.sg/jkt.

Switzerland
Jalan H.R. Rasuna Said Kav X3/2, tel: 021 525 6061.

United Kingdom
Jalan M.H. Thamrin 75, Menteng, tel: 021-2356 5200, www.ukinindonesia.fco.gov.uk.

United States
Jalan Medan Merdeka Selatan 5, tel: 021-3435 9000, www.jakarta.usembassy.gov.

Emergency numbers

Jakarta
Ambulance Tel: 118/119
Fire Tel: 113
Police Tel: 110

Etiquette

Indonesians are remarkably friendly and courteous, but they are also staunchly conservative. Travellers who observe a few basic rules of etiquette will be assured of a warm welcome.

Using the left hand to give or to receive anything is taboo (the left hand is reserved for hygiene acts), as is pointing or crooking a finger to call someone.

Don't make any offers to purchase unless you intend to buy. When bargaining, start at half the asking price and then work out a compromise. Rp 1,000 can mean the difference of a day's meal, so avoid quibbling over small sums. Many Indonesians are still very poor, so be prudent and don't display large sums of money.

A small contribution at a temple, a village or a cultural conservation centre is appropriate and will be appreciated.

Do not give candy, money or pens to children, which promotes begging. Share smiles instead.

Hands on the hips indicates defiance or arrogance, especially when also standing with legs apart.

When sitting, feet should be tucked away, not propped up with the soles facing another person.

When visiting mosques and other places of worship, dress modestly and remove shoes.

Health and medical care

Yellow fever vaccinations are required if arriving within six days of leaving or passing through an infected area.

Determine if you will be travelling in a malaria-infected area (not all of Indonesia is). Use insect repellent and wear long trousers and long-sleeved shirts around dawn and dusk. Sleep under a mosquito net in infected areas.

Dengue fever, carried by daytime mosquitoes, is far more prevalent in Indonesia than malaria is, especially during the rainy season (November–April). There is no prophylactic; take the precautions described above.

Healthcare in Western-standard hospitals in large cities is good. However, in villages sanitation and health provisions are poor. Health insurance allowing air evacuation is recommended.

Indonesian tap water is undrinkable. Bottled water is widely available. Street food is risky. Avoid salads, ice and unpeeled fruit outside Western-standard hotels and restaurants.

Hospitals and clinics

International-standard medical facilities are available in large cities. However, some expatriates living in Indonesia prefer to fly to Singapore for medical treatment and carry medical insurance that also covers emergency airlift evacuation. The following hospitals and clinics, all open 24 hours, have English-speaking staff.

Jakarta
SOS Medika Klinik Cipete
Jalan Puri Sakti 10, Cipete, Jakarta, tel (appointments): 021-750 5980, tel (24-hour emergencies): 021-750 6001, www.sosindonesia.com
SOS Medika Klinik Kuningan
Menara Prima 2nd Floor, Jalan Lingkar Mega Kuningan Blok 6.2, Jakarta, tel: 021-5794 8600, www. sosindonesia.com

Yogyakarta (Jogja)
Rumah Sakit Panti Rapih
Jl. Cik Ditiro 30, tel: 0274-514 014/ 514 845/563 333, www.pantirapih. or.id

Bali
BIMC Hospital Bali
Jalan Bypass Ngurah Rai No. 100X, Kuta, tel: 0361-761 263, www.bimcbali.com

Public holidays

Many public holidays are based on the lunar calendar and these dates are therefore variable (indicated by *)
January 1 New Year's Day
January* Chinese Lunar New Year
February/March* Hindu New Year or Seclusion Day (Nyepi), Birthday of the Prophet Muhammad
March/April* Good Friday
April/May* Ascension of Jesus Christ
May/June* Birth, Enlightenment and Death of Buddha (Vesak)
July/August* Ascension of Prophet Muhammad
August 17 National Independence Day
September* Ramadan
November* Muslim Day of Sacrifice
December 25 Christmas Day
December* Islamic New Year

SOS Medika Klinik Bali
Jalan Bypass Ngurah Rai 550X, Kuta, tel (clinic): 0361-720 100, (24-hour alarm centre): 0361-710 505, www. sosindonesia.com

Internet

Public kiosks, called *warnet*, and cyber cafés, provide Internet access, as do large hotels and resorts. WiFi hot spots are found everywhere in major cities.

Media

The Jakarta Post is the major English-language newspaper. In addition, most international newspapers – English-language and others – are available at the newsstands of large hotels and major airports. *Tempo* magazine, published in Indonesian and English, is a good source of political and business news. Several magazines list events and restaurants, such as *Jakarta/Java Kini*, *Hello Bali*, and *Bali and Beyond*, which are distributed free in rooms of large hotels but can also be found at newsstands.

Money

Indonesia's national currency, the rupiah, comes in banknote denominations of 100,000, 50,000, 20,000, 10,000, 5,000, 2,000 and 1,000. Coins come in 1,000 (rare), 500, 200, 100, and 50 (rare) rupiah. At the time of going to press, there were 11,356 rupiah to the US dollar.

Changing money

Bring only new notes (no coins), as practically no one will change dirty

Bali has many fascinating temples to visit.

or marred bank notes. The best exchange rate is usually obtained at moneychangers. Hotels often offer a lower rate, and banks often offer even worse rates. It is advisable to change most currencies in the cities. Rupiah may be freely converted to foreign currencies when leaving. Be sure to ask for small notes for taxis and tipping.

Travellers' cheques

Good at major hotels and banks in cities only.

Credit cards

MasterCard and Visa are accepted at most large hotels, restaurants and shops. American Express and Diner's Club cards are less prevalent. Adding 3–5 percent to the bill for credit card use is an accepted practice.

ATMs

These are ubiquitous in large towns and cities.

Tipping

Major hotels add a 10 percent service charge to bills. If it is not included in upscale restaurants, a tip of 5–10 percent is appropriate if the service has been satisfactory.

In small town eateries, tipping is not expected. Airport and hotel porterage is Rp 5,000 per piece. Tipping taxi and hired-car drivers is not mandatory, but rounding up the fare to the nearest Rp 1,000 is standard. However, if you are travelling with a hired-car driver and/or a guide, tips to both are appreciated if the service was good.

Opening hours

Government offices 8am–3pm weekdays, except Friday when they close at 11.30am. On Saturdays, they are often open until around 2pm. **Business offices** weekdays 8–9am until 4–5pm. Some companies work on Saturday mornings as well. Banks 8am–3pm on weekdays.

Postal services

Regular airmail to Western countries takes 7–10 days, whereas express airmail delivers in as little as 3 days. Domestic mail is fast and generally reliable except to outer islands. Post offices are generally open Mon–Thur 8am–2pm, Fri 8am–noon and Sat 8am–1pm. The central post office in larger cities may stay open later.

International courier services like DHL (tel: 0800-133 3333/021-

THAILAND
MYANMAR
LAOS
CAMBODIA
VIETNAM
MALAYSIA
BRUNEI
SINGAPORE
INDONESIA
PHILIPPINES

7917 3333), FedEx (tel: 0800-188 8800/021-7590 1800) and UPS (tel: 0807-187 7877/021-526 5353) offer reliable overseas deliveries.

Telephones

Telephone services are rapidly being modernised and overhauled, particularly in urban areas. Don't be surprised to see telephone numbers with as few as six or as many as eight digits. As the phone system is brought into the 21st century, telephone numbers often change. Although every effort has been made to ensure that telephone numbers in this guide are correct, if a number listed doesn't work, it has probably been upgraded – and changed.

Hotels offer international direct dialling (IDD) services, with the usual surcharges. International calls can also be made from public phone kiosks called *wartel*. Dial 001, 007, 008, 009 or 017 for an international line, although not all these numbers connect with all countries. Dial 102 for international directory enquiries in English.

If calling Indonesia from overseas, dial the country code 62, followed by the area code (leaving out the zero), then the telephone number. When calling from one province to another in Indonesia, dial the area code with the zero in front of it.

Mobile phones

Indonesia uses GSM 900 and 1800 networks. Coverage may be limited to main towns and cities, depending on the provider. Prepaid domestic and international cards can be easily found in all cities.

Tourist information

Tourism information is now generated by provincial and regional authorities rather than the central government. The national Ministry of Culture and Tourism website gives links to provincial offices and their websites, but note that some government websites are better than others. Also, be aware that provincial and regional tourism information centres are not knowledgeable about destinations outside their areas.

Indonesian Ministry of Culture and Tourism
Sapta Pesona Building, Jalan Medan Merdeka Barat No. 17, Jakarta 10110, tel: 62-21-383 8167, www.indonesia.travel

Bali Culture and Tourism Office
Jalan S. Parman No. 1, Niti Mandala, Denpasar 80235, tel: 62-361-235 200, 780-6200

Central Java Culture and Tourism Office
Jl. Madukoro Blok BB/1D, Semarang 50144, tel: 62-24-354 6001, www.central-java-tourism.com

Jakarta City Government Culture and Tourism Office
Jalan Kuningan Barat No. 2, Jakarta 12710, tel: 62-21-520 5455 (culture), 520 9703 (general), 520 5454 (information), 5263922 (tourism)

West Java Culture and Tourism Office
Jalan R.E. Martadinata No. 209, Bandung 40114, tel: 62-22-727 3209, 710 3605

West Nusa Tenggara Provincial Tourist Office (Lombok and Sumbawa)
Jl. Singosari No. 2, Mataram, Lombok

83127, tel: 62-370-631 730, 633 886, 635 8474, 638 7828

Yogyakarta City Tourist Information Office
Jl. Malioboro No. 56, Yogyakarta, tel: 62-274- 936-5952, www.jogjapages.com

Visas and passports

All travellers must possess a passport valid for at least six months after arrival and tickets proving onward passage.

Visa regulations are constantly changing. At the time of writing, free 30-day visas are given to citizens of only 12 countries. Visas-on-arrival are given to 65 other countries (US$10 for a 7-day stay; US$25 for a 30-day stay). All others must apply to the Indonesian embassy or consulate in their home country for a visa before travelling. Visas for 60-day stays are available to all countries if applied for at the Indonesian embassy or consulate in their home country for a visa before travelling.

A *surat jalan* (travel permit) is required for visits to certain destinations, such as Nanggroe Aceh Darusalam and Papua.

Websites

Building websites and furnishing the public with complete, current travel information has been a slow process. Some of the better websites are:
Bali Tourism Board: www.Bali-Tourism-Board.com
Bandung (West Java) tourism, hotel and travel information: www.VisitBandung.net
Borobudur (Central Java): www.BorobudurPark.co.id and www.BorobudurCorner.com
Central Java Province Tourism Office: www.Central-Java-Tourism.com
East Java Tourism Office: www.EastJavaTourism.com
Kupang (Timor) travel information: www.KupangKlubHouse.com
Lombok Network Interactive: www.Lombok-Network.com
Maluku (the Moluccas) diving: www.DivingMaluku.com
Maps – general and national parks: www.IndonesiaTraveling.com
Medan (Sumatra) travel information: www.MedanKu.com
North Sulawesi diving and travel information: www.North-Sulawesi.com
Raja Ampat (Papua) diving: www.IrianDiving.com
Unesco World Heritage Sites (Java, Komodo, Sumatra and Papua): http://whc.unesco.com

Preparing for a temple festival at Pura Besakih in Bali.

PHILIPPINES

TRANSPORT, ACCOMMODATION, EATING OUT, ACTIVITIES AND AN A–Z OF TRAVEL INFORMATION

FACT FILE

Situation An archipelago of 7,107 islands separating the South China Sea from the western Pacific Ocean
Area 300,000 sq km (116,000 sq miles)
Population 98.5 million people, 12 million of whom live in the greater Metro Manila area
Languages Pilipino (derived from Tagalog) and English
Religion The main religion is Christianity: 80 percent of all Filipinos are Roman Catholic, 11 percent Protestant/other Christian, seven percent Muslim, two percent Buddhist/other.
Time zone Eight hours ahead of Greenwich Mean Time (GMT), so New York is 13 hours, Los Angeles 16 hours and London eight hours behind, Australia two hours ahead. Sunrise and sunset are at about 6am and 6pm.
Currency Peso (P). Approx P43 to US$1
Weights and measures Metric
Electricity 120 volts at 60 Hz

TRANSPORT

Getting there

By air

More than 500 international flights arrive in Manila weekly. The **Ninoy Aquino International Airport** (NAIA) has four terminals. Terminal 1: NAIA Terminal serves international flights, except for Philippine Airlines; Terminal 2: Centennial Terminal, is reserved for Philippine Airlines, both domestic and international; Terminal

3: NAIA International Terminal, also serves international flights, particularly those of other Philippine carriers, such as Cebu Pacific. The Domestic Terminal serves all domestic flights other than Philippine Airlines. International flights also arrive at airports in Cebu, Davao, Laoag, Subic and Clark.

Getting around

Getting out of Manila by car can be a problem, as traffic is often heavy. Going north, the renovated North Luzon Expressway provides much easier access than in years past. Some bus companies, as well as taxi operators, have security problems, such as hold-ups, so check carefully before using public transportation. Hotels and established car rental companies can provide hired vehicles with drivers that provide safe, fast transport to the north and southern Luzon area. Manila has an elevated rail system that is fast and efficient, but crowded during peak hours. The country's rail system is not recommended, as it is painfully slow. Unless you have plenty of time, flying is the only realistic way of travelling to the Visayas from the capital.

By air

There are flights to all large cities from Manila and Cebu. Flying is relatively cheap, with domestic airlines spanning much of the archipelago and offering competitive fares through online booking. Domestic flight schedules are in constant flux; check airline websites for updates. There is usually a departure tax ofP550 (international) and P200 (domestic) at most airports.

Philippine Airlines, tel: 02-855 8555, www.philippineairlines.com
Air Philippines, tel: 02-855 9000, www.airphils.com
Cebu Pacific, tel: 02-702 0888, www.cebupacificair.com
South East Asian Airlines, tel: 02-849 0100, www.flyseair.com
Air Asia, tel: 02-742 2742, www.air asia.com

At the airport: arrival and departure

Arrival: Manila's **Ninoy Aquino International Airport** (NAIA) is one of the trickier airports in Southeast Asia for arrival. There is no modern public transport system linked to the airport, and metered 'street' taxis are at their most predatory when working the airport. The two safest, and most convenient, options are to either arrange airport transportation to your hotel or hire a fixed rate or 'coupon' taxi. The coupon taxis are significantly more expensive than street taxis ($10–20 compared to under $5) but the fixed rate taxis are safe and regulated. Trying to save a few dollars on a taxi is not recommended when arriving in Manila with your passport, cash and valuables all in tow. Avoid offers of rides, and 'colorum' taxis – those people offering rides in their private vehicles.

Departure: It is easiest to reach the airport by private car or taxi. If using a street taxi, have your hotel hail the cab and record their licence plate. Give yourself plenty of time, especially during rush hour and inclement weather. Most airline counters open 3 hours prior to departure and check-in lines can be very long, depending upon the destination. The Manila airport departure tax is P550 (about US$11), payable in peso or US dollars.

THAILAND · MYANMAR · LAOS · CAMBODIA · VIETNAM · MALAYSIA · BRUNEI · SINGAPORE · INDONESIA · **PHILIPPINES**

Water transport

Inter-island boat travel in the Philippines can be something of an adventure. Many lines are now attempting to offer comfortable cabins and international standard accommodations, but most of the ships criss-crossing the country have spotty safety records and tie up at gritty ports. But for those with some time on their hands, and who want to see another side of the Philippines, hopping on a ferry boat for an inter-island journey can be a memorable experience.

Some of the larger shipping companies sell tickets online (upscale cabins are inexpensive but sell out quickly, so book early). Tickets can also be bought at travel agents and in stands at shopping malls nationwide. **2Go Travel** (tel: 02-528 7000, http://travel.2go.com.ph) is owned by the Chinese government, 2Go Travel has swallowed many of its competitors and is now the largest ferry company in the Philippines. Based in Cebu with ports of call across the entire country.. **Cokaliong Shipping Lines** (tel: 032-232-7211, www.cokaliongshipping.com) is based in Cebu with ports of call that include Dapitan, Dumaguete, Iloilo, Larena, Maasin, Sindangan, Surigao and Tagbilaran.

By bus

The areas surrounding Manila and provincial capitals are relatively well serviced by a reasonably good network of roads. Potholes are a problem, and traffic usually moves at a snail's pace – especially through cities. However, the improved North Luzon Expressway – the single main artery heading north – has greatly reduced travel times. Dozens of

bus companies operate services to the main tourist centres and fares are low. Long-distance buses make frequent stops at rest stops along the way, which offer snacks and 'comfort rooms' (toilets), usually requesting a donation of P1 for their upkeep. Look for 'express' buses whenever possible.
BLTB – Batangas Laguna Tayabas Bus Company (tel: 02 913-1525) goes to Calamba, Nasugbu, Lucena, Legaspi, Naga and multiple destinations in Leyte and Samar.
Dagupan Bus Lines (tel: 02 727 2330) goes to Dagupan, Alaminos, Lingayen, Baguio City and various locations in Benguet province.
Dangwa Tranco Company Incorporated (tel: 02 731 2879) goes to Benguet and Ifugao areas.
JAM Transit (tel: 02 541 4409) goes south of Manila to Batangas, Quezon and Laguna provinces.
Philippine Rabbit (tel: 02 734 9836) goes to Abra province, Laoag City, San Fernando in La Union Province, Tarlac and Vigan.
Victory Liner (tel: 02 833-5019-20; www.victoryliner.com) goes north to Olongapo, Iba, Tarlac, San Fernando (La Union), Baguio City, Alaminos, Bolinao, Dagupan, Tuguegarao and Aparri.

Car rental

Cars may be rented without a driver, but opting for a driver is highly recommended. As in many developing countries, the roads are chaotic, traffic laws are optional for most drivers, and traffic police are corrupt and predatory. Hiring a reliable car, with driver, solves most of these problems and opens the country to travel in ways different than public

transportation. Make sure that fuel, tolls and the driver's food and lodging, if travelling overnight, are discussed before you begin your road trip. Most drivers will accept a relatively small fee per night to find their own lodging and food on overnight road trips.
JB Rent a Car (tel: 02-526-6288) has offices in the Midland Plaza Hotel in the Ermita section of Manila.
Nissan Rent A Car (tel: 02-854-7099) has outlets in Makati, Ortigas and many other areas of Manila.
Avalon Transport Services (tel: 02-890-8667) has offices in Makati.
Filcar Transport Services (tel: 02-817-8346) has offices in Makati and Ermita.
Avis (www.avis.com.ph)
Budget (www.budget.com.ph)
Dollar Rent-A-Car (www.dollar.com)
Safari Rent-a-Car (www.safarirentacarinc.com)
Hertz Rent-A-Car (www.hertzphilippines.com)
National Car Rental (www.nationalcarph.ukf.net)

By train

Train travel is slow and not recommended. Manila's sole line runs from Tutuban Station in Tondo south to Legaspi City, and north to San Fernando in La Union province.

Public transport in Manila

Complaints of travel by public transportation are slow city traffic, and hot and crowded conditions in the vehicles. In Metro Manila, non-air-conditioned bus and jeepney rates are minimal, as are air-conditioned buses.

The jeepney is the Philippines' most colourful mode of transport, originally constructed from American jeeps left behind after World War II. Routes are fixed, and can be complicated to figure out. But for the adventurous, a jeepney ride through Manila is the quintessential Philippine experience.

Air-conditioned buses travel major thoroughfares and the South and North expressways. Air-conditioned bus terminals are located in Escolta, in Binondo, Manila, Ayala Center (Makati) and in Cubao, Quezon City.

Motorcycles with sidecars, called tricycles, may be available for short trips on the smaller streets. Ask local residents the costs of your journey, as tricycle drivers are not averse to profiting on a foreigner's ignorance.

Manila's elevated rail system consists of two Light Rail Transit lines: LRT1 (yellow line) and LRT2 (purple line), and the Metro Rail

Motorbike taxis are a popular way of getting around.

The Shangri-La chain has made inroads in the Philippines, as at this resort on Mactan Island.

Transit line: MRT3 (blue line). The oldest and most crowded of the light rail systems is the LRT1, which runs along Taft and Rizal avenues between Baclaran (near the airport) and Monumento, providing access to many of Manila's historical attractions. The newest of Manila's light rail systems, the LRT2, has 11 stops running east-west along Aurora Avenue from Recto to M.A. Roxas in Marakina, meeting the LRT1 by Doroteo Jose Station, and the MRT3 at Cubao (Aurora) Station. Finally, the MRT3 runs from Taft Avenue along EDSA until North Avenue in Quezon City. The final gap from North Avenue to link with the LRT1 station in Monumento is being constructed. During peak hours, the elevated trains are crowded, with a crush of people at ticket booths, and packed train cars. If you can get on during off-peak hours, it is an inexpensive, fast and interesting way to the see the city – from above.

Cultural center

The sprawling **Cultural Center of the Philippines (CCP,** tel: 02-832 1125, www.culturalcenter.gov. ph**)** complex on Roxas Boulevard houses theatres, museums, a library, restaurants, galleries and exhibition rooms. Most of Manila's plays, ballets and concerts take place here. The building was constructed as the pride and joy of former first lady Imelda Marcos nearly 50 years ago.

ACCOMMODATION

There is a wide range of accommodation for every budget, from beach resorts and pensions to luxury hotels.

The Makati and Ortigas areas of Manila, where most of the high-end restaurants and shopping malls are located, has most of the country's top hotels. Stay in these areas for an 'insulated' visit to the country.

The grittier Ermita/Malate area of the city offers more affordable accommodation, with Malate hosting numerous popular hostels and budget hotels. Ermita is home to several pub-style hotels with low rates, as well as lively Australian-run pubs.

Preparing drinks in Manila.

Quezon City, which links to Manila's sprawling middle-class suburban area has many affordable lodging options, but few are located near tourist areas – something of a problem in this congested city.

In provincial areas, there are a scattering of luxury options and a large number of international-standard accommodation. Many expatriates have moved to the Philippines to run small resorts and hotels, and they can often be found in the most remote areas. Friendly, family-run Filipino-owned establishments can also offer a good alternative to the often rather grim hotels in provincial areas.

EATING OUT

Dining is not one of Manila's strong points. Filipino cuisine is an interesting blend of Malay, Spanish and Chinese influences, but it is often an acquired taste. It is less spicy, and heavier on meat, than most other Southeast Asian cuisines.

Manila and Cebu have a fairly wide range of dining options, but in many cities and virtually all provincial areas, the fare offered is often very basic. But there are a few gems out there, even in small towns and beach areas.

Dining is usually very inexpensive – even the high-end establishments are a bargain compared to other cities in Asia. Expect to pay anywhere from a few dollars to not much more than $10 for a main course. Restaurants are generally open from lunchtime to 9 or 10pm, with few 24-hour dining options in most places.

Dining options can primarily be broken down into three groups: local establishments, international restaurants and fast food.

Local establishments vary greatly. Some have fancy menus and nearly inedible food, while others are not much more than a grass hut, but offer excellent fresh fish dishes and roasted chicken. A stroll through the restaurant to glance at what's on the plates of others is one way to get an idea of what you might get before ordering.

International restaurants – those catering to tourists, foreign residents and wealthier Filipinos – offer most major cuisines in Manila, and generally good service and food. Places with hands-on owners are usually the best.

There are plenty of American fast food restaurants (McDonald's, KFC, Pizza Hut, etc), and the Philippines has a host of local varieties, such as Jollibee (burgers), Chow King (rice and noodles) and Greenwich (pizza and pasta). While no one goes on vacation to eat fast food, it is sometimes your safest option in provincial areas.

ACTIVITIES

The arts

Buying tickets

For information about concerts, plays and other events, check out **Ticketworld** at www.ticketworld.com. ph, which allows online booking. Tickets can also be purchased at the customer service areas of SM department stores around the city.

Aside from concerts and plays at the Cultural Center of the Philippines, Ticketworld handles Philippine Basketball Association (PBA) games at Ultra in Pasig City, and Pasay's Cuneta Astrodome. The website is a good clearing house for just about anything in the city that requires a ticket.

Dance

Ballet Philippines is the country's foremost company, followed by the **Philippine Ballet Theater**. The **Bayanihan National Dance Company** and **Ramon Obusan Folkloric Group** excel in cultural and folk dancing.

Theatre and concerts

The following venues also host theatrical and musical performances:
gsis Theater
GSIS Building, CCP Complex, Manila, tel: 02-891 6161,
Manila Metropolitan Theater
Liwasang Bonifacio, Manila, tel: 02-527 0892, http://manilamet. webs.com
Philippine Ballet Theater
Schedules plays and musicals year-round, Ortigas Avenue, Pasig City, tel: 02-631 2222 x 8201
Tanghalang Pilipino
CCP Complex, Roxas Boulevard, Manila, tel: 02-842 0137, 832 3704, www.tanghalangpilipino.org.ph

Music

The Philippine Philharmonic Orchestra, Philippine Madrigal Singers and UST **Symphony Orchestra** perform regularly at the Cultural Center of the Philippines (CCP, tel: 02-832 1125, www.cultural center.gov.ph). Call for information

on open-air concerts held around the city.

Movies

Cinemas are a great respite from the heat and chaos of Manila. Hollywood movies are very popular and widely available, while local Filipino films are coming into their own, particularly in the horror genre.

With the opening of **Mall of Asia**, the Philippines has its first IMAX movie theatre, with an eight-storey screen and bone-shaking sound. For tickets, call 02-556 IMAX.

For information about movies at the various **Robinsons Malls** around the country, check out www.robinsonmovieworld.com. For movies at **SM Malls**, check out www. smcinema.com.

Nightlife

Manila is one of Asia's great nightlife cities. The Filipinos' love of music (you'll find Filipino musicians performing throughout Asia) and the general fun-loving attitude in the country translates to a broad range of night-time activities.

The business district of Makati is one nightlife hub, where bars such as Havana, in Greenbelt shopping centre, bring a lively mix of foreign residents, Filipinos and visitors for dancing and drinking. The nearby Fort Bonifacio area has several similar clubs, including The Embassy.

For great music, head across town to Malate, which hosts many excellent music nightclubs in Adriatico Circle area, and Ermita, which is home to the Hobbit House, Manila's most famous folk bar and a favourite of Filipino folk legend Freddie Aguilar. In the Ortigas

Shopping malls in Manila

Shopping malls abound in Metro Manila, most offering daily air-conditioned comfort (10am–8pm) and reasonable prices for the foreign visitor. In the Malate–Ermita tourist belt is **Robinson's Place**. North of the Pasig, check out the flea market-esque **Tutuban Center**, in the dense urban area of **Divisoria market**.

The Ortigas area of Manila is the largest concentration of upscale malls, with the huge **SM Megamall**, Robinson's Galleria, **Shangri-La Plaza Mall**, and the Podium concentrated together in walking distance.

In Makati, the **Ayala Center** includes department stores such

area, where shopping malls abound but nightclubs are rare, Chef & Brewer puts on great bands nightly.

The hotels in Makati, Ortigas and Malate all have lounges that offer better than average singers (after all, Manila is where most of Asia's lounge singers come from). The Sky Lounge, at the Diamond Hotel along Roxas Boulevard, has a good lounge act in an elegant setting overlooking the city.

There are several excellent cigar bars in Manila, including Kipling's in the Mandarin Oriental Hotel in Makati, where a top-rated selection of cigars can be enjoyed with an impressive selection of single malt scotch.

Quezon City nightclubs offer an insight into local comedy acts, as well as the city's booming original pop music scene and the ubiquitous karaoke bars. Many bars are located in the Timog/Morato area, as well as along the Quezon Ave area.

Manila also has its share of 'go go' bars, which feature girls dancing in skimpy bikinis. Bars oriented toward foreigners can be found along P. Burgos Street in Makati and at the ESDA Entertainment Complex in Pasay. Local nightclubs, which offer more risqué performances, can be found along Roxas Boulevard and in Quezon City, but bring along a Filipino friend if venturing into these establishments or you might get a nasty surprise when your bill arrives.

Shopping

What to buy

Basketry
Popular Philippine baskets are found everywhere. Made from natural rattan,

as **Landmark**, **SM Shoemart** and **Rustan's**. Greenbelt Shopping **Complex** and **Makati Cinema Square** (with its indoor firing range) round out the list of regular malls, while the upscale boutiques of **6750 Ayala Avenue** carry internationally known brands.

The huge **SM Mall of Asia**, built in Pasay at the end of EDSA, offers ice-skating and an IMAX theatre. Southwards, the residential community of Ayala Alabang in Muntinlupa City offers the **Ayala Town Center, Festival Mall** (Corporate Avenue corner Civic Drive, Alabang) and **SM Southmall**.

Police preparing for festivities on Cebu's Founders' Day.

nipa, bamboo, abaca and palm, the baskets come in a range of sizes and purposes, and are both functional and decorative.

Handicrafts

Abaca hats, placemats, coasters, bamboo trays, shells, ceramic pots and *gewgaw* are ubiquitous in airport tourist shops, the **Makati** commercial centre and **Ermita** tourist belt. Newer developments include lovely handmade paper, picture frames made from coconut husks and bamboo, and capiz-shell Christmas ornaments. Native woven pieces are always popular.

Embroidery

The no-tie-required *barong Tagalog* is beloved by casual tourists and foreign expatriate businessmen. Ask the hotel concierge to suggest a tailor. Choose either the translucent pineapple fibre, *piña*, with the finest hand embroidery, or the cheaper *ramie* or cotton with machine-embroidery. For women, there are the embroidered *terno* dresses, with matching scarves, bags and handkerchiefs.

Jewellery

Aside from pearls, the most typical Philippine jewellery is made of shell and silver. Mother-of-pearl is perhaps the most popular. Don't purchase items made from coral or tortoise shell, as supporting such unsustainable trade contributes to the degradation of the Philippine environment.

The best silver jewellery is found in **Baguio**, where the guild-like training of St Louis University has engendered fine craftsmanship.

You can also find wood and vine jewellery in the specialty shops of **Ermita** and **Makati**, as well as beadwork from the tribes, notably the necklaces, earrings and ornamental hair pieces of the T'boli, Mangyan and Ifugao people.

Pearls

Quality pearls from Mindanao are for sale at V-Mall in Greenhills, San Juan, Manila. Most of the strands are freshwater pearls in irregular shapes, exotically beautiful and selling for prices that are just as other-worldly. Cultured pearls are available as well. Also look for South Sea black pearls sold at bargain prices compared to the international market. Serious pearl shoppers can drop by Jewelmer's showroom in Megamall B. Jewelmer (www.jewelmer.com) is the world's second-largest producer of salt-water

Furniture

Wicker and rattan furniture normally weighs little enough to ship without spending large amounts of money. Angeles City is the shopper's best bet and offers made-to-order items, while Cebu has emerged as the country's main source of export-quality furniture. In Manila, drop by a FIRMA Home Accessories shop (www.firma.com.ph) for the latest in decor.

Brassware

The first craftspeople of the Philippines are from Mindanao. To this day, they still make gongs, jewel boxes, betel nut boxes, brass beds, and cannon replicas. Ermita's tourist belt area hawks a fair amount of

brassware, though the true collector will head to Mindanao.

Woodcarving

Giant hardwood carvings of the mountain-dwelling Ifugao were among the first local items that the Americans brought home. What they missed were other, more fascinating items, such as carvings of the rice granary god (*bulol*) and the animal totems from Palawan that can now be found in the Ermita tourist belt. Visit the woodcarving village in **Baguio**, or make your way through the Central Cordillera, especially **Banaue**.

A–Z

Budgeting for your trip

The Philippines is a very affordable travel destination, though some things are surprisingly expensive. In general, food, lodging and transport are inexpensive by international standards with a budget trip easily possible on US$40 a day, and a fairly luxurious one for US$200 a day or less. Though the Philippine government markets the country as a shopping destination, luxury goods are generally more expensive than in nearby Singapore or Hong Kong. Handicrafts, and local products, particularly those purchased in provincial areas, are very affordable. Here are average prices for common expenses:

Coffee, juice or beer: P21–P80 per can or bottle
Glass of house wine: P100–P200
Restaurant meal, per person: P200 budget, P500 moderate, P800 expensive
One night in a hotel: P800 cheap, P1,500 moderate, above P3,500 deluxe
Taxi fare from Manila's airport complex to downtown: P275
In-town tricycle-taxi and jeepney fares: P7–P15

Foreign currency is best exchanged in the capital city, where the rates are highest. Travellers' cheques are difficult to cash and offer lower rates nationwide. ATM machines charge fees per transaction, and have fairly low per-transaction limits (often $200 or less) but they often use competitive exchange rates.

Climate

Broadly speaking, the climate of the Philippines can be divided into three seasons. The southwest monsoon – and the typhoons it brings – predominates from June to October. A dry, cooler season during the northeast monsoon period lasts from November to February. Year-round daytime temperatures range from 77°F (25°C) to 90°F (32°C); mean annual humidity is at 83 percent. A hot, dry season – more pronounced in the north – runs from March to May.

There are four main climate zones: **Zone 1** has two seasons, dry November–May and wet June–October. Type 1 areas are found mainly in the western half of Luzon (including Manila), Palawan, Coron, Cuyo and the lower part of Antique, Iloilo and Negros.

Zone 2 lacks a distinct dry season but has a pronounced maximum rain period December–February. Areas include eastern Bicol, eastern Mindanao, northern and eastern Samar and southern Leyte.

Zone 3 areas, which do not have a pronounced maximum rain period but a short dry season of 1–3 (November–January) months, include central Luzon, Visayas and western Mindanao.

Zone 4 sees even rainfall throughout the year and is found in the eastern coast of Luzon, Leyte and Bohol, and in central Mindanao.

The Philippines are affected by about 15 typhoons each year. High season is June–October, with the peak in July–September. The worst-affected areas are in the east – Samar, Leyte and eastern Luzon, while the deep south sees very few.

What to wear/bring

Loose, light clothes are best. Outside the cities, shorts and T-shirts are fine, but there is a degree of formality expected in Manila and other big cities. Signs saying, 'No shorts or sandals' can be seen on government offices and nightclubs alike. The

right clothes to bring would be best described as 'smart casual'. Bring any specialised prescription medicine needed. Other than that, Manila's vast malls sell just about every product you can think of.

Crime and safety

Manila and other major cities in the Philippines are rife with con artists, who exploit the Filipino friendliness to foreigners. Filipinos are generally a very hospitable and welcoming people, and 99 percent of those who approach you will have good intentions. But the remaining one percent cause real problems for travellers. Don't accept rides, invitations to card games or drinking sessions, business or property purchase proposals or any other kinds of solicitations from strangers.

Pickpocketing and theft are also a real problem, particularly in crowded places such as bus and railway stations. Thieves work in teams and are skilful. One bumps into you and apologises profusely, while the other approaches from behind while you are distracted to grab your purse, wallet, camera, etc. Carry valuables tightly fastened to your body in urban areas, and, of course, never leave valuables unattended.

In parts of Mindanao, in the deep south, separatist groups continue to fight the government with bombings, kidnappings and other acts of terror. Seek the latest travel advice before considering a trip to Mindanao.

Customs regulations

Each arriving passenger is allowed 400 cigarettes (20 packs) or two tins of tobacco, and two 1-litre bottles of alcohol.

Filipinos living overseas bring home huge amounts of goods – many of them dutiable – to their families

Emergency numbers

For an updated list of Manila emergency numbers, check www. manilacityph.com/emergency.html
Key emergency numbers include:
Police/Fire/Medical Emergency Tel: 117
Philippine National Police SMS Text Message No: 2920
Tourist Security (24 hrs) **Tel:** 02-524 1660, 524 1728
Police Headquarters (24 hours) **Tel:** 02-723 0401. Camp Crame, edsa, Metro Manila
Manila Police Tel: 02-523 3378
Makati Police Tel: 02-899 9014
Pasay City Police Tel: 02-831 8070
Quezon City Police Tel: 02-921 5267

back in the Philippines. As a result, you will see passengers walking stacks of boxes through the 'Nothing to Declare' Customs line at the Manila airport. In general, customs regulations are not strictly enforced but officials will sometimes use the rule of law on a selective basis, particularly when it comes to bringing electronics into the country.

Etiquette

Filipinos are justly famous for their hospitality. All levels of society exude friendliness and generosity toward visitors. The poorest family will give their last meal to a visitor, while the wealthiest people will invite a foreign traveller to their tennis club for the afternoon. It is the responsibility of visitors to the Philippines to respect this generosity and not take advantage. Filipinos also tend to be very respectful, with honorific titles for family members based on age, and a tendency to call visitors 'sir' or 'madam'. Elderly family members are greeted with the respectful sign of putting the forehead to their hand, while children will offer this greeting to visiting adults. Learning and participating in this ritual is always appreciated.

The people of the Philippines, like other Southeast Asian cultures, seek to avoid confrontation, or loss of face. Many visitors from Western countries, who favour more direct forms of speaking and addressing issues, face challenges when communicating with Filipinos. Most of these issues can be overcome with politeness and patience.

Embassies in Manila

Australia: Level 23, Tower 2, RCBC Plaza, 6819 Ayala Avenue, Makati, tel: 02-757-8100, www.australia.gov.ph
Canada: Levels 6–8, Tower 2, RCBC Plaza, 6819 Ayala Avenue, Makati, tel: 02-857-9000, www.philippines.gc.ca
New Zealand: 23/F, BP1 Buendia Center, Sen. Gil Puyat Avenue (Buendia Avenue Extension), Makati City, tel: 02-891-5355, www.nzembassy.com/philippines

Singapore: 35/F, Tower One, Enterprise Center, Ayala Avenue, Makati City, tel: 02-751-2345, www.mfa.gov.sg/manila
Thailand: 107 Rada /Thailand Street, Makati, tel: 02-815-4219
United Kingdom: 120 Upper McKinley Road, Taguig, tel: 02-858-2200, www.ukinthephilippines.fco.gov.uk
United States: 1201 Roxas Boulevard, Ermita, tel: 02-528-6300, http://manila.usembassy.gov

Boracay is the Philippines' playground.

Health and medical care

Yellow fever vaccination is necessary for those arriving from an infected area. There is a risk of malaria year-round in remote areas below 600 metres. Check on the malaria situation before travelling to remote areas.

As well as malaria, rabies is also prevalent in the Philippines. If bitten by any mammal, seek medical treatment immediately. Bilharzia (schistosomiasis) is another problem, so avoid swimming in fresh water. Chlorinated swimming pools are safe.

Drinking water is generally safe in Metro Manila, although it is wise to drink mineral or bottled water (readily available everywhere).

Mercury Drug is one of the most widely-found pharmacies in Manila; some branches are open 24 hours.

For medical treatment, payment must usually be guaranteed in advance at major hospitals, though a credit card can often be used. Travel insurance that covers medical is recommended. Healthcare standards are poor in many parts of the Philippines, but there are several excellent hospitals in the country.

Manila hospitals

Asian Hospital: Filinvest Corporate Center, Alabang, tel: 02-771-9000.
Cardinal Santos Medical Center: Wilson Street, Greenhills, San Juan, tel: 02-727-0001–46.
Makati Medical Center: 2 Amorsolo corner de la Rosa Street, Makati City, tel: 02-888-89991, 892-5544.
Manila Doctor's Hospital: 667 United Nations Avenue, Ermita, tel: 02-524-3011–77.
Medical Center Manila: 1122 General Luna Street, Ermita, tel: 02-523-8131/65.
Philippine General Hospital: Taft Avenue, Manila, tel: 02-521-8450.
St Luke's Medical Center: 279 Rodriguez Boulevard, Quezon City, tel: 02-723-0301, 723-0101.

Davao hospital

Davao Doctors Hospital, General Malvar Street, tel: 082-222-0850, local tel: 106.

Cebu hospitals

Ching Hua Hospital, Fuente Osmeña, tel: 032-253-9409
Cebu Doctors Hospital, President Osmeña Boulevard, tel: 032-255-5555.

Media

The Philippine Daily Inquirer, *Manila Bulletin*, and other English-language newspapers are circulated widely, with in-depth national news about corruption, accidents, and celebrity gossip. The papers carry foreign news from overseas wire services. Newsstands sell *Newsweek*, *Time*, and internationally circulated consumer magazines with focuses such as automotive and high-tech. Radio stations from abroad include the BBC World Service and Voice of America. BBC broadcasts often appear on hotel TVs.Money
The Philippines' currency, the peso (P), is divided into 100 centavos. The US dollar, pound sterling, euros, Canadian dollar, Australian dollar and Japanese yen are all easily convertible. Outside Manila the US dollar is the most easily converted, but at lower exchange rates than in the capital.

Major credit cards are generally accepted in Manila, though some establishments tack on 3 to 5 percent on some cards.

Tipping

Larger establishments will add a service charge, though this is usually taken by the owner, and not given to the waiter. Smaller establishments leave tipping to discretion, but it is usual to give something. A P20 bill is a good standard tip for simple tasks and small establishments. The local habit is to leave a token fee rather than a percentage of the total bill, usually less than P100. Of course, the relatively low cost of travel here makes it easier for foreign visitors to be generous.

Opening hours

Offices Government/business hours are Mon–Fri 8am–5pm and workers break for lunch from noon–1pm. The lethargic Philippine government bureaucracy is improving, but still don't expect much performance around lunch times or near closing time. Some private offices are open on Sat 8am–noon.
Banks are open Mon–Fri 9am–3pm, but a few modern banks are open in shopping malls now with later hours.
Small shops Mon–Sat 9am or 10am–7pm.
Larger shops Most shopping centres, department stores and supermarkets are open 10am–9 pm every day.

Postal services

Post offices are open Mon–Fri, 8am–5pm, Sat 8am–noon. The Philippine Postal Corporation is at Lawton Plaza (Liwasang Bonifacio), Intramuros, Manila. Hotel desks provide the most convenient services for purchasing stamps and posting letters. At Ninoy Aquino International Airport, the post office is in the arrival area.

The Philippine mail system is slow and unreliable. It is fine for postcards but not much use for anything else. Private courier services like **DHL** (tel: 1800-1888-0345), **Fedex** (1800-10-855-8484), **UPS** (tel: 1800-10-742-5877), and **TNT** (tel: 02-551-5632) offer inexpensive and reliable mail service within the Philippines, as well as speedy overseas deliveries.

THAILAND

MYANMAR

LAOS

CAMBODIA

VIETNAM

MALAYSIA

BRUNEI

SINGAPORE

INDONESIA

PHILIPPINES

Post offices in Manila

Manila Post Office Liwasang Bonifacio, Manila
Makati Post Office corner Gil Puyat Avenue (Buendia) and Ayala Avenue
Pasay Post Office F.B. Harrison, Pasay
San Juan Central Post Office Pinaglabanan, San Juan
For other branches, see www.philpost. gov.ph.

Public holidays

The current government of the Philippines is known (with admiration by some workers, and disdain by some employers) for a tendency to declare impromptu holidays. National holidays can be called at any time, and sometimes with only a day or two of notice, so monitor the media if you need to visit a bank or other official establishment. Regular national holidays include:
January 1 New Year's Day. Fireworks and celebratory gunfire ring in the New Year. Take cover and enjoy.
April/May Maundy Thursday, Good Friday. Flagellants in the streets, processions and *Cenaculos* (passion plays). In Pampanga and elsewhere, devout Catholics are voluntarily crucified.
April/May Easter Sunday Morning processions; family celebration.
April 9 Araw ng Kagitingan (Day of Valor/Bataan and Corregidor Day). Bravery of Filipino soldiers during World War II commemorated at Fort Santiago in Intramuros.
May 1 Labour Day. A tribute to the Philippine worker.
June 12 Independence Day – from Spain in 1898. Parades at Rizal Park in Manila.
October/November Hari Raya Aidilfitri. Marks the end of Ramadan.
November 1 All Saints' Day. Most Filipinos travel home to visit ancestral tombs and spend the day with their family.
November 30 Bonifacio Day celebrates the birth of nationalist leader Andres Bonifacio.
December 25 Christmas Day.
December 30 Rizal Day. Wreath laying ceremony at National Hero's Monument in Rizal Park (Manila), in honour of the revered José Rizal.

Telephones

Most Philippine hotels have over-priced international long-distance and fax services, as well as Internet access for a small charge. Very inexpensive Internet telephone services are now available at Internet cafés around the country.
The ubiquity of mobile phones makes it possible buy a cheap cell phone (as low as $30) and load it with minutes, which is cheap and requires no registration, for use during your visit. It can be resold, or better yet, given to Filipino friends, upon departure. You can also try to use a local SIM card (sold for less than $1) on your home mobile phone.

Tourist information

The best place to start when looking for tourism information on the Philippines is the excellent Department of Tourism website at www.wowphilippines.com.ph. The Department of Tourism's main office in **Manila** is on Kalaw Street in Ermita, call also be visited or called at tel: 02-524 2345 or 525 6114.
Singapore
Philippine Tourism Office, 400 Orchard Road, 13-08 Orchard Towers, Singapore 238875, tel: (65) 67387165, www.philippine-embassy. org.sg
United Kingdom
Philippines Department of Tourism,

Telephone codes

International access code: 00
International operator Tel: 108
Domestic operator Tel: 109
Directory assistance Tel: 114 or 187
Philippines country code: 63
City codes:
Manila: 02
Angeles: 045, 0455
Bacolod: 034
Baguio: 074
Batangas: 043
Boracay: 036
Cagayan de Oro: 088, 08822
Cebu: 032
Clark: 045
Davao: 082
General Santos City: 083
Iloilo: 033
Subic: 047

146 Cromwell Road, London SW7 4EF, tel: +44 207 835 1100, www. wowphilippines.co.uk
United States
Philippine Tourism Center, 556 Fifth Avenue, New York 10036, tel: (1) (212) 575-7915, www. experiencephilippines.org

Visas and passports

All foreigners must have valid passports. Except tourists from countries with which the Philippines have no diplomatic relations and nationals from restricted countries, everyone may enter without visas and stay for 21 days, provided they hold onward or return tickets.
Visitors who wish to extend their stay to 59 days should contact the Bureau of Immigration and Deportation, Magallanes Drive, Intramuros, by Jones Bridge (Mon–Fri 8am–5pm). Longer visas can also be applied for at Philippine embassies.

Philippino money.

CREDITS

Photo Credits

Alamy 268
Anefo 153B
Brunei Ministry of Tourism 265T, 265B, 266, 269
Chris Stowers/Apa Publications 2/3, 4ML, 5TR, 9TR, 10BL, 14/15, 226BL, 260/261T, 261TR, 338/339, 340/341, 342, 343T, 343B, 344B, 346, 347, 348, 349, 352, 353, 355T, 355B, 356, 357, 358, 359, 360, 361B, 361T, 362T, 362B, 364, 365, 366, 367T, 367B, 368, 369, 370, 371T, 372/373T, 372BR, 440, 441T, 441B, 443, 445, 446
Corbis 115, 159, 262/263
Corrie Wingate/Apa Publications 1, 4ML, 5ML, 5BR, 6ML, 6BL, 8BR, 8M, 11T, 12/13, 19, 20, 70/71T, 71TR, 72/73, 74/75, 76, 77T, 77B, 79, 80, 81, 82, 83, 84, 85, 86, 87, 88, 89, 92, 93, 94, 95T, 95B, 97, 98, 99, 101, 102, 103, 105B, 105T, 106T, 106B, 107, 108, 109B, 109T, 111T, 111B, 112T, 112B, 113, 114, 145TR, 178BL, 178/179T, 179BR, 179TR, 227ML, 227BR, 227BL, 260BR, 261BR, 294/295, 298, 299T, 299B, 302, 303L, 303R, 304L, 304R, 305, 306BL, 306/307T, 307ML, 307BR, 307TR, 308, 309, 311, 312, 313T, 313B, 314, 315, 316T, 316B, 317, 318, 319T, 319B, 320, 321T, 321B, 322, 323, 324, 326, 327, 328T, 328B, 329, 330, 331T, 331B, 334T, 334B, 335B, 335T, 336B, 372BL, 374,

388, 389, 390, 391, 392, 431, 432, 433, 434, 435, 437, 438
Dreamstime 7TL, 31B, 32, 144BR, 145BL, 153T, 172, 173T, 175, 235, 280, 296/297, 373ML
Fotolia 421
Georges Erhard/Rainbow Divers 373TR
Getty Images 345, 363
Indonesia Ministry of Culture and Tourism 336T
iStock 4BR, 4BL, 5TL, 35, 40, 48T, 57, 58T, 58B, 66T, 68T, 70BL, 78T, 123B, 123T, 134, 150, 151T, 151B, 169, 171B, 171T, 173B, 174T, 174B, 179ML, 206B, 261BL, 277, 282, 287T, 371B, 373BL, 404, 439
James Tye/Apa Publications 5MR, 9BL, 9BR, 10BR, 16/17, 23, 144BL, 228/229, 230/231, 232, 233T, 233B, 234B, 236, 237, 238, 239, 240, 241, 244, 245T, 245B, 247, 248B, 249, 250, 251, 253, 254T, 256, 257, 258, 259, 260BL, 307BL, 337, 413, 416, 417, 419
John Ishii/Apa Publications 28, 63, 66B, 67, 68B, 69, 255
Leonardo 401
Library of Congress 31T, 276T, 301T, 301B, 344T
Negara Muzium, Malaysia 234T
Nikt Wong/Apa publications 62, 64, 65T, 65B, 248T, 254B, 306BR
Peter Stuckings/Apa Publications 6T, 6MR, 6BR, 7BL, 7MR, 7BR, 8BL, 10TR, 11B, 18, 21, 22, 26/27, 29T, 29B, 33, 34, 36, 37, 38, 39, 41, 46,

47, 48B, 49, 50T, 50B, 51T, 51B, 52, 53, 54, 55, 56, 59, 60B, 60T, 61, 70BR, 71ML, 71BR, 71BL, 116/117, 118/119, 120, 121T, 121B, 124, 125, 126, 127, 130, 131, 132T, 132B, 133, 135, 136, 137, 138, 139T, 139B, 140B, 140T, 141, 142, 143T, 143B, 144/145T, 145BR, 146/147, 148/149, 154, 155, 156, 157, 158, 162, 163, 164B, 164T, 165, 166, 167, 176, 177T, 177B, 178BR, 179BL, 180/181, 182/183, 184, 185T, 185B, 186, 188, 189, 190, 191, 192, 193L, 193R, 194, 195, 196, 197, 200, 201, 203B, 203T, 204, 205B, 205T, 206T, 207, 208, 209T, 209B, 210T, 210B, 211T, 211B, 212, 213T, 213B, 214T, 214B, 215, 216, 217, 219T, 219B, 220, 221T, 221B, 222T, 222B, 223, 224, 225, 226/227T, 226BR, 227TR, 261ML, 373BR, 376, 378, 379, 380, 382, 383, 384, 387, 395, 396, 397, 400T, 400B, 405, 406, 409, 412
Public domain 30, 78B, 122, 152, 187, 276B, 300
Robert Harding 100, 168, 264
Singapore Tourism Board 5ML, 145ML, 274, 275B, 278, 279, 285T, 287B, 290, 291, 292BL, 292/293T, 292BR, 293ML, 293BR, 293BL, 293TR, 424, 425, 426, 427, 430
Vincent Ng/Apa Publications 270/271, 272/273, 275T, 281, 283, 285B, 286, 288
Visit Philippines 7TR

Cover Credits

Front cover: Pura Ulun Danau Bratan Temple on Lake Bratan, *AWL Images*
Back cover: (top) Thailand, Phi Phi island, *Dreamstime*; (middle) Students perform the ancient play Sovannahang, *Peter Stuckings/Apa*

Publications
Front flap: (from top) Elephant trekking, *Peter Stuckings/Apa Publications* ; Legong, Pura Gunung Lebah, *Corrie Wingate/Apa Publications*; Orangutan (Orang utan) , *James Tye/Apa Publications*;

description *credit*
Back flap: Rice Terraces *iStockphoto*
Spine: Artifacts in Trowulan museum, East Java, *Corrie Wingate/ Apa Publications*

Insight Guide Credits

Distribution

UK
Dorling Kindersley Ltd
A Penguin Group company
80 Strand, London, WC2R 0RL
sales@uk.dk.com

United States
Ingram Publisher Services
1 Ingram Boulevard, PO Box 3006,
La Vergne, TN 37086-1986
ips@ingramcontent.com

Australia and New Zealand
Woodslane
10 Apollo St, Warriewood,
NSW 2102, Australia
info@woodslane.com.au

Worldwide
Apa Publications GmbH & Co. Verlag
KG (Singapore branch)
7030 Ang Mo Kio Avenue 5
08-65 Northstar @ AMK
Singapore 569880
apasin@singnet.com.sg

Printing
CTPS-China
(C) 2014 Apa Publications (UK) Ltd
All Rights Reserved
First Edition 1995
Fourth Edition 2014

www.insightguides.com

Project Editor
Sarah Clark
Series Manager
Rachel Lawrence
Author
Adam Bray
Picture Editor/Art Editor
Tom Smyth/Shahid Mahmood
Map Production
Original cartography Berndtson & Berndtson, updated by Apa Cartography Department
Production
Tynan Dean and Rebeka Davies

Legend

City maps

	Freeway/Highway/Motorway
	Divided Highway
	Main Roads
	Minor Roads
	Pedestrian Roads
	Steps
	Footpath
	Railway
	Funicular Railway
	Cable Car
	Tunnel
	City Wall
	Important Building
	Built Up Area
	Other Land
	Transport Hub
	Park
	Pedestrian Area
	Bus Station
	Tourist Information
	Main Post Office
	Cathedral/Church
	Mosque
	Synagogue
	Statue/Monument
	Beach
	Airport

Regional maps

	Freeway/Highway/Motorway (with junction)
	Freeway/Highway/Motorway (under construction)
	Divided Highway
	Main Road
	Secondary Road
	Minor Road
	Track
	Footpath
	International Boundary
	State/Province Boundary
	National Park/Reserve
	Marine Park
	Ferry Route
	Marshland/Swamp
	Glacier Salt Lake
	Airport/Airfield
	Ancient Site
	Border Control
	Cable Car
	Castle/Castle Ruins
	Cave
	Chateau/Stately Home
	Church/Church Ruins
	Crater
	Lighthouse
	Mountain Peak
	Place of Interest
	Viewpoint

Contributors

This new edition was comprehensively updated by **Adam Bray**, a transplanted American freelance writer, who has lived in Vietnam since 2003 and written extensively about the Southeast Asia region. His work builds on the earlier content of many excellent Asia specialist writers who contributed to this and other *Insight Guides* titles. These include **David Abram, Floyd Whaley, Mark Beales, Andrew Forbes, Siew Lyn Wong, Joan Koh, Linda Hoffman, Aviva West** and **Samantha Coomber**.

The book was a collaborative effort, commissioned and managed by **Rebecca Lovell, Catherine Dreghorn** and **Sarah Clark. Jonathan Gilbert** copyedited the text and the index was provided by **Penny Phenix**.

About Insight Guides

Insight Guides have more than 40 years' experience of publishing high-quality, visual travel guides. We produce 400 full-colour titles, in both print and digital form, covering more than 200 destinations across the globe, in a variety of formats to meet your different needs.

Insight Guides are written by local authors who use their on-the-ground experience to provide the very latest information; their local expertise is evident in the extensive historical and cultural background features. All the reviews in **Insight Guides** are independent; we strive to maintain an impartial view. Our reviews are carefully selected to guide to you the best places to stay and eat, so you can be confident that when we say a restaurant or hotel is special, we really mean it.

INDEX

Abbreviations: T = Thailand; My = Myanmar; L = Laos; C = Cambodia; V = Vietnam; M = Malaysia; S = Singapore; Br = Brunei; I = Indonesia; P = The Philippines. City abbreviations: KL = Kuala Lumpur; BSB = Bandar Seri Begawan

I

J

K